# Macworld
# Networking Bible
## 2nd Edition

# Macworld
# Networking Bible
## 2nd Edition

by Dave Kosiur
and Joel M Snyder

# IDG
# BOOKS

IDG Books Worldwide, Inc.

An International Data Group Company

San Mateo, California ◆ Indianapolis, Indiana ◆ Boston, Massachusetts

# Macworld™ Networking Bible, 2nd Edition

Published by
**IDG Books Worldwide, Inc.**
An International Data Group Company
155 Bovet Road, Suite 310
San Mateo, CA 94402

Library of Congress Catalog Card No.: 94-77528

ISBN: 1-56884-194-9

Printed in the United States of America

10 9 8 7 6 5 4 3 2 1

2B/QX/SR/ZU

Distributed in the United States by IDG Books Worldwide, Inc.

Distributed in Canada by Macmillan of Canada, a Division of Canada Publishing Corporation; by Computer and Technical books in Miami, Florida, for South America and the Caribbean; by Longman Singapore in Singapore, Malaysia, Thieland, and Korea; by Toppan Co. Ltd. in Japan; by Asia Computerworld in Hong Kong; by Woodslane Pty. Ltd. in Australia and New Zealand; and by Trans Publishers Ltd. in the U.K. and Europe.

For general information in IDG Books in the U.S., including information on discounts and premiums, contact IDG Books at 800-434-3422 or 415-312-0650.

For information on where to purchase IDG Books outside the U.S., contact Christina Turner at 415-312-0633.

For information on translations contact Marc Jeffrey Mikulich, Foreign Rights Manager, at IDG Books Worldwide; FAX NUMBER 415-286-2747.

For sales inquiries and special prices for bulk quantities, write to the address above or call IDG Books Worldwide at 415-312-0650.

For information on using IDG Books in the classroom, or for ordering examination copies, contact Jim Kelly at 800-434-2086.

 is a registered trademark of IDG Books Worldwide, Inc.

The text in this book is printed on recycled paper.

# About the Author

**Dave Kosiur** has been involved with computers in one form or another since he was a freshman in college (back in the "dark ages" of 1969, when mainframes were mainframes and PCs hadn't been invented yet). Kosiur, a contributing editor for *Macworld* magazine for the past five years, has been writing for the magazine since 1987. Kosiur, who also contributes to *InfoWorld*, founded *Connections, the Newsletter for Macintosh Networking* in 1987 and served as Publisher until the end of 1991.

Before working with *Connections*, Dave, who received his Ph.D. in Geochemistry from UCLA, worked as a research geochemist for Chevron Oil Field Research Co. (COFRC). During his tenure with Chevron, he was one of the few hardy souls who brought their own personal Macs to work to replace what he'd been doing on mainframes and minicomputers. Dave also worked with an employee computer club and wrote an "unofficial" company newsletter about Macs for three years.

Even before he got hooked on computers, Dave has been an avid reader, particularly of science fiction, mysteries, and historical fiction. If he's not in front of his Mac these days, you'll likely find him in a bookstore or record store, unless he's out driving around Virginia with his top down or spending time in the Blue Ridge Mountains.

Dave now works as the head of strategic services for InterCon Systems Corp. in Herndon, Virginia, where he helps plan the next new great TCP/IP-based software for Mac and MS Windows. Dave and his wife live with their cat, Riley, in Reston, Virginia, where they're trying to cope with humid summers, which are nothing like those in California.

**Joel Snyder** is a senior partner with Opus One, a consulting firm in Tucson, Arizona. Joel spends most of his time on the road helping people build larger, faster, better, and more reliable networks. His professional travels have taken him from San Francisco to St. Petersburg, where he always carries his trusty Macintosh and modem, neither of which have cute names.

Joel has been working with networks since 1980, when he signed on with CompuServe Research and Development, and has been a member of the ISO and ITU committees which write network standards for over a decade. He has authored over 100 articles for technical publications and has been a network consultant since 1984. At home, his seven-node Ethernet network has run all of the protocols described in this book — except SNA and token ring, mostly for religious reasons.

Joel's baccaulureate degree is in Latin, and his Ph.D. is in Management Information Systems. His dissertation is on computer networks in the former Soviet Union. Almost everything he wrote in graduate school is now classified, and he's not allowed to read it anymore, which is good because it wasn't very interesting to begin with. His favorite Crayola™ crayon color is Burnt Sienna.

Joel lives in Tucson with Jan Trumbo and their cat, Romeo Y Julieta, who is the only feline in the Internet Network Information Center's databases to be listed as an administrative point of contact for an Internet domain.

Welcome to the world of IDG Books Worldwide.

IDG Books Worldwide, Inc., is a subsidiary of International Data Group, the world's largest publisher of business and computer-related information and the leading global provider of information services on information technology. IDG was founded more than 25 years ago and now employs more than 5,700 people worldwide. IDG publishes more than 200 computer publications in 63 countries (see listing below). Forty million people read one or more IDG publications each month.

Launched in 1990, IDG Books is today the fastest-growing publisher of computer and business books in the United States. We are proud to have received 3 awards from the Computer Press Association in recognition of editorial excellence, and our best-selling ...*For Dummies* series has more than 7 million copies in print with translations in more than 20 languages. IDG Books, through a recent joint venture with IDG's Hi-Tech Beijing, became the first U.S. publisher to publish a computer book in the People's Republic of China. In record time, IDG Books has become the first choice for millions of readers around the world who want to learn how to better manage their businesses.

Our mission is simple: Every IDG book is designed to bring extra value and skill-building instructions to the reader. Our books are written by experts who understand and care about our readers. The knowledge base of our editorial staff comes from years of experience in publishing, education, and journalism — experience which we use to produce books for the '90s. In short, we care about books, so we attract the best people. We devote special attention to details such as audience, interior design, use of icons, and illustrations. And because we use an efficient process of authoring, editing, and desktop publishing our books electronically, we can spend more time ensuring superior content and spend less time on the technicalities of making books.

You can count on our commitment to deliver high-quality books at competitive prices on topics customers want to read about. At IDG, we value quality, and we have been delivering quality for more than 25 years. You'll find no better book on a subject than an IDG book.

*John J. Kilcullen*

John Kilcullen
President and CEO
IDG Books Worldwide, Inc.

# Dedication

To the networking engineering and development team at Apple Computer. We have met only a handful of you, but we use your knowledge and your ideas every day. You have made the lives of countless network managers easier and we thank you for that!

— Dave Kosiur and Joel Snyder

For Jan,

Amabo, mea dulcis Ipsitilla,
meae deliciae, mei lepores,
iube ad te ueniam meridiatum.
et si iusseris, illud adiuuato,
ne quis liminis obseret tabellam,
neu tibi lubeat foras abire,
sed domi maneas paresque nobis
nouem continuas fututiones.
uerum si quid ages, statim iubeto:
nam pransus iaceo et satur supinus
pertundo tunicamque palliumque.

— Catulli Carmina XXXII

— from Joel Snyder

# Credits

**Publisher**
David Solomon

**Managing Editor**
Mary Bednarek

**Acquisitions Editor**
Janna Custer

**Production Director**
Beth Jenkins

**Senior Editors**
Sandy Blackthorn
Diane Graves Steele
Tracy Barr

**Production Coordinator**
Cindy L. Phipps

**Associate Acquisitions Editor**
Megg Bonar

**Project Editor**
Andy Cummings

**Editorial Assistants**
Rebecca Forrest
Laura Schaible

**Editors**
Michael Simsic
Kathy Simpson
Laurie Ann Smith
Pam Mourouzis
Bill Barton

**Technical Reviewer**
Chris Janton

**Production Staff**
Kent Gish
Angie Hunkler
Drew R. Moore
Steve Peake
Carla Radzikinas
Patricia R. Reynolds
Robert Simon
Kathy Schnorr
Gina Scott

**Proofreader**
Michelle Worthington

**Indexer**
Sherry Massey

# Acknowledgments

When IDG Books said that they wanted a book on networking that wasn't obsolete before it hit the shelves, I knew that I was going to be relying heavily on the kindness of both friends and strangers.

In Tucson, friends Chris Janton, Aaron Leonard, Ehud Gavron, Mark Basinski, Deb McClellan, and Jan Trumbo all helped me wrestle through the dark dungeons of networks and networking to make sense out of piles and piles of literature, software, and other information.

On the Indiana end, Andy Cummings and the production staff at IDG Books Worldwide worked overtime to put this together as quickly as possible — without sacrificing quality.

If you like the style of writing, you should join me in thanking the many editors who have taught me how to write. Colleagues Charlie Babcock, John Cox, Kyle Nitzche, Elizabeth Dougherty, Tova Fliegel, Patricia Schnaidt, Eric Bowden, Dave Taylor, Mark Cappell, Peter Clegg, Charlie Bruno, Charlie Piller, Tim Sylvester, Daniel Dern, Michael Neubarth, Margie Wylie, and Fritz Nelson have all taken their turns crafting my writing into readable prose.

At the other end of the world are all the people who work with all your favorite Macintosh vendors. They have helped me understand their products. Starting with Apple's John McCreadie, Emilio Robles, Keri Walker, and Doedy Hunter and including folks at nearly every company mentioned in this book, I say "Thank you, all of you, for working overtime to help me on all of the research which went into this book. Without your assistance, this simply would not exist."

Finally, I owe thanks to both Dave Kosiur and Nancy Jones. What you read here is one-third Joel Snyder, but that means it's two-thirds Dave and Nancy. Revising a book this well written to begin with is much easier than starting from scratch. I'm privileged to have been allowed to tromp through the first edition and build upon what was already a fine text.

Joel Snyder
Tucson, Arizona

(The publisher would like to give special thanks to Patrick J. McGovern, without whom this book would not have been possible.)

If I have seen farther than others, it is because I was standing on the shoulders of giants.

— Isaac Newton

If I have not seen as far as others, it is because giants were standing on my shoulders.

— Hal Abelson

In computer science, we stand on each other's feet.

— Brian K. Reed

# Contents at a Glance

# Table of Contents

# Part II: Installing an AppleTalk Network ......107

## Part III: Managing a Network .....................295

CHAPTER

# 13 Configuring, Monitoring, and Fixing AppleTalk Networks ...............................................297

CHAPTER

## 14 Managing AppleTalk Networks for Management ......................................................351

CHAPTER

## 15 Securing an AppleTalk Network ............................375

# Part VI: Appendixes

# Foreword

The Macintosh is still the only personal computer that comes with built-in networking capability. Apple's foresight in 1984 has made it possible for the Mac to take the lead in personal computer networking.

The proliferation of add-on network architectures in the DOS/Windows world has created barriers to networking that the Mac world has never known. Couple that with the Mac's ease of configuration, and Mac system administrators have it easy, right?

Well, almost. Administering any network is a daunting task. Very few managers understand the level of expertise needed to run a successful network, yet everyone in the company depends on the network as they do the telephone. It's a truly thankless job. Since you have purchased this book, you are someone who understands the need to constantly hone your knowledge and skills. The political side of your job is as important as the technical side. This is true of any job involving mission critical technology.

Moving from a pure AppleTalk environment to a mixed one is today's challenge. This means that you need to digest a great deal of new information and turn it into useful knowledge. This book is packed with information. How can you best use it? Here are a few hints:

First, computers and networks are like cars; you can't learn to drive from a book. So dive in and work with your network. Learn how it behaves while it's working properly. Become familiar with the concepts in this book, then use them to explore your network. As you learn what "normal" is, you gain the judgment to spot abnormalities. How can you fix a problem when you don't know what "broken" looks like?

Also, very few people take technical books to bed with them. It's unlikely that you will ever read this book straight through from cover to cover. On the other hand, it's full of "gold nuggets" that can save you major time and prevent big embarrassments.

The technique that has worked best for me is to quickly scan-read the entire book. Just expose yourself to each page for maybe a second or two. Do it in a few sessions of 15 minutes or so each. It's amazing what you'll pick up on this pass, but the real payoff comes later. In the heat of battle, you'll say to yourself "Hey! I saw something about this in that in the *Macworld Networking Bible*." Between your right brain, the contents, and the index, you'll often find that nugget you need. Something that just fits the bill.

In the next few years, you'll probably be tasked with tying your company's network to the Internet. The difference is enormous. Addresses are statically assigned, the naming system covers both machines and mail routing, and must be synchronized with the worldwide Domain Name Service. There's much more. Start becoming familiar with TCP/IP. Install MacTCP on a few machines and get familiar with how it works. Set up a Worldwide Web server (MacHTTPD) in your company and give out copies of Mosaic or MacWeb so your users can begin to learn about this new and exciting Internet service. Get yourself access to the Usenet newsgroups that deal with Macintosh networking issues.

There's no end in sight to the networking explosion. It's my feeling that we're just beginning. Don't trust the marketing hype, don't trust the big company salesmen that want to throw a warm blanket over you. Your direct experience, knowledge, and problem-solving skills are a valuable asset to your company. Make sure they know how valuable you are. Sell the network. Put on in-house seminars. Teach people how best to use the tools they have. Experience, knowledge, and exposure are the keys to success.

And remember, AppleTalk is a plug-and-play network, not a play-and-plug network. You'll see what I mean.

— Robert Denny
Pasadena, California

Denny, with Bill Northlich of Kinetics, developed the first implementation of AppleTalk over Ethernet. His company also pioneered the Mac-VAX connectivity technology.

# Introduction

We believe that a Macintosh network, with its ease of use, friendly interface, and powerful capabilities, is more exciting to see in action than any other network system. Network users easily become proficient at collecting and distributing information. To provide this easy interface, however, the network administrator must deal with many complex concepts that are unseen to the end-user. This book is intended to help the administrator understand networking concepts in order to design and manage Macintosh networks that run at their highest performance potential.

## Why You Need This Book

There are very few sources of detailed information on the construction and management of Macintosh networks. This book aims to fill that gap. It doesn't make any difference whether you're a user of a network, a designer of a new network, or a manager of a large established network — this book explains both the background concepts and the working details of Mac networks so that you can put the information to good use. If you're interested in making a network work better — or even just making one work! — this book will help.

## Whom This Book Is For

This book is aimed at two groups of network administrators: beginning Macintosh network administrators, who may need help in understanding how to design a simple AppleTalk network for sharing printers and files, and administrators of large, challenging networks, who need information on the various aspects of managing multiple routers, servers, modems, and other network equipment.

We have written this book for a wide audience because we believe that the network administrator of a small network often finds himself or herself becoming the network administrator of a large network. So this is a book you can grow with.

To get the most from this book, you should already be familiar with the basic pieces of the Macintosh interface, such as volume icons and opening the Chooser. You should also have an understanding of the basic use of the Macintosh — manipulating the mouse, and so on. If you do need to learn more Macintosh fundamentals, please study the manual *Getting Started With Your Macintosh* or the disk *Your Tour of the Macintosh*. Both come with every Macintosh computer. You can also consult other IDG books on the Macintosh for additional information. Suggested titles include *Macworld Complete Mac Handbook Plus CD* by Jim Heid; *Macworld Guide to System 7* and *Macworld Guide to System 7.5* by Lon Poole; and *Macworld Read Me First Book*, by Jerry Borrell, *et al.*

The first section of this book covers network fundamentals to provide background if you have never worked with a network before.

## How This Book Is Organized

Material in this book has been organized as much as possible to lead you from simple and fundamental concepts to the more advanced complexities of networking. Although you may be tempted to read this book from cover to cover, we think you will get more out of it if you jump around a little more. Although we tried to build each chapter on the foundation of the previous, there are lots of places — particularly in the last half of the book — where that just didn't work out. Your best bet is to give the detailed table of contents some study and use that as a guide to plan your reading. Because we want you to use this book as you grow as a network manager, you may want to put off reading some chapters for quite a while.

You should also use the index of this book; it will be your best friend when it comes to finding information. The limitations of a paper book keep us from organizing the *Macworld Networking Bible* in more than one way. That means that as you read through this book, you're going to have to use the index to find the best path to complete coverage of each topic.

## Part I: Introducing Networking

In Part I, we discuss why we think networking is so important and introduce the many exciting things that you can do with a network. We describe how information is transmitted across a network and how network protocol suites are used. You'll find that these fundamentals are very important for understanding the material presented in later sections.

Chapter 1, "Understanding Connectivity," explains what a network can do for you and your company and why we recommend the AppleTalk protocol system for Macintosh networking.

Chapter 2, "Understanding Networks," describes how signals work over your networks cable to transmit information and the basics of how the various pieces of your network, such as transceivers, repeaters, bridges, and routers, function. This chapter also introduces some basic network vocabulary that you can refer to as you continue in the book.

Chapter 3, "Understanding AppleTalk Protocols," explains network protocols, the OSI Reference Model, and the AppleTalk protocol suite.

Chapter 4, "AppleTalk Protocols in Action," gives you examples of several of the AppleTalk protocols in action. You learn, for example, which network protocols are used when a Macintosh sends a print job to a LaserWriter.

# Part II: Installing an AppleTalk Network

Part II takes a close look at putting together AppleTalk networks, starting out with the basics of network designs and layout. In this part, we cover LocalTalk and EtherTalk network design as well as the design of large (20 or more zones) networks. You'll find tips on what types of cable and connectors to purchase and what topology pitfalls to avoid. We also cover the new and growing area of remote access in this section.

Chapter 5, "Network Design 101," describes the various topologies you can use for designing your network and the advantages and disadvantages of each. We also introduce you to the concept of fault-tolerant network design.

Chapter 6, "Designing a LocalTalk LAN," builds on the concepts introduced in Chapter 5 and describes in detail the relationship between LocalTalk and other topologies. After covering the physical limits of LocalTalk network topologies, the chapter then goes on to show you what devices, such as repeaters and bridges, you can use to extend the limits of those networks.

Chapter 7, "Installing a LocalTalk LAN," explains how to select connectors and cables for your LocalTalk network and then tells you how to install a LocalTalk LAN in either the daisy-chain, bus, passive star, or active star topology. You learn the importance of testing your network.

Chapter 8, "Designing an Ethernet LAN," describes Ethernet standards and the types of cables and topologies that can be used for Ethernet networks. The chapter then moves on to describe the hardware that's available for connecting Macs and printers to Ethernet and what kind of performance you can expect from Macs on Ethernet networks.

Chapter 9, "Installing an Ethernet LAN," is the Ethernet parallel to Chapter 7, as it explains how to select Ethernet cables and connectors and how to wire them together to create a LAN using either coaxial cable or unshielded twisted-pair wire. The chapter also walks you through the procedures for setting up an Ethernet connection for your Mac.

Chapter 10, "Using Modems with Networks," introduces you to the terminology of modems and telephone systems, including error-detection-and-correction and data-compression protocols. The chapter then discusses how you can share modems on a network. Chapter 10 also has a discussion of remote access, showing you how to bring remote users back to your AppleTalk or TCP/IP LAN.

Chapter 11, "Designing an AppleTalk LAN," explains Apple's concept of internetworking and how you can use routers to join networks together to form larger internetworks.

Chapter 12, "Designing an AppleTalk WAN," is an overview of the methods you can use to connect geographically separated networks, WANs (Wide Area Networks), using some of the newer high-speed transmission services, such as frame relay, ISDN, and ATM. Chapter 12 also shows you how to link up AppleTalk networks over a TCP/IP WAN, such as a corporate backbone.

# Part III: Managing a Network

Part III covers many of the aspects of managing a local area network, from troubleshooting physical cable problems to maintaining security for your data files. In this part, we present procedures for troubleshooting network problems, monitoring network traffic, configuring routers, maintaining security, and keeping track of software usage on your network.

Chapter 13, "Configuring, Monitoring, and Fixing AppleTalk Networks," shows you how to configure an AppleTalk network for optimum performance. You learn about SNMP, the emerging standard in network monitoring tools and how you can use SNMP and other tools to monitor the performance of your AppleTalk network. We also discuss what a network protocol analyzer is, how to find a good one, and how to use one. Finally, we show you some techniques we've learned for fixing AppleTalk networks when they break. It's a long, but worthwhile, chapter.

Chapter 14, "Managing AppleTalk Networks for Management," describes how to handle the nontechnical aspects of network management. This includes disaster recovery plans, network accounting and auditing, keeping track of what hardware and software are on your network, and working with vendors.

Chapter 15, "Securing an AppleTalk Network," shows you how to use routers and other tools to maintain security in an AppleTalk network. Chapter 15 also gives you some guidance in dealing with computer viruses in a network environment.

# Part IV: Integrating Macs into Other Networks

Part IV covers the wide world of networks when AppleTalk and Macintoshes just aren't enough. We show you how to extend AppleTalk networks and network services to non-Macintosh computers. Then we dive into the wide, wide world of protocols (apologies to Marlin Perkins) and show you how to integrate Macintosh computers into TCP/IP, SNA, and OSI networks.

Chapter 16, "Bringing AppleTalk to the Masses," explains how you can integrate Macintosh and non-Macintosh computers in a microcomputer style local area network. We show the many options for extending the reach of AppleTalk file and disk services beyond just Macintosh hardware — to MS-DOS, UNIX, and OpenVMS systems.

Chapter 17, "The World of Protocols," gives you a quick overview of some of the many protocols you can expect to see in networks today. We show you what TCP/IP, DECnet, SNA, and ISO protocols are, as well as the most popular micro-computer LAN protocols, such as Novell's Netware and Banyan's VINES. After reading this chapter, you are at least partially prepared for what comes after!

Chapter 18, "Macs in the World of TCP/IP," shows you how to integrate Macs into a TCP/IP network. We show you some of the software options available to you and tradeoffs in different connection strategies. Chapter 19, "Macs in the World of SNA," and Chapter 20, "Macs in the World of OSI," do the same thing for mainframe-based SNA networks and networks which use OSI services, such as X.400.

# Part V: Using Networks

Part V covers the various types of applications that you may run on your network. We discuss the setup and usage of printers, file servers, and databases, as well as the types of electronic mail and groupware currently available for Macintosh LANs. We also discuss the value of connecting to the world through the Internet.

Chapter 21, "Printing on AppleTalk Networks," describes the differences between print spoolers and print servers and how they should be installed on a network.

Chapter 22, "Sharing Files on AppleTalk Networks," explains how you can use file-transfer utilities and file servers on a LAN, and how distributed and centralized file servers differ from each other. This chapter also includes hints for setting up a centralized file server.

Chapter 23, "Using Groupware," shows you what software is available for users so that they can work together as a group over a network. Groupware includes such items as group schedulers, document editing programs, and document tracking and retrieval programs.

Chapter 24, "Using Electronic Mail," explains how e-mail programs work and the important features that you should look for in an e-mail program. This chapter also introduces you to the types of gateways you can use to link different e-mail systems together.

Chapter 25, "Using the X Window System," shows how you can use a Macintosh as either a server or as a client in a network using the X window system. Chapter 25 also shows you the options for running UNIX on a Macintosh computer.

Chapter 26, "Exploring Mac LANs and the Internet," discusses the issues involved in connecting a Macintosh LAN to the Internet.

# The Stuff in the Back: Appendices

Because you may want to know more details about AppleTalk and TCP/IP, we show you the format of the most popular packets in Appendix A.

Appendix B will show you how to convert your network from a Phase I AppleTalk network to a Phase II AppleTalk network — if you haven't already.

Appendix C will be your resource list of names and addresses of companies we mention throughout the *Macworld Networking Bible*, Second Edition. Macintosh networking often comes down to finding the right software and hardware to put together a working system. Use this appendix to lead you through the Macintosh networking maze.

Appendix D and Appendix E will help you with the acronym filled-world of networking by summarizing the definitions and acronyms we've used. The networking glossary helps define the terms in the ways you will encounter them every day.

# Conventions Used in This book

Certain conventions are used in this book to help you better understand the discussions.

## Sidebars

Certain discussions in this book are expanded with sidebars. These are shaded boxes that contain background information, expert tips and advice, network areas where caution is needed, and other helpful information.

Each sidebar features an icon, or symbol, that hints at the information contained in the sidebar. These icons are designed to alert you to the type of information you will find. Here's what to look for:

The information in this type of sidebar provides background detail on the networking issue under discussion. This is the kind of information and detail that you may not need when skimming the chapter. But the sidebars are most valuable when you require more information on a given topic.

The information in this type of sidebar points out a useful tip (or tips) that can save you a great deal of time and trouble.

The information in this type of sidebar alerts you to potential problems with a networking issue under discussion. Solutions and ways to avoid the scary situation are also included.

The quotables appear at the beginning of most chapters. We selected quotes we believe help set the tone for the material covered in the chapter.

As you'll soon find out, networking involves some complicated systems. The step-by-step boxes provide detailed, stepwise instructions that show you how to perform specific tasks or procedures.

## Concepts and Terms

Each chapter concludes with a helpful concepts and terms section.

---

### CONCEPTS AND TERMS

- In this *concepts* section, the major topics discussed in the chapter are summarized.
- Several bulleted items provide a concise review of the major points.
- The concepts section is also a helpful index when referring to the chapter at a later time.

**Terms Section**
In this section, the important terms covered in the chapter are defined. Each term will be introduced in alphabetical order and followed by an *expanded* definition.

**More Detailed Definition**
If you come across a new term in the chapter, and the brief definition there doesn't satisfy you, jump ahead to the Concepts and Terms section for a more detailed description.

---

## Special notations

The dollar sign ($) represents the start of a string of hexidecimal numbers. For example, an Ethernet address would be written like this: **$0800899a724b.**

Note that hexadecimal numbers, on-screen information, code, and commands you type in are indicated in **bold type.**

## Feedback, Please!

We appreciate your feedback. Please feel free to contact us in care of IDG Books Worldwide with questions or comments. Of course, being a networked world, we prefer you send e-mail. You can send to "mnb@Opus1.COM" and it will reach the *Macworld Networking Bible* team.

# I

# Introducing
# Networking

# Understanding Connectivity

IN THIS CHAPTER

- Definition of a computer network
- Evolution of computers and networks
- Examples of computer networks in use
- Special qualities of AppleTalk networks

During the Industrial Revolution, machines augmented, enhanced, and replaced the power of human and animal muscles. If you had better machines, you were able to leverage the power of your people to make goods with greater precision, speed, accuracy, and durability. The world economy turned upside down in 100 years because of the utilization of machines. Businesses that adapted to this new machine-driven era survived and prospered. Those that continued to depend on the direct labor of people could not compete.

The drive for better, faster, and more reliable machines took a dramatic turn in the late 1930s.

In 1937, a professor at Harvard University named Howard Aiken made a convincing proposal to International Business Machines Corporation. Aiken wanted to build a new, revolutionary machine: a stored-program digital computer. He won IBM's support and created the Automatic Sequence Controlled Calculator, later known as the Harvard Mark I. The machine was built at IBM's Endicott Development Laboratories, and became operational in August, 1944.

Sometime between 1937 and 1944, the Industrial Revolution ended and the Information Revolution began.

Information is power, wealth, and security. For the past 50 years, organizations have gathered, stored, and used information as an integral part of their businesses. They can't live without it.

QUOTABLES

"Nothing in life is to be feared. It is only to be understood."

— Marie Curie

Today, computer networks are vital to a successful organization. In this book, we're going to go deep into the world of networks and show you how you can link computers in your organization to build networks. We're going to start at the very bottom, with the wires, connectors, boards, and cards. And we'll work our way all the way to the top in order to show you how to use networks to pass around information and make your organization more successful.

# What Is a Computer Network?

A network is a collection of devices that share a common purpose and are interconnected in some way. A *computer network* is a collection of computing devices, such as personal computers, large mainframe computers, printers, and modems. This collection of devices is interconnected so that all devices can share information. Such information might include stock quotes, a printed report, or even a typed message about the next intramural baseball game. It is important to remember three key words from this definition: *collection, interconnected,* and *sharing.*

A single personal computer connected to a printer is not a network. Neither is a computer attached to a modem. But if you connect more than one computer to a cable to use a printer and share information with each other, you have created a network.

What can be connected to a network? We mentioned the basic devices — personal computers, printers, and modems. You may also connect larger computers, such as minicomputers, mainframes, and supercomputers, to your network. Or you may use a cellular modem to link a portable computer to a network. The possibilities are nearly endless. In this book, we'll introduce you to many of the common networked devices, as well as the common applications of Macintosh networks.

Before we show you examples of Macintosh networks, we'll take a look at the evolution of computer networks from the first electronic computers to the sophisticated multiplatform networks of the present day.

# A Short History of Networking

The first electronic computers were huge beasts of vacuum tubes and relays that required air-conditioned rooms and teams of workers just to keep running. Not just anyone could go into the computer room and start programming the computer to solve a problem. In fact, very few people even knew how to program these computers. Usually, a group of workers strived day and night to coddle the big computers — called *mainframes* — as the machines solved the assigned problems. Often, the computers and their support teams were in a large room all by themselves, isolated from the rest of the workers or users.

Because the computers represented a large corporate investment, these rooms often had large glass windows so that executives and other visitors could see the results of their investment. (The situation hasn't changed much today — the glass rooms and large computers are still around. And most experts believe they are likely to stay around for some time to come.)

As these large computers became more sophisticated, they could actually process more than one job at a time — a capability known as *time-sharing.*

Time-sharing led to the first attempts at networking, more properly known as *terminal networking*. Each user could sit at a computer terminal located somewhere in the building and submit jobs to the computer for processing. The computer queued jobs according to the job's requirements and available resources. The computer then ran a few jobs at the same time, spitting back results to the users at their terminals (or on a printer).

As the technology of computers improved, it became possible to move computing resources from glass houses and onto desktops. The new computers weren't just smaller and faster versions of their mainframe and minicomputer cousins. They had fundamental differences in architecture.

These new systems were called *personal computers*, which is to say that they were not meant to be shared at all. Whereas a minicomputer might have hundreds of terminals capable of displaying characters and symbols, every personal computer had a single display tube with color, graphics, sound, and animation. Personal computers today are often called *workstations*. There are some distinctions between the two terms, but the differences are mostly the subject of cocktail party arguments.

Until LAN systems came along, each personal computer was fairly isolated from the other personal computers. In fact, *sneakernet* was the main transport for exchanging data (see related backgrounder called "Transferring Files the Old-Fashioned Way").

With the introduction of *local area networks* (LANs) composed of personal computers, a major change in the control of communications occurred. With mainframes, most, if not all, of the intelligence and communications control was located at the mainframe and not at the terminals. With personal computer LANs, however, the computing intelligence and communications control could be distributed among the computers. As a result, communications control was built into the network itself.

BACKGROUNDER

### Transferring Files the Old-Fashioned Way

Sneakernet is a common term denoting a non-network method for transferring files between computers. With sneakernet, you transfer the files by walking — in your sneakers, of course — from computer to computer with a floppy disk containing the files.

Although we often put down the idea of sneakernet, noted networker Andrew Tanenbaum reminds us that a computer network is not always the best way to transfer huge amounts of data: "Never underestimate the bandwidth of a station wagon full of magnetic tapes hurling down the highway."

There's a tendency to associate the term networking with the smaller Mac- and MS-DOS-based computers and workstations. This reflects a frequent pairing of the term network with LAN. But there's more to connectivity than just networking as we've defined it here. Connectivity means connecting to and exchanging data with any kind of computer, small or large, wherever it may be. So although most of this book focuses on LANs, we will devote an entire section to using a Mac to connect to mainframe computers, with or without a LAN (see Chapter 19, "Macs in the World of SNA.")

# Sharing Information and Resources

In today's competitive work environment, working with other people, either in your own company or with your customers, is a must. That means that if you're not networked now, you probably soon will be.

Networks are built for two main purposes: sharing resources and sharing information. Resources can include such tangible items as expensive computer peripherals — laser printers, imagesetters, slide makers, and so on. Information, on the other hand, is likely to be the lifeblood of your enterprise. All those sales reports, parts inventories and orders, sales contacts, and personnel histories are integral requirements of business.

You may assert that you can share all this information without a network; after all, you've already got sneakernet, so you can copy your files to a floppy disk and take them down the hall to someone else's Mac.

That philosophy may work in some situations. But what about the times when the person you're sharing data with is in another building, another city, or in another country, and the person needs the information *right now*? In these cases, sneakernet just won't cut it. You need a real live network to make data exchange easier, regardless of the scale.

One of the most important advantages of sharing information on a network is the capability to continually update information. As an example, imagine what the New York Stock Exchange would be like if every stock transaction had to be hand-carried to a computer operator, who entered the transaction and then printed out a report for every interested party. Even worse, imagine that this manual exchange had to be accomplished with the interested parties residing all over the country, and that each party required delivery of the information at the same time. That's what would happen without a network. By the time some of the reports were printed, they would most likely be out of date.

With a network, the transaction can be entered once and that data is shared immediately with everyone who needs it. You can get the same type of interaction by sharing data in special files (usually in a database installed on a file server) with the other members of your workgroup. The data may include your company's current inventory, and by using a network everyone gets the same data at the same time. This sharing of information from one central source also ensures that duplicate, perhaps incorrect, data isn't being circulated.

In our opinion, sharing information is a more important justification for networks than sharing resources. It's true that not everyone has a personal LaserWriter, and networks are an effective way to share printers. But printing reports and memos is only a small portion of what networks can help you accomplish. Information sharing can help you and your business accomplish a great deal more.

In addition, future networks are likely to offer even more opportunities to share and use information than you thought possible. But for now we're not going to get starry-eyed here about future prospects. We're concerned here with what networks can do to help you and your business right now.

Versatility is one of the greatest appeals of networking. You can do so many different things with a computer network. If you surveyed a group of network users, you'd probably get different responses from each of them, where each pointed out different ways that the network worked to his or her benefit. We'll go through a few examples to give you a flavor of how networks help you work.

## Using electronic mail and groupware

Electronic mail, commonly called *e-mail*, is just what its name implies: an electronic form of paper mail that follows the same type of conventions used by intercompany mail or the U.S. Postal Service. You type a note on your Mac, select the names of the people it's supposed to go to, and send it over the network. (We give more details of e-mail in Chapter 24.)

A new class of computer software, called *groupware*, is similar to e-mail. Groupware is designed to make the exchange of information among a group of workers easier by having the networked computers take care of some of the details. For example, the computer network can keep track of a group's schedules. The network may also track different versions of a report and automatically update changes to that report that anyone in the workgroup makes. We'll discuss groupware in Chapter 23.

## Relieving telephone tag

When Steve Jobs introduced the Macintosh computer at Apple Computer, he claimed that he wanted to make the Mac an information appliance as simple to use as the telephone. But, the downside of telephone calls is that the person you're trying to reach sometimes isn't there to take your call. Often, we're left talking to an answering machine or voice mail. Conversely, even if a human being is answering phones for you, your desk may get covered with slips of paper from past phone calls that you weren't able to take.

Fortunately, computer networks don't suffer from the same problems as telephone networks. With products like electronic mail, your computer can take care of relaying information to others whether or not they're available at the time. So instead of passing telephone messages back and forth as you try to talk to each other (rather than each other's voice mail), you can compose a lengthy discussion of a subject and mail it to your co-worker. The co-worker can sit down, read your message, think about it, and compose a suitable reply. Each of you gets to do this at your leisure, and you'll have accomplished something when the process is finished. If nothing else, the hassle level is greatly reduced when compared to playing telephone tag.

Of course, you can't always avoid telephone tag, even if everyone in your company uses e-mail. The system may not include all of your clients and contacts in the outside world. But electronic mail is still helpful in these cases. A receptionist answering your phone can use e-mail to send you all the telephone messages, rather than writing them down and adding them to the pile of papers on your desk.

## Scheduling and holding meetings

Meetings are one of the most common activities of businesses. Keeping track of all the meetings you have to attend as well as their agendas can often seem like an overwhelming task. But there are ways to use a computer network to keep track of and schedule meetings more easily than with paper-based systems.

You can use e-mail to send notices to your co-workers about a proposed meeting. You might include the agenda for the meeting or even attach a spreadsheet or graphics to be discussed at the meeting. When the other workers receive their e-mail, they can read your proposal and send back a reply. They may confirm that they'll be there, give you an excuse why they can't make it, or even offer comments on your agenda. All this can be done via e-mail, without using a single piece of paper.

As mentioned previously, groupware software can accomplish the same thing. One type of groupware handles meeting schedules by searching workers' schedules for open time slots and identifying a feasible date and time. A product called Meeting Maker XP (ON Technology) does this for networked Macintoshes and MS-DOS personal computers.

Groupware can do more than just schedule meetings. Many companies are working on network software to help you conduct meetings electronically. Today, a meeting is a bunch of people in a room waiting for the meeting to end. With *electronic meeting systems*, a kind of groupware, the entire definition of a meeting is changing. Meetings can be held at any time, in any place, with people participating from many separate locations. In addition, electronic assistants can help the process of idea generation, decision making, and problem solving — all using computer networks.

# Using a shared database

Databases have become a common way to store and share information over a network. That's because everyone who accesses the data stored in a database sees the same data, and any changes are extended to everyone else using the database. Databases also offer security options which you can use to control access to the data. For instance, some users may be able to change or update the data, while others may only use the data to generate reports.

### Passing around sales contacts

If you work in a sales department, you probably have a method for sharing new sales contacts. For example, if you receive or find leads meant for someone else's territory, you may have a way to distribute the information to the right person. Or it may be that the sales manager distributes the workload of new leads.

Although you may feel that this system works (with a few glitches now and then), this is another area where networked computers can help. One way of maintaining a collection of sales information to be shared is to set up a shared database on a file server. This database can compile essential information about each sales lead and may even include assignments. Because this shared database is centrally located on the network, sharing data is easier than if each salesperson were to store sales information in a separate database on his or her own Mac.

### Tracking inventory

Tracking your company's inventory is another effective use of a shared database. The inventory database might be more complicated than our previous example, as it probably contains information on parts availability, suppliers, pending orders, and many more items.

Users access this centralized database in various ways. The level of access to the information is usually determined by groups within the company. The receiving department can update new parts shipments, and the accounting department can generate billings directly from the same database. Sales can check the status of previous orders, and managers can track the product flow into and out of the company. The basic data that everyone sees is the same; it's just that each user is allowed to access the data that's specific to the user's needs. Because data is stored in a central location, it's easier to verify that everyone's talking about the same numbers, and that everything's up to date.

# Sharing files

Assume that it's time to prepare a special sales report that requires input from a group of your co-workers. Here again, using the network can make your job easier.

First, you should realize that what we mean by "the network" isn't geographically restricted. Your co-workers may be all in the same building or may be scattered around the city, the state, or even the world. With a properly designed network, this geographic scatter makes no difference.

The basic function of the network is to exchange ideas and files among workers. You may choose a simple file-transfer program to send word processing and graphics files to the other worker, or you may decide to keep all the files necessary for the report on a file server that everyone can access. Tracking files is a bit easier if everyone works on the files from a central location, as on a file server.

There are also some groupware products designed to make some steps of report generation easier. With these products, you can work with the rest of your co-workers on a report document at the same time, and everyone can see changes as they occur. Such a process might be difficult to coordinate if the work team were located all over the world, though. Another way is to use groupware that coordinates different versions of the document, showing the changes suggested by each team member to the document's owner. (If these items sound interesting, you may want to jump ahead to Chapter 23 where we talk about exciting groupware products.)

We hope that this gives you a feel for what you can do with a computer network, with a minimum of hype — we work with networks every day, so we know that the hype doesn't do anything to improve connectivity.

# Macs and Connectivity

We live in a multinational world. In similar fashion, our businesses run in a multicomputer world. It's more common for companies to have a network using more than one vendor's computers than it is to see only one type of computer throughout the company. In this multicomputer world, no vendor's computer can afford to be an island unto itself. Connectivity, or the ability to share information with other types of computers, is *de rigueur*. Like many other computers, Apple's Macintosh computers offer many ways to connect to other computing systems and different types of networks to exchange data. Throughout this book, we'll show you how Macs can be connected to each other using their built-in networking support, and how Macs can connect to other systems and computers.

## AppleTalk and networking

The first half of this book is primarily about AppleTalk. Why? The answer's fairly simple — when someone begins the process of connecting Macs, the first network they try is AppleTalk. This preference stems from two reasons. First, AppleTalk support has been built into every Mac since the first one rolled off Apple's assembly lines. Second, the user interface to networks provided by AppleTalk is probably the easiest to use of any currently available.

Don't underestimate the advantage the Mac has provided by including a built-in interface to networking. This support has made it easy for users to experiment with networking. In this way, they can discover what works, what doesn't work, and whether a network will solve their problems or create new ones.

By incorporating AppleTalk within the Mac, Apple also gave developers a single standard to use when creating network applications. Developers no longer have to worry about the type of network interface being used or whether any network drivers (the interface to the network card) are installed. Network support comes with each Mac, and activating it is as easy as clicking a button in the Chooser. This feature makes some parts of network development easier than before.

Even though developers have benefited, the real winners from Apple's technology are the users. One of the distinguishing features of the Macintosh is Apple's attention to detail regarding the user interface. The interface makes it as easy and intuitive as possible to do things without reading many manuals. Apple has paid a great deal of attention to the user interface for networking from the beginning. It was a natural outgrowth of creating the Macintosh itself and its distinctive user interface. Apple wanted to make sure that the ease of use that the Mac is known for would extend to networking as well.

One of the principal mechanisms for making the network interface more understandable for the user is AppleTalk's use of *named entities*. This means that with AppleTalk, you choose the networked devices, such as laser printers and file servers, by their names, not by some cryptic number, as is common in other networking systems. Your Mac also has a name on the network, which makes it easier for others to identify the Mac in order to send information or to deal with a problem.

AppleTalk also allows you to create logical subdivisions of your network, called *zones*, making it easier for users to find services on the network. These subdivisions can be named appropriately for your company, such as zones for Accounting, Marketing, Sales, and Engineering; or zones may be Bldg. 1: First Floor, Bldg. 2: First Floor, and Bldg 2: Second Floor. (For details, see Chapters 2 and 11.)

## Connecting to other computers

We said that no computer can afford to act as an island. The Mac is no exception. That's why the second half of this book is about the other types of networks — other than AppleTalk networks — that the Macintosh can connect to. Fortunately, both Apple and third-party vendors have seen to it that the hardware and software you may need to connect to other computers are easily available and inexpensive. This is true whether the computer is a personal computer running DOS, a larger computer running Digital's OpenVMS operating system, one of IBM's mainframe-based operating systems, or one of the many flavors of UNIX. The Mac can connect to and communicate with them all.

### The Many Flavors of UNIX

The UNIX Operating System started as a project of Ken Thompson at Bell Telephone Laboratories in 1969. The first version of UNIX ran on a Digital PDP-7 computer and was written entirely in assembly language It was rewritten in a language called "B" the next year. Dennis Ritchie, another Bell Labs researcher, led the development of a new language called "C" (because it came after "B"), and a version of UNIX that could be easily ported to different machine architectures was completed in 1973.

Since then, literally dozens of different operating systems have been developed, all of which are based, at least a little bit, on the original UNIX operating system from Bell Labs. When people bandy about the word *UNIX*, they are speaking of one of the many different operating systems which look more or less alike. To keep things straight, we will refer to this whole confusing puzzle as "UNIX-flavored Operating Systems."

Apple has worked to persuade other vendors to provide support for connectivity from Macs to other computers. At the same time, Apple has also attempted to guide vendors in the use of the Mac interface and its approach to networking. Thus, when using the Mac, you see that you may use a variety of network services on other types of computers, but the interface to those services will probably look very much like the same one you use on an AppleTalk network with your Mac. This perhaps gives the Mac the most transparent interface to multivendor networking available at this time, making the Mac a *universal client* to all kinds of network services. Later in this book, we will demonstrate how this *universal* connectivity can be achieved.

# CHAPTER 1 CONCEPTS AND TERMS

- A network is a group of devices that are interconnected for a common purpose.

- Computer networks are only one of many different kinds of networks that we come into contact with on a daily basis.

- The main reasons for networking are sharing resources and sharing information.

- Every Mac has built-in support for Apple's AppleTalk networking system.

- Tools are available for connecting the Mac to almost every kind of major computer.

## AppleTalk
The network architecture for printer, disk, and information sharing developed by Apple Computer for their Macintosh systems. AppleTalk runs over different kinds of LANs, including **LocalTalk** and **EtherTalk**.

## electronic meeting systems
This is a kind of groupware that makes meetings possible at any time, in any place, with people participating from many separate locations.

## groupware
A new class of computer software, similar to e-mail. Groupware is designed to make the exchange of information among a group of workers easier by having the networked computers take care of some of the details. For example, the computer network can keep track of a group's schedules.

## LAN
A **local area network** with some special characteristics, such as very high speed, very low error rate, and small geographical area.

## network
A collection of computing systems, such as computers, printers, resource servers, and the wires which connect them all; interconnected for information and resource sharing.

## sneakernet
Common term denoting a non-network method for transferring files between computers. With sneakernet, you transfer the files by walking — in your sneakers — from computer to computer with a floppy disk containing the files.

## terminal networking
Describes a system where each user can sit at a computer terminal located somewhere in a building and submit jobs to a central computer for processing. The computer queues jobs according to the job's requirements and available resources. The computer then runs a few jobs at the same time, spitting back the results.

## workstation
Also **personal computer**, a computer with display, storage, and network connections all devoted to the needs of a single user. Contrast this with a **mainframe**, **supercomputer**, or **minicomputer**, where multiple users share the resources of a single system.

## UNIX
An operating system developed by Bell Telephone Laboratories. There are many variations that fall under the UNIX label. Macintosh networks can (and often must) work with the many different types of UNIX.

# Understanding Networks

IN THIS CHAPTER

- The components of a network
- How a computer connects to the network
- The electrical basics of network signals
- How a networking system controls network traffic
- What devices can be used to build larger networks
- Some unique features of AppleTalk networks

So far we've introduced you to some examples of how you can use networks in your business. But a network isn't just something you install and forget about. The networks themselves are far from transparent — aside from doing such tasks as transferring files or sending faxes differently, you're usually aware of the wires and connectors that have been added to your computer to connect to the network.

In this chapter, we focus on the various aspects of any physical network: the cables, the electrical signals transmitted on those cables, how your computer is attached to the network's cables, and how your computer communicates with other computers. We also introduce you to the basics of other network devices that are used to build networks larger than those found on a single floor of a building or contained in a single building. Then we point out some of the concepts of AppleTalk networking.

## The Components of the Network

A network needs both hardware and software to work. On the hardware side are the cables used to carry the network's signals, the connectors between a computer and the network cable, and any electronics required to interface the computer to the network. As you'll see when we discuss networking protocols in Chapter 3, "Understanding AppleTalk Protocols," these items form what's known as the *physical layer*.

In order for these electronic items to do something useful, you need some software on your computer to communicate with the network hardware — this is the job of one or more software drivers that work with your computer's operating system. The most basic functions of the drivers form a network's *data link layer*, but drivers can also perform network functions that are defined by other protocol layers.

QUOTABLES

"Purgamentum init, exit purgamentum."
(Garbage In, Garbage Out)

# Network media

Networks can be constructed out of almost anything that can transmit a signal (excepting smoke signals, but including avian carriers — the famous *PigeonNet*). Copper cabling is the most common means of carrying network signals, but there's an increasing use of fiber optic cables that use photons, or light signals, rather than electrons to carry the signals. Wireless local area networks, which use infrared light or radio frequencies to transmit signals in a large room or a small building, are also becoming very popular. Large networks are often created using microwave, spread spectrum, or satellite links to connect smaller geographically distant networks, such as when a large multinational corporation needs to link together all of its branch offices.

Throughout this book, we focus on the various types of cables that use electrical signals for a network because cables make up the majority of networks today. We don't cover fiber optic or wireless networks, except in passing.

The two most common cable types for networks are *coaxial* cables and *twisted-pair* cables (see Figure 2-1). Coaxial cable looks like the cable for your cable-TV hookup. These cables use a center conductor for transmitting a signal and are surrounded with insulation and a wire braid or a similar conductive sheet to shield the conductor from outside interference.

This shielding makes these types of cables ideal for use in noisy environments, such as factories. Shielding also reduces the strength of the signal that is broadcast out of the wire, reducing the chance of interception and snooping. Any wire carrying an oscillating electrical signal acts as an antenna, broadcasting the signal to the space

BACKGROUNDER

## What Is Spread Spectrum?

Spread spectrum is a technology for transmitting signals using radio frequency in the presence of noise. It was developed for the military because the spread spectrum transmission techniques provide resistance to jamming, interference, and interception. Spread spectrum also minimizes interference to other users.

There are two commonly used types of spread spectrum: frequency hopping and direct sequence.

In frequency hopping systems, the transmitter abruptly changes (hops) in accordance with a pseudo-random pattern synchronized between transmitter and receiver. The receiver tracks these changes.

In direct sequence systems, a more complex algorithm for frequency changes provides greater bandwidth and resistance to interference.

Spread spectrum is commonly used in short-haul building-to-building networks at speeds of 1M bps or more.

(air or vacuum) outside the wire. High-tech snoops can use radiated signals to eavesdrop on your network from across the street without ever entering your building. In Chapter 15, "Securing an AppleTalk Network," we show you some ways of guarding against high-tech snooping.

Twisted-pair cables are constructed just as their name suggests. These cables are pairs of insulated copper wire wound around each other, much like strands of DNA. These pairs are placed with other twisted-pairs inside a larger insulated casing. The twists within a pair (measured by the *pitch*, or number of twists per foot) help reduce the electrical interference between signals transmitted on the wires (this interference is called *crosstalk*). Simple twisted-pair cable may contain only two or three pairs, but the heftier twisted-pair cable, such as that used for corporate phone installations and networks, may contain 25 or more pairs. The telephone wires you see on telephone poles start at 500 pairs and go up from there.

Networks use two types of twisted-pair cable — *unshielded* and *shielded* (refer again to the diagram in Figure 2-1). The shielding performs the same function as the shielding in coaxial cable — it reduces the interference from electrical sources outside of the cable. In general, however, the electrical interaction (*capacitance*) between the shielding and the cable it protects means that a signal cannot be transmitted as far in a shielded cable as in a similar cable without the shielding. Therefore, when deciding between unshielded and shielded cable, your choice should be guided by the amount of noise in your network environment, as well as by the length of your network cabling. Don't be deceived by cable vendors who tell you that shielded cables increase your ability to send a signal over longer distances; that's usually not true. (See Part II, "Installing an AppleTalk Network," for more details.)

The wire used in twisted-pair cable is solid, not stranded, copper wire. The thickness of the wire is most often expressed as American Wire Gauge (AWG). The diameter of a wire is inversely related to the AWG number. For example, 24 AWG wire is thinner than 22 AWG because the AWG number is the number of wires of that size that can fit in a standard area.

## Cable connections

The purpose of the network cable is to transmit electrical signals, which are received and processed by each computer's electrical interface to the network. We go into detail on the nature of these signals in the following section. What we want to emphasize here is that each computer, or other networked device (such as a printer), requires an electrical interface between itself and the cable. In a local area network, this interface is known as a *transceiver* because it both transmits and receives the network signals.

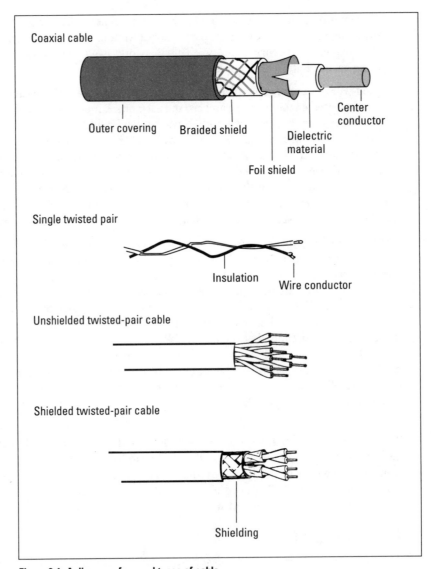

**Figure 2-1: A diagram of several types of cable.**

Part of the transceiver's job is to distinguish between true network signals and noise. The transceiver also converts the analog electrical signals traveling on the network cable to the binary 0s and 1s (digital bits) that computers can understand and process.

QUICK TIPS

## Keeping Twisted-Pairs Straight

Twisted-pair cable uses a color code to help everyone keep things straight. No matter how many pairs are in your cable, you'll see some variation on the same color coding. Wires are marked as pairs, each pair having two colors. For example, the first pair is usually colored blue and white. One wire in the pair is white with blue stripes and the other is blue with white stripes. To keep things simple, there are ten colors used, always in the same order in every cable. Five of the colors are major colors; the other five are minor colors. Each major color is paired with all five minor colors before the next major color is used. For example, the first pair in a cable is White/

Blue, the second White/Orange, the fifth White/Slate, the sixth Red/Blue, and the twenty-fifth Violet/Slate.

| Major Colors | Minor Colors |
|---|---|
| White | Blue |
| Red | Orange |
| Black | Green |
| Yellow | Brown |
| Violet | Slate |

In many cases, the transceiver is a small box connected by a cable to the *Network Interface Card* (NIC), also called the *Network Interface Unit* (NIU), that's installed in your computer. This describes the setup for one type of Ethernet cable, called *thick-wire* Ethernet (see Chapter 8, "Designing an Ethernet LAN," for more information). Network interface boards for the remaining two major types of Ethernet, *thin-wire* Ethernet and *10BASE-T* (also called *twisted-pair* Ethernet), almost always use a transceiver that's part of the NIC. With Apple's LocalTalk wiring scheme, the transceiver is built into each Mac and LaserWriter; an external connection box is connected to the network cable, and a cable connects this box to the transceiver's port on the Mac or LaserWriter (see Figure 2-2).

BACKGROUNDER

## What Is a Transceiver?

A *transceiver*, which transmits *and* receives the network's signals, distinguishes between true network signals and noise and also converts analog signals to binary signals.

The external connection device that connects to the network cable is also often called a *Medium Attachment Unit*, or MAU. This term is usually restricted to external connection devices that include a transceiver, such as the one just described for thick-wire Ethernet. A MAU connects to the NIC or NIU via an *Attachment Unit Interface* (AUI) cable, or *drop cable*, which plugs into the AUI socket on the NIC.

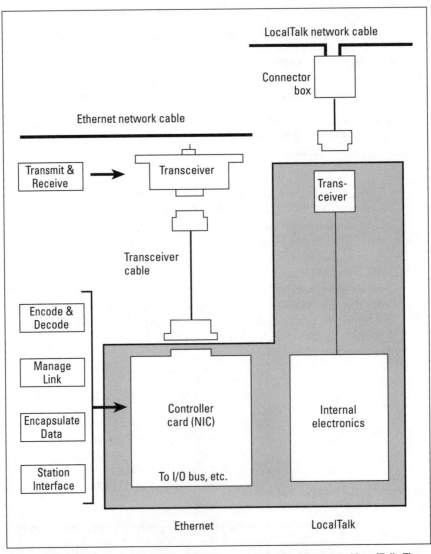

**Figure 2-2: A block diagram of a typical workstation connection for Ethernet and LocalTalk. The shaded area represents the computer's hardware.**

## What's in the station?

On a LAN, it doesn't really matter what kind of device is attached to the network. Printers, computers, and all sorts of other systems are called *stations*, which is a generic term for anything on a LAN that can send and receive network traffic. Whether or not the network transceiver is located outside of your computer, the remainder of the electronics for processing a network signal is found within your computer.

Macintoshes and LaserWriters have a chip on the motherboard that can interpret LocalTalk signals and communicate with the microprocessor and its operating system. For Ethernet, most Macs require an interface card (or an external box using the SCSI or a serial port), which includes buffers for storing incoming and outgoing packets and the rest of the processing electronics. The newer Mac Quadras have Ethernet built into the motherboard.

In either case, the operating system must include software that can communicate with, and control, the network interface. This type of software is called a *driver*.

BACKGROUNDER

### What Is a Driver?

A driver (sometimes called a device driver) contains the computer instructions to process incoming bits and to recognize their patterns according to certain rules known as *protocols*. When the computer is sending data to the network, the driver also ensures that the outgoing bits are properly arranged so that your computer can communicate with other stations on the network.

# An Introduction to Network Signals

The electrical signals that are transmitted over network cables are much more complex than the alternating current that's flowing in your home's electrical wiring. In this section, we discuss the basics of how network signals are created and how to combat the problems of noise and other interference.

## Creating signals

We've said that signals are transmitted throughout a network by cables. These signals resemble the alternating current in your home's electrical supply. The signals change, or *oscillate*, continuously from one voltage to another in a regular manner.

Electrical signals are usually specified with two numbers. The first number is the signal's *amplitude*, or the difference between the maximum and minimum voltage. The second number is the signal's *frequency*, or how many times per second it cycles from maximum to minimum voltage and back again. A signal that has a smooth oscillation between the voltages is called a *sine wave*, which resembles a smooth-topped hill next to a broad, smooth valley.

But computers deal with binary digits — the 0s and 1s that have no values between them. If the maximum voltage of a sine wave means "1" and the minimum voltage means "0," what do all the rest of the voltages in the sine wave mean?

In order to make electrical signals represent 0s and 1s on a cable, engineers have combined sine waves together to form a *square wave*. The trick is to use a number of varied sine waves, each with a different amplitude and a different frequency (see Figure 2-3). The resultant square wave now remains most of the time at either the maximum or minimum voltage, and the transition from one to the other is very rapid compared to the period the wave spends at the maximum or minimum.

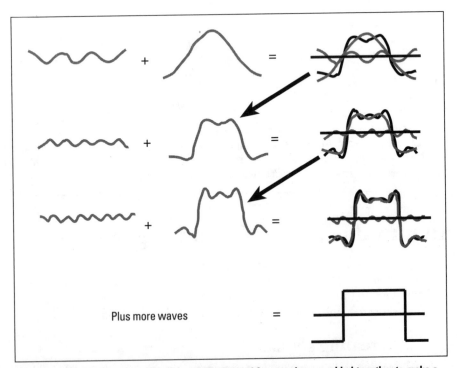

Figure 2-3: These sine waves of various amplitudes and frequencies are added together to make a square wave. The horizontal black line represents the result of adding waves together.

To take this concept further, we can use the maximum of the square wave to represent a binary 0 or a 1 from the station and the minimum of the square wave to represent the other value of the binary 0 or 1. Figures 2-4 and 2-5 are diagrams of this concept. The maximum and minimum threshold values indicated by the jagged lines in Figure 2-4 represent the maximum and minimum voltages that the transceiver's electronics can detect as a signal. Any wave that falls between the maximum and minimum threshold values (as shown in Figure 2-5) is not detected by the transceiver because the wave is smaller than either the maximum or minimum threshold value.

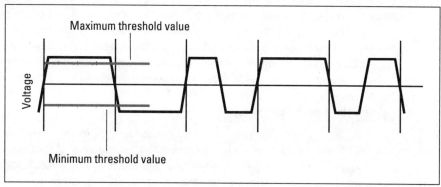

**Figure 2-4: A typical square wave used for a network signal.**

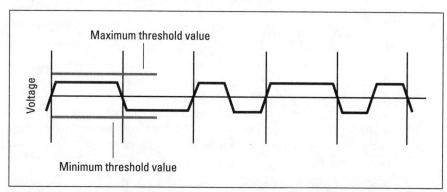

**Figure 2-5: An example of a weakened square wave signal that is lower than the transceiver's threshold.**

# Erroneous signals

Nothing in life is perfect, and neither are electrical wires and cables. The laws of physics are such that wires resist the flow of electrons from one end of a wire to the other. This property is called *resistance*, which is measured in *ohms* and varies from one kind of wire to another. Wires also resist changes from one voltage to another, such as when a sine wave passes through. This phenomenon, called *impedance*, is also measured in ohms, partly because impedance is electrically related to the resistance.

Resistance and impedance are two of the reasons why a network station's signal may never make it to another station on the network. Both of these cable properties act to absorb a signal, weakening it and dissipating the absorbed energy as heat. If the cable's length between the two stations is too great, your signal may be reduced to a low enough voltage that the receiving station never "hears" it (refer to Figure 2-5). That's why all networking schemes have limits to the maximum distance between the first and last stations on the network. There are also devices called *repeaters*, which can boost, or *amplify*, the network signals. We explain these devices later in this chapter.

Electrical signals don't always retain their original shape as they pass through a wire because the impedance of a wire changes with the frequency of the signal. Let's go back to our square wave, which is composed of multiple sine waves, each having a different frequency. A wire's impedance acts with different strength on the waves making up the square wave in a process called *attenuation*. With enough attenuation, the signal may no longer resemble a square wave, and the transceiver may not recognize it as a network signal (see Figure 2-6).

# Encoding signals

A transceiver can have problems even with a good strong signal. That's because a transceiver receiving a signal has to be synchronized with the transceiver that sent the signal, meaning that the receiving station must know where the signal starts and where the signal ends. If the receiving transceiver doesn't detect the beginning of a signal at the right time, chances are good that it will eventually miss one of the bits in the frame — this problem is most likely to happen when there's a long string of binary 0s or 1s.

A transceiver with an extremely accurate clock might carefully measure the width of the square wave representing a 0 or a 1 and thereby keep track of the signal, counting binary digits as it goes along. But any drift or inaccuracy in the clock eventually causes the transceiver to lose track of a digit. It's not only difficult to create a clock that is this accurate, it's also expensive. Fortunately, there are *encoding* methods that keep one transceiver synchronized with another transceiver.

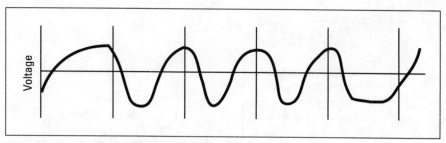

**Figure 2-6: An example of an attenuated square wave.**

Rather than depending on the width of a square wave signal to represent a bit, most network systems rely on different representations, or *encodings*, of 0s and 1s. A basic encoding method is called NRZ, or *Non-Return to Zero* (see Figure 2-7). In NRZ, two separate voltage levels, one positive and one negative, are used to represent the two binary digits, 0 and 1. One form of NRZ encoding, NRZ-level or NRZ-L, uses a negative voltage to represent a binary 1 and a positive voltage to represent a binary 0.

However, all the NRZ encoding methods make it difficult to detect where one bit ends and another begins. A more popular and reliable encoding method is *Manchester encoding* (see Figure 2-7), which is used, for example, by Ethernet networks. Manchester encoding always has a transition from high to low voltage (or vice versa) within the signal that represents one bit. By detecting this additional transition, a transceiver can always tell that it has detected one bit. The presence of this predictable transition within each bit's representation makes it possible for transceivers to remain synchronized. Such encodings are called *self-clocking codes*.

# Getting the Message Through

Imagine that you're in a crowded room, perhaps at a cocktail party, with a group of people, all of whom are talking at the same time. In this chaotic scene, your chances of holding a decent conversation for any length of time are pretty slim. But now imagine something even worse — each person in the room is talking non-stop, without taking a breath, and not bothering to listen at all (which may not be uncommon at such gatherings). At this kind of party, your best bet is to grab a glass of wine and simply nod your head from time to time.

Networks have to deal with the same sort of communication problems. Two conditions are necessary on a network to ensure that two stations can communicate with each other reliably. First, no station can transmit data on the network endlessly. Second, each station must have a system for giving way to another station so that other stations can transmit data on the network.

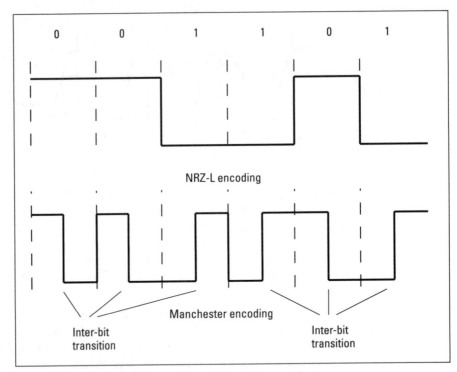

**Figure 2-7: An example of NRZ-L encoding and Manchester encoding**

Networks deal with the first problem by dividing your computer's data into groups of bits called *frames*, or *packets*. In addition to the data that you send from your computer, a frame contains information about the source and destination of the data — the network address of the stations on the network.

The frame, or packet, also contains information about which rules, or *protocols*, were used by the computer to create the frame. If you send more data than will fit into one frame, your computer divides the data into smaller groups and sends as many frames as necessary to transmit all the data. So now you've got your computer saying something but still taking a breath every so often.

We still haven't dealt with the problem of having more than one station transmit on the network at the same time. If a group of computers started transmitting their signals simultaneously on the network, the signals would mix together unintelligibly, much like the commotion at the cocktail party. None of the computers could distinguish the original signals.

Network designers have developed a number of ways to deal with this problem, which is commonly called *contention*. We'll briefly describe the two most common ways of overcoming network contention. These methods are known as *carrier sensing* and *token passing*.

BACKGROUNDER

## What Are Frames, Packets, and Messages?

Bits, Bytes, Frames, Packets, and Messages are all used to describe the passing of information across a network. What's the difference? It depends on the network you're talking about, but a good rule of thumb is that *bits* and *bytes* are the lowest level of data, usually at the wire, or physical, layer. Above that come *frames* which are at the data link layer. For everything above that, you can usually use the term *packet*, until you get all the way to the top of the network, where *message* is most often used.

For example, in the world of TCP/IP, you would say "Bits on an Ethernet segment," "an Ethernet frame," "an IP packet" (or datagram), "a TCP segment," "a UDP packet," or "an SMTP message." (TCP/IP is discussed in detail in Chapters 17 and 18.)

Each station on the network has a specific network address. This address identifies the computer as the sender or receiver of a frame. You may wonder why contention is a problem if every station has an address — can't a signal be sent from one station to the right destination much as you'd drive a car from your house to a friend's?

Unfortunately, electrical signals don't work that way. Electrical signals are transmitted in both directions along a cable from their source. Therefore, every station's transceiver on the network must listen to the network cable to see whether the frame that's passing by is meant for it. If it is, the transceiver copies the frame and passes it on to the computer (see Figure 2-8). This process is similar to having a party line for your telephone; everyone's phone rings for an incoming call. You know whether the call is for you only when you answer the phone.

What follows is a closer look at the different methods that networks commonly use for dealing with contention problems.

## Carrier sensing

The idea behind carrier sensing is that a station can listen to the network to see that no signal is being transmitted before it transmits its own signal. When the network is idle, the station transmits its own packet, while continuing to monitor, or *listen* to the network.

In some cases, two or more stations may decide to transmit at about the same time. Their packets will interfere with each other, a situation known as a *collision*. What a station does to prevent or detect a collision is the distinguishing factor for the two major types of carrier-sensing networks. These types are called *Carrier Sensing Multiple Access with Collision Detection (CSMA/CD)* and *Carrier Sensing Multiple Access with Collision Avoidance (CSMA/CA)*. The words *multiple access* in this terminology simply mean that more than one station is operating on the network.

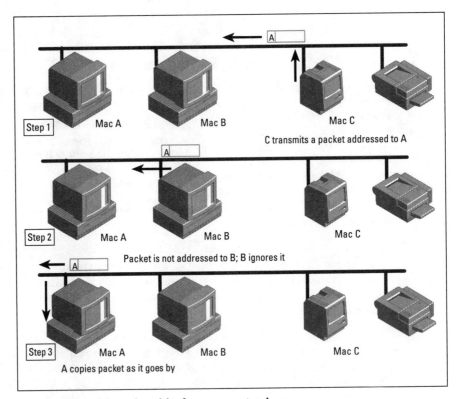

**Figure 2-8: Transmitting and receiving frames on a network.**

In CSMA/CD, a transmitting station stops transmitting its data on the network when it notices that a collision has taken place (see Figure 2-9). If you think back to our cocktail party analogy, this is like a person who waits silently for a period before saying anything; if anyone else starts talking when he does, he stops talking.

CSMA with collision avoidance (CSMA/CA) parallels our cocktail party with a new twist. Rather than simply waiting for a silence, our speaker now says "excuse me" or coughs to alert the others and then starts talking. The key here is that the speaker does something to grab everyone's attention before speaking. Drawing a comparison to a network, the stations each listen for such an attention-getting signal in the form of a particular packet, called a *carrier burst*, to see whether the cable is going to be used by another computer. If a station detects this packet, it knows that another station is going to use the cable and that data will follow; if there is no carrier burst, the first station can send one of its own to start a conversation.

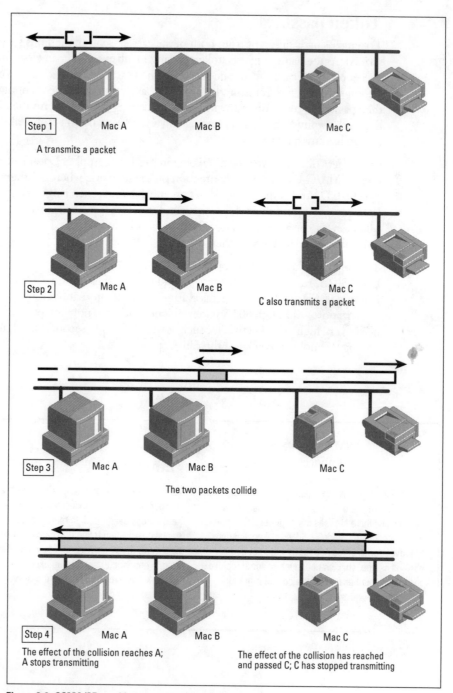

**Figure 2-9: CSMA/CD working on a network.**

# Token passing

Token passing is different from both of the carrier-sensing methods we just described. As the name suggests, token passing involves sending an electronic *token* packet on the network from one station to the next; this token gives the receiving station permission to transmit data. When that station is finished sending its data, it then passes the token on to the next station (see Figure 2-10). This method is much like going around a table at a meeting and asking each person at the table if that person has anything to say.

Of the networks that we'll be discussing in this book, Apple's LocalTalk network uses CSMA/CA to deal with contention on the network, whereas Ethernet uses CSMA/CD. And, although we don't say much about token ring networks, many IBM computers and their clones are wired together using token passing rings. Macs can also be attached to token ring networks and use the TokenTalk driver to communicate with each other.

The original token ring network, developed by IBM and later standardized as IEEE 802.5, runs at either 4M bits/second or 16M bits/second. (IEEE stands for Institute of Electronic and Electrical Engineers, an international standards-setting organization.) Although 802.5 token ring networks are not very popular any more, newer very high-speed networks, such as the 100M bits/second FDDI, use token passing technology to achieve their high speeds.

BACKGROUNDER

## Token Ring or Ethernet?

Networking types like to argue about whether token ring or Ethernet is better for local area networks. Technically, there are reasons to prefer either one for certain very narrowly defined kinds of applications. However, for all office networks, Ethernet is the obvious choice. This isn't because of some technical superiority, but because of the cost of materials and supplies.

As the market leader, Ethernet-based LAN hardware has become quite inexpensive, while token ring hardware is overpriced. In many cases, it's cheaper to pull out existing token ring cards and connecting hardware, throw it away, and buy new Ethernet gear than to continue expanding an existing token ring network. "We've always done it that way" is never a good reason to do anything.

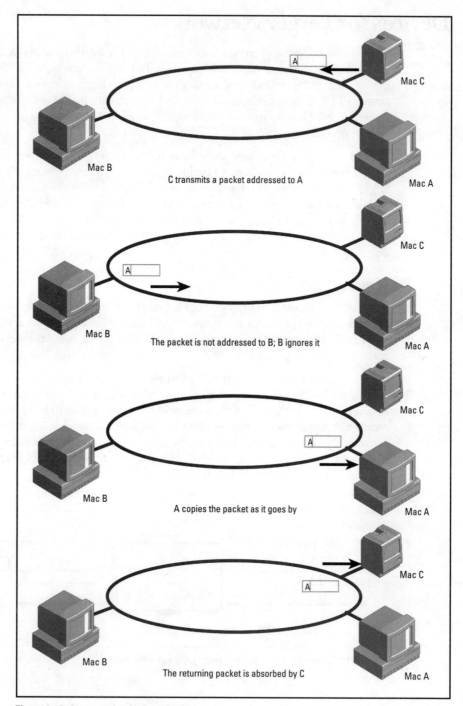

Figure 2-10: An example of token passing.

# Devices for Larger Networks

So now you know that such conditions as noise and resistance place both distance and node limitations on your network cables. But suppose you need for Mary to talk to Paul, and they're at opposite sides of a long building, or even across the street. All LANs have limits on distance and the total number of nodes which can be connected. How do you overcome these limitations? In other words, how do you create a larger network?

You can go beyond these limitations by using any of the devices known as *repeaters*, *bridges*, and *routers*. These devices enable you to connect cables together to form larger and larger networks. Each device type in its turn is a step up in performance and flexibility, but also a step up in complexity for the network administrator. We'll explain each of these devices in order of their increasing complexity. We'll show you how and when each device can be used and point out the limitations of each device as well.

## Repeaters

You can use a repeater to link two network cables of the same type. AppleTalk networks use two primary cable types: LocalTalk and Ethernet. A repeater can link two LocalTalk cables to make a longer LocalTalk cable, or two Ethernet cables to make a longer Ethernet cable.

The primary purpose of a repeater is to amplify and reclock the electrical signal (see Figure 2-11). A signal traveling along a cable is gradually weakened by the resistance of the path, making the voltage of the wave too low to be heard by the receiver. A repeater solves this problem by reissuing the signal at full strength across to the second cable. Obviously, the placement of the repeater is important. The repeater must be located at some place along the cable where it can still detect the incoming signal (even though it may be weak).

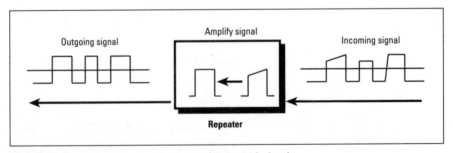

Figure 2-11: An example of a repeater processing network signals.

A repeater has two primary limitations. The first is that a repeater strengthens a signal, but can only do so a few times. Every time a signal passed through a repeater, some noise is added — not on purpose, but as a side effect of the process. Once a signal has gone through a few repeaters (where "few" depends on the kind of network you're building), the signal has too much noise in it to be repeated once again.

Secondly, a repeater does not solve the problem of too many collisions. The number of collisions goes up with the number of nodes in use on a segment. When the number of collisions causes the network to fail or to slow to a crawl, you need to move up a step and install a bridge.

## Bridges

A bridge also combines two like cable segments, but it does so in a different way than a repeater. A repeater doesn't know anything about networks; it simply reshapes and amplifies the signal it receives. A bridge actually receives each frame from the network, looks at it, and decides what to do with it. A bridge maintains a table that informs it about which nodes are located on either side of it.

As a frame travels on the network, the bridge retrieves it and checks its header. If the frame and its destination are on the same side of the bridge, the bridge does nothing, dumping the frame into the bit bucket. But when the destination is on the other side of the bridge, the bridge passes the frame across (see Figure 2-12). In this way, only the traffic that is destined for the other side gets across. Local traffic stays local. Bridges, sometimes called *learning bridges*, collect information that they need for the address table from the network itself. The only time a network manager has to change parameters in a bridge is if the normal behavior isn't adequate.

The simplicity of bridges makes them popular with network managers. They are a way of reducing excess network traffic and extending network segments. As bridge prices drop to about $1,000 each, a bridge is a simple way of handling the problem of an overloaded network. All you have to do is drop it in, turn it on, and forget it.

Newer bridges support an IEEE standard called *802.1 Spanning Tree*, which lets bridges learn about each other and automatically form a network without loops. Consider that a network with bridges in a big circle can't automatically learn which side frames are on because everyone is on both sides. Spanning Tree bridges detect this and elect one of the bridges to shut down. If there is a break in the network, the bridges automatically discover it, and the shut-down bridge starts processing frames, restoring service immediately.

Like repeaters, there are two primary limitations to a bridge:

❖ First, a bridge only looks at the address to determine whether the frame should be passed across. Certain types of frames, called *broadcast* and *multicast frames*, aren't aimed at a single station but at a group of stations or even every station. As your network grows, such multicast frames can overwhelm the network, and the bridge can do nothing to limit them. As your network traffic increases, you need to put routers in place.

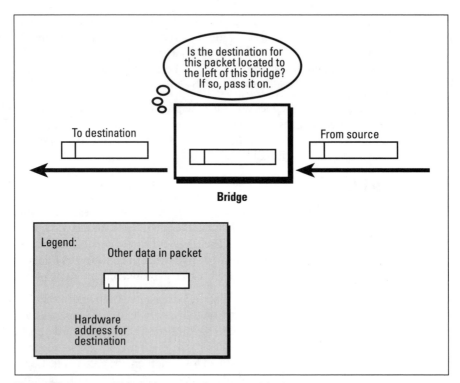

**Figure 2-12: An example of a bridge processing a network packet.**

❖ A second limitation of a bridge is that it can join only like segments. If you want to connect a LocalTalk cable to an Ethernet cable, you need to use a router.

Bridges also introduce delay in your network, because they normally receive an entire frame before deciding what to do with it. There are no hard and fast guidelines about the number of bridges you can have in a network. However, a good rule of thumb, is that any two stations should have at most seven bridges; the reason is that some LAN protocols cannot tolerate the delay which many bridges introduce.

Some newer bridges, which are called *switching bridges*, make the decision whether to forward a frame before receiving the entire frame and can start retransmitting frames more quickly. This process decreases delay and can increase the total throughput of your network as well as the number of bridges you can have between any two stations.

# Routers

A router does more than link two cable segments together and filter traffic. A router actually links two networks together. When you put a router in place, it creates a separate designation for each cable and calls each a network. Each network then has its own designator — a network number — so that the router can keep track of it (see Figure 2-13).

With bridges and repeaters, you make a single larger network. But with a router, you are joining multiple networks. So what does this mean to you? With a router in place, the administrator can define areas physically. In addition to source and destination node addresses, each packet now contains network addresses for both source and destination. If you place another router as a link between network cables on a second floor and third floor, for example, you can look at any packet and identify the source floor or destination floor. If you used a bridge and not a router, there would be no network address. You would have only the node address, so the packet wouldn't tell you whether the node was from the second or third floor.

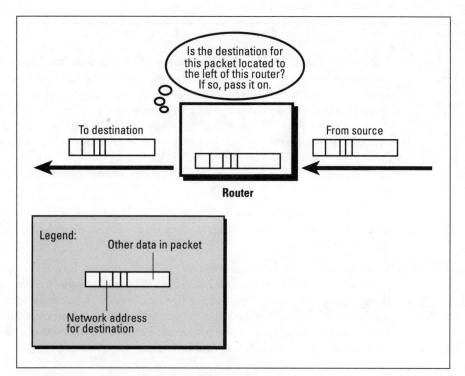

**Figure 2-13: An example of a router processing network packets.**

QUICK TIPS

## Repeaters Versus Bridges Versus Routers

A bridge works at the frame level of a network, looking at the hardware address encoded into each device as it left the factory. Bridges don't know anything about protocols, such as AppleTalk or NetWare or TCP/IP; they are *protocol independent*.

A router works at the packet level of a network. To properly handle traffic, the router must be configured by the network manager for every protocol being used on the network. Routers are more powerful than bridges, but require a great deal more management.

A *brouter* is a combination of a bridge and a router. It routes some protocols and bridges others.

Avoid using repeaters unless you absolutely have to, such as in 10BASE-T networks (see Chapter 9, "Installing an Ethernet LAN") or for very long reaches with only a few stations. For LocalTalk, you should have no more than 48 active nodes.

Use a bridge in busy but small physical areas to separate a work group from the rest of the network.

Use a router when the network's physical area is large, when the number of stations is very large, or when you need to join together two dissimilar cable segments (such as LocalTalk, Ethernet, and token ring).

A router is capable of performing many advanced traffic-flow procedures. As we mentioned previously, a router does not pass broadcast traffic. If information in a broadcast packet is needed on the other side, the router itself creates a packet, using its own hardware address as the source and then sending the information. In some cases, multiple devices may be sending out information in a broadcast format. With a router, this information goes across only once. Information regarding node addresses also is not passed on by the router. The router looks at the network-address destination portion of a packet and passes it across when the destination-network number matches.

Because a router joins two separate networks, it can also join two different types of cable segments. The router changes the packet as necessary and sends it across in the new format.

Although routers can link networks that are countries apart by using telephone serial links, routers do have traffic limitations. A router is usually slower than a bridge because the router does more processing of packets, maintaining network numbers, and filtering packets. Also, routers add to the data traffic on the network. On networks with more than one router, the exchange of route information among the routers creates additional overhead.

# A Basic Networking Vocabulary

In this chapter, the focus has been on the physical aspects of a network. Occasionally, we've used some terminology that deals more with the logical or organizational aspects of networking, such as network addresses. We will deal extensively with the logical organization of networks throughout the book, so we'll take some time now to introduce some of the vocabulary that you'll need to know. Remember also to check Appendix D, "Glossary of Networking Terms," for further reference.

Previously, we referred to *network devices* and *stations*. It should be fairly obvious by now that a station is just about any type of computing device that you can attach to a network. These devices include Macs, MS-DOS computers, file servers, printers, and even modems.

When any device is attached to a network, it is commonly referred to as a *network node* and has several addresses. Addressing is a particularly hairy problem in networking and can be rather confusing. If you think about the physical setup of a network, a wire attaches each station to the shared LAN media. That wire goes to a *network interface*, and each network interface has a different network address. In the world of Ethernet and token ring, network addresses are 48 bits long (about 250 trillion possibilities), assigned by the IEEE, and are guaranteed to be unique throughout the world.

Network software running on top of the hardware also needs addresses to keep things straight. These addresses are usually called *network addresses*. This network address is unique for each node in a particular network. Many network systems require an administrator to assign the network address to the node; some, like AppleTalk, allow the node to select one for itself. We say more about AppleTalk's method later in this chapter. If a network node has multiple sets of network software, we say it is running multiple *protocol stacks*. For example, a Mac might use both AppleTalk and TCP/IP (Transmission Control Protocol/Internet Protocol — a very popular standard for network connections) at the same time. In this case, it has a single hardware address and two network addresses, one for AppleTalk and one for TCP/IP.

Inside of a particular kind of protocol, which is itself inside of a network node, things are divided once more. The common term for the next division is *socket*. Each socket has its own identifying number or name for tracking purposes. In addition, each socket on a network node is associated with a single process or application on that node. Therefore, if you're printing a document on a networked printer and using electronic mail, the network sees two sockets defined on your computer: one for the print job, the other for your electronic mail.

In summary, the hardware address identifies a particular station on the network, the network address identifies a protocol stack within the node, and the socket identifies a process running on top of a protocol stack.

Networkers also have a specific name for most of the networking tasks that your computer performs; each task is called a *session*. It's convenient to think of a session as a conversation between your computer and another node on the network. For example, to complete a printing task and read e-mail simultaneously, your computer is running one session between itself and the printer and another session between itself and the mail server.

In a previous section in this chapter titled "Devices for Larger Networks," we introduced you to networking devices that can be used to create larger networks. In our discussion of routers, we mentioned that routers connect two or more networks to form a larger network. How does the router know which network is which? When you install a router, you assign a unique network number to each network. Then, packets are directed to their destination by the router, based on both the network number and the network address of the destination. (For convenience, many network systems, such as AppleTalk, combine the node's network address and network number into a single internet address.)

## Not All Network Tasks Are Sessions

Note that we said that most, but not all, of your computer's network tasks are sessions. Occasionally your computer searches the network for a particular device — it may be looking for *any* file server, for example. To do this, the computer sends a *multicast* over the network. This multicast is just what its name implies; it is not addressed to any node in particular, but to multiple nodes. A special kind of multicast is called a *broadcast*, which is addressed to every single node on a network. Multiple nodes on the network receive multicasts and each decides how to respond separately, if it responds at all, based on the contents of the multicast. Because the multicast isn't directed to one node in particular and there may be no response, a conversation doesn't take place between two nodes. For this reason, multicasts and broadcasts aren't considered sessions.

# An Overview of AppleTalk Networks

The first half of this book focuses on AppleTalk networking. Before going into the detail of the AppleTalk networking protocols, wiring, and applications, here are some basic concepts of AppleTalk networks.

## Dynamic network addressing

As we explained in the section about networking vocabulary, AppleTalk uses both a network address and socket number to identify a network task. Devices using AppleTalk are designed to select their node addresses *dynamically*. This means that the first time a device is attached to an AppleTalk network, it randomly selects a tentative network address from a range of numbers, as defined within the AppleTalk specifications.

The device broadcasts that address to the network. If no other node is already using that address, the new device uses the selected address and stores it for future use. If another node already has the desired address, the new device selects another address at random and tries the process all over again until it selects an unused address.

Because an AppleTalk device stores its selected network address, it tries to use the same address the next time it is turned on (or when it is reattached to the network, if the device is a Mac PowerBook). This usually means that, after the device is attached to the network and the selection process is completed, the same address is used over and over again. On occasion, however, an AppleTalk device may need to go through the process of selecting a new address.

When a new device is attached to the network and turned on, the new device may select an address formerly used by an older device. Also, if you reconfigure your network, possibly by adding a router, your AppleTalk devices will go through the process of selecting new addresses.

Note that because each Mac stores its network address in PRAM (Parameter Random Access Memory), the address will be cleared if you replace the Mac's battery. So the Mac will need a new address when it's reattached to the network.

## AppleTalk names

Even though AppleTalk networks transmit and route network traffic based on numeric addresses, we human users are more comfortable working with named objects. AppleTalk relies on converting, or *mapping*, node addresses to names to make network access easier for users. AppleTalk also lets network administrators logically group nodes into *zones* to make navigation through a network easier.

Here is a brief look at AppleTalk's named services. When a device is attached to the network and provides a network service for other users, or *clients*, to use, the type of service usually has a name associated with it. These names, which represent types of services, usually show up in your Mac's Chooser with an associated icon. Some examples are AppleShare, which is a file server, LaserWriter, which is a networked laser printer, and MS Mail, which is an electronic mail server.

When installing any of these services on the AppleTalk network, an administrator has the option of giving the device a name. Therefore, you may have on your network AppleShare servers named "Finance," "Legal," and "Marketing." Or your LaserWriters may have names like "Word Processing," or "Bldg. 3," "1st Floor," or "Naco." In any case, these names show up in the Chooser when you're looking for a particular server or printer, so you don't need to know the device's numeric address in order to use it.

We also said that AppleTalk lets a network administrator combine nodes into a logical group (provided your network has a router installed). These named groups are called *zones*. The main idea behind zones is to make it easier for a user to navigate through the network. For example, you may have a network that runs through three stories of a building (see Figure 2-14).

If your network includes a router or two, you could decide that all devices on the first floor would be in a zone called "1st Floor," all devices on the second and third floors are in the "Upper Floors." (Note that the "Upper Floors" zone includes two routers.) When a user on the second floor starts looking for a laser printer on the upper floors, he can use the Chooser to see a list of zone names, select the "Upper Floors" zone, and select the LaserWriter icon to find all the laser printers in that zone (see Figure 2-15). If no zones were created (even if a router is part of the network), the user would see all of the laser printers in one list (see Figure 2-16).

## The AppleTalk internet

Recall that the router calls each cable segment that is attached to it a *network*. If each of these segments is called a network, what do you call the entire network? A network of networks? Or a Network with a big N? That's a bit awkward. Besides, you'd have problems discussing the "big-N" Network, as opposed to one of the router's "little-n" networks. Apple chooses to call the entire aggregate of networks connected via routers an *internet*.

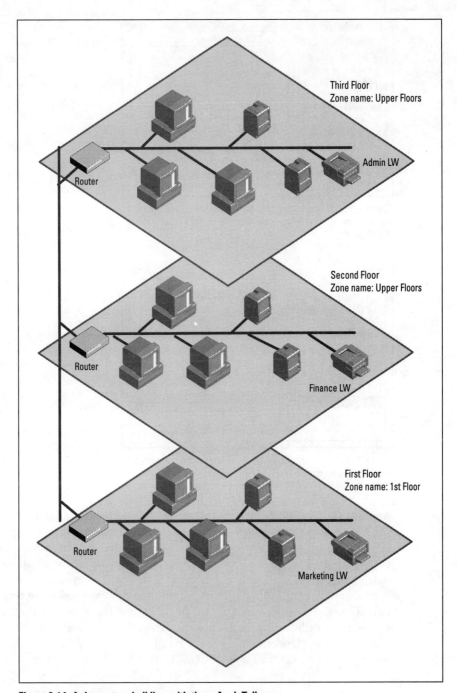

Figure 2-14: A three-story building with three AppleTalk zones.

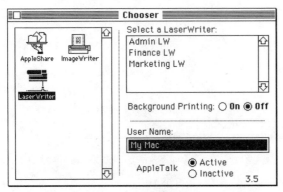

**Figure 2-15: The user sees only the Admin LaserWriter and Finance LaserWriter when selecting the Upper Floors zone in the Chooser.**

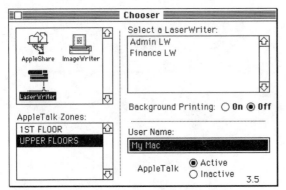

**Figure 2-16: The user sees all three laser printers because the network has no zones.**

Apple's use of the term *internet* is not the same as *the Internet*, which is a network of networks stretching around the world (read more about the Internet in Chapter 26). Within an AppleTalk internet, each cable segment has one or more network numbers associated with it. The original AppleTalk specifications allowed only a single network number per cable. When AppleTalk specifications were upgraded to Phase 2 in June 1989, Apple allowed Ethernet and token ring cables to have more than one network number. In either case, the AppleTalk router is responsible for maintaining the list of network numbers and their associated cables. (See Chapter 3, "Understanding AppleTalk Protocols," and Chapter 11, "Designing an AppleTalk LAN," for more detail.)

QUICK TIPS

## The AppleTalk Internet

It's important to keep your letters and capitalization straight. An AppleTalk internet is a collection of network segments. The Internet is a single collection of networks. And, the AppleTalk Internet is a collection of AppleTalk internets which have been linked over the Internet to form a huge AppleTalk network-of-networks. If you're on the Internet and have an AppleTalk router, you can join the AppleTalk Internet as well.

If you want to join an AppleTalk internet, all you need to do is read Chapter 12 and buy an AppleTalk router. In that case, you'll be linking multiple AppleTalk network segments, usually ones which belong to you.

To join the Internet, read Chapter 26 and get a connection with an Internet service provider. Here,

you'll be linking your corporate network with a world-wide TCP/IP network. Of course, you'll also have to run TCP/IP on your network.

To join the AppleTalk Internet, you'll need to do both of the above and get a copy of Apple's AppleTalk Internet Router with TCP/IP extensions. This will allow you link your corporate AppleTalk internet with other AppleTalk internets all over the world — over the Internet!

*Note:* Good reference guides for connecting to and exploring the Internet are *The Internet For Dummies* by John Levine and Carol Baroudi, *More Internet For Dummies* by John Levine, and *The Internet For Dummies, Mac Version* by Charles Seiter (all published by IDG Books Worldwide).

# CHAPTER 2 CONCEPTS AND TERMS

- The most common networks use coaxial cable or twisted-pair cable. Some also use fiber optic cabling or wireless connections, such as infrared or radio frequency.

- A computer requires both hardware and software to connect to a network. The hardware includes both a cable connector and a transceiver to understand network signals. The software is called a driver.

- These network signals can be weakened by the cabling, or interfered with by external noise sources.

- Networks use either a carrier-sensing technique or token passing to control communications between computers. Ethernet and LocalTalk are examples of the former; token ring and FDDI of the latter.

- A repeater can be used to amplify the network signal. A bridge can link networks using the same type of cabling to create larger networks. A router can link networks using dissimilar cables to create larger networks and control traffic on the network.

- AppleTalk uses names to identify networked services to the user. It also uses names to show the user logical divisions of the network. AppleTalk addresses are picked dynamically and automatically, unlike most other network addresses.

- A session runs between two sockets on a network node. The node has at least one network address for each protocol stack it uses and at least one hardware address for each network interface.

**bridges**
An electronic device that connects two networks so that devices on one network can communicate with devices on the other network. Bridges only work with networks using the same communications protocols.

**crosstalk**
The electrical interference between signals transmitted on wires.

**carrier sensing**
A method used by network devices to gain access to a single channel on the network. Each device listens to the traffic on the network (or senses the carrier) and thus detects whether the network is clear.

**data link layer**
The layer of the OSI Reference Model that defines protocols governing data packets and transmissions.

**driver**
Software for using a peripheral hardware device attached to a computer. For example, to control a printer from a Macintosh, the print driver program for that type of printer has to be added to the Mac's System Folder.

**frames**
A series of bytes of data encapsulated with a header. The data link layer sends frames back and forth. Term is used interchangeably with packet.

**network interface card (or controller)**
A card (or set of chips) that fits inside a computer so that the computer can connect to a network. Often called just the interface card. Different types of networks require different cards.

**network node**
An addressable device on a network, such as a LaserWriter or a Macintosh.

**packets**
A group of bits, including address, data, and control elements, that are switched and transmitted together.

**protocol**
A procedural rule or convention for sending information over a network. Each network has its own way of transmitting data and divides the entire process into a series of specific functions. Each function requires a complete set of operating rules (or protocols).

**repeaters**
A hardware device that repeats signals on a network. As signals pass over a line, they lose some of their power and pick up static. A repeater amplifies and conditions the signals on a network line.

**routers**
A device that connects two networks together and maintains addressing information for each network. Workstations can pass information from one network to another by sending information through the router.

**session**
Term used to refer to the logical stream of data flowing between two programs that are communicating over the network. There are usually many different sessions originating from one particular node of a network. In AppleTalk, each session in a node has its own socket.

*(continued on the next page)*

*(continued from the previous page)*

**socket**
Any addressable entity in a node on an AppleTalk network. Sockets are "owned" by the software processes that create them. For example, if a communications program obtains a socket for receiving messages, that socket can only be used to receive messages for that program.

**the Internet**
A collection of networks with a common routing backbone which encompasses such public networks as NSFnet (National Science Foundation Network) as well as private networks such as those at various universities.

**token passing**
Involves sending an electronic *token* packet on the network from one station to the next; this token gives the receiving station permission to transmit data. When that station is finished sending its data, it then passes the token on to the next station. This method is much like going around a table at a meeting and asking each person at the table if that person has anything to say.

**transceiver**
A device used as an interface between a workstation and the network to which it is attached. The transceiver performs the task of transmitting frames onto the cable and receiving them from it. It also monitors signal levels on the medium and detects collisions and other error conditions.

# Understanding AppleTalk Protocols

IN THIS CHAPTER

- The OSI Reference Model for classifying network protocols

- The function of each AppleTalk protocol

- The interrelationships of the AppleTalk protocols

- The differences between AppleTalk Phase 1 and Phase 2 protocols

Understanding networks means answering three basic questions:

1. What is a network?

2. What are protocols?

3. Why do we layer?

Everything else is just wires and acronyms! The first two chapters provided the details to answer the first question. In this chapter, we cover questions two and three.

## Understanding Protocols

Love may make the world go 'round, but network operations are set in motion by *protocols* — the rules that determine everything about the way a network operates. Protocols are the rules for talking between two entities in a network. We use the term *entities* instead of computers because entities may be bits of hardware in a transceiver, micro codes on an Ethernet controller board, or some abstractions of a process inside of a computer. Protocols govern how applications access the network, the way messages from an application are divided into packets and then frames for transmission through a cable, and which electrical signals represent data on a network cable.

QUOTABLES

"I had the story, bit by bit, from various people, and, as generally happens in such cases, each time it was a different story."

— from *Ethan Frome* by Edith Warton, 1911.

Protocols support two basic kinds of messages, *data transfer* and *signaling*. Data transfer is the actual talking where data is passed between two entities, presumably for the purposes of doing some useful work. Protocols also spend a lot of time signaling, which is all of the overhead of networks. Protocol signaling includes functions such as setting up connections and sessions; error detection, control, and correction; routing and relaying; and congestion control. All of these are required for the network to work, even if they don't pass any real data.

You can accomplish a good deal on a network without being aware of protocols. But knowing about protocols can help if you're ever called upon to troubleshoot a network or if you want to understand what's happening with a router, a laser printer, or a mail server. Each protocol is assigned a different network function, so that you can use the protocol definitions to see how the parts of a network relate to one another or to understand the steps that an application must go through in order to perform on a network.

When the guts of a networking system are designed, a suite of protocols is defined so that the proper hardware can be manufactured and programmers can adopt a standardized method of communicating with that hardware. Protocols may be defined by a single vendor as with AppleTalk, or by a group of vendors, as with Ethernet. In other cases, an international committee defines the protocols for a network, as with the ISO (International Organization for Standardization) and ITU-T (International Telecommunications Union) protocols.

More than one kind of networking system is currently available for computers — names such as Ethernet, TCP/IP, SNA, DECnet, AppleTalk, and FDDI come to mind. Each system has its own rules for how the network should work. And, as you might expect, the rules aren't interchangeable from one network to another. However, there are many cases where a single computer can run multiple protocols and where a single physical network can support multiple protocols.

# Introducing the OSI Reference Model

In an effort to standardize a way of looking at network protocols, the International Organization for Standardization (ISO) created a seven-layer model that defines the basic network functions (see Figure 3-1). This model is known among network folk as "two apartment buildings with garage." It is officially called the *OSI Reference Model*. The letters OSI stand for *Open Systems Interconnection*.

In many network operating systems, you can pigeonhole each protocol into one layer of this reference model. In other cases, it's not so easy. Occasionally, a protocol spans more than one layer of the model. In most cases, some layers are missing entirely. But once you categorize the protocols according to the OSI Reference Model, you'll find it easier to compare the component functions of the various networks.

The OSI Reference Model is just what its name implies, a model for how you look at networks. It doesn't actually describe how to build networks, and no one has ever built a network which conforms exactly to the model — not even the ISO itself! But it is important because the model provides a common vocabulary of terms and concepts that network managers can use to talk about networks.

The OSI Reference Model depends on the concept of *peer-to-peer communications*, which means that data created by one layer in the OSI Reference Model (such as the network layer) and transmitted to another device on the network pertains only to the same layer on that device. In other words, intervening layers do not alter the data; the other layers simply add to the data found in a packet to perform their assigned functions on the network.

Protocol suites are designed in distinct layers to make it easier to substitute one protocol for another (see Figure 3-2). You can say that protocol suites govern how data is exchanged above and below each protocol layer. (In fact, the graphical representation of these protocols in vertical layers is why protocol suites are sometimes called *protocol stacks*.) When protocols are designed, specifications set forth how a protocol exchanges data with a protocol layered above or below it. As long as you follow those specifications, you can substitute a new, supposedly better, protocol for one currently in the suite without affecting the general behavior of the network.

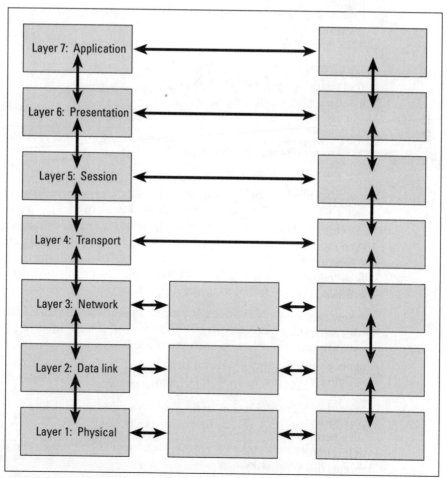

**Figure 3-1: The OSI Reference Model shows how a network can be built using standard interfaces and functions.**

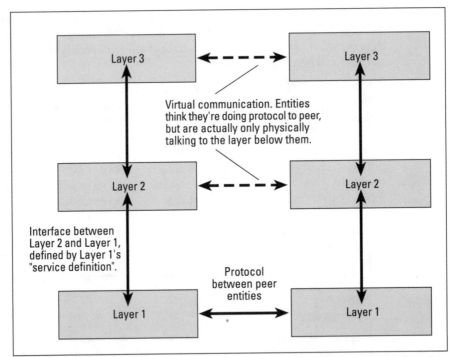

**Figure 3-2: In a layered network, peer entities communicate with each other by passing information across the service boundary of the layer below.**

You see this effect in AppleTalk quite well: the AppleTalk network stack runs over a LocalTalk physical layer, an Ethernet physical layer, or a token ring layer without any changes. As long as the lower layer provides the exact service expected by the upper layer, it's possible to swap out the actual protocols. In the network world, we write *service descriptions* which say what one layer will do for another. The analogy in the programming world is the API (Application Programming Interface), which describes services a subroutine library will provide to a program.

The following are some examples and explanations of the purposes of each layer, which are listed here in descending order. For now, you can think of the layers as dealing with the following questions and concepts:

**Layer 7 — The application layer:** What data do I want to send to my partner? These are the actual programs which use the network.

**Layer 6 — The presentation layer:** What does the data look like? Virtual terminals, code conversion, and security all commonly happen here.

**Layer 5 — The session layer:** Who is the partner? How are sessions established? Who will pay for this connection?

**Layer 4 — The transport layer:** What is the far end of the connection and what kind of transfer do I need to do? How do I break up the messages from the application layer? This layer is the lowest-numbered end-to-end layer. Everything below this layer is replicated in every machine along the way; everything above this layer is one end of the connection talking only to the other end.

**Layer 3 — The network layer:** Which route do I follow to get there? How do I break the transport layer packets up into network layer packets? How will the network be managed?

**Layer 2 — The data link layer:** How do I make each step in that route appear to be error free? How do I break up the network layer packets into frames?

**Layer 1 — The physical layer:** How do I use the medium for that step? How do I transmit bits over a raw channel?

To further explain the OSI Reference Model, here is a noncomputer example — the process of a fax communication — to illustrate what happens in different layers of the model, starting from the top and working down the layers.

Suppose that you want to fax a report to a correspondent in another, non-English-speaking country. Deciding to send the report is your job as the user, but the actual job of setting up the report for transmittal is the job of your staff, which compares here to Layer 7, the *application layer*. The report itself and any translations necessary are part of Layer 6, the *presentation layer* (see Figure 3-3).

BACKGROUNDER

### Why Learn about OSI?

The seven layers of the OSI Reference Model group network functions into general categories; comparing various protocols to this standard model will help you understand various networking systems.

Even if you think that your own favorite kind of networking—AppleTalk, TCP/IP, SNA, or whatever—is the way to go, you need to understand the OSI model and how it relates to your network protocol. Many organizations are not interested in implementing ISO-designed networks. However, **every** network vendor and author now uses the OSI model as a way of looking at their network. Even if they don't conform to the model directly, they usually explain how their vision differs. By having a common base and a common set of terms to look at all different networks, you can understand better the similarities and differences between them.

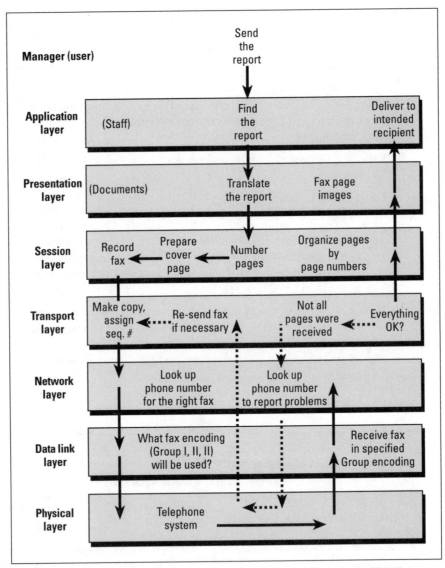

**Figure 3-3: The steps used in sending a fax correspond to the protocol layers in the OSI Reference Model.**

The preparation of this report for fax transmission is a good example of how the top two layers, the application and presentation layers, work together. The various tasks assigned to the presentation layer — finding the report, translating the report, and then preparing the fax page images — may be handled by different members of your staff as discrete functions within the application and presentation layers. Storing the original report and its final translated copy is the job of the presentation layer, for example, but it's the job of the application layer to find and track the report. In short, there's a continual conversation going on between the staff at the application layer and the documents at the presentation layer.

When the document is ready to be transmitted, someone has to prepare the cover page. This is the job of Layer 5, the *session layer*. The session layer also has the responsibility of recording and checking pertinent details of the fax, such as the address of the recipient, the recipient's correct title, and the size of the fax document. This is an important task because lower protocol layers will request information from the session layer in order to maintain a two-way conversation between the sender and the recipient.

The next lowest layer in the model, Layer 4, the *transport layer*, takes care of numbering the pages of the fax document in sequence, copying the fax for storage, and assigning a sequence number for easier tracking. These tasks are necessary to ensure reliable transmission of the fax. If something goes wrong with the transmission, the transport layer can recover a copy for re-sending. Also, numbering the pages ensures that the pages are sent and received in the proper order. Numbered pages also make it easier to determine whether a page was not received and identifies an unreadable page that needs to be sent again.

Now you have a fax document, and you know what to do if all of it or parts of it don't make it to the intended recipient. Which fax do you call to get the document to intended recipient? The transmittal sheet may simply say that the report is from Bill in the Billing Department and that it is to be sent to Coral in Corporate Finance. Layer 3, the *network layer*, keeps track of people's locations according to department and location in the company. But someone needs to look up the phone number for Coral's fax number. This is a function called *mapping*. A logical address is mapped to a physical address by Layer 2, the *data link layer*.

Actually getting the report pages sent from one fax to the other requires that both faxes use the same data format. We're not talking about the format of the fax document with such considerations as pagination and paragraph setup, but the way that the bits representing the image of the fax page are sent. This *encoding* (and *decoding* on the receiving fax) of the bit patterns is also a part of the data link layer.

Layer 1, the *physical layer*, is pretty much what its name implies. Following the fax example, the physical layer becomes the physical wiring scheme or the telephone service between the two offices.

In a later section, you'll see that real data exchange on a network isn't very different from this fax example with one notable difference. The form that data takes as it is passed from layer to layer, or protocol to protocol, is different. Each protocol adds some information to the original data on the sending computer so that the receiving computer knows the rules to follow as it decodes the data packets and reconstructs the original data (see Figures 3-4 and 3-5). This added protocol information is either prepended or appended to the data in the form of *headers* and *footers*. Under no circumstances is your raw data transmitted on a network.

| top layer, n | | | | | original message | | | | |
|---|---|---|---|---|---|---|---|---|---|
| layer n-1 | | | | n-1 hdr | original message | n-1 end | | | |
| layer n-2 | | | n-2 hdr | n-1 hdr | original message | n-1 end | n-2 end | | |
| layer n-3 | | n-3 hdr | n-2 hdr | n-1 hdr | original message | n-1 end | n-2 end | n-3 end | |
| layer n-4 | n-4 hdr | n-3 hdr | n-2 hdr | n-1 hdr | original message | n-1 end | n-2 end | n-3 end | n-4 end |

**Figure 3-4: Each protocol adds information to the original data.**

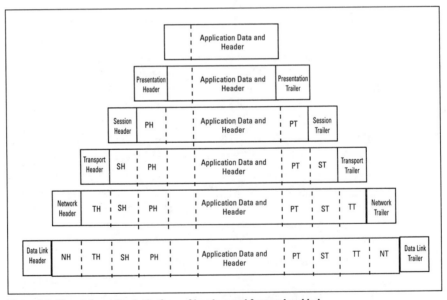

**Figure 3-5: More information in the form of headers and footers is added.**

In the next section, we'll discuss the protocols in greater depth. We'll first give you an overview of AppleTalk protocols, and then we'll examine each of the protocols in sequence, according to the layer their functions belong to.

# Introducing AppleTalk Protocols

AppleTalk, the name for Apple's proprietary network architecture, is a layered suite of protocols that easily fits the OSI Reference Model. As you see in Figure 3-6, the AppleTalk suite includes quite a few protocols. Although they fall into distinct layers according to the OSI model, it's useful to further classify the protocols according to their functions. These functions can be described as follows, in order from bottom to top:

1. The physical and data link functions

2. The end-to-end data flow functions

3. The named entities functions

4. The reliable data delivery functions

5. The end-user services

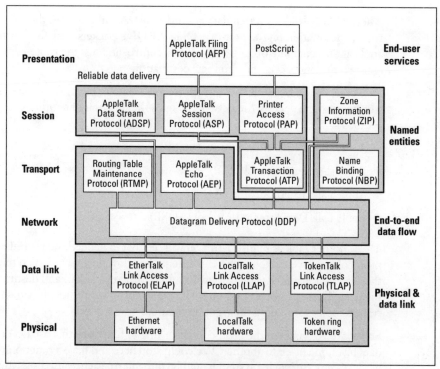

Figure 3-6: The AppleTalk protocol stack is arranged here by function.

Looking at Figure 3-6, you'll see the physical and data link functions grouped together at the bottom of the diagram. This physical and data link category contains the Link Access Protocols, or LAPs. Think of this category as the network hardware interface — the network's cable and the hardware needed to communicate with that cable (see Chapter 2, "Understanding Networks"). The AppleTalk Address Resolution Protocol (AARP) also belongs in this category because it's intimately linked to the Ethernet and token ring LAPs (AARP is not shown in the protocol layer diagram, as this protocol is usually included within the definition of each LAP).

Moving upward on the diagram, notice the end-to-end data flow category. End-to-end data flow (the flow of data from one network socket to the other) is controlled by the following three protocols:

❖ Datagram Delivery Protocol (DDP)

❖ Routing Table Maintenance Protocol (RTMP)

❖ AppleTalk Echo Protocol (AEP)

These protocols see to it that data are properly transmitted from the source to the correct destination on the network. Only the DDP packets actually transmit your application's data; the other two protocols control and test the route your computer's data packets take to their destination.

However, the end-to-end data flow protocols are not concerned with reliability in transmitting the data on the network. That's the function of another group of four protocols:

❖ AppleTalk Transaction Protocol (ATP)

❖ Printer Access Protocol (PAP)

❖ AppleTalk Session Protocol (ASP)

❖ AppleTalk Data Stream Protocol (ADSP)

Take another look at Figure 3-6. You will see that in general the preceding four protocols are layered above the end-to-end data flow protocols, which means that they ensure reliable data delivery without knowing the source and destination of the data. These protocols pass on their data to the lower protocols, which take the responsibility for finding the right destination.

So far, we've classified the protocols according to functions that are needed to get data from one place to another. We could stop here and have a functioning network system. But such a system would be difficult to use because users must select other destination nodes by a numeric network address that would be difficult to remember.

## BACKGROUNDER

## End Systems and Intermediate Systems

End-to-end data flow means getting the data from one network socket to another; AppleTalk protocols in this category make certain that data are transmitted to the right destination.

There is an important difference between end-to-end data flow and system-to-system data flow. This explains the presence of the garage in Figure 3-1. At Layers 1, 2, and 3, data flow is from one system to

the adjacent relaying or routing system. At Layers 4 and above, the data flows from one end all the way to the other without being explicitly processed by the intermediate systems.

On a LAN, of course, there are no intermediate systems and everything is end-to-end. But in a WAN or a LAN with routers, gateways, or bridges, not all traffic is end-to-end.

Apple's solution is to assign names to every network device or service. The two protocols responsible for handling these named devices and services so that they are easy to use and so that the network understands what the users want are the Name Binding Protocol (NBP) and the Zone Information Protocol (ZIP). We explain these further in the section on the Name Binding Protocol later in this chapter.

The final category, end-user services, represents what the user will probably want to do with the network. AppleTalk defines two fundamental user services: file sharing and printing. File sharing is defined by the AppleTalk Filing Protocol (AFP); printing is covered by PostScript. Although PostScript isn't owned by Apple (it's patented by Adobe Systems), it is included in the protocol stack because it's a common interface for networked printer output on Macs. (Apple's first laser printers mainly supported PostScript as the page description language.)

Beyond file sharing and printing, the whole area of *IPC* (Inter-Process Communication) or *PPC* (Process-to-Process Communication) is also a big part of most networks. Although technologies such as Novell's NetWare have put blinders on the eyes of many network managers, the availability of more interesting services, such as graphics (see Chapter 25), electronic mail (see Chapter 24), and groupware (see Chapter 23) can make networks more than just printer and disk sharing tools.

If you're new to AppleTalk or don't need to figure out what each protocol is doing on the network, you may want to stop here. Up to this point, the chapter has presented a broad overview of the various protocols and their functions. You can skim the rest of the chapter if you're interested. But if you're curious about how the protocols accomplish their functions, or if you need to understand their operations for troubleshooting purposes, continue with the next section, which covers the AppleTalk protocols in more explicit detail. (Details on the AppleTalk packet formats are found in Appendix A.)

# A Detailed Look at the AppleTalk Protocols

The next sections provide an in-depth look at AppleTalk protocols. Users, who are mainly concerned with end-user services, generally deal with protocols from the top of the stack downward; from Layer 7, the application layer, down to Layer 1, the physical layer. We'll start our discussion of the protocol suite, however, with the lower layers (see Figure 3-7) and work our way upward. It's more effective to proceed in this direction; as you get to the higher layers in the protocol stack, you'll find that many protocols often use the same protocol in a layer below them. Working our way up from the bottom, makes tracking these relationships easier and reduces repetition.

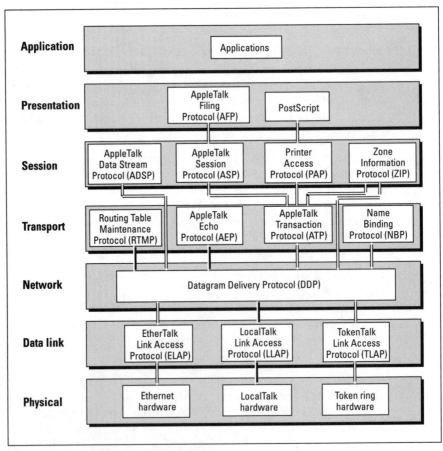

**Figure 3-7: The complete AppleTalk protocol stack.**

## Layer 1: The physical layer

Referring again to Figure 3-7, notice Layer 1, the physical layer of the protocol stack, which is responsible for handling the network hardware. Standard network hardware, such as that defined for Ethernet and token ring networks can be used with AppleTalk. Apple has also defined its own network hardware, called *LocalTalk*, which uses a synchronous RS-422A bus for communications. Bits are encoded on the cable using FM (Frequency Modulation) 0 encoding (see Figure 3-8).

FM 0 is a biphase encoding technique that provides self-clocking (see Chapter 2, "Understanding Networks" for more information). With this method, a transition occurs at the beginning and end of each bit; 0s also have a transition in the middle — the 1s do not. LocalTalk's transmission speed in the absence of any special hardware is 230,400 bps (bits per second). Several manufacturers have made special LocalTalk connectors that increase the bit rate of LocalTalk, but these were never very reliable in the first place and are hardly necessary now that Ethernet is widely and inexpensively available.

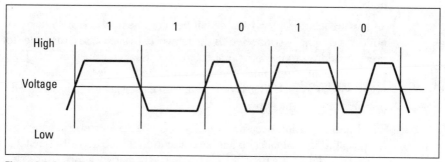

**Figure 3-8: LocalTalk uses FM 0 encoding.**

To prevent unwanted reflections of the LocalTalk signals, Apple's network connectors contain an internal 100-ohm resistor for unused ports. Farallon's PhoneNET connectors do not include internal resistors, but require insertion of a 120-ohm resistor into unused ports to counter reflections. In each case, the transformers used within the connectors provide ground isolation as well as protection from static discharge.

## Layer 2: The data link layer

The next layer upward in the AppleTalk protocol stack is Layer 2 — the data link layer. The data link layer, which is responsible for interfacing to the network hardware, includes three protocols called LAPs (for Link Access Protocols). The original LAP defined by Apple was the ALAP (AppleTalk Link Access Protocol).

With the passage of time, ALAP was renamed LLAP (LocalTalk Link Access Protocol) to distinguish it from other LAPs that were defined for Ethernet (ELAP) and token ring (TLAP) hardware. A few other LAPs have been defined by third-party vendors; the most notable ones are the ARCNet LAP and the PPP (Point-to-Point Protocol) LAP.

Each LAP is designed to handle what is known as *dynamic node ID assignment*. Simply put, this means that a node picks its node number whenever it starts up. This is the same address we called the *network address* in the previous chapter. This also means that a node does not necessarily have the same ID each time it starts up.

The procedure for dynamic node ID assignment is relatively simple. When a node starts up, it randomly assigns itself an ID. The node then tests this ID by transmitting a control packet on the network to discover whether another node has that ID. If the ID is not being used, the node keeps that ID. If the ID is in use, the node must select a new ID and try again. As you might guess, this procedure can lead to heavy traffic on a large network. Nodes joining the network late in the game have more existing node IDs to conflict with and may retry a number of times to get an unused ID.

Things are a bit simpler if a node has been on the network previously, as when the node was originally connected to the network. In such cases, the Mac stores its previous address to use as its first try for dynamic node assignment. Therefore, a previously configured, unchanged network should experience only one round of node requests as each Mac is restarted, with each Mac using its assigned ID from its previous time on the network.

The LocalTalk Link Access Protocol is a CSMA/CA protocol, which means that it uses collision avoidance to handle contention on the network (see Chapter 2, "Understanding Networks"). LLAP expects the network cable to be clear for an Interdialog Gap (IDG) of 400 microseconds plus a random wait period before a transmission is initiated by a node. Each packet in the transmission is separated by no more than 200 microseconds (the Interframe Gap, or IFG).

LLAP can choose to send packets either to a single node in a *directed transmission* or to all nodes in a *broadcast transmission*. In both cases, LLAP sends a Request-to-Send packet (lapRTS) to the destination node. For a directed transmission, the destination is the node ID; for the broadcast transmission, the node ID has the address of $FF in hexadecimal (or 255 in decimal). When the transmission is directed, LLAP waits for a Clear-to-Send packet (lapCTS) from the destination node and then transmits a data packet to the destination. In the case of a broadcast, however, the source node simply waits for one IFG and then broadcasts the packet.

The LocalTalk LAP defines two types of packets, which are specified in the LLAP type field (see Appendix A). If the type field contains a value in the range 128-255 ($80-$FF), the LLAP packet is a control packet and does not contain a data field. On the other hand, if the value is between 1 and 127 ($01-$7F), the LLAP is a data packet. Data packets can contain up to 600 bytes of data.

Two other LAPs are worth noting at this point. These are the EtherTalk LAP (ELAP) and the TokenTalk LAP (TLAP). *EtherTalk* is Apple's name for Apple-Talk protocols running on Ethernet, whereas *TokenTalk* is Apple's name for AppleTalk running on token ring networks. In each case, because of the modularity of the AppleTalk protocol stack, all the protocols above the data link layer function independently of these LAP definitions. In other words, once you get to the protocols starting at the network layer and above, it doesn't matter what network medium you're working with.

One advantage of working with layered protocols is that switching among the different media is handled within the data link layer by the LAP Manager (see Figure 3-9). The most common interface to this at the user level is the Network Control Panel which is found in Macintosh System 7 (see Figure 3-10).

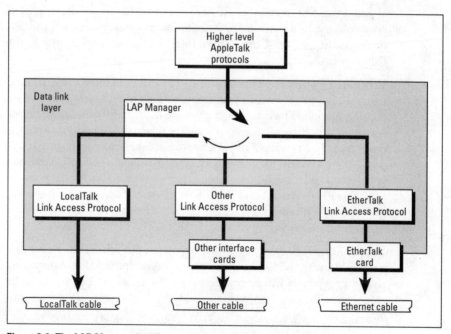

Figure 3-9: The LAP Manager handles switching among the different media.

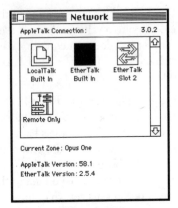

**Figure 3-10: The Network control panel lets you choose which kind of network AppleTalk will use. Most Macintoshes are only connected to one network, but many, such as PowerBooks, have several.**

When Apple first introduced EtherTalk as an extension of the AppleTalk Phase 1 protocols, the Ethernet version 2 definition was used, as defined and promulgated by Digital Equipment Corporation, Intel, and Xerox (see Chapter 8, "Designing an Ethernet LAN").

When Apple upgraded its protocols to Phase 2, it adopted the IEEE standards for Ethernet and token ring, so that the EtherTalk packets now followed the IEEE 802.3 definition. The two packet types are defined differently. That means that a computer expecting to receive one packet type will not necessarily recognize the other type. The two types of packets are not inherently confusing. It would be possible for a system to receive both types, but most vendors have chosen to allow you to send and transmit only one of the two types. This is one reason you can have EtherTalk Phase 1 and EtherTalk Phase 2 Macs on the same network, but they cannot communicate with each other unless a transition router is present (see Appendix B, "Converting Phase 1 AppleTalk Networks to Phase 2").

In both EtherTalk types, Apple has registered the EtherTalk packet as Ethernet type $809B with the IEEE, the organization responsible for maintaining the international registry of Ethernet packet types. In the Phase 1 data packet, the Ethernet type field follows the hardware source address, as shown in Figure 3-11.

However, because EtherTalk Phase 2 packets use the IEEE 802.2 Logical Link Control (LLC) to promote connectivity over different data links, the Ethernet type is contained in the SNAP type field. (SNAP is the acronym for Sub-Network Access Point.) The SNAP field requires added information, namely an organization code, which is $080007 in Apple's case. (The full protocol type, which combines the organization code with the Ethernet type, is $080007809B.)

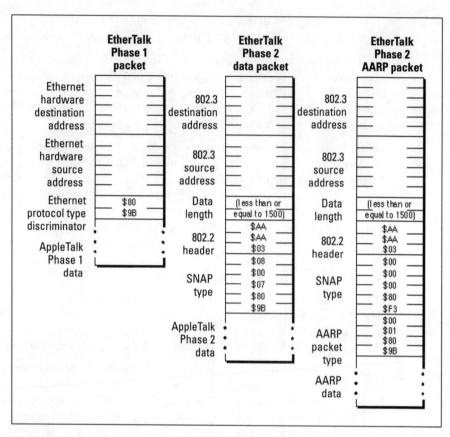

**Figure 3-11: A diagram of the types of EtherTalk packets.**

The TokenTalk LAP did not exist before the introduction of AppleTalk Phase 2, and there's only one definition of token ring packets. Consequently, TokenTalk doesn't suffer from the packet-typing problems just discussed for EtherTalk. AppleTalk follows the IEEE 802.5 standard for token ring packets. By supporting the 802.5 and the 802.2 LLC standards (in addition to 802.3 for Ethernet), AppleTalk can transmit data over an internetwork composed of LocalTalk, Ethernet, and token ring networks.

When Apple introduced EtherTalk, it also had to create a protocol that could map a hardware address to an AppleTalk protocol address. This protocol is known as the AppleTalk Address Resolution Protocol, or AARP. One reason for the existence of this protocol is AppleTalk's use of dynamically assigned 8-bit addresses for LocalTalk media, whereas Ethernet and token ring use a statically assigned 48-bit address.

Under AppleTalk Phase 2, which also added AARP support for token ring, the SNAP protocol type defined for AARP is $00000080F3. AARP lets an AppleTalk node multicast the question: "What is the Ethernet address of AppleTalk node

117?" When AppleTalk node 117 sees its number in an AARP request, it sends back its Ethernet address so that the two AppleTalk nodes can communicate.

AARP uses an Address Mapping Table (AMT) to simplify mapping between hardware addresses and protocol addresses. By keeping the most recently used addresses in the AMT, AARP can efficiently map addresses as needed. If an address is not contained in the AMT, AARP sends a request to the protocol address desired and adds the appropriate information to the AMT when the desired device replies.

AARP is also used to register a node's dynamically assigned address on the network (for non-LocalTalk networks). To accomplish this, AARP first assigns a tentative random address (one that's not already in the AMT), and then AARP broadcasts AARP probe packets on the network to determine whether another node is using the tentative address. If no other node is using the selected address, the address is made permanent. If another node is already using that address, however, AARP randomly picks another address and repeats this procedure until a usable address is found.

## Layer 3: The network layer

The third layer in the AppleTalk stack, the network layer, is responsible for accepting data from the layers above it and dividing the data into packets that can be sent over the network. Because the network layer creates the packets, it's also used to define the way packets should be treated if they've been damaged in transit.

Only one protocol, the Datagram Delivery Protocol (DDP), is present in the AppleTalk Network Layer. DDP is an important protocol because it communicates between two sockets on the network. The datagram defined by DDP is limited to 586 bytes of data and includes a checksum so that the destination node can verify the integrity of the data.

Prior to the introduction of AppleTalk Phase 2, only one type of DDP header existed — the *short DDP header*. The short DDP header uses both the source and destination sockets for addressing and is still used when both sockets are on the same network. (Remember that the internet address is the 8-bit socket number and the 8-bit node ID, as defined in the LAP.)

Phase 2 introduced the *long DDP header*, designed to accommodate Apple's extended network addressing scheme. The extended network internet address is defined as the 8-bit socket number, plus the 8-bit LAP-assigned node ID, plus the 16-bit network number assigned by DDP. In this way, AppleTalk Phase 2 overcame the restriction of 256 nodes per network, raising the limit to a nearly astronomical 16 million. Note, however, that the socket number assignment hasn't changed, still allowing only 256 sockets per node. Of the 256 sockets, only 128 are available for actual use because the first 64 ($01 through $3F) are reserved by Apple, and the next 64 ($40 through $7F) are set aside for unrestricted experimental use.

## Differences between AppleTalk Phase 1 and Phase 2

AppleTalk Phase 1 used *short DDP headers,* which addressed source and destination sockets by their 8-bit socket numbers and 8-bit node numbers.

AppleTalk Phase 2 uses the *long DDP header,* an extended address of the 8-bit socket number, 8-bit node ID, and 16-bit network number.

Each DDP packet contains the *hop count,* which is AppleTalk's way of tracking the number of routers the packet travels through from source to destination. In AppleTalk, a packet can traverse no more than 15 routers, which is to say that 15 is the maximum hop count. Every time a DDP packet passes through a router, the router increments the hop count by 1 hop as the router regenerates the packet.

# Layer 4: The transport layer

The next layer up from the network layer is Layer 4, the transport layer. Layer 4 includes four protocols. This is the first end-to-end layer. Layer 3 DDP packets are passed from router to router, with each router looking inside and sending it to the next router along the way. At the transport layer, the stations talk to each other directly - the transport layer headers are not changed as Layer 4 packets are passed around inside of Layer 3 packets.

Referring again to Figure 3-6, notice that two of these protocols are for end-to-end data flow, one is for reliable data delivery, and the last is for using AppleTalk's named entities. The four protocols are as follows:

❖ Routing Table Maintenance Protocol (RTMP)

❖ AppleTalk Echo Protocol (AEP)

❖ AppleTalk Transaction Protocol (ATP)

❖ Name Binding Protocol (NBP)

In the following sections, we explain each of these protocols in detail.

## The Routing Table Maintenance Protocol (RTMP)

The RTMP maintains information about internetwork addresses and connections between the various networks. Most of this protocol's work is performed on what is known as an *internet router.* RTMP defines the rules for information exchange between routers so that they can maintain their routing tables, as well as the rules for the information contained within each routing table.

## The Maximum Diameter of a Network

An AppleTalk network can have, at most, 15 routers between any two stations. Anything larger than that, and the packets will be discarded by the network router when the hop count in a DDP packet reaches 15. Apple's Internet Router software product can be used to get around this problem; it will reset hop counts when linking two different AppleTalk internets. Unfortunately, there is no equivalent for protocols such as TCP/IP, which have a similar problem.

Take a brief look at the AppleTalk routing table shown in Figure 3-12. Each entry within a routing table consists of five items:

❖ The network range

❖ The distance in hops to the destination network

❖ The port number of the destination network

❖ The node ID of the next router (also called the *entry state*)

❖ The status of each port

The routing table contains an entry for each network that a datagram can reach, within 15 hops of the router. The table is aged at set intervals as follows:

1.  First, the status of all entries is changed from good to suspect.

2.  Then the router sends an RTMP packet to all routers within its tables.

3.  If a response is not received within a set period of time, the entry for the nonresponding router is set to bad and removed from the routing table.

The data contained in the routing table is cross-referenced to the Zone Information Table (ZIT), which is needed to map networks into zones (see Figure 3-13). We'll go further into the relationship between the routing table and the Zone Information Table when we discuss the Zone Information Protocol later in this chapter.

The RTMP was originally assigned three packet types: the RTMP Request packet, the RTMP Data packet, and the RTMP Response packet. A fourth packet type was added in AppleTalk Phase 2 — the RTMP Route Data Request packet (RDR). The Route Data Request can be used by a nonrouter node (such as a network management program) to acquire the routing table of a specific router, or this request can be used by a router to load a routing table without waiting for the other routers to update their tables at the usual interval of 20 seconds.

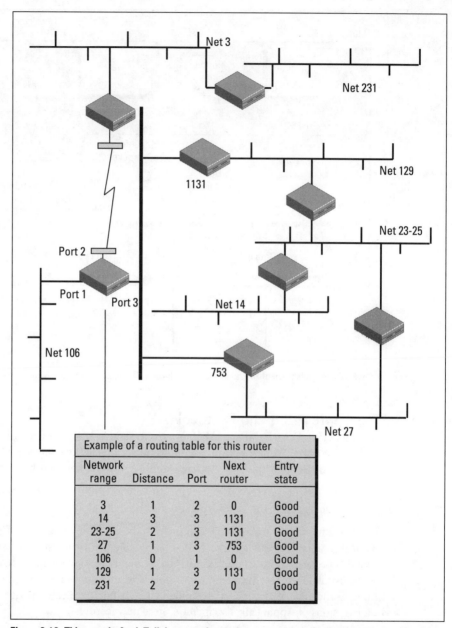

| Example of a routing table for this router | | | | |
|---|---|---|---|---|
| Network range | Distance | Port | Next router | Entry state |
| 3 | 1 | 2 | 0 | Good |
| 14 | 3 | 3 | 1131 | Good |
| 23-25 | 2 | 3 | 1131 | Good |
| 27 | 1 | 3 | 753 | Good |
| 106 | 0 | 1 | 0 | Good |
| 129 | 1 | 3 | 1131 | Good |
| 231 | 2 | 2 | 0 | Good |

**Figure 3-12: This sample AppleTalk internet shows the construction of a routing table for one of the routers.**

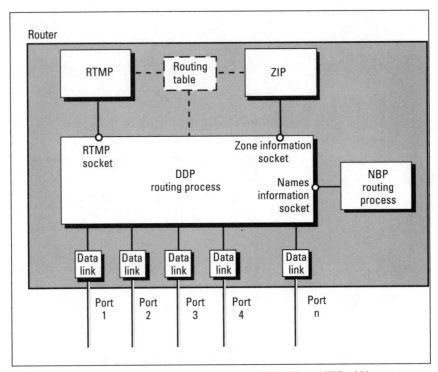

**Figure 3-13: An illustration of the relationships between RTMP, ZIP, and NBP within a router.**

## The AppleTalk Echo Protocol (AEP)

The AppleTalk Echo Protocol (AEP) is used to send a datagram from one node to another and cause the destination node to return, or *echo*, the datagram to the sender. To implement this process, each AppleTalk node has an echo socket.

Because the function of the AEP is comparatively uncomplicated, this protocol has only two packet types: the Echo Request and the Echo Reply.

Yet despite its simplicity, the AEP can prove to be useful on a network. First, this protocol can determine whether a node is accessible before any sessions are started. Second, a programmer can use the AEP to estimate the round-trip delay time for a data transmission between two nodes. (Apple now includes other mechanisms for timing round-trip delay times with AppleTalk version 56, released with System 7. Later versions of AppleTalk also include these new features.)

## The AppleTalk Transaction Protocol (ATP)

The AppleTalk Transaction Protocol (ATP) uses three types of transactions: the ATP Transaction Request (TReq), the ATP Transaction Response (TResp), and the ATP Transaction Release (TRel). The ATP is one of the methods that

AppleTalk uses to ensure that DDP packets are delivered to a destination without any losses (the other is the AppleTalk Data Stream Protocol). ATP accomplishes this result by requiring a reply to every ATP transaction. In other words, every time that ATP is requested to send a packet, the receiver socket must report the outcome of the transfer. The first action is referred to as a *transaction request*, and the report of the action is a *transaction response*.

Because ATP maintains a conversation between two sockets by pairing transaction requests with transaction responses, ATP can deal with three possible network errors:

1.  A transaction request is lost on the network.

2.  A transaction response is lost or delayed on the network.

3.  A responder becomes unreachable.

ATP determines whether these conditions occur by using a timer; if the timer expires before a response is received, ATP retransmits its original request. ATP will stop trying to retransmit when it gets a response or when the maximum retry count is reached.

Because ATP can retry packet transmissions that are required due to a lost packet, data may not arrive in its original sequence. This condition can lead to problems in protocols which do not automatically resequence transmissions. For example, if the transactions are database transactions and they both update the same record, then without a strict sequence, the database would not know which value to use as the final value.

One way of handling the problems of lost or delayed transactions is to enable an automatic retry mechanism. If a response is not received within a set period of time, the requester will retransmit a Transition Request (TReq), and the process is repeated until the response is received or the maximum retry count is reached. (If the maximum retry count is reached, the requester is notified that the responder is unreachable.) This approach is called the ALO (*At-Least-Once*) transaction. If ALO transactions are used, it is up to the responder to handle retransmission of responses to duplicate requests.

To counter the difficulty of handling duplicate requests, ATP can be programmed to operate in XO (*Exactly-Once*) transactions. By maintaining a transactions list, ATP can filter out duplicate transaction requests (caused by a lost transaction response, for example) and re-send transactions as needed. On small networks, such as a single AppleTalk network, ATP XO transactions can be quite effective. In an internet, however, packets may arrive at their destination in an order different from the order in which they were sent (by traveling through different routers, for example). This situation requires additional program control to ensure proper sequencing. Alternatively, a different protocol, such as ADSP, can be used.

The third ATP transaction, the ATP Release, is used to close a transaction session once all data has been transferred and acknowledged. Each of the transaction types — request, response, and release — is represented by a TID (Transaction Identifier), which appears in the ATP request packet and has a maximum size of 16 bits. The limited size of the transaction identifier ($2^{16}$ = 65,536) can lead to *roll-over*, or repeated use of the same TIDs for transactions involving large numbers of packets. ATP can send more than one ATP response packet in sequence as a reply — the maximum number of ATP response packets for a single request packet is 8.

## The Name Binding Protocol (NBP)

The Name Binding Protocol (NBP) is important in the AppleTalk scheme of things. As you recall, to maintain communications, the network itself operates with *numeric internet addresses*, but the AppleTalk user works with *named entities*. AppleTalk internally represents any named entity, which is a network service such as a file server or a network device such as your Mac, according to the following conventions:

**object:type@zone**

In this line, *object* is the name of the user or service name, *type* is the entity classification, and *zone* is the logical zone of the AppleTalk internet.

Given these conventions, then, consider the following line:

**Bldg. 3 Printer:LaserWriter@California**

In this line, Bldg. 3 Printer represents the *object*; LaserWriter represents the *type*; and California represents the *zone*. These conventions are only used internally by AppleTalk protocols; the Chooser serves as the user's interface to named entities (see Figure 3-14). When you select one of the icons shown in the Chooser, you're selecting the device *type*; the *zone* list is shown below the list of icons, and the list of *objects* matching the selected type is displayed in the right half of the Chooser.

The Name Binding Protocol handles the translations between the numeric internet addresses and alphanumeric entity names. The NBP maintains a table of *mappings* (a names table) between internet addresses (a node) and name socket clients (named entities) that reside in that node. Because each node maintains its own list of named entities, the names directory within an AppleTalk network is not centralized, but is a distributed database of all nodes on the internet.

This approach to storing entity names requires a socket that needs to communicate with a named service to first find out where the service is by requesting its location. This request is made via the NBP Broadcast Request (BrRq) packet, which names the desired entity and requests the network address for that named entity. On a single network, each node responds to the NBP Broadcast Request (BrRq) and searches its internal names table for a match. When a match is found, NBP sends a LookUp-Reply to the requesting socket, including the address of the named entity (see Figure 3-15). If the request is made on an internet, the router forwards the BrRq to each network in the specified target zone, causing the affected nodes to perform the search of their names tables.

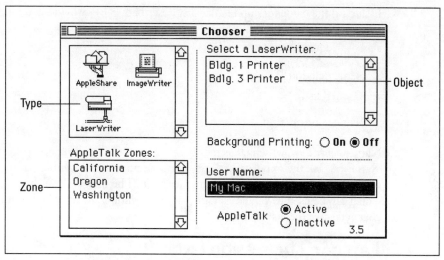

Figure 3-14: The Chooser is the user's interface to selecting named entities on AppleTalk.

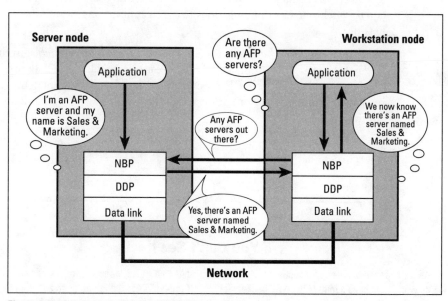

Figure 3-15: An example of the name binding process.

In the example in Figure 3-15, the workstation sends an NBP LkUp for AFP servers. The server node named Sales & Marketing then replies that it is an AFP server and supplies its network address.

Including the name lookup feature just described, NBP provides a total of four services to accomplish this search:

1. Name registration

2. Name deletion

3. Name lookup

4. Name confirmation

Name *registration*, which takes place on each node, is used to build the names table. Name *deletion*, the opposite of registration, occurs when an entity has its name and socket number removed from the names table. The final is name *confirmation*, which can be used to validate a name-address binding, to see whether it has changed since the last lookup.

## Layer 5: The session layer

Situated atop the transport layer is Layer 5, the session layer. The main purpose of this layer is to manage the conversations among end users (hence the word *session*) and to synchronize communications between applications located throughout the network.

As with the transport layer, the session layer contains four protocols. In this case, three of the protocols (AppleTalk Data Stream Protocol, AppleTalk Session Protocol, and Printer Access Protocol) are related to reliable data delivery. The remaining protocol, the Zone Information Protocol, is used for handling named entities on the network.

QUICK TIPS

### If You Can't See It . . .

A very common technique for security in AppleTalk networks is to have a router filter NBP packets for a certain kind of device. For example, if the Check Printing laser printer was on one side of a router and J. Random Hacker was on the other, the router could filter out all NBP requests for devices named "Check Printing." Even though traffic to and from the printer could still flow through the router, blocking NBPs means that Mr. Hacker can't find out the address of the printer to send data ... because he cannot see it!

## The AppleTalk Data Stream Protocol (ADSP)

Like the AppleTalk Transaction Protocol, the AppleTalk Data Stream Protocol (ADSP) is responsible for reliable transmission of data between two sockets. Unlike ATP, however, ADSP provides full-duplex byte-stream delivery, which means that a conversation between two computers can take place in both directions at the same time. ADSP also includes flow control, so that a fast sender does not overwhelm a slow receiver.

ADSP uses the concept of a *connection-to-connection* data exchange between two nodes. Only when both nodes have established a connection end by using ADSP can data be exchanged between them. If only one node is able to establish a connection end, the connection is called *half-open* and can be automatically closed by that node if a second connection end at the other node fails to be established within a preset time interval.

After a connection is established, ADSP uses a 32-bit sequence number to ensure the sequential flow of data between connection ends (compare this number to ATP's 16-bit transaction ID). ADSP also uses packet sequencing to make certain that packets are received in the correct order. Every ADSP data packet contains a number identifying the packet's sequence in the data stream — the receiving node compares this number with its own counter to track the next expected packet. If the two numbers coincide, the packet is accepted; otherwise, the packet is discarded.

ADSP is also capable of controlling the rate at which data is sent from one node to another, a process known as *flow control*. Flow control keeps a data transmitter from overwhelming the buffer space of a slower receiver. To accomplish this controlled rate, the receiving node periodically updates the transmitting node by reporting the amount of available buffer space. As a side benefit of this mechanism, two nodes participating in a connection can negotiate a suitably sized window to take advantage of larger bandwidth networks (which is something ATP cannot do).

### Understanding ADSP Packets

ADSP uses two types of packets to set up and maintain connections: *control packets* and *data packets*. Control packets can be used to probe or acknowledge a connection, open or close a connection, or negotiate a retransmission of a series of data packets. The second type of packets, data packets, are just what the name suggests: These are packets designed to exchange data using DDP. Up to 572 bytes of data can be stuffed into a packet. (The DDP type field equals 7 for ADSP packets.)

When a device such as a LaserWriter is busy processing a job, it's doing very little on the network. Under such circumstances, the client of the LaserWriter periodically sends out *tickler packets* (which are a kind of control packet called a *probe* packet) to the LaserWriter to make sure that it's still working.

## The AppleTalk Session Protocol (ASP)

Many AppleTalk communications between a workstation and a server occur during a session between the two. Once a connection is made between a workstation and server, it's up to the AppleTalk Session Protocol (ASP) to pass the commands that make up a session. ASP ensures that the commands are delivered in the same order as they were sent and returns the results of these commands to the workstation.

The AppleTalk Session Protocol uses two protocols in the transport layer to do its job. ASP employs NBP to obtain the address of the server's session listening socket so that it knows to which address it should direct commands. ASP also uses ATP to provide the transport service for its packets. ASP does *not* perform two important tasks: First, it does not ensure that consecutive commands are completed in the order they were sent to the server; and second, ASP does not allow the server to send commands to the workstation, as it can only use the attention mechanism to alert the workstation.

Within ASP, four basic processes occur. The first two are rather obvious: these are the processes of opening and closing a session. The third, called *session request handling*, conveys the commands from workstation to server and returns the replies from the server. Fourth, there's *session management*, which, in this case, uses a tickler packet to make sure that both ends of the connections are still operational. The following discussion of PAP will give more information on tickler packets.

## The Printer Access Protocol (PAP)

As its name implies, the Printer Access Protocol, or PAP, takes the responsibility for maintaining communications between a workstation and a printer (or print service). PAP functions include setting up and maintaining a connection, as well as transferring the data and tearing down the connection on completion of a job.

When a connection is established, either socket client can send or receive data. This two-way communication is necessary because printers often must control the amount of data sent (by asking for the next page) or reply with the printer's status.

As with other protocols in the session layer, PAP relies on NBP to find the addresses of named entities. PAP also depends on ATP for sending data (see Figure 3-16). On a workstation, the application uses the Print Manager software to communicate with the PAP. The client, or workstation, side of PAP then maintains a session with the networked printer (a PAP server) to print the required pages.

The Printer Access Protocol covers five basic processes: opening a connection, transferring data, closing a connection, determining a print service's status, and filtering duplicate requests. (Because PAP uses ATP, duplicate packets can be received from a node; see the previous description of ATP for an explanation of the problems involved.)

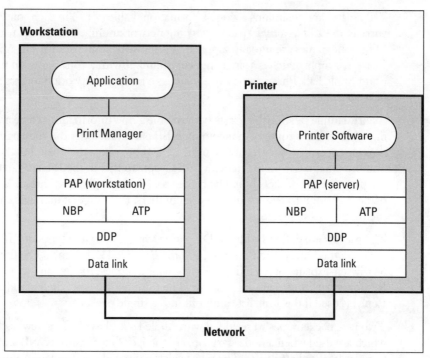

**Figure 3-16: A workstation prints to a server using AppleTalk's PAP protocol.**

One of PAP's capabilities is to handle half-open connections, which occur when one side of the connection goes down or terminates without informing its partner. To cope with half-open connections, PAP maintains a connection timer at both ends. If the connection timer expires before any packets are received, the connection is terminated.

To assist in maintaining a connection, PAP also sends tickler packets periodically. As you might expect, ticklers are used to keep the other end informed that the device is actually still on-line, even if it otherwise appears that nothing's happening. Many printers spend most of their time processing the data, while ignoring nearly everything else; sending a tickler tells the user that something is happening and that the printer hasn't gone down.

## The Zone Information Protocol (ZIP)

One of the unique features of AppleTalk is its use of logical groupings of networks. These logical groupings are presented to the user as names. The groupings are called zones — each AppleTalk zone consists of a collection of AppleTalk networks. Working in concert with the Routing Table Maintenance Protocol (RTMP), the Zone Information Protocol, or ZIP, helps routers maintain a mapping of network numbers to zones for the entire internet.

ZIP creates and maintains a Zone Information Table (ZIT) in each router. Each entry in the ZIT is a *tuple* (pair), matching network numbers and zone names. (The zone names are initially supplied by a network administrator.) In AppleTalk Phase 1, a tuple matches a single network number with a zone name. In routers using AppleTalk Phase 2, the tuple matches a range of network numbers and a list of zone names.

A fairly simple relationship exists between the Zone Information Table and a routing table within a router: An incoming NBP packet includes the zone name, which the router compares with entries in the ZIT. The router then matches the network number obtained from the matching ZIT tuple to that in the RTMP table to find the port that the packet should be routed to. (With AppleTalk Phase 2, a zone name may point to a range of network numbers; this range of numbers still directs the router to a single port.)

ZIP packets are defined with a DDP packet type of 6. Three types of ZIP packets are used: the Query, the Response, and the Extended ZIP Reply. The first two are nearly self-explanatory; a ZIP Query contains a request for a zone list, and the Response packet returns the zone list. The third packet type, the Extended ZIP Reply, is used if the zone list cannot fit into a single packet.

Two new packet types were added with AppleTalk Phase 2. The new packet types, which are used when a node starts up, are the ZIP GetNetInfo (GNI) and the ZIP GetNetInfoReply (GNIR). The new packet types make it simpler for nonrouter nodes (such as your workstation) to obtain the name of any zone on the internet. ZIP GetNetInfo tells the node which zone it has chosen to be in (from the node's original setup); otherwise, the zone name is set to local (*zone* = *), and a GetNetInfoReply (GNIR) from the router tells the node which zone to use (if it's not specified). ZIP GetNetInfoReply also provides a multicast address for the zone.

## Layer 6: The presentation layer

The next-to-last layer is the presentation layer, which handles issues related to data files and formats. In addition to file formats and translations between formats, tools such as data encryption and data compression are part of the presentation layer.

Only two protocols, the AppleTalk Filing Protocol (AFP) and PostScript, are part of the presentation layer. The first protocol is used to provide remote access to files on a network. The second, PostScript, is the well-known page description language used by many printers. We won't be covering PostScript in any detail in this book. If you want to learn more about PostScript, you should get a copy of the *PostScript Language Reference Manual*, published by Addison-Wesley for Adobe, Inc.

The AppleTalk Filing Protocol provides both Mac and non-Mac workstations with a means of accessing files on a file server's shared disk while still using a workstation's native file system commands. To accomplish this, AFP employs an AFP translator to convert native file system commands into AFP calls that will be understood by the server (see Figure 3-17).

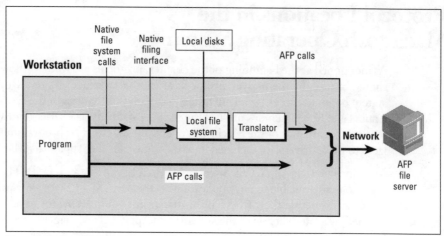

**Figure 3-17: The AFP file access model.**

A program can either directly issue AFP calls, or the AFP Translator can translate calls from the native file system to AFP calls. Only AFP calls are transmitted on the network to the AFP server.

It's up to the application developer to design a translator for the native file system in use. Apple currently includes translators for the Macintosh, Apple II (ProDOS), and MS-DOS file systems.

AFP uses the AppleTalk Session Protocol to open and maintain a session between the workstation and the server. Before this occurs, the workstation uses the Name Binding Protocol to look up the file server's name and obtain its address. Once a connection is established, the workstation uses AFP to log onto the server, after which the server and workstation exchange information regarding the level of access to the server's files that has been granted to the workstation.

Many details of AFP, especially as they pertain to servers, will be discussed later in this book in the chapter on file sharing (see Chapter 22, "Sharing Files on AppleTalk Networks").

# Layer 7: The application layer

The top layer of the OSI model is the application layer, which is the layer of most interest to you as a user. This is the layer at which all of your programs are going to work. And at this level you'll decide if an application is going to use the network to access other files or to send and receive electronic mail. AppleTalk has no specific protocols for the application layer, since printing and file service are all carried at a lower level. Other network systems, such as TCP/IP, have protocols for file transfer, remote terminal emulation, and other network services at Layer 7.

# Protocol Locations in the Macintosh Operating System

As mentioned at the beginning of the chapter, protocols are rules for how networks should behave. By themselves, protocols are not software. It's up to the operating system or application to implement the protocols in software. In the case of AppleTalk, Apple includes most of the network software as a series of driver resources that are part of the Macintosh operating system. The programming interfaces to these drivers are included in what Apple calls the AppleTalk Manager.

Macs include four AppleTalk drivers: .MPP, .ATP, .XPP, and .DSP. These drivers are resources available to any application on the Mac. Most Macs already have these drivers within their ROM; if the drivers are not in ROM (or have been patched by a later version of the system), the AppleTalk Manager software is read from disk and loaded into the system heap.

As you can see from Figure 3-18, the .MPP driver implements the LocalTalk Link Access Protocol for connecting to the network hardware, as well as the DDP, AEP, and NBP protocols. The .ATP driver has only one protocol associated with it, the AppleTalk Transaction Protocol, handling both transaction requests and transaction responses.

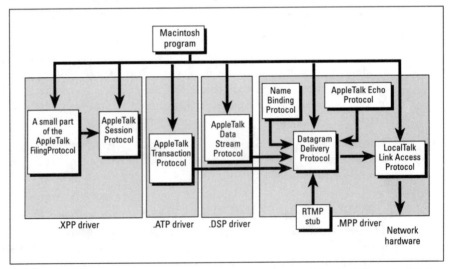

Figure 3-18: This schematic shows which Mac drivers contain the code for the different AppleTalk protocols.

The .XPP driver is the Extended Protocol Package. Within the .XPP driver are the workstation (or client) side of ASP and a portion of the AppleTalk Filing Protocol, the part responsible for sending AFP commands to the file server. Other software has the responsibility for translating native file system calls to AFP calls. With the introduction of AppleTalk Phase 2, the .XPP driver also includes part of the Zone Information Protocol functions.

Because ADSP was introduced as a protocol after the initial roll out of AppleTalk, ADSP was usually added as a separate system file when needed. (Often the programs that used it included ADSP as part of the installation process on the Mac.) Macs which run System 7 have a built-in .DSP driver; this implements ADSP and removes any need for the separate ADSP file found in System 6.

A Macintosh can also include additional AppleTalk connection files, such as those used for EtherTalk and TokenTalk. An AppleTalk connection file has the file type adev and contains the code for a specific type of LAP for that data link (ELAP for EtherTalk or TLAP for token ring, for instance). When you're using the Network panel in the Control Panel to select a different network interface, you're asking the LAP Manager to select and load a new adev file.

# The Evolution of AppleTalk Protocols

Networks are dynamic systems, and the protocols used to define them can change. These changes are often introduced to take advantage of new technology or to address limitations in the original specifications. First, we'll look at how Apple altered its protocol suite with the introduction of AppleTalk Phase 2, and then we'll move on to an overview of some of the mechanisms that Apple is currently using to introduce new protocols.

## AppleTalk Phase 2

When Apple first created AppleTalk, its designers defined the network protocols for small networks that would be easy to install and maintain. But AppleTalk quickly grew in popularity, and its easy installation encouraged networks to a point that they outgrew the expectations of AppleTalk's architects.

A variety of problems began to crop up on the larger networks that used multiple routers and corporate backbones, notably on those using Ethernet. To resolve the inadequacies of the original AppleTalk release, AppleTalk Phase 2 was released in 1989 with a redesigned suite of protocols.

Prior to the development of Phase 2, AppleTalk networks were restricted to 254 nodes per physical cable. For users with a large Ethernet backbone and Macs scattered throughout the plant, this arrangement quickly became unsatisfactory. Now,

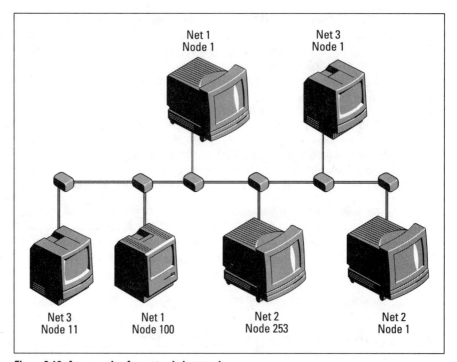

Net 1
Node 1

Net 3
Node 1

Net 3
Node 11

Net 1
Node 100

Net 2
Node 253

Net 2
Node 1

**Figure 3-19: An example of an extended network.**

with Phase 2, AppleTalk uses the concept of *extended addressing*. Rather than relying on the limited 8-bit node identification number, Phase 2 networks using
extended addressing employ a network address that consists of the 8-bit node number plus a 16-bit network number. This expands the network node limits to $2^{24}$
addresses, or over 16 million nodes on a single network. Note that each workstation can be assigned to a different network number, even though all workstations
are on the same cable (see Figure 3-19).

But not all networks running Phase 2 are extended networks. LocalTalk does
not implement extended addressing, for example. EtherTalk and TokenTalk networks, however, do implement extended addressing. This means that LocalTalk
networks are still limited to 254 nodes per cable.

Along with the extended addressing scheme just described, extended networks
enable you to assign a range of network numbers to each network. In the past, all
nodes on a single physical cable were assigned one network number. Under Phase
2, that's no longer the case.

The coexistence of extended and nonextended networks also prompted a change in
the way AppleTalk DDP packets are defined. For nonextended networks, especially LocalTalk networks, the DDP packet format remained as it was and became

known for containing the short DDP header. Short DDP headers are also used when the source and destination sockets have the same network number. The newer long DDP packets, containing the long DDP header, are meant for extended networks and include the full internet addresses of the source and destination sockets.

The dynamic aspect of addressing AppleTalk nodes has also changed somewhat from Phase 1 to Phase 2. In the past, a node selected a provisional address when it started up on the network. Now under Phase 2, this provisional address includes both the node's ID number and network number.

If a node must start with a provisional address, it communicates with the nearest router to determine whether the network number found in its provisional address falls within the network range of the router. If not, it selects one of the network numbers supported by the router. If there is no router on the network, the node uses the provisional address as its final address. This method makes it easier for large networks, such as those entirely on Ethernet or token ring, to function without using a router to assign network numbers.

AppleTalk Phase 2 introduced several new mechanisms for reducing traffic. One of these is the way the AppleTalk routers periodically exchange data packets, called RTMP Data packets. RTMP Data packets contain routing tables to create an up-to-date map of the internet; this map tells the router what the best path is to forward a data packet on to its destination.

Phase 2 also uses a routing technique called *split horizon*. Split-horizon routing is much more efficient than the routing method used in Phase 1, which was to send out routing information regarding what all routers know about all ports. With split-horizon routing, the router recognizes that a different set of information is needed for each port (the "horizon"). The router therefore "splits" the routing information. It only sends information out a port that is needed by networks listening to that port.

An example of split-horizon routing is shown in Figure 3-20. In the figure, router X has two ports: port B and port A. Three routers are attached to the Ethernet cable that is attached to port A. The three routers each have one LocalTalk network attached. Off port A, router X therefore has a total of four reachable networks: three LocalTalk networks (Net 1, Net 2, and Net 3) and one EtherTalk network (Net 4). Off port B, router X has two reachable networks: one LocalTalk network (Net 5) and one EtherTalk network (Net 6).

Router X will advertise the two routes that are reachable via its port B only out of port A. In other words, the RTMP Data packet that router X sends out of port B will *not* contain routing information regarding the networks that are reachable via port B (Nets 5 and 6). Likewise, router X will not send an RTMP Data packet with routing information regarding the four networks (Nets 1, 2, 3, 4) reachable via port A out of port A.

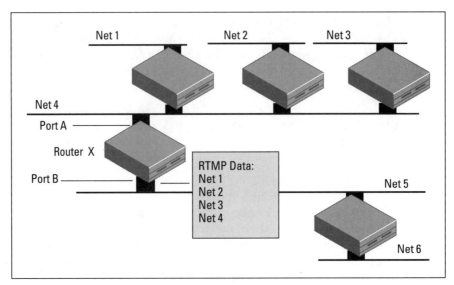

**Figure 3-20: An example of split-horizon routing.**

Another method that reduces traffic and provides convenience for users is the Phase 2 support for *multiple zones per network cable*. Multiple zones on one network enable the administrator to set up logical areas to group services. For example, putting all of the Engineering department's Ethernet file servers in a zone called Engineering will enable users to quickly find their file servers in the Chooser. The reduced traffic benefit comes because the name lookup requests (NBP LkUp) are sent only to nodes in a particular zone rather than to all the nodes on the Ethernet. For more information about AppleTalk routers, see Chapter 2, "Understanding Networks," and Chapter 11, "Designing an AppleTalk LAN."

AppleTalk Phase 2 uses another mechanism — called *directed broadcasting* — for reducing network traffic. In the past, AppleTalk devices would broadcast packets to all nodes on a given network. On an Ethernet network, for example, broadcast packets would be received by AppleTalk nodes as well as non-AppleTalk nodes (VAXes, UNIX boxes, and so on). These non-AppleTalk nodes had to receive the broadcast packets and then process and discard them, thereby reducing the node's efficiency.

With directed broadcasting, AppleTalk nodes register to receive packets from a multicast address (defined by DDP). Non-AppleTalk nodes do not register on that address, so they cannot receive or be interrupted by AppleTalk broadcasts. Routers on Phase 2 internets can also assign various zone multicast addresses to the network nodes. Using these zone multicast addresses, a router can then multicast packets to nodes within selected zones on the network.

Finally, AppleTalk Phase 2 includes support for certain networking standards. This support includes IEEE 802.3 for Ethernet and 802.5 for token ring. Also, for internets requiring more than one network media (such as networks containing both Ethernet and token ring), AppleTalk Phase 2 uses the IEEE 802.2 Logical Link Control specification, enabling AppleTalk packets to be sent over the entire network.

## Introducing the new AppleTalk protocols

When Apple introduced the Phase 2 protocol suite, no protocols were added other than those in the physical and data link layers. Most of what Apple changed in Phase 2 was accomplished by changing definitions and variables within the existing protocols.

Since then, Apple has added several new protocols to the Macintosh. The *AppleTalk Update-Based Routing Protocol* (AURP) has been designed to make it easier for users to connect LANs into wide area networks (WANs) and reduce routing table updates over the WAN link. We discuss AURP's capabilities in detail in Chapter 12, "Designing an AppleTalk WAN."

At the physical and data link layers, Apple developed a new protocol for using tele-communications links between a single user and a network. Introduced at the same time as the Mac PowerBooks in late 1991, Apple Remote Access Protocol (ARAP) lets a Mac user dial into a network and use any of the network services as if the Mac were physically attached to the network. You can read more about remote access and ARAP in Chapter 10, "Using Modems with Networks."

Finally, Apple has also decided to implement another foreign, or non-AppleTalk, protocol to assist in network management. Apple has been working on MIBs (Management Information Base) for both Macs and AppleTalk routers for use with the Simple Network Management Protocol (SNMP), which was originally defined for use with TCP/IP networks. SNMP and Macintosh systems are covered in Chapter 13, "Configuring, Monitoring, and Fixing AppleTalk Networks."

# CHAPTER 3  CONCEPTS AND TERMS

- The OSI Reference Model is a seven-layer model that defines basic network functions.

- Protocol specifications set forth how a protocol exchanges data and sends signaling information to its peer at the other end of the network. Service definitions define how a layer interacts with the protocols in the layer above and below it.

- The AppleTalk protocols fall into distinct layers according to the OSI Reference Model, but they can be further classified according to their functions.

- The physical layer of the protocol stack handles the network's hardware.

- The data link layer contains the AppleTalk Link Access Protocols (LAPs), which are responsible for interfacing to the network hardware.

- The network layer, containing the AppleTalk Datagram Delivery Protocol (DDP), is an important layer that is responsible for accepting data from the layers above it and dividing the data into packets that can be sent across the network.

- The transport layer includes four protocols that are responsible for end-to-end data flow, reliable data delivery, and the use of AppleTalk named entities.

- The session layer, which contains four protocols, manages network conversations among end users.

- The presentation layer handles issues related to data files and formats, and includes two protocols.

## directed broadcasting
AppleTalk nodes register to receive packets from a multicast address (defined by DDP). Non-AppleTalk nodes do not register on that address, so they cannot receive or be interrupted by AppleTalk broadcasts. Opposed to broadcast.

## dynamic node assignment
This means that a node picks its node number whenever it starts up. This is the same address we called the *network address* in the previous chapter. This also means that a node does not necessarily have the same ID each time it starts up.

## EtherTalk
The name given to AppleTalk protocols transmitted over Ethernet media.

## LocalTalk
The name for Apple's low-cost connectivity products consisting of cables, connection boxes, cable extenders, and other equipment.

## mappings
The redirection of local resources to network resources.

## OSI reference model
A model for the modularization of network protocols and their functions. Each layer communicates only with the layer immediately above and below it. The OSI Reference Model has seven layers: physical layer, data link layer, network layer, transport layer, session layer, presentation layer, and application layer. OSI stands for Open Systems Interconnection.

## peer-to-peer communications
Networks that let workstations and other nodes communicate with each other as equals.

## protocol stacks (suites)
The implementation of a specific protocol family in a computer or other node on the network. The stack refers to the visual analogy of all of the layers of a set of protocols — a stack of protocols.

## signaling
Protocols spend a lot of time signaling, which is all of the overhead of networks. Protocol signaling includes functions such as setting up connections and sessions; error detection, control, and correction; routing and relaying; and congestion control. All of these are required for the network to work, even if they don't pass any real data.

## split horizon
Phase 2 uses a routing technique called *split horizon*. Split-horizon routing is much more efficient than the routing method used in Phase 1, which was to send out routing information regarding what all routers know about all ports. With split-horizon routing, the router recognizes that a different set of information is needed for each port (the "horizon"). The router therefore "splits" the routing information. It only sends information out a port that is needed by networks listening to that port.

## tickler packets
A kind of control packet called a *probe* packet used in ADSP.

## TokenTalk
Apple's name for AppleTalk running on token ring networks.

## zone
A collection of networks on an AppleTalk internet. A zone can consist of a single network or a number of networks. One of the main reasons for breaking a network into zones is to reduce the amount of searching a user has to do to find a resource on the network.

CHAPTER FOUR

# AppleTalk Protocols in Action

IN THIS CHAPTER

- We discuss the sequence of AppleTalk protocols for a variety of actions, including the following:

- Registering your Mac on the network

- Selecting a printer

- Printing on the network

- Using an AppleShare server

With so many protocols in the AppleTalk stack, a number of activities may result from each simple action that you perform on a network. Some of the protocols discussed in Chapter 3, such as RTMP and ZIP, are invisible to you as a user because they are meant primarily for such network devices as routers. But you do use the information that these protocols maintain on the network, even if you use it indirectly. We selected a few common network actions that you or your Mac ordinarily perform to show you which protocols are used for these actions and to illustrate how the protocols are used.

This chapter will discuss the following network tasks and answer the appropriate questions:

❖ **Registering your Mac on the network:** What procedures does the Mac follow for dynamic node addressing when you first turn on your Mac?

❖ **Selecting a printer:** What happens when you open the Chooser and select a LaserWriter on the network?

❖ **Printing on the network:** What is the sequence of protocols used in printing to a LaserWriter?

❖ **Using an AppleShare server:** What protocols are used when you select an AppleShare server, log onto it, and mount a volume?

QUOTABLES

"Those Macintoshes aren't the cute little boxes you think they are."

— Elizabeth Zwicky

To help explore which protocols are used and in what sequence, we've included two charts that help explain each session. The first, Figure 4-1, is a simple flow chart showing the flow of control and data through the AppleTalk protocol stack. The second, Figure 4-2, is a network activity chart, which shows you what protocol data is exchanged between the devices involved in that task.

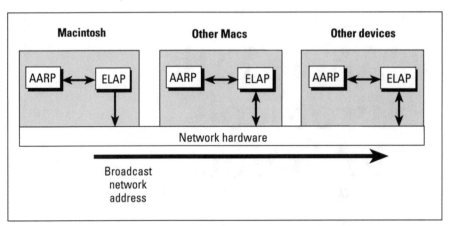

Figure 4-1: This diagram shows the protocol flow for dynamic node number assignment.

# Registering Your Mac on the Network

For the first action, we'll look at the protocols used when your Mac attempts to assign itself a node number dynamically, using the AppleTalk Address Resolution Protocol (AARP) over EtherTalk.

Remember that a Mac randomly picks an address the first time it's used on the network; if the Mac has already succeeded in obtaining a legitimate network address from a previous connection to the network, it attempts to use that address first. Either way, your Mac must broadcast its selected address on the network to ensure that there are no conflicts.

The part of AARP used for network addressing is the AARP Probe. As an example, we'll discuss how the AARP Probe is used on Ethernet (see Figure 4-1). If the node is on a LocalTalk network, LLAP Enquiry packets are used to determine if the node address is unique.

When you turn on your Mac, the operating system instructs the AppleTalk Address Resolution Protocol (AARP) in your Mac's network interface (in this case, Ethernet, as signified by ELAP in Figure 4-1) to broadcast an AARP probe packet with the selected address. Any other AppleTalk node on the network receives the AARP Probe and compares your Mac's suggested address with its own. If the two addresses do not coincide, the node does nothing further. If the two addresses are identical, the node sends an AARP reply to the originator node of the AARP probe, informing it that the desired address is already being used.

As you work your way through the network activity diagram (see Figure 4-2) for the AARP procedure, note that the Mac first looks for its selected address ten times. After ten broadcasts, if the Mac does not receive notification from another device on the network that the address is already in use, the Mac uses that address for further communications.

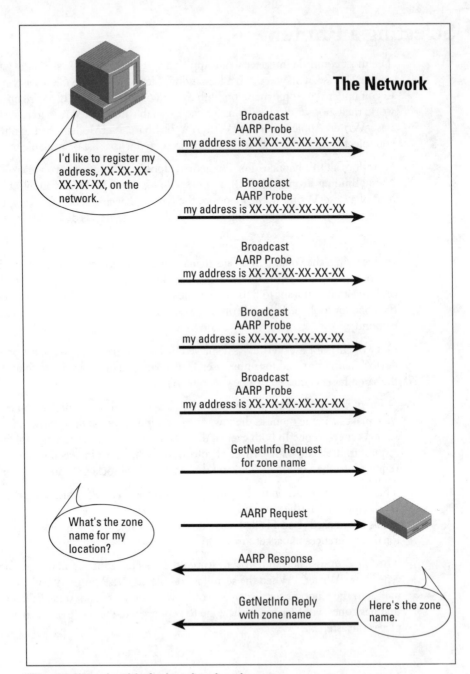

Figure 4-2: Network activity for dynamic node assignment.

# Selecting a Printer

The most common interface to an AppleTalk network that you see is the Chooser on the Mac (see Chapter 2, "Understanding Networks"). The Chooser is available to you under the Apple menu on both System 6 and System 7. If you're on a network, the Chooser displays icons for each available networked resource, such as the LaserWriter, AppleTalk ImageWriter, AppleShare, NetModem, and so on. When you select the LaserWriter icon, you're presented with a list of available printers.

How does all this happen? For this activity, most of the action revolves around the Name Binding Protocol (NBP), as you see in Figure 4-3. When you select the icon of a LaserWriter in the Chooser, the type of device is set (in this case, to LaserWriter). A character string for controlling the search is defined, as follows:

```
"=:LaserWriter@*"
```

In this string, the equal sign means that any name is allowed, and the @* refers to the local zone. The name inserted between the colon and the @ (at sign) is the type of device that you want to find. The name lookup request now goes to all nodes in the zone for lookup. Any node (in this case, any LaserWriter) that has a match will respond.

Once the list of LaserWriters is displayed by the Chooser and you select one, that device's name is stored for future use. That's why you don't always have to select the same LaserWriter every time you want to print.

Note in Figure 4-3 that the top diagram indicates the flow of information as the Mac makes a name request; the lower diagram indicates the flow during the LaserWriter's reply. In both events, the Name Binding Protocol sends the name request to the Datagram Delivery Protocol (DDP), which inserts the name lookup request into the DDP data field and then attaches the socket number of your Mac.

This data is then sent on to the Link Access Protocol (LAP), which adds the node ID of your Mac to the data and constructs a packet according to the network protocols being used (LocalTalk, Ethernet, or token ring, for example; see Appendix A for the differences in packet formats).

The Chooser instructs the NBP to search the selected zone for all devices of the type "LaserWriter." When the search is completed, NBP presents a list of the names to the Chooser for display. If you're working within an AppleTalk internet that has zones, you also select the zone to be searched; the name of the zone replaces the asterisk.

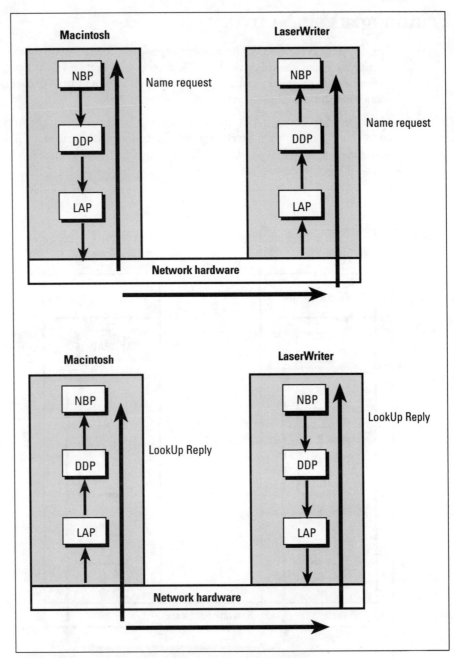

Figure 4-3: The protocol flow for finding a LaserWriter with the Chooser.

# Printing on the Network

Printing a file on a LaserWriter involves other protocols, particularly the AppleTalk Transaction Protocol (ATP), as you see in Figure 4-4. When you issue a command to print a document, your application uses the Print Manager to establish a connection with the printer.

First, the Print Manager uses the Name Binding Protocol to find the AppleTalk address of the currently selected printer. This is done by issuing an NBP broadcast with the name, device type (that is, "LaserWriter"), and zone name of the desired

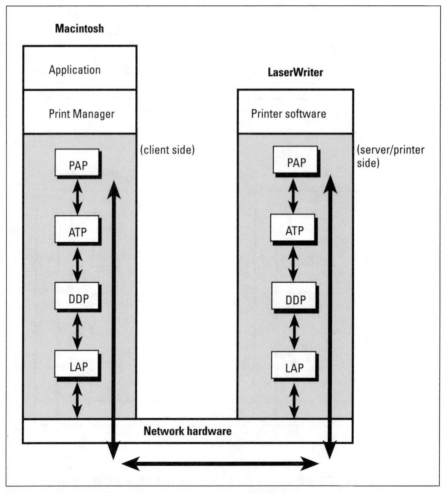

Figure 4-4: The protocol flow diagram for printing on a LaserWriter.

LaserWriter. When the LaserWriter replies with an NBP packet containing its node address and socket number, the Printer Access Protocol (PAP) then opens a connection with the printer and proceeds to send the data to the printer. PAP uses the AppleTalk Transaction Protocol to send the print file to the printer.

Once the data is divided into a size that ATP can deal with (a maximum of 578 bytes of data per packet), ATP keeps track of the necessary number of packets and sends the data on to the Datagram Delivery Protocol. Next, DDP adds the socket number for this session, followed by the Link Access Protocol, which adds the node ID and forms the final packets that are transmitted on the network cable.

Figure 4-5 summarizes the process of selecting a LaserWriter and starting to print to that LaserWriter. If a router is present on the network, the router intercepts the NBP BrRq (Broadcast Request) and propagates NBP LkUp packets to create a list of LaserWriters, which it then forwards back to the Mac. If there is no router, the Mac will send an NBP LkUp packet on its own.

In the upper two-thirds of the diagram, you see the flow of packets as the user's Mac selects the LaserWriter named "Bldg. 3" in that Mac's zone, and then initiates a session for transferring the printing data. Once the LaserWriter indicates that it's ready to print (the next-to-last packet in the diagram, an ATP Response containing the SendData Response), the Mac uses ATP packets to send the data created by the Printer Access Protocol (PAP).

# Using an AppleShare Server

When you use an AppleShare server, the initial procedure is much the same as for selecting a printer. First, you use the Chooser to find the list of available file servers in the selected zone, and then you select the appropriate server from the list. This mainly involves the Name Binding Protocol, as with the printer selection (see Figure 4-6). The only difference is that the NBP data contains a string that directs a search for file servers in the zone named MyZone:

```
"=:AFPServer@MyZone"
```

Here, we've used the term "AFPServer" to remind you that AppleTalk network file servers run a protocol called AFP, AppleTalk Filing Protocol. We discuss AFP in much greater detail in Chapter 22, "Sharing Files on AppleTalk Networks." Note in Figure 4-6 that the top diagram shows the protocols involved in sending out a name request for an AFP server on the network (along with its interception by an AFP server). The lower diagram shows the flow back to the requesting Mac from the AFP server, telling the Mac the server's name.

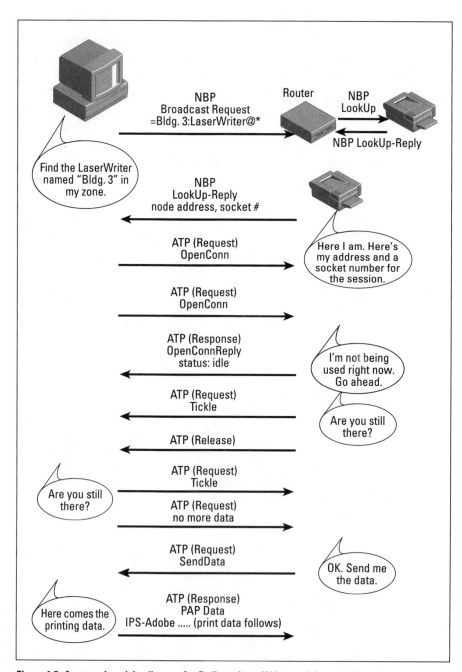

Figure 4-5: A network activity diagram for finding a LaserWriter and then printing to it.

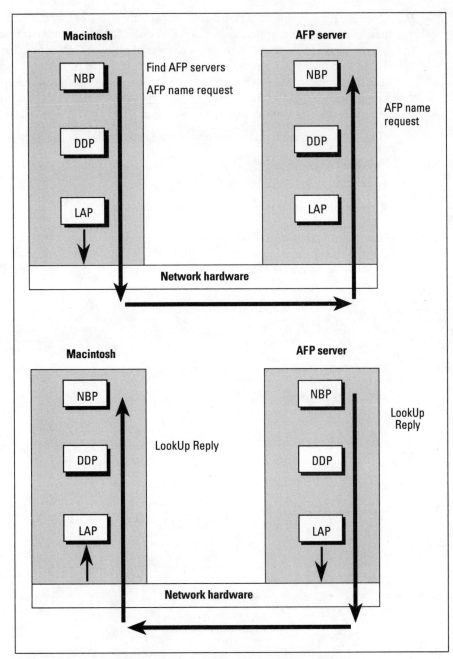

**Figure 4-6: A protocol flow diagram for selecting an AppleShare file server.**

Once the AppleShare file server is selected, you then proceed through a log-in session, in which the AppleTalk Session Protocol (ASP) handles the transmission of your name and a password from your workstation to the server (see Figure 4-7). Then ASP delivers a list of the available server volumes to your Mac. Once you select the volume that you want to mount and use with your Mac, the AppleTalk Filing Protocol (AFP) takes over and shows you which folders can be accessed and what files are in any folder that you open.

Figure 4-8 summarizes the major parts of the session:

❖ Selecting an AppleShare file server.

❖ Logging in to the file server.

❖ Mounting a server volume on your Mac's desktop.

Note that the session as illustrated does not include actually selecting and opening a file on the server. Note that, as in Figure 4-5, when a router is present, the router is used to acquire a list of available servers in response to the Mac's NBP Broadcast Request (BrRq).

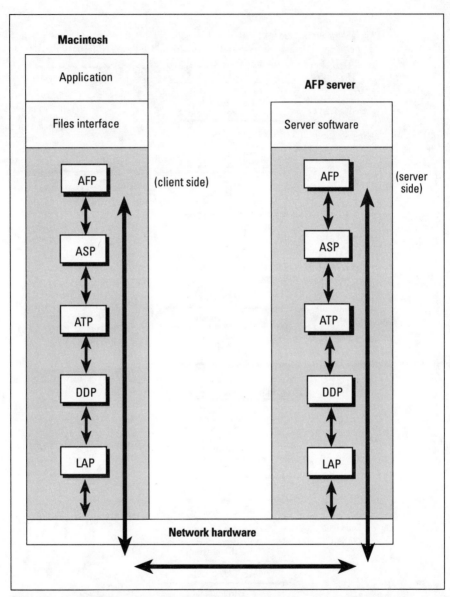

Figure 4-7: A protocol flow diagram for selecting an AppleShare file server and then using the selected server.

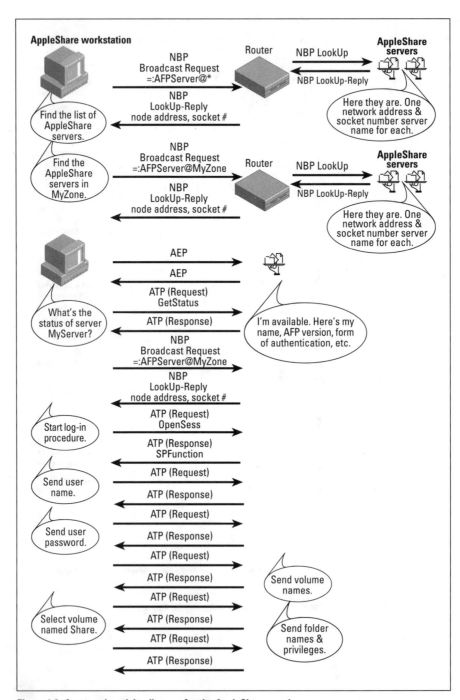

Figure 4-8: A network activity diagram for the AppleShare session.

# CHAPTER 4 CONCEPTS AND TERMS

- AppleTalk protocols are used in a certain well-defined sequence when the Macintosh starts.

- When the Mac registers itself on the network, the AARP (AppleTalk Address Resolution Protocol) is used to discover its network number and to let other nodes know its hardware (Ethernet or token ring) address.

- During printer selection, the NBP (Name Binding Protocol) starts the process by sending a name request to look for LaserWriters on the network.

- The protocols involved in the execution of printing commands include NBP, PAP (Printer Access Protocol), and ATP (AppleTalk Transaction Protocol). All these run over DDP (Datagram Delivery Protocol).

- Selecting a file server is similar to selecting a printer. AFP (AppleTalk Filing Protocol), ASP (AppleTalk Session Protocol), and ATP are used over AppleTalk's standard data transfer protocol.

**AFP (AppleTalk Filing Protocol)**
The presentation-level protocol that governs remote file access in an AppleTalk network.

**ASP (AppleTalk Session Protocol)**
Protocol that handles the transmission of a name and a password from your workstation to a server. Then ASP delivers a list of the available server volumes to a user's Mac.

**ATP (AppleTalk Transaction Protocol)**
The protocol that is integral to printing on an AppleTalk network. When a user starts to print, ATP keeps track of the necessary number of data packets and sends the data on to the Datagram Delivery Protocol for the next step in the printing process.

**broadcast transmission**
A message sent over the network to all network devices. A network administrator planning to shut down the network for maintenance may send a broadcast transmission so that everyone on the network will know when the interruption will occur.

**Chooser**
A desk accessory included with the Macintosh system software. The desk accessory is used to select network services by service types (such as LaserWriter or AppleShare), device name, and zone name.

**DDP (Datagram Delivery Protocol)**
Responsible for ensuring delivery of datagrams between AppleTalk sockets.

**LAP (Link Access Protocol)**
AppleTalk protocols for controlling the hardware interface to different network media, including ELAP for Ethernet and LLAP for LocalTalk.

**NBP**
Protocol responsible for translating device names to addresses.

**node**
An addressable device on a network, such as a LaserWriter or a Macintosh. Network processes running within a node are called sockets and are assigned socket numbers.

**PAP (Printer Access Protocol)**
The protocol that opens a connection with the printer and proceeds to send data to the printer on an AppleTalk network.

**protocol**
A procedural rule or convention for sending information over a network. Each network has its own way of transmitting data and divides the entire process into a series of specific functions. Each function requires a complete set of operating rules (or protocols).

# II
# Installing an
# AppleTalk Network

# Network Design 101

IN THIS CHAPTER

- Checklists you can use to determine the network needs of the users
- Different network topologies for wiring your network
- Advantages and disadvantages of each topology
- Fault-tolerant network design

D esigning a network requires care and attention to detail. When you plan your network, you have to consider both physical and human factors. You must deal with the cables and devices that make up the physical network, and you must consider the people who use the network as well. This chapter presents the fundamentals of network design that are applicable to almost any type of network — even those not using AppleTalk. The material covered in this chapter forms the basis of knowledge you can apply to network design and installation, as detailed in the rest of Part II, "Installing an AppleTalk Network."

## Using a Top-Down Approach to Network Design

Although we can talk of network functions in terms of the layered protocols found in AppleTalk and the OSI Reference Model, the fundamentals of network design don't involve all the OSI protocols. Rather, the basics of network design involve the two extreme ends of the network: Layer 1, the physical layer, and some layer above 7: namely, the user of the network.

The best network design philosophy takes a top-down approach, beginning with the people who will use the network. Despite the fact that installation starts at the bottom, with cables and the physical apparatus of the network, you'll get the best results from your network if you start with the needs of the network users (the "top" in "top-down") and design your network from there.

QUOTABLES

"Education, c'est délivrance."
(Education is delivery from bondage.)

— André Gide,
Journal (1889)

As you investigate what your network users need, or what you *think* they need, you'll need to ask questions about individual Mac use and what your users will expect from the network. To assist you in making a thorough evaluation, we've drawn up several lists of questions that you'll need to ask, beginning at the individual level.

### Layers 8, 9, and 10

Although the OSI Reference Model handles networks up to and including Layer 7, the Application Layer, it is obvious that there's a lot more to networks than that. One long-time observer in the world of networks has identified what he calls Layers 8, 9, and 10, consisting of Economics, Religion, and Politics. These layers, as you may agree, tend to dominate all lower layers. For example, the strongly held feelings of managers will almost certainly drive a decision between, say, token ring and Ethernet, rather than any substantive technical discussion. Unfortunately, the scope of this book precludes us from extensive discussions of economics, religion, or politics. You're on your own with those layers.

## Determining the needs of the network users

Only rarely are users active on a network for the entire day or even most of their working day. Network traffic is usually sporadic, so many small as well as large networks do well even at the relatively low speeds of LocalTalk (230,400 bps). Installation of larger bandwidth networks, such as Ethernet, is usually driven by the need for large file transfers, access to large databases, and support for many users. Access to other computers using Ethernet, such as a UNIX or an OpenVMS computer, may be another justification for installing Ethernet. Consider the following questions as you judge the adequacy of network types for your work environment:

❖ **Will LocalTalk speeds suffice for the user?**

The occasional use of e-mail and networked printing doesn't necessarily require faster networks.

❖ **Are transfers of large amounts of information routinely involved?**

If so, consider an Ethernet segment on your network for those users who transfer large amounts of information.

❖ **Must the network design accommodate multiple protocols and architectures?**

Although LocalTalk can be used as a LAN medium for multiple platforms, Ethernet is a better choice when more than Macs need to work together.

## Setting up the network for print services

Often, the reason for installing a network is to share expensive printers among members of a workgroup. Depending on your workgroup, you may have to select printers with multiple paper trays, color output, or envelope feeders. When selecting your printers and how they'll be connected to the network, consider these questions:

❖ **What kind of printing will these users need?**

Will their finished output be mainly business correspondence and reports? Lots of graphics? The answers to these questions will govern the quality and speed of printer you use.

❖ **Will the users require any color output?**

Most color printers are expensive — restricted access to these printers may be required.

❖ **Will your workgroup need special paper, such as company letterhead or transparencies?**

If so, you should consider printers that include multiple paper trays or can be used with special paper-feeder attachments.

❖ **Will your users be addressing envelopes?**

Again, a special tray or feeder attachment may be required.

❖ **Does your network need central or individual control over printer queues?**

If you need centralized control, consider installing a print spooler.

❖ **Will users on Ethernet require access to a printer?**

Some PostScript printers, including some made by Apple, now include Ethernet connections. Others can be connected with special adapter boxes, or you can use a print spooler that connects to both Ethernet (for the users) and LocalTalk (for the printers).

## Providing for modem sharing and remote access

Your users may need access by modem to such outside telecommunications services as an e-mail system, a stock quotation service, or an information bank. Or the users may need a modem to dial into another computer. Your company employees may travel with notebooks or other portable computers and need access to network services, possibly a database or printer. Consider the following modem issues:

❖ **Will the users require a modem?**

If many of your users have a need to access outside telecommunications services, computers at other sites, or network services such as a printer or company databases, you will want to consider network-based modem services.

❖ **Will employees use the modem frequently or can one be shared on the network?**

Modem-sharing devices and modem servers are a good solution for sharing one or more modems on a network. Heavy users of a modem probably should have their own.

❖ **Do you want users on the road or in other building sites to access your network?**

Some of the devices for sharing modems allow dial-in access to the network. The Shiva NetModem and Farallon Liaison are two examples of modem-sharing devices. A few of the newer ARA (Apple Remote Access) servers also allow for outgoing connections. Plus, there's the whole brave new world of wireless computing.

## Evaluating file-sharing needs

Next to printing, the most common use of a network is to share files. Your file sharing may require either point-to-point file transfers or group sharing of files on a file server. Dedicated servers use a computer solely to provide the services, whereas *distributed* servers, also called *peer-to-peer* servers, allow your Mac to be both server and client at the same time.

These questions will help you evaluate your file-sharing needs:

❖ **What kind of file server will be appropriate?**

Servers come in various flavors: dedicated (centralized), distributed (peer-to-peer), or background.

❖ **Will the file sharing in System 7's peer-to-peer file services suffice (see Chapter 22, "Sharing Files on AppleTalk Networks"), or will a dedicated file server be required?**

System 7's file sharing is good for small workgroups of fewer than ten users. A dedicated file server is appropriate for larger workgroups databases.

❖ **Will the users be accessing a database? And will the database file be shared among the users?**

The more complicated a database becomes, the more essential it is to install the database file on a dedicated server.

❖ **Are point-to-point file transfers enough?**

You don't need a dedicated file server for users to send files occasionally to one another. File-transfer programs or e-mail can do this job.

❖ **Will services such as electronic mail, group calendars, or group scheduling systems be used?**

If you depend on these types of services, you probably don't want to have your file services on a Mac that someone is using as a workstation.

After you resolve these questions to the satisfaction of yourself, your management, and your users, you can move on to questions regarding the physical plant, or the physical layout of the network. In the next sections, you'll find a few questions worth asking to help you make decisions in this area.

## Planning for the distribution of users and services

Designing the physical layout of your network depends on such matters as the distance between users, the location of wiring closets, and the availability of existing wiring. Try to answer these questions when planning the physical layout of the network:

❖ **How close are each of the users to one another? How closely do they work together?**

You may have to install routers and repeaters to get everyone on the same network. Assigning zone names to different areas of the network can make it easier for members of a workgroup to work together and use the networks resources.

❖ **Are the users grouped together?**

Again, physical groupings make it easier to connect networks to a backbone to form a larger network.

❖ **Is the distance between groups large or small?**

Even backbone networks may not be enough. You may need to use repeaters, or you may have to plan a wide area internet (usually called a WAN, for *Wide Area Network*.).

## Evaluating the physical plant

The actual installation of the network depends on a number of factors, many of which you may not be able to control. Here are some of the installation factors:

❖ **Will you use existing wiring or install new wiring?**

Someone has to check the integrity of the wiring. Special connectors may be needed if you use existing wiring systems.

❖ **Is there space in the existing utility closets for your planned network equipment, such as StarControllers and routers?**

Everyone jostles for space in utility closets; hopefully there's some room left for your new network. Make sure other users of this space know what belongs to the network.

❖ **Who will install the wiring?**

The installer should be certified to handle network (or data) wiring. A regular phone installer usually is not aware of the problems associated with data transmissions at high speeds — that is, networks. Have all the network wiring checked after installation to make sure everything works, and have these checks done in your presence and *before* you approve payment for the job.

❖ **Who will be responsible for maintenance of the wiring?**

Your original wiring contractor may be called in if you need to rewire an entire floor of a building. But someone within the company should be responsible for reassigning wall jacks or changing wires at a hub without calling a contractor.

❖ **Where can you set up print stations?**

Because so many people use printers, ready access to printers is a must. Give some thought to the procedures for maintaining the printers, including paper and toner refills. Make sure that your users know the rules.

❖ **Where can you install file servers, mail servers, or networked modems?**

All these services require some degree of security and should probably be in a locked room, or at least one with limited access.

❖ **Are there any noise sources (fluorescent lights, faxes, copy machines, motors, and so on) near the wiring?**

Watch out for these noise sources, especially if you're using unshielded twisted-pair (UTP) wiring for your network.

❖ **Is there sufficient air flow or air-conditioning in the utility closet?**

Routers, modems, and other network equipment can generate a lot of heat and should be cooled to run well. If these devices overheat, their lives will be shortened, and the network may go down. A cool network is a reliable network.

After you work your way through these lists of questions, you should have a good idea of what the users expect to do with the network, as well as some of the equipment or services that youll have to install on the network.

# Introducing Network Topologies

Network design is a compromise between what your users want and what you can provide. When it comes to connecting all the users into a network, the main constraint in designing a network is not the users needs, as we outlined in the top-down approach, but how you can wire the network. The various layouts that you can follow to wire a network are called *network topologies*, which is the focus of this section of the chapter.

When you design a network, you will choose from four basic network topologies: the daisy-chain, bus, star, and ring. Not all of these work with all network media, so you're going to start out constrained. We'll begin with the daisy-chain.

# The daisy-chain network topology

The *daisy-chain* network topology is a simple one that's easy to set up, but one that should be restricted to small workgroups. This topology consists of separate links between each device on the network, with a terminating resistor at each end of the chain (see Figure 5-1).

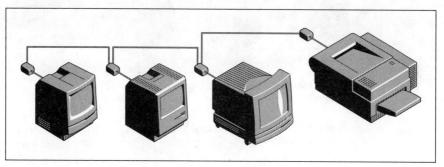

Figure 5-1: An example of a daisy-chain network topology.

Daisy-chain topologies are used in LocalTalk and PhoneNET networks, in thinwire 10BASE2 Ethernet networks, in token ring LANs such as the IEEE 802.5 4 Mb and 16 Mb token ring, and in 100 Mb FDDI. More advanced technologies, such as FDDI, have very tight requirements on interconnection hardware that reduce the risk of network failure as a result of equipment malfunction.

One problem with a daisy-chain topology is its fragility. If someone disconnects one of the network cables from a connector, for instance, the original network is broken in two. Also, because the network connector is the link between two neighboring cables, the connector must stay in place even when you move a device on the network. Daisy-chains are good only for shorter length networks because the introduction of so many interfaces (two for each connector) weakens the signal on the cable.

Daisy-chain topologies do have a few advantages, though. They're easy to set up and therefore don't cost much. You only have to buy the network cables and connectors. Daisy-chains are particularly useful for small networks, such as networks of two or three Macs and a LaserWriter.

A better network topology, even for small networks, is the bus network topology.

# The bus network topology

A straightforward network configuration is the *bus*, or *backbone*, network topology. Simply think of the bus as a linear cable with each device attached directly to this central cable. The connection is often called a *tap*. Just as with any straight line, there are two ends to the bus — these ends must be terminated electrically with a resistor to complete the bus (see Figure 5-2).

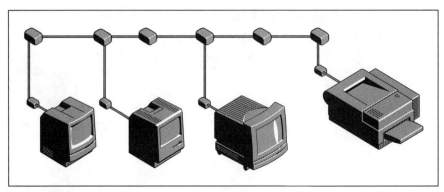

**Figure 5-2: An example of a bus network topology.**

The major difference between daisy-chain and bus network topologies is the continuity of the main cable of the bus. Because the bus can be a single length of cable, there are fewer interfaces on the cable to weaken a networks signal. Also, you can attach taps (almost) anywhere along the length of the bus and leave them unused (in wall jacks, for example) without affecting the signal of the bus. Therefore, you can lay out a bus cable and place taps anywhere that you may want to install a network device. Then you can use the taps you need now and leave others for later expansion.

Bus-based network topologies are good for small- to medium-sized networks. Also, they are very useful when you're planning to install the wires within a wall and want to allow for expansion of the network. If you make connections available (in wall jacks, for example) in currently unused offices as you install the bus, you'll be able to add users to the network without added wiring. A good way to extend a bus network is with a repeater (not by soldering two lengths of cable together).

Bus topology networks suffer from some of the same disadvantages as daisy-chains. A break in the network cable disrupts the entire network. Note, however, that these breaks are less likely to occur than with a daisy-chain. The daisy-chain network cable leads right to the network connector for your Mac, so someone may accidentally break the network by unplugging a cable from the connector. By contrast, the bus cable will most likely be hidden in the wall, out of someone's errant reach. Also, the network connector is part of the wall jack, which further reduces the chances of disconnecting the connector from the network cable.

The most common bus network is the thickwire 10BASE5 Ethernet LAN. We show you how to put together a 10BASE5 bus topology network in Chapters 8 and 9.

## The star network topology

Many people are already using a type of *star* network topology, although they probably dont realize it. Most phone systems are wired in a star topology. Your phone is wired to a central location in a utility closet, as are all the other phones on

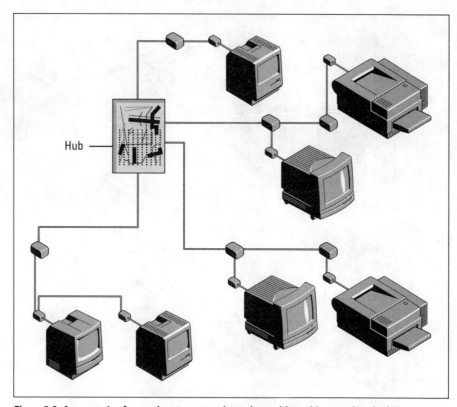

**Figure 5-3: An example of a passive star network topology with a wiring panel as the hub.**

your floor. The main thing to remember is that each device has its own set of wires that attach it to the central location, commonly called a *hub* in networking.

This hub may be no more than a wiring panel or punchdown block for gathering all the wires in one place. Such an arrangement is called a *passive star* (see Figure 5-3).

In an *active star*, the hub is an active device on the network that amplifies any signal it receives before passing the signal on to other wires connected to it (see Figure 5-4). The amplifying device is usually called either a *concentrator* or a *multiport repeater*. Active stars are popular both for LocalTalk and Ethernet networks, as you'll learn in later chapters.

One advantage of a star network topology is that its easier to troubleshoot than other networks. Its a fairly easy matter to determine which device is having or causing problems by testing the different wires making up the star. These wires are commonly called *branches* or *legs*. Usually, there is one device per branch, so finding the problem wire isolates the problem device. The hubs used for active stars generally include electronics for testing each branch and for disconnecting a branch if necessary, as when there is too much noise on the branch.

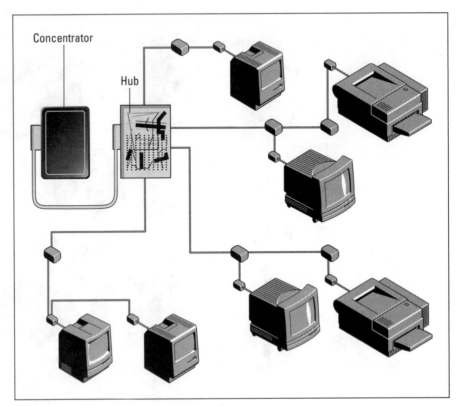

**Figure 5-4: An example of an active star network.**

The one disadvantage of a star network is that the network doesn't work when the hub fails. Fortunately, a failure is rare with a passive star because only wiring connections and no additional electronics are involved in the hub. On the other hand, an active star uses a multiport repeater as the hub and it contains electronics that will, at some point in time, fail.

The most common star network is the 10BASE-T Ethernet wiring scheme. LocalTalk (and PhoneNET) can also be wired in a star configuration, as can IEEE 802.5 token ring.

## The ring network topology

With LocalTalk, PhoneNET, and Ethernet networks, you're told time and again not to create a closed loop in the network cable. But other networks, such as the token ring, require a closed loop in order to work. As you may expect, these are called *ring topologies*. Mac users are likely to encounter this topology if they're using TokenTalk, which sends AppleTalk protocols over token ring networks (see Figure 5-5).

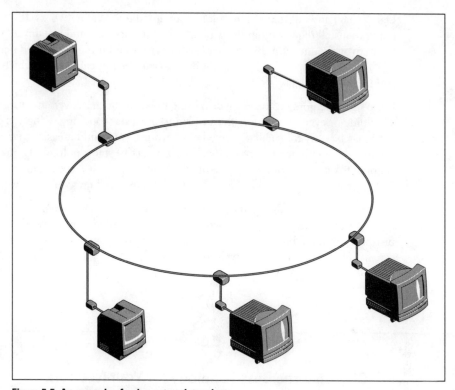

**Figure 5-5: An example of a ring network topology.**

Because the ring network topology depends on a closed ring, any break in the network cable stops the network from working. Newer ring networks, such as FDDI, have a "self-healing" dual-ring topology which lets them recover from any single break in the ring.

# Selecting a Network Topology

Deciding which topology, or set of topologies, to use for your network isn't a cut-and-dried decision. But here are a few suggestions and points to consider when you're designing your network.

You will probably find that your network uses a combination of these topologies for different environments. For example, it is common to see a star topology used to distribute network connections around a wiring closet, while the wiring closets themselves are connected using a bus or daisy-chain topology.

Daisy-chain and bus network topologies are good for small networks. If you're going to install the wiring in the wall, use the bus topology and install wall jacks for the network connection. Bus networks also work well for medium-sized networks of 10 to 40 Macs, provided you don't have to run the bus cable every which way to connect all the cubicles or offices.

If the users are going to be fairly dispersed, however, such as over an entire floor of a building or even on multiple floors, plan to use a star topology. Whereas passive stars may be okay for small dispersed workgroups, you'll find it easier to trouble-shoot and reconfigure a network if you have an active star topology. If you're running token ring, you don't have much choice but to use a combination of ring and passive star topology — because that's the only topology you're allowed to use!

Remember that only the smallest networks are configured as a single topology. As networks grow, they eventually incorporate more than one topology. With growth prospects in mind, bus and active star network topologies are best suited for expandability. And they work well together.

QUICK TIPS

## Choosing the Best Topology for Your Network

When designing your network, you should keep the following issues in mind. Each has a bearing on what topology or topologies you select:

❖ **Determine the average distance between nodes.**

This distance will quickly tell you if you're exceeding recommended wiring limits or if installation will be more costly for a given topology. For example, wiring a dispersed work-group for a bus topology will probably cost more than wiring the same workgroup for a star topology.

❖ **Decide whether certain network services, such as a file server or printer, will be centrally located with users located at peripheral sites.**

If so, a star topology is probably your best bet.

❖ **Determine the density of workstations.**

A network where every office has three LAN taps should be configured very differently from one where every office has a single workstation. A combination of star and daisy-chain topologies, such as Farallon's EtherWave, or a pure

daisy-chain, such as 10BASE2, is economical when each office has multiple taps.

❖ **Determine how many sites (or workgroups) will be connected via the network.**

A series of stars connected to a backbone, or a series of stars connected to a centrally located star, will be best when you have more than two or three sites.

❖ **Determine whether you're going to use existing wiring or install new wiring.**

If you use some existing phone cables (which PhoneNET allows, for example), a star topology is best because the topology matches that used by the phone companies.

❖ **Keep in mind how difficult it may be to install new wiring in some locations.**

Also remember that, someday, you or someone else will probably have to access the network wiring to repair it.

# Designing Fault-Tolerant Networks

*Fault tolerance* is the capability of a system to continue functioning when some component of the system fails. This concept is most often applied to file servers on networks, but it also applies to network design in general. (See Chapter 13, "Configuring, Monitoring, and Fixing AppleTalk Networks," for more information on these issues.)

The basic precept of fault-tolerant network design is this: the network manager should plan to provide users with alternate paths to crucial services. If a fault-tolerant design is in place, and one path between a user and a file server — such as through a router — goes down, the user is left with an alternate way of reaching the server. The alternate path may be another, slower network (LocalTalk instead of Ethernet, for instance) or even a modem link. But as long as such a path is available, the path allows users to continue with their work even if part of the network goes down.

An integral part of any fault-tolerant network is an honest analysis of where the weak links in the network are located. If you can identify single points of failure, you can minimize them and be prepared for the problems that will take down the entire network. Table 5-1 shows some areas where you may not have realized you were vulnerable.

Here are some examples of fault-tolerant network design:

❖ If your network spans more than one building, plan more than one link between each building; don't install all the links in the same conduit.

❖ Try to run an extra pair of wires to each workstation (this is especially easy in twisted-pair cables) for use in case the original connection is broken.

❖ When wiring to a hub, wire as many devices as possible with their own wiring runs; in other words, avoid daisy-chains and, if possible, buses.

❖ If you're wiring together more than one hub in a larger network, provide a second connection between the hubs as a standby connection; if possible, also provide a standby hub to take over the network if one of the hubs goes down.

Table 5-1
**Weak Links in Network Designs**

| Vulnerability | Analysis |
| --- | --- |
| Power supplies | Because power supplies need fans to keep them cool, they are more susceptible to failure than almost any other nonmoving component in a system. Watch for places where a single power supply failure will bring down a server. |
| Power sources | Uninterruptible Power Supplies (UPS) fail much more often than you think. Make sure that you constantly test your UPS to make sure that the batteries are in good condition and that it can take the load you have plugged into it. If you have diesel generators, don't forget to keep the tanks topped off. |
| Wiring closets | Redundant wiring doesn't do you much good if all of the cable passes through the same conduits or wiring closets. Fires in wiring closets can be devastating. |
| Cables and connectors | The most unreliable part of any system is the internal cabling. Many cables are rated for only a few insertion/removal cycles. Make sure that you have a spare for every kind of cable in use inside and outside your network systems. If you're buying cables, don't skimp on connectors. Cheap connectors fail sooner than quality ones. |
| Water | Look around your computer room and ask what would happen if the fire sprinklers were to go off or if water were to start pouring in the ceiling. Few computer room floods are the result of rain; almost all are the result of human or equipment error. You should make sure that any and all wires and equipment are at least a foot off the floor. |
| Air conditioning | If the air conditioner goes off, your computer room may overheat and will quickly shut down. If your computer room doesn't have windows, buy a few fans to have around in case of an emergency. |
| Clumsy people | Lots of computer rooms have single points of failure accessible to someone who doesn't know what they're doing or where they're going. Is the switch on the UPS easily bumped? Is equipment stacked up where it can be knocked over? Are there cables which can be tripped over? Forget liability problems, we're talking about your network here! |
| Barry the Backhoe | If a backhoe operator starts slicing through the ground around your computer room, can all the lines leaving the building be cut in a single scoop? |

# CHAPTER 5 — CONCEPTS AND TERMS

- Plan your network with a top-down approach that keeps the users' needs in mind.

- When designing your network, keep in mind the types of services that need to be installed. Such services can include print services, modem sharing, remote access, and file-sharing needs.

- Keep the physical layout in mind when designing a network.

- Network topologies are the various layouts used to wire a network. Four basic network topologies are the daisy-chain, the bus, the passive star and active star topologies and the ring topology.

- Fault-tolerant network design involves planning for alternate paths to crucial network services and paying attention to the single points of failure in a network.

**active star**
A network topology which depends on a powered repeater at the hub for each branch of the network. Each station is on a separate branch.

**backbone**
The core of the network. All packets from one branch to another pass over the backbone. Not every network has a single backbone.

**branches**
Segments of a network which physically and logically are separate from one another. A repeater, for example, links different branches. In a passive network topology, the branches are electrically connected but logically separate.

**bus network**
A network where all stations connect to the same branch of the network.

**daisy-chain network**
A topology where the network wiring of a single branch chains from one station to another. Any failure of a station to pass on network signals causes all systems downstream of that station to lose network connectivity.

**fault tolerance**
A design principle which includes the analysis of probable system, human, and equipment failure and procedures, hardware, and software to keep the system running (even in degraded operation) when a component fails.

**hub**
A central point used to link branches in a network.

**multiport repeater**
A multibranch hub used in active star networks, such as 10BASE-T Ethernet or some LocalTalk configurations, which electrically isolates each branch from every other branch.

**network topologies**
Options for design of networks based on where the wires physically (rather than logically) go.

**passive star**
A network topology which depends on an unpowered hub (such as a patch panel or punchdown block) connecting each branch of the network. Each station is on a separate branch.

**ring network**
A daisy-chain network with both ends connected.

**star network**
A network topology in which individual stations have their own wiring branch to a hub.

**tap**
Used to connect a station to a network (usually a bus network, such as 10BASE5 Ethernet).

# Designing a LocalTalk LAN

IN THIS CHAPTER

- Using different topologies with LocalTalk
- Selecting hardware for your network
- Calculating wiring limits for LocalTalk and PhoneNET wiring
- Choosing devices to extend your network

We have introduced you to how networks operate, particularly AppleTalk networks. Now we will begin the discussion of how to install a network to use AppleTalk and the services it provides. In this chapter, we'll cover rules and tips for designing networks using LocalTalk and related media, such as PhoneNET. The next chapter will provide the details of installing the network you have designed.

Remember that AppleTalk is the entire suite of networking protocols developed by Apple and is *not* just a network cable or connector. If this sounds a bit confusing, it's because Apple originally used the term AppleTalk to refer to both the network protocols and the network wiring. Apple changed the name of the wiring when the company adapted AppleTalk to run over Ethernet.

The original transmission medium developed by Apple to run AppleTalk protocols is called LocalTalk, which uses shielded twisted-pair cable. A popular alternative to LocalTalk cabling is PhoneNET, originally developed by Farallon Computing, which uses unshielded twisted-pair cabling similar to that used by your telephone system. Today, you can buy both LocalTalk cabling connectors and PhoneNET cabling connectors from many different vendors. In this chapter, we'll talk about designing networks with these two transmission media.

## Getting Acquainted with LocalTalk and PhoneNET

Apple's LocalTalk networking system is designed to run at a speed of 230,400 bits per second over shielded twisted-pair cable. The specifications for LocalTalk are a part of the physical and data link layers of the AppleTalk protocol suite (see Chapter 3, "Understanding AppleTalk Protocols").

Farallon Computing pioneered a similar wiring scheme, using unshielded twisted-pair cabling to transmit at LocalTalk speeds — the original idea and the connectors actually began with a group of students from the Berkeley Mac Users Group (BMUG).

Since the first Mac rolled off the assembly lines in 1984, each Mac has had built-in networking support for AppleTalk. In LocalTalk, this was accomplished by the Serial Communications Controller (SCC) chip that controls the two serial ports found on each Mac. Later Macs, starting with the IIfx, used a custom chip for controlling the serial ports. The resulting LocalTalk support stayed the same.

# Selecting a Network Topology

As discussed in Chapter 5, "Network Design 101," four main types of topologies are used for wiring networks: daisy-chain, bus, star, and ring. Because we're concentrating on LocalTalk here, which doesn't support a ring topology, we'll cover only the daisy-chain, bus, and star networks in this chapter.

To help guide you as we discuss the ins and outs of the various network topologies, we've set up an example of a building with 15 offices and one copier room. All but two of the offices have Macs, but you'll also need to support Macs in the two empty offices at some later date. The laser printer and a Mac for print spooling and file services are installed in the copier room. Now let's look at the different ways in which you can wire these offices for LocalTalk.

### Is It BPS or Is It Baud?

You may hear the term *baud* to describe the speed of a modem or of a transmission line, such as a LocalTalk cable or an Ethernet cable. Technically, baud is used to refer to transitions of a signal per second. When 300 *bits per second* (bps) modems first came out, they were called 300 baud modems because there were 300 signal transitions (or symbols) per second. For every common modem introduced since then, the baud rate is much lower than the bits per second rate because each symbol conveys more than 1 bit of information. For example, the 2400 bps modem is really a 600 baud modem where each symbol can take one of 16 different values, conveying 4 bits of information per baud. In the other direction, the FDDI (Fiber Distributed Data Interface) ring operates at 125M baud, conveying 100M bits per second of information.

You're better off always using the term bits per second unless you happen to be an electrical engineer.

## The daisy-chain topology

The daisy-chain network is the simplest to construct, especially if you're using LocalTalk or PhoneNET connectors. Just plug the network connector box into each Mac, connect a network cable from one box to the next, then from that box to the next, and so on (see Figure 6-1). But remember that if one of the cables breaks or is disconnected from the connector box, you now have two networks, neither one of which can talk to the other. We use the term *partitioned* to describe this situation.

Daisy-chain networks are good for small networks, but when they get beyond 10 or 12 devices, this type of network becomes difficult to troubleshoot and maintain. Also, note that the daisy-chain network is the only network topology that you can create with LocalTalk, unless you use adapter cables, which we will cover in Chapter 7, "Installing a LocalTalk LAN."

## The bus topology

If you don't like the idea of wires hanging around your cubicles, you're better off using a bus, or backbone, topology for your network. In the bus topology, you use one cable for the entire network and tap into the main cable with another wire that leads to your network connector. Often, these backbone cables are run through the walls of your building, and the taps are made at wall jacks — much like the phone system. As this means stringing a new cable in the wall, the bus topology is also recommended for small workgroups. You can also install the wire along the baseboard and attach new jacks to the wall if you want — it's all a question of neatness and available resources.

If you plan to install a bus network, plan also on using PhoneNET connectors or their clones. Apple's LocalTalk connectors are not meant for any topology other than a daisy-chain network. PhoneNET has two other advantages: it's less expensive, and your telephone installers will easily understand its telephone-like wiring scheme.

Figure 6-2 shows the example network as a bus network. Note that the two empty offices also have been wired to the bus, as indicated by the circles marked WJ (for wall jack). You can connect a new computer to the network in those offices simply by plugging a PhoneNET connector into the wall jack.

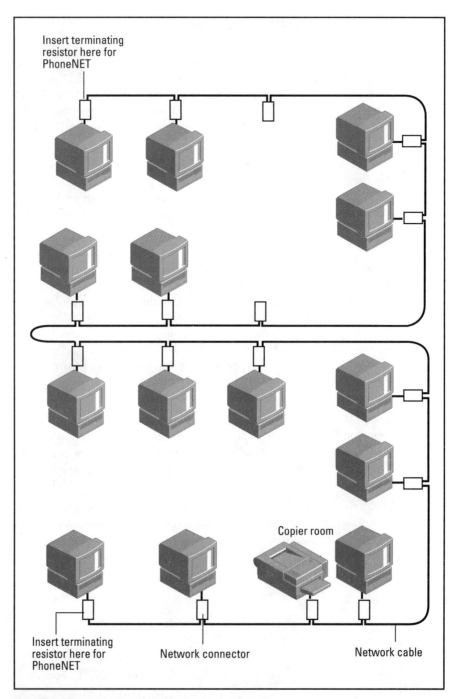

Figure 6-1: An example office network wired as a daisy-chain.

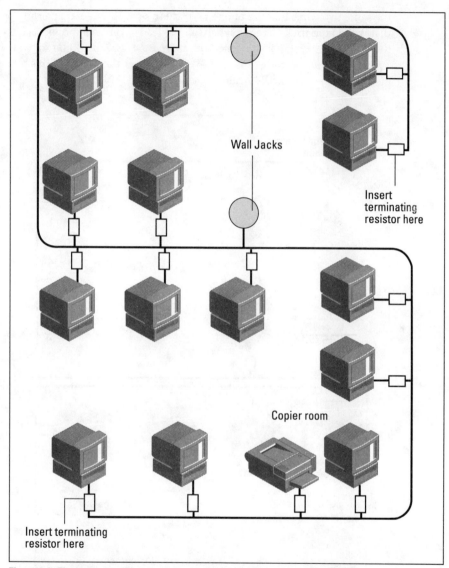

Figure 6-2: The example office network now wired as a bus network.

## The passive star topology

Phone wiring in most buildings meets the specifications for PhoneNET wiring, so you can use the existing phone wiring to create a PhoneNET network. To do this, all you need to do is attach each Mac to a phone jack and reconnect the phone jack to the utility closet, just as if you were installing a phone. Of course, you don't use the same two wires that the phone uses; there's usually an extra pair in the cable that will do the trick. Then you wire all the leads from each phone jack together in the phone closet, at a device called the *punchdown block*. By doing so, you've created a passive star network (see Figure 6-3). We'll cover the details of this part of the installation in Chapter 7, "Installing a LocalTalk LAN."

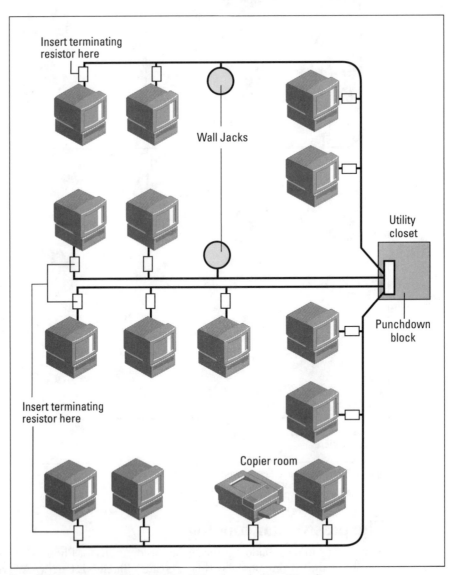

Figure 6-3: The example office network wired as a passive star network.

Note in Figure 6-3 that each branch of the passive star has more than one device attached to it. In this example, we wired each branch as a bus, but that's not required. Note that the two empty offices also have been wired to the bus, as indicated by the circles marked WJ. You can connect a new computer to the network in those offices simply by plugging a PhoneNET connector into the wall jack.

Passive stars can be very limiting when designing a PhoneNET network. This is mainly because the ends of the network wires are joined in a passive star. When a signal from a Mac on one branch reaches this common connection point, the signal's power is divided among all the branches of the passive star. Because the passive star doesn't provide any means to amplify the signal, the network signal becomes weaker each time it reaches the common connection point.

When you're designing a passive star network, try to use no more than four branches, and don't attach other passive stars to any of the branches. To determine the maximum length of each of your passive star's branches, divide the wiring limit (which is 3,000 feet for 24 AWG wire) by the number of branches in your star. The answer is your branch's maximum length. The following is the same procedure in a formula:

```
maximum branch length = (wiring limit/number of branches)
```

If you're going to attach other cables to a branch, you should also subtract four times the length of those cables from the remaining length to determine the maximum branch length:

```
maximum branch length = (wiring limit/number of branches) - (4 x
length of added cables)
```

In both formulas, if you're using 24 AWG wire, the wiring limit is 3,000 feet, whereas the wiring limit is 4,500 feet for 22 AWG wire and 2,000 feet for 26 AWG wire. If you use more than four branches, you still use the same formulas, but for installation, you should use no more than a total of four terminating resistors on the network.

We have explained that passive star networks are limiting because each branch of the passive star is not electrically isolated from the others, and the branches have to be limited in length. There is a further limitation to passive star networks.

A passive star network limits the number of devices you can install on it because the connection of each branch to the others reduces the network signal. For example, Farallon recommends no more than 16 devices on a 3-branch passive star network of 1,800 feet. By contrast, a backbone network of the same length can support 48 devices.

From our discussion, you can see that passive stars networks are limited. In fact, they can often be more trouble than they're worth. If you have a small network in which the users are not located centrally, a passive star network can be a simple start to creating a network. But as you expand your network, either by adding more devices or incorporating more-distant users, you should be prepared to convert your passive star to another topology, usually an active star.

## The active star topology

Because of the wiring-length limits for a passive star network, you're usually better off using an active star topology. Doing so will create a more reliable network, even though it is more expensive to set up.

Buy a Farallon StarController LocalTalk hub (or one of the compatible competitors) and install it in your phone closet. You can wire your active star just as we described for the passive star, connecting the wires from each device into a punchdown block in the utility closet.

The difference is that you then plug a feeder cable from the punchdown block to the active hub. Now, instead of each wire contributing to the length of your network (as it did in the passive star), each Mac's cable is electrically isolated from the other. This is important because the network signal is now amplified when it passes through the active hub. This means that you're not stuck with calculating branch limits (as you were with the passive star), In addition, each branch of an active star can be set up following the rules for a daisy-chain or bus network, depending on how you want to connect devices to the active hub — also called a *multiport repeater*.

Note that in Figure 6-4, the example network wired as an active star, the branches drawn in the center of the diagram, as well as the two at the top and bottom of the drawing, have multiple devices attached to them. Four computers at the right of the drawing are attached individually to the active star. Also note that the two empty offices also have been wired to the bus, as indicated by the circles marked WJ. You can connect a new computer to the network in those offices simply by plugging a PhoneNET connector into the wall jack.

QUICK TIPS

### One Device per Wiring Run Makes Troubleshooting Easy

The best approach when planning for network troubleshooting is to keep as few devices as possible on each wiring run. Therefore, it's better to use a separate wiring run for each device and connect it to the desired port at the punchdown block or patch panel than to use one wiring run for the same four devices. As a result, when something goes wrong, you can physically disconnect and isolate a problem wire or device without adversely affecting the rest of the network. Of course, if you're planning to connect more than four devices per port, you have no choice but to use some wiring runs for more than one device. And in some cases, you may not be able to run enough wires to use one run per device.

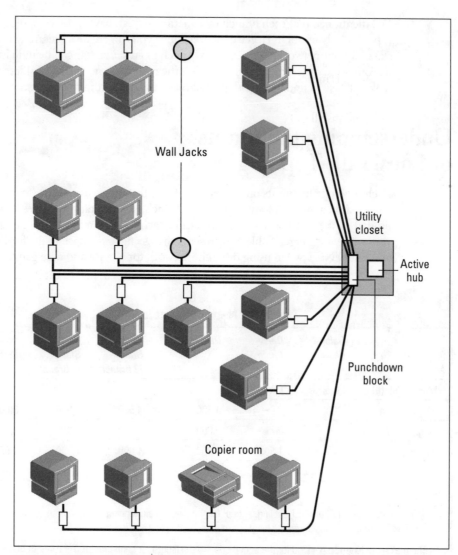

**Figure 6-4: The example office network wired as an active star network.**

Because each active star's branch is electrically isolated from the rest of the network, you're free to make any of the branches a daisy-chain, a bus, or even a passive star or another active star network. The active hubs available for LocalTalk are designed for a maximum of four wire runs for each port. Therefore, if you're planning to wire more than one device per port (the StarControllers have 12 or 24 ports), you have a great deal of flexibility in choosing your wiring runs.

We mentioned that each branch of an active star can have its own topology. This is particularly useful in larger networks, since you can create a hierarchy of active stars for your network. Because each branch of an active star can be individually disconnected or tested without affecting the rest of the network, this hierarchy makes it easy to find a network problem and isolate it from the others.

# Understanding the Limits of LocalTalk Topologies

Each topology has limits on the length of wire that can be used, either for the entire length, as in a bus topology, or for each branch, as with star topologies. You're also limited by the number of devices you can attach to a given topology. These limits vary with wire gauge. Table 6-1 presents the wiring and device limits for LocalTalk and PhoneNET when using different network topologies and wire gauge.

| Table 6-1 | | | | | | |
|---|---|---|---|---|---|---|
| **Limits for Network Topologies*** | | | | | | |
| | *Daisy-Chain* | *Daisy-Chain* | *Backbone* | *Passive Star (3 branch)* | *Passive Star (4 branch)* | *Active Star*** |
| Max Length (ft) | LocalTalk | PhoneNet | | | | |
| 22-gauge wire | 1,000 | — | 4,500 | 4,500 | 4,500 | 3,000 |
| 24-gauge wire | — | — | 3,000 | 3,000 | 3,000 | 2,000 |
| 26-gauge wire | — | 1,800 | 1,800 | 1,800 | 1,800 | 1,500 |
| Max nodes | 32 | 24 | 48 | 16 | 12 | varies*** |

Notes:

* All limits are cited for PhoneNET cabling, except for the daisy-chain topology, where both LocalTalk and PhoneNET wiring are considered. All lengths are measured in feet.

** The maximum lengths specified for the active star are the length for each branch. Total length of the network should be the maximum length of each branch times the number of ports in the active hub.

*** The maximum number of nodes depends on the networks attached to each port of the active hub and on the number of ports in the active hub.

Before you start calculating whether or not you can fit the number of Macintoshes you've got into the topology you've chosen, you should ask yourself an important question: Is LocalTalk the most appropriate medium for my network? As the cost of an Ethernet card drops below $100, you may find that your total cost for an Ethernet network is not much higher than the equivalent LocalTalk network. There are additional advantages to an Ethernet network:

❖ Non-Macintosh computers will be able to share your network more easily.

❖ You will have better choices of suppliers for Ethernet-style network components and connectors.

In conclusion, LocalTalk is fine for small numbers of Macintoshes, but try not to get carried away with it.

# Extending Network Limits

If the network length limits we mentioned in Table 6-1 aren't long enough for your needs, you may want to consider using a repeater to extend the reach of your network. If you only want to extend the length of one network cable, a single-port repeater will do the trick. On the other hand, if you want to wire a star topology and use long network cables, you can use either a multiport repeater, such as the Farallon StarController or Nuvotech Turbostar, or a multiport bridge, such as the Tribe LocalSwitch.

Multiport repeaters (we've also referred to them as *active star hubs*) amplify and reclock any network signal as it passes through the hub, retransmitting the signal to all other ports of the hub. A multiport repeater handles network traffic much like a conference call — everyone hears every conversation on the network. A multiport bridge (sometimes called a packet switching hub), on the other hand, works more like the phone system and is able to isolate network traffic on one port from traffic on other ports, exchanging packets between ports only as necessary. The multiport bridge is able to do this because it inspects each network packet to determine the destination of the packet; it then forwards the packet to the appropriate port and only the devices attached to that port will see (or "hear") the packet. In the world of Ethernet, this style of bridge has become very popular recently.

When should you use each device? Multiport repeaters deal only with electrical signals and retransmit the amplified signal to all network branches attached to the repeater. So a multiport repeater cannot be used to isolate traffic on one wiring branch from traffic on another wiring branch. But multiport repeaters are good for extending the scope (or length) of your network because they amplify signals.

Multiport bridges can be used in the same way as multiport repeaters, because they also amplify the signal. But you should plan to use these devices for more than just repeater replacements, as they're more expensive. Multiport bridges are good for isolating network traffic on one wiring branch from that on another branch. Before investing in a multiport bridge or router, consider whether you want to move to Ethernet instead.

The traffic isolation provided by a multiport bridge or router is good for improving the performance of your network if you meet two qualifications:

❖ Users aren't continually accessing centralized services; and

❖ Users are more likely to exchange information in reasonably well-defined workgroups.

Therefore, if you have a single laser printer or file server and everyone on the network must use those devices, a multiport bridge won't help increase network performance to those devices. On the other hand, if you have a number of users running the Personal File Sharing feature under System 7, or if each workgroup has its own printer and/or file server, a multiport bridge will most likely increase the network's performance. This happens because each branch of the network is isolated from the other and only those packets that need to get from one branch to the other are passed on by the bridge. Multiport repeaters won't make any difference in such cases.

To further illustrate this point, we've constructed a network with multiple workgroups wired in a star topology. Notice in Figure 6-5 that the network has a multiport repeater installed at the hub. The figure illustrates where various network packets go. If the Macintosh labeled A is printing to LaserWriter B, the packets it generates travel throughout the network and are seen by Macs C, D, E, F, and H, and LaserWriter G as well. That means that any traffic to and from C, D, E, F, G, and H will have to share the network with A and B. If A is sending a lot of data to B, then any traffic between the other systems will be slowed down somewhat (depending, of course, on just how fast B can take data from A).

A similar network is shown in Figure 6-6, but this one has a multiport bridge in the middle of the star. In this case, the packets generated by Mac A printing to LaserWriter B are not transmitted beyond the bridge, so the other devices don't see these other packets.

Therefore, as you can see in the figure, Mac C can exchange a file with Mac D on a cable that's attached to the bridge because that cable is isolated from the cable connecting Mac A and LaserWriter B. The other network task, Mac E printing to LaserWriter G, is also unaffected by the other two uses because the multiport bridge can relay the packets between the two cables involved without transmitting those packets to the other cables. This means that the total throughput of the network can be higher than if all devices are sharing bandwidth. Only in a case where Mac H wants to send a file to Mac F, which is on the same cable as Mac E, will the multiport bridge not show any improvement.

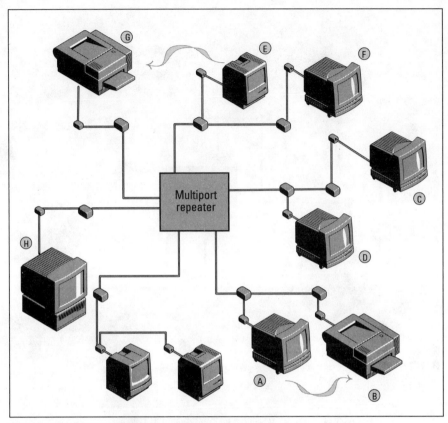

**Figure 6-5: Network traffic with a multiport repeater installed.**

Although we'll cover the subject of routers in more detail in Chapter 11, "Designing an AppleTalk LAN," it's worth noting here that you can also use routers to isolate traffic between networks. This can be a more cost-effective solution than the multiport bridge if you only have a few workgroups or networks. But be aware that multiport bridges can process network traffic faster than routers and that a router may become a bottleneck in your network.

Bear in mind that your network's performance can be greatly affected by where you locate your network services, such as print spoolers, file servers, and e-mail servers. We touched on that point when discussing multiport bridges, and we'll be concentrating on that aspect of network design and optimization in Chapter 13, "Configuring, Monitoring, and Fixing AppleTalk Networks."

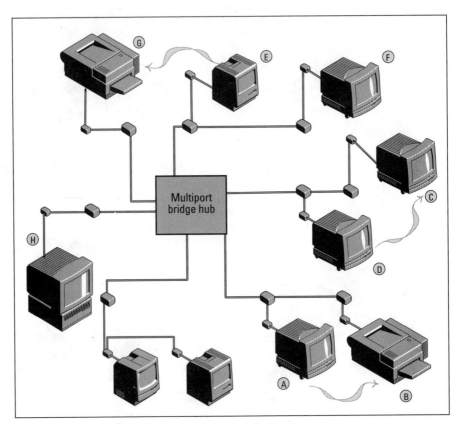

Figure 6-6: Network traffic with a multiport bridge installed.

# CHAPTER 6   CONCEPTS AND TERMS

- LocalTalk is Apple's hardware for installing your network. AppleTalk is Apple's protocol stack for networks. AppleTalk runs over LocalTalk and other types of networks, such as Ethernet (called EtherTalk when AppleTalk is running over it).

- An alternative to Apple's LocalTalk cabling is PhoneNET, originally developed by Farallon Computing.

- You can lay out LocalTalk networks in the daisy-chain, bus, and star topologies.

- Each network topology has limits on the length of wire used; you can calculate these wiring limits for both LocalTalk and PhoneNET.

- You can use repeaters and multiport bridges to extend your network, or you can make a transition to an Ethernet network at that time.

### active star topology
A network wired in a star topology with a concentrator or multiport repeater located at the center of the star. All wiring runs lead to the concentrator, which is responsible for retransmitting the network signal from one wiring run to other wiring runs attached to it.

### baud rate
Describes the number of signal changes per second when talking about a modem's speed in transferring data.

### bus (or backbone) topology
A network topology in which a single cable is used to carry the network's signals. Computing devices are attached to the central cable via taps.

### contention
A problem that results from having more than one computer transmitting on the network at the same time. If a procedure is not implemented, the signals will mix together unintelligibly.

### daisy-chain topology
A topology where the network wiring of a single branch chains from one station to another. Any failure of a station to pass on network signals causes all systems downstream of that station to lose network connectivity.

### LocalTalk
The name for Apple's low-cost connectivity products consisting of cables, connection boxes, cable extenders, and other cabling equipment for connecting computers and other devices.

### multiport repeater (or multiport bridge)
A unit where each wire from a Mac (or network) is connected. This is important because the network signal is now amplified when it passes through the repeater (also called an active hub).

### partitioned
A situation that happens in a daisy-chain network if one of the cables breaks or is disconnected from the connector box. The result is two networks, neither one of which can talk to the other.

### passive star topology
A network topology which depends on an unpowered hub (such as a patch panel or punchdown block) connecting each branch of the network. Each station is on a separate branch.

### PhoneNET
A popular alternative to LocalTalk cabling is PhoneNET, originally developed by Farallon Computing, which uses unshielded twisted-pair cabling similar to that used by your telephone system.

### punchdown block
A wiring device used by phone companies and network installers for connecting many wires together in one location. A typical punchdown block (type 66 block) has 50 rows of four contacts, or pins. Wires are pushed, or "punched down," onto a pin to make electrical contact.

### router
A device that connects two networks together and maintains addressing information for each network. Workstations can pass information from one network to another by sending the information through the router.

# Installing a LocalTalk LAN

In Chapters 5 and 6, we covered some of the details of planning and designing a network. Now we'll show you how to install and test both simple networks as well as the larger, more complicated LocalTalk networks. Before you read this chapter, you should read Chapter 6, "Designing a LocalTalk LAN", which deals with the basic types of LocalTalk networks.

## Selecting Cables and Connectors

The first thing you should know about your Macs is it has built-in support for networking. Apple calls its networking system *AppleTalk*. You don't need to buy any special software to make a network of Macs work together. But you do need some hardware. You can choose either Apples own cabling system, called *LocalTalk*, or a popular alternative called *PhoneNET*.

### Using standard cabling and wiring kits

Apple offers LocalTalk connectors and wiring kits for use with Macs and LaserWriters (see Figure 7-1). The LocalTalk kit uses shielded twisted-pair cables, which are less affected by outside interference, or *noise*, but are limited to maximum lengths of 300 feet. The standard LocalTalk cable that comes with each Apple LocalTalk connector is 2 meters (6½ feet) long. If you need longer cables, you can buy a LocalTalk wiring kit and make your own cables. The LocalTalk connectors for your Mac are self-terminating, which makes it easier to set up or change a network without added pieces. (We'll describe the process of terminating your network cables shortly.)

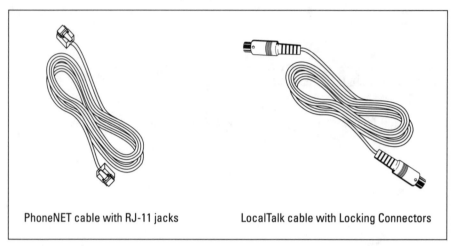

PhoneNET cable with RJ-11 jacks          LocalTalk cable with Locking Connectors

Figure 7-1: Both PhoneNET and LocalTalk cabling types can be used for an AppleTalk network.

The most popular wiring scheme for Mac networks is PhoneNET, mainly because it can use existing phone wires. This wiring scheme is particularly convenient if you have a spare pair of wires in your phone cable that can be set up for the network, especially in prewired buildings with wiring closets and such. In a small office, though, you can get by just as well with the modular cords that come with the PhoneNET connectors. The modular cords are thinner and a bit easier to bend than Apples LocalTalk cables. Other custom-made cables for PhoneNET can extend over distances as great as 1,000 feet. Because they are not shielded as LocalTalk cables are, PhoneNET cables are not recommended for high-noise environments, such as in factories or near electrical motors or elevators.

Because most modular cable is not twisted-pair, you shouldn't use it for long network wiring runs; we suggest lengths of not more than 50 feet. If you need longer wiring runs, use a cable that is known to contain twisted-pair, such as *station cable*, which is the 22-gauge twisted-pair often used by phone companies. (See the next section for details on making your own cables.) If you are in doubt as to whether the cable you have is twisted-pair, look for yourself. Strip off a foot or so of insulation, and you can easily see whether the wires are twisted together in the cable. If they're not, it's not twisted-pair.

If you must combine two or more existing networks and some of the networks use LocalTalk cabling and others use PhoneNET, you can use a LocalTalk-PhoneNET adapter cable to link the two types of cables together. This adapter cable is also handy when you're installing an active star network because you can use it to connect existing LocalTalk daisy-chains to the phone jacks for the star. Remember, though, whenever you mix cables in this manner, your total length is limited by the LocalTalk cable specifications.

### Jacket and Tie Required

We offer a word of warning here about the insulation used for these cables. Buildings use one of two methods for circulating room air — either through the airspace within the buildings ceiling, often called *plenum air returns*, or through air ducts. Most cables can be purchased with either of two types of insulation: polyvinyl chloride (PVC) or fluoropolymer (usually called Teflon, although Teflon is just one type of this cable category).

If you're planning to install network cables within a plenum air return, you must not use PVC-insulated cable. PVC releases poisonous gases when burned, and the plenum return can carry flames and the poisonous gases rapidly through the building. Cable insulated with a fluoropolymer such as Teflon usually costs about three times as much as PVC-insulated cable, so you probably only want to use it where you have to. If you have any questions about the type of network cable that you should install in air spaces, check your local fire codes.

The Apple LocalTalk 2-meter and 10-meter cables are PVC-coated and must be run through metal conduit when they are installed in plenum ceilings. The LocalTalk Custom Wiring Kit uses Teflon-coated cable.

## Making your own cables

Stock cable lengths usually fall in the range of the 2-meter (6½-foot) length provided with connectors, up to the 50-foot modular cables. These lengths still may be too short for your network. For a bus or star network, you may not be able to purchase the proper twisted-pair cables in the lengths you need, complete with connectors or terminators. You may also find that running premade cable in ceilings and through walls is a good way to ruin the connectors. Your best bet then is to make your own cables.

There is more than one type of telephone wiring, and not all of it is twisted-pair. Most older homes (and some newer ones) are wired with a 4-wire cable with red, green, black, and yellow conductors that is not twisted-pair. Another common cable is called *silver satin* wire, a flat cable often used between telephones and wall jacks. Most silver satin is not twisted-pair (although there is silver telephone wire that is twisted-pair). These cables are not suitable for high-speed (10M bit/sec) LANs, but they can be used at LocalTalk speeds. If you use existing wiring, find out as much as possible about its electrical characteristics before using it.

If you make your own modular extension cables, such as for a PhoneNET daisy-chain, you can use modular cable from a supplier like Radio Shack, which offers the cabling in a variety of lengths and reels for longer cabling. Farallon Computing also offers a modular cable construction kit for creating custom cable lengths. Once you cut the cable to the lengths you want, you'll need to trim away the outer jacket of the cable from the four wires in the modular cable. Place the wire ends within the four slots of an RJ-11 connector and then use a crimping tool to drive the connector's pins into the wire. Above all, be consistent — always match the same color wire to the pin number of the connector. (Each wire in the cable can be distinguished from the others by the color of its insulation.)

If you have to buy all the equipment you need to make the cables, don't scrimp when buying the crimping tool. We've found that the cheaper crimping tools don't always push the RJ-11 connector pins into the wires evenly, meaning that you can end up with an intermittent connection. Try contacting Specialized Products, Time Motion Tools, or Jensen Tools for a modular plug crimp tool. Expect to pay about $185 for one. Our personal favorite is made by Futureonics and has replaceable dies so you can make 4-, 6-, and 8-position cables.

As we said previously, if you're planning to make your own cables for a bus or a star network, use 22-gauge or 24-gauge twisted-pair cable that contains solid wire. The 22-gauge version (which often has an outer tan-colored jacket) is often called *station cable* by phone installers. You can use the typical four-conductor (two-pair) cable to create a bus or to run a branch for a star, leaving the extra pair as a replacement in case the first pair malfunctions. If you use normal station cable, use the black and yellow conductors for LocalTalk wiring (since the red and green ones are normally used for telephone wiring).

Remember that the maximum distance for reliable use of PhoneNET cables is a function of the wire thickness used within the cables. A common wiring, especially for telephone installations in businesses, is 24-gauge. The tan-colored, 22-gauge phone cable just mentioned is most often found in homes. Network buses and branches for stars should be installed with 22-gauge quad cable, which has a solid copper core for each wire.

You can also make your own LocalTalk cables, using wiring kits from either Apple or third-party vendors. For LocalTalk, you'll need a soldering iron instead of a crimping tool because you have to solder each wire of the cable to the pins found in the LocalTalk connector. It's a bit more work than crimping RJ-11 jacks for PhoneNET, but a soldered connection is more reliable.

## Setting up connectors

Each type of cable, whether LocalTalk or PhoneNET, requires its own special connector box. The LocalTalk connector boxes have two ports for connecting network cables. Each port is *self-terminating*, which means that you don't have to add a terminating resistor at the end of each network cable segment (see Figure 7-2).

The most common PhoneNET connectors and their clones also have two ports for the network cables but require a terminating resistor at both ends of the network segment. You'll get into the details of placing terminating resistors later in this chapter, during the discussion of specific network topologies. Each connector, whether LocalTalk or PhoneNET, connects to a Mac's printer port with a short cable. There's a third type of connector, Farallons StarConnector, which is internally terminated and has only one port for connecting a network cable — this connector is designed only for star topologies with one device per wiring run.

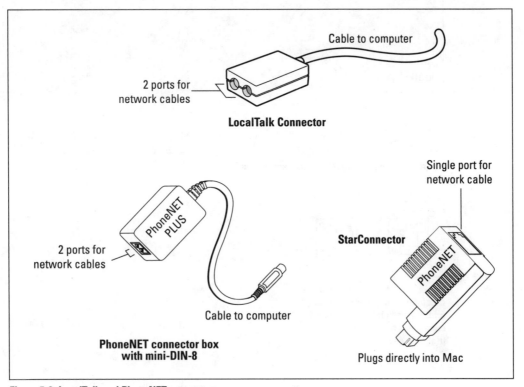

Figure 7-2: LocalTalk and PhoneNET connectors.

No matter which wiring system you choose, you may need to buy more than one type of network connector. All the newer Macs and LaserWriters use the smaller mini-DIN-8 connector for their printer ports, which is where the network connects to the Mac. The older LaserWriters from Apple and some other PostScript printers, as well as the venerable Mac 512, use a larger DB-9 connector (see Figure 7-3). The DB-9 connector is also used for older LocalTalk cards for DOS computers. Check the printer port of each of your Macs and LaserWriters before you purchase your connectors. In any case, make sure that you use the printer port (not the communications port) on the back of the Macintosh for connecting LocalTalk. Figure 7-4 shows the icons that Apple uses to mark the communications and printer ports.

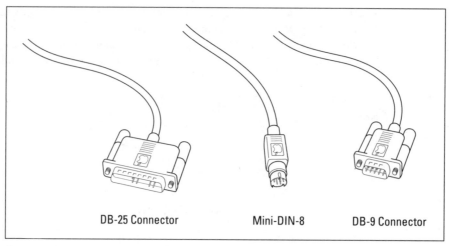

DB-25 Connector        Mini-DIN-8      DB-9 Connector

**Figure 7-3: Connector types for connecting to a Mac.**

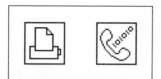

**Figure 7-4: Apple marks each
Macintosh serial port as either a
printer port (left-hand icon) or a
communications/modem port
(right-hand icon).**

Other types of connectors are available for use with the PhoneNET system.
Nuvotech offers a PhoneNET-compatible connector that includes an internal
terminating resistor. In this case, the resistor is not the normal 120-ohm resistor
but a smaller resistor that attempts to weaken, or *dampen,* the reflected signals suffi-
ciently so as not to interfere with the original network signal.

The problem here is to decide what is sufficient dampening. The 120-ohm resistor
used with PhoneNET connectors absorbs enough of the signal to prevent a reflection and thereby prevent interference with the original signal. Resistance values of
less than 120 ohms, such as those used with the Nuvotech connectors, don't completely absorb the signals energy. Although this may not be a problem on a short
cable with a strong signal, reflections from lower-value terminating resistors can
lead to interference with a weak signal, as you may have on networks with long
cable lengths.

### Mixing and Matching Connectors

All PhoneNET and PhoneNET clones are designed to work together. However, there are always variances in manufacturing style and design that can cause minor incompatibilities, particularly as your network begins to stretch its limits. If possible, try to pick a single manufacturer for your connectors and buy from that same manufacturer as you expand your network. This advice holds true for cable as well: it's better to buy all of the cable you'll use at once to ensure that its electrical characteristics are even throughout.

## Choosing wiring accessories

If you're going to install either a passive or an active star network, you'll choose from various wiring devices that organize your wiring and make installation easier. Devices that you'll need to know about are the *harmonica block*, the *punchdown block*, and the *patch panel*.

Harmonica blocks are good for small networks. They come in 12-port models and have sockets for RJ-11 jacks (see Figure 7-5), which means that you can use them with modular cables. Changing a cable is as easy as plugging a new one into the proper RJ-11 socket. One end of the harmonica block has a socket for a 50-pin Amphenol connector — you use a cable with Amphenol connectors on both ends to connect the harmonica block to a concentrator (a StarController, for example).

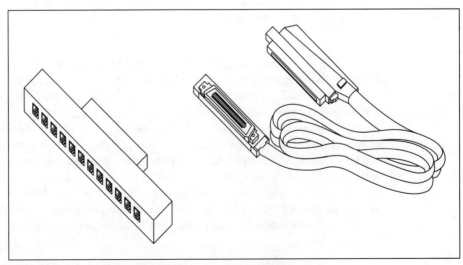

Figure 7-5: A typical 12-port harmonica block with mating Amphenol cable.

Instead of a harmonica block, you can use a punchdown block (see Figure 7-6) for connecting your wiring runs to the active hub. The most common type of punchdown blocks are the *Type 66 block* and the *Type 110 block*, as named by AT&T and used in many phone installations (some companies also call them *telco splice* blocks). Type 66 blocks are older and are slowly being phased out in favor of the Type 110 blocks, mostly for reasons of wiring density.

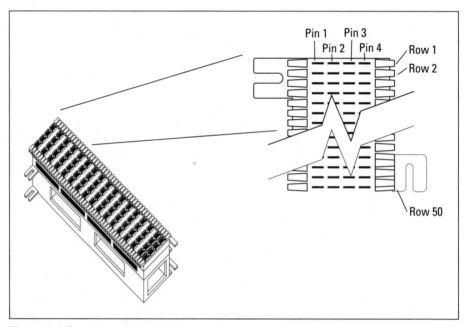

Figure 7-6: A Type 66 punchdown block.

Better wiring technologies than the AT&T blocks exist. For example, Krone has designed a punchdown system which has even higher density and a more reliable contact. A typical Type 66 punchdown block has 50 rows of four insulated contacts; in each row, contacts 1 and 2 are electrically connected, as are contacts 3 and 4. This is called a *split* block. A *full* block looks the same, but all four contacts are wired together. To connect a wire to a contact, you place the wire between the jaws of a retaining clip that's attached to the contact and then use a special punchdown tool to *punch* the wire *down* into the retaining clip — hence the name *punchdown block*. As you force the wire into the clip, the clip slices through the wires insulation to make electrical contact with the wires conductor. This gives the punchdown block its technical name: IDC, for Insulation Displacement Connector.

Punchdown blocks are especially useful if you're working with network cables that are collected in a wiring closet. Wiring closets are usually short on space, so using a compact, wall-mounted wiring device like a punchdown block helps to keep your cables organized and makes it easy to add or exchange wires in a star network.

Punchdown blocks are available in a variety of configurations and wirings. For example, they can be purchased prewired with a 50-pin Amphenol connector so that you can run a cable from the punchdown block to your stars multiport repeater or a packet-switching hub.

If you decide to use punchdown blocks, you'll need to know the secret wiring code used by telephone installers to keep hundreds of little wires straight. If you missed it, go back to Chapter 2, where we explained the code.

The third device, the patch panel, is a cross between the harmonica block and the punchdown block. Like the harmonica block, the patch panel is designed to accept RJ-11 jacks. But like the punchdown block, the patch panel has places for connecting more than one wire per port. Patch panels usually offer four RJ-11 jacks per hub port (see Figure 7-7). Because a patch panel has more jacks per port, you can use one for easy connection of multiple wiring runs to each port of an active hub. Again, like the harmonica block and punchdown block, the patch panel has an Amphenol 50-pin socket for connection to an active hub.

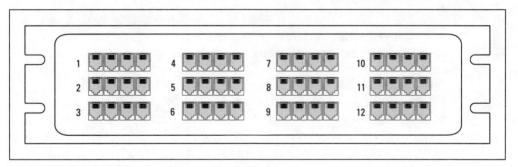

Figure 7-7: A typical patch panel with four RJ-11 jacks per port. This extended view shows contacts, or pins.

If you're running only one device per port, you don't really need a patch panel, but you may want to use one for future expansion capabilities. If you have multiple wiring runs to a single port, with or without a patch panel, just remember that the total length of the runs attached to one port is subject to the usual wiring limits and number of nodes of a passive star network (with four branches if you use all four jacks on the patch panel).

Patch panels have a distinct advantage if you have to rewire your network because they don't require special tools to connect the wires to the panel. (Of course, you need wiring runs ending in RJ-11 jacks in order to make the connections.)

There are some differences in installing any of these devices for passive and active stars, but we cover these differences later in this chapter when we discuss installing these types of network topologies.

# Installing a Daisy-Chain Network

The simplest network to create is a daisy-chain. All you need to do is connect the network connectors with network cables; then plug the connectors into the computers, and you're done. Well go through this procedure step by step.

The following is a shopping list of the items you need:

❖ One Apple LocalTalk or Farallon PhoneNET Plus connector for each Mac.

❖ One similar connector for each LaserWriter.

❖ LocalTalk or PhoneNET cables (depending on connectors).

We'll assume that all of your Macs and your LaserWriter are installed relatively close to one another. That proximity, although it's certainly not a requirement, makes installation a bit simpler.

If you decide to use LocalTalk wiring, all you need to do is plug the network connectors into each Mac and LaserWriter and then plug the LocalTalk cables into the connectors. Of course, you should never wire up a device to the network when the device is powered on. You don't have to take down the entire network, but you should make sure that the Mac or LaserWriter you are connecting is turned off. The connectors should be plugged into the printer port of each Mac. Make sure you connect to the one with the printer icon .

Start with one Mac. First plug a cable into its network connector and then plug the other end of that cable into the next Macs network connector. Repeat the process until all of the Macs and the LaserWriter are connected. You've just created a *daisy-chain* network (see Figure 7-8).

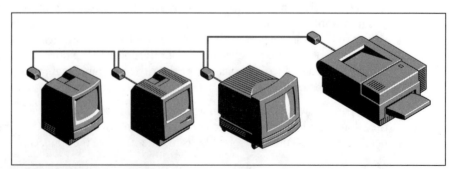

Figure 7-8: A daisy-chain network.

If you are installing a PhoneNET system, you need to take an extra step. As described previously, you plug the connectors into your Macs and run cables from each network connector to the others. You also have to *terminate* the network. To terminate the network, you use special resistors that come with the PhoneNET connectors (see Figure 7-9). You need two RJ-11 jacks with terminating resistors for a PhoneNET installation.

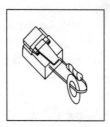

**Figure 7-9: An RJ-11 jack with terminating resistor.**

If you connected all the cables correctly, you should have a PhoneNET connector with an open socket at each end of the daisy-chain. These two connectors define the ends of your network. To make the network run smoothly, you should install terminating resistors on these connectors. Take the resistors that are soldered to the clear plastic RJ-11 jacks and place one jack into each PhoneNET network connector that has an empty socket. Your network is now terminated.

We'll move on to a network that is more complicated, but one that offers more expandability options — the bus network.

# Installing a Bus Network

We present a sample layout for a bus network in Chapter 6, "Designing a Local-Talk LAN." In that example, we explain how to use wall jacks and place taps in the bus cable to form the network. Now, we'll show you a way to wire those wall jacks to the bus to form the network.

The bus network is a fairly custom installation because the length of the bus is determined by your building's layout. You'll probably start with a reel of cable that you need to cut to your specifications. First, check the cable while its still on the reel. Use an ohmmeter, a cable tester, or a Time Domain Reflectometer (TDR) to verify the continuity of the cable (see Chapter 9 for use of these instruments). Ohmmeters are the simplest tools for this task, but they don't indicate the position of a break if one has occurred in the cable. On the other hand, cable testers can locate the break to within a few feet, and TDRs can pinpoint the break, with an error factor of within an inch or two.

Once you pull the cables to their locations, be sure to test the cables again for shorts or breaks that may have occurred during the installation. Mark the cable every five meters with white tape and a cable number. (Do this beforehand if the cable is being pulled through conduit or inaccessible areas.) Then add colored labels bearing the cable number in a neighboring location, such as a baseboard, and mark the location of the cables on a building plan. This way, when you have a break in the cable, a TDR or other cable tester can pinpoint the break, and your systematic labeling of cables will lead you right to the problem.

You can use wall-mounted phone jacks for tapping into a PhoneNET bus network. Once you've pulled your cable through the wall, leaving some slack in the cable, remove the phone jacks where you intend to tap into the bus cable. Strip the outer insulation from about two inches of the cable and then strip about one inch of insulation from the two wires in the cable that will be used to carry network signals.

Be careful not to cut any of the wires. If you accidentally cut a wire, solder the two ends together; do not simply twist them back together. Take the two stripped lengths of wire and wrap them around the screw terminals in the phone jack.

Be consistent in following the color schemes of the wires and the labels of the phone jack. For example, as the red and green wires are usually used for the phone system, use the yellow and black wires (the remaining colors in a quad cable) for your network.

If you picked twisted-pair wiring, use the second pair (the one with orange stripes on it, not the one with blue stripes). Attach the stripped black wire to the terminal marked B, and the stripped yellow wire to the terminal marked Y (see Figure 7-10). Mount the phone jack back into the wall and continue with the rest of your phone jacks. Be sure to install a 120-ohm terminating resistor between the black and yellow terminals of the wall jacks at each end of the bus cable, as shown in Figure 7-10. The wall jack on the right-hand side of the drawing shows where to install a terminating resistor.

## You Can Never Have Enough Labels

What's obvious now won't be obvious a few days, months, or years from now. We suggest getting a good stock of cable marking tools, including permanent marking pens (such as the Sharpie), cable ties with label tags, white electrical tape, and key tags with string attached. Take a few extra minutes to label your cable at both ends and at several points in the middle.

The same advice goes for wall jacks and any other part of your cabling plant. Write all over everything, and you will find your efforts well rewarded years later.

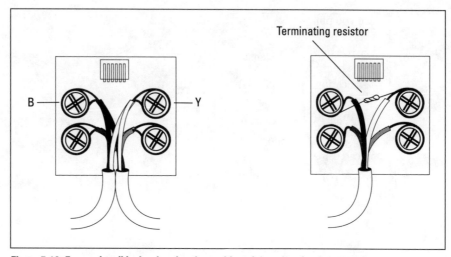

**Figure 7-10: Exposed wall jacks showing the position of the wires for the network.**

To use the bus that you installed in the wall, all you need to do is plug a PhoneNET connector into your Mac (or other network device) and run a modular extension cable from the connector to the wall jack. You're now ready to use the network.

Note that because you've installed a terminating resistor at each end of the bus, you don't need any further terminating resistors. Thus, if you use regular PhoneNET connectors to connect a Mac to the wall jack, the unused RJ-11 socket in the connector should remain empty. **Hint:** put a piece of tape over it to remind yourself that no resistor is needed. Also, remember that you shouldn't use StarConnectors to connect devices to a bus.

In some cases, you may want a dual wall jack for your network connection so that you can use one plug for a phone and the other for the network. The process of connecting the wires is the same as described above, except that only the network wires are connected to one jack, whereas the phone wires are connected to the other jack (see Figure 7-11).

As we've said before, star networks easily have the most versatile topology and make troubleshooting simpler. Well explain next what it takes to install both passive and active star networks.

# Installing a Star Network

If you're installing either a passive or an active star network, you'll most likely be using the wiring, or utility, closets of your building. The utility closet is where the phone installers connect your office phones to the phone system. As we pointed out

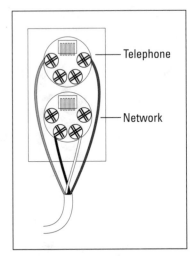

**Figure 7-11: An exposed dual wall jack showing wire positions for the network and for the phone.**

in the preceding chapter, the phone system also uses a star network to link together the phones in a building.

Initially, we'll assume that you are installing only one device per branch. Later, we'll explain the stars wiring options when you use more than one device per branch, but for now you won't add party lines. To set up a star, you need some type of wiring distribution block for connecting the network branches — we'll say that you're using a punchdown block rather than a patch panel.

Install the punchdown block on a wall in the utility closet; then pull a separate length of cable from the block to each wall jack that you intend to use. Wire each wall jack. For the moment, because you are installing one device per wall jack, you can simply cut the wire, strip the ends, and attach the wire ends to the terminals. If you're using regular PhoneNET Plus connectors, attach a terminating resistor to the wall jack terminals (refer again to Figure 7-10). If you use the newer StarConnectors, which are already terminated, you can't use a resistor in the wall jack.

We advise putting a symbol on each jack with an internal terminating resistor so you know that you can't use a StarConnector without removing the resistor — or, if you use a normal PhoneNET connector, you must not put its terminating resistor on.

If you want to connect a few wall jacks together to support more than one device per branch, you should wire the intermediate wall jacks using the same method as described for the bus, stripping the wires without cutting them. The last wall jack in the branch can be connected to the cut ends of that wire run. Only the last wall jack in the run — the one farthest from the utility closet — should be terminated.

Most of what we've just described applies to both passive and active stars. But recall that in Chapter 6 we explained that there can be no more than four terminating resistors on a passive star, regardless of the number of branches. So take care not to exceed this limit if you're installing a passive star.

Back at the punchdown block, connect the wires coming from each wall jack to the block (see Figure 7-12). Yellow wires should be connected to one row of pins; black wires should be connected to the next row of pins. Remember to use the pair with orange stripes if you used twisted-pair cable. Now use a jumper wire to connect all the yellow wires together and use a second jumper to connect all the black wires together. You now have a passive star. Farallon also offers a passive wiring kit, which includes a special jumper plug that mates with the punchdown block's Amphenol socket and eliminates the need for the jumper wires.

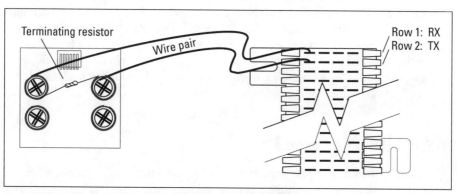

Figure 7-12: Wiring run from the phone jack to the punchdown block.

You may not be able to pull each wire pair separately, as you may have a number of wires that are simply connected to unmarked pins on a punchdown block in the utility closet. If so, you'll need to determine which wire pair goes to which wall jack or room.

The best way to do this is to emulate telephone installers. Obtain a tone generator and a listening unit. We use a set made by Progressive Electronics which costs about $95. The first time you save a few hours tracing unknown wires, you'll appreciate the value of this investment.

Attach the tone generator to the wire pair in one room and then return to the utility closet with the listening unit. If you wave the listening unit like a wand over the pins of the punchdown block, you'll hear a tone. The tone gets louder as the listening unit gets closer to the pair that's connected to the tone generator. When you touch the wires with the listening unit, the tone is ear-splitting. You've just located the wire pair that leads to the desired room. You need to move the tone generator to another wall jack and repeat the process until you've identified and labeled all pairs on the punchdown block.

If you've just completed a wiring layout for an active star network rather than a passive one, you don't run any jumper wires on the punchdown block. All you do is mount your active hub (a StarController, TurboStar, or LocalSwitch) nearby. Then run a cable with Amphenol-style 50-pin plugs from the socket on the punchdown block to a similar socket on the active hub. Plug in the active hub, turn on the power, and your active star is ready for action.

Whether you use punchdown blocks or patch panels to create your star network, you can create a hierarchy of networks by combining active stars. This combination is especially effective when it comes to troubleshooting the physical layers of your network. For example, you may use one or more active stars to wire the networks on each floor of a building and then connect each of those stars to a master hub for the entire building. A problem that occurs with one branch on a particular floor can be isolated from the rest of the network by shutting down that branch at its active hub. If the problem involves an entire workgroup wired to one active hub, you can isolate the workgroup by shutting down the branch that leads from the workgroups hub to the master hub.

# Testing the Network

Some of the simplest, but most useful, cabling tests that you can perform involve only an ohmmeter. Under the right conditions, you can use this instrument to determine if a cable is damaged or cut. Here are two exercises using an ohmmeter that will test your network cables.

If you don't have an ohmmeter, acquire one with a continuity buzzer or beep and some extra sets of probes. We normally buy Fluke digital multimeters, such as the Model 10, which costs about $70, although you can find less expensive models with continuity buzzers as well. Most ohmmeters come with rather coarse probes. You'll probably want at least two more sets: a set with finer clips and a set with test lead clips on them to attach to network wires. This will set you back another $40 or so.

If you're testing wires that are connected to wall jacks, the first thing you should do is create a test cable from a small piece of modular extension cable, of one to three feet in length. Install an RJ-11 plug on one end; strip one inch of insulation from the yellow and black wires at the other end.

Then after attaching the yellow and black leads to your ohmmeter, you can insert the RJ-11 end into the wall jack that you want to test. If you want a heavier-duty test set, combine a female-to-female RJ-11 connector, a short RJ-11-to-spade-lugs cable from Radio Shack, and some inexpensive alligator clips. If you're really flush, both Harris and Mod-Tap make heavy-duty versions for about $10.

Because you cannot have any PhoneNET connectors attached to the network when you're performing an ohmmeter test, its a good idea to perform this test right after installing the cables. If you must use this test at a later time, you'll have to disconnect all your users from the network, a situation which can be bothersome to everyone. You can use diagnostic software to perform other tests that check a cable's continuity and do not involve physical changes to the network. Such tests are particularly useful for a fully installed network. For more information on such tests, see Chapter 13, "Configuring, Monitoring, and Fixing AppleTalk Networks."

To test a bus network, simply plug your test cable into a wall plug and measure the resistance (see Figure 7-13). The resistance should measure 60 ohms, plus about 30-50 ohms for every 1,000 feet of cable. If the resistance is infinite, your cable is cut or has suffered other damage. It may also simply be lacking a terminating resistor, so check this out before jumping to conclusions about the condition of your cable.

On the other hand, if the measured resistance is near zero or just 30-50 ohms per 1,000 feet of cable, you either have a shorted cable or you've left a PhoneNET connector plugged in somewhere along the cable. Obviously, the ohmmeter is not an infallible, definitive test, but it can point you in the right direction if you're checking cables.

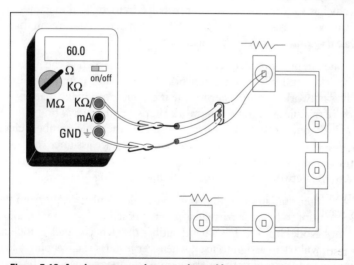

**Figure 7-13: An ohmmeter used to test a bus cable.**

With a star network, you can perform similar tests, except that you test at the punchdown block instead of at the wall jacks. Measure the resistance across the two pins that correspond to one wiring run; the resistance should measure 120 ohms, plus the usual 30-50 ohms for every 1,000 feet of cable. Again, if the resistance is infinite, the cable is either cut or lacks a terminating resistor. If your cable has been shorted, as with a bad crimp, the resistance will be near zero or approximately 30-50 ohms for every 1,000 feet of cable on the run. Don't forget that you may have left a PhoneNET connector plugged into the wiring run.

If you go back and plug a PhoneNET connector into the wall jack at the end of the wiring run, you should be able to measure a resistance between 0 and 100 ohms. If the resistance is more than 100 ohms, either you have a bad connection or the cable is too long.

When you work with punchdown blocks, there's always a chance that the wiring installer has confused a network run with a phone line. If you can measure the DC voltage of a wiring run (using a voltmeter), you should measure no voltage on a network wire pair. On the other hand, if you're testing a live phone line, there will be some measurable voltage (not enough to harm you), and you know that someone has connected the wrong line to the network.

# Setting Up Your Computers

Now that your network wiring is in place, you can start connecting your Macs and other network devices to the network. Remember that when you're using wall jacks that already have a terminating resistor installed in them, you must not install another terminating resistor in the PhoneNET connector. Also, recall that you can not use a StarConnector in such a case.

As mentioned in previous chapters, AppleTalk devices such as the Mac and LaserWriter dynamically poll the network to assign node numbers to themselves. This makes network startup easier for the user, but it can make matters trickier when you're troubleshooting the network later — and you *will* find yourself doing some troubleshooting later. A network doesn't see the node numbers change after the first time the devices are used and node numbers are assigned, because each device tries to use the same node number it had the last time it was turned on and attached to the network (see Chapter 2, "Understanding Networks").

You may be interested in assigning your own node numbers right from the start; perhaps you want to follow a particular scheme based on location. Farallon Computings NodeHint INIT is a handy utility that lets you pick a node number that the Mac will try to assign to itself whenever it starts up. Keeping a log of all node numbers and assigning them every time you attach a Mac to the network can work particularly well with LocalTalk and PhoneNET networks. This technique doesn't work with LaserWriters, of course, because you cannot install the INIT on a LaserWriter.

You may also want to assign specific names to each Mac and LaserWriter that is part of the network. In fact, if you have more than one LaserWriter, you *must* assign names to them.

QUICK TIPS

## Name that Mac

Assigning a name to a Mac is easy. For Macs running System 6.x, simply select the Chooser DA and enter an appropriate name in the space provided (see the figure). If you're running System 7 on your Mac, you need to choose Control Panels from the Apple menu and then open the Sharing Setup control panel. The part labeled Network Identity in the Sharing Setup window (see the second figure) contains a field where you enter the name for your Mac.

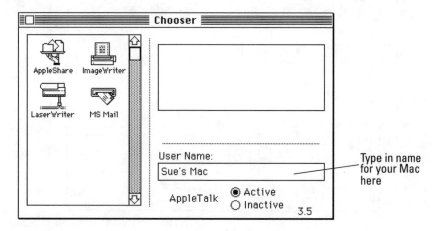

Now turn on all your Macs and the LaserWriters. When your Mac is ready, select the Chooser program from the Apple menu on the far left of your screen. At the lower right-hand side of the Chooser window, you see the word AppleTalk with two buttons, one marked Inactive, the other marked Active (see Figure 7-14). If the Active button isn't checked, check it. This step activates your Macs built-in support for AppleTalk networking so that your Mac now becomes part of the network that you built. If you started your Macintosh without AppleTalk, you will need to re-start now to activate the network software.

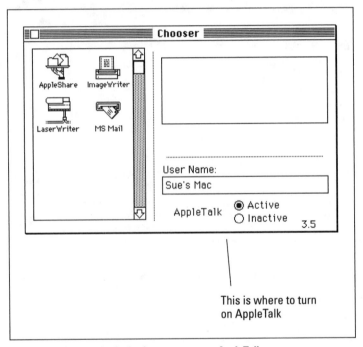

This is where to turn
on AppleTalk

Figure 7-14: Choose the Active button to turn on AppleTalk.

To assign names to LaserWriters under System 6, use the Namer application that comes with the LaserWriter. Install this application on one Mac that is attached to the network. Turn on one LaserWriter at a time and run Namer to assign a new name to that LaserWriter; simply cycle through each of the LaserWriters on your network. System 7 has a new application for naming LaserWriters. This applica-tion is called the LaserWriter Utility 7.0 (and 8.0), but it does the same job as the Namer.

So far, we've talked only about attaching Macs and LaserWriters to your network. You may want to connect some DOS-based computers to your network as well. If you do, you'll need to install a LocalTalk card in each PC. These cards are available from Dayna Communications, Daystar Digital, and Farallon. The cards include software that allows a PC user to print to a LaserWriter and log into AppleShare file servers. Some readers may be familiar with the AppleShare PC card and software from Apple. This product was turned over to Farallon Computing in 1990 for further development and is now being sold by Farallon as part of its PhoneNET Talk line.

# CHAPTER 7  CONCEPTS AND TERMS

- When selecting the cables and connectors for your network, you can choose from Apple's own LocalTalk kit or a popular alternative, PhoneNET.

- Making your own network cables may be your best bet especially if your network doesn't fit the standard lengths of cable offered in the ready-made kits.

- Wall jacks can be wired for bus and star networks.

- Various wiring devices, including the *harmonica block*, the *punchdown block*, and the *patch panel* can organize your wiring and make installation easier.

- Certain types of networks require terminating resistors to make the network run smoothly.

- You can assign a network name to individual Macs using Sharing Setup control panel (System 7) or Chooser DA (System 6).

**AppleTalk**
Apple's networking architecture. Built-in to every Macintosh.

**full block**
A punchdown block (Type 66) where all four punch positions in a horizontal row are electrically connected.

**harmonica block**
Used to convert a 50-pin Amphenol-style connector on the end of a 25-pair phone cable to one or more RJ-style jacks.

**PhoneNET**
Farallon Computing's name for a LocalTalk cabling system which uses RJ-11 style jacks and a single pair of wires instead of Apple's self-terminating LocalTalk connectors which use a DIN-3 style connector. The primary advantages of PhoneNET over Apple's LocalTalk Connector are cost and easy installation.

**plenum air return**
A building construction technique where the space above a suspended ceiling is used, without ducts, as an integral part of the air handling system, usually to return air for circulation through the HVAC system.

**punchdown block**
A system designed by the telephone companies to terminate and join cables without explicit mechanical splices. A typical punchdown block (Type 66 block) has 50 rows of four contacts, or pins. Wires are pushed, or "punched down," onto a pin to make electrical contact using a special tool called a punchdown tool.

**self-terminating port**
A LocalTalk port which will automatically apply proper termination resistance whether it is connected or not connected to another station. A self-terminating port does not require the network manager to add termination resistance.

**silver satin wire**
A kind of non-twisted-pair wire (normally) used for connections between a wall jack and a telephone, or, in LocalTalk, between PhoneNET connectors.

**split block**
A punchdown block where each half of the block, divided vertically, is independent. On a split block (sometimes called a "half block"), the leftmost two connectors on each horizontal row are connected to each other, the rightmost two connectors on each horizontal row are connected to each other, but connecting the left half to the right half will require an external connection, usually through a bridging clip.

**Type 66 block**
An older type of punch-down block, very common in buildings wired before 1988 (and many wired after). The Type 66 block is distinguished by a relatively low density (compared to later technologies), low cost, and simple tools.

**Type 110 block**
A replacement for the Type 66 block devised by AT&T. It boasts a higher wiring density, but relatively more difficult wiring technology. Type 110 blocks can be used for 100M bps wiring (Category 5), while Type 66 blocks cannot. Other manufacturers, such as Krone, have developed alternatives to the 110 block which have similar or better densities and similar or better electrical characteristics.

# Designing an Ethernet LAN

IN THIS CHAPTER

- The standards that have been developed for Ethernet networks

- The differences among Ethernet standards

- Cabling types used for Ethernet networks

- Topologies for Ethernet networks

- Hardware for connecting Macs to Ethernet

- Hardware and software for connecting LaserWriters to Ethernet

- Typical Mac performance on Ethernet networks

Running a network at the LocalTalk speed of 230 k bps may not be fast enough for your needs, even on a well-designed network. LocalTalk was designed for a different era and a different kind of network, where Macintoshes were the only computers and AppleTalk the only protocol.

In the world of multiprotocol and multiplatform networks, Ethernet is the standard for networking from the desktop to the wiring closet. With Ethernet interface cards widely available for all Macs at prices of less than $100 per system, you will probably find that Ethernet is the best and least expensive network for all but the smallest of installations.

## An Introduction to Ethernet

Ethernet is a set of protocols for only the lowermost part of the OSI Reference Model. Ethernet includes a physical layer and part of the data link layer from the OSI model. The rest of the network protocols, such as AppleTalk or TCP/IP, are then layered atop Ethernet to form a complete network.

With only a few exceptions, Ethernet is a *multiple–protocol medium*. This means that a single physical Ethernet network can have many different protocols operating on it without causing any problems.

QUOTABLES

*"Gratis anhelans, multa agendo nihil agens."* (Breathless for no reason and busy doing nothing.)

— Phaedrus

Ethernet packets include data about protocol types in order to distinguish among the various network operating systems. Therefore, you can have an Ethernet network with AppleTalk, DECnet, IPX, XNS, and TCP/IP protocols all being transmitted on the same cable without any extra effort on your part — although network management may be an issue. The AppleTalk machines know which protocols are for them, the DEC computers know that they should be handling DECnet (or TCP/IP or LAT), and so on down the line.

**BACKGROUNDER**

### So What's the Exception?

Actually, we know of only one case where you could have a problem when running multiple network protocols stacks on the same wire: Novell's Netware. It's a long story, but the bottom line is that Novell, in its infinite wisdom, has four different ways of putting Netware IPX packets into an Ethernet frame (*encapsulating* is the term for this): three of which are compatible with international standards and one which isn't. Every Novell NetWare network has to pick one of these four, usually at random, and every station on the same network segment must use the same encapsulation method. As Dave Barry is fond of saying, "We are not making this up."

You may ask yourself, as so many people have asked Novell, why they continue to this day to support an encapsulation method which is incompat-ible with protocols running on the same wire. Novell claims that it's because Novell was ahead of its time and kept releasing software to its customers before the standards committees had made up their minds.

Perhaps closer to the truth is that Novell was sloppy and failed to keep up with the status of the network standards because it felt that only Novell networks ought to exist and didn't mind causing headaches for any network manager so audacious as to try and run multiple protocols on the same wire. Fortunately, no self-respecting NetWare manager would be caught dead reading a book about Macintosh networking, so we Mac managers can have a quiet chuckle at Novell's expense. Try not to giggle out loud next time you hear a NetWare-running colleague complain about encapsulation problems, would you?

Three companies, Digital Equipment Corp. (DEC), Intel, and Xerox (known in networking circles collectively as DIX), were responsible for formulating the first working Ethernet networks and publishing the specifications in the 1970s. These specifications have been upgraded since their original publications and are now known as the *Ethernet version 2 specifications*, or *Ethernet V2* for short. You don't have to worry about Ethernet V1, which is not compatible with Ethernet V2 and was never used widely. If you do run across some Ethernet V1 gear in a dusty closet, throw it out immediately — it can only cause you trouble if you try to use it.

The IEEE (Institute of Electrical and Electronics Engineers, pronounced I-triple-E) is a standards-making body that depends on the participation of many company representatives. Companies such as DEC, Intel, Xerox, and Apple, among others, cooperate in the formulation of electrical, communications, and networking standards.

The IEEE is an international standards organization and can obtain broader support for a standard from a variety of companies than if a similar standard were suggested by a single corporation, a set of corporations such as DIX, or even the U.S.-based ANSI (American National Standards Institute). Most of the Ethernet standards defined by the IEEE eventually find their way into the ISO (International Organization for Standardization; see Chapter 3, "Understanding AppleTalk Protocols"), which has delegated primary responsibility for development of Ethernet to the IEEE.

Although the DIX Ethernet specifications predate those from the IEEE, we'll take a look at the IEEE specifications first, primarily because we discuss these most frequently in this book. The IEEE Ethernet standards fall within a category called the Project 802 standards, which include Ethernet, token ring, and all the other local area networking standards. These standards are structured in a typical layered scheme, as in the OSI Reference Model (see Figure 8-1). The Ethernet standards are labeled *802.3* in the diagram (pronounced eight-oh-two-dot-three). Note the layer labeled *802.2: Logical Link Control*. This is an optional specification that has two primary functions:

❖ It extends the interoperability of LANs so that multiple protocols can all run on the same media through *protocol identification*. (This feature was present in Ethernet V2.)

❖ It brings many of the traditional functions of the network layer closer to the LAN. You will find that this second feature is not often used in most microcomputer network software (such as AppleTalk or NetWare).

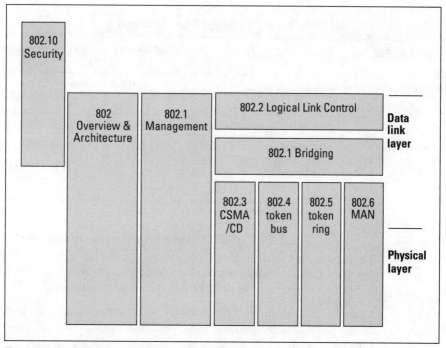

Figure 8-1: The IEEE LAN family standards work together to create a complete LAN environment.

AppleTalk's transition from Ethernet V2 to IEEE 802.3 with LLC protocol identification came in Phase 2 and is discussed in Chapter 3, "Understanding AppleTalk Protocols."

The IEEE 802.3 Ethernet standards currently include six LAN implementations:

❖ 10BASE5, sometimes called *thicknet*

❖ 10BASE2, sometimes called *thinnet* or *cheapernet*

❖ 10BROAD36, sometimes called *broadband Ethernet*

❖ 1BASE5, sometimes called *Starlan*

❖ 10BASE-T, sometimes called *UTP Ethernet* or *twisted-pair Ethernet*

❖ 10BASE-F, sometimes called *fiber Ethernet*

See Table 8-1 for a summary of the main features of these standards.

## Table 8-1
## IEEE Ethernet Specifications

| Specification | Medium | # Devices | Max. Segment Length (meters) |
|---|---|---|---|
| 10BASE5 (thickwire) | RG8 coaxial cable | up to 100 per segment | 500 |
| 10BASE2 (thinwire) | RG58A/U or C/U coaxial cable | up to 30 per segment | 185 |
| 10BASE-T | 22 to 26 AWG unshielded twisted pair | 1 per branch | 100 |
| 10BROAD36 | RG9 coaxial cable | 1,024 | 3,600 |
| 10BASE-F | 62.5/125 μ fiber optic | 1 per branch | 2,000 (FL), 2,000 (FB), 500 (FP) |

The 10BASE-F standard actually includes three fiber-based Ethernets, all of which replace the older FOIRL (Fiber Optic Inter-Repeater Link), which was a kind of connection that allowed the use of fiber optic segments between Ethernet repeaters. The three types of fiber optic Ethernet include the following:

❖ 10BASE-FL (FL means Fiber Link). This Ethernet replaces the FOIRL standard directly and is designed to work with existing FOIRL repeaters you may already have. 10BASE-FL allows two repeaters to be separated by a fiber segment of 2km (unless a 10BASE-FL device is connected to a FOIRL device, in which case a distance of 1km is allowed). 10BASE-FL connections are allowed between repeaters, between two LAN stations, or between a station and a repeater.

❖ 10BASE-FB (FB means Fiber Backbone). This Ethernet is a special kind of fiber segment between repeaters that allows the rules on the number of repeaters in an Ethernet to be broken. 10BASE-FB links may only be run between special 10BASE-FB repeaters and may be up to 2km long. 10BASE-FB is used in special cases where distance is a problem.

❖ 10BASE-FP (FP means Fiber Passive). This Ethernet is a star Ethernet that lets you link up to 33 stations over fiber segments up to 500 meters long. The 10BASE-FP network requires a special passive fiber star coupler to which all segments are connected. No repeaters are used in a 10BASE-FP network.

The labels used by the IEEE to distinguish the different types of Ethernet (10BASE2, 10BASE-T, and so on) form a shorthand notation for the salient features of each specification. Each label includes the data rate in M bps, the transmission style, and the maximum segment length (in 100 meter units):

```
<data rate in M bps><medium type><maximum segment length
(x 100m)>
```

Thus, a 10BASE5 network is a 10 M bps network on a baseband medium with a maximum segment length of 500 meters. The following paragraphs explain these three parts in greater detail.

The number prefix represents the transmission speed in Megabits per second (M bps). Most Ethernet networks run at a speed of 10 M bps. An older version that currently is used very little is the Starlan network, which has a transmission speed of 1 M bps.

Ethernet networks can propagate signals in one of two ways — baseband or broadband transmissions. *Baseband* means that the signal is transmitted at its original frequency without modulation. Baseband uses digital signaling, as opposed to the analog signaling used by broadband systems. *Broadband* networks use the same type of cables and transmission devices as cable TV and implement a range of frequencies for transmission.

In the IEEE labels, *BASE* tells you that the network uses baseband transmission, whereas *BROAD* tells you that this is broadband. Any electrical engineers out there will have to pardon us for simplifying this a little bit, but the real details aren't all that interesting to most network managers. If you really want to learn more about the down-and-dirty aspects of Ethernet, you should get a copy of the ANSI/IEEE standard 802.3, "Carrier sense multiple access with collision detection (CSMA/CD) access method and physical layer specifications."

The suffix after BASE or BROAD tells you the approximate maximum length of a network segment in 100s of meters (some rounding of numbers is used in assigning the labels, as you can see for 10BASE2 in Table 8-1. The 10BASE-T and 10BASE-F LAN types have dashes in their names to remind you that this describes the medium type rather than the transmission style. In the 10BASE-T specification, the *T* stands for *twisted*, as in twisted-pair wire, so this is a qualitative term rather than a distance limit. 10BASE-T is commonly referred to as *UTP Ethernet*, where *UTP* stands for Unshielded Twisted-Pair. In 10BASE-F, the *F* stands for *fiber*.

Although the IEEE labels do not include information about the number of devices that you can install on an Ethernet network, certain limits exist that vary with the medium you use. These limits are shown in Table 8-1. 10BASE5 and 10BROAD36 can accommodate the largest number of devices per network segment. As you'll see, 10BASE-T networks are multibranch star networks, where the only limit on the number of devices is the capacity of the active hub used for the star.

We mentioned previously, that there are actually two different standards for Ethernet — the IEEE 802.3 standard and the DIX, or Ethernet version 2, standard. An important difference between the IEEE 802.3 and Ethernet version 2 standards is the packet format. If you compare the two packet types, as shown in Figure 8-2, you'll see that the Type field used in Ethernet version 2 to specify protocol types (XNS, AppleTalk, DECnet, and so on) is located where the Length field is in the IEEE 802.3 packets. Fortunately, the designers of IEEE 802.3 and Ethernet V2 picked a set of legal packet lengths and a set of legal protocol types such that you can always tell what kind of packet you're looking at just by examining that field.

There is no ambiguity or overlap — the length field from 802.3 and the protocol type field from Ethernet V2 overlap, but all legal Ethernet V2 protocol types are greater than 1500, which is the maximum 802.3 data length. Some implementations of Ethernet drivers are smart enough to handle both types of Ethernet packets at the same time, although most protocols support one or the other.

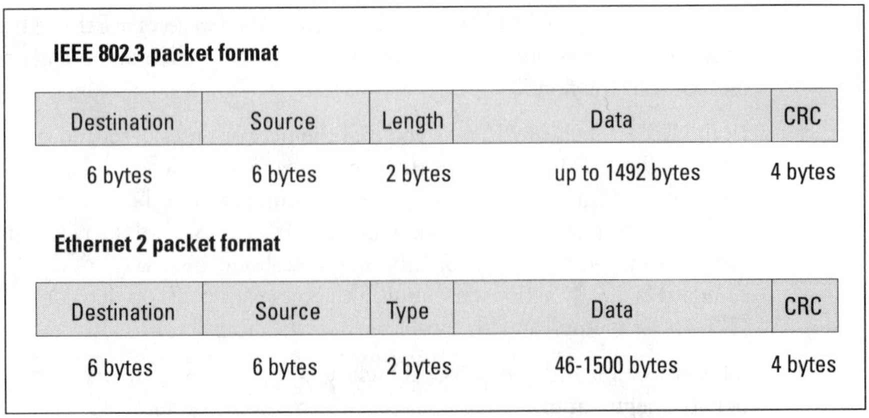

**IEEE 802.3 packet format**

| Destination | Source | Length | Data | CRC |
|---|---|---|---|---|
| 6 bytes | 6 bytes | 2 bytes | up to 1492 bytes | 4 bytes |

**Ethernet 2 packet format**

| Destination | Source | Type | Data | CRC |
|---|---|---|---|---|
| 6 bytes | 6 bytes | 2 bytes | 46-1500 bytes | 4 bytes |

Figure 8-2: A comparison of the Ethernet 2 and IEEE 802.3 Ethernet packet formats.

This difference in packet format can cause problems in AppleTalk networks. Apple's original specifications for EtherTalk used the Ethernet version 2 packet format; then Apple switched to IEEE 802.3 for AppleTalk Phase 2 (see Figure 8-3). This becomes a problem when you use an Ethernet bridge, as is common in large corporate networks, to filter out AppleTalk packets and then switch some or all of your AppleTalk networks to Phase 2. If you want to continue filtering AppleTalk, you'll have to reconfigure the filtering bridge for the IEEE 802.3 packets carrying AppleTalk data. (See Appendix B, "Converting Phase 1 AppleTalk Networks to Phase 2," and Chapter 13, "Configuring, Monitoring, and Fixing AppleTalk Networks," for more details.)

Now that weve reviewed the different Ethernet standards and the differences in packet formats, we'll explain what cables can be used for Ethernet and what network topologies you can build with these cables.

# Cabling and Network Topologies

Ethernet packets are routinely transmitted over both electrical media, such as coaxial cable and twisted-pair wires, and optical media, such as fiber optic cable. You can create larger networks by connecting Ethernet networks with microwave or laser links. And, within the past year, vendors such as Motorola, with its Altair system, have made it possible to use wireless (radio-frequency) links within offices to tie together workstations using Ethernet technology.

Four transmission media for Ethernet are currently popular: thick coaxial cable (10BASE5), thin coaxial cable (10BASE2), twisted-pair cable (10BASE-T), and fiber optic cable (10BASE-F), each shown in Figure 8-4. Each of these media poses restrictions on the network topologies you can use for your Ethernet network.

When 10BASE5 thick coaxial cable was first standardized for Ethernet, there were few, if any, workstations and PCs around. Network installers routinely ran thick coaxial cable as a bus for connecting a series of mainframe computers or minicomputers. Thick coaxial cable is still used primarily as a bus or backbone network to connect either subnetworks or buildings. In many cases, newer installations are using fiber optic cable for Ethernet (among other protocols, such as FDDI) as a backbone cable or are created with no backbone at all, using a *collapsed backbone*. In this topology, a single device, such as a multiport transceiver or a router acts as the backbone of the network — the backbone has been *collapsed* to something a few inches long, internal to the new backbone device.

Thin coaxial cable, or 10BASE2 thinnet, is also primarily used to create bus networks, although it is restricted to shorter lengths than 10BASE5. In addition, thinnet multiport repeaters can also be used to create stars out of thin coaxial cabling. Because 10BASE2 is simple to work with and readily available, it is an ideal medium for a laboratory or small office where many systems need to be connected to the network all at the same time.

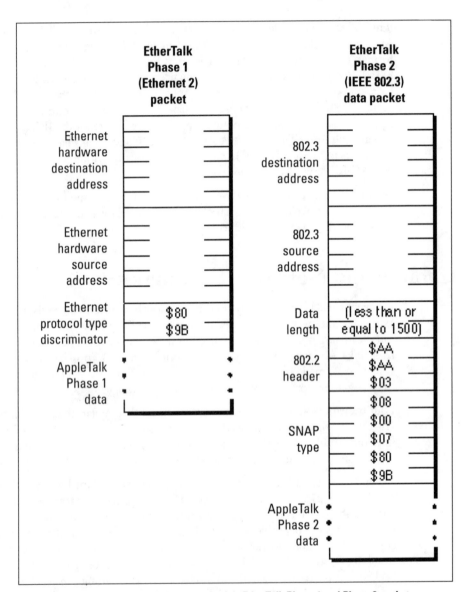

**Figure 8-3: The format differences between Apple's EtherTalk Phase 1 and Phase 2 packets.**

An appealing Ethernet medium for an office environment is unshielded twisted-pair cable, a wire similar to that used in many phone installations. However, unlike thicknet or thinnet Ethernet, UTP Ethernet requires an active controller, or *hub*, to create a complete network. This hub contains control circuitry for monitoring the condition of each UTP branch, as well as the repeater circuitry for amplifying the Ethernet signal for each port.

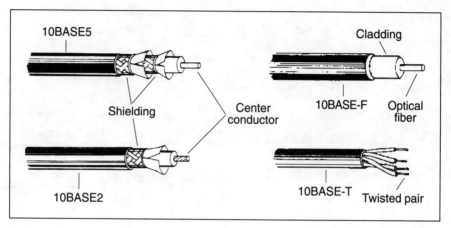

**Figure 8-4: Types of cables for Ethernet.**

Each device in an Ethernet network (called a DTE, for Data Terminal Equipment) follows the same model, no matter what type of cabling scheme is chosen. In Figure 8-5, you can see the Ethernet model for connecting a device to some LAN medium.

The medium in Figure 8-5 that is used to carry LAN traffic between systems is the real wires being used: coaxial cable, twisted-pair, or fiber optic cabling. To attach to the medium, you use the *MDI* (Medium Dependent Interface). The MDI together with the *PMA* (Physical Medium Attachment) make up the *MAU*, the Medium Attachment Unit. The MDI is a piece of hardware which makes the physical connection to the medium.

For example, in 10BASE-T LANs, the MDI is an RJ-45 telephone connector. (RJ-45 jacks have 8 conductors; RJ-11 jacks have four). The MAU (called a transceiver in DIX Ethernet V2, because it transmits and receives signals onto the medium) is responsible for converting the digital signals transmitted and received by the actual device into whatever kind of signals the particular LAN media require.

The MAU connects to the station (DTE) using the AUI, Attachment Unit Interface (called a transceiver cable in DIX Ethernet V2). The DTE itself is responsible for physical layer signaling onto the MAU and for handling collisions and media contention through the MAC, Media Access Control, layer.

In the following sections, we discuss the characteristics and pitfalls of each of the three most common types of Ethernet networks. In Chapter 9, we go into greater detail on how to install and use these media.

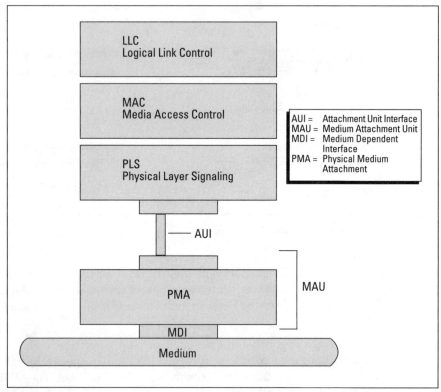

**Figure 8-5: The Ethernet model for connecting a device to a LAN has many parts, but you'll typically only see one or two.**

# Thick Ethernet: Type 10BASE5

Thick Ethernet is relatively unusual today, mostly because it's so much more difficult to work with than thin Ethernet or 10BASE-T systems. However, you will find thick Ethernet in building backbones, older Ethernet installations, or where long segments are required.

In thick Ethernet, the AUI port is a 15-pin connector to which you attach a transceiver cable. The transceiver cable, which cannot be any longer than 50 meters, goes to a transceiver which has been clamped directly onto the coaxial cable (see Figure 8-6). Some companies, such as Digital, sell "office" transceiver cables which are thinner and more flexible than normal Ethernet transceiver cables. We use these cables when attaching Ethernet equipment in a single location, such as an equipment rack, to other equipment very nearby. Office transceiver cables cannot be as long as normal transceiver cables because of signal loss. Digital, for example, doesn't sell cables longer than 5 meters.

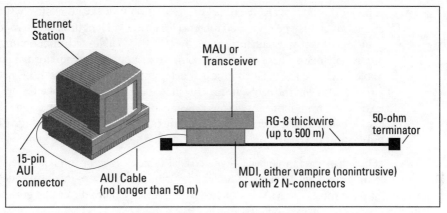

**Figure 8-6: The thick Ethernet 10BASE5 connection requires a MAU (transceiver) attached to the Ethernet cable and a 15-pin AUI cable to connect the MAU to the station.**

QUICK TIPS

## Who Came Up with that 15-Pin Connector?

If you've ever had a chance to work with thick Ethernet, you've probably also met the worst connector in the computer business: the 15-pin Ethernet AUI connector. Actually, the connector isn't so bad — it's the standard DB15 shell you've seen in lots of other environments. It's the hold-downs that can be troublesome. In the Ethernet specification, a special kind of latch between the male and female 15-pin connectors is required. Instead of the screws most other DB-style connectors use, the Ethernet connector uses slide locks to hold the cable in.

Unfortunately, manufacturers have not come up with a way of making the slide lock a very secure holding system. These connectors tend to not fit very well when mixing vendors. Even worse, they tend to fall apart because transceiver cables are so heavy and thick. We don't know a network manager who is using thickwire Ethernet who hasn't had some sort of network emergency caused because an AUI cable

slowly worked its way out of contact with the computer it was serving.

If you have to use these connectors, here's some advice:

❖ If at all possible, secure the transceiver cable to the coaxial cable (on the transceiver end) or the DTE (at the other end) so that it has no strain and will not easily come out.

❖ Double- and triple-check any slide lock connection in an Ethernet network. It's easy to make mistakes when mating cables of this type. Give each cable a good strong pull to make sure that it is seated and locked down properly.

❖ Where possible, replace the slide latches with screw-down terminals to provide a more secure connection.

Thick Ethernet uses RG8 coaxial cable, a 50-ohm thick and relatively stiff cable, which may be up to 500 meters (1,640 feet) in length between repeaters. Thick Ethernet is usually bright yellow (for PVC cable) or bright orange (for fluoropolymer or Teflon cable) in color, to distinguish it from normal power cables. Because the most common attachment method for thick Ethernet involves drilling a hole in the cable, it was considered a good idea to make Ethernet cable easy to tell from more dangerous power cables. Thick Ethernet also has black bands painted on it every 2.5 meters. Any transceiver attached to thick Ethernet cable must be located on one of these black bands, give or take 5 cm.

Thick Ethernet cable has N-type coaxial cable connectors on it and needs a 50-ohm terminating resistor at each end. A single segment of thick Ethernet cable can have, at most, 100 MAUs attached to it. A thick Ethernet must be grounded at exactly one place along its length.

# Thin Ethernet: Type 10BASE2

Thin Ethernet, sometimes called *cheapernet*, is electrically very similar to thickwire Ethernet. The major differences are in packaging:

❖ Thin Ethernet normally includes the AUI and MAU on the Ethernet card itself, eliminating the need for an external transceiver cable and transceiver.

❖ Thin Ethernet cable is thinner and easier to work with than thick Ethernet cable.

The Ethernet signals used in thin Ethernet are the same as those used in thick Ethernet, which means that it is technically possible to link a thin and thick Ethernet segment purely by means of a cable adapter. This type of configuration is highly undesirable and not recommended because the signal reflections caused by linking dissimilar media significantly shortens the maximum network topology and contributes to a less reliable network.

Thin Ethernet cable uses BNC connectors and must be terminated with a 50-ohm terminator at each end (see Figure 8-7). The actual cable specifications for thin Ethernet can be a problem. Although thin Ethernet is normally described as RG-58 coaxial cable, true RG-58 cable does not conform to the requirements for thin Ethernet. RG-58 A/U and RG-58 C/U cables should be used for thin Ethernet. As with most other cabling schemes, it is a good idea to buy all your Ethernet cable from the same source at the same time in order to ensure that your network will have a minimum of problems caused by slight mismatches in impedance of media. The specifications for thin Ethernet cable and for some common substitutes are provided in Table 8-2.

In thinwire Ethernet, the Ethernet medium is brought right to the station and attached to it with a T-style connector. Unlike thickwire Ethernet, the thinwire is cut and BNC connectors are used to join it to the T. You may have no more than

30 stations on any single thinwire Ethernet segment, and a segment can be no more than 185 meters in length. Pieces of a thinwire Ethernet may be no *shorter* than ½ meter (about 20 inches).

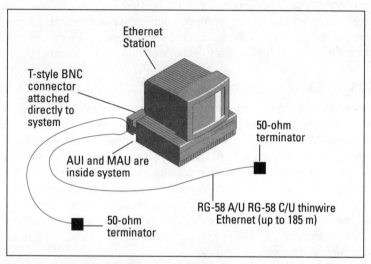

Figure 8-7: A thinwire 10BASE2 connection only requires a T because the MAU is normally built into the NIC card.

## Table 8-2
## Comparison of Specifications for 10BASE2 Thinwire Cable and Commercial Coaxial Cables

| Cable Type | Conductor | Foil Shield | Braided Shield | Jacket | Outside Diameter | Impedance |
|---|---|---|---|---|---|---|
| IEEE 802.3 Specification | Stranded | Not Specified | 95% coverage | PVC | .193" +/- .012 | 50 +/- 2 |
| Digital Thinwire | Stranded | Yes | 93% coverage | PVC, with NEC CL2 | .183" +/- .007 | 50 +/- 2 |
| Belden Thinwire | Stranded | Yes | 95% coverage | PVC, with NEC CL2 | .182" +/- .003 | 50 +/- 2 |
| Belden RG-58A | Stranded | No | 95% coverage | PVC, with NEC CL2 | .198" +/- .004 | 50 +/- 5 |
| Belden RG-58A | Stranded | No | 95% coverage | PVC | .193" +/- .004 | 50 +/- 3 |
| Belden RG-58C | Stranded | No | 95% coverage | PVC | .195" +/- .003 | 50 +/- 2 |
| Belden RG-58 | Solid | No | 95% coverage | PVC | .193" +/- .003 | 53.5 |

Cable grounding is an important part of an Ethernet network. Most vendors ship their Ethernet cards with uninsulated T-style connectors. Any Ethernet must be grounded at exactly one point and cannot make contact with your building ground system anywhere else. For this reason, the Ethernet standard requires that the T-style connectors and BNC connectors be fully insulated so that when you are connecting and disconnecting them you don't make accidental contact with the frame ground of a station. You also must make sure that any connectors don't contact building metal, plumbing, air ducts, or any other conducting material.

## Unshielded twisted-pair (UTP): Type 10BASE-T

Thick and thin Ethernet are the original Ethernet media. 10BASE-T is a relative newcomer but has since become the most popular Ethernet medium for new installations. 10BASE-T overcomes many of the annoying features of 10BASE2 and 10BASE5 by substituting a lot of repeaters for a passive bus. In a 10BASE-T network, each device is connected in a star configuration directly to a multiport repeating hub, usually in a wiring closet somewhere. The massive market for 10BASE-T hubs has brought the price-per-port down to less than $50, even for small numbers of ports. Compare this to the original price for a multiport repeating hub for thinwire of $300 per port, and you see why 10BASE-T is a relatively inexpensive alternative.

The original goal of the UTP (*unshielded twisted-pair*) Ethernet standards was to allow the use of existing building wiring as an Ethernet transmission medium. The idea was that most buildings had more than enough 25-pair telephone cable run to each office and that the rise of the digital PBX left about 22 of those pairs unused. Engineers were also entranced by the idea of having telephone installers handle Ethernet as well as telephone. Unfortunately, it didn't work out quite that well. UTP Ethernet usually can't be run in existing 25-pair bundles, but it does use relatively inexpensive cabling called EIA/TIA Category 3, as Table 8-3 shows.

CAUTION

### How Long Can the T Be?

We have met many system managers who would like to put a wire between the T connector in the Ethernet cable and the station. Do not do this under any circumstances.

The T connector with the cable on it must be connected directly to the station, or the network will not work properly. Actually, the IEEE 802.3 standard does allow for a stub between the T and the device, so long as it is no longer than 4 cm. If a single cable connection between a wall jack, for example, and a station is desired, there are cabling systems which build a "round trip" into the cable between the wall and the DTE. These systems, from vendors such as Digital and AMP, are usually rather expensive.

| Table 8-3<br>Standard Wiring Types for 10BASE-T | |
| --- | --- |
| *EIA/TIA Category* | *Planned Use* |
| 3 | 10 M bps Ethernet |
| 4 | 16 M bps token ring |
| 5 | 100 M bps networking |

The specifications for 10BASE-T Ethernet are made in terms of cross-talk, loss, coupling, and a host of other parameters. In general, you will find that you can run up to 100m of unshielded, twisted-pair cable with 24 AWG conductors. If you want to push the limits, you may find Table 8-4 helpful.

| Table 8-4<br>10BASE-T Link Segment Characteristics | |
| --- | --- |
| *UTP Cable Parameters* | *Value* |
| Insertion loss | no more than 11.5 dB between 5.0 MHz and 10 MHz |
| Impedance | between 85 ohm and 111 ohm |
| Jitter | no more than /- 5.0 ns |
| Delay | no more than 1000 ns. Propagation speed of at least .585c |
| Coupling (NEXT, Near End Crosstalk) | Depending on circumstances, but in general at least 23 -15 log(BASE10)(f/10), f=5 MHz, 7.5MHz, and 10MHz |
| Noise | No impulses greater than 264 mV for longer than 0.2 sec |

10BASE-T uses an 8-position RJ-45 connector, similar to the ones you see in telephones (see Figure 8-8 for the female RJ-45 connector). Four conductors in this connector are used, two for transmittal and two for reception. Table 8-5 shows the mapping between contacts in Figure 8-8 and signals.

Notice that to give a margin of safety for people who accidentally plug 10BASE-T connectors into telephone jacks, the middle two pins aren't used. Because the telephone ringer generates up to 175 Vac and 56 Vdc current, plugging a device directly into a telephone jack with the middle pins connected fries your hardware the moment the phone rings. Table 8-6 may help you plan for future wiring of buildings.

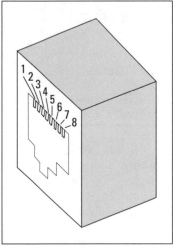

**Figure 8-8: Pins used on a 10BASE-T Ethernet connector**

| Table 8-5 Mapping of 10BASE-T Ethernet Connector | |
|---|---|
| Contact | Signal |
| 1 | Transmit Data + |
| 2 | Transmit Data − |
| 3 | Receive Data + |
| 4 | Not used |
| 5 | Not used |
| 6 | Receive Data − |
| 7 | Not used |
| 8 | Not used |

| Table 8-6 Current and Future Uses for 8-Pin RJ45 Connectors | | | | |
|---|---|---|---|---|
| Application | Pins 4,5 | Pins 3,6 | Pins 1,2 | Pins 7,8 |
| Voice (PBX) | X | O | O | O |
| ISDN | X | X | O | O |
| Token ring | X | X | | |
| 10BASE-T | | X | X | |
| TP-PMD | | | O | O |

X - in use
O - optional use, or planned for future development
Note also that the connection of all 4 pair for ATM connectors and for 100BASE-T and 100BASE-VG are under study.

In wiring 10BASE-T, each link must have at exactly one crossover, where the transmit and receive leads are switched. Because both the station and the hub repeater are transmitting on pins 1 and 2, for example, the two pairs must be swapped to connect the transmitter of each to the receiver of the other. However, the 10BASE-T standard suggests that you don't do this in the cable because it's hard to keep track of. Instead, wire your cables "straight through" and either make the transition at the very end (where you connect from the phone blocks to the repeater) or by purchasing 10BASE-T hubs which have internal crossovers. You can tell an internally crossed hub because each connector must be marked with an X.

Recently, some manufacturers have taken to putting *two* RJ-45 jacks on each hub for each port, one crossed over and one not. The idea is to run your wiring, plug the device in, and try each jack until a little LED lights up to say that you've got it right. Now that's user friendly! Most repeater vendors also detect and automatically correct polarity problems you may have introduced by swapping the individual wires for transmit or receive.

Normally, only one device can be connected to each port of the hub, so no daisy-chaining of devices is allowed with 10BASE-T. Recently, Farallon introduced a product line called EtherWave, which includes transceivers, cards, and adapters. Each EtherWave device has two self-terminating RJ-45 8-pin ports which allow you to daisy-chain up to seven devices to an existing 10BASE-T hub port. This technology brings much of the power of a 10BASE2 network (daisy-chaining in a small area) to 10BASE-T. However, when you use this type of product, make sure you understand thoroughly how you affect the total distance budget for your network.

The hubs currently offered for 10BASE-T Ethernet offer further advantages to the network designer. Because the hubs can be connected to each other, several star networks can be arranged in a hierarchy, so network management and trouble-shooting can progress from the top downward to the subordinate networks. Many hubs are built on a chassis that contains extra slots for modules that connect to other media, making it a simple task to connect your UTP Ethernet star network to fiber optic or thicknet Ethernet backbones.

QUICK TIPS

## Connecting Different Kinds of Network Devices

It is not uncommon to discover that your all-10BASE-T or all-10BASE2 network suddenly has to accommodate a foreigner in its midst. This is usually not a problem. Most Ethernet cards have a 10BASE5 AUI connector on them in addition to a thinwire or 10BASE-T connector. You can get external MAUs for about $40 which connect directly to the 10BASE5 AUI connector (without a cable) and allow you to add the device to either a 10BASE-T or 10BASE2 network. This works because the 15-pin AUI connector includes power from the device to operate the transceiver electronics.

Connecting a device which has only a 10BASE2 or only a 10BASE-T connector to the other kind of network is much more difficult. In this case, you need to have a repeater with external power to change signal types. These can be quite small, but they're expensive, usually about $200 each. In addition, they're not very convenient to use because they require external power.

If you need to connect a 10BASE2 or 10BASE-T device to a 10BASE5 network, don't think you can just get a gender-bender and use a $30 external MAU. That just won't work. You're going to have to spring for a repeater.

Before you think seriously about using your existing phone wiring for a 10BASE-T Ethernet network, look carefully at your wiring. Older cabling may not be of sufficient quality to support the full 100 meters between a device and the hub. Or your wiring contractor may have used substandard wiring thats not capable of transmitting the 10M bps Ethernet signal without heavy noise and other interference.

Once again, good planning can help prevent problems in the future. If you're working with an existing wiring plant, be sure that each run you plan to use for the network is capable of handling Ethernet signals. Making the proper measurements with a 10BASE-T wiring tester can tell you how much you should expect from your existing wiring. Make sure that you know where the wires go. Do they pass sources of intermittent noise, such as heavy machinery or elevators? Checking each length at different times of the day helps to discover problems now, so that you won't have to deal with them later. Some substandard wiring may still be used if its length is less than the maximum recommended by the 10BASE-T standard. But if you have any doubts about the wire, dont use it — you'll save yourself much grief later.

When wiring up 8-pin RJ-45 jacks, you have several common standards to contend with, including the older USOC RJ-45 and Bell's 258A as well as the newer TIA 568A standards. Refer to Figure 8-9 to see the subtle, but important, differences. TIA 568A is recommended for new buildings, but you will probably find mostly TIA 568B (Bell 258A) used if your wiring is more than a few years old. That's not a problem; you just need to know what's going on. If you've got a building full of Bell 258A, it's probably not a good idea to switch wiring schemes.

QUICK TIPS

### The Advantages of UTP Ethernet

Because UTP Ethernet connects nodes at an active hub or *concentrator*, this type of Ethernet network is advantageous for network management. The star topology joins the legs to a common hub, so diagnosis of network problems is simple. Each leg of the star can be individually isolated and tested at the hub to determine which one is causing the problem. Then the defective leg can be disconnected for repairs without affecting the rest of the network. The bus topology, used for thickwire and thinwire Ethernet, is more complex to troubleshoot because it requires continuity of the entire network; disconnecting any segment breaks all network operations.

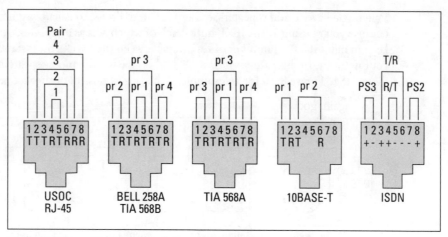

**Figure 8-9: Different wiring standards for the RJ-45 8-position connector**

# Designing Large Ethernets

For any of the cabling schemes described, you can install a repeater to amplify the signal whenever excessive length of the network becomes a problem. Recall that the repeater is a physical layer device (see Chapter 2), and as such, does not filter network addresses or any of the network signals. When you must subdivide the network to control network traffic, you can use routers or bridges, which we discuss in more detail in Chapter 11, "Designing an AppleTalk LAN."

A working Ethernet network is the result of some careful engineering on your part to make sure that all the limits are properly met. An Ethernet network is governed by two important limits that ensure that all components operate properly: the *maximum round-trip signal propagation delay* and the *minimum inter-packet gap*. If your network is longer than the maximum allowed, the whole CSMA/CD system won't work because it assumes that each device on the network will be able to hear every other device's transmissions and detect collisions within a certain window of time. Inter-packet gap is a different kind of measurement. Packets transmitted on an Ethernet must be separated by a certain amount of time, called the inter-packet gap. As you add Ethernet repeaters, you shrink the inter-packet gap, meaning that the number of repeaters on a network must be limited.

The most important cable length and station limits are summarized in Table 8-1. Many network managers keep adding on to thinwire Ethernets without noticing that they've exceeded the limits of the wire. As you add any segment to a thinwire or thickwire Ethernet, make sure that you label both ends with the length of the cable and keep documentation on how long your cable is and how many stations are on it.

When you have to add repeaters, either for length limits, to isolate segments, or because you're using 10BASE-T hubs, each of which acts as a repeater, you need to keep in mind the total number of repeaters between the two furthest stations on your network. In this case, *furthest* is defined as "having the most repeaters between them." (See Figure 8-10 for an example of the largest possible Ethernet network.)

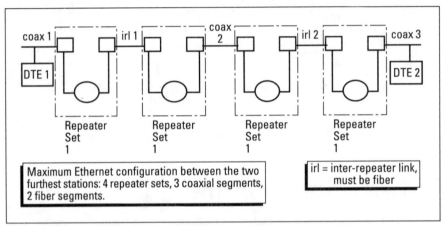

**Figure 8-10:The maximum Ethernet configuration between the two furthest stations would include 4 repeater sets, 3 coaxial cable segments, and 2 fiber optic cable segments.**

The basic rules for configuring large Ethernets are as follows:

❖ Any two segments must be linked with a real 802.3 repeater. Remember that each 10BASE-T hub is a repeater. If you decide to add a *hublet* at the end of an existing 10BASE-T segment, that's another repeater. Don't let vendors tell you that a piece of equipment doesn't count as a repeater.

❖ The maximum distance between two stations is five segments with four repeater sets (but see rules below for more information).

❖ When you use four repeaters and five segments, two of the segments must be inter-repeater link segments, such as fiber optic. Three of the segments may be *mixing* segments, which implies that they can have more than two devices on them. For example, a piece of thinwire cable is a mixing segment. If you are in a maximum configuration, the fiber segments may not exceed 500 meters.

❖ When the maximum distance between two stations is four segments and three repeaters, all segments may be mixing segments, but the fiber segments are limited in length.

If you're confused about these limits, enlist the services of a good network consultant to help in the design of your Ethernet. If you don't get it right, you may not know it right away and you can spend a lot of time chasing network gremlins that you cannot reproduce.

# Selecting Macintosh Ethernet Hardware

When we described the options for connecting Macs to a LocalTalk network in Chapters 6 and 7, you can see that options for making a connection depended only on the wiring you select — you only have to select the proper connection box. One reason for this is Apple's inclusion of the LocalTalk transceiver within every Mac.

With Ethernet, the story is a bit more complicated because the type of Ethernet cable you use determines what type of network interface you'll need. Ethernet transceivers are designed differently for each type of cable.

You can use one of three approaches for connecting a Mac to Ethernet. You can use a router to connect a LocalTalk network to Ethernet; you can use an external device that connects to a single Mac via either the SCSI port or a serial port; or you can use an internal card for a single Mac. In addition, for newer Macs, such as the Mac Quadras, Apple has included an Ethernet adapter on the CPU board. We'll briefly explain each of these alternatives.

## Using a router to connect LocalTalk to Ethernet

If you're interested in connecting two or more LocalTalk networks via an Ethernet backbone, you should use a router. Routers available for this are the Shiva FastPath, Cayman Systems GatorBox, Compatible Systems EtherRoute, NRC LT2000E, and Apple's AppleTalk Internet Router. The first four are hardware routers, and the latter two are software for installation on a Mac. Each product is capable of sending and receiving AppleTalk packets inside Ethernet packets. In general, you will find it better to use dedicated hardware for all but the smallest of networks.

## Using an external adapter

The second alternative, which is to use an external box that connects to either the Mac's SCSI port or its printer port, is designed with a single Mac in mind. Most of these devices are designed for use with the Macs SCSI ports; some are also available for connecting to your Mac's printer port. For the SCSI-based devices, you either plug the box into your Mac's SCSI port or make the box a part of your daisy-chain of SCSI devices; then install the Ethernet driver software and plug the box into your Ethernet network. Installing a serial-based box is much the same, except that you plug the box into the Mac's printer port and then install the software.

When should you use one of these external interfaces? First, think of all those Mac
Pluses and Classics with no expansion slots in them. Second, you may have a Mac
SE or SE/30 with its single slot already allocated to another board, possibly an
accelerator or a second monitor. The external boxes are excellent choices for
Ethernet connectivity in either of these cases. Also, you may want to select an ex-
ternal box for a Mac Portable or PowerBook, as no vendors currently offer an
internal Ethernet board for the 1xx and 2xx series of portable Macs without built-in
Ethernet adapters.

## Choosing an external adapter

Many companies market external SCSI-to-Ethernet adapters, including Asante,
Cabletron, Inc., Compatible Systems, Dayna, Farallon, Focus Enhancements,
MaCNet, Technology Works, and Xircom. Prices range from as low as $200 to
as high as $625.

Most of the external adapters are roughly the same. All but one (from Xircom)
come with an external transformer to provide power. For the PowerBook user, the
external transformer is a hefty weight — and it means that an AC outlet has to be
available at all times. All of the external adapters have an Apple-style standard 25-
pin SCSI connector. All allow you to select SCSI device number, and all come with
drivers that support the most popular network applications, AppleShare and
MacTCP.

Watch out for another PowerBook gotcha. Apple's 1xx and 2xx series of Power-
Books require an unusual cable to connect the SCSI port to any of the adapters.
Some companies include the proper cable, selling PowerBook and "standard" Mac
versions of their adapters, usually at a higher price for PowerBook owners. Others
sell the cable as an extra-cost add-on, for as much as $50. Asante has the best cable
policy of all. It includes both PowerBook and standard Mac cables with every
adapter.

Some of these adapters include multiple media (such as 10BASE-T, 10BASE2, and
10BASE5 connectors), while others are more limited. When selecting an adapter,
keep your application firmly in mind. Will this be for a network manager to connect to a PowerBook to be used as a network analyzer? Or is this a desktop unit for
someone who will never move it?

Dayna is the most flexible in this area with their DaynaPORT SCSI/Link-3. The
SCSI/Link-3 is the only SCSI-to-Ethernet adapter which has all three media available in one small box: a thinwire, a thickwire, and a 10BASE-T port.

For fiber-to-the-desk networks, the Cabletron EA414 is the only choice. No other
company sells an adapter that connects to fiber. Cabletron chose the FOIRL (Fiber
Optic Inter-Repeater Link) fiber standard (part of 10BASE-F), which is widely
supported among Ethernet equipment manufacturers.

Performance is a tricky issue. In general use, all the adapters give equivalent performances because of the speed of the SCSI driver software, the speed of the SCSI bus itself, and the speed of the disk connected to the Macintosh.

The SCSI bus is not a limiting factor. The Macintosh SCSI bus is far faster than any normal Ethernet adapter. All Macintosh SCSI busses transfer data at up to 600K bps for normal (*nonblind*, in SCSI terminology) transfers and up to 1,200K bps for *blind* transfers. (With nonblind transfers, the SCSI chip is polled, or checked for the successful transfer of each byte.) Newer high-end Macintoshes have even faster busses. This means, in theory, that a Macintosh SCSI bus can transfer data as fast as 4.8M bps, 48 percent of Ethernet's 10 M bps speed. SCSI bus protocol aspects, such as bus arbitration, reduce that figure somewhat.

For pure data transfers from memory on one Macintosh to memory on another, you can achieve greater than .5M bps transfer rates using these SCSI-to-Ethernet adapters. Unfortunately, that figure is meaningless because Macs never transfer large amounts of data from memory to memory. A disk always gets into the picture. And that slows things down to a snail's pace. In general, for TCP/IP and AppleShare network applications, it doesn't matter what adapter you buy. They all run at about the same speed. For special-purpose applications, such as Ethernet protocol analysis, look at Asante's Mini series adapters, which performed fastest in some tests we ran recently.

## Using an internal card for a single Mac

Last, but most important, are the internal Ethernet cards for any of the Mac LC, Mac SE, Mac SE/30, or NuBus based Macs. Your Mac can achieve its best Ethernet performance by using an internal card.

Common Ethernet adapter cards support two Ethernet media, usually 10BASE5 and either 10BASE2 or 10BASE-T. It is not a good idea to get cards that *only* support 10BASE2 or 10BASE-T, as they severely limit your flexibility.

If you're short of internal slots, as with the Mac Performa series, you can now purchase multifunction cards from some of the video monitor manufacturers, such as E-Machines and Mobius Technologies; these cards combine the video interface for an external monitor with Ethernet support.

## Using Apple internal Ethernet adapters

With its new Ethernet Cabling System, Apple anticipated that you may on occasion want to change your network media. The new Apple EtherTalk cards and built-in Ethernet adapters do not include an on-board transceiver or socket for a particular Ethernet cable; instead the cards have a special interface port called the AAUI (Apple Attachment Unit Interface) into which you plug a special media adapter/transceiver box. This approach lets you change network media just by changing the external adapter/transceiver box.

Note that Apple's AAUI is the standard method for connecting the new Mac
Quadras, high-end PowerBooks, and newer high-end LaserWriters to Ethernet.
These devices have built-in support for Ethernet but do not include transceivers.

# Connecting Laser Printers to Ethernet

One of the most popular devices on any network is the laser printer. But most laser
printers, including Apple's LaserWriters, include only a LocalTalk port for connection to a network. If you're working with a mixed network of LocalTalk and
Ethernet, that's all right because you can always place your laser printers on a
LocalTalk segment of the network.

But what do you do if you're using only Ethernet cabling? A few laser printer models are now available with built-in Ethernet support, such as the Apple LaserWriter
Select series and the Hewlett-Packard LaserJet 4si. However, most laser printers
on the market require another method for connecting to Ethernet. For those laser
printers without built-in Ethernet connections, you can use either software installed on your Mac or self-contained hardware to connect a laser printer to an
Ethernet network.

The software for connecting laser printers to Ethernet is a software router for
AppleTalk — Apple's AppleTalk Internet Router. This can be installed to run in
the background on a Mac that has both LocalTalk and Ethernet connections. The
Ethernet connection is the connection normally used by the Mac, whereas the
LocalTalk connection is used for the laser printer. This is a reasonable, low-cost
solution, but bear in mind that the availability of the link depends on the reliability
of the Mac running the router software; if the Mac becomes unavailable, as during
a system crash, users will be unable to access the laser printer.

A more reliable solution is to use hardware that is solely dedicated to the task of
linking LocalTalk-based laser printers to an Ethernet network. The EtherPrint/
EtherPrint Plus series from Dayna Communications and EtherWrite from Compatible Systems are examples. They contain anywhere from one to six LocalTalk
ports for laser printers and one Ethernet port for attaching to the network. These
are not full-functioned AppleTalk routers (see Chapter 11, "Designing an
AppleTalk LAN"), so they shouldn't be used for other devices (such as Macs), but
they do the job of connecting laser printers to an Ethernet quite well.

Of course, you can also buy AppleTalk routers to perform the same function as
these printer interfaces, but the routers generally are two to four times more expensive and aren't worth considering for this task unless you have devices other than
laser printers to attach to the LocalTalk ports.

Another solution, which we discuss in detail in Chapter 21, "Printing on AppleTalk
Networks," is to use a computer as the print server, attaching the computer to the
Ethernet network and the laser printer to the print server/computer.

# Understanding Ethernet Performance

When you're transferring large graphics images or CAD files, using a large multi-user database, or simply adding more users to your network, the 10M bps speed of Ethernet can be mighty appealing. But be careful. Just because Ethernet transmits data 44 times faster than LocalTalks 230K bps speed, file transfers between two Macs aren't accomplished 40 times faster because many of today's computers cannot send or receive data that quickly.

If you read articles about Ethernet board performance for MS-DOS computers, you'll note that the authors spend much time discussing buffer sizes, bus architectures, and the width of the data bus. Partly because of the uniformity of the Macs bus architecture, there's less variation in Ethernet board performance among Macs than for MS-DOS systems.

While working with Macworld Labs, we noted little difference in performance among the various Ethernet boards for a given type of Mac. Despite differences in data bus width (16 bits vs. 32 bits) and RAM buffers for caching packets (8K to 32K), all the boards performed about the same under such typical conditions as transferring data from a hard disk. In general, you can use Ethernet to increase your data throughput by a factor of five over the throughput rate for LocalTalk.

The cause appears to be the Mac operating systems control of the SCSI bus and the hard disk. As long as data is transferred through the Macs SCSI Manager, the rate of data transfer from a hard disk through the CPU and onto the Ethernet is fairly constant. Even when we tried using a SCSI accelerator card — one employing DMA (Direct Memory Access) to the CPU — we noted little improvement in the transfer rates. This means that there's very little reason to pick one Ethernet interface card over another because of its features.

In certain situations, the more advanced cards, such as those using a 32-bit data path, can be used to good advantage. When we tested the boards by transferring data directly from the RAM of one Mac to the RAM of another, there was a noticeable difference between boards. Thus, if you're using a database or other distributed application that loads much of its code and data into memory, your best bets for an Ethernet card are those from Asante, Cayman, and Interlan. These cards all have a data bus width of 32 bits.

This advantage can also extend to Macs running A/UX, which doesn't use the SCSI Manager to control disk access. Some programs that do depend more on Ethernet card speed and CPU speed rather than file-access rates are windowing software, such as MacX (Apple Computer, Inc.) and eXodus (White Pine Software, Inc.). These X Windows server programs receive a large number of commands and data over the network from the X Windows client in order to create a display.

Another thing to keep in mind when considering board performance is the type of network you'll be on. For a large network with heavy traffic performing large file transfers (24-bit color images, for example), you may receive slightly better performance from boards with larger buffer sizes. Some vendors offer boards with at least two sizes. Regular applications don't need the extra buffer, but large file transfers, A/UX and X Windows, can benefit from the increased buffer size.

# CHAPTER 8    CONCEPTS AND TERMS

- IEEE 802.3 and Ethernet version 2 use different packet formats. Multiple protocols can usually be accommodated on a single Ethernet cable.

- For Ethernet, you can use two types of coaxial cable or unshielded twisted-pair (UTP) or fiber optic cable.

- Thicknet and thinnet Ethernet are usually wired in bus topologies, whereas UTP Ethernet uses an active hub and is wired as a star.

- Each type of Ethernet cabling scheme has different requirements for length, number of stations, termination, and grounding.

- Planning ahead lets you mix and match different devices on your chosen Ethernet media without great expense or bother.

- There are very strict limits on the configuration of large Ethernets that must be carefully followed. To keep your network "in spec," good documentation and a thorough understanding of the rules is a must.

- Macs can be connected to an Ethernet network with a router, an external box using the SCSI or serial port, or an internal card. Laser Printers are best attached using dedicated *printer routers*.

- Macs on Ethernet perform network tasks about five times faster than on a LocalTalk network.

**baseband**
A type of network transmission that uses the entire bandwidth of a network to transmit a digital signal. The cables of a baseband network only carry one set of signals at a time. (See *broadband*, a type of transmission that can send multiple signals simultaneously.)

**blind transfer**
A SCSI transfer in which the SCSI master sends the data without explicit acknowledgment of each byte.

**broadband**
A method of transmitting data so that a single wire or cable can simultaneously carry many different channels of information. Cable television uses the broadband method to carry as many as 100 channels on a single coaxial cable. (Compare with *baseband*.)

**cheapernet**
Implementation of the Ethernet IEEE standard on thin coaxial cable, a baseband medium, at 10 M bps. The maximum segment length is just under 200 meters (185 to be exact). Also known as **thinnet**

**collapsed backbone**
A new network topology where the backbone of the network is collapsed into a single multiport transceiver or router backplane.

**encapsulation**
A generic networking concept where one protocol is contained within another. For example, AppleTalk can be encapsulated inside of IP.

**Ethernet V2**
A data link protocol jointly developed by Intel, Xerox, and DEC.

**fiber Ethernet**
Ethernet run over fiber optic cable.

**hublet**
A hub normally placed remotely from a wiring closet, as in an office.

**MAU**
Medium Attachment Unit, used to attach to the network cable.

**maximum roundtrip signal propagation delay**
The maximum length of time a signal can take to go from one end of an Ethernet to the other and back.

**minimum inter-packet gap**
The minimum length of time between the end of one Ethernet frame and the beginning of the next.

**multiple protocol medium**
A LAN medium which can have more than one set of protocols running on it. For example, the coaxial cable used in Ethernet can have Ethernet and IEEE 802.3 frames as well as different higher layer protocols, such as AppleTalk, DECnet, TCP/IP, and something else like IPX.

**nonblind transfers**
A SCSI transfer mode where the SCSI chip is polled after each byte is transferred.

**protocol identification**
A network technique where the next higher-layer protocol is identified in the header of a lower-layer protocol. For example, in Ethernet, the next higher-layer protocol is indicated in a field just after the source and destination addresses.

**router**
A device that connects two networks together and maintains addressing information for each network. Workstations can pass information from one network to another by sending the information through the router.

*(continued on the next page)*

*(continued from the previous page)*

[Routers are often confused with bridges. A bridge physically connects two networks, but a bridge does not maintain the network addressing information. The router maintains a table of network addresses and is more effective in sending data to nodes on the different networks.

**Starlan**
A type of LAN cabling and transmission not often found. 1BASE5 network.

**thicknet**
10BASE5 network. The original Ethernet medium, an implementation of the Ethernet IEEE standard on coaxial cable, a baseband medium, at 10 M bps. The maximum segment length is 500 meters

**UTP Ethernet**
10BASE-T network. An implementation of the Ethernet IEEE standard on 24 gauge unshielded, twisted-pair wiring, a baseband medium, at 10 M bps.

CHAPTER NINE

# Installing an Ethernet LAN

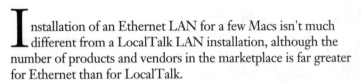

**IN THIS CHAPTER**

- Selecting the proper cables and connectors for an Ethernet network
- Installing 10BASE-T wiring
- Installing an Ethernet MAU (transceiver)
- Testing your cabling
- Setting up a 10BASE2 LAN
- Setting up a 10BASE-T LAN
- Setting up an Ethernet connection for your Mac

Installation of an Ethernet LAN for a few Macs isn't much different from a LocalTalk LAN installation, although the number of products and vendors in the marketplace is far greater for Ethernet than for LocalTalk.

Chapter 8, "Designing an Ethernet LAN", introduces you to the types of cables that can be used to create Ethernet networks. In this chapter, you get into the details of installing the cables and the connectors that you need to connect your Macs to Ethernet. Then we'll discuss the types of Ethernet MAUs (known as transceivers in Ethernet V2 terminology), how to connect these MAUs to the cables, and then how to connect your Macs to Ethernet.

This chapter ends with a discussion of the future — what's *beyond* Ethernet and just around the corner.

## Installing Ethernet Media

When you install an Ethernet network, you need to consider three aspects of the network hardware: the type of cabling that you want to use, the methods that you'll use for attaching to the network cable, and the type of MAU (transceiver) you'll use for your Mac. First, you learn how to select and install Ethernet cables and connectors, and then how to attach various types of cables, taps, and MAUs to the Ethernet cable.

**QUOTABLES**

"Our systems, perhaps, are nothing more than an unconscious apology for our faults — a gigantic scaffolding whose object is to hide from us our favorite sin."

— Henri Frederic Amiel, 1865.

It's very important that you read both Chapters 8 and 9 before using any of the advice in either one. Chapter 8 deals with general issues and design goals of Ethernet networks, while Chapter 9 is aimed at the specifics of installing an Ethernet network yourself. You need the information from both chapters if you want to have a reliable LAN.

# Installing Cables and Connectors

As we point out in Chapter 8, there is more than one cabling standard for Ethernet networks — thick coaxial, or *thickwire*; thin coaxial, or *thinwire*; and Unshielded Twisted-Pair, or UTP. Fiber optic cable is also used with Ethernet networks, although usually between repeaters rather than between stations.

This section concentrates on three popular media for Ethernet: thick coaxial cable for 10BASE5, thin coaxial cable for 10BASE2, and twisted-pair cable for 10BASE-T. Fiber optic cable isn't included in this discussion. Although fiber optic cable has advanced to the point where you don't have to have a special installer in every time you want to put a connector on, we think that you need more training than we can give you in this book to properly install fiber optic cabling.

## 10BASE5 coaxial cable

Thick coaxial cable for 10BASE5, the original Ethernet medium, uses a 50-ohm coaxial cable as the backbone for the network. The cable has an outer diameter of 0.375 to 0.405 inches, depending on whether it has a plenum-rated fire resistant jacket or a normal PVC jacket (see Figure 9-1). Many vendors offer 10BASE5 cable according to the DEC cable number as a cross-reference. In this case, the cable is called BNE2A (plenum cable) or BNE2B (PVC insulation).

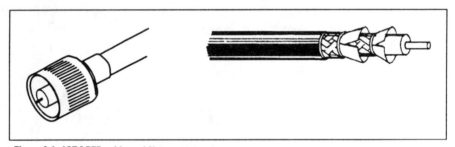

Figure 9-1: 10BASE5 cable and N-type connector.

Thick coaxial is available in either premade standard lengths or on a reel for making your own cables. When cable sections are joined together (both in thickwire and thinwire), each joint causes reflections of the signal back and forth on the cable. To reduce the possibility of these reflections adding together to cause interference, the IEEE has recommended that all thickwire segments be odd multiples of the half wavelength of the cable at 5 MHz. For this reason, they recommend making thickwire segments with lengths of 23.4, 70.2, 117 (+/- 0.5m) or, of course, 500 meters (See Table 8-1 for more information).

Thick coaxial cable has a few limitations. First, its harder to install, especially around corners, than other cable types because it is more difficult to bend without damaging the internal wires. When you purchase your thickwire cable, ask the supplier what the *minimum bending radius* of the cable is. Then make a jig out of a piece of wood or wire which you can use to make sure you don't bend the cable any more tightly than this. For example, if the minimum bending radius is 8 inches, then make a circle 16 inches in diameter. Use that circle whenever you have to bend the cable, such as around a corner. After the bend has been made, secure the cable using some tie wraps to make sure that it won't be easily knocked out of place.

Thick coaxial also requires a MAU (transceiver) and a carefully placed tap to link a device to the network, as mentioned in Chapter 8. If you're using thickwire cable, you must also run an AUI cable (transceiver cable), or *drop cable*, from your Macs Ethernet interface board to the MAU that's attached to the coaxial cable. The drop cable can be no longer than 50 meters in length for standard AUI cables; it needs to be less than that for "office style" AUI cables.

Thick coaxial cable uses N-type connectors. Adding the N-type connectors to the ends of cables is a somewhat complicated process. To connect an N-type connector to thick coaxial, you need cable cutters, wire strippers, and a soldering iron; you may also need a crimping tool, as you'll see in a moment. You should also get a few extra feet of cable and a few extra connectors to practice with. It generally takes one or two test runs on any coaxial cable to get a good connection if you haven't terminated cable recently.

The dielectric separates the shielding (foil or braid) from the central conductor. The amount of shield and dielectric you cut away to reveal the central conductor depends on the manufacturer of the connector, so check the specifications that come with the connectors. After stripping the outer insulation, you need to roll back the braid to expose the dielectric and central conductor; the braided shield makes contact with the outer sleeve of the connector through a series of washers that are squeezed together when you screw the outer sleeve over the end of the connector assembly. The central conductor is either soldered or crimped to a central pin, depending on the connectors manufacturer.

You should carefully test any termination you make for electrical shorts or for physical weakness. Give it a good strong pull before hiding it in the ceiling forever.

## 10BASE2 coaxial cable

Coaxial cable for 10BASE2, or thinwire, is quite popular because it is more flexible and less expensive than thickwire and because it can be used without large MAUs (transceivers) and taps (see Figure 9-2). Thinwire coaxial cable is also a 50-ohm coaxial cable, but it has a smaller diameter than thickwire coaxial — thinwire coaxial is 0.20 inches in outer diameter.

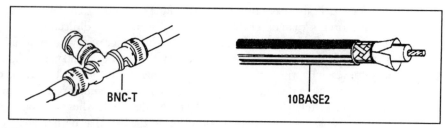

Figure 9-2: BNC T-style and 10BASE2 cable connectors.

Thin Ethernet cable has a maximum limit of 185 meters, with fewer stations permitted on the cable than for a thickwire segment; thin Ethernet cable allows 30 devices, as compared to 100 devices for thickwire. Note that a T-style connector (for a MAU, or transceiver) and a barrel connector both count as a device. There must be a distance of at least 0.5 meters between MAUs.

You can purchase thin coaxial either in premade standard lengths or on a reel for making your own cables. Adding the BNC connectors to the ends of cables is also a fairly involved process. After stripping the outer insulation, you have to roll back the braid to expose the dielectric and inner conductor and then solder the conductor to the BNC connector. Then you screw down the outer sleeve of the connector over the braid. As with the N-type connector, the central pin can be either soldered or crimped to the central conductor of the cable. The process takes some time until you become accustomed to doing it and certainly isn't as easy as crimping RJ-11 or RJ-45 jacks onto twisted-pair cable.

As with thickwire, make sure you test your cable both with an ohmmeter and by giving the connector a good strong tug.

## 10BASE-T unshielded twisted-pair

10BASE-T networks are designed to be installed only as an active star. Each branch of the star from the network device to the 10BASE-T hub, or *concentrator*, is limited to 100 meters in the best case. If you're using existing wire, your mileage will vary. The wiring normally used in 10BASE-T is 26 to 22 AWG with solid copper conductors, a wiring setup which corresponds to many telephone twisted-pair cables. Remember that you need two pairs of wiring for each node (see Figure 9-3).

Be sure to check any preexisting cable that you intend to use for 10BASE-T. Older cabling may not be of adequate quality to support the full 100 meters between a device and the hub. Or you may have substandard wiring that cannot transmit the 10M bps Ethernet signal without interference.

When you're wiring your network, you should take care not to run any other data traffic (especially from another network, such as token ring) on the same cable; the unshielded twisted-pairs are not protected from interference from other non-Ethernet signals that may be generated within the same cable bundle.

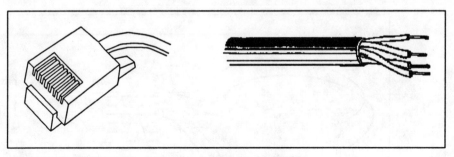

**Figure 9-3: An RJ-45 8-position jack and two-pair twisted-pair cable.**

If you use standard phone wire to install your 10BASE-T Ethernet network, the insulation color codes for each wire in the bundle make it easy to keep pairs together. All telephone pairs are color coded, as discussed in Chapter 2. (If you plan to use 10BASE-T wiring for your Ethernet LAN, you probably want to copy the table in Chapter 2 that gives the color code for paired telephone wire.)

When wiring your connections, take precautions against splitting pairs. In other words, be sure that you maintain the same color mates for each pair used within the cable. If you don't follow a common color pairing, you'll most likely mix up the wires, and the Ethernet signal won't be transmitted. This is particularly important with 10BASE-T Ethernet, which uses one pair of wires as the transmitting pair and the other as the receiving pair.

Connections are made with 8-position RJ-45 plugs, cousins of the familiar RJ-11 plugs (see Figure 9-4). Your home phone system probably uses at least one RJ-11 jack. Be careful when selecting the plugs; without careful examination, the two plugs look confusingly similar. Their main distinguishing feature is the number of conductor blades at the end of the jack. The RJ-11 jack has either four or six positions; the RJ-45 jack has eight. 10BASE-T specifications expect the transmitting pair to be connected to pins 1 and 2 and the receiving pair to pins 3 and 6 (see Figure 9-5).

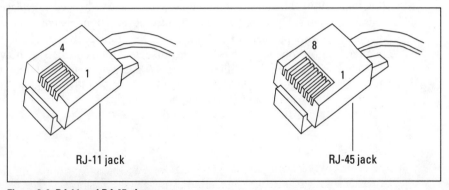

RJ-11 jack                                      RJ-45 jack

**Figure 9-4: RJ-11 and RJ-45 plugs.**

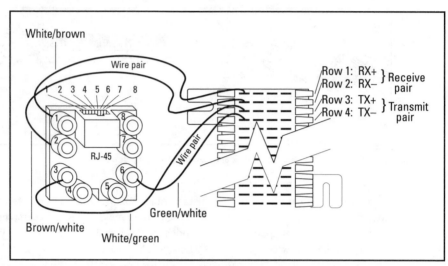

**Figure 9-5: A wiring run from a wall jack to a punchdown block.**

As shown in Chapter 8, you need to make a choice between several different standards for wiring 8-position RJ-45 jacks. Most new installations use EIA/TIA T568A, as this is the preferred system. However, there are no performance reasons to prefer T568A over T568B. If your building is already wired with T568B, you don't need to spend a lot of money rewiring all your phone jacks.

If you want to go crazy figuring out exactly how to wire your building, Table 9-1 provides a number of nifty standards and regulations that you may want to check out.

## Installation tips

When you're installing coaxial cables of over 50 meters, especially 10BASE2 cables, it's a good idea to divide the cable into shorter segments (remembering, of course, the 23.4 meter multiple used in 10BASE5 coaxial cables) with barrel connectors (see Figure 9-6). Then if something goes wrong, you only need to replace a short segment of cable. Dividing the network into short sections also makes it easier to diagnose network problems. For a diagnostic test, replace the barrel connector with two terminators (one for each cable, of course) and then check to see how the two new networks perform. We call this the *divide-and-conquer* method of network diagnosis (see Chapter 13, "Configuring, Managing, and Fixing AppleTalk Networks").

| Table 9-1 Wiring Standards for LAN Managers | |
| --- | --- |
| *Standard Designation* | *Description* |
| ANSI/EIA/TIA-568 | Commercial building telecommunications wiring standard |
| IEC 603-7, Part 7 | Detail specification for connectors, eight-way, including fixed and free connectors with common mating features |
| FCC CFR 47 | Part 68, Subpart F of the code of federal regulations; telecommunications |
| ANSI/NFPA 70 | The National Electrical Code |
| TIA/EIA TSB40A | Technical systems bulletin — additional transmission specifications for unshielded twisted-pair connection hardware |
| UL 1863 | Standard for safety, communications circuit accessories |
| ISO 8877 | Interface connector and contact assignments for ISDN basic access interface located at reference points S and T |
| IEEE 802.5 | Token ring data transmission |
| IEEE 802.3 | Ethernet data transmission (including 10BASE-T) |
| ANSI/TIA/EIA 606 | Administration standard for the telecommunications infrastructure of commercial buildings |

When you're wiring your network, remember that coaxial cable Ethernet segments must be terminated at both ends with 50-ohm resistors, and that one and only one end of the network should be grounded. Dont bother making your own terminators — many vendors offer ready-made terminators that mate with the connectors for either thick or thin coaxial cable. Some of these premounted terminators also include a wire on the end that can be used to make your grounding connection.

Another point about grounding is that you should not ground a cable segment in more than one place. If you do, you're likely to create interfering currents in the cable because of differences in the ground voltage. Even in the same building, all electrical grounds may not be at the same voltage level. In general, coaxial cable should not be used for any type of connection between two buildings.

Two types of cable insulation — plenum and non-plenum — are offered for most cable types. Generally, you must use plenum cable in any air plenum in the building; if you wish to install PVC-insulated cable in these areas, the cable must be installed within a conduit. For more detail, see Chapter 7, "Installing a LocalTalk LAN."

When you install Ethernet cabling, place the cables perpendicular to any power wiring and at least six inches away from power cables. Also, keep cables at least six inches away from lighting fixtures.

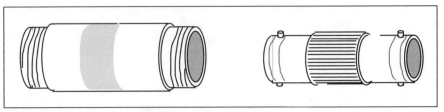

Figure 9-6: Barrel connectors for 10BASE5 (left) and 10BASE2 (right).

# Attaching to the Media

Very few Macs have built-in support for Ethernet (only higher-end Macs, such as Quadras, Workgroup Servers, Power Macs, and some PowerBooks), and none of them include built-in MAUs (transceivers) for Ethernet. To make the physical link between your Mac and the Ethernet cable, you need to tap the cable and attach an Ethernet MAU (transceiver) to the tap.

There are two types of taps: *intrusive* and *nonintrusive*. A nonintrusive tap does not disrupt cable operations, so you can install this tap while the network is running. Many MAU tap devices for 10BASE5 Ethernet are nonintrusive (also called vampire tap) because they require drilling only through the cables outer insulation and dielectric and because they use a needle-like spine to connect to the center conductor of the coaxial cable (see Figure 9-7).

During installation of an intrusive tap, you must disrupt, or break, the cable connection. An example of an intrusive tap is the BNC T-style connector for thinwire cabling, which connects two cable segments together at two ends of the T-style connector and provides the connection to the MAU (transceiver) at the remaining end of the T (see Figure 9-8).

## 10BASE5 MAUs (transceivers)

For 10BASE5 Ethernet, the MAU itself includes the *tap*, which is a needle-like protrusion (also called a *spine*) that connects the MAU to the cable. Because the spine must make contact with the center conductor of the cable and no other conductor (such as the shielding, or braid), MAUs are designed for specific cable diameters. Make sure that you order MAUs and cables that match.

To connect the 10BASE5 tap to your Ethernet board, you'll have to run a special AUI cable (transceiver cable, also called a *drop cable*) between the two. This AUI cable offers a great deal of design flexibility. For example, you can install the MAUs in the ceiling and run AUI cables in two segments: one from the MAU to a special wall socket and the second from the computer to the wall socket.

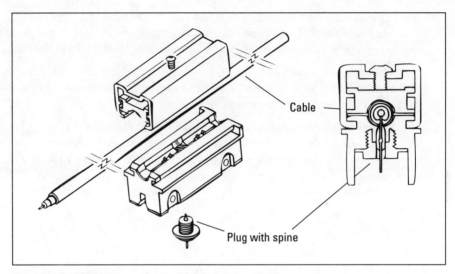

Figure 9-7: A 10BASE5 transceiver and detail showing spine tap.

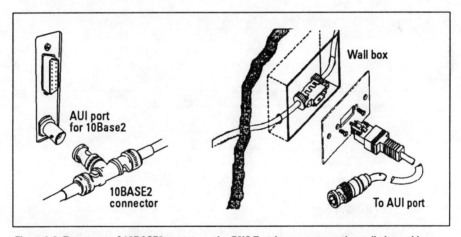

Figure 9-8: Two types of 10BASE2 taps: a regular BNC T-style connector and a wall plate with a special connector.

Installing a tap usually requires that you use a tapping tool for clamping and aligning the cable, along with a screw-in device for piercing the shielding and dielectric of the cable to get to the conductor (see Figure 9-7). As mentioned previously, the dielectric separates the shielding (foil or braid) from the central conductor.

In some cases, you can use a drill bit to pierce the cable. Never, however, use an AC-powered drill, as the power drill can cause a ground loop throughout the cable, shorting out and ruining every MAU (transceiver) connected to the cable.

The spine, as shown in Figure 9-7, is then screwed into the cable from the side opposite the clamp (the top assembly in Figure 9-7), and then the drop cable is screwed into the plug containing the spine.

The final connection needed for a thickwire installation is the AUI cable (transceiver cable) that runs from the MAU (transceiver) to the Ethernet controller in the computer (see Figure 9-9). Most AUI cables are relatively thick, stiff 15-pin cables with a D-style connector that attaches to the MAU. Some AUI cables use screws to lock the connector, but most now have a sliding-lock system.

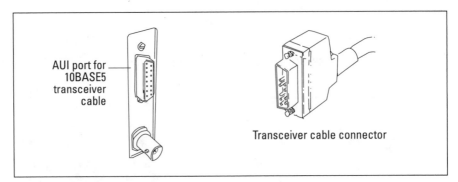

AUI port for
10BASE5
transceiver
cable

Transceiver cable connector

**Figure 9-9: A 10BASE5 transceiver cable and AUI on an interface card.**

Carefully check the locking mechanism: occasionally, the controller cable with a sliding-lock system does not stay attached to the wall box used for an AUI cable connection, even when the units have compatible sliding locks.

## 10BASE2

For thinwire connections, a BNC T-style connector most frequently serves as the tap (see Figure 9-8) and plugs directly into the on-board BNC socket for the MAU (transceiver) that is part of the Ethernet controller.

Because the BNC T-style connector is intrusive, you should be careful when connecting and disconnecting workstations. Because each workstation is directly connected to the network cabling, its a good idea to physically anchor the cable to the workstation so that an energetic user moving the workstation won't be able to rip apart the connector or controller board. In order to maintain the continuity of the network, you should disconnect your workstation from the network by unplugging the T connector from the BNC connector on the controller board. Never disconnect your workstation by unplugging one end of the T from the thinwire cable.

It's also a good idea to tape the cable to the T connector to discourage anyone from breaking a thinwire segment. We like to put signs on the cable, too. Something like "disconnect this and die" is usually a good deterrent.

Although the most common way of setting up a simple thinwire network is to use coaxial cables with T and barrel connectors, some wiring vendors offer systems for installing special in-wall taps (see Figure 9-8). The end of the tap is connected to a faceplate mounted on the wall; a special 50-ohm coaxial cable has the usual BNC connector for plugging into your interface card on one end and a locking connector that mates with the faceplate on the other end. This is an expensive approach, but it provides greater assurance that someone won't inadvertently take down your network.

There are a few other ways to install 10BASE2 cabling. In 10BASE2, the MAU (transceiver) is most often located on the interface card. (Some cards, like the newest ones from Apple, use an external MAU for all Ethernet connections.) If you don't like the idea of stringing thinwire cables to each computer, you can use an external thinwire MAU, which allows you to keep the thinwire coaxial cable closer to the wall. Then you just run a small AUI cable (transceiver cable) from the thinwire MAU to the interface board in the computer, much as you would with thickwire MAUs. With the growing popularity of the in-wall wiring systems we just described (see Figure 9-8), the added cost of external MAUs usually isn't worth it.

Apple's Ethernet Cabling System is a self-terminating system. If you use Apple's cabling and MAUs throughout, you'll be assured that a user won't accidentally open up a segment and take down all stations on both sides of his workstation.

You can also use multiport MAUs (transceivers) for 10BASE2 coaxial to connect a cluster of workstations to a single tap. This approach is expensive, so a better approach is to use unshielded twisted-pair cable and a 10BASE-T hub.

# 10BASE-T

10BASE-T is a star-based network that allows only one device per branch, so there is no tap for connecting an interface card to the network. All you need to make the network connection is an RJ-45 8-pin plug on the end of the wiring run; insert this plug into the RJ-45 socket on the interface card.

Many sophisticated wiring systems for buildings allow you to run a 10BASE-T cable to a wall jack. When you need to attach a computer to the network, you simply use a length of twisted-pair cable with RJ-45 plugs on both ends to connect one end to the computer and the other to the network through the wall jack. Just remember that the total length of the wiring run, including the cable from the concentrator to the wall jack, plus the cable from the wall jack to the computer, must be less than the 100-meter limit of 10BASE-T.

If you want to change over to 10BASE-T wiring without losing your investment in 10BASE2 or 10BASE5 Ethernet cards, you need to use external MAUs (transceivers), as discussed in Chapter 8.

# 10BASE-T hubs

As mentioned previously, 10BASE-T networks require an active repeating hub to work properly. Remember that 10BASE-T hubs and hublets count towards your Ethernet repeater budget. If you're not sure whether you're legal or not, check Chapter 8. As you'd expect, all hub hardware is not alike.

First, consider the construction. A hub may be a closed box with a fixed set of ports, or it may be a rack-like box with slots for different modules. Also, hubs may feature an added built-in port for 10BASE5 thickwire or 10BASE2 thinwire Ethernet or even fiber optics; others may require you to purchase a special card or module in order to connect to different Ethernet media. Some especially nifty new hubs have 16 or 20 slots into which you can put your choice of Ethernet AUI connectors (male and female), 10BASE-T, 10BASE2, and 10BASE-FL fiber optic connectors.

Another consideration is the method of connecting the hub to the network cables. Depending on your situation, you may get by with RJ-45 jacks on the hub, which is good enough for small networks. Or you may want a hub that can connect directly to a punchdown block with an RJ-21 50-wire connector (sometimes called an Amphenol connector).

Another difference in hubs is in the way they implement the 10BASE-T specifications. Some specifications designate only minimum requirements, giving vendors a great deal of latitude in design. An example of this latitude is the way a hub is designed to handle a line that has too many collisions on it (too many collisions may indicate a problem on the line). That line, by specification, is to be disabled after 30 or more consecutive collisions, but different vendors have chosen to disconnect the line after anywhere from 30 to 90 collisions. Some hubs try to reenable the line after a set period of time; others do nothing but turn on an LED to indicate that a problem has occurred.

A final consideration is that you can buy hubs that perform only the most basic network management functions: disconnecting noisy lines, flashing LEDs, and so on. Other hubs support extensive software packages for managing a network. The most advanced hubs include SNMP (Simple Network Management Protocol) support. See Chapter 13 for a description of SNMP and Mac third-party vendors.

One thing is certain: The number of hub vendors is enormous. In early 1994, over 350 different companies were selling labeled hub products. This number is sure to decrease somewhat, but there will always be tremendous variety in hub equipment to meet your needs.

# Installing an Ethernet LAN

To set up your own Ethernet network for a group of Macs, your best choices for cabling are either thinwire or 10BASE-T UTP (Unshielded Twisted-Pair). At the moment, a thinwire network is cheaper than an unshielded twisted-pair network. It's not that the cable is cheaper, but the added cost of a hub for 10BASE-T to run Ethernet on unshielded twisted-pair wire adds significantly to the network cost.

A small workgroup can do without that added cost, especially because the network management options of many 10BASE-T hubs are usually not required for small workgroups. This situation may change quickly, though. At the time of this writing, low-end 10BASE-T hubs are being introduced at prices under $50 per port.

## Installing 10BASE2

If you decide to go with 10BASE2 thinwire Ethernet, remember that the network will be laid out in the bus topology (see Chapter 8, "Designing an Ethernet LAN"). This means that you'll be stringing a thinwire cable from workstation to workstation, tying cables together with T connectors, and plugging those Ts into the network interface. This method is what we use in our offices. Because we're constantly getting new equipment in for testing and evaluation, it's important to be able to change the network topology without having to punch down wires or expand hubs.

But what if running two coaxial cables, thin as they may be, to your Mac is too disruptive in your office?

Remember that there's a cable coming from the Mac to the left of you that connects to the T-style connector on the back of your Mac; then the cable continues the network connection from your T to the Mac to the right of you. If you're concerned about these two cables, you can buy an external thinwire Ethernet MAU (transceiver) that connects to the 15-pin AUI port of your interface card, which lets you put the thinwire connection farther away from your Mac. This port is usually meant for a 10BASE5 AUI cable, but it works for any external MAU. Because most Ethernet cards already have an on-board thinwire MAU, the extra MAU is a bit of a wasteful expense. An extra MAU, however, is one of the few ways you can put a greater distance between your Mac and the network connection. Or you may find the new in-wall systems more to your liking.

Don't forget those terminating resistors — one at each end of the thinwire bus. For Ethernet, the terminating resistor is 50 ohms. Don't make them; buy them to be sure that you have the proper resistance. If you use Apple's new Ethernet Cabling System, the terminators are built into the thinwire connectors.

When it's time to add other Macs to your Ethernet network, first make sure that no one is using the network. Then disconnect the cable from one of the T connectors and add the lengths of cables and the T connectors for the new workstations. When we first installed our office network, we purchased premade 15-foot and 20-foot thinwire cables from a network vendor and connected the cables with T-style connectors instead of barrel connectors. Any time we have to add a new device to the network, all we need to do is plug the device into one of the unused Ts — we don't even have to bring down the network to do this. Remember that the shortest distance between T connectors is 0.5 meters.

Another handy device to use with thinwire Ethernet installations is the multiport MAU (transceiver). Even though the Ethernet adapter for your Mac probably has a built-in thinwire MAU, you may find it more convenient to install a multiport thinwire MAU in locations where three or four Macs are close to one another. To set this up, plug the multiport MAU into your thinwire network and then run AUI cables (such as those used for thickwire MAUs) from the multiport MAU to each of your Macs. These AUI cables have to be shorter than the normal 50 meter limit; your multiport MAU vendor can tell you exactly how much shorter. Some vendors also refer to multiport MAUs as *fan-out transceivers* or by the name for the first of these devices, Digital's *DELNI*. (Note: These MAUs are not strictly part of the Ethernet specifications, so you should use them with caution.)

## Installing 10BASE-T

If the idea of having thinwire cables lying all around doesn't appeal to you, or if your Macs are scattered throughout the site, making it next to impossible to stay with a simple bus topology, you'll probably want to set up a network using unshielded twisted-pair.

Remember that if you plan to use existing twisted-pair wire (such as the extra pairs in your phone cable), you'll need to have two pairs of wire available for the connection, not the single pair that PhoneNET requires. Lay out your network with a star topology and place the hub in your wiring closet or a similar location.

As we caution in Chapter 8, you are limited to one network device per hub port. You can buy many types of hubs, choosing from 4-port hubs, 8-port hubs, 12-port hubs, and so on. Some hubs are self-contained boxes with no expansion options; others give you an empty rack enclosure with a built-in power supply and slots for the boards that you want. Some hubs have no network management software whatsoever; others offer all the bells and whistles you'll ever need. The market for 10BASE-T hubs has become highly competitive, so shop around for your exact needs. Almost all hubs have a second network connection of some type so that you can connect them to a backbone network, which may be thinwire, thickwire, or fiber optic cable. (See Figure 9-10).

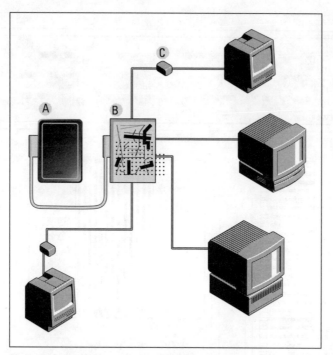

**Figure 9-10: A typical workgroup 10BASE-T installation.**

If you're using 4-wire twisted-pair cable running from your workstations (or wall plugs) to the wiring closet, your cables most likely terminate at a punchdown block. This situation is similar to a typical PhoneNET installation (see Chapter 7), except that you're using four wires for each connection instead of two; also note that each wire is connected to a row of its own (refer again to Figure 9-5).

Normally, you use a 25-pair cable to attach the punchdown block to your hub (see Figure 9-11), just as the PhoneNET StarController, TurboStar, or LocalSwitch is connected to a punchdown block for LocalTalk networks. If you're not working within the existing telephone company wiring system, you may find it just as convenient to run 4-wire cable from your workstations directly to a patch panel feeding the hub or to the hub itself; some hubs have RJ-45 receptacles built in for this particular purpose.

Before you get into hub wiring, make sure you review the information on connectors, wire pairs, and crossovers, in Chapter 8.

Now that you've covered some ways that you can construct your Ethernet network, you'll move on to a crucial aspect of the installation — testing the network.

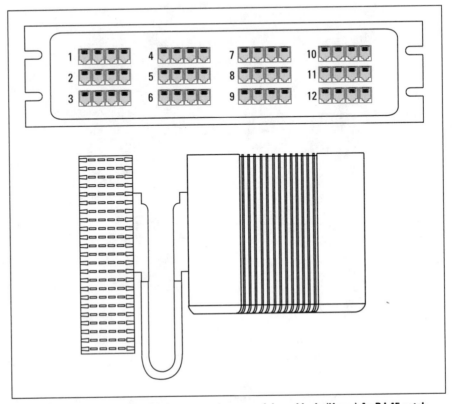

Figure 9-11: (Lower) A 10BASE-T hub connected to a punchdown block. (Upper) An RJ-45 patch panel.

# Testing the Network

When you're installing a new network, its wise to test the cabling before its installed. For large installations, check the cable while it's still on the reel. You can perform a simple test with an ohmmeter, but a better method is to use a *time domain reflectometer* (TDR). The TDR sends electrical pulses down the cable and checks for returned signals. Electrically flawless cables take an infinite time to return a signal. If return signals are received, the TDR can tell you the exact distance to the fault in the cable.

You can run a similar test with a simple box called a *cable scanner*, but the scanner is not as accurate in pinpointing a problem as the TDR. The downside of the TDR is that it uses an oscilloscope monitor to display signals. Although the signals give you a great deal of information, the monitor usually requires training to interpret properly.

After the cable is installed, its advisable to test again to verify that the cable is solid. Because repeated bending of coaxial cable can cause shorts, a short or a break may have occurred during installation. As you install the cable, its a good idea to mark the cable every few meters with a piece of white tape indicating the distance from the end and the cable number. Then place colored labels with the cable number written on them in a neighboring location, possibly the baseboard or ceiling. Next, mark the location of the cables on a building layout. Should you have a break in the cable, a TDR can indicate the exact distance of the break from your test location, and the systematized labeling of your cables will lead you to the problem area.

Should you have reason to doubt the integrity of your MAUs (transceivers) — either a thickwire box or the thinwire ones mounted directly on your controller board — you'll need to construct a loop-back connector (see Figure 9-12). These connectors are fairly simple to make and can prove quite useful for eliminating some components from the checklist as you work your way toward isolating a net-work problem. To use the loop-back connector, all you have to do is disconnect the suspected computer from the network, plug the loop-back connector into the in-terface card, and run the interface cards diagnostic software. If the card passes all the diagnostic tests, you can be sure that the problem is not with the card, and then you can reattach the computer to the network.

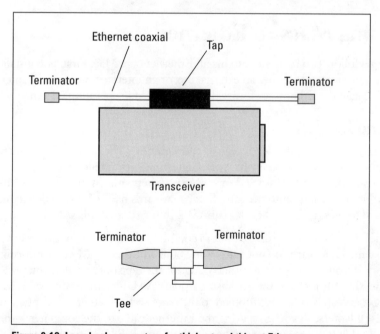

**Figure 9-12: Loop-back connectors for thicknet and thinnet Ethernet.**

Other test instruments are simpler, such as the hand-held TDR with a digital display and fewer functions, sometimes called a *hand-held scanner*. These simpler devices can usually tell you whether a twisted-pair cable is acceptable for use with token ring or 10BASE-T Ethernet, although they don't report actual measurements for the appropriate parameters. Instead, hand-held scanners flash messages like Good or No Good on the digital display when you're testing a cable. Table 9-2 shows when to use these devices for testing network wiring problems.

| Table 9-2 Capabilities of Testing Instruments | | | |
|---|---|---|---|
| | *Ohmmeter* | *Hand-Held Scanner* | *TDR* |
| Resistance | ● | ● | ● |
| Split pairs | | ● | |
| Open cables | ● | ● | ● |
| Shorts | ● | ● | ● |
| Cable length | ● | ● | ● |

# Connecting Macs to Ethernet

You'll follow two basic steps to install Ethernet on a Mac. First, you install the hardware interface, either an external box or an interface card (see Chapter 8); then you install the Ethernet software drivers in the Mac operating system.

## The hardware

Ethernet cards for the Mac come in two varieties. First, there's the standard adapter card, which usually has two connector ports: one for a 10BASE5 AUI cable and one for either a 10BASE2 or 10BASE-T network. In this case, the MAU and AUI cable are built into the card. Some new cards have all three connectors onboard — 10BASE5 AUI cable, 10BASE2 thinwire, and 10BASE-T.

The second kind of cards are built to comply with Apple's new Ethernet Cabling System. These cards do not feature any built-in Ethernet MAUs (transceivers). Instead, you purchase an external MAU for the type of cable that you plan to use. The MAU attaches to the card using Apple's AAUI latching connector. Most network installers are accustomed to the older style of Ethernet adapters; with these adapters, all you do is bring the Ethernet cable to the computer — or use an AUI cable (transceiver cable) when you're using 10BASE5 thickwire.

The adapters for the Apple Ethernet Cabling System have two relatively minor advantages. First, if you change your network medium, all you need to do is change the external media adapter rather than the card. Second, Apple's media adapters for 10BASE2 thinwire Ethernet are self-terminating, just as with its LocalTalk Cabling System. This means that you won't worry about installing the proper terminating resistor at each end of the thinwire bus. (This is not a great advantage because we've never found that to be much of a problem.) Apple's Ethernet Cabling System does make it more convenient to attach the newer LaserWriters and Macs with built-in adapters (such as Quadras, Power Macs and high-end PowerBooks) to Ethernet.

The Mac has always been designed for easy use. Installing Ethernet on a Mac is no exception. An Ethernet adapter board is simple to install in the Mac II and Quadra family because of the NuBus bus architecture, which frees you from setting board switches to register the boards slot address on the system. Older-style compact Macs (such as the Mac Classic and SE/30) require that installation of internal boards be done by trained personnel because disassembly of the Mac is necessary.

## The software

Some board vendors include a simple diagnostic program so that you can check the status of the board after it's installed. Usually, the diagnostic program tells you whether the board is electrically sound and whether it can see the Ethernet network. Some diagnostics let you send a sample packet to another computer on the Ethernet, which should return a reply to verify that your computer can use the network. If you cannot find a diagnostic program for your Ethernet board, try Neon Software. Neon includes a program as part of its Netminder Ethernet package that tests all Ethernet boards in contact with Netminder.

BACKGROUNDER

### A Caution about the Apple Ethernet Cable System

All the 10BASE2 and 10BASE-T MAUs (transceivers), Apple Ethernet Thin Coaxial Transceiver, and Apple Ethernet Twisted-Pair Transceiver, draw power from the Mac. However, the external 10BASE5 MAU, Apple's Ethernet AUI Adapter, has its own six-foot power cord and requires an electrical outlet nearby. That's not a very nice solution — why hang this huge thing on the side of your Mac, add a power transformer, and still need another electrical cord? It's because Apple didn't provide enough power on the AAUI connector to power a transceiver.

## You can't teach an old board new tricks?

Watch out for older Ethernet boards which require you to select the Ethernet medium you're going to use. Some of these old dogs have an internal switch that you must set; others have a socket with a multipin jumper that you must change. The better ones place the switch near the connectors, at the outside of the boards, so that you can make a change after the board has been installed or let you change the port with software. (After working with many vendors' cards, we've found that each installation step is clearly explained in the vendors' instruction manuals and shouldn't pose any problems.) Still better are *auto-sensing* boards, which automatically sense the port being used. If you can, buy this type.

All board manufacturers have settled on using Apple's Installer program for installing their Ethernet driver software. This compatibility makes it a simple matter to complete installation of your Ethernet board and its software. In keeping with the trend toward AppleTalk Phase 2, most Installer scripts install only the Phase 2 drivers. If you need Phase 1 support over Ethernet, you must execute a special Installer script for the Phase 1 driver — provided the board manufacturer supports it. In Apple's case, for example, you can copy the EtherTalk Phase 1 file to your system folder after you've used the Installer to install the Phase 2 driver.

If multiple network device drivers are installed, you can select between them by using the Network Control Panel. In Figure 9-13, the System 7 Network Control Panel lets you select either LocalTalk (labeled Built-in) or EtherTalk as your network for the AppleTalk stack. If you've got both Phase 1 and Phase 2 installed, the icons in the Network Control Panel distinguish between the Phase 1 and Phase 2 EtherTalk drivers — the Phase 1 driver has single-headed arrows, and the Phase 2 driver has two-headed arrows within the icon (see Figure 9-14 for what this looks like under System 6).

In most circumstances, you'll probably have only one Ethernet card installed in your Mac. But on some occasions, you'll want more than one card. The Mac may, for example, be configured to be a router (using Liaison or the AppleTalk Internet Router). Or perhaps you're setting up the Mac as an Ethernet packet analyzer and want to use one card for the analyzer and another for your regular network functions.

Prior to System 7, you were restricted to using boards from the same manufacturer if you installed more than one Ethernet board in a Mac. The .ENET driver in System 7 (EtherTalk 2.2.1) has been rewritten to allow mixing of boards from different vendors in the same Mac.

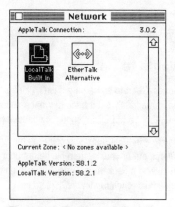

**Figure 9-13: The Network Control Panel lets you pick which medium you will use for AppleTalk.**

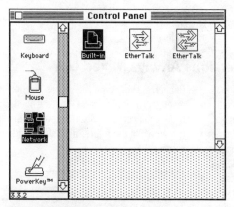

**Figure 9-14: The Network Control Panel, showing the LocalTalk driver (labeled Built-in) and two EtherTalk drivers, one for Phase 1 (middle) and one for Phase 2 (right).**

# Thinking Beyond Ethernet

Everybody knows that faster is better, particularly with networks. As Ethernet has permeated the culture of almost every corporation, network managers have taken it far beyond its original goal of a "local" area network by extending single Ethernets to entire campuses with dozens or even hundreds of buildings.

## DECnet Always Wants to Be Last.

If you run DECnet on your Macintosh, you'll notice that it stops working every time you upgrade almost any network software. It does this because DECnet insists on changing the Ethernet address of your Mac (you don't want to know why, but Digital has fixed this in the DECnet Phase V). If DECnet has given up the ghost for you, try bringing up the NCP program and using the menu options to reset your node

address. Set it to something it isn't, like 50.16, and then immediately set it back to what it should be. Then reboot and DECnet should be happy again.

If you're a ResEdit guru, you can grab the EADR resource out of your system file before upgrading and putting it back afterwards. But why go through such a fuss when running NCP is so easy?

## Why Are the Versions Always Mixed Up?

As you install different network applications on Macintoshes, you will discover that not everyone ships the latest and greatest versions of Apple products, such as the AppleTalk stack, the Ethernet driver, or MacTCP. This means that when you add some terminal emulation program, for example, you may be going backwards in time, software-wise. We find it very helpful to have a copy of the latest versions of Apple's Network Software Installer and MacTCP floppies around at all times. Any time we install new network software, we go ahead and reinstall the AppleTalk and Ethernet drivers (from the Network Software Installer floppy) and MacTCP (from the MacTCP floppy) just to make sure.

We download the Network Software Installer off of the Internet. Apple keeps it on **ftp.apple.com** in the system software directories. If you don't have access to the Internet, you'll have to work with your dealer or Apple to make sure you have a steady supply of software.

Of course, every time you do this you may have to reset your TCP/IP address, so it's a good idea to have a copy of your MacTCP setup screen on paper (as shown in the figure) filed along with those floppies.

Setting up MacTCP with its control panel means answering a lot of questions

To handle all this traffic, vendors have begun work on three copper-based LAN technologies designed to make the jump from 10M bps transmission speed to 100M bps transmission speed. These new LAN-style technologies are in competition with many other very high speed networks, such as the fiber optic based FDDI (Fiber Distributed Data Interface) or the packet-switched ATM (Asynchronous Transfer Mode) networks.

CDDI, the Copper Distributed Data Interface, is a copper version of FDDI. FDDI is a LAN which uses dual counter-rotating token rings to achieve a very survivable network. In FDDI (and CDDI), if a wire is cut, the network self-heals to continue operation. Both FDDI and CDDI operate at 100M bps. CDDI uses Category 5 UTP cable, which is more difficult to install and work with than the Category 3 UTP required by 10BASE-T networks. The real down side of CDDI is that it's an expensive network, one which managers accustomed to $100 Ethernet NIC cards and $400 10BASE-T hubs won't be interested in. For certain environments, such as interbuilding backbone networks, CDDI and FDDI are ideal.

The other two LAN-style networks are both aimed at replacing the standard Ethernet technology with 100M bps technology at around two or three times the cost of existing Ethernet gear. This cost prediction, as you may have guessed, has a lot of network managers interested. The IEEE 802.3 committee is working on a version of Ethernet that operates at 100M bps, which they call "Fast Ethernet." The standards for this 100BASE-T system are in the 802.3u series (see Table 9-3).

Fast Ethernet works very much like Ethernet; it is a CSMA/CD style of network technology. To accommodate the requirements for such speed, 802.3 has provided two different kinds of physical media. 100BASE-TX specifies two-pair Category 5 UTP, Type 1 STP (Shielded Twisted-Pair), and fiber optic cabling. To handle the enormous installed base of Category 3 UTP wiring, 100BASE-T4 specifies a transmission scheme using four-pair Category 3 UTP wiring.

| Table 9-3 Fast Ethernet Standards | |
|---|---|
| **Standard Number** | **Description** |
| 802.3ua | Medium Access Control |
| 802.3ub | Medium Independent Interface |
| 802.3uc | Repeaters |
| 802.3ud | 100BASE-X physical layer |
| 802.3ue | 4T+ media specification |

In the other corner is another IEEE committee, IEEE 802.12, which has created the 100VG-AnyLAN system. This is essentially a token ring network operating at 100M bps that can run over four-pair Category 3 UTP wiring. A normal RJ-45 8-position jack has positions for four pairs of wires, which the 100VG-AnyLAN people are using to their advantage.

Both these standards are getting a lot of media attention currently, which is creating an exciting rivalry between the two groups. Much of the discussion is in terms of religious issues, such as the differences between CSMA/CD and token passing in networks, rather than on technical ones. Which will win? The marketplace will decide (or it may be based on which group has the better public relations firm, rather than which has the technically superior product.)

Table 9-4 compares the 100VG-AnyLAN system with the 100BASE-T system.

| Table 9-4 Comparing Fast Ethernet and 100VG-AnyLAN | | |
|---|---|---|
| | **100BASE-T** | **100VG-AnyLAN** |
| Data Rate | 100M bps | 100M bps |
| Access Protocol | CSMA/CD | Demand Priority (similar to token ring) |
| Physical Topology | Star (as in 10BASE-T) | Star (as in 10BASE-T) |
| Cabling | UTP Category 5, STP Type 1, Fiber, UTP Category 3 | UTP Category 3, 4, or 5 |
| Distance between hub and device | 100 meters | 100 meters on Category 3 or 4; 200 meters on Category 5 |
| Initially available | Summer, 1994 | Summer, 1994 |
| Cost, compared to standard Ethernet | 2 to 3 times more | 2 to 3 times more |

## Why Four Pair?

Both 100VG-AnyLAN and 100BASE-T have an option to use Category 3 cable, rated at only 10M bps, for transmission of 100M bps LANs. However, both require more than the two pair we're accustomed to seeing. That's because they use all four pair for transmission and receiving, de-multiplexing a 100M bps signal across multiple lower-speed signals, and multiplexing (recombining) it at the other end to add up to 100M bps.

In 100VG-AnyLAN, this is called *quartet signaling*. It divides the data into four parallel streams and transmits all four simultaneously over the four pair of UTP Category 3 wire. As a result, each of the four streams has a data rate of only 30M bps (after adding in necessary overhead), which works just fine over Category 3 cable.

# CHAPTER 9  CONCEPTS AND TERMS

- 10BASE5 coaxial cable (thickwire) is best used for bus networks in a building infrastructure, such as between floors or in the ceilings. This type of cable requires that you use a MAU (transceiver) with a tap to connect a workstation.

- 10BASE2 coaxial cable (thinwire) is easier to install and uses a BNC T-style connector to connect to your network interface card; thinwire is also best suited for small bus networks in offices.

- 10BASE-T twisted-pair cable requires a star network with a concentrator at the center of the star; 10BASE-T requires two pairs for each connection and an RJ-45 jack to plug into your network interface card. A 10BASE-T network can use existing telephone wires — maybe.

- A TDR (Time Domain Reflectometer) can give you the most information about wiring problems, but it requires some skill and training to use; simpler hand-held cable scanners are often sufficient for diagnosing network wiring problems.

- Connecting Macs to Ethernet with Apple's cabling system is simple, although the 10BASE5 connector is bulky and inconvenient.

- New Ethernet technologies, such as Fast Ethernet and 100VG-AnyLAN, will eventually raise the standard from 10M bps to 100M bps.

**AAUI (Apple Attachment Unit Interface)**
The name used for Apple's new Ethernet physical interface, which uses a special connector and requires an external transceiver to complete a connection to the network.

**auto-sensing boards**
A network board which detects which type of cabling system it is connected to and uses that media, automatically.

**coaxial cable**
An electrical cable that contains two separate wires. One wire is solid, and the other is a tube. The solid wire is inside the tube. Both wires have the same center point, or axis, which is why the cable is named *coaxial*. The solid wire carries data while the tube wire acts as a shield for the solid wire. The solid wire is surrounded by insulation to isolate it from the tube wire. The tube

wire, which is made of a braided mesh, screen material, is in turn surrounded by insulation. Coaxial cables, also called *coax*, are the familiar wires used for cable television connections. Terminals used on IBM networks frequently have coaxial cables for their connections; many Ethernet networks also use coaxial cables.

**drop cable**
Used to connect a device to the network cable.

**fan-out transceiver**
A non-standard device which connects multiple stations to the network cable through a single network connection. Fan-out transceivers, also called *multi-port transceivers*, are not repeaters. The most popular transceiver was the Digital DELNI, and many manufacturers refer to their product by that nomenclature.

**intrusive tap**
An Ethernet tap which requires you to physically break the cable to attach the device. Most all 10BASE2 taps are intrusive; very few 10BASE5 taps are. Compare with *nonintrusive*.

**minimum bending radius**
The radius of the smallest circle you can safely make with your network cable. If you run the network cable with a tighter bend than the manufacturer-specified minimum, then you risk breaking the wires or changing the impedence or shielding characteristics inside of the cable.

**Network Interface Controller (NIC)**
A card (or set of chips) that fits inside a computer so that the computer can connect to a network. The card has a connector for attaching the network cable. Sometimes the Network Interface Controller is called simply the *interface card*.

Different types of networks require different interface cards. The connectors are different sizes to accommodate the cables of different networks, and the chips on the card contain the hardware and software needed to implement the various protocols for a specific type of network.

**nonintrusive tap**
An Ethernet tap which attaches to an existing cable without causing a break in the cable. In 10BASE5, this usually means a "vampire tap," which requires drilling a hole through the cable insulation and shielding but not through the center conductor (a precise job which requires a jig to prevent nicking the center conductor).

**segment**
Any section of cable that is attached to a port of a repeater, bridge, or router.

*(continued on the next page)*

*(continued from the previous page)*

**thicknet**
Ethernet 10BASE5 cabling scheme using 50-ohm coaxial cable with N-type connectors. Thicknet uses a 50-ohm coaxial cable as the backbone for the network. The cable has an outer diameter of 0.37 to 0.41 inches, depending on the type of insulation; also note that thicknet cable has two layers of shielding.

**thinnet**
Ethernet 10BASE2 cabling scheme using 50-ohm coaxial cable with BNC-type connectors — thinnet coaxial is 0.20 inches in outer diameter and has a single layer of shielding. Sometimes called *cheapernet*.

**transceiver**
A device used as an interface between a workstation and the network to which it is attached. The transceiver performs the task of transmitting frames onto the cable and receiving them from it. It also monitors signal levels on the medium and detects collisions and other error conditions.

# Using Modems with Networks

Telecommunications, a technology that uses devices such as modems and PBXs, is a science deserving a book or two of its own. In fact, just mention the word network to some people, and they start thinking about statewide or nationwide networks involving telephone company services. For an investigation of the ties between some of these services and internetworks, see Chapter 12, "Designing an AppleTalk WAN." For the moment, this chapter focuses on using modems on your LAN.

QUOTABLES

"To understand this important story, you have to understand how the telephone company works. Your telephone is connected to a local computer, which is in turn connected to a regional computer, which is in turn connected to a loudspeaker the size of a garbage truck on the lawn of Edna A. Bargewater of Lawrence, Kansas.

"Whenever you talk on the phone, your local computer listens in. If it suspects you're going to discuss an intimate topic, it notifies the computer above it, which listens in and decides whether to alert the one above it, until finally, if you really humiliate yourself, maybe break down in tears and tell your closest friend about a sordid incident from your past involving a seedy motel, a neighbor's spouse, an entire religious order, a garden hose, and six quarts of tapioca pudding, the top computer feeds your conversation into Edna's loudspeaker, and she and her friends come out on the porch to listen and drink gin and laugh themselves silly."

— Dave Barry, "Won't It Be Just Great Owning Our Own Phones?"
Dave is a syndicated columnist for the *Miami Herald*.
[reprinted with permission]

## An Introduction to Modems

Modems exist because of the fundamental difference between the way computers work and the way the telephone system works. Computers work with the 0s and 1s of digital signals (see Chapter 2). Telephones work with analog signals.

Digital is discrete: everything is either a 0 or a 1, and that's it. (Any of you purists who insist that there is no such thing as real digital electronics are correct, but that's not important here.) The opposite is true of analog. Analog is continuous. Something could be 0, or 1, or ½, or anything in between (or above or below).

Most of the world is analog; only in the artificial land of computers is everything so black and white. Because sound is essentially analog, telephone lines use analog signals (see Figure 10-1). These analog signals look like the sine waves illustrated by the figures in Chapter 2. To enable one computer to communicate with another over a phone line, you need a device that can convert digital signals into analog signals and analog signals into digital signals. This is the function of the modem.

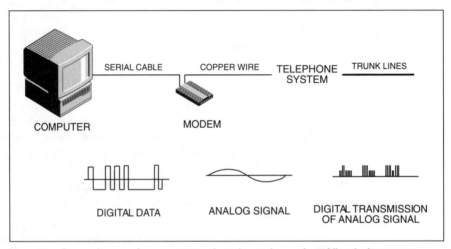

Figure 10-1: Data as it moves from a computer through a modem to the public telephone system.

The word *modem* derives from *mo*dulate and *dem*odulate, both of which describe a modem's primary functions. First, a modem modulates a digital signal, or data from the computer, into analog form so that it can be transmitted over a phone line. The analog wave is called a *carrier wave*. Second, the modem demodulates a received analog signal back into digital form so that the computer can understand it. Each modem does both functions: modulates transmitted data, and demodulates received data. The specific techniques that a modem uses to transform digital signals into analog signals and vice versa are called *modulation protocols*, distinguishing them from network protocols, such as those covered in Chapter 3, "Understanding AppleTalk Protocols."

Whether you're sending an e-mail message or transferring a large file from a remote file server, it's best to work with the fastest modems possible. When you're trying to connect to a network, the timing of network protocols can cause transmission failures if you use a slow modem. Also, faster modems mean that your connection time is shorter, so your cost for the call is less. In addition to the speed gained by modulation techniques, you'll see how error correction and data compression can affect a modem's speed.

# Modem terminology

You should be familiar with some terms that you're likely to run into time and again in discussions of modems. First, there are the terms *baud rate* and *bits per second (bps)*, both of which are used to explain a modem's speed. *Baud rate* describes the number of signal changes per second. In a simple system where a signal change represents a single bit of information, baud rate and bits per second measure the same thing. However, when special modulation techniques are used — all contemporary modems use them — baud rate and bits per second are not identical because a signal change can represent more than one bit.

As we explain in Chapter 6, when 300 *bits per second* (bps) modems first came out, they were called 300 baud modems because there were 300 signal transitions (or symbols) per second. For every common modem introduced since then, the baud rate is much lower than the bits per second rate because each symbol conveys more than 1 bit of information. For example, the 9600 bps modem is really a 2400 baud modem where each symbol can take one of 16 different values. Because four bits can represent any one of 16 values, each baud represents four bits.

Modems can communicate with each other in either of two modes: *half-duplex* and *full-duplex*. In half-duplex mode, data is sent over the connection in only one direction at a time; the sending modem must wait for the receiving modem to acknowledge receipt of the data before sending the next block of data. But in full-duplex mode, data can be sent in both directions at once. You will find that most of the modems you encounter are full-duplex modems. The only modem standard you'll likely see which is half-duplex is the one which fax machines use. Because faxing is actually a unidirectional data transfer, half-duplex modems are ideal for fax machines.

It's entirely possible that two modems can exchange data at a rate faster than the attached computers can process it. To ensure that no data is lost in such cases, the modem-computer connection uses some type of *flow control*. Flow control is usually accomplished by either a *software handshake* or a *hardware handshake*. The software handshake, or *in-band flow control*, inserts the special characters Control-S (also called XON) and Control-Q (also called XOFF) in the data stream to control data transmission and prevent data loss. For example, a modem transmits XOFF to the host computer if the computer is sending data too quickly to be transmitted or stored in the memory buffer. The modem transmits XON when it's ready for more data.

The hardware handshake, or *out-of-band flow control*, uses an electrical signal sent from the modem to the computer over a wire in the modem cable. The EIA-232 specification does not include symmetrical flow control, which may be a problem for modem manufacturers. It is possible for the modem to tell the computer to stop sending data, but there is no defined way for the computer to tell the modem to stop sending data. For computers using the standard EIA-232 interface to a modem, the device (called a DTE) tells the modem (called a DCE) that it wants to send data by raising a line (called RTS, for Request To Send). When the DCE is prepared to receive data from the DTE, it raises CTS, or Clear To Send. By dropping CTS, the modem can tell the computer not to send any more data.

## DCE versus DTE

Before you dive into modem terminology, it's essential to get two very common acronyms straight. DCE, for *Data Circuit-terminating Equipment*, is what you commonly think of as a modem. DCE is really a more generic term, especially in the digital world where not everything that looks like a modem does what a modem does. A DCE is the thing at the end of the phone line, more or less. DTE, for *Data Terminal Equipment* is whatever you attach to a DCE. In the early days, DTEs were dumb terminals. Nowadays, a DTE is more likely to be a computer, such as a Macintosh.

We will use these terms quite often when talking about modems because they're both shorter and more precise. It pays to memorize these and keep them straight in your head because they get used (not entirely correctly, but usefully enough) in lots of other networking discussions. Remember that the DTE is the device at the end of the line and the DCE is the device which connects the DCE to the network.

One other bit of network knowledge we file away with DCE and DTE is the correct sex of DB-25 EIA-232 connectors. A DCE must always be a female DB-25 and a DTE must always be a male DB-25. Many poorly designed MS-DOS systems have the wrong sex connector on them, but most modems get it right. If you ever have to match a male to a male, you need to do more than change the connectors — you also need to use a null modem which moves the signals around so that each device gets its signals on the pins it expects. Of course, the range of sloppy design is so great that we also keep a bag of gender changers (usually called *gender benders*), which do not have a null modem function, around just to make the connection.

If you really get into EIA-232 connections, you should invest in a *universal cable*, which is a cable which has both male and female ends at both ends.

To accommodate the needs for a computer to slow down a modem, most manufacturers change the meaning of these lines slightly and treat the RTS line as a CTS for the DTE. When the computer is ready to receive, it turns on RTS. When the modem is ready to receive, it turns on CTS.

You will find that the standardized definitions of the EIA-232 signals don't have much relationship to the reality of modems and communications. However, if you can figure out from the description of the signal what your computer and your modem want, then you can probably make it work. You should, however, be prepared for a little work with a soldering iron and some small jumper wires. The main reason for hardware handshaking is to eliminate any confusion of the software handshake control characters with actual data; some encoding methods process control characters as well as data characters, leading to errors.

Table 10-1 provides a quick summary of commonly used EIA-232 signals. Remember that in this table DTE is the Macintosh while DCE is the modem. EIA-232 calls for the DTE to have a male DB-25 connector and the DCE a female one. Of course, Macs with their 8-pin connectors pay no attention to this rule.

| | | |
|---|---|---|
| **Table 10-1** | | |
| **Commonly Used EIA-232 Signals** | | |
| *Signal Name* | *DB-25 pin* | *Notes* |
| Protective Ground | 1 | Attached to the frame of the equipment. This should never be attached to pin 7, and should only be connected at one end. |
| Transmitted Data | 2 | Transmitted from the DTE to the DCE. |
| Received Data | 3 | Received by the DTE from the DCE. |
| Request to Send | 4 | From the DTE; often usurped for DTE flow control. |
| Clear to Send | 5 | From the DCE; indicates that the DTE may transmit. |
| Data Set Ready | 6 | From the DCE; indicates that the modem has power turned on and can be used by the DTE. |
| Signal Ground | 7 | Bidirectional; this is the reference ground for all other signals. |
| Carrier Detect | 8 | From the DCE; indicates that the modem has established carrier with a remote modem. Think of this as the hardware equivalent of a CONNECT message. |
| Data Terminal Ready | 20 | From the DTE; indicates that the DTE has power turned on and wants the modem to be alive. A modem should not answer the phone if DTE is not active. |
| Ring In | 22 | From the DCE; the phone line is ringing. |
| Transmit Timing | 15 | From DCE; used in synchronous communications for timing. |
| Receive Timing | 17 | From DTE; used in synchronous communications for timing. |
| Data Speed Indicator, Data Signal Rate Selector | 12, 23 | From DCE; used in some tiny percentage of modems to tell the DTE the speed the modem is communicating. |
| External Transmit Clock | 24 | From DTE; used in synchronous communications for timing. |

Many modem cables offered for Macintosh modems are not wired to use hardware handshaking. If you plan to configure a modem to use hardware handshaking, be sure that the cable for connecting your modem and the Mac has the RTS and CTS signals wired as described. If you buy Mac modems with a Mac cable, you usually get what you need.

All Macs have EIA-422 ports, not EIA-232 ports, for communications. EIA-422 is a newer standard that is capable of transmitting and receiving data much faster than EIA-232 and over longer cable distances in the presence of greater noise. Most Macs have two ports with a round 8-pin mini-DIN connector; the PowerBook 100 only has one, and really old Macs and the original LaserWriter use a DB-9 connector.

The wiring diagram for a Macintosh EIA-422 port is given in Figure 10-2.

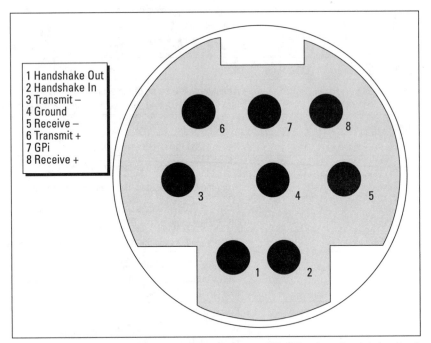

1 Handshake Out
2 Handshake In
3 Transmit –
4 Ground
5 Receive –
6 Transmit +
7 GPi
8 Receive +

**Figure 10-2: The Macintosh mini-DIN-8 connector supports EIA-422 and two handshake signals.**

A normal Macintosh serial cable appears in Figure 10-3. A Macintosh serial cable for hardware flow control is shown in Figure 10-4. If you can't decide which to use, you could also try connecting the Macintosh HSKo pin to *both* RTS and DTR. It shouldn't hurt anything, but you could find that you'll have to tell the modem to ignore DTR if you want to use RTS for Macintosh-initiated flow control. The GPi signal is unused in all but the newest AV Macintoshes; Apple recommends connecting it to CD (Carrier Detect, usually pin 8 on an EIA-232 cable).

## Telephone terminology

Telephone systems have a vocabulary all their own. You'll need to know a few terms that are pertinent to the following discussion of modems. Primarily, these terms concern the types of phone lines used for modem-based communications.

The most common phone line, such as the one in your home, is the dial-up line, or switched *circuit*, which uses two wires to connect your phone jack to the phone network. Because only two wires are used, this type of line is also referred to as a *2-wire circuit*, or a *2-wire connection*. The telephone network, called the PSTN (Public Switched Telephone Network), is based on the principle of providing 2-wire analog circuits for voice transmission. Inside of the PSTN, you may find lots of digital gear. But at your house, it's all analog.

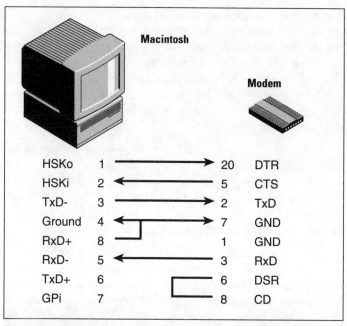

**Figure 10-3:** Wiring diagram for a Macintosh-to-Modem cable which supports software flow control.

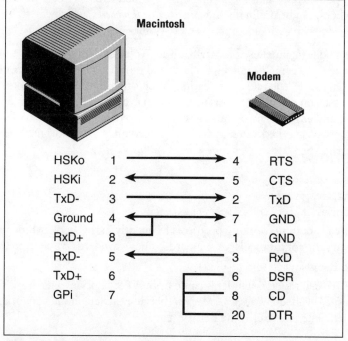

**Figure 10-4:** Wiring diagram for a Macintosh-to-Modem cable which supports hardware flow control.

A decade ago, before the development of modems capable of transmitting at speeds faster than 9600 bps, speedy data transmission required a 4-wire circuit. Why four wires? One pair was used for transmitting data and one pair for receiving. That's because the bandwidth of one pair of wires was only sufficient for 9600 bps transmission. Consider that a 2400 bps full-duplex modem on a 2-wire circuit actually requires 4800 bps of bandwidth: 2400 in one direction and 2400 in the other. During the dark ages of data, one phone line could barely fit 9600 bps. And 14,400 bps would be really pushing it.

All 4-wire circuits are dedicated. Rather than two wires going to a switch that can be connected to any other two wires in the world, the telephone companies dedicate four wires — two pair — between two points. These lines are also known as *leased* or *private* circuits. Not all leased lines are 4-wire; it's possible to get a single pair as well. Four-wire circuits are sometimes called by their AT&T moniker, 3004 lines. Likewise, 2-wire circuits are sometimes called 3002 lines.

These data circuits have amplifiers and signal regenerators built into them. Therefore, a circuit from Tucson to Phoenix has the same amount of noise and signal loss as one from Tucson to Tokyo. Occasionally, you may find a need for *bare copper* circuits between two points, usually in a very limited geographic area such as a campus or small neighborhood. Your phone company may or may not be interested in selling or leasing you bare copper circuits. It turns out that it's more difficult for them to do this because they have to go through the length of the circuit and pull out any amplifiers. These lines, called LADA (Local Area Data Access) lines, can be useful if you have *short haul modems*, which can transmit at very high speeds (such as 56,000 bps) over a few miles of copper wire.

The telephone channel used for transmitting voice or data signals can transmit frequencies between 300 and 3400 Hertz and thus has a bandwidth of only 3100 Hertz. Originally, the rate of oscillation in repeating signals (see Chapter 2), such as those used on phone lines, was measured in cycles per second. Over 20 years, the scientific and engineering communities agreed to name the unit of oscillation as the Hertz (abbreviated Hz), after a scientist who did much of the original research on electromagnetic waves.

# Modem Protocols

You've read about networking protocols frequently in this book. Modems have their own series of protocols, or standards. These standards come from three major sources:

❖ The original modem standards came from AT&T, prior to its breakup. These are usually called *Bell modem standards* because the telephone network in the United States was called the Bell System.

❖ Most modem standards in current use were developed by the ITU's (International Telecommunications Union) Telecommunications Standardization Sector and are called ITU-T Recommendations. You may have heard of these described as CCITT Recommendations. In 1993, the CCITT was reorganized and renamed as the ITU. CCITT is a French acronym; in English it is rendered as the International Consultative Committee on Telegraphy and Telephony.

❖ The commonly used standard for an interface between a modem (DCE) and a computer or terminal (DTE) is defined by the EIA/TIA (Electronic Industry Association/Telecommunications Industry Association). If you've ever heard of RS-232-C, you're thinking of what is now known as EIA-232.

Today, most new modem standards are created by the ITU Telecommunications Standardization Sector, which is a Geneva-based United Nations agency concerned with standards for radio and data communications. Modem data communications standards from the ITU are in the V-series. Other series of standards include the X-series (protocols and data representation), Q-series (telephone signaling systems), I-series (ISDN, Integrated Services Digital Network), T-series (many things, including fax), and E-series (other aspects of telephony).

Contemporary modems use four types of standards: modulation standards, command standards, error detection and correction standards, and data-compression standards. You'll look at each type separately.

BACKGROUNDER

### Why *bis* and *ter*?

If you hang around ITU standards long enough you'll notice some interesting things about their terminology. For one thing, they're not called standards. They *are* standards, but in the ITU they are only called *Recommendations*, and "Recommendation" is an official part of the title. Another important part of the title is the year the standard was adopted. Many data communications standards change from edition to edition (usually once every four years, called a *study period*) and it's vital to keep the year with the title. If you support, for example, the 1984 version of Recommendation X.25, that's very different from the 1992 version of X.25. Given all of that, you can now build the official title of a standard. For example, a standard for multicast one of the authors wrote is known as *Recommendation X.6 (1992)*.

A second bit of confusion is the use of the terms *bis* and *ter*. These are not used to denote different versions of a standard, but are used to indicate standards which are very closely related. The first closely related standard gets the designation *bis* and the second closely related standard gets *ter*. So far, there are only two *ter* recommendations we know of: V.27*ter* and V.26*ter*, neither of which are in common use. Thus, Recommendation V.32 is very similar to V.32*bis*.

The designation of what has become known as V.fast modems as V.34 rather than V.32*ter* was done because V.34 modems are fundamentally different than V.32 modems. The V.32terbo industry standard is much more similar to V.32 than to V.34.

### If the Network is Digital, Who Needs a Modem?

Although the telephone network started as an analog system, much of it has been replaced by digital electronics. In most cities, your computer's signal is translated from digital to analog, goes out over the phone wires, travels a few miles to a central office (CO), and is then digitized. The digital signal is multiplexed with other phone calls and transmitted over digital lines, switched, packetized, and shunted along, until it hits the final CO at the other end of your call. Then the signal is converted back from digital to analog for that last mile of transmission to the modem at the other end, where it goes back into digital for the final hop into the computer.

If all this is going on, why not throw out the modems and digitizers and simply transmit things digitally? It's not impossible.

Phone companies are now prepared to sell direct digital service, usually in one of two ways: circuit-switched and packet-switched. The circuit-switched alternatives will be familiar to any telephone user because the telephone network is a circuit-switched network. The digital equivalent of a 2-wire or 4-wire circuit is called a DDS line (Direct Digital Service). Telephone companies also offer digital service on a switched basis, where you "dial" a phone number to connect your digital circuit to someone else participating in the digital network. You will probably hear this called *switched 56* (for 56,000 bps transmission) or even switched T1.

Packet-switched services from telephone companies have been around for a while but are now available as direct digital services. These services include SMDS (Switched Multimegabit Data Service), frame relay, and ISDN (Integrated Services Digital Network). More about these technologies later in this chapter.

ISDN is a telephone system that replaces all analog services with digital services. With ISDN, *all* signals are digital, whether they originate from your home phone or computer or are cross-country carrier signals. Because all signals are digital, ISDN does not require a modem. An ISDN adapter, which formats the data for the ISDN phone lines, takes the place of a modem to connect a computer to the phone system. The home-style ISDN service (called the *Basic Rate Interface,* or BRI) includes two multiplexed 64k bit/second channels and a 16k bit/second channel used for signaling, such as placing calls.

The Regional Bell Operating Companies (RBOCs) have started to offer ISDN services to homes and businesses in the last few years, but only in restricted geographic areas. Although ISDN looked as though it was simply going to die out a few years ago, aggressive marketing and pricing actions by companies such as Pacific Bell (in the California coastal cities) have led to strong demand for the service.

## Modulation standards

As explained previously, a modem works by modulating digital data into an analog carrier wave. To represent the digital data, the modem alters the frequency, amplitude, and phase of the carrier wave. Low-speed modems, 2400 bps and slower, split the approximately 3000 Hz bandwidth of a telephone line into two parts: an upper and a lower part. One of the two modems at each end transmits on the upper part and the other modem transmits on the lower part. Each modem has a relatively simple filter that separates the transmitting signal from the receiving signal. This technique is cheap, but has a drawback — you're only using half of the theoretical bandwidth of the phone line.

Higher speed modems are based on DSPs (Digital Signal Processors), which allow both modems on the circuit to use the entire bandwidth of the phone line to send and receive data. We'll explain the technique used by high-speed modems, called echo cancellation, in just a few paragraphs. A summary of common modem types is in Table 10-2.

## The Facts on Fax

Fax modems and machines use several terms that can be confusing if you're not paying careful attention. Fax modems transmit at one of four speeds: 300 bps (using V.21 signaling); 4800 bps (using V.27*ter* signaling); 9600 bps, the most common (using V.29 signaling); or at 14,400 bps, the newest speed (using V.17 signaling). The most common speeds used by fax machines and fax modems are 9600 bps (V.29) and 4800 bps (V.27*ter*); the higher rates allowed by V.17 are still rather rare.

Many fax modems advertise themselves as 14,400 bps fax and data modems. Check the specifications carefully when buying that kind of modem. These modems probably use V.32*bis* for the high-speed fax communications, which may or may not be compatible with the system at the other end. We have found such variation in the 14,400 support by fax machines that we've set our fax modem to attempt no speed higher than 9600 bps.

Fax machines are sometimes listed by *group*, which identifies a particular version of the ITU-T (CCITT) fax Recommendations. Fax standards define the method of scanning the document, the coding of the data, and the speed of transmission. Group 1 faxes are never found anymore; they use purely analog

encoding (which really means they don't work as modems!) and transmit one page every 6 minutes. Group 2 fax machines are also very rare. Group 2 fax, standardized in 1976, still uses analog encoding, and can transmit one page every 3 minutes. Group 3 fax, the first digital fax encoding system, was standardized in 1980. Group 3 are the most common fax machines in use today and can transmit one page in less than one minute. Group 4 fax, standardized in 1984, uses digital transmission at 56,000 or 64,000 bps to send fax data.

Fax modems may also conform to an EIA/TIA *class* designation, which defines the computer-to-modem interface. This designation is the fax equivalent of the Hayes de facto "AT" command set. A Class 1 fax modem uses only a basic set of six commands to transmit fax data from the CPU to the modem and puts most of the burden of processing on the CPU. Class 2 fax modems have an extended command set with forty functions, moving more of the work into the modem and freeing up the CPU. Class 3 fax modems, not yet approved by the EIA, add file conversion to the modem for more efficient operation. You probably won't see a Class 3 fax modem for a while — which is good because you won't be able to confuse Class 3 with Group 3.

|  | Table 10-2 **Popular Modem Types** | |
| --- | --- | --- |
| **Modem Standard** | **Maximum Speed** | **Notes** |
| Bell 103 | 300 bps | 300 baud (see also V.21). |
| Bell 212A | 1200 bps | 600 baud PSK coding; also known as ITU-T V.22. Each symbol is a di-bit. |
| ITU-T V.22*bis* | 2400 bps | 600 baud QAM coding. Each symbol is a quad-bit. |
| ITU-T V.32 | 9600 bps | 2400 baud QAM and TCM coding with 64-point constellation. |
| ITU-T V.32*bis* | 14,400 bps | 2400 baud QAM and TCM coding with 128-point constellation. |
| V.32terbo | 19,200 bps | 2400 baud QAM and TCM coding with 512 point constellation. |
| ITU-T V.34 (V.fast) | 19,200 bps to 28,800 bps | 4D 16-, 32-, or 64-state TCM with constellation points representing a variable and noninteger number of bits; 2400, 2743, 2800, 3000, 3200, and 3429 baud signals; 2 center frequencies at each symbol rate; -9 to -7 dBM transmit power. |

The original low-speed modem was manufactured by AT&T and went by the model number 103. The Bell 103, as it was known, supported a full-duplex link of 300 bps across a standard telephone line. The 103, in addition to being a 300 *bps* modem, was also a 300 *baud* modem. Standardization was simple: either your modem worked with the Bell 103, or it didn't. Actually, it was even simpler for the first few years, as you weren't allowed to attach modems to the PSTN from anyone but AT&T. Judge Greene, of course, changed all that (Greene is the judge who ruled that AT&T must break into the "baby bells.").

The Bell 103 was followed by a four-times increase in performance with the Bell 212A. The 212A was a similar product, except that it was four times faster. Eventually, the technology used in the 212A was standardized by the CCITT (also called the ITU) as Recommendation V.22, as the 600 baud differential PSK (Phase-Shift Keying) modem. The ITU eventually came out with a 300 bps international standard called Recommendation V.21, but you will probably only run into that in the backwaters of Europe.

Recommendation V.22*bis* is a standard closely related to V.22 which raised the speed to 2400 bps. In order to transmit data at 2400 bps, modems using V.22*bis* use two carrier signals, or states — one for the originating modem and one for the answering modem. The originator transmits at a frequency of 1200 Hz; the answering modem transmits at a frequency of 2400 Hz. Each carrier is QAM (Quadrature Amplitude Modulation) modulated at 600 baud so that the modem sends four bits of data per baud (remember that baud equals signal change).

BACKGROUNDER

### A Modem, a Floor Wax, and a Dessert Topping?

One commonly held misconception is that modems, such as the 2400 bps V.22*bis* modem, must also work with other types of modems, such as the lower speed 1200 bps V.22. In the eyes of the ITU, a V.22*bis* modem doesn't have to talk to anything but another V.22*bis* modem at 2400 bps. In fact, if you've listened to a high-speed modem sync up with it's cousin at the other end of a phone line, you've probably noticed that as speeds get higher and higher, the time to sync up gets longer and longer.

Manufacturers believe that a *universal* modem is what people want, and their engineers are working overtime to come up with a way for two modems to figure out the fastest speed at which they can talk.

The upshot of all this is that as modems are asked to magically figure out which of five different models are at the other end of the phone line, users and network managers will have to figure out how to handle more and more compatibility problems.

The ITU standard for full-duplex 9600 bps communications on dial-up lines is Recommendation V.32. To send data at 9600 bits per second, V.32 modems use two techniques, QAM and TCM (Trellis Coded Modulation).

In full-duplex mode, modems can handle simultaneous signal transmission. With each modem transmitting its signals at the same time as the other, each modem must sort out its transmitted signal from the signal it receives. *Echo cancellation* is a technique in which the modem remembers the most recently transmitted signal and uses that stored signal to recognize and cancel out the near and far echoes of the transmitted signal. Effectively, each modem takes up the entire communications pipe and is able to subtract its own transmitted signal from the received signal. Think of it as two people talking at once with total comprehension because each person only hears what the other is saying.

Modems based on V.32 still make the same assumptions about the quality and bandwidth of the telephone line as older, slower modems do, which is why they use 2400 baud as the signaling rate. To get around this narrow channel, QAM was developed to pack more bits into a single baud.

In its most basic form, QAM combines amplitude and phase, with each component representing half the signal. Each symbol then has two bits that can be either on or off (or high or low). V.22*bis* modems use this technique. For 9600 bps, though, two bits isn't enough. Instead, V.32 and faster modems use a *constellation* plotted on a two-dimensional graph that represents specific amplitude and phase combinations. A point in a constellation may, for example, select a particular combination of amplitude and phase shift. The V.32 constellation has 64 points; higher speed modems, such as the nonstandard V.32terbo 19,200 bps modem, have as many as 512 points.

To improve the immunity of a modem from noise, V.32 and faster modems include the TCM (Trellis Coded Modulation) technique. TCM takes the two dimensional constellation of QAM and adds a third to it: time. Each point in the constellation only has a small number of transition points it can go to. If a receiving modem knows this, it can better interpret noisy data. A good analogy may be a hypothetical rule that says you cannot place the number zero in the middle of a w0rd.

Naturally, things haven't stopped at 9600 bps. Recommendation V.32*bis* uses a denser constellation than V.32 to achieve a 14,400 bps transmission rate. A proposed extension to V.32*bis*, called V.32terbo (that's a joke, you see, because if there had been a real standard based on V.32*bis*, it would have been called V.32*ter*) increased the V.32*bis* constellation from 128 points to 512 to achieve a 19,200 bps signaling rate.

Recommendation V.34 (formerly known as V.fast) takes things in a little different direction. Although V.34 builds on the echo cancellation and trellis coding technology from the V.32 family, there are strong engineering differences. First, and most important, is that V.34 assumes that telephone lines are getting better and better and that a standard telephone line has more than 3000 Hz of bandwidth.

More importantly, the V.34 modem builds on the work of companies such as Telebit by letting two modems adapt their transmission signal to accommodate potential phone line differences. V.34 modems support six signaling rates (from 2400 Hz to 3429 Hz), two center-band frequencies for each signaling rate, three different data encoding schemes that can encode a variable and noninteger number of bits per symbol, and a choice of transmission power. The V.34 modem is designed to seek out and use the best parts of each phone line. The result is a modem that can perform at speeds between 19,200 bps and 28,800 bps (in 2400 bps chunks), maximizing throughput based on available facilities. If you're calling from the outback of Window Rock, Arizona, you probably won't get 28,800 bps. If you're calling cross-town in San Francisco, you may.

If you want to send as much data as possible in the least amount of time, you can keep improving modulation schemes, but this isn't the only way to get better throughput rate on a telephone line. Two further important processes are *error correction* and *data compression*.

## Command standards

The D.C. Hayes Corporation (now Hayes Microcomputer Products, Inc.) became a dominant player in the modem business in the early 1980s. At that time, Hayes modems used an in-band command language to control the modem. This language, now often known as the *AT Command Set*, has become a de facto standard for the computer industry.

BACKGROUNDER

## The Rise of the Single-Chip Modem

In most modems produced prior to approximately 1985, each modem manufacturer designed their own electronics and signaling system out of discrete components. When the cost of VLSI technology dropped, several chip manufacturers began to create single-chip modems. These components can be used by modem manufacturers to greatly decrease the chip count of their product and lower the production costs of most modems. At the same time, the Hayes AT command set became a de facto standard for the modem industry. The Hayes AT command set was unusual for the era, in that it allowed the user to configure the modem directly from the attached terminal or computer, rather than require the use of hardware switches. These commands give both the manufacturer and the end user a great deal of flexibility in configuring modem parameters.

Chip manufacturer Rockwell became a strong supporter of both the Hayes AT command set and the VLSI modem chips. Rockwell built the Hayes commands into their extremely successful V.22bis (2400 bps transmission speed) modem chip set, which was adopted and used by many of the modem manufacturers of the time. To make their modem chips as attractive to manufacturers as possible, Rockwell made them very configurable. This ease of configuration was then passed on to the end user.

The dominance of the Rockwell chip sets (now in V.32 and V.32*bis* modems as well) has good and bad sides. It increases compatibility because the inside of the modem (the *data pump*) is virtually all from the same company, even if the outside looks different. On the other hand, any defects in the common data pump appear in most modems, and finding a modem which doesn't have the defect means spending a lot more money. Companies such as Zyxel and AT&T do not use the Rockwell chip sets; they start from scratch.

Although most modems now support the same basic set of Hayes commands for dialing numbers, resetting the modem, and controlling whether or not the modem answers the phone, very little else is consistent from manufacturer to manufacturer. You'll find that dialing a number works beautifully from modem to modem, but anything else you want to do requires a careful study of the relevant manuals.

## Error detection and correction standards

Error detection and correction has been an integral part of most modems since Microcom added it to the firmware inside of their modem products in the early 1980s. Although protocols such as Kermit, X-, Y-, and Z-modems, the CompuServe B protocol, and UUCP (UNIX-to-UNIX CP), all include built-in error detection and correction facilities during file transfers, users doing simple terminal emulation to a host are at the mercy of any noise on the telephone line. Including error detection and correction in the modem itself makes the whole process more efficient and can actually increase bandwidth. For example, Microcom's MNP4 protocol uses only 8 *modem* bits to transmit a standard 8-bit ASCII character. Most modems use 10 bits: the 8 data bits plus a stop and start bit. MNP4 can therefore deliver performance at rates slightly above the signaling rate, even with the overhead of packetization.

In 1983, Tymshare, Inc., introduced a protocol and software product called *X.PC*. At that time, Tymshare was operating Tymnet, the world's second largest public data network, now called BT Tymnet. They had created a research program to examine models for a reliable communication protocol that provided value-added PSN (Packet-Switched Network) services to personal computers. Tymshare's rationale was that personal computers, once used only as dedicated and isolated systems, were increasingly being used in applications requiring reliable communication with other personal and host computers. The protocol they designed, X.PC, was a derivative of Recommendation X.25 and provided reliable communication over dial-up, asynchronous communications links between personal computers and PSNs.

In response to X.PC, Microcom Corporation introduced MNP, the Microcom Networking Protocol, in 1985. MNP was a combination of hardware and software built into modems that both increased bandwidth and decreased error rates. MNP differs from X.PC in one substantial way: X.PC was exclusively a software product, while MNP required changes to the modems. In a nutshell, MNP would sell more modems and X.PC would not.

Two major error detection and correction standards are currently in use. The newest is ITU-T Recommendation V.42; the oldest is a family of Microcom protocols known as MNP (Microcom Networking Protocol). There are currently 10 different MNP protocols (see Table 10-3), although only a few have come into wide use. MNP has become a popular ad hoc standard because of its wide-spread implementation by Microcom and other vendors.

As modems push more and more data through the limited bandwidth of a telephone line, smaller and smaller amounts of line noise will show up as errors in transmission. To compensate for noisy lines, the ITU-T V.42 error detection and correction system (called LAPM for Link Access Protocol Modem) packetizes all data transmitted over the telephone line, verifies the integrity of each packet at the remote end, and retransmits packets that have become corrupted. The main drawback to V.42, as with most packetizing error control protocols, is that the packets themselves have an overhead and add to the latency (delay) of data transmitted over the line.

As a compromise that recognizes the political power of Microcom and the lack of backbone of the U.S. Department of State, the ITU included MNP Level 4 as an option in Recommendation V.42. Therefore, two modems that only support MNP can claim compliance to V.42, even though they don't implement the V.42 error detection and correction protocols. The fear that modem manufacturers wouldn't support V.42 because of an enormous installed base of MNP modems has turned out to be groundless. The entire modem plant of the United States (the world's largest consumer of modems) has turned over twice since V.42 was approved, as everyone upgraded first from 2400 to 9600 bps modems and then from 9600 bps to 14,400 bps equipment. Most modems built today support both MNP and V.42.

| Table 10-3 Microcom Networking Protocol Levels | |
| --- | --- |
| **MNP Level** | **Purpose** |
| 1 | Not used. |
| 2 | A character oriented protocol, where complete asynchronous characters are transmitted along with a sliding window protocol. This results in a throughput of about 84 percent of modem speed. Relatively few modems incorporating hardware-based Level 2 MNP have ever been sold. |
| 3 | A bit-oriented protocol, where asynchronous characters are converted to a synchronous data stream stripping off start and stop bits. The protocol efficiency is about 108 percent of modem speed. Virtually all MNP modems today utilize Level 3. Both Level 2 and Level 3 are public domain protocols. |
| 4 | Level 4 is nearly identical to Level 3, except that it yields a slightly better throughput. The Level 4 protocol is flexible about the size of blocks that are transmitted, and by monitoring the data transmission quality, will permit larger blocks during times of lower error quality. These larger block transmissions can increase the protocol efficiency to about 120 percent. |
| 5 | Level 5 includes the features of levels 3 and 4 and also uses data compression techniques to increase throughput. Depending on the type of data transmitted, the throughput of a Level 5 MNP modem can be about 200 percent of modem speed. |
| 6 | Not widely distributed. Level 6 was used in a proprietary signaling scheme involving half-duplex V.29 modems. |
| 7 | Not widely distributed. |
| 8 | Not widely distributed. |
| 9 | A proprietary compression scheme not released by Microcom to the general public. Class 9 modems are claimed to have a potential throughput efficiency of 400 percent. |
| 10 | Used primarily to handle special characteristics of cellular telephone lines. |

BACKGROUNDER

## Why LAPM?

LAPM is the latest child in a long line of acronym-rich data link layer error detection and correction standards. If you're really interested in impressing your date with your knowledge of obscure data communications history, read on.

The original data link layer for ITU Recommendation X.25, the oldest internationally standardized network-to-computer interface, was called LAP — Link Access Protocol — and was a subset of an ISO protocol called HDLC, for High-Level Data Link Control. HDLC, of course, was based on an IBM standard called SDLC (Synchronous Data Link Control). As X.25 matured, LAP was modified and became LAPB. LAPB was so simple to implement and so popular that it was chosen as the data link protocol for ISDN's signaling channel (the D channel) and was renamed LAPD. When it came time to select an internationally standardized data link protocol for modems, it was obvious to all (except Microcom) that it should be called LAPM.

Besides the ITU standards, some ad hoc standards for modems are still in use. The most notable of these is PEP (Packetized Ensemble Protocol), a proprietary error-control and data-compression protocol developed by Telebit for use in its modems. PEP slices the phone line up into little pieces that the Telebit modem combines to maximize throughput in whichever direction needs it at the moment. PEP is very popular with UNIX system managers who depend on a poorly designed protocol, UUCP, which insists on treating a full-duplex data communications line as a half-duplex resource. PEP modems are, by their nature, half-duplex modems. They are poor choices for dial-up terminals but excellent for UUCP "g" protocols. The Telebit optimizes this protocol, offering exceptionally good throughput for this environment (and endearing Telebit to UNIX system managers around the world forever).

PEP modems employ a multicarrier modulation scheme called DAMQAM (Dynamically Adaptive Multicarrier Quadrature Amplitude Modulation). A sliding window protocol using a standard scheme for error detection and selective retransmission known as CRC-16 runs on top of this modulation scheme for error detection and retransmission. DAMQAM divides the voice bandwidth into 511 individual channels, each capable of passing two, four, or six bits per baud based on the measured characteristics of the individual frequencies associated with each channel. Telebit reports that in the United States, their modems typically use about 400 of those channels — the remainder are too noisy for data transmission.

Each time a PEP modem connects to another over the PSTN, the modem measures the quality of the connection and determines the usable subset of the 511 carriers. The aggregate sum of bits modulated on this subset of carriers multiplied by the baud rate yields a bit per second rate for that particular connection. In the United States, Telebit reports that typical connections modulate at 18,031 bps. Telebit's protocol overhead is roughly 20 percent. Reduce 18,031 bps by 20 percent and you have the true end-to-end throughput (about 14,425 bps).

The PEP modem allocates the 511 channels (or as many as are appropriate for a particular call) in a half-duplex way. Therefore when half-duplex data transmission is going on, 100 percent of the telephone line is used for transmission, and virtually none of the bandwidth is wasted in the back channel. PEP modems contrast strongly with ITU-T standardized modems, which use a static allocation of bandwidth to ensure predictable full-duplex operation.

## Data-compression standards

Technically, data compression uses mathematical algorithms to eliminate redundancies by re-encoding data using fewer bits. This process is possible because it takes far more bits to represent data than the information content requires. For example, although eight bits (256 distinct values) is reserved for the ASCII character set, most ASCII data is composed of the lowercase characters, spaces, punctuation, and an occasional uppercase character. That's only about 50 distinct values, which could easily be represented in six bits — a 25 percent decrease in data size. This is only the simplest kind of compression.

In practice, compression algorithms use a code table with a variable number of bits per character. Therefore, very common characters, such as the space or lowercase *e* take only a few bits, while very uncommon characters, such as the accent grave ( ´ ) may take many more than the usual eight bits. All of this compression is very non-deterministic, meaning that *compression ratios* as stated on the box that the modem came in are rarely indicative of the actual increase in throughput you'll see when you actually use the modem. For example, a compression ratio of four to one (sometimes written as 4:1) implies that the raw data can be compressed to one-fourth of its original size. However, an algorithm which advertised a four to one compression ratio would probably only deliver that throughput in very special circumstances.

The amount of real compression depends on the type of data being transmitted. Not every data stream is equally compressible. All of this is governed by something called *information theory*. Although the fundamental details of information theory have been long understood, they were firmed up in 1948, when Claude E. Shannon published two papers on "A Mathematical Theory of Communication" in *Bell System Technical Journal*.

Information theory measures how much information is contained in a given data stream. For example, a file of 1,000,000 spaces has very little information in it: its content can be represented in less than a dozen characters. A file of 1,000,000 binary random numbers, however, probably has very little chance at compression. Generally, compression ratios for such files as graphic images, spreadsheets, and ASCII text fall in the range of 2:1 to 4:1.

ITU-T Recommendation V.42*bis* provides the first *official* method for compressing and decompressing data in modems. Several proprietary techniques, such as Microcoms MNP Level 5 protocol, have been available for some time. Because they gave such a significant edge to the first developer, they were considered highly undesirable in

BACKGROUNDER

## How Low Can You Go?

According to Shannon, ordinary English text of eight-letter words has information content of about 2.3 bits per letter. Therefore, a list of words could be compressed from 64 bits per word to about 18 bits, a ratio of 3.5 to 1. Phrases and sentences have an even lower information content per letter, somewhere between 1.2 and 1.5 bits, which means that a document like this one that has an average word length of seven characters could be represented in about 10 bits per word rather than 56. In theory, anyway.

Of course, no compression algorithm has perfect knowledge about a document. Typically, to achieve such a compression would require an analysis of the entire document before transmitting any piece of it. Because modems don't have that opportunity, they have to modify their compression parameters (usually called a dictionary because it maps symbols to bit patterns) on the fly and can never achieve the maximum theoretical compression ratio.

the marketplace. Where the originator held a protocol to be proprietary, it was difficult, if not impossible, for different vendor's modems to communicate.

As an international standard, Recommendation V.42*bis* addresses this very problem. V.42*bis* uses an algorithm similar to computer programs that produce compressed files, such as ARC and ZIP files on a DOS computer, or StuffIt files on the Mac. Again, as with V.42, V.42*bis* is applied to *all* data communications, not just file transfers. Although it is difficult to claim a compression ratio for V.42*bis* as typical, V.42*bis* is fundamentally a better compression algorithm than MNP Level 5. So if your modem supports both, you should use V.42*bis*. If you haven't bought a modem yet, make sure that it supports both V.42 and V.42*bis*. Because data compression requires an error-free channel, you must have an error detection and correction protocol running under your data compression protocol.

# How Modems Are Used on a Network

You can use modems with networks through two types of access. First, you can share modems for dialing out of the network, thus reducing the cost of telecommunications for your network. You can also use a modem to dial into a network, which is a convenient way to access files and network resources while you're on the road.

## Sharing modems on a network

If you've used a modem with a terminal emulator program such as TCP/Connect II (Intercon Systems Corp.), MicroPhone II (Software Ventures), VersaTerm (Synergy Software), or MacTerminal (Apple), to connect to another computer or bulletin board service, you can imagine what it would be like to give all your network users a modem to do the same. Even for use of only a few minutes a day, buying modems for everyone is an expensive proposition.

You can offer modem services to your users with another method. You can set up modem sharing via the network by installing a product like Shiva's NetModem or a NetSerial with an attached modem. Using these systems, your networked users can access those networked modems just as if they were locally attached to the modem port of their Mac. If the one modem becomes heavily used, you can always add another networked modem or two to create a modem pool for users. In a *modem pool*, a waiting user is automatically directed to the next available modem.

The NetModem has only one RS-232 modem port per box; therefore, you must buy one NetModem for each modem that you plan to attach to your network. When you access the NetModems via the Chooser, you select the NetModems by name to create the pool that you want. If the first modem selected is busy, the NetModem software tries the second, then the third, and so on, until you reach an available modem.

## QUICK TIPS

### Accounting for Modem Usage

Network managers usually want logs of modem-related phone calls so that they can calculate the phone charges and keep track of illegal attempts to access the network. But its usually difficult to collect all the logs, especially if you have more than one modem that's used for connecting to the network. You can either arrange for the keepers of those modems to send you the logs, or you can use a program like Timbuktu to log onto the controlling Macs and obtain a copy of the logs yourself.

An advantage of the NetSerial over the NetModem is flexibility. If you use a NetSerial, you can start out with low-speed V.22*bis* modems and switch to higher speed V.32, V.32*bis*, or V.34 modems as the demand requires. In the meantime, you continue to use the same device as the point of attachment to the network; you then need only to buy a new modem. If, on the other hand, you start out with a NetModem, you'll need to buy an entirely different unit when you want to upgrade to a higher speed.

If you plan to set up networked modems, you're always likely to face one problem — that of immediate access to a local (directly connected) resource, as opposed to queued access to a shared resource. Will your users always be content to wait for a networked modem to become available for their use? Or will users be impatient and want the immediate turnaround offered by a modem directly attached to their Macs?

## Gaining remote access to the network

Even in the age of PowerBooks and palmtops, terminal emulation is the rule rather than the exception. The main reason for this is straightforward. System administrators understand terminal servers and modem banks, and they know how to install and manage them. End-users have figured out terminal emulation software. It's easy, straightforward, and cheap. The whole scheme reeks of simplicity. But if your e-mail or spreadsheets are stuck where you can't read them, terminal emulation is also useless.

To support remote access to your network, you'll need high-speed modems (such as the V.32*bis* ones discussed above) and a *remote access server*.

### Selecting a remote access server

Remote access servers aren't always dedicated boxes. Originally, in the Macintosh world, a remote access server was a modem hanging off your desktop Mac. Apple still supports this style. More and more, though, vendors are meeting the need for remote access servers by building them in the same format as terminal servers, with multiple ports designed to be connected to modem banks as a shared resource among a group of users.

When Apple introduced the PowerBook series of portable Macintosh computers, they knew that they couldn't just leave the chaos of remote access the way it was. So they created AppleTalk Remote Access (ARA), a set of protocols, hardware, and software products that makes remote access simple for both managers and end-users.

ARA's success is a testament to the pent-up demand for an easy-to-use remote access system. Apple started the ball rolling with the ARA client/server software. Third parties have taken the idea and run with it. There are now at least a dozen ARA servers available, all of which are very easy to use.

ARA isn't the only way to bring Macintosh users back to their electronic home base. The TCP/IP and DECnet worlds have long had dial-up access to basic networking services. For Mac users, however, there has always been a gap. Terminal emulation and file transfer are possible over these networks, but the friendly remote disk and printing services of AppleTalk have been unavailable.

A brand new protocol, called *PPP* (Point-to-Point Protocol), is designed to change all that. PPP is a generic link-layer protocol that can support multiple higher level protocols. Most people think of TCP/IP over PPP, but LAN protocols are also supported, including AppleTalk, Netware's IPX, and others.

Table 10-4 provides a list of ARA servers now available from a variety of vendors.

BACKGROUNDER

## The ABC of PPP

TCP/IP was born in a Wide Area Network (WAN) world, but it wasn't until recently that a standardized protocol for WAN links was created. For many years, TCP/IP networks depended on proprietary or highly specialized interfaces between routers for wide area connectivity. This standard, called PPP (for Point-to-Point Protocol), describes how to use a point-to-point WAN link as a transport for multiple protocols.

PPP is applicable to a broad spectrum of links and protocols. PPP will operate over both asynchronous and synchronous links and can be used to transport multiple protocols over the same link. At this time, standards for transporting IP, DECnet Phase IV, Netware IPX, AppleTalk, and the OSI Network Layer protocol over PPP are all readily available.

PPP isn't set in stone, but it isn't far from it. The most recent version of PPP, dated December 9, 1993, is not yet an Internet standard. PPP is firmly on track, currently classified as a draft standard. More importantly, many routers and network software packages for personal computers and workstations now include a version of PPP.

TCP/IP users are switching from SLIP (Serial Line IP) as PPP has become available. For dedicated lines and TCP/IP applications, PPP doesn't go much beyond SLIP. For dial-up lines that need authentication or anyone who wants to use high-speed synchronous lines or run multiple protocols over the same link, PPP can be a big improvement.

Table 10-4
## ARA Servers and Vendors

| Product Name, Vendor | Ports | LAN Media | ARA | MacIP | Proprietary | PPP+ AT | PPP+ IP | PPP+ IPX | SLIP | Term. Server | IPX | Comments |
|---|---|---|---|---|---|---|---|---|---|---|---|---|
| Cayman Systems GatorLink | 3 | 2/5/T | ● | ● | | | | | | | | Lowest cost-per-port when we looked at them |
| APT DialServer | 3 | 2/5/T | ● | | | | | | | | | |
| Webster MultiPort/LT | 4 | 2/5/T | ● | ● | | | | | | | | Any port can also be a LocalTalk routing port |
| Shiva LanRover/E | 4 or 8 | 2/5/T | ● | ● | | | | | | | | Comes w/ client SW; can also be used as a dial-out server |
| Shiva NetModem/E | 1 (with V.32bis modem) | 2/T | | | ● | | | | | | | Works with Mac and MS-DOS; can also be used for dial-out |
| Telebit NetBlazer PN | 2 or 4 | | ● | | | N | ● | ● | ● | ● | | Wouldn't interoperate w/ MacPPP using AppleTalk |
| Digital Equipment DECServer 700 | 8 or 16 | 5/T | | | | ● | ● | ● | ● | ● | | |
| Asanté Remote Access Server | 8 or 16 | 2/5/T | ● | | | | | | | | ● | Management software not included; must be bought separately. |
| Global Village OneWorld Remote Access | 2 (with V.32terbo modems) | "T, LT" | ● | | | | | | | | | |
| Xyplex MAXserver 1600 | 8 to 20 | 5/T | ● | | | | ● | | ● | ● | ● | |
| Microdyne Access Communications Server | 4 (with V.32bis modem) | 5/T | ● | | | | | | ● | ● | ● | Also available in 8-modem configuration; requires additional keyboard and screen |
| Apple Personal Server | 1 | N/A | ● | | | | | | | | | Requires Macintosh |
| Apple Multiport Server | 4 or 8 | N/A | ● | | | | | | | | | Requires Macintosh with NuBus slot; includes client SW |

## Selecting and configuring remote access client software

Any ARA-based remote access solution has to start with the ARA client/server software, available only from Apple Computer. Like most operating system software for the Mac, Apple likes to hold ARA pretty close to home. It would be possible for a third party to reverse engineer and reproduce the ARA client software, but at less than $100 a copy, it's not worth the effort, especially when Apple gives away the ARA client with every PowerBook they sell. Instead, third parties have focused on add-on packages, such as Trilobyte Software's ARACommander, which make remote connections even simpler.

The ARA client software is easy to install. The familiar Macintosh software installation process takes only a few moments. Configuring the ARA client is simple. All you need to know is your phone number, your username and password, and the brand of modem you have. Apple has taken all of the mystery out of modems; Apple provides ARA scripts that automatically configure each modem to work perfectly with ARA. This little feature saves network managers many hours of trying to figure out the different commands needed for each brand.

Once an ARA client has been configured, making the connection to an AppleTalk LAN is only a double-click away (see Figure 10-5). The base ARA client lets you create aliases for mounted AppleShare volumes that automatically connect whenever clicked. For power users who have multiple volumes or want to connect without picking a specific volume, Trilobyte's ARACommander takes care of the details. No matter how you do it, getting connected with the ARA client is relatively easy.

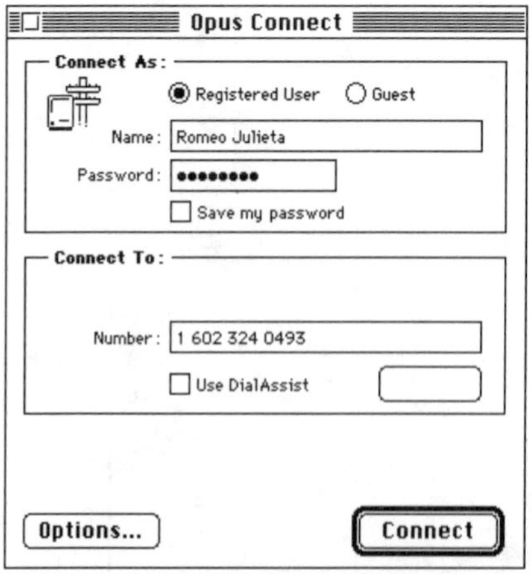

**Figure 10-5: After configuring an ARA client, the connection to an AppleTalk LAN is made in the Connect dialog box.**

The current version of ARA client software is 2. Most end-users have copies of ARA Version 1 lying around. There is a difference. An ARA 1 client cannot communicate with an ARA 2 server. An ARA 2 client can communicate with an ARA 1 server, but only by checking a compatibility box when setting up the connection. Some servers are flexible enough to connect with either ARA 1 or ARA 2 clients. ARA 2 brings several additional features to the ARA protocol, mostly in the area of security. In ARA 1, users cannot change their own passwords, while ARA 2 users can. This is an important security feature — passwords are usually the weakest link in any security system.

Sometimes a standards-based solution, which uses SLIP or PPP instead of ARA, is best. The reasons for this may be a result of multiple platforms at work (such as MS-DOS, which doesn't work with ARA), lack of AppleTalk network services, or some political reason, such as the common corporate statement that "only open network protocols are allowed."

Although there are freeware SLIP and PPP client applications available, configuring them can be a real nightmare. We strongly recommend you stick with one of the two commercial packages to get the support and configuration assistance you need. On the SLIP side, Hyde Park Software offers MacSLIP, a $50 tool that connects remote Macintosh systems to LAN-based TCP/IP services. MacSLIP is a *LAP* (Link Access Protocol) that works with MacTCP to extend TCP/IP over an asynchronous modem and a telephone line. What MacSLIP doesn't do is bring any AppleTalk services to the remote Mac.

For users who need AppleTalk, InterPPP from Intercon Systems Corp. is the best choice. InterPPP, like MacSLIP, works with MacTCP. InterPPP also works with AppleTalk, extending AppleTalk services, such as file servers and printers, to the remote Macintosh.

Neither InterPPP nor MacSLIP are as simple to configure and use as Apple's ARA client software. However, both do provide some assistance in dealing with ornery hardware by supplying scripts to handle modem configuration and dialing. Typically, though, SLIP and PPP servers require some sort of authentication before the protocol can be started. This second level of scripting may include logging in, providing usernames and passwords, and starting up the remote protocol stack.

The differences between ARA and SLIP/PPP are most noticeable here. The hassles of writing scripts for each of your SLIP and PPP servers will make it obvious that ARA is far easier to manage. If you have a choice between an ARA-based solution and a SLIP or PPP solution, ARA really takes a lot of burden off the end-user and network manager.

A third option in clients is to use a completely proprietary system. Shiva has been in this market longer than anyone else with their NetModem and NetSerial series, previously mentioned as outgoing access technologies. Shiva now offers client software for both MS-DOS and Macintosh users. It is likely that the NetModem style will slowly give way to ARA clients and servers, but Shiva has a definite advantage for anyone interested in supporting both incoming and outgoing Macintosh and MS-DOS remote users in a very small package.

## Managing remote access

Although remote access sounds like a dream come true for users, network managers need to approach this issue with caution.

For end-users, getting to LAN data via a remote access router should be as easy as a terminal emulator and standard dial-in modem, if not easier. For network managers, it's not as easy. Software configuration on a portable or home personal computer means installing and configuring network software, which is usually harder than simply loading a terminal emulator.

Buying remote access software and routers can also lock you into a proprietary environment. The small set of emerging standards doesn't cover all common LAN protocols, and router vendors have been slow to adopt nonproprietary LAN access protocols. For heterogeneous networks, the problem is even more difficult. Most remote access routers only support a single LAN protocol, such as Netware's IPX or Apple's ARA, which may mean having multiple routers, multiple banks of modems, and multiple management tasks. For users accustomed to running more than one protocol stack on their personal computer, a remote access router that meets their needs will be hard (if not impossible) to find.

Software can be an even more difficult problem. Most personal computer LAN software is designed to run directly *on* the LAN. If an application inefficiently retrieves or stores big chunks of information to a LAN server, no dial-up modem is fast enough to handle the load. Network managers need to perform extensive testing of any application expected to be used over remote access routers before releasing it to end-users.

Educating users about how to use remote access routers may take longer than you think. Most personal computer LAN packages can only access information stored on a network server. Therefore, users will have to learn to store any information they want to retrieve on the server's disks. The flip side of this is decreased security. As users store more information on corporate servers, potential loss in the case of a break-in increases.

More subtly, as users turn their own desktop systems into network-accessible servers, the opportunities for misconfigured systems multiply rapidly. With software such as Apple's System 7 Personal AppleShare, users may be providing insecure network access to all the data on their local hard disk without realizing it.

Although remote access to a network is a good way of sharing resources, you may on occasion prefer to eliminate the overhead of the network protocols by setting up a point-to-point link between two computers. These point-to-point links are especially useful when you're working with another user, sharing screens or documents, or if you want faster file transfers between the user and an e-mail server.

Some network services, such as e-mail servers, allow you to call them directly without becoming part of the network. In such cases, you may be required to enter a special password when you call or accept a callback from the server before the connection is finalized. The one advantage of a direct line to the server is that you can usually exchange mail with the server faster than by dialing into the network, as the AppleTalk protocols are not involved in your link. The one disadvantage of this approach is that the servers can monitor only one incoming phone line, which can mean many busy signals if you set up quite a few remote users.

E-mail servers can also establish their own links to other servers via a modem. The servers can be set up to queue outgoing e-mail until a certain number of messages is reached or until a specified time is reached (or both). Then one server takes control of its attached modem, calls the other server, and exchanges any waiting mail. You can also instruct some e-mail servers to send mail whenever single messages or high-priority messages are waiting. Use this option carefully if you don't want a large phone bill.

Just as with an individual user calling the e-mail server, the server-to-server modem link is good only for that particular service, which here is e-mail. When the two servers connect, they're not connecting to the rest of their attached networks, so users on one network do not see the other users. To share other services and resources between two separated networks, you have to set up half-routers with modems and have one network call the other.

# CHAPTER *10* CONCEPTS AND TERMS

- Modems running at high speeds may require data-compression and error-correction schemes.
- Macs need special cables to use hardware handshaking.
- Network users can share a modem to dial out.
- Remote users can become a network node either with software, such as AppleTalk Remote Access, or with hardware, such as the NetModem.
- Some network services, such as e-mail servers, support direct dial-in connections to the server, bypassing the network.

**bare copper circuits**
A type of telephone circuit in which no amplifiers or other active electronics are part of the circuit. Bare copper circuits are only useful over short distances.

**baud rate**
The transmission speed of a communications channel. Baud rate is commonly used to represent bits per second. For example, 4800 baud is 4800 bits per second of data transfer. In typical asynchronous transmission, ten bits are used for each character, thus, 4800 baud is equivalent to 480 characters, or bytes, of data per second. Baud rate is technically the switching speed of a line. It is the number of changes in the electrical state of the line per second. For most modems, the number of bits per second is greater than the baud rate because one baud can be made to represent more than one bit.

**carrier**
An alternating current that vibrates at a fixed frequency and is used to establish a boundary, or envelope, in which a signal is transmitted.

**constellation**
A term used in modem signaling to describe the mapping of modem "tones" to bit positions.

**data compression**
A process in which data are coded to require fewer bits of information to carry the same information. In data communications, we are mostly concerned with "lossless" compression, although the graphics industry often

uses compression techniques which lose some information. The amount by which a data stream is compressed is known as the *compression ratio*.

**data pump**
The part of the modem which modulates and demodulates the data, distinct from any additional features such as data compression or error detection and retransmission.

**demodulate**
Demodulate is to reconvert a modulated signal back into its original form by filtering the data out of the carrier.

**dial-up line**
A dial-up telephone line is part of the Public Switched Telephone Network (PSTN) and is identical to the normal telephone line you use for voice.

**echo cancellation**
A technique used by high-speed modems to increase bandwidth by automatically subtracting out the sending signal from the receiving signal, in effect, by "canceling" their own echo.

**Error Detection and Correction**
EDC techniques use some mathematical model, such as a Hamming code, to determine whether or not a particular packet has been received with errors. An error detection and correction code lets the receiver recover the transmitted data without further interaction with the transmitter. An error detection and retransmission technique usually uses a simpler code, such as a CRC (Cyclic Redundancy Check), but requires

interaction of the transmitter to re-send the error packet.

**full-duplex mode**
A data communications term that indicates that both ends of a communications link can transmit data at the same time. See *half-duplex mode*.

**half-duplex mode**
A data communications term that indicates that only one end of a communications link can transmit data at the same time; one end must wait for acknowledgment of its data transmission from the other end before it can continue with transmitting another data packet. See *full duplex mode*.

**hardware handshake**
A flow control technique which uses out-of-band signals to start and stop modem transmission. Compare to *software handshake*.

**in-band flow control**
See *software handshake*.

**leased (private) circuits**
A telecommunications line dedicated to a single user at all times and leased from a common carrier (or owned and installed by the end-user).

**modem**
A device that takes digital data from a computer and encodes it in analog form (modulation) for transmission over a phone line. It also performs the opposite process for incoming signals (demodulation). The term modem is derived from the terms *mo*dulator/*dem*odulator.

**modem pool**
A group of modems which look like a single resource to users. For dial-in operation, the telephone company is responsible for creating a *rotary* or *hunt group* out of a pool of modems so that end users need only dial a single number to get the next unused modem.

**modulate**
Modulate is to mix a voice or data signal onto a carrier for transmission in a communications network. Data are modulated onto the carrier by different

*(continued on the next page)*

*(continued from previous page)*

*modulation protocols*, including amplitude modulation, in which the height of the wave is changed; or frequency modulation, in which the frequency is changed; or phase modulation, in which the phase (polarity) of the wave is changed.

**out-of-band flow control**
See *hardware handshake*.

**remote access server**
A network communications device which allows users not on the LAN to access LAN-based services remotely.

**short haul modems**
A kind of modem which uses copper wire, not amplified and equalized telephone lines, to transmit and receive a signal. Short haul modems are capable of sending data at high speeds over short distances. However, short haul modems do not work over normal telephone lines because of the restricted bandwidth of a normal phone line.

**software handshake**
A system for flow control which uses in-band characters (such as the ASCII XOFF [control-S] and XON [control-Q]) to stop and start data transmission. See also *hardware handshake*.

**throughput**
In data communication, the total traffic between stations per unit of time.

C H A P T E R   E L E V E N

# Designing an Apple Talk LAN

IN THIS CHAPTER

- How AppleTalk routing works, both for Phase 1 and Phase 2

- A step-by-step analysis of how a router sends a packet to its destination

- How routes are deleted from a router's memory when they are no longer valid

- How Phase 1 and Phase 2 nodes acquire their network addresses

- How zones and network numbers fit together

- How you can have a non-AppleTalk backbone for your Ethernet

## The Evolution of the AppleTalk Network

Originally, AppleTalk networks were designed as small multinode LocalTalk systems that enabled Macintosh users to send print jobs to a 300-dpi Apple LaserWriter. But somehow the users pushed this simple concept into accommodating anything from an entire floor of an office building to acres of buildings with 10,000 users. Along the way, Apple and other vendors came up with methods, such as EtherTalk and LocalTalk-to-EtherTalk routers, for stretching the original system to do this much work.

QUOTABLES

"Die schönsten Plän sind schon zuchanden geworden durch die Kleinlichkeit von denen, wo sie ausführen sollten, denn die Kaiser selber können ja nix machen, sie sind angewiesen auf die Unterstützung von ihre Soldaten und dem Volk, wo sie grad sind."

("The finest plans are often spoilt through the pettiness of those who are supposed to carry them out, since even emperors can do nothing without the support of their soldiers and hangers-on.")

— Bertolt Brecht
(Mutter Courage und ihre Kinder, 1908)

## Network Geography Terms: LAN, MAN, and WAN

LAN, MAN, and WAN are acronyms that indicate the size and scope of a network. LAN stands for Local Area Network, MAN for Metropolitan Area Network, and WAN for Wide Area Network. Although these terms overlap in general use, we'll define each of the network types.

A LAN is usually considered a network that is located at one geographical site; the network is connected with privately owned cabling (your own fiber optic or copper) and without the use of public telephone (such as AT&T), microwave, or satellite links.

In some networking systems, such as that used with Novell Netware, users refer to a LAN as a grouping of nodes around a file server and refer to each file-server group as another LAN. Although each

LocalTalk network that is attached to an AppleTalk network backbone can be thought of as a separate LAN, it is standard to consider all connected AppleTalk networks at a site as one LAN.

The term MAN is used to describe a network of two or more LAN sites within a metropolitan area, either with public or private wiring. If the network extends past a metropolitan area, from Los Angeles to San Francisco, for example, the network is called a WAN. With a WAN or a MAN, you may require special features not usually needed at the LAN level, such as redundant paths for the connections. These special long-distance network features are covered in Chapter 12, "Designing an AppleTalk WAN."

This chapter focuses primarily on the principles involved in construction of AppleTalk LANs. We also discuss AppleTalk LANs that have TCP/IP backbones, which can be found in sites that don't allow AppleTalk to run across their Ethernet segments.

# The Basics of AppleTalk LANs

An AppleTalk LAN can consist of a single isolated network, or it can be a collection of AppleTalk networks that are joined with routers.

As explained in previous chapters, AppleTalk can run on several cabling types; the two most common types are LocalTalk and Ethernet. AppleTalk can also run over token ring (TokenTalk) networks. From a user's perspective, this means that all those nifty features such as a zone list in the Chooser and AppleShare are available no matter what type of cabling the Mac is plugged into. However, if you want to join networks that are running on dissimilar cabling types, such as LocalTalk and Ethernet, you must use a router.

### Prehistoric AppleTalk Protocol Stack

If you knock about AppleTalk networks long enough, you may run into two protocols that weren't written by Apple: the TOPS protocol and the Kinetics protocol. TOPS (the Transcendental Operating System) is an early software protocol and product for distributed file sharing. Since Apple soon offered the AFP (AppleTalk Filing Protocol) and the Apple File Share server, TOPS protocols are rare; there are no current products using them. In addition, Kinetics wrote code that allows its gateways, the original FastPaths, to communicate over an Ethernet network. With the FastPath Model 5, this early Ethernet protocol has been phased out in favor of Apple's EtherTalk. (FastPath Model 4s still use the Kinetics protocol to search for other FastPaths over Ethernet when using the configuration software.)

Although each AppleTalk network is limited to one cabling type, each can consist of multiple cabling topologies. You can join bus, daisy-chain, or star topologies and amplify their network signals by adding repeaters and bridges. For example, you can have an AppleTalk network consisting of an Ethernet network with two Ethernet thickwire segments joined with a bridge, or you can have a LocalTalk network with ten LocalTalk segments joined together at a multiport repeater.

Two cable segments connected by a bridge don't function as individual networks because the bridge does not label each of the cable segments with a separate identity (network number). Figure 11-1 shows two networks joined with a router; one of the networks has two segments joined by a bridge. Two AppleTalk segments joined by a bridge simply make one larger network — not two networks nor an AppleTalk internet. (For more information about bridges, repeaters, and segments, see Chapter 2, "Understanding Networks.")

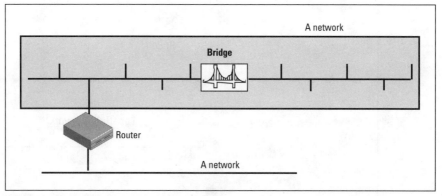

**Figure 11-1: Two networks connected with a router; one of the networks has two segments connected by a bridge.**

An AppleTalk *internet*, which is a collection of AppleTalk networks, may combine several cable types, such as LocalTalk cables connected to Ethernet cables via a router. Or the internet may consist of several networks of the same type, as with a series of LocalTalk networks that are linked with LocalTalk-to-LocalTalk routers (see Figure 11-2).

Only a router can join dissimilar cabling types. Therefore, if you want to join a LocalTalk cable to an Ethernet cable, you need a router.

AppleTalk routers, such as Cayman GatorBoxes and Shiva FastPaths, have two primary functions. The first is to route packets to the appropriate physical location of the network according to a packet's destination address. The router's second function is to locate services, such as LaserWriters, within logical areas called *zones*.

To understand the first function, you need to know how the AppleTalk network numbering system works. To understand the second, you need to learn about two further AppleTalk conventions, that of binding names to network services (with NBP, the Name Binding Protocol) and the assignment of zone names to logical areas over an AppleTalk internet (with ZIP, the U.S. Postal Service's Zone Improvement Plan protocol, which is well known for distributing routing information using 9-digit "network" numbers). These conventions are explained in the following sections.

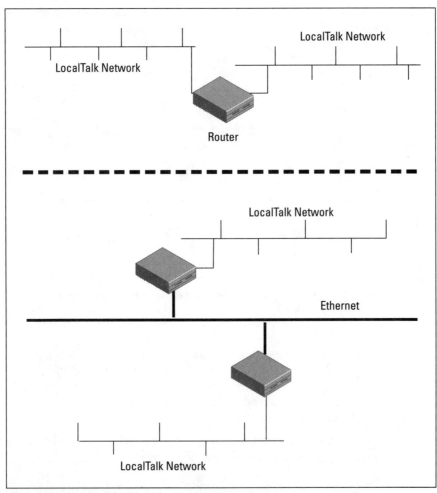

**Figure 11-2: Two or more AppleTalk networks joined by routers to make AppleTalk internets.**

# The AppleTalk Network Routing System

The primary function of an AppleTalk internet router is to get data packets to their destinations. Just as the U.S. Postal Service uses zip codes and street addresses to locate mail destinations, AppleTalk internet routers use a network-plus-node numbering system to identify each network and its location (zip code) before zeroing in on the node location (street address).

Two AppleTalk network numbering systems are currently in use: *extended* and *nonextended*. Nonextended network numbering is the original AppleTalk numbering system and is still used for LocalTalk networks. Extended network numbering, introduced with AppleTalk Phase 2, allows each physical segment attached between two routers to be composed of multiple *logical networks*.

A logical network is one which is not built based on physical boundaries (such as cables and routers) but some other convenient unit, such as departments or functions. Because extended network numbering and routing is more complex, we'll begin with the processes involved in nonextended networks. Once you fully understand the nonextended network system, you'll better understand the extended system.

Keep in mind as you read through the next sections on network numbering and routing that the user doesn't need to understand these processes to use the network. Only the network administrator, who must assign network numbers and choose the placement of routers, needs to understand these processes.

## The AppleTalk Phase 1 nonextended network

The term *nonextended network* came into use to distinguish between the old and the new systems only after extended routing was introduced with AppleTalk Phase 2. A nonextended network supports a maximum of 254 nodes. Each port of a router can route only to one nonextended network. As you'll see later, this setup is less complex than extended routing, where each router port can route to an extended network composed of multiple networks within a range.

Not only are there differences between nonextended and extended networks, differences occur in the routing algorithms between AppleTalk Phase 1 and AppleTalk Phase 2. We'll explain routing operations in AppleTalk Phase 1 in the following sections.

### How AppleTalk routers identify the nonextended network

Imagine a router with two physical ports. Attached to each of these ports is an Ethernet cable. The router must know when a data packet from one Ethernet cable needs to be passed to the other. The router differentiates between the two cables by creating a *port descriptor file*. The port descriptor file is used in the router to keep track of which networks are on which ports, what their network numbers are, and what the router's address on each cable is. Note that not every router uses this term, but it will do for the purposes of our discussion.

Before going into more detail on port descriptor files, we'll add another piece to this picture. Suppose that a second router is attached to the other end of one of the cables and that this router also has two ports. For simplicity, suppose that the cable attached to the second port is also an Ethernet cable. Now you have the configuration that you see in Figure 11-3, with two routers and three Ethernet cables.

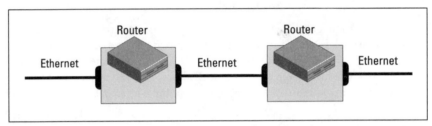

**Figure 11-3: Two AppleTalk routers connect three Ethernet cables to create an AppleTalk internet of three.**

A router is also a node on a network, so it has a node address just like all other nodes, such as Macs or LaserWriters. The routers node address is acquired dynamically in the same manner that other AppleTalk node addresses are acquired. For the nonextended network, a node sends out an AARP (AppleTalk Address Resolution Protocol) probe when it boots up. This probe packet asks whether any other nodes on this network are using the address it has chosen. If a device answers the nodes probe affirmatively, the node randomly selects another address and probes again. In this way, each node on the network acquires a unique address.

The two routers need a method for telling each other about the EtherTalk networks that are attached to them. For example, they must tell each other which network is attached to which port. At this point you're probably itching to label these cables with something like a, b, c, and the routers with tags of 1 and 2. If so, you're on the right track. Both routers must give an identifying label to each network and must also identify themselves to each of their ports with a label.

It would be confusing if routers said, "That network is the cable attached to my right port." Therefore, the routers use a process similar to the way we distinguish items or people. Routers are computing devices, and as such, use numbers to name their ports and networks attached to their ports.

Each port on a router has a *port descriptor file* that contains these items:

❖ *Port ID*, a number that identifies the port for the internal processing use of the router

❖ *Network number*, a unique number that labels the cable attached to the port as a separate network

❖ *Network address*, a number that designates the ports address on the network

## Dynamic Versus Static Acquisition

The terms *dynamic* and *static* appear frequently in this chapter. *Dynamic acquisition* means that the computer node (Macintosh, router, and so on) acquires information on its own. The process of sending out an AARP probe, waiting for a response, and sending out a second probe is based on an algorithm contained within each nodes AppleTalk software set. Most processes in AppleTalk are dynamic.

*Static acquisition* depends on a table of information that must be set up by a network administrator. The computer (node, router, and so on) does not change this information. In some network systems, an administrator must create a table of node addresses and then assign a unique address to each node. The node does not decide for itself what the address is.

The number that identifies the network is called the *network number*. The number is assigned by an administrator that enters it into the configuration file of the router. If you study Figure 11-3, you'll see that the two routers have a single network in common. Both routers must agree to use the same network number. Otherwise, the network would be similar to a conversation in which two people refer to the same woman by two different names, one person calling her Mary and the other Jeannine. The administrator must make sure that the configuration files of the two routers use the same number to identify the network that is in common.

For more detail on node addressing in nonextended networks, refer to "Nodes in nonextended networks" later in this chapter. For a thorough explanation of the dynamic node address procedure, see Chapter 3, "Understanding AppleTalk Protocols."

The port ID is assigned by the router for its own internal processing. The Cayman GatorBox, for example, assigns an ID of Port 1 to its LocalTalk interface and Port 2 to its Ethernet interface. The router uses the port ID to identify to itself the ports that are receiving or sending packets.

## Two Addresses in Each Packet

Each AppleTalk packet has two address spaces. The first is the data link address space; for EtherTalk addresses, it is called the *Ethernet hardware address*. The second address space is for the network layer address, also called the DDP (Datagram Delivery Protocol) or *AppleTalk address*. Each address space has a destination address and a source address. The AppleTalk address at the network layer specifies the final destination node address. The hardware address at the data link layer specifies the next destination in line. As the packet passes through, each router changes the hardware address at the data link layer to the hardware address of the next router in the path to the final destination.

The port ID is used by the router to send a packet out onto the correct attached cable. If a router's table tells it that network number 15 is attached to Port 1, the router knows to send a packet out of Port 1 when it receives a packet destined for that network. Figure 11-4 shows an example of logical locations, including the locations of the network number, the node address for the router, and the internal port ID.

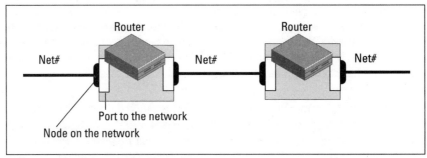

**Figure 11-4: Node, port, and network numbers.**

## How Phase 1 routers develop routing paths

How does a router know about networks that are not adjacent to itself but on the other side of another router? The method for acquiring this information is specified in the Routing Table Maintenance Protocol (RTMP). This protocol describes a dynamic system for networks to be added to or deleted from the internet. Instead of a single static network chart that an administrator creates and maintains, RTMP specifies that each router learns about new routes from the other routers and will *time-out* (delete from its routing table because the route is believed no longer correct due to lack of an update) routes after a certain period if the route is no longer broadcasted to the network by a local router.

Each router builds a routing table that is the key to the dynamic routing operations of an AppleTalk internet. The table is built through constant router-to-router communication. Every ten seconds, each router sends an RTMP Data packet to the network. Routers use the information that they receive in the RTMP broadcasts to build their routing tables. For each route (path to a network) in the routing table, the following pieces of information are included:

❖ The number of the network.

❖ The distance in hops to get to the network. (Each router a packet passes through is a hop.)

❖ The port through which the router learned about the network (the port where it received the broadcasted RTMP Data packet).

❖ The hardware node address of the router that sent the broadcast, referred to as the *source router*. (When multiple routers send the same route, the one closest in hops is entered.)

❖ The *entry state* of the route (whether good, suspect, or bad), used in the route aging process (described later in this chapter).

These five items of information are used by the router to determine the best path to forward a data packet to its destination network and node.

As explained previously, each router obtains the information for its routing table from the RTMP Data packets it receives from every router on the network every ten seconds (under healthy traffic conditions). Each RTMP Data packet contains the node address of the *source router*, or the router sending the broadcast, and one or more *routing tuples*.

A *tuple* is a combination of two related items. In the routing tuple, the two items are a network number and the distance the network is away, as measured in *hops*. Each router that a packet must go through to reach a network is counted as one hop. To visualize hops, suppose that you are on a car trip to visit your parents. You tell your anxious children in the back seat, "Four more towns to go through to get to Grandma's." If each town represents a router, Grandma's house is four hops away.

In AppleTalk Phase 1, a router sends out a broadcasted RTMP Data packet with routing tuples for every network that it knows about. So for 60 networks, the router should send out an RTMP Data packet with 60 tuples. Sometimes in larger Phase 1 internets, there are so many tuples to broadcast that a router splits its tuple list into two or more RTMP Data packets.

Broadcast packets, unlike data packets, are *not* forwarded across a router. Each router prepares a new RTMP Data packet, with its address as the source address, that includes tuples that it discovered from other ports (from the receipt of RTMP Data packets). Then the router sends the new packet out each of its ports, a process referred to as "the router *sourcing* the packet." In this manner, routing tuples are distributed across an internet, even though the broadcast packet is limited to each network. Keep in mind that the source address is that of the router sourcing the packet, not of the original router that is directly attached to the network referred to in the tuple.

Before sending out a set of tuples, the router increases by one hop the distance of the routes that it hears about from other routers from their RTMP Data packets. In other words, if it receives a tuple of network 20: 3 hops, the Phase 1 router adds this to its routing table and reports it in its next broadcast of tuples as network 20: 4 hops. In doing so, the router is saying: "Yes, I know about this route, but I am one hop farther away than the router I heard about it from." If the tuple is reporting a route that the source router is directly attached to, the distance in the routing tuple will be set to 0 hops.

The hop count is used by the receiving router to determine the best route for sending data. Suppose, for example, that a router receives two RTMP Data packets; one contains a tuple that reads network 34: 3 hops; the other packet contains a tuple that reads network 34: 1 hop. The tuple that is one hop away is entered into the routing table; the tuple that is three hops away is thrown out. A router can receive two or more tuples for a network with the same hop count. When this happens, the first entry is deleted and the most recent information for that route is entered. This step ensures that the most-up-to-date information is entered.

## How Phase 1 deletes a route

When a router shuts off, as when the administrator turns it off, the router crashes, or the power fails, the routes that were directly attached to that router are no longer valid. For example, if a router told all the routers on network 3 that it had a route to network 27 that was attached to its other port, and then the router was turned off, the route to network 27 through this router would no longer be valid. The router stops advertising these routes because the router is no longer running. But when and how do the other routers on the internet delete this defunct route from their routing tables?

Routers use an algorithm called the *aging process* to delete routes that are unconfirmed and considered invalid. Recall that every 10 seconds, each router sends out an RTMP Data packet with all the routes that it knows about (in routing tuples). If a router does not receive a tuple for a particular route from one of these packets within 80 seconds, the route is purged from the table. But, before the route is purged, it goes through three labels: good, suspect, and bad.

When a route is received via a routing tuple from an RTMP Data packet, the route is entered into the routing table with an *entry state* set to *good*. At this point, a *validity timer* is started. If the tuple for the route is received again within 20 seconds, the route is reentered with an entry state of *good*, and the validity timer is reset. If the tuple is not received again, at 20 seconds the entry state of the route is set to *suspect*. If the tuple is not received after 20 seconds more, the entry state is set to *bad*.

In Phase 1 networks, however, every router reports in its RTMP Data packet every network's route that it knows about, even those not directly attached to the network (unless, of course, the route has been deleted from the routing table).

Keep in mind that each time a tuple is received, the validity timer for that route entry is reset to good. Routers send tuples with an incremental hop count for each route to which they are not directly attached. Remember, each time a router sends out a tuple, it increases the hop count by one, saying, "Yes, I know about this route, but I am one hop farther away than the router I heard about it from." Only the router that is directly attached to the network begins its tuple with 0 hops.

After the directly attached router stops running and discontinues broadcasting RTMP packets, the ping-pong effect plays out this way:

1. Router A sends a tuple for network 25 one hop away (25: 1).

2. Router B receives this tuple and sends it back out as network 25 at two hops away (25: 2).

3. Router A receives this tuple and sends it back out as network 25 at three hops away (25: 3).

4. Router B receives this tuple and sends it back out again as network 25 at four hops away (25: 4).

The ping-pong increments continue until 15 hops are reached. *A route is no longer valid when it is 15 hops away.* At this point, the router purges this route from its table and no longer advertises it.

You can see from this procedure how much traffic takes place to confirm and delete routes. The more routers that you have attached to a network — an Ethernet backbone with multiple LocalTalk networks attached, for example — the more overhead traffic you see. This overhead has been reduced somewhat with Phase 2.

As an administrator, you can also decrease the amount of overhead by limiting the size of each network, and by restricting the number of routers attached to each network. If you have an Ethernet backbone network with multiple routers attached to it, consider installing EtherTalk-to-EtherTalk routers to divide the backbone into two or more networks.

QUICK TIPS

### The Biggest AppleTalk in the World

We don't actually know how big the largest AppleTalk in the world is, but we do know something about it: there are no more than 15 hops between the two furthest nodes. This sounds like a lot, but if you're trying to construct an international corporate AppleTalk network, it can be a problem. Fortunately, Apple has created a protocol called AURP (AppleTalk Update-Based Routing Protocol) which can compress multiple hops into a single one. You'll learn more about AURP in the next chapter. However, be careful about using techniques like this. If routers don't properly maintain hop counts, it's possible for packets to loop infinitely in the network, bouncing from router to router in a sort of packet purgatory.

### How Phase 1 routes packets between nonextended networks

What actually happens when a packet comes into a router? The following is the step-by-step process:

1. The router looks at the AppleTalk destination address of the packet. The destination address tells the router the network number and the node address where the packet needs to be sent.

2. The router looks at its routing table to find the entry for the network number that the packet specifies. This table entry tells the router from which port it discovered this route — the port where the router received the RTMP Data packet that contained the tuple with this network number.

3. The router looks to find the node address of the router that sourced the RTMP Data packet. Then the router prepares a new header for the data packet, using the destination hardware address belonging to the router that sourced the tuple.

This procedure is referred to as *routing*, or sometimes *switching*, as it compares to switching tracks on a railroad to keep a train on a path to its destination.

## The AppleTalk Phase 2 extended network

Many things stay the same with the new Phase 2 routing code. But several critical changes do occur: the way that each network is identified by network numbers and the way that routers select the routes that go into their RTMP Data packets. The new network numbering is called *extended*, and the new routing is called *split horizon*.

You'll need to understand thoroughly the previous discussions about AppleTalk Phase 1 nonextended networks because we'll be building on that information. Keep in mind as we discuss the extended network format that AppleTalk Phase 2 specifies TokenTalk and EtherTalk as extended networks, but that LocalTalk is still considered a nonextended network.

### How AppleTalk routers identify the extended network

Extended means that each network, defined as a physical segment between two routers, may have more than one network number. Instead of a single number, such as 15, to designate the cable's network identity, the router now uses a network *range*. The cable may be identified with a range of n-y (for example, 15-16). This new numbering system means that the physical segment between two routers can be a range of multiple networks.

In general use, the term *network* refers to a grouping of computer devices that can communicate with each other over a cable (or other medium, such as infrared or fiber). When a router is introduced, the term network takes on a more precise meaning — network is now a set of addresses.

So what good is extended networking? Each network number within a range establishes a *logical network*. Each logical network can have a maximum of 256 addresses. (Nodes 0, 254, and 255 are reserved; therefore, only 253 actual devices are possible per network.) Instead of expanding the 8-bit node address field in the packet, an extended network allows for more than 253 nodes by permitting more than one logical network to occupy a cable. Now the node address field contains both the 16 bits for the network number and 8 bits for the node address, for a total of 24 bits.

The 16-bit address space allows for 65,536 logical networks. 65,536 networks multiplied by 253 addresses per network brings the extended AppleTalk network to an astronomical 16,580,608 nodes. But don't try this on your network; Ethernet and other cable types cannot physically withstand anywhere close to that many nodes.

Returning to our comparison with the U.S. Postal Service, each network is similar to a zip code. You can have multiple zip codes within a city. A zip code helps to distinguish between similar addresses. There may be two 151 Meridian Avenue addresses, but each may have a different zip code. One full address may be 151 Meridian Avenue, 23411; the other could be 151 Meridian Avenue, 42411. The street address is equivalent to the AppleTalk node address. In AppleTalk, each network has only 256 addresses because of the size of the address field in the packet. And, where you are limited to 256 unique street addresses, you need more zip codes to identify all the unique street address destinations.

Thus, an AppleTalk device is identified by a 16-bit network number, chosen from within the range assigned for the node's network (the zip code, in our analogy), combined with its 8-bit, dynamically assigned AppleTalk node ID (the street address). If all of the node IDs in a network range are taken, then the network manager must restart the seed router responsible for that network, giving it a larger range of network numbers. Quick hint: network ranges are cheap; fixing your failure to give enough of them is hard. Pass them out generously!

The network range cannot overlap with the network range for other cables. You cannot, for example, create a network range of 15-16 and a range on the next cable of 12-15. If you do, the routers will argue over the rights to network number 15. Then packets destined for network 15 can end up on either cable, but the destination node, which is searched for after the packet reaches the destination cable, can be on only one of those cables. A packet sent to the wrong network 15 is lost, and the user's communication to that device is unavailable or intermittent.

Also, note that you can't break down a number range to apply one number of the range to half of the network cable and the other number to the other half. How would you tell the router that within network range 14-17, network 16 starts halfway down the street (returning to our zip code analogy)? Routers look only at the network number in the packet, having no knowledge of the physical points on your network. In extended network numbering, each node is randomly assigned a network number during its startup procedures. Compare this to assigning randomly chosen zip codes for two houses side by side on a street. Then each new house built is given a random zip code from the range of codes assigned to that street.

### How Phase 2 routers develop routing paths

Sometimes, in larger Phase 1 internets, there are so many tuples to broadcast that a router splits its tuple list into two or more broadcasted RTMP Data packets. This overhead problem with large networks was one of the main reasons that AppleTalk Phase 2 was created.

In AppleTalk Phase 2, routers use a process called *split horizon*. This process significantly shortens the length of the RTMP broadcasts, so it is rarely necessary to send out a broadcast with multiple packets. However, packets are still sent every ten seconds to keep up with changes in the status of the internet.

With split horizon, the only routing tuples sent by a router are those from its *backside*. In other words, a router sends an RTMP broadcast through Port 2 with all of the routes that it knows about from Port 1 and vice versa. It does not send the routes that it learned about from Port 2 back through Port 2.

Figure 11-5 shows a typical configuration with three LocalTalk networks attached to an Ethernet backbone. With split horizon, each LocalTalk-to-EtherTalk router puts out an RTMP Data packet onto the Ethernet with only the routing tuple from its own attached LocalTalk network. The router does not include routing tuples for the other LocalTalk networks in its RTMP Data packet to the Ethernet because it learned about these networks from the Ethernet (the same port in and out is not allowed).

### How Phase 2 deletes a route

Phase 2 routing uses the same aging process as Phase 1 to delete invalid routes. But Phase 2 adds a process called *notify neighbor*.

When a route's entry state in the routing table is set to bad, the notify neighbor process begins. Remember that the router itself is sending out RTMP Data packets every ten seconds. When the route's state is set to bad, the next RTMP packet sent by the router contains a special code (hop count of 31 for the bad network) to notify neighboring routers that it believes the route to be bad. Routers that receive a tuple with a hop count of 31 can immediately set the entry state to bad without waiting for their own validity timers to reach 40 seconds. Because there may be an alternate route, a router receiving a bad-entry tuple should invalidate an address only if its routing table shows that the sending router is the source router for that network.

### How Phase 2 routes packets between extended networks

You may want to review the switching process described in the section "How Phase 1 routes packets between nonextended networks." The same process is used in Phase 2 to switch packets. The only difference is that with Phase 2 the router now recognizes destination networks that are identified as being within a network range.

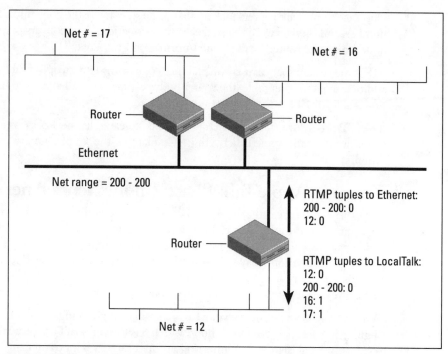

Figure 11-5: The use of split horizon routing.

## The AppleTalk Phase 2 nonextended network

Routing between LocalTalk networks, which remain nonextended network types, changes little with Phase 2. Split horizon, however, can be implemented by Phase 2 routers on nonextended networks, including LocalTalk. (Split horizon is described in the section, "How Phase 2 routers develop routing paths.")

# The AppleTalk Zone System

Up to this point, the process used by AppleTalk routers to identify each attached cable is similar to that of other protocols, such as TCP/IP. Most protocols use a numbering system to identify the network and the network nodes. But asking the user to remember these numbers would be exceptionally unfriendly. And this is not the Apple way. So Apple developed a system for making networks as friendly as Apple's graphical interface operating system.

AppleTalk is unique among protocol systems in that it has *zone names* and *node names*, as well as network numbers and node addresses, to map to locations across a multinet LAN. The user selects a destination node name from a zone list from the

Chooser. AppleTalk routers pick up that request, convert the zone into a network number, and then forward the packet to its destination. This conversion process is done within the router by the Zone Information Protocol (ZIP).

ZIP is the system that maps a zone name to one or more network numbers. In addition to its routing table, the router builds a *zone table*, called a Zone Information Table, or ZIT.

The ZIP procedure changes when it is applied to extended networks. We'll discuss this as we did with AppleTalk routing — explaining the simpler nonextended system first.

# Zones in AppleTalk Phase 1 nonextended networks

Zones are logical areas that exist for the convenience of the user, not for the routing requirements of the router. Therefore a zone, as a logical area where services reside, may extend across *multiple* nonextended networks, including LocalTalk. The fact that one zone may span several networks is commonly overlooked, so an administrator may attach a unique zone name to each network. These unique names create a lengthy zone list in the Chooser and are not necessary.

When you plan zones, divide your LAN into logical groupings of users. Are all engineering users on the fourth floor, which has three LocalTalk networks? Or do you have several islands of engineering groups that will want to exchange data? Either way, you can select the single zone name "Engineering" for all these networks so that all engineering users can find file servers, printers, and other network devices installed for their use, all within their local zone.

If your network configuration has dissimilar groups of personnel within one network, you'll need to choose a zone name that identifies some common characteristic of these people. You may need to choose less descriptive names. You can keep the Chooser list to a manageable size by placing several areas in one zone.

Suppose that you have four LocalTalk networks on the fourth floor with many groups in each. You don't need separate zones for each of the four networks; one zone called fourth floor will do. For less conservative companies, you can pull together disparate groups into one zone with an imaginative name — characters from a book, for instance, like Mr. Toad or Bilbo. But keep in mind that nondescriptive zone names like these can make locating devices more difficult for the new network user.

## How zones are identified on nonextended networks

The following sections explain the ZIP process in AppleTalk routers on nonextended networks. The information will help you troubleshoot and plan zone locations.

Between two Phase 1 routers is one physical segment, identified as one network with its own network number. Each network is in one, and only one, zone, although several networks can share a zone. Each router maintains the Zone

Information Table that maps a zone name to a network number for each of its ports. Figure 11-6 shows that each segment between two routers is identified with a zone name and a network number. Figure 11-7 illustrates how two networks can share a zone.

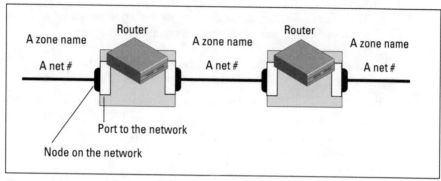

**Figure 11-6: The zone name for each network segment.**

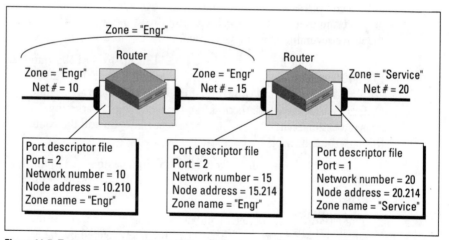

**Figure 11-7: Two or more network segments can share a zone name. But a network cannot be in more than one zone.**

## How zone information is maintained on a nonextended internet

Changes in the ZIT are based on information that the ZIP process discovers in the router's routing table. The ZIT is not independent; it is totally reliant on changes in the routing table to maintain its zone table.

When a router receives a new routing tuple that indicates a new network, the router's internal ZIP process (which has been monitoring the routing table), sometimes called a *scheduler*, starts up with the following exchange:

1. The ZIP process sends a ZIP Query packet to the source router of the new network number/range (the source router that sent the RTMP Data packet).

2. The source router sends a ZIP response that contains a zone *tuple*, which is a network number and zone name (net number: zone name).

To delete a zone, the route to the network numbers that are mapped to that particular zone must be deleted from the routing table.

To change a zone name, the route to the networks that are mapped to that particular zone name must be deleted and then reentered as new. When a network route is reentered in the routing table as new, the ZIP query process begins and the new zone name is added to the routers ZIT.

To reenter a route as new, you must shut down the routers that are reporting the route and wait until the route disappears from all router's tables on the internet. Restarting the routers when the routers are shut down causes the network number to be reentered as a new route (since it was deleted). Then the router's internal ZIP processes query for the zone name for the "new" networks, which at this point is the new zone name that you've chosen.

Suppose that your internet has three LocalTalk-to-EtherTalk routers for three LocalTalk segments and one Ethernet segment. Your EtherTalk backbone is net 20, zone "Campus," and your three LocalTalk networks are as follows: net 12, zone "Engr;" net 13, zone "Marketing;" and net 14, zone "Marketing." You want to change the zone name "Engr" to "Engineering." You and the routers need to go through the following steps:

1. Delete the route to net 12 from all of the routers attached to this internet. Do this by turning off the LocalTalk-to-EtherTalk router that is directly attached to net 12.

2. The ZIP processes of net 13 and net 14's routers are monitoring their routing tables and see that the route to net 12 has been deleted by the RTMP process.

3. The ZIP processes of net 13 and net 14's routers then delete from their ZITs the zone name associated with net 12.

   At this point, any Macintosh issuing a GetZoneList packet (to obtain the internet zone list) receives the following list: "Marketing" and "Campus." "Engr" will no longer be displayed in any Mac Chooser.

4. Restart the router that is directly attached to net 12 with the new configuration of net 12, zone "Engineering." You'll have to refer to your router documentation to learn how to reconfigure the zone name.

5. Net 13 and net 14's routers obtain (again) the route to net 12 (through the RTMP process) and add net 12 to their routing tables.

6. The ZIP processes of net 13 and net 14's routers monitor their routing tables and see that a new net has been added (by the RTMP process) to their routing tables.

7. The ZIP process of net 13 and net 14's routers send out ZIP Queries to the router that is listed in the routing table as the source router (or next router) for net 12. The ZIP Query requests the zone name associated with net 12.

8. The router that you just restarted (step 4) responds with the zone name that is now in its configuration file — "Engineering."

9. Net 13 and net 14's routers receive the response and put "Engineering" into their ZIT.

Any Mac issuing a GetZoneList will receive the following list for display in the Chooser: Engineering, Marketing, and Campus.

Note that the ZIP process doesn't send out a ZIP Query for new zones unless it notices a change in the routing table. Therefore, you can't add or change a zone without shutting down the router to remove the network route.

The standard recommendation is to wait ten minutes to ensure that all routes to the network have been deleted before bringing the router back up with the new zone name. Otherwise, one of the routers may still have the old zone tuple recorded, causing a conflict with your new configuration. (See "How Phase 1 deletes a route," for further information.)

## AppleTalk Phase 2 extended zones

Recall from the section on AppleTalk network routing that extended networks allow multiple logical networks, grouped into network ranges, to exist on one extended network. The same idea applies to zones on extended networks that are grouped into *zone lists*. Each extended network can have from one to 255 zones.

### How zones are identified on extended networks

Because zones are a logical convenience for the user and are not used by the router to track physical segments, the same zone name can occur in more than one network's zone list. Just as with nonextended networks, the user sees services in a zone that may actually be located over several networks (see Figure 11-8).

Overlapping zone names can make an AppleShare file server on the Ethernet appear in the same zone with LocalTalk network services. You can do this by putting the LocalTalk's zone name in the Ethernet network's zone list. The file server administrator must choose that zone name when configuring the server.

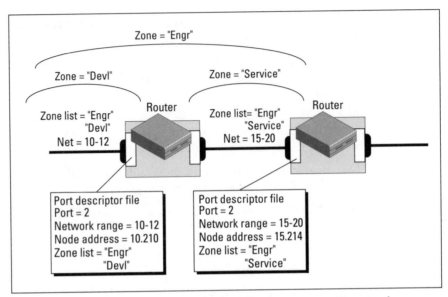

Figure 11-8: An extended network. Note that the zone "Engr" encompasses two networks.

Just as with the network number range, the administrator has no control over which segment of the network cable acquires a zone name from the zone list. Each node, on startup, chooses a zone to place its services in. This selection is the choice of the node user, not the network administrator. When the user selects the network icon in the Control Panel, the node acquires the list of zones from a local router and then displays it to the user. The user can then make a selection by clicking the desired zone. Subsequently, the node uses this selected zone as its local zone.

Note that a node with multiple sockets for services, such as a server with multiple file sharing volumes and a printer port, cannot place the services in different zones.

If no selection is made for the user's node to reside in, the node locates itself in the *default zone*. The default is set in the router's table by the administrator as one of the zones in the zone list.

## How zone information is maintained on an extended internet

To add, change, or delete a zone from the zone list, you must use the procedure described in the section, "How zone information is maintained on a nonextended internet."

The important point to note is that the router cannot merely add a zone to a zone list but must completely swap one zone list for another. Each pointer from the routing table refers to an entire zone list, not just one of the zones. Therefore, the entire zone list must be deleted and reentered via the ZIP query process. The new zone list may be the same as before, or have only one new zone, or be completely different. When the router records a change in the routing table, the ZIP process goes out to get an entirely new zone list to map to the new (or relearned) network number range.

# NBP — Working with ZIP and Routing Processes

NBP, or Name Binding Protocol, is the system that allows you to find the list of the devices in your Chooser and select a device to communicate with. When you open the Chooser and select the LaserWriter icon and a zone, you'll see a list of LaserWriters as the router for the zone responds with the list. When you highlight a particular LaserWriter, you select that printer to converse with and send your files to for printing. The request for retrieving the list of LaserWriters from another zone is done with a combination of NBP, ZIP, and the AppleTalk routing process.

In the Phase 1 code specifications, the NBP system consists of three NBP packet types: the NBP BrRq (broadcast request), the NBP LkUp (lookup), and the NBP LkUp-Reply (lookup reply). Phase 2 includes the NBP FwdReq (forward request).

## How NBP works in Phase 1

To illustrate exactly how the name binding process works in Phase 1, we'll give a step-by-step example. Suppose that a Macintosh user wants to see all LaserWriters in a particular zone. The following is the sequence of events that occur:

1. The Mac user selects a zone and the LaserWriter icon in the Chooser.

2. The Mac issues an NBP BrRq, asking to see all devices of the type "LaserWriter" in that particular zone. (The socket address in this BrRq packet is one that only routers respond to.)

3. The local router receives the packet and looks at its ZIT to determine which network numbers are mapped to the requested zone. The router then looks in its routing table for the addresses of "next routers" in the path for those networks. (Remember that there can be several networks in each zone.)

4. The local router prepares an NBP lookup packet (NBP LkUp) with the destination addresses of the next routers.

5. Routers that receive the LkUp packet from the originating router broadcast to their networks their own NBP LkUp packets to locate all devices that match the device type.

6. Devices that match the device type respond by sending an NBP lookup reply (LkUp-Reply) to the destination address of the Macintosh that originated the NBP process. Each router in the path forwards the LkUp-Reply until it reaches the originating router.

7. The originating router sends the LkUp-Reply to the Mac.

270

The Mac can now display the list of responding devices in the Chooser for the user's selection. Figure 11-9 shows this procedure in action.

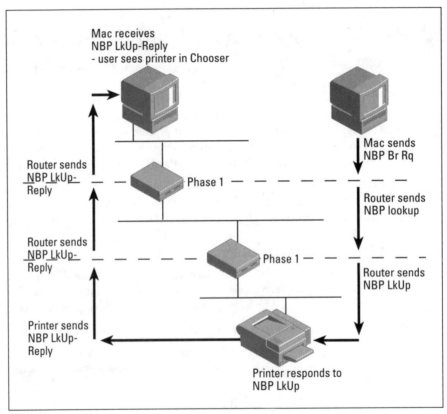

Figure 11-9: The NBP process over an internet with Phase 1 routers. A Mac sends a broadcast request; the local router sends an NBP lookup to the target network; the devices respond with a LkUp-Reply.

## How NBP works in Phase 2

For Phase 2, the NBP process is the same as with Phase 1 routers, with one exception. The local router that sends the NBP packet to the next router over an internet now sends an NBP FwdReq (forward request) packet instead of an NBP LkUp. With the addition of the NBP FwdReq, there now is a distinction between sending an NBP request from one router to another router (using FwdReq) and sending an NBP request from a router to a device (using LkUp). Figure 11-10 diagrams this procedure.

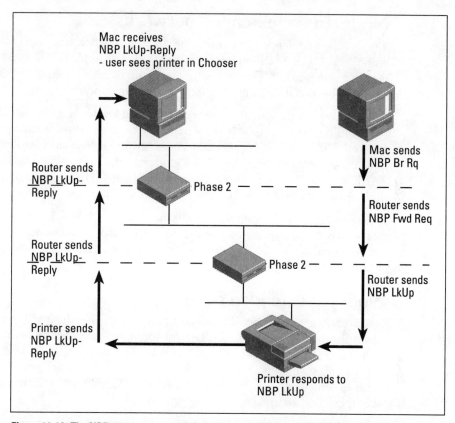

Mac receives
NBP LkUp-Reply
- user sees printer in Chooser

Router sends
NBP LkUp-Reply

Phase 2

Mac sends
NBP Br Rq

Router sends
NBP Fwd Req

Router sends
NBP LkUp-Reply

Phase 2

Router sends
NBP LkUp

Printer sends
NBP LkUp-Reply

Printer responds to
NBP LkUp

Figure 11-10: The NBP process over an internet with Phase 2 routers. A Mac sends a BrRq; the local router sends an NBP FwdReq to the target network router; the devices respond with a LkUp-Reply.

# The AppleTalk Node Boot-Up Procedure

The following sections explain what happens when a node boots up. First, you'll learn how a node boots up on a nonextended network and then how it is done in the more complex extended network with multiple zones and networks. Youll see how a node chooses a zone from the zone list or a network from the network range.

It is helpful to review the AppleTalk Address Resolution Protocol (AARP) process before we start this explanation. On Ethernet, an additional process called the AARP determines the hardware address if it has the AppleTalk node address. AARP uses three packet types: probe, request, and response. The probe is used to verify a unique address on booting; the request is used to obtain the hardware address of a node; and the response is used to return the hardware address. The AARP process is required for Ethernet node compatibility with other Ethernet devices on the cable.

# Nodes in nonextended networks

A node on a nonextended Ethernet cable starts up and then sends out an AARP probe packet. The AARP probe contains the tentative AppleTalk node address that the node wishes to use. The node either picks this number randomly or uses the same number that is saved in PRAM (nonvolatile memory).

The node repeats the AARP probe every ⅕ second for two seconds (actually, ten probes). These probes are sent to the multicast hardware broadcast address $090007ffffff. Every AppleTalk node on the network receives this broadcast. Any node that already has the address given in the new nodes probe packet returns an AARP response. On non-Ethernet networks, such as FDDI or token ring, the number of probes and their frequency may be different.

If the new node is on LocalTalk, it sends out multiple LLAP Enquiry (ENQ) control packets to the broadcast address (255) to verify that its node address is unique. If a node on this network is already using the address, it returns an Acknowledge (ACK) control packet.

# Nodes in extended networks

Nodes booting up on extended Ethernet networks also use the AARP probe to verify that their address is unique. Because the node address is now a combination of "net.node," the node also needs to verify that it is using a valid network number (a net number within the range established by the routers). The node also needs either to verify that the zone name it chose from PRAM is still valid or to know what the default zone is.

Each zone on an extended network has a unique broadcast address, called a *multicast address*. Nodes can use this address to look up services within a zone without disturbing devices located in other zones. The booting node also needs to know the multicast address for the zone that it has chosen or for the default zone.

The multicast zone address, the validity of the network number, and the validity of the zone name are all verified by sending a GetNetInfo (GNI) packet. A router replies to the node with a GetNetInfoReply (GNIR) packet to verify or flag as invalid the nodes assumptions. If the node has not chosen a zone, the GNIR packet provides the default zone name and its multicast address.

If the information that the node has chosen is valid, the following sequence occurs:

1. The node sends an AARP probe to the hardware multicast broadcast address to verify the uniqueness of its net.node address (the AARP probe is sent up to ten times, once every ⅕ second).

2. The node sends a GNI packet containing its "net.node" address and desired zone to the hardware multicast broadcast address.

3. The router sends an AARP request to the hardware multicast broadcast address (a request for the hardware address of the node sending the GNI).

4. The node sends an AARP response to the hardware and node address of the router to return the node's hardware address.

5. The router sends a GNIR to the hardware and node address of the node. (This packet validates the zone and network number and provides the zones multicast address).

The following sequence occurs when the information chosen by the node is not valid because the node is from another internet:

1. The node sends an AARP probe to the hardware multicast broadcast address to verify the uniqueness of the "net.node" address (up to ten times, once every ⅕ second).

2. The node sends a GNI to the hardware multicast broadcast address (this packet contains its "net.node" address and desired zone).

3. The router sends a GNIR to the hardware multicast broadcast address; the router must use the broadcast because it has no route to the invalid network that the node is using as its address. (The GNIR packet contains the valid network range and the default zone with its multicast address).

4. The node sends an AARP probe to the hardware multicast broadcast address to verify the uniqueness of its "net.node" address. (This packet contains its new address selection with a net number in the valid range).

5. The node sends a GNI to the hardware multicast broadcast address. (This packet contains its new "net.node" address and the default zone).

6. The router sends an AARP request to the hardware multicast broadcast address. (This packet requests the hardware address of the node sending the GNI).

7. The node sends an AARP response to the hardware and node address of the router (returning the node's hardware address).

8. The router sends a GNIR to the hardware and node address of the node (validating zone and network number).

The following sequence occurs when the information chosen by the node is not valid because the node is new to an internet:

1. The node sends an AARP probe to the hardware multicast broadcast address (up to ten times, once every ⅕ second); the node uses a network number in the *startup range* of 65,280-65,534.

2. The node sends a GNI to the hardware multicast broadcast address. (This packet contains its "net.node" address and desired zone).

3. The router sends a GNIR to the hardware multicast broadcast address: the router broadcasts because it has no route to the startup range network. (This packet contains the valid network range and the default zone with its multicast address).

4. The node sends an AARP probe to the hardware multicast broadcast address to verify the uniqueness of its "net.node" address. (This packet contains the new address selection with a net number in the valid range).

5. The node sends a GNI to the hardware multicast broadcast address. (This packet contains its new "net.node" address and the default zone).

6. The router sends an AARP request to the hardware multicast broadcast address (requesting the hardware address of the node sending the GNI).

7. The node sends an AARP response to the hardware and node address of the router (returning the nodes hardware address).

8. The router sends a GNIR to the hardware and node address of the node (validating the zone and network number).

# Non-AppleTalk Ethernet Backbones for Macintosh Networks

This chapter focuses on AppleTalk routing as the mechanism for linking separate AppleTalk networks. Another method, sometimes referred to as *tunneling*, enables a backbone to route TCP/IP between individual LocalTalk networks. You can use this routing method when you want to keep all AppleTalk traffic off the Ethernet. We discuss tunneling in detail in Chapter 12, "Designing an AppleTalk WAN."

Keep in mind, however, that this method restricts you to AppleTalk end nodes residing only on LocalTalk networks. As soon as you put a Macintosh with an Ethernet card on the backbone Ethernet, you'll need AppleTalk-over-Ethernet routing services for that node to share such AppleTalk services as file sharing with other networks, including other LocalTalk networks. When tunneling hides traffic, it really hides traffic. A Macintosh has no way of peeking inside of some other protocol's packets to see if it happens to have AppleTalk packed away inside. An Ethernet-connected Macintosh must use TCP/IP end-node software for network communications in a tunneled environment or must have a router able to unpack tunneled packets for it.

## CHAPTER 11 CONCEPTS AND TERMS

- LAN, MAN, and WAN are terms that describe the geography of a networks configuration.

- A collection of AppleTalk networks joined with routers is called an AppleTalk internet.

- The primary function of an AppleTalk internet router is to get data packets to their destinations.

- A Phase 1 router operates on a nonextended network; a Phase 2 router operates on an extended network.

- AppleTalk is unique among networking protocol systems in that it uses zone names and node names, as well as network numbers and node addresses, to map to locations across a multinet LAN.

- You can change, add, or delete zones from the zone list displayed in the Chooser.

- You can use a non-AppleTalk Ethernet backbone for your AppleTalk Network.

### address
A name, set of numbers, or sequence of bits used to identify devices on a network. Each computer, printer, server, or other device on the network must have a unique address. Addresses are necessary so that information transmitted on the network will get to the right destination. The network software keeps track of the addresses.

### aging process
A technique where routes which have not been updated are moved progressively from suspect status to bad status and then deleted.

### default zone
The zone to which any node on an extended network will automatically belong until a different zone is explicitly selected for that node.

### dynamic acquisition
A technique where information is gathered dynamically from the running network rather than requiring pre-configuration by the network manager.

For example, an AppleTalk node determines its address by dynamic acquisition.

### entry state
Every entry in a routing table has a state: good, suspect, bad, or deleted.

### extended network
An AppleTalk network that allows addressing of more than 254 nodes and can support multiple zones.

### hop count
The number of routers that a packet passes through between source and destination. Each router counts as one hop.

### multicast address
A destination address used to indicate a subset (although not necessarily a proper subset) of the nodes on the network. A protocol entity within a node must register with the network layers below it to receive multicasts directed at a particular address. Compare with *broadcast address*, a kind of multicast

address which means "all nodes on a network" or *unicast address*, a kind of address which identifies a specific node on a network and no other.

### network number
A 16-bit number used to indicate which AppleTalk network a node is connected to. Nodes chose their network number from within the network number range assigned to their network.

### nonextended network
An AppleTalk network which can only support 254 nodes and does not use multiple zones.

### port descriptor file
A file maintained by a router for network-related information for each of the router's ports. The port descriptor file includes the *port ID*, a number that designates the identity of the port for the internal processing use of the router; the *network number*, a number that labels the cable that is attached to the port with a unique number that identifies it as a separate network; and the *network address*, a number that designates the port's address on the network.

### router
A device that connects two networks together and maintains addressing information for each network. Workstations can pass information from one network to another by sending the information through the router.

Routers are often confused with bridges. A bridge physically connects two networks, but a bridge does not maintain the network-layer addressing information; bridges maintain data-link layer addressing information (sometimes called MAC, for Medium Access Control, addresses). The router maintains a table of network-layer addresses and gives greater flexibility and control than a bridge (at greater overhead cost).

*(continued on the next page)*

*(continued from previous page)*

**split horizon**
A technique for maintaining routing tables of individual routers. If router A is attached (via a network) to one port of another router (B), then router B only informs router A of networks that are reachable through the other ports of router B. Router A is thus not informed of networks that are attached to the same port of Router B as the one router A is attached to.

**static acquisition**
Contrast with *dynamic acquisition.* A technique where status and configuration information must be entered before operation can begin.

**tunneling**
Encapsulating messages of one protocol inside of another for transport. Common examples include tunneling AppleTalk packets through a TCP/IP network and tunneling IBM's SNA through an X.25 network.

**tuple**
A term from the field of databases; a tuple is a single record of related fields in a database.

**ZIP (Zone Information Protocol)**
The AppleTalk protocol used to exchange information on zone names and locations between routers.

**ZIT (Zone Information Table)**
Table maintained within an AppleTalk router, relating zone names to the router's ports.

**zone**
A collection of networks on an AppleTalk internet. A zone can consist of a single network or a number of networks.

One of the main reasons for breaking a network into a zone is to reduce the amount of searching a user has to do to find a resource on the network. For example, to use a particular printer on the network, the user can search various zones instead of searching the entire network.

Although grouping an internet into zones is usually done on some logical basis such as work loads or business departments, the zones do not have to be physically contiguous. A network in one building might be part of the same zone as a network in another building.

# Designing an AppleTalk WAN

IN THIS CHAPTER

- How to put together a wide area network

- The building blocks of wide area networks

- The advantages and disadvantages of point-to-point circuits, X.25, frame relay, and other circuit types

- Issues in routing AppleTalk between two LANs

A WAN, or *Wide Area Network*, is an internetwork that extends between two or more LANs, usually across long distances, such as between cities and even across continents. Wide area network connectivity for AppleTalk users means that when you, as a user, select any device in the Chooser, such as a LaserWriter, you can use a device in a zone that is located tens, hundreds, or thousands of miles away on the other side of a wide area link. Connectivity for the network means that routing information such as zone names/lists and network numbers/ranges is communicated across the wide area link so that routing tables and zone information tables are maintained and packets are forwarded to their destinations.

In this chapter, we'll help you understand the basics involved in using and managing a wide area network. Note that the security issues involved in managing wide area networks are covered in Chapter 15, "Securing an AppleTalk Network."

QUOTABLES

"Brace yourselves. We're about to try something that borders on the unique: an actually rather serious technical book which is not only vehemently *anti*-solemn but also takes sides. I tend to think of it as 'Constructive Snottiness'."

— *Elements of Networking Style*, M. A. Padlipsky, (Englewood Cliffs, New Jersey: Prentice Hall, 1985), xi. [printed with permission]

## Building Wide Area Links

The full amount of information and background that you need to make decisions about setting up your WAN is beyond the scope of this chapter. We will, however, provide you with some of the basics so that you will be better informed when you begin considering the design of your WAN. For more detailed information, we suggest that you talk with carrier vendors and WAN router vendors. Both types of vendors have excellent literature available for the new WAN network administrator and designer.

## Setting up WAN services

For best results, you need to select and integrate into your existing AppleTalk LAN topologies a WAN service setup that adds the greatest value to your LANs in the most cost-effective manner. Many choices are available for WAN services. You can build a WAN using phone or satellite links, but phone links are most commonly used because the satellite links are slower.

The following are some of your other choices:

❖ You can choose a private WAN that you manage yourself, or you can have the carrier you select manage your private WAN for you.

❖ You can choose a public Value Added WAN (called a VAN).

❖ You can choose from a number of carriers; AT&T, US Sprint, WilTel, MCI, CompuServe, and BT (Tymnet) all have WAN offerings.

❖ You need to select one of the following circuit types: point-to-point circuits, circuit-switched service, or packet-switched services. This choice depends on how often you will use the line, whether occasionally or 24 hours a day.

❖ Finally, you need to select the amount of bandwidth you need: 56K bps, 1.544M bps (which is referred to as T1), or 45M bps (sometimes referred to as T3).

To summarize your choices, you need to select between public or private services, and then select a carrier, the quantity of line usage, the circuit type, and the bandwidth.

QUICK TIPS

### Bridge Versus Router

We recommend that for connecting AppleTalk LANs, you always use a router-to-router connection instead of a bridge-to-bridge connection. A router broadcasts one RTMP Data packet every ten seconds; a bridge forwards all broadcasted RTMP Data packets from *all* the routers on the LAN.

For example, if ten LocalTalk-to-EtherTalk routers are connected to an Ethernet backbone that has a bridge going over a wide area link, and ten LocalTalk-to-EtherTalk routers are on the other side, 200 RTMP Data packets will be sent every ten seconds. This type of overhead will drown your bridged wide area link at a certain point, especially if you are also bridging other Ethernet protocols, such as IPX, DECnet, or TCP/IP, over the same link.

# The building blocks of a WAN

To explain all of your WAN options, we need first to describe how a WAN is put together. A router that connects a LAN to another remote LAN with a port attached to a wide area link is called an *exterior router*. An exterior router is usually a router that is on an Ethernet cable (as opposed to LocalTalk). An exterior router then typically connects to a specialized high-speed device called a CSU/DSU (Channel Service Unit/Data Service Unit). A CSU/DSU is like a modem, in that it interfaces your device to the telephone network.

However, CSU/DSUs are used to connect to *digital* lines, not analog lines, which means they don't actually modulate and demodulate the signal. It's bits all the way. The CSU/DSU is connected to a switch that brings the network into a carrier's system. At the destination or termination point, the carrier's switch is connected to a CSU/DSU and then again to an exterior router.

The exterior router must perform a specialized function called *packet encapsulation*. Because the data traffic in a WAN is leaving Ethernet's data link and physical characteristics, the data must be encapsulated into a data link format for the physical conditions of the wide area link. (Encapsulation is the sandwiching of a packet inside of a new type of header and trailer.) The most common encapsulation type for wide area links is HDLC (High-Level Data Link Control). LAPB (Link Access Protocol B) is also used for the data link layer of a packet-switched network protocol using ITU Recommendation X.25, which we'll cover in an upcoming section. Data packets are encapsulated into either HDLC or LAPB by the exterior router and de-encapsulated by the termination end exterior router.

# Point-to-point circuits

Despite a recent substantial decrease in its use, one of the most common ways to build an AppleTalk WAN is by using a *point-to-point circuit*. A point-to-point circuit is a permanently dedicated circuit between two end points (see Figure 12-1). The carrier's equipment that constructs the circuit does not manipulate the data traffic in any way. The point-to-point circuit is therefore said to be *transparent* to the end LAN protocol (such as AppleTalk).

Point-to-point circuits are available in a variety of speeds. Analog leased lines will work with V-series modems (such as those described in Chapter 10) at speeds of up to about 20,000 bps. Digital leased lines start at 56K bps (64K bps in Europe) and go on up from there. Typical speeds you'll deal with are 56K bps, 256K bps, 1.5M bps ("T1" speed), and 45M bps ("T3" speed).

Because AppleTalk routing currently requires constant broadcasting of RTMP Data packets (every ten seconds), we recommend that you do not connect two AppleTalk LANs with anything less than a 56K bps line. Preferably, you should connect the LANs with a T1. For the sake of reference, a 56K bps line is 0.05 percent of Ethernet's 10M bps bandwidth, and a T1 is 10.544 percent of Ethernet's 10M bps bandwidth.

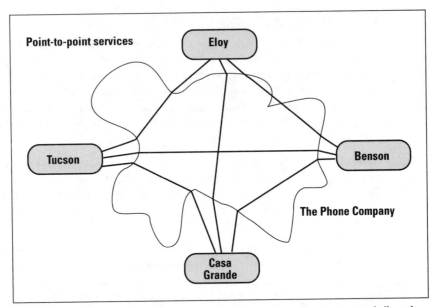

Figure 12-1: Using point-to-point circuits, linking four sites will require six separate dedicated circuits.

*Note:* A point-to-point circuit that you lease from a carrier is usually priced at a monthly flat charge. The cost is based on the distance of the circuit and its bandwidth.

## Circuit-switched services

With a circuit-switched service, a fixed amount of bandwidth is allocated and reserved between two end points, but only for the duration of the call (see Figure 12-2). This call can either be made automatically with software, or manually by a person dialing the phone line. *Dial-up service*, another name for circuit-switched service, is appropriate when you need to establish LAN-to-LAN connectivity only for short time periods. For example, you might use dial-up service when you need a connection only one day of the month, possibly to send sales reports to your corporate office.

The most common bandwidth available for a circuit-switched service is called "Switched 56" and offers a 56K bps channel. Switched T1 is also available in some areas. Calls using switched services such as these usually can be set up in 10 to 30 seconds, significantly faster than using standard dial-up modems, although not as fast as services such as ISDN.

Circuit-switched services are highly recommended — they can be much more useful and more cost effective than their point-to-point cousins. If you have networking applications such as video conferencing that don't require access 24 hours a day, 7 days a week, you can use switched DS-0, T1, and T3 circuits to connect only when you have data to send. Think of it as a grown-up version of a dial-up modem. The cost to connect many sites for a few hours a day is much lower than the equivalent private lines.

One of the big advantages of switched circuits and private lines over the packet-switched services (discussed next) is that you rent the wire (figuratively speaking) from point to point. There's no network to delay or drop your packets, and you can run any obscure protocol you want over the wire. On the other hand, this means that you don't realize any economies of scale by sharing facilities with other customers of the network provider — even if you don't know who you are sharing with.

### Of Disco Suits, Point-to-Point Circuits, and SONET

Although point-to-point circuits are the most common way of linking networks, they have fallen into disfavor with network cognoscenti (gurus). Point-to-points are becoming the white polyester disco suits of the networking world. DS-0 (56K bps), T1 (1.5M bps), E1 (European T1, that's 2M bps), and T3 (45M bps) lines are all over the place, but they don't fit well with the networking style of the 1990s.

Despite the advantage of being well-known technologies and having a great deal of off-the-shelf equipment available, point-to-point circuits have some serious shortcomings. They're too expensive and they take too long to set up. Also, when you put in a private line, you pay for a point-to-point circuit between exactly two buildings, and that's a costly proposition if you've got to help a lot of sites to communicate with each other.

Therefore, point-to-point circuits may be the most common, but they're no longer the best way to link medium- to large-sized networks.

#### SONET is the exception
However, there is a place for dedicated point-to-point circuits — when you have to go really fast. That means fiber optics and SONET, the Synchronous

Optical Network (SONET is SDH in Europe, Synchronous Digital Hierarchy).

When the phone company divides up copper, it thinks in terms of a 64K bps voice channel. So T1 and T3 lines are multiples of that same 64K bps channel. Dividing up a fiber channel at such small speeds didn't make much sense, so SONET begins with a 51.84M bps building block, usually called an OC-1 (Optical Carrier) channel. That size is a chunk you can work with. SONET currently goes up to OC-48, which has 48.51M bps channels — about 2,488M bps.

SONET is being standardized by ANSI, the United States standards group. AT&T has been testing SONET since 1991. The other major players (MCI and US Sprint) entered the SONET game in 1992.

SONET is nearly ready; it is certainly developed enough for there to be real products out there. Nevertheless, you may have a hard time finding someone who offers SONET between the two cities you need because it's still not available everywhere. It's also expensive — that much bandwidth comes with a hefty price tag.

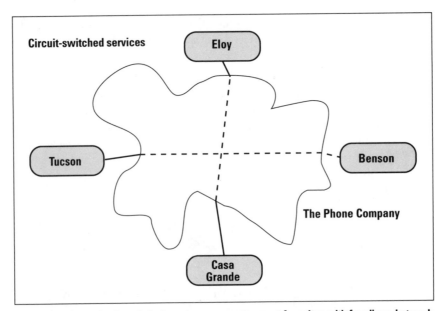

Figure 12-2: Using circuit-switched services, you can connect four sites with four lines, but each site can only talk to one other site at a time. In this case, Eloy is talking to Casa Grande and Tucson is talking to Benson. If Tucson wanted to talk to Eloy, it would have to disconnect from Benson and wait until the Eloy-Casa Grande connection was over.

Nevertheless, circuit-switched services are beneficial because network traffic, in general, is bursty, and there's few organizations who can really fill a T1 circuit 24 hours a day. So we suggest that you don't pay for something you're not using.

*Note:* The cost of circuit-switched service is based on bandwidth, distance, and the amount of connect-time during which a call is actually established.

## Packet-switched services

Packet-switched services are quite a bit different from either circuit-switched or point-to-point. For packet-switched networks, you have a network-layer protocol, such as X.25, frame relay, or SMDS (Switched Multimegabit Data Services). When the protocol allows for virtual circuits, such as in X.25, routers make a connection only when there is actual data to transmit (RTMP, ZIP, and the other overhead packets of AppleTalk are considered data to the packet-switched protocol, which is a good reason not to use a protocol such as X.25 with out-of-the-box AppleTalk routing). Within a packet-switched network are store-and-forward switches that will send data traffic to its destination (see Figure 12-3).

You can set up a packet-switched network to be *multipoint,* with one port on your LAN's exterior router connecting to multiple termination or destination points. For example, one port on an exterior router in Los Angeles may connect your LAN to a packet-switched network and send data to Chicago, New York, and

Denver — one connection, three destinations. This setup can be very cost-effective because you don't need to purchase a port on your exterior router for every destination, as you would with point-to-point circuits.

The throughput of a packet-switched circuit cannot be equated to its bandwidth, as can point-to-point or circuit-switched links. Delay is incurred for processing at each store-and-forward switch, and, for X.25, delay is incurred for error-recovery and flow control. Bandwidth is also taken up by protocol overhead that must be added to the data packet. The bandwidth of a packet-switched circuit is therefore described in terms of the bandwidth for the area between the exterior router and the network switch that puts the data out over the wide area link, rather than the bandwidth between source to destination.

The area between the exterior router and the network switch is referred to as the *access line*. Access line bandwidth for packet-switched networks is available at 300 bps to 56K bps and T1 all the way up to T3 (45M bps), depending on which protocol is used.

*Note:* The fee for a packet-switched service is usually based on the amount of traffic, but distance and connect-time can also be factors in the cost. Note that the AppleTalk protocol has a great amount of overhead for routing and for NBP searches to zones. The pay-per-usage charge for a packet-switched circuit may be higher for an AppleTalk WAN than for multiple point-to-point circuits.

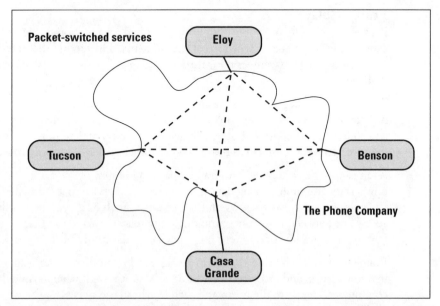

**Figure 12-3: Using packet-switched services, only the four physical connections between each site and the phone company can carry on multiple logical conversations. Any site can talk to all other sites, all at the same time.**

The next sections deal with the various types of packet-switched services: X.25, frame relay, and SMDS.

## X.25

X.25 is a network-layer protocol that is used to connect a device to a network. Using X.25, your two routers can connect to each other over a network and get a clear data channel. X.25 supports either *Permanent Virtual Circuit* (PVC) or *Switched Virtual Circuit* (SVC) operations.

In SVC operations, your routers make a data *call* to each other whenever they have data to transfer. The network brings the circuit up, you transfer data, and you *clear* the call (hang up) when you're done.

PVC operation is the X.25 equivalent of a leased line. A network carrier administratively configures a path through the store-and-forward switches of the network and that path is available to you 24 hours a day. X.25 delivers a perfect data path — everything shows up in sequence and without corruption. (Actually, there's a subtle difference. X.25 guarantees that your data will be properly sequenced *and* uncorrupted *or* it will at least tell you that data was lost.)

A LAN protocol, such as AppleTalk, is encapsulated into X.25 by the LAN's exterior router for transmission over the wide area link. Bandwidth for X.25 links is available at 300 bps to 2M bps — although you would never want to run AppleTalk at only 300 bps!

## Frame Relay

Because packet data networks built using X.25 had a reputation for being very slow, experts decided to take a close look at the elements. They found that the design of X.25 pretty much guarantees poor throughput and response time at speeds above 9.6K bps.

To build fast packet protocols, designers took a look at what it would take to make X.25 faster. To do this, they took X.25, ripped out the parts which slow it down, and ended up with a pretty fast way to get bits from point A to point B. in this way, they created what is known as frame relay, another packet-switched protocol.

As a result of this improvement, frame relay is a hot new *fast packet* technology. It is now a statistical multiplexing data communications service that's available in most cities across North America. With frame relay, as with X.25, you have a single access line between your router and the frame relay network. On that wire, you're free to multiplex lots of different high speed circuits (from 56K bps to 1.5M bps).

Frame relay is much faster than X.25 because it does not have overhead for providing flow control and error-recovery of data. X.25 was built when terminal-to-host communications were the norm and such overhead was necessary. Now, with the proliferation of LAN protocols, such as TCP/IP and AppleTalk, the extra overhead is not necessary and is, in fact, redundant with the error-control features of LAN protocols.

The down side is that frame relay means sending your data through someone else's network, which could mean packet delays and loss.

Frame relay is a permanent virtual circuit (PVC) network right now. That means that you have to call up your frame relay provider and tell it: "I want a 256K bps circuit between Eloy and Tucson," (that's called *provisioning* a circuit) and the provider can take anywhere from a few minutes to days to set it up. The switched virtual circuit (SVC) form of frame relay is on the standards table now and should be available in the next year or two.

Frame relay's biggest advantage is its cost. It's much cheaper to run ten 56K bps circuits over a frame relay line than to install the equivalent private lines. Also, frame relay is available from many different companies, so the competition is keeping prices down. For example, one of the authors uses a frame relay line to connect his house to the Internet at 56K bps. The total cost of his portion of the line is $73 per month — a fraction of what a dedicated 56K bps circuit would cost.

In general, though, frame relay is only recommended for environments where you expect to have more than one PVC on each access line. For example, if you had a mesh (every system connected to every other system) network of five sites, you would probably find it much cheaper to use frame relay to connect them than the equivalent number of dedicated private lines.

## SMDS

AppleTalk applications of SMDS were demonstrated for the first time in networking shows in early 1992. Like X.25 and frame relay, SMDS is a packet-switched service protocol, so you can configure an SMDS network to be multipoint. In a multipoint network, one connection can have multiple destinations; the data is sent through store-and-forward switches within the SMDS network. Like frame relay, SMDS does not provide error control or flow control.

SMDS differs from both X.25 and frame relay in that SMDS is a connectionless type of packet-switched circuit. Connectionless service does not guarantee that packets will be delivered in the same sequence as they were sent. This also means that there is no concept of a virtual circuit between two sites — each packet passed from your network to the SMDS network has to have the destination address in it so that the SMDS network will know where to send it. SMDS is fast, with bandwidth speeds available at a low end of T1 to a current high end of T3 and projections of future speeds of 150M bps.

## ATM

Asynchronous Transfer Mode (ATM, not to be confused with Automated Teller Machines) is breathing hot and heavy at frame relay's heels. Frame relay may be slower than ATM, but ATM is only available in a very few areas. As ATM becomes widely available, it will quickly overtake frame relay for high speed applications.

ATM is an evolving technology and since it is still in the prototype stage, not all standards are in place. In any case, ATM is the official network buzzword of the decade. Everyone wants to get into ATM because it promises real speed. While networks such as frame relay top out at about 45M bps, ATM starts well above that level (although the initial offerings by most vendors are using T1 speeds of 1.544M bps). ATM is unique because of a process called *cell switching*. Data is divided into 53-byte cells, and these cells are switched through the network.

If you divide up the world into circuit-switched pipes (like a phone call) and packet-switched pipes (like the IP part of TCP/IP), ATM fits somewhere in between. Unlike Ethernet, every cell is the same size. This provides two advantages. First, because the cell size is known in advance, switching and routing are easier and faster. It's easier to write the software for an ATM switch than for a TCP/IP or DECnet router. Second, because the cell size is small, it's easy to guarantee bandwidth to applications that need it, such as video and audio. There may be two million CompuServe subscribers out there who could use a faster data channel to send and receive e-mail, but there are 50 million cable TV homes that are potential buyers of ATM-delivered HD-TV (High Definition Television).

ATM uses multiplexing technology in the same way as frame relay. You buy one access line to the ATM network, and run as many ATM virtual circuits over that as your line will allow.

Most people think of using ATM on top of a fiber network, such as SONET (described in the preceding section) or over broadband ISDN (described in the following section), but there's no requirement for that. The basic ATM protocol could be run over a copper wire, if you can get one that goes fast enough.

Vendors are also starting to push ATM as a technology for LANs. ATM is fundamentally different from networks such as Ethernet or LocalTalk. ATM is not a broadcast network. Each device in an ATM network talks only to the ATM switch. The switch looks at frames coming in and sends them only to the destination device. It remains to be seen whether the hype will convince anyone to run "ATM to the desk," as such a process is called.

## ISDN

ISDN is the Integrated Services Digital Network. To really understand ISDN, you have to zoom out and look at the big picture of the world of telephony. Consider *The Phone Company*. You may think that data networks or the Internet are large, but the telephone network is orders of magnitude larger. The telephone network has many switches, standards, computers, wires, and fibers. Somehow all these end up in a little 4-wire jack in your house. When you plug your phone in that jack, you're connected to the largest network in the world.

ISDN is The Phone Company's plan for the next generation telephone network. Looking ahead 50 years, the goal of the world's telephone companies is to replace the current mostly-analog telephone network with a mostly-digital telephone network. So instead of an analog jack at your home, you'll have a digital jack — and a digital telephone. The phone companies have already begun implementing portions of ISDN in limited areas.

For most people, the transition to ISDN will be almost transparent. After you have bought your new digital phone at Wal-Mart, the only differences are that the jack you will plug into is bigger and you won't hear dial tones or touch tones (because ISDN doesn't use them).

ISDN is a comprehensive telephone system, not just a transmission technology. It deals with everything: how you build and network telephone switches; how digital phones connect to the phone company; even what ISDN phone numbers look like.

But for those of us who care about data, the world according to ISDN will be very different. The ISDN digital wall jack is really a 192K bps all-digital circuit, divided up into two chunks of two 64K bps and one of 19K bps. This is *Basic Rate ISDN* access, called BRI.

The basic ISDN unit is a 64K bps channel, called a B channel (don't ask what the B stands for; it doesn't officially stand for anything). A B channel can carry a voice telephone call, or a single point-to-point data call — at 64K bps. ISDN basic access is the bottom-of-the-line service. Basic access, called 2B + D, gets you two B channels, and a low-speed D channel, which is used to set up calls on the B channels and can be used for data. The whole thing adds up to a single 192K bps channel, with overhead, framing, and the like.

A call on an ISDN phone works like this. You dial the number into a keypad. The ISDN phone sends a digital message on the D channel to the phone company asking for a connection between one of your B channels and some remote subscriber's B channel. The other end gets a message on its D channel, and (presumably) accepts the call. At that point, the phone company opens up a circuit between the two B channels, and you can talk.

You may also send data. The phone company doesn't really care. The other end can be a computer data port just as easily as a person holding a handset. You're free to run any protocol you want over the wire, because all signaling is done on the D channel. When you're done, send another D channel message, and the connection is closed.

Basic rate isn't the only way to bundle together B and D channels. A common alternative called *Primary Rate ISDN* (PRI) access can be plugged directly into a router or remote access server. PRI access is 23 B channels and one 64K bps D channel in the United States (T1 speed) or 30 B channels and one D channel in Europe (E1 speed). ISDN also defines higher speed H channels of 384K bps, 1,536K bps and 1,920K bps, for those with a real need for speed.

Although ISDN doesn't *require* any specific protocol over the B channel, it does define a set of *Bearer Services*. These vary from a vanilla 64K bps divided into bytes to 64K bps for voice to special data services like X.25 and frame relay (both described above).

Even though ISDN is not available in many places, the basic ISDN concepts are about ten years old. So in order to keep up with technology, a second generation of ISDN technology, called Broadband ISDN (B-ISDN), is already under development. Many parts of B-ISDN have already been defined, and the rest are nearing completion. (The original ISDN is now usually called Narrowband ISDN. Or, if you like soft drinks, you can think of one as ISDN Classic and the other as New ISDN). One of the key pieces of B-ISDN is Asynchronous Transfer Mode (ATM), described above.

As we noted before, Narrowband ISDN works in chunks of 64K bps, which is a pretty good speed for voice and simple data transfer. B-ISDN is designed to handle high-resolution video, such as HD-TV, which means it needs a much larger size — about a thousand times larger!

Although B-ISDN is designed to move data much faster than Narrowband ISDN, it's still part of the same family of standards. That means that B-ISDN is controlled in the same way as ISDN, and is supposed to be totally compatible with ISDN. If you're lucky enough to have Narrowband ISDN, your phone company could be using a mix of B-ISDN and ISDN technologies to transmit Narrowband ISDN data.

You can use either or both types of ISDN to link AppleTalk LANs over a wide area, although ISDN is becoming increasingly affordable for small branch office connections.

## Public and private WAN links

All the WAN circuits described in the preceding sections — point-to-point, circuit-switched, and packet-switched — are available from carriers, which means your links share the circuits with other customers on a public network. If you prefer, you can build your own private network with your own circuits.

A public network has the advantage of being controlled and monitored by the carrier. With a public network, you can concentrate on your business, not on your wide area network. Also, hooking up to a public network does not require a large capital expenditure in equipment that may soon become obsolete.

However, public networks have two drawbacks. First, public networks are not as secure as private networks. With a public network, it is possible (although difficult) for an unauthorized entity to call into the network. (For more information on security procedures for networks, see Chapter 15, "Securing an AppleTalk Network.")

The second drawback is that upgrades to new technology take place at the carrier's schedule, which may not be as fast as you'd like.

Private networks commonly connect privately owned switching equipment to point-to-point circuits leased from a carrier. It is possible to build a completely private network if you can obtain your own right-of-way for installing circuits (possibly with satellite links). Private networks can be more cost-effective over time, when compared to the monthly charges of a public network. Also, with a private network, you can control the timing of any moves to a new technology, such as SMDS.

All these technologies — point-to-point, circuit-switched, and packet-switched — connect two or more AppleTalk LANs. But there are several ways to get AppleTalk out onto the WAN, as we'll describe next.

# Routing AppleTalk across a Wide Area Link

Because corporate networks are moving with great alacrity towards TCP/IP backbones, most of the work on improving wide area AppleTalk performance has focused on a mixed AppleTalk and TCP/IP environment, with AppleTalk extended between sites over TCP/IP backbone networks.

In 1989, Cayman Systems Corp. introduced Cayman Tunnels (now called SEDI) to the AppleTalk world. Using Cayman Tunnels, a router can encapsulate AppleTalk packets in TCP/IP packets for transmission across a TCP/IP network. Cayman Tunnels aimed to solve problems network managers found in building very large AppleTalk networks. Apple has always known about the these problems. In *Inside AppleTalk*, the reference bible for AppleTalk networkers, Apple warns managers that the features which make AppleTalk so usable on small networks will cause problems in very large ones. AppleTalk is a verbose protocol. Its routing protocol, RTMP (Routing Table Maintenance Protocol), requires every AppleTalk router on an extended LAN to broadcast its routing table every ten seconds. If a route goes for twenty seconds without an RTMP packet advertising its presence, AppleTalk considers it gone.

In small networks, AppleTalk's approach to routing means that any topology is discovered quickly. New networks, down networks, and adaptive routing all happen without manager intervention, network downtime, or reconfigurations. In large networks, though, RTMP traffic can get out of hand. An extended AppleTalk network with 100 routers will burn up almost 25 percent of Ethernet's 10M bps just handling routing updates. That much routing traffic has another side effect: routers will spend all their time passing around routing information and won't have any time left for the more important task of routing data packets.

AppleTalk routing breaks down in large networks for another reason. AppleTalk supports no more than 15 *hops* between any two AppleTalk systems. With an extended backbone of sufficient size, it may be simply impossible to use AppleTalk from one end of the network to the other.

There are other problems which show up in wide area AppleTalk. You must be careful not to duplicate network numbers when joining one AppleTalk LAN to another. In some cases, you must change all the router configuration files of one of the LANs to new, non-conflicting numbers. In addition, AppleTalk, as a purely hop-count-based protocol, has no way of establishing that one parallel path is better than another. Even if you have two point-to-point links, with one at 9.6K bps and the other at T1's 1.544M bps, the AppleTalk protocol looks at these links as equal because both are one hop away.

AppleTalk can also run into political, rather than technical problems, in large networks. Many network managers don't like running AppleTalk routing on the corporate backbone. In large networks, keeping a DECnet, SNA, or TCP/IP backbone running is hard enough without adding support for personal computer networks. Adding AppleTalk to a backbone means additional configuration and management complexity in routers. That overhead can be out of the question for a network manager already stressed by budgetary and resource constraints.

AppleTalk tunneling was introduced to solve these problems (and more.) Simple tunnels such as Cayman's SEDI or Cisco Corporation's GRE (Generic Route Encapsulation) let a network manager build a virtual AppleTalk network over a TCP/IP network. Simple tunnels are simple indeed. A tunneling router on one AppleTalk network picks off AppleTalk's DDP packets, places them into IP packets on the TCP/IP network and sends them to a tunneling router at the other end of the TCP/IP network. The router at the other end unpacks the DDP packet out of the IP packet for transmission on the other AppleTalk network. (See Figure 12-1).

## Simple encapsulation techniques

Cayman's SEDI (Simple Encapsulation of DDP in IP) has become an industry standard. Network routers from Cayman Systems, Farallon Computing, Inc., Compatible Systems, Inc., and Cisco Systems, Inc., all support SEDI and can work with each other. Cisco's GRE can encapsulate other protocols, such as IPX and IP, in addition to AppleTalk. No other vendor supports GRE yet.

Although SEDI and GRE both solve the basic problem of connecting AppleTalk networks over a TCP/IP backbone, neither one does anything to reduce the amount of RTMP traffic that AppleTalk routers generate. To solve that problem, Cayman has introduced TREDI (Traffic Reduced Encapsulation of DDP in IP) as an extension to the older SEDI protocol. The main difference between SEDI and TREDI is in the routing. A TREDI router at one end of an AppleTalk tunnel only transmits RTMP packets when there's a change in the network topology.

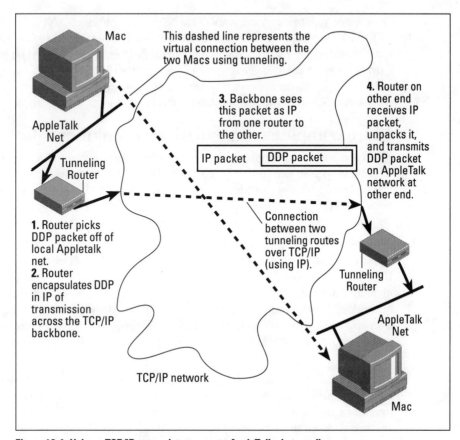

Mac

This dashed line represents the
virtual connection between the
two Macs using tunneling.

**3.** Backbone sees
this packet as IP
from one router to
the other.

**4.** Router on
other end
receives IP
packet,
unpacks it,
and transmits
DDP packet
on AppleTalk
network at
other end.

AppleTalk
Net

| IP packet | DDP packet |

Tunneling
Router

Connection
between two
tunneling routes
over TCP/IP
(using IP).

**1.** Router picks
DDP packet off of
local Appletalk
net.
**2.** Router
encapsulates DDP
in IP of
transmission
across the TCP/IP
backbone.

Tunneling
Router

AppleTalk
Net

TCP/IP network

Mac

Figure 12-4: Using a TCP/IP network to transport AppleTalk via tunneling.

For a stable network, this means that the IP tunnel isn't jammed with routing packets carrying redundant information. When a topology change occurs, the TREDI
router passes the RTMP packet to its counterpart at the other end of the tunnel.
If there is no change, the TREDI router discards the RTMP packet. At the other
end, it is the responsibility of the counterpart TREDI router to generate *fake*
RTMP packets for transmission on its local AppleTalk network. This technique
allows the network manager to link AppleTalk networks without wasting TCP/IP
backbone bandwidth.

TREDI is backwards-compatible with SEDI, meaning a TREDI router that connects to a SEDI router will fall back to SEDI operation. Cayman has announced
that it will be shipping TREDI-compatible routers later this year.

Dr. Pepper, published by the AppleTalk Networking Forum (ANF), is very similar to TREDI. Dr. Pepper, which has also been called AppleTalk Low Overhead Encapsulation (ALOE), Fresca, and TunnelTalk, has been implemented by Shiva Corporation in the latest version of its AppleTalk network router software. At this time, the ANF is working on a new version of their tunneling protocol which incorporates elements from Cisco's GRE as well.

## More complex encapsulation techniques

SEDI is designed for simple tunnels where size is not a problem. Dr. Pepper and TREDI both go a step further by reducing the amount of routing traffic. The high end of AppleTalk encapsulation approaches was designed by Apple and has been published as AURP (Apple Update-Based Routing Protocol). Apple sells this software AURP router, the Apple Internet Router which runs on Macintosh computers.

AURP is the next step in AppleTalk routing, a feature-rich extension to the AppleTalk protocol family. AURP defines AppleTalk tunnels through both TCP/IP and point-to-point links (using PPP, the Point-to-Point Protocol). AURP also includes a mechanism for reducing routing traffic, additional security through network and device hiding, and network number remapping and clustering. AURP is a tool for constructing huge AppleTalk networks. AURP lets different organizations build larger AppleTalk internets without making changes to the existing network.

One powerful feature of AURP allows network managers to re-map AppleTalk network numbers into unused ranges. Each zone in an AppleTalk network must have a unique number. Connecting two networks which haven't been administered as one usually means numbering conflicts. AURP solves this problem with number remapping. Network number 100 is automatically translated to network 3,000 across an AURP tunnel to avoid a collision, and only the local router needs to know this.

To demonstrate the power of AURP, Apple has established The AppleTalk Internet (not to be confused with an AppleTalk internet). Any AppleTalk network connected to the TCP/IP Internet can join the AppleTalk Internet simply by installing Apple's Internet Router software and building a tunnel over the TCP/IP Internet. Today, the AppleTalk Internet links many different sites, ranging from huge universities to tiny software vendors. All together, the AppleTalk Internet has over 200 AppleTalk zones. It's an impressive demonstration of the power of AURP.

## Other reasons to tunnel

Tunneling AppleTalk through TCP/IP is a useful tool in handling incremental growth of an AppleTalk network. Because the traffic in an AppleTalk tunnel is completely transparent to the TCP/IP network, organizations can use AppleTalk tunneling to build experimental, private, and virtual AppleTalk networks. A virtual AppleTalk network would allow the network manager to give access to new, untested protocols and services to testing centers without fear of disturbing production systems. Tunneling can also be used as part of an outsourcing program to link AppleTalk networks across a public or private TCP/IP backbone.

Tunneling can solve problems, but it can create them as well. Tunneling, especially complex protocols such as Dr. Pepper, AURP, and TREDI, places a load on routers that may require CPU or memory upgrades. Tunnels can also be a security problem. A network *firewall* which is designed to stop AppleTalk traffic and let TCP/IP traffic through won't necessarily keep tunneled AppleTalk data from getting through. Tunneling has implications for routing as well. A careless network manager could end up routing traffic from San Francisco to Los Angeles via Tokyo if network topology isn't carefully constructed.

## Picking the right tunneling technology

If you think there are too many tunneling technologies to choose from, you're right. For small networks with high speed backbones, SEDI products are available from several vendors. Network managers who don't want to waste backbone bandwidth are in a quandary. With TREDI and Dr. Pepper providing nearly identical service, and vendors such as Cisco sitting the battle out by establishing proprietary tunneling protocols, the choice is a hard one. TREDI is being promoted by the AppleTalk tunneling leader, Cayman, while Dr. Pepper is a vendor-neutral specification from a consortium of networking companies.

Apple's non-proprietary AURP remains the high-end solution, but Apple is the only vendor to have included AURP in a router product. Others are sure to follow, but choosing AURP today means a lonely start and a single vendor. Despite these concerns, AURP-based routers are the only reasonable choice for very large and multiorganizational networks.

# CHAPTER *12* CONCEPTS AND TERMS

- You can use three types of circuit services to build wide area networks: point-to-point, circuit-switched, and packet-switched.

- There are many new packet-switched services, including X.25, frame relay, SMDS, ATM, and ISDN.

- Speeds below 56K bps are not recommended for connecting one AppleTalk LAN to another.

- Connecting two or more large AppleTalk LANs can be a cause for concern. Tunneling is used by many network managers to keep things in synchronization, provide security, and prevent numbering conflicts.

**access line**
A circuit between a device, such as a router, and a network, such as a frame relay, X.25, or ATM network. This is the line by which that router *accesses* the network. A physical access line may have many virtual circuits over it.

**ATM**
Asynchronous Transfer Mode, a broadband ISDN transmission technology which uses 53-byte fixed length cells to provide very high speed data rates, up to several gigabit per second.

**Basic Rate Interface**
A style of ISDN access with 2 B channels and 1 D channel.

**circuit-switched service**
A network technology where the end user has a clear channel between two network entities without visible processing by the network. Compare to packet-switched.

**frame relay**
A packet-switched technology based on Recommendation X.25 which includes multiplexing, permanent and switched virtual circuits, but which does not include error or congestion control.

**hop**
A network connection which passes through a router is said to have made a hop. The number of hops between two end systems is usually the number of routers between them, although this can vary widely depending on context.

**ISDN (Integrated Services Digital Network)**
An international communications standard that allows the integration of voice and data on a common transport mechanism.

**multipoint**
A single circuit which connects more than one site. Multipoint circuits require some sort of addressing scheme to keep things straight.

**packet-switched**
A network technology where data are broken up into units called packets and the packets have a meaning to the network. Compare to circuit-switched.

**permanent virtual unit**
A logical connection through a network between two entities brought up and down only through an external management interface.

**point-to-point circuit**
A dedicated circuit between exactly two locations.

**SMDS**
Switched Multimegbit Data Services, a connectionless packet-oriented network technology

**switched virtual circuit**
A logical connection through a network between two entities brought up and down in real time.

**tunneling**
A technique for networking which involves packing the packets of one protocol into the packets of another protocol (or the same protocol) for passage over a backbone network. For example, AppleTalk packets may be placed in IP packets.

**X.25**
A standard for data communications, ITU-T Recommendation X.25, which specifies the interface between a computer and a network at Layers 1, 2, and 3.

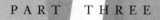

PART THREE

# Managing
# a Network

# Configuring, Monitoring, and Fixing AppleTalk Networks

IN THIS CHAPTER

- Planning and configuring AppleTalk networks

- Managing your AppleTalk network configuration

- Configuration monitoring and reporting tools

- Using SNMP in AppleTalk and TCP/IP networks

- Using network protocol analyzers to find and solve problems in your network

- Monitoring AppleTalk networks, and using your performance data to design better networks

- Fixing AppleTalk networks

I n earlier chapters, we present rules for building and installing LocalTalk and Ethernet networks. This chapter discusses the issues involved in managing bigger networks. Most of these issues aren't specific to AppleTalk, but are discussed in the context of the Macintosh-oriented network manager. The first issue with which you, as a network manager, must deal is the configuration of your network. And this issue concerns not only the basic wiring between one station and the next, but also the larger question of the entire network's topology. If you must wire an entire building, for example, how do you go about it? How are the routers configured? And how is the system as a whole managed?

After you install and begin managing a larger AppleTalk network, you soon begin to have questions about what's going on inside: How much network bandwidth is in use? Who is talking to whom? And, most important, just when am I going to hit some limit on my existing network and need to install something bigger? This chapter answers these questions.

QUOTABLES

"I like having a machine called 'elvis' on the network because that way, I can say 'ping elvis' and have it come back with 'elvis is alive'."

— Carl Shipley
[printed with permission]

Finally, this chapter discusses how to handle broken networks. Every network breaks down sooner or later, and you must know how to locate the problem and fix it as soon as possible. After describing some general problem solving principles, including how you can use the information in the first part of this chapter to help diagnose network problems, we provide examples of problems we encountered and how we found and fixed them.

In Part II of this book, you learned how to wire up LocalTalk and Ethernet networks. The focus in those chapters is on the individual station and how to connect it to an existing network. In Part III and in this chapter, we step back and take a more holistic view of network configuration. You should find such a view especially helpful as your Macintosh network grows and reaches out to touch other corporate networks running other applications.

# Planning LocalTalk Network Configurations

For small LocalTalk network installations — those that fill a single floor in a building or so — you can use any of several configurations: the *daisy-chain*, the *bus*, the *passive star*, or the *active star*. Each of these topologies has its own pluses and minuses, as discussed later in this chapter. (Limitations on a network's length are further discussed in Chapter 6, "Designing a LocalTalk LAN," and Chapter 8, "Designing an Ethernet LAN.")

If you manage a very small network, you may opt for the simplest network configuration, which is the daisy-chain. This topology, though, is fraught with performance pitfalls. Daisy-chains are particularly susceptible to bad crimps in their wires, which can cause network problems. (See Chapter 7, "Installing a LocalTalk LAN.") Consequently, you should avoid daisy-chains for networks of more than ten nodes, including printers and file servers.

The next step up is the bus topology. With this configuration, each node is joined separately to the network cable so that disconnecting a node doesn't cause network failure (see Chapter 7). An Ethernet bus requires more planning than a LocalTalk bus does, because the Ethernet network can be tapped into only at specific distances (see Chapter 9, "Installing an Ethernet LAN"). LocalTalk networks, can also be configured as a passive star, which is simply several bus segments joined in a star formation (see Chapter 6, "Designing a LocalTalk LAN"). A bus topology, however, is still a simple style that allows for only minimal network traffic. Remember the rule of only one network conversation at a time on a segment.

After your network grows past ten nodes, you need to resolve two issues: which topology to change to and whether to use a centralized wiring closet. Wiring closets can be used for bus, passive star, and active star networks as well as for Ethernet star hubs. Installing a wiring closet can make your network more stable — if you can afford to add one. A wiring closet is similar to a phone closet in that it is a special room dedicated to switching equipment. Often, the same room can be used for both data and phone equipment. Pairs of wire are run from the office locations to the closet, where they can be cross-connected to the desired equipment (such as a LocalTalk repeater). Wiring closets are a definite advantage for effective performance management, as they enable you to adapt the network quickly to new service needs simply by moving cross-connects.

With or without a wiring closet, however you can also install an active star repeater to strengthen your network. The repeater enhances performance by isolating signals that could disrupt the network. Each port on a repeater can isolate any signal that seems to cause a problem. Further, the repeater amplifies the physical signal as the signal moves from one port to the next, a capability that enables you to exceed the 32-station limits on a different topology, the simple bus LocalTalk network.

The rule of one conversation at a time, however, still applies even to a network divided by a repeater. So be cautious about putting a large number of users on a network with a repeater. Examine the traffic statistics and determine how long your users must wait for a service. On a lightly used network, you probably can go ahead and connect more than 32 users.

The next step up from a repeater is to divide your segments by adding either a *bridge* or a *router*. Your choice depends on what kind of use your network sees. For a widely distributed traffic pattern with many nodes exchanging and sending packets frequently, a *packet-switched bridge*, such as the LocalSwitch (from Tribe Computer Systems) is a good addition to the network. (Figure 13-1 shows an example of a LocalTalk bridge configuration.) On the other hand, using routers to divide segments makes sense under other conditions. You should consider routers if, for example, much of the traffic must travel across an AppleTalk internet because of expensive shared services or because many users are tied into one service system, such as a corporate e-mail system. (At this point, you're making decisions about internet configurations, which is the subject of the following section.)

If you decide to use routers, you still need to establish a topology for the router-connected networks. Such networks can be bridged segments configured as a star, bus, or daisy-chain system, depending on your performance requirements, as described in the following sections.

# Setting up Internet Configurations

An *internet*, a collection of AppleTalk networks joined by routers, can be configured in either of two ways: combining two or more networks serially in a row (a *serial configuration*) or connecting them in a star layout with a *center hub* and one or more *legs*. We recommend the star topology if your LAN internet is a collection of networks at one physical site (an Ethernet or fiber optic internet located in one or multiple buildings rather than extended across a city).

See Chapter 11, "Designing an AppleTalk LAN," for descriptions of LANs, MANs, and WANs and some LAN configuration strategies. See Chapter 12, "Designing an AppleTalk WAN," for MAN and WAN configuration strategies.

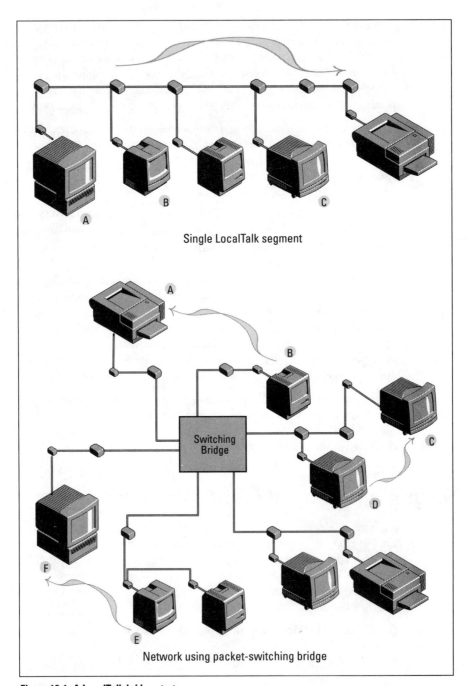

Single LocalTalk segment

Network using packet-switching bridge

Figure 13-1: A LocalTalk bridge strategy.

A star topology offers several advantages over a serial approach. With a serial configuration, a packet may travel through several routers to reach its destination. This approach can be seriously detrimental to your network's performance. With a star topology, however, packets travel through a single router to reach a *backbone* and then through another router if necessary to reach a second network. A backbone, as discussed previously, is a central network that connects a number of networks.

A typical serial network uses LocalTalk routers to connect three or four LocalTalk networks in a row. To expand this serial network, the *leg* can be routed to an Ethernet, which may also connect to other legs. This interconnection creates a combination serial/star topology. Any packet that needs to reach the Ethernet from the end LocalTalk network must travel through four routers. This brings up the problem of where to place centralized services, such as e-mail servers or high-speed printers. With a star topology, such services are easily placed on the backbone, which is central to all network users. Figure 13-2 compares a serial network to a star network.

In very large networks, you may need to place routers between sections of the Ethernet for better fault management. Should this become necessary, follow the star topology, as shown in Figure 13-3, and plan for an Ethernet backbone with the various Ethernet segments branching off it. This arrangement still allows centralized placement of services.

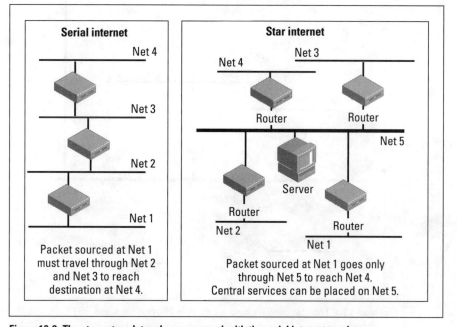

Figure 13-2: The star network topology compared with the serial internet topology.

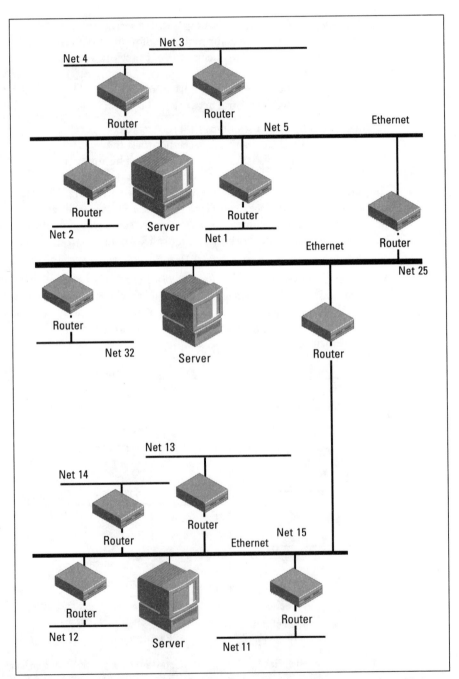

Figure 13-3: This star network includes multiple Ethernet branches. Net 5, 25, and 15 are Ethernet networks.

# The configuration management of network devices

This section discusses configuration management with respect to the following types of devices: routers, Ethernet filtering bridges, and servers.

Managing the configuration on your internet is the most critical element of configuration management. If you configure the devices at the network layer incorrectly or inefficiently, the layers of applications above the network layer suffer as they cross from one network to another.

The configuration of Ethernet filtering bridges is another important consideration. You can use Ethernet bridges to filter out AppleTalk traffic. By preventing AppleTalk from crossing from one network to the other (through the bridge), you have an effective tool which you can use to segregate one area from another.

The configuration of the network's server also is important. As *ADSP*, a sophisticated data-transfer protocol, became available with the Macintosh operating system in System 6.0.4, many new server-based applications came to the AppleTalk market. These applications also must be configured correctly and efficiently for the health of the network.

# The configuration of AppleTalk routers

Configuration management for AppleTalk routers consists of the following three activities:

❖ *Monitoring*, or using software tools to view the configuration

❖ *Reporting*, in which software tools report the configuration to you along with any discrepancies or errors that the tools find

❖ *Control*, in which you manipulate the configuration of the router

You can perform all three activities by using various applications. As in other discussions of software applications, the following sections concentrate on pointing out the features you should seek in such software tools instead of identifying specific applications.

## Router configuration monitoring tools

Monitoring is built into almost every router application available. This feature may variously be called *diagnostics*, *error reporting*, or *debugging*. Monitoring features enable you to view the condition of the router at any time, and these tools perceive and report certain errors or unusual conditions.

A typical condition identified by a monitoring tool is a multitude of GNI (GetNetInfo) packets sent to the multicast broadcast address. This condition occurs if a node starts up on an extended network in the Phase 2 startup network range. (For details on GNI broadcasting, see Chapter 11, "Designing an AppleTalk LAN.") Well-written tools also tell you if a router is misconfigured in relation to the configurations of other routers on an internet.

### Router configuration control tools

You're probably already familiar with tools that control configuration. Such tools are, by necessity, built into every router. Configuration control tools are currently all proprietary software, but future SNMP network management should offer control capabilities for AppleTalk. (We're not holding our breaths, however, as explained later in this chapter.) As an administrator, you must control two sets of information on the AppleTalk router: the zone name and list and the network number and range for each port.

See Chapter 11, "Designing an AppleTalk LAN," for information on selecting appropriate network numbers or ranges; see the section on Fault Management, "Fixing AppleTalk Networks" later in this chapter, for the consequences of incorrect selection.

### Controlling zone name changes

In addition to controlling the installation of new zone names and lists, the network administrator controls any changes to a zone name and list. Currently, no easy way exists to change a zone name or zone list on an internet.

For now, you can use the method described in the following Step-by-Step section called "Changing a Zone List."

## Changing a Zone List

The administrator must keep a careful watch over the network zone names and lists. The following steps show how to make changes to that list.

1.  **First, shut down all routers that are attached to the cable;** If ten LocalTalk-to-Ethernet routers are attached to the backbone, you must shut off *all ten*.

    At this point, no established routing exists on the network. Traffic can occur locally — between two Macintoshes with Ethernet cards, for example — but no traffic can cross the routers into other networks. And users on this cable see no zones showing up in Choosers.

2.  **Next, go to one of the routers and change the configuration by entering the new zone information.**

3.  **Reboot the router.**

    This router thus becomes the first router on the network and is the router that establishes the network range and number and the zone name and list.

4.  **Continue around the network, rebooting each router with the new configuration.**

    This method doesn't work with the network running, however, if what you want to change is just the zone list. The reason for this is that no change has occurred in the network range and number. Remember that the router checks its routing table to make changes in the ZIT (Zone Information Table). To do this, you'll have to shut down all the routers in the network before rebooting any of them.

Currently, no mechanism exists for dynamic zone list assignments across a network. And, if you try to change the network range while the network is running, the newly configured routers conflict with the old routers. (For more information about how zone names and lists are generated across an internet and about shutting off routers for this process, see Chapter 11, "Designing an AppleTalk LAN.")

## Controlling router startups

Besides controlling network numbers and zone names, you also can control the router startup procedure. Specifically, you can choose for a router to start up as either a *seed* or *nonseed* router.

Seed routers *seed*, or initialize, the internet with the configuration information the administrator enters (network number and range, zone name and list). Nonseed routers wait and listen for a seed router and then take this configuration initialization information from the first seed router they hear. After a nonseed router obtains a network configuration, it begins to participate in the routing of the network. This participation effectively makes that router a seed router for any new nonseed routers coming on line. Seed and nonseed determinations, therefore apply only as a router starts up.

A router, whether nonseed or seed, first obtains a unique node address for each port through the AARP probe procedure (see Chapter 11). Next, if the router is nonseed, it begins a *discovery* process. A seed router, on the other hand, begins the process of *verification*.

These processes either verify or discover the network number or range, the zone name or zone list, and, for extended networks, the default zone. After this discovery and verification phase is complete, the router can begin the actual routing process by sending out RTMP Data packets every ten seconds, answering queries (such as those found in the ZIP protocol), and forwarding packets to their destination networks.

Completing the process of verification or discovery before the router begins functioning is important so that misinformation does not travel onto the internet. If the verification phase for seed routers is not completed correctly because of a conflicting configuration, Apple recommends (in *Inside AppleTalk*, their specifications of the AppleTalk protocol suite) that the router not use that seed information and alert the network administrator in some way.

We've seen vendors use several methods for handling a seed router that attempts to start up in a network with a configuration different from its own (whether a zone name and list, a default zone, or a network number range). Unfortunately, because most routers are not monitored, there's often no one listening when the router complains that it cannot start up correctly.

Apple's recommendation in *Inside AppleTalk* is that the router alert the administrator if it detects a different configuration for either a network or zone on the network and not to route until the administrator eliminates the disparity. Farallon Computing, Cisco, Apple, and Digital currently take this approach. To eliminate the difference, the administrator may either change the configuration file to match the existing configuration or find the other router and change its configuration. The administrator can also change the router to nonseed status so that it can discover the correct network and zone information.

A second method, first implemented by Cayman Systems, is called *soft-seed*. Using this method, a router starts up as a seed router. If the router detects a conflict during the verification phase, however, the router switches to discovery mode, acting as a nonseed router. The router then obtains the information it needs from the other seed routers on the network. A drawback to this method is that the administrator loses control over network configuration.

Another problem to using this approach is that an administrator may not discover an undesired configuration for some time. Most soft-seed implementations don't report to the administrator whether any changeovers occur from the administrator's selected seed information to information from another router.

A third method was initiated by Kinetics (now Shiva) in its FastPath and is now copied by many vendors. This method circumvents the verification process entirely and begins routing with the seed information found in the configuration file, regardless of the configuration in use on the internet. We consider this practice dangerous, however, because it could result in a loss of connectivity to parts of the internet — some stations may not be able to talk to other stations, even though the hardware part of the network is fine. Even simple mistakes such as typos in the seed configuration can jeopardize the entire network (see Chapter 14). And without a verification phase, the administrator cannot be alerted to a configuration problem — because the router has not checked for one.

BACKGROUNDER

### Choosing Between Seed and Nonseed Routers

Selecting whether to make a router a seed router or a nonseed router depends on two rationales. Making all routers except one nonseed guarantees that all routers obtain the same configuration information, as this information issues from a single seed router. Such a setup is especially helpful if you use a long zone list.

If you often experience power-failure problems, however, consider buying a *UPS* (Uninterruptible Power Supply). If you don't want to (or can't) install a UPS, consider making most or all of your routers seed routers. Then, if two areas fail and only one comes back up, the area that comes back up isn't waiting for a second router containing the seed information to come back up, too.

## The configuration of Ethernet filtering bridges

As network manager, you can also control the configuration of *Ethernet filtering bridges* which are installed between Ethernet segments. An Ethernet filtering bridge lets you filter the flow of packets between two (or sometimes more) Ethernet segments based on protocol type. The bridge discards any packets of a type you specify to be filtered. If you establish AppleTalk filtering, for example, no AppleTalk connectivity exists over that bridge. Some bridges also enable you to establish priority settings that take effect whenever their buffers become full and overflow packets must be discarded. A low-priority packet type is discarded first.

If you decide on any of these configurations, carefully consider that the AppleTalk protocol needs timely AARP probes for startup devices as well as RTMP Data packets to maintain routing tables. Never eliminate Ethernet broadcasts if you want to maintain AppleTalk Phase 1 connectivity over the bridge — or AppleTalk multicasts if you want to maintain AppleTalk Phase 2 connectivity. *Multicasting* is a critical part of the functioning of the AppleTalk protocol (RTMP, for example). For this reason, we also suggest that you don't assign AppleTalk packets a low priority. Assigning AppleTalk a low priority can cause zones to disappear and reappear on the network because of the RTMP time-out procedure.

To specify AppleTalk Phase 1 packets, you must identify their *type field*. Two types of packets are available: 809b and 80f3. To specify AppleTalk Phase 2 packets, you must identify in an 8-bit string that the packet is 802 LLC; then you identify the vendor code and type. These two strings are **aaaa03080007809b** and **aaaa0300000080f3.**

## The configuration of AppleTalk servers

A third type of device the configuration of which you control is the AppleTalk server. You can configure only a few settings on AppleTalk servers, and these settings are on servers that automatically establish network conversations, such as e-mail servers and workflow-management servers. On most e-mail servers, you can set the timing for the distribution of names lists. On most e-mail servers and workflow management servers, you can also establish the time for forwarding data. The time interval you set directly affects the performance of your network. Check with vendors for their recommendations. Monitor your network, too, and adjust these settings as necessary.

With some servers, you can determine security restrictions regarding passwords. Standard practice among network managers is to require that all users have passwords of a certain length and that passwords be alphanumeric. Although AppleShare servers are currently limited to eight-character passwords, other vendors' products can use longer ones. If your software allows it, avoid using passwords containing fewer than six characters or passwords composed only of alphanumeric characters. Such passwords are too easy to guess by using the existing password-breaking software easily available to computer hackers.

## Other tips for configuration management

Following are several additional tips to help you avoid problems on your network:

❖ Never test a new configuration on-line during normal business hours. Test it on a "lab network" first and then test on the real network after hours.

❖ Make sure that you have tools to monitor your devices after you bring the devices on-line.

❖ Keep the vendor's tech-support phone number and policies handy.

And, finally, here's a tip from our technical editor with which we heartily agree: Never make a major change just before you go on vacation — you may not have a job when you return.

# Tools for Network Management

All craftsmen need tools to do their jobs — the better the tools, the better the end product. This section discusses several classes of tools that we find exceptionally useful in network management: network monitoring tools, network reporting tools, network management stations based on SNMP, and network protocol analyzers. Some of these tools stretch far beyond the goals of simple AppleTalk managers and are general purpose products that can help you manage much larger networks with greater success.

## Open network management for AppleTalk managers

Today, AppleTalk network managers must continue to manage their network configuration primarily by using *proprietary* software tools. *Open*, the opposite of *proprietary*, refers to a set, published standard to which everyone has access and can implement. But open network management software tools for AppleTalk are still merely chalk on the drawing boards, voices in meeting rooms, and bits on e-mail systems.

Why do network managers need open network management tools? Recall the discussion in Chapter 11 of all the processes that take place on the internet. ZIP, RTMP, and NBP all deliver an easy communications interface to the users of an AppleTalk internet. Remember that the workings of an AppleTalk internet can become highly complex, with multiple types of components: Macintosh and PC workstations, routers, servers, bridges, and repeaters.

Quick, no peeking. How many different brands of equipment are in *your* network? Now take a minute to think about it. Did you remember all those different hubs? Ethernet cards? Servers and routers? Modems? If you ran out of fingers before you ran out of equipment, you probably should start thinking more seriously about network management. You could currently have a heterogeneous, multivendor, multiprotocol, multibuzzword network on your hands — and not even realize it.

Traditional multivendor network management requires many different software tools, as we showed in the section above on "Configuration Management of Network Devices" — one for configuring brand X hubs, one for brand Y, one for Macintosh software updates, one for servers, and so on.

The advantage to this approach is that the management tools are highly customized to handle each proprietary network interface. Each tool works beautifully with the equipment it's designed to manage — but not at all with everything else. The problem to this approach is that you can end up with a disk full of tools but no coherent picture of the entire network. Which vendor, for example, made the hub on the third floor? Is a bridge installed in the computer room, or did we put in a router? Does that printer support AppleTalk or TCP/IP? As the network grows, so do your headaches.

Network management tools can be broken down along two main functions: *monitoring*, and *configuration*. A management tool monitors a network by periodically polling each device and taking some action if a problem arises. Some tools simply test reachability: Is the device still up and running? Others can make more sophisticated queries, checking error rates, throughput, and other significant indicators of network health. If a problem appears, the management tool can initiate many different actions: writing to a log file, sounding a beep or playing a sound, sending out e-mail, and even paging the network manager with the bad news.

The other side of management is configuration. As new devices are added to the network, and as the network status changes, you invariably must change the configuration of most network devices from the defaults given to them at the factory. The AppleTalk zone name, for example, must be configured for each router; Phase 2 AppleTalk routers must be assigned AppleTalk zones before these devices are used.

You need to keep in mind that a network management tool isn't like "After Dark;" it's not a fluffy piece of software you pick up on sale because it looks like fun. Management tools are expensive applications that take time to learn and configure. A good set of network management tools can save you time and frustration, but only if you're already trying to manage a sizable network without one. If your network domain is limited to five Macintoshes and a LaserWriter, these tools are not necessary.

To effectively use network management tools, you must take the time to seriously consider which parts of your network are critical, how you can determine whether the network is healthy, and what you need to do should a problem arise. You must be willing to invest sufficient time to learn the software, configure it to your environment, tune it as you use it, and actually use the data such a setup provides after you collect it.

# AppleTalk network monitoring tools

Several tools are available that help monitor the entire configuration of your AppleTalk (or multiprotocol) internet. Neon Software makes a configuration overview tool called LANsurveyor to map and monitor AppleTalk networks. LANsurveyor's forte is map drawing. (Neon also makes Router Check, a complementary tool that helps keep an eye on AppleTalk routers.)

Set LANsurveyor loose on an AppleTalk network, and the program identifies all the network's routers, picks appropriate icons for the routers, and tries to lay them out into a logical map of the network. You can also instruct LANsurveyor to find every AppleTalk node on the network, not just the routers. Such a tactic is not as useful as you may think, however, because AppleTalk end nodes, such as individual Macintoshes or LaserWriters, can change node numbers every time they boot.

After you build a map by using LANsurveyor, securing information on the configuration of each device is easy. Simply double-click a device icon and a window opens, enabling you to view that device's AppleTalk information, SNMP MIB information, and any notes and comments you may have added to the map.

LANsurveyor isn't a very full-featured program in the areas of monitoring and notifications, but it does incorporate a few monitoring features. LANsurveyor can watch a list of network devices and send out notifications if a device becomes unavailable or if AppleTalk traffic error rates go above a threshold you define. Notifications can take the form of an entry to a log file, the appearance of dialog boxes, and other visual changes to the map, sounds, transmitted pages, or mail sent to any address via QuickMail.

One nice feature of LANsurveyor is its capability for linkage to other Macintosh applications. You can associate any device mapped by LANsurveyor with a Macintosh application. Then, if you press the Option key and double-click the device's icon, that application is launched. (We used this feature to link Compatible Systems' configuration utility to their RiscRouter 3000. Press Option and double-click a RiscRouter 3000 icon on the LANsurveyor map, and up comes the configuration utility.)

Without a doubt, the coolest part of LANsurveyor is its automated mapping capability. We took LANsurveyor to a multihundred node AppleTalk network, and set it loose. A day later, we had a full map of the network, complete with device names, links between routers, and other nifty information.

# AppleTalk network reporting tools

Tools that report differ from tools that monitor a network. Reporting tools are self-initiating: they don't wait for you to open the software to search for errors but send a report to you on their own.

One kind of reporting tool is an SNMP workstation. SNMP management stations (discussed in the next section in this chapter on SNMP tools) can gather information as a background task on the health and status of your network. The central station can then present the network manager with up-to-the-minute conditions of an entire internet.

One of the best examples of a configuration reporting package is Caravelle Networks Corporation's NetWORKS network-management package. Originally designed to report on an AppleTalk network, NetWORKS can now provide reports on a network of computers and devices that talk AppleTalk, Novell's IPX, Digital's DECnet, TCP/IP, SNMP/TCP/IP, and SNMP/AppleTalk. NetWORKS is only a reporting tool, however; it doesn't let you make any changes to the network configuration.

The NetWORKS approach to network monitoring is based on two elements: a device list and a list of *notifications*. NetWORKS checks the devices in the device list as often as you want, and if a problem appears, the program activates a notification. This device list is made up of virtually anything on the network — hubs, routers, workstations, printers, modems — running virtually any protocol: AppleTalk, IPX, DECnet, or TCP/IP. Unfortunately, you must create the device list yourself, one device at a time — a time-consuming process.

Notifications are what NetWORKS uses to tell you that something is wrong on the network. The network manager is free to choose for each notification from NetWORKS' broad repertoire. Possibilities include displaying a dialog box on-screen of the Mac running NetWORKS; using MacinTalk to "say" a message at that Mac; playing a recorded message or sound; sending a message to a pager; sending a message via modem to another computer or bulletin board (such as CompuServe); and sending mail by using QuickMail, Microsoft Mail, SMTP mail, or Apple's AOCE (Apple Open Collaborative Environment) mail.

By using NetWORKS, the network manager can keep a pretty close eye on a very large multivendor network. We set up NetWORKS to query a particular SNMP MIB variable in one of our network routers every 30 seconds, play a recorded message at the Macintosh if the variable went over a certain threshold ("Hey, the router is real busy now"), and page the network manager if the variable went too high into the danger zone. Because NetWORKS supports both numeric and alphanumeric pagers, the network manager could actually see the router name and the traffic level as part of the page.

## The simple network management protocol

*SNMP*, the Simple Network Management Protocol, is being promoted as a way to break out of proprietary network management tools. The SNMP vision is simple: one common management language for every computer, workstation, and network device; many management stations that talk that language; and much more free time for network managers.

SNMP's roots lie in the management of the Internet, a TCP/IP-based network. As the Internet moved to a multivendor backbone in the late 1980s, efficient management became a serious problem. SNMP is a very simple protocol designed to run over TCP/IP networks. SNMP has become a de-facto standard for network management, and almost all network equipment vendors now include some type of SNMP capability in their equipment.

The SNMP model is based on three basic pieces: *MIBs* (Management Information Bases), *management stations*, and *agents*.

MIBs sit in each network device. A MIB (pronounced "mib," not em-eye-bee) is similar to a database; it stores configuration and status information about a device. An entry in a MIB is called a *MIB variable*. One common MIB variable, for example, is "sysDescr," the system description. Retrieve (or *Get*, in SNMP terms) the "sysDescr" for a Macintosh, and you see something like "Macintosh Quadra 800, System 7.1."

Information in a MIB variable can also be stored (or *Set*, in SNMP terms). One MIB variable, for example, is "sysLocation." You may set the "sysLocation" on a particular Macintosh as "Opus One World HQ, Room 117." That way, if someone reads that variable later, he or she knows where the system is located.

A management station is where the network management software runs. Management stations, also called *consoles*, are usually UNIX-based workstations. Think of the management stations as the control seats for the entire network; using a management station, the network manager can watch over, troubleshoot, and configure any SNMP-capable device in the network. Depending on your network management style, you may have a single management station or more than one.

Agents are pieces of software located in each network device. The agent software responds to requests sent by the management station to retrieve information from MIB variables for its device (see Figure 13-4). The agent acts as a translator, peering into the inside of a proprietary device to pass status information out using an open protocol.

Besides the basic Get and Set operations, SNMP supports *traps*, which are notifications sent by a network device's agent after some event occurs. Traps help to keep an eye on the network without constantly asking every device for status information. One kind of trap, for example, is the *Cold Start trap*. A router that speaks SNMP sends out a Cold Start trap every time it boots up. A management station that receives that trap could simply log the information to a file, notify a network manager via e-mail or a pocket pager or set up that trap to trigger some other action, such as downloading device-configuration information.

Many different kinds of MIBs are defined for SNMP. The basic MIB, called MIB-II (because it replaced MIB-I), contains a variety of system, network protocol, and SNMP parameters and counters. Other MIBs are defined for different types of devices, such as bridges, hubs, terminal servers, and routers. Many vendors also

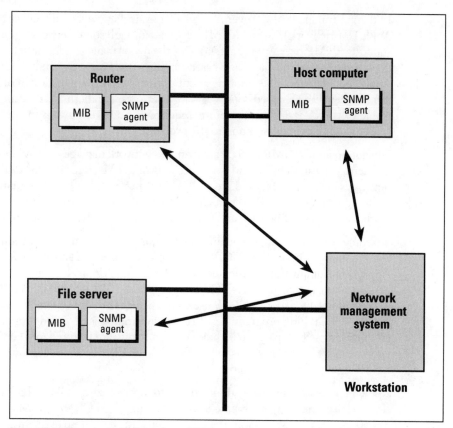

**Figure 13-4: This schematic shows how SNMP agents and a network management system interrelate.**

define a private MIB that works only with their own equipment to handle special statistics or configuration options.

Most network devices support more than one MIB. Apple's SNMP agent for the Macintosh, for example, includes almost all of MIB-II, an AppleTalk MIB, and a new MIB called the Macintosh System MIB. The Macintosh MIB reports on almost every aspect of the Macintosh. In the next chapter, "Managing AppleTalk Networks for Management," Table 14-2 shows the information available in the Macintosh MIB.

## SNMP over AppleTalk

SNMP was first defined and used on the TCP/IP Internet, with the UDP protocol used for data transfer. Nothing about SNMP *requires* it to run over TCP/IP, however, which has led to the development of standards for running SNMP over AppleTalk's DDP protocol (as well as others, such as Netware's IPX and pure Ethernet).

In theory, running SNMP over AppleTalk means that you could manage an AppleTalk network by using SNMP. In fact, although some network equipment supports SNMP over AppleTalk, none of the major management station software does. You must use a Macintosh-based management station to handle the AppleTalk network. These management stations aren't as sophisticated or as powerful as their UNIX-based cousins. A large network with both TCP/IP and AppleTalk SNMP devices, therefore, requires two different management stations — not the best solution to the problem.

The idea behind SNMP is to create a unified network management system. In such a system, you can monitor and configure networked Macintoshes and all the network's connecting bits and pieces by using one single application, running on anything you want: UNIX, OpenVMS, MS-DOS, or Macintosh. That is, you *could* do this if you could find such an application. Unfortunately, it doesn't exist yet.

To add to the confusion, Apple introduced four SNMP-compatible products in 1993: TCP/IP Connection, TCP/IP Administration, AppleTalk Connection, and AppleTalk Administration. Included in the two TCP/IP products are MacTCP version 2 and an SNMP-over-TCP/IP agent for the Macintosh. TCP/IP Connection is designed for most TCP/IP users and includes not only those two products, but also a TCP Ping program. TCP/IP Administration is designed for network administrators. This package includes the same software featured in TCP/IP Connection, as well as applications for configuring MacTCP and the Macintosh SNMP agent, plus some additional documentation.

Apple's idea is for a network administrator to buy one copy of TCP/IP Administration and use that to create floppy disks containing MacTCP and the Macintosh SNMP agent, for distribution to TCP/IP users. Each of those users must have a TCP/IP Connection license (which Apple sells in quantity at a discount).

AppleTalk Connection and AppleTalk Administration bring SNMP to the AppleTalk-connected Macintosh. The main goal of these AppleTalk packages is to expose the masses to the latest and greatest AppleTalk. These new versions have an important plus: they include Apple's new SNMP-over-AppleTalk agent as well.

If you want to add Apple's SNMP agent to your Macintosh computers, you need TCP/IP Connection or AppleTalk Connection. For such minor extras as documentation and administrator tools, you also need at least one copy of TCP/IP Administration or AppleTalk Administration.

Apple wasn't the first to develop an SNMP agent for the Macintosh. But by including SNMP in the basic TCP/IP package, Apple is pushing SNMP for everyone. This package, combined with the new Macintosh MIB, enables you to manage and monitor networked Macintoshes remotely. (Or you could if you were willing to buy and configure a smart enough management station.)

## SNMP in AppleTalk networking devices;

SNMP has extended its reach into virtually every bit of network hardware. For Macintosh users, however, the "SNMP-compatible" label isn't enough. You need to read the fine print of the device specifications to see just how SNMP is included and which of the protocols it runs over — TCP/IP, AppleTalk, or something else. In particular, you must know whether the protocols used under SNMP are compatible with your diagnostic and management software.

Most high-end routers and workstations support SNMP over TCP/IP only. Network equipment sold in the Macintosh marketplace could support SNMP over TCP/IP, SNMP over AppleTalk (sometimes referred to as "SNMP over DDP"), or both. Table 13-1 lists several Macintosh networking vendors and how their products support SNMP.

| Table 13-1 | | | | | |
|---|---|---|---|---|---|
| **Macintosh Networking Vendors and Product Support for SNMP** | | | | | |
| **Vendor** | **Product** | **Device type** | **MIBs Supported** | **Transports** | **Get/Set or Get Only** |
| Apple Computer | TCP/IP Connection for Macintosh | Macintosh | MIB-II, Macintosh System MIB, AppleTalk MIB | UDP | Get/Set |
| | AppleTalk Connection for Macintosh | Macintosh | MIB-II, Macintosh System MIB, AppleTalk MIB | DDP | Get/Set |
| APT Communications | ComTalk | router | MIB-II, AppleTalk MIB, Ethernet MIB, Generic Interface MIB | UDP, DDP, Ethernet | Get/Set |
| Asante | 1012 hub and 1012 bridge | Ethernet hub | MIB-II (subset), Asante MIB, Ethernet Hub MIB, Bridge MIB | UDP | Get/Set |
| | 2072 hub | Ethernet hub | MIB-II (subset), Asante MIB, Ethernet Hub MIB | UDP | Get/Set |
| Cayman | GatorStar | router/ | MIB-II, AppleTalk MIB, Ethernet hub Cayman MIB | UDP, DDP Ethernet MIB, | Get Only |
| | "Gatorbox EX, CS, GX" | router | MIB-II, AppleTalk MIB, Ethernet MIB, Cayman MIB | UDP,DDP | Get Only |
| Compatible Systems | EtherRoute TCP | router | MIB II, AppleTalk | UDP,DDP | Get Only |

*(continued on the next page)*

| Vendor | Product | Device type | MIBs Supported | Transports | Get/Set or Get Only |
|---|---|---|---|---|---|
| | RiscRouter 3000 | router | MIB II | UDP,DDP | Get Only |
| Farallon | InterRoute/5 | router | MIB II, Farallon MIB, Farallon StarRouter MIB, AppleTalk MIB, Ethernet MIB | UDP,DDP | Get/Set |
| | StarRouter | router/ | MIB II, Farallon MIB, Ethernet hub Router MIB, AppleTalk MIB, Ethernet MIB | UDP,DDP Farallon Star | Get/Set |
| | Ether10-T StarController Hub | Ethernet hub | Farallon MIB | UDP,DDP | Get/Set |
| Network Resources Corporation | MultiGate Hub 2 | hub | MIB-II, Repeater MIB, Bridge MIB, PPP MIB, NRC Hub2 MIB | UDP | Get/Set |
| | MultiGate Hub | hub | MIB-II, Repeater MIB, Bridge MIB, NRC Hub1 MIB | UDP | Get/Set |
| | MultiGate Hub 1 and Hub 1+ | hub | MIB-II, Repeater MIB, NRC Hub1 MIB | UDP | Get/Set |
| Shiva | FastPath 5 | router | MIB-II, AppleTalk MIB, Ethernet MIB, Shiva MIB | UDP, DDP | Get/Set |

Table 13-1 *(continued)*

## SNMP management stations

Two SNMP workstations are available for the Macintosh. The first is InterCon Systems Corporation's Watchtower. Watchtower supports SNMP only over TCP/IP. Watchtower starts out as any good SNMP management station should; it enables the network manager to draw a simple map of the network. Unfortunately, it does little else. Network monitoring is severely restricted in this product. No automatic device polling is available either; to determine if a device is up and running, you must double-click the device's icon on the map each time you want to learn its status.

Watchtower does feature some nifty graphs that show trends for TCP/IP nodes. But these plot only five real variables over time (the TCP and UDP input and output rates, as well as IP input rates), and that's not very much help. Watchtower can also create bar graphs of some traffic, but even here its choices are extremely limited and not all that useful.

Watchtower's configuration capabilities are even more restricted. To configure a device by using Watchtower, you must know exactly what SNMP variable to change and what its legal values are. You configure the device by opening up a window that displays that one variable and then changing the variable — not a very useful way to run a network.

The other SNMP management station is Network Resource Corporation's MultiGate Manager. MultiGate Manager is a good base-line product for the network manager who wants to monitor TCP/IP network devices and has an interest in querying SNMP MIB information.

MultiGate Manager does not draw network maps. Instead, network devices are listed in tabular format, along with device interface status, network address, any device traps, and an alarm status field.

MultiGate Manager does enable you to find devices on a TCP/IP network automatically — a very useful feature. You provide a range of network numbers and MultiGate Manager returns a list of all the devices running TCP/IP in that range. You can then move the devices to one or more MultiGate Manager network windows.

MultiGate Manager also enables you to view and set individual MIB variables. Most network managers, however, are more likely to consider MultiGate Manager for its network monitoring capabilities. MultiGate Manager keeps an eye on your network in two ways. First, devices in the network manager window are polled at whatever rate you specify. If a device becomes unavailable, its status appears on the display. MultiGate Manager is also designed to display the status of hubs and routers. A series of spots appears by each device, one spot per interface. If the interface is up, the spot is green. If the interface is down, the spot is red. Even if your network contains many hubs, MultiGate Manager provides a quick visual check of each port on each hub without the need for further customization.

MultiGate Manager also features *trend/threshold* windows for network monitoring. A trend/threshold window is a continuously monitored strip chart of one or more SNMP variables from one or more devices. You could, for example, create a strip chart that shows the throughput of each interface on a single router to give you an idea of where the heaviest load is. MultiGate Manager can use Apple events to tie into the Notify! pager software. MultiGate Manager enables you to indicate a particular SNMP MIB variable, a threshold value and frequency, someone to page when the variable crosses the value or frequency lines you set up, and what to send to the person being paged. In plainer terms, MultiGate Manager let's you say "Page me with code 117 if the AppleShare server's free disk space falls below 1MB more than four times in an hour."

Neither MultiGate Manager nor Watchtower, however, are full-fledged network management stations. Perhaps by the next edition of this book, we can tell you about a complete Macintosh-based tool that can solve all your network management problems by using SNMP.

### If Not the Mac, Then What?

The sad part about using SNMP to manage AppleTalk networks is that you can't manage it on a Macintosh. A Macintosh can be managed by an SNMP manager, but there are no good management station packages for the Macintosh. The top three network management packages are SunConnect's SunNet Manager, Hewlett-Packard's Network Node Manager, and IBM's Netview/6000. If you're serious about using SNMP, check out one of these three programs.

## Network protocol analyzers

We'll come right out and say it: Every LAN manager needs a protocol analyzer. The most popular ones run on MS-DOS laptops, cost a ton of money, and feature pretty poor user interfaces. Fortunately, an alternative exists — and it runs on the Macintosh. You can put together a network analyzer package for less than $4,000, including the cost of the PowerBook on which to run it.

*Protocol analyzers* are tools for looking at networks. They "watch" a wire, capture all the data that passes over the wire, and can display (and sometimes explain) each bit of data. Protocol analyzers exist both for LAN links, such as Ethernet and token ring, and for WAN links, such as RS-232 lines. Protocol analyzers are the last word in network diagnostic tools. With an analyzer in place, the network to which it is applied holds no secrets. Every frame, every packet, can be viewed and reviewed. If a serious problem exists on a network, a protocol analyzer is the tool to use to find it.

The primary use of a protocol analyzer is to help the network manager solve network anomalies. Analyzers can also be used to check network usage levels. (See Figure 13-5 for an example of protocol analyzer statistics.)

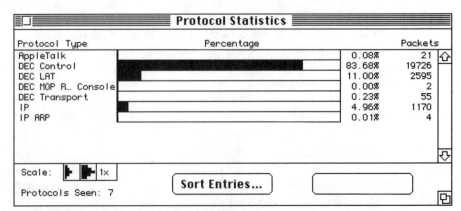

Figure 13-5: A protocol analyzer's statistics report can show which protocols are being used.

Protocol analysis is a three-step process. First, you decide which traffic you need to examine. Then you use the protocol analyzer to capture that traffic. Finally, you examine the captured frames to determine the problem. (Ideally, however, you should be able to swap the first two steps. Capturing all the traffic on the network and then whittling it down from there until you locate the problem usually is easier than determining from the start where the problem lies.)

Three companies have staked out the Macintosh protocol analyzer territory for their own. The AG Group's EtherPeek, Cabletron Systems' MacLANVIEW, and Neon Software's NetMinder Ethernet all offer Macintosh-based analyzers for Ethernet networks. All three also offer LocalTalk versions; AG Group's and Cabletron's analyzers can also monitor token ring LANs. Only Cabletron, however, includes all three in the base package; Neon Software and AG Group charge for each LAN media separately. No Macintosh-based WAN protocol analyzers are currently available.

Using a protocol analyzer is pretty simple. You simply click the Start button, and away it goes. A main window scrolls by as frames are captured, giving you quick information on each frame. Analyzers also make available during these captures such statistical information as the frame type, the network bandwidth used, and which nodes are sending and receiving traffic. (See Figure 13-6 for an example of a protocol analyzer's main window, and refer to Figure 13-5 for some sample statistics.)

```
┌──────────────────────────────── EtherPeek ────────────────────────────┐
│ ☐                                                                      │
│ Packets received:   23705                                              │
│ Packets filtered:   23573                                              │
│ Packets processed:  23573        ┌──────────────┐  ┌──────────────┐    │
│ Bytes available:    9037188      │ Start Capture│  │ Initiate Send│    │
│ Bytes used:          614432      └──────────────┘  └──────────────┘    │
│                                                                        │
│ Packet   Source         Destination      Flag  Type    Size  Time-stamp│
│  22457  tennis          Piano_dlc              DEC Cont  96   0:00:00.022│
│  22458  Piano_dlc       tennis                 DEC Cont  96   0:00:00.003│
│  22459  tennis          Piano_dlc              DEC Cont  72   0:00:00.000│
│  22460  Piano_dlc       tennis                 DEC Cont 584   0:00:00.001│
│  22461  tennis          Piano_dlc              DEC Cont  96   0:00:00.013│
│  22462  Piano_dlc       tennis                 DEC Cont 192   0:00:00.002│
│  22463  Piano_dlc       tennis                 DEC Cont 192   0:00:00.000│
│  22464  tennis          Piano_dlc              DEC Cont 192   0:00:00.001│
│  22465  Piano          ACC Router             TCP        64   0:00:00.002│
│  22466  08:00:2b:0e:08:49  tennis             DEC LAT   184   0:00:00.036│
│  22467  tennis          08:00:2b:0e:08:49     DEC LAT    64   0:00:00.001│
│  22468  tennis          Piano                 TCP       310   0:00:00.001│
│  22469  08:00:2b:0e:08:49  tennis             DEC LAT   184   0:00:00.079│
│  22470  tennis          08:00:2b:0e:08:49     DEC LAT    64   0:00:00.002│
│  22471  Piano_dlc       tennis                 DEC Cont 192   0:00:00.072│
│  22472  tennis          Piano_dlc              DEC Cont 192   0:00:00.001│
│  22473  Piano_dlc       ab:00:00:03:00:00     DEC Tran   64   0:00:00.002│
│  22474  08:00:2b:0e:08:49  tennis             DEC LAT   184   0:00:00.005│
│  22475  Piano_dlc       tennis                 DEC Cont 192   0:00:00.001│
│                                                                        │
│  ┌──────────────────────┐        ═══════ EtherPeek ═══════             │
│  └──────────────────────┘                                              │
└────────────────────────────────────────────────────────────────────────┘
```

Figure 13-6: The main window of a protocol analyzer should show source, destination, and protocol type for each packet.

If you plan to run a protocol analyzer on your regular Macintosh, a second
Ethernet interface is a requirement. Because the analyzers intercept all network
traffic, anything else using your normal Ethernet interface (such as AppleTalk or
TCP/IP) is disconnected. If you try to skimp on this, expect numerous crashes of
the protocol analyzer.

On a multiple protocol Ethernet, capturing only the frames you seek can be difficult. To help keep the amount of captured data to a minimum, protocol analyzers
offer two capabilities called *triggering* and *filtering*. Triggers are used to begin capturing frames only after a specific event occurs, such as after a particular type of
packet goes by ("Next time the Jan router sends an RTMP update packet, start
capturing") or after a certain time has passed ("Start capturing at 1:17 a.m.").

Filters tell the protocol analyzer which frames to keep and which to discard. Protocol analyzers enable you to define filters based on a variety of criteria, such as
protocol type, hardware address, or socket number.

*Protocol decoding* is the most important function of a protocol analyzer and the one
by which a protocol analyzer can really make your life easy. Figure 13-7 shows a
network frame decoded by EtherPeek.

```
═════════════════════ Packet #4 ═════════════════════
 Flags:         0x80  802.3
 Status:        0x00
 Packet Length:64
 Timestamp:     17:25:52.353
 Filter:        AppleTalk
802.3 Header
 Destination:   09:00:07:ff:ff:ff  AT Ph2 Broadcast
 Source:        aa:00:04:00:45:c8  (50.69)  Piano_dlc
 LLC Length:    31
802.2 Logical Link Control (LLC) Header
 Dest. SAP:     0xaa  SNAP
 Source SAP:    0xaa  SNAP
 Command:       0x03  Unnumbered Information
 Protocol:      0x080007809b  AppleTalk
Long DDP Header - Datagram Delivery Protocol
 Unused:        %00
 Hop Count:     %0000
 Datagram Length: 23
 DDP Checksum:  0x0000
 Dest. Network: 0
 Source Network: 2320
 Dest Node:     255   0.255      AppleTalk Broadcast
 Source Node:   162
 Dest. Socket:  1  RTMP Socket
 Source Socket: 1  RTMP Socket
 DDP Type:      1  RTMP Response or Data
RTMP - Routing Table Maintenance Protocol
 Router's Net:  2320
 ID Length:     8
 Router's Node ID: 0xa2  162
RTMP Tuple #1
 Range Start:   2320
 Range Flag:    %100  Extended
 Distance:      0
 Range End:     2321
 Version:       0x82
 ---------------   00 00 00 00 00 00 00 00 00 00 00 00 00 00 00 00
Frame Check Sequence:  0x792a6317
```

Figure 13-7: The innards of an AppleTalk RTMP packet, laid bare by
EtherPeek.

### How to use a protocol analyzer

The following sections outline our rules of thumb to help you on your coming adventures through the nebulous muck of network protocol analysis.

#### Move from the known to the unknown

That may seem an obvious statement, but a couple of stupid mistakes taught us how important this concept really is. Don't just sit down, plug in, program a complex filter, and press the Monitor button. We got cocky a couple of times, and tried this, wasting about an hour before figuring out that the Ethernet cable to the analyzer wasn't even plugged into anything. Whenever you decide to actually attack a problem, set up the analyzer and grab a few frames first — just to make sure that everything is working.

Most problems you may encounter require multiple filters to capture the exact packets you need to examine. Test each filter individually before combining them. Mistyping an address is easy to do — but often hard to catch. If you can, generate a few test packets to make sure that your filters are actually doing what you want them to do. If all else fails, turn off all your filters and try again.

#### Get a clear, reproducible definition of your problem

If someone calls you and complains that "The printers are responding slowly," resist the temptation to immediately whip out your analyzer and rush to the "scene of the crime."   Spend as much time as you need to extract from the caller an exact description of the problem — and then to figure out how to reproduce it. After securing this information, you should be able to restate the problem in such terms as "Whenever I try to do *this*, I expect it to say *that*, but instead it says something else." Learn the exact command to type to reproduce the problem and the resulting error condition. If you don't have a clear problem definition before you attempt to fix it, you're just wasting your time.

Finding a similar case in which the problem *doesn't* occur, however, may prove even more useful to you. Then you can capture that traffic and compare it to the problem traffic for any differences between the two.

In any event, take your protocol handbooks with you and set up your protocol analyzer — with you in front of it — next to a workstation from which the problem can be created. Nothing's worse than trying to diagnose a problem over the phone or running back and forth between your analyzer and a workstation. You paid for the portability; use it.

#### Understand the protocol suite you're viewing

A good protocol analyzer can save you hours of frustration by decoding packets for you — a notoriously error-prone process if attempted manually. But even with the help of an analyzer, *you* must understand what all the fields mean, how the protocols work, and what sequence of packets is the correct one. Everything can appear so simple on-screen, but when the going gets tough, understanding the protocols is critical. And that means securing the complete documentation for every protocol you want to support.

Unfortunately, few problems are caused by what protocol analyzers are best at spotting — badly formed packets. Instead, we find most problems involve subtle differences in interpretation of the protocol description; optional features that somehow are interpreted as mandatory; information that is somehow too long or too short; and systems that generate perfectly formed packets — with entirely bogus information. All such mishaps are impossible to discover without a good set of protocol documentation.

Whenever the fingers start pointing, nothing helps so much as calling someone up and reading the solution to them straight from the protocol specification. ("Section 3.2.1.7 says that this bit must be zero. You are setting it to be one. Your software is broken and needs to be fixed.")

For a short introduction to major protocols, the *Network Protocol Handbook* (McGraw-Hill), by Matthew Naugle, offers a good overview of most major LAN protocols.

### Practice before a problem arises

Protocol analyzers look easy to use, and they often are. But real detective work takes expertise. Don't skimp on self-training time. After you buy an analyzer, set time aside to really learn the software. Make up some simple problems and try to solve them before a broken network and angry users cause you to make dumb mistakes with unfamiliar software. Try capturing all the passwords on your network; that's a good start.

Another reason to practice on a working network is that doing so helps you get a feel for its normal activity. Networks often carry a very different traffic mix than we may imagine. Spending practice time on it while the network is healthy shows you what to expect during normal operations and thus enables you to focus your energies better and avoid wasting time if a real problem arises.

### *A network doesn't look the same everywhere*

Most LANs now contain much more than a single piece of Ethernet cable. With hubs, repeaters, bridges and routers, different locations on the network provide different views of the data in transit. If a problem appears somewhere on the network, try to locate yourself as close physically to the location of the problem as possible. Such proximity often helps you to discover examples of poor network topology or installation, which can cause sporadic failures in a LAN.

Be aware, however, that an Ethernet protocol analyzer does not necessarily see every packet on the network. Packets can pass by too fast for many analyzers. Both Ethernet and token ring are *datagram networks* — frames can be lost or corrupted at any time on such networks, without detection. If possible, reduce network traffic on any segment you're trying to analyze.

### Use the right tool for the job

Protocol analyzers can be fun to use. Peering into the guts of your LAN is both cool and mysterious. Don't be tempted, however, to use a protocol analyzer for every situation. Even with an expensive portable protocol analyzer at hand, you still have no excuse for failing to check configurations, addresses, and reading error log files. Most network problems don't require a network analyzer to diagnose or to fix. At certain times, however, a protocol analyzer is the *only* way to solve some problems.

### Don't get bit by byte order

The bits on the wire don't always look how you'd expect them to look from the protocol documentation. *Network byte order* usually specifies that the most significant byte (or octet) of an integer is transmitted first (this ordering is called *big endian* in geek-speak) on the LAN. Some machines, however, don't represent data internally in the same way the data is transmitted. (These machines are known as *little endian* machines).

To further complicate matters, token ring and Ethernet transmit bits on the wire backwards from one another — one puts bit 1 of each byte (octet) on the wire first, while the other puts bit 8 on first. This especially complicates bridging or routing between the two types of networks. Together, these factors provide you ample opportunity for confusion about which byte goes where in the protocol. We got lost on this a couple of times ourselves, and so could you.

You should also invest in a pocket calculator that converts between decimal, octal, hexadecimal, and binary numbers. Casio sells one for about $20 (solar powered, even), or you can go for the deluxe Hewlett-Packard version for about $70.

# Tuning AppleTalk Networks

*Throughput* is one of those words born in the age of technology. Quite simply, throughput is the amount of data that can be transferred through a device. In discussions about performance, flashy terms such as *packets per second, speed,* and *response time* often are tossed into the conversation. But before you go racing off in search of the *fastest* network, we should caution you that performance should never be obtained at the price of stability. A fast network that frequently crashes is not the gleaming achievement you envisioned.

To examine the steps toward making your network a hot performer, we break the subject down into two sections. The first section deals with service ratios, some of which are based on traffic patterns and traffic volume. In the second section, we talk about network configuration.

We start with services first because services are the driving forces of your network. Just ask any network manager — does a manager hear from the users if a router slows down? Maybe. But does the manager hear from the users if a file transfer "takes forever"? You bet! After examining the needs of your network services, we examine ways to configure your network so that it becomes the strong framework you require.

We analyze the decisions you need to make about features by expressing them as three ratios:

❖ Services per network

❖ Services per device

❖ Users per service

After you determine these ratios, you know whether stepping a segment of your internet through the following progression of possible setups is appropriate:

❖ Build the network by using a daisy-chain

❖ Build the network by using a bus or passive star

❖ Build the network by using a repeater

❖ Build the network by using a bridge

In the section on network configuration, we discuss these options so that you can make a decision appropriate to your needs. Most of this discussion deals with LocalTalk networks, but the general concepts also apply to Ethernet networks.

As your network grows and takes up more space, you also must decide when to begin joining networks together with routers. These decisions lead you to a plan for your internet configuration. A backbone internet, for example, is a popular choice. We also discuss how to plan an internet in a star configuration, a design popularized by the 10BASE-T twisted-pair wiring system and now commonly used by almost all new Ethernet networks.

## Using traffic statistics to determine service ratios

To make effective performance decisions, you need to know several important facts about your network services:

❖ What network services are available?

❖ Who uses these services?

❖ How much traffic is generated between the users and the services?

You probably already know the answers to the first question, and may know the answer to the second. If you don't, you may wish to gather that information on the disaster recovery chart we suggest in Chapter 14, "Managing AppleTalk Networks for Management." In the following sections, you learn about tools that gather traffic statistics. These tools help you determine the volume of traffic between network services and their users.

Several traffic monitoring tools are available in the Macintosh network market. Among the important features of these tools are their capabilities for plotting the following aspects of network traffic:

❖ Traffic patterns established by the entire network over a period of time

❖ Statistics on the amount of traffic between specific nodes, such as individual workstations and printers

❖ The amount of traffic generated by specific services and measured against the network's full bandwidth

In the following sections, we examine these important plotting capabilities.

## Statistics plotted over time

The capability for plotting statistics over a period of time is an important feature in a traffic statistics tool. A snapshot gives you an idea of what's going on at any given time, but even more important is the capability to determine the busy or peak times for each network service. An effective traffic statistics tool should enable you to establish which are the busy times during the day — and throughout the week. If your business uses projected monthly work schedules, these schedules also may help you locate peak periods for your network.

## Statistics on specific node-to-node traffic

Another statistic you can gather with these tools is a plot of the usages between specific nodes. These tools tell you which users and services are taking up a specific amount of the bandwidth.

### Looking for Traffic Patterns

We suggest that you monitor your network traffic over a period of several weeks before deciding on a new network configuration. Your best course is to establish long-term traffic patterns rather than just to rely on an occasional heavy week to make configuration decisions.

After running the statistics program, for example, you may see that users Mary and Jon are using one of the LaserWriters at a rate of more than 60 percent of the total traffic going to that node. If the statistics tell you only about sending and receiving traffic in separate charts, instead of showing specific node-to-node usage, you would know from these figures only that Mary and Jon are busy users on the network.

The limited nature of such statistical information is why establishing a correlation between users and services is so important. Further investigation may show, for example, that Mary and Jon should either spool their print jobs for after hours or that a new high-end printer should be purchased for their needs. On the other hand, gathering additional statistics may show that their heavy use was atypical and resulted from an additional task added to that week or day. Determining these correlations is another important reason to plot statistics over time.

### Statistics plotted against traffic

The capability to plot each service's traffic against the full traffic level of the network also is a useful convenience. Here, you're looking at the percentage of the *traffic* on the network, not the *bandwidth*. A station which takes 20 percent of the traffic may account for 0.0001 percent of the bandwidth. Some programs plot each node's traffic only against the total traffic, so you may see a node producing 30 percent of the total traffic on the network. Unfortunately, that statistic doesn't tell you whether that node is actually causing performance difficulties on your network. After all, the total network traffic may be low. If, however, you see that a service node is sending 20 percent of the network's total bandwidth, you can more readily pinpoint a performance problem.

## Using service ratios to design your AppleTalk internet

After you obtain statistics about your network's traffic conditions, you can start making decisions about service ratios, according to the following categories:

❖ Services per network

❖ Services per device

❖ Users per service

Although these three ratios depend greatly on the amount of traffic the service receives, some general guidelines to follow do exist. Keep in mind that sometimes a slowdown in response from a service is not network related. The culprit may be an incorrect balance of the system configuration, such as with INIT conflicts or insufficient RAM on the user's Mac. (See the *Macworld Complete Mac Handbook Plus CD* by Jim Heid published by IDG Books Worldwide, for more information on configuring a Macintosh.)

QUICK TIPS

## Watch Collision Rates During High Traffic Periods

As a rule, most Ethernet and LocalTalk networks never exceed a 10 percent usage of their total bandwidth at peak times. If you have a busy network and see that the traffic rate is approaching 50 percent or more during peaks, you will probably also notice that the collision rate has gone way up. Because packets must be re-sent after a collision, your network's throughput decreases in proportion to an increase in traffic. So watch your network's traffic use, and make sure that you closely watch the collision rate to get a total performance picture.

## Services per network

Each network in an AppleTalk internet can support multiple services, including services that are distributed across all users' Macintoshes (or other computers). Remember that the more traffic you have on a network, the more collisions you have and, therefore, the less throughput. In any case, the user perceives that the network is slow.

In the following sections, we offer some rules of thumb to help you decide how many services to place on each network. We divide this discussion into two groups of service ratios — those for LocalTalk networks and those for Ethernet networks.

### LocalTalk networks

If we define a LocalTalk network as a cable with its own network number, rather than as a zone extending over several networks, we can say that the number of primary services on this network should not exceed three. *Primary services* can include central file servers, printers, and other devices that are shared by a significant portion of the network's users. Examples of *secondary services* are distributed file-share systems that see only occasional use and file-transfer programs. For more information on file-sharing and file-transfer programs, see Chapter 22, "Sharing Files on AppleTalk Networks."

Even with as few as three primary services on the network, you should be vigilant in watching for traffic overload. Reduce the number of services as necessary to prevent network throughput from slowing down.

If you use a LocalTalk bridge, you may decide to put heavily used primary services on their own segments and have users access these services across the bridge. Although this method does cause some slowdown as traffic goes through the bridge, it also frees up other segments for secondary traffic.

On LocalTalk, all traffic from all conversations is seen by all stations in the network. This means that if two stations are using the network, the total bandwidth available to all the other stations is reduced. LocalTalk, which is slow to begin with, can crawl along if lots of stations want to talk at the same time. (A multiport repeater does not create multiple segments that enable separate simultaneous conversations the way a bridge does.) You may also want to split up the users into groups on different segments (see Figure 13-8). That way, if a user from one group accesses a primary service, other groups are not affected. For more about LocalTalk network segments, see Chapter 6, "Designing a LocalTalk LAN."

Figure 13-8 demonstrates that on a single LocalTalk network (top diagram), any traffic from one session is seen by all nodes in the network. If Mac B is printing to the LaserWriter, Mac A and Mac C also see the traffic. This reduces the total bandwidth available for sessions from Mac A to Mac C, as they must share the network with Mac B and the LaserWriter. With a LocalTalk bridge, multiple sessions can take place without any reduction in bandwidth, as shown in the lower diagram. In this example, Mac B is printing to LaserWriter A, while Macs C and D are exchanging information and Mac E is using server F. All three network sessions have the full bandwidth of their own network available to them, yet can communicate through the bridge with complete transparency.

When planning how many primary and secondary services to put on a network and how much traffic to load on that network, think about what the user sees. In the first example in Figure 13-8, only one user can access a printer. That user obtains the print job quickly. But if another user decides to print at this time, this second user sees only that the job takes a long time to get printed. Behind the scenes, the AppleTalk software on the computer keeps resending the job until its packets get across the network. That's a good way to frustrate users. So make sure that you keep your users' requirements in mind as you plan your network loading.

### Ethernet networks

Ethernet networks are similar to LocalTalk networks in that they enable only one network conversation at the same time. The two networks differ greatly, however, in bandwidth. Ethernet, at 10MBper second, can complete a conversation much faster than LocalTalk can at its 230.4K per second (only 2.3 percent the speed of Ethernet). And you can add many more services to an Ethernet network than to a LocalTalk network without seeing a significant drop in performance.

After you add more than a half-dozen Macs to a LocalTalk network, you are almost certain to want to upgrade your entire network to Ethernet. As the costs of Ethernet hardware and wiring drop dramatically, the increased performance you realize by switching to Ethernet actually costs you less and less. Certainly, you should buy all new Macintosh hardware, either with built-in Ethernet adapters (as in the Quadra series) or with an Ethernet card.

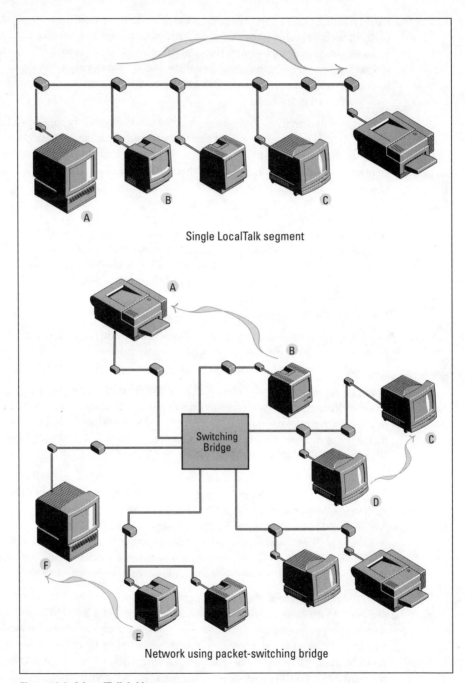

Single LocalTalk segment

Network using packet-switching bridge

Figure 13-8: A LocalTalk bridge strategy.

Staying with LocalTalk is possible, however, as long as your usage is occasional or light. In such a case, you may want to postpone moving to Ethernet until after you add a service that accepts a significant number of large file transfers, such as a file server. Remember, however, that graphics files are almost always large files, so switching to Ethernet is a good idea for networks with servers that handle a significant number of graphics files.

Even constant activity from a small group of users may justify the use of Ethernet. If possible, move power users and their servers onto Ethernet networks to keep them on the same network. If you put a heavily used server on Ethernet and keep its users on a LocalTalk network, all that traffic must be transmitted through a LocalTalk-to-EtherTalk router.

## Services per device

Another consideration in your high-performance network design is how many services to put on one device. Many network server applications, including certain e-mail servers, file-share servers, and print servers, can be doubled up on a Macintosh. (Some applications that require servers are AppleShare, Meeting Maker XP, almost all e-mail programs, and ODMS — Odesta Document Management System.)

Doubling up functions on devices is a popular cost-cutting strategy. You can, for example, run some of these server applications on Macs that individuals use for personal workstation tasks, such as word processing and spreadsheets.

A similar strategy is to combine a software router application, such as Apple's Internet Router, and a server application on one Macintosh. Another alternative is to run a server application on a router that has its own hardware platform, such as GatorShare running on the GatorBox router, a Webster Computer Corp. MultiPort/LT, or a Compatible Systems RISCrouter.

Doubling up on services this way saves money but costs you in performance. Unless the usage of any of these server applications is minimal, we don't recommend such strategies. One service per platform (as in one server application per Macintosh) is a safe bet for getting the best performance out of that platform. This approach is also a good fault-management practice, enabling you to more easily detect the origin of errors. Moreover, a limit of one service per device minimizes the effect on your users if you need to shut down a device to work on it.

If your AppleTalk internet consists of more than a few networks, putting anything else on a Macintosh running a software router is never a good idea. Keep in mind that, if you put a software router on a user's Macintosh and that user locks up the Macintosh, the routes the software router was advertising are gone and must be reestablished. After less than a minute of silence, other routers purge that route through the RTMP process. (See Chapter 11, "Designing an AppleTalk LAN.")

On the other hand, routers with their own optimized hardware platforms and operating systems (such as FastPaths, Ciscos, and GatorBoxes) can multitask several services. Even as you load up these routers with different tasks, however, make sure that you monitor their diagnostics for any errors or buffer-overflow occurrences.

### Users per service

The third service ratio listed in this chapter indicates the number of users per service. This particular ratio depends heavily on the type of traffic statistics you obtain. Having 14 people accessing the same file-share server may work just fine if all are occasional users. Yet, for most work environments, 14 active users to a printer is not a workable number. We suggest that administrators of larger networks use a planning model for networks, allocating, for instance, four users per printer. (Obviously, this number can vary depending on whether you use 4 ppm — pages per minute — Personal LaserWriters or 17 ppm Hewlett-Packard LaserJets.) Then vary the model as conditions require. (Monitoring the network's collision rate can help you determine this.) You may, for example, want to share a higher performance print server among a larger group of users.

In looking at users per service, consider as well where those users are located in relation to the services. A user shouldn't need to go through more than one bridge, router, or other network device to access an often-used service. In fact, going through *no* network device is best, wherever possible. Printing services, usually the most burdened network service, should be placed within the same network as the user whenever possible.

An exception is in your placement of a high-end Ethernet printer, such as a DEC LPS40 or Hewlett-Packard LaserJet IIIsi, which prints many pages per minute. These devices are expensive items, so most administrators plan on sharing them with as many networks (or network segments) as possible. Locating this kind of device centrally is best, spacing the majority of users an equal distance from the service. For more information on this subject, refer to the section "Setting Up Internet Configurations," earlier in this chapter.

# Fixing AppleTalk Networks

The term *proactive* has a special meaning for network managers. A proactive network manager has the right tools and skills to stay on top of a disaster. The best fault-management plan enables the network manager to avoid noticeable network downtime by catching the problem before the users do. To do so, you must monitor your network. Monitoring your network is also one of the quickest ways to determine what has changed. To determine what has changed, you must know how it looked before.

If your network monitoring shows that a failure has occurred, you need good troubleshooting skills to get you through. Some say that troubleshooting is an art. But troubleshooting is also a skill you can develop. Troubleshooting is the application of a logical, consistent, step-by-step analysis of the problem.

Before we get farther into troubleshooting, consider the following network manager's classic mistake. The troubleshooter looks at a system, picks the area with which the troubleshooter has the least contact or understands the least, and then decides that this area should be the starting point for any network repair work — instead of following a logical, systematic approach, in which the starting point is always the same.

Not only is the former approach ineffective, but it can be somewhat threatening to the person who is responsible for and who does understand the chosen area. Thus, without a logical framework for the failure analysis, the network manager puts that person on the defensive. This approach can even turn network repair into a quagmire of "Who screwed up?" finger pointing.

Network repair should always be approached logically. To help you keep your thinking along logical paths, the section "Troubleshooting the network," later in this chapter, offers a series of steps you can follow. Even as top-level managers breathe down your neck — some companies claim that each minute of network downtime costs them as much as a million dollars — you must remain unemotional. So don't panic. Take a few deep breaths and begin at the beginning. The repairs may seem to proceed more slowly at first, but you almost always arrive at a solution faster by remaining calm and working through the problem step by step.

One technique that really helps in troubleshooting difficult network problems is to keep a notebook about what you've done and how you've done it. Get a notebook with bound and numbered pages and carry it with you whenever you go problem solving along your network. For each experiment or problem-solving step you take, document what you've done and how you've changed the configuration. You may be surprised at how this kind of documentation focuses your thinking and keeps you from making dangerous assumptions about what is broken and what is working.

As you either monitor your network or step your way through troubleshooting a network failure, keep in mind, too, that a network is a system of related parts. Each part or component can be described separately; in action, however, each integrates with other components to fulfill its function. In your mind's eye, you need to visualize these component relationships as you step through the problem.

## Monitoring the network

You can monitor an AppleTalk network by using several sets of special-purpose AppleTalk-specific tools. The most predominant tools today are those that use NBP (Name Binding Protocol) and AEP (AppleTalk Echo Protocol). Also available are the diagnostic tool sets that come with most AppleTalk routers, bridges, and repeaters. Some of these tools now even implement features that send alarms to you via a modem or e-mail. For information on using a protocol analyzer to monitor your network, or to learn about other monitoring tools, refer to earlier sections in this chapter. For more information on NBP and AEP, see Chapter 3, "Understanding AppleTalk Protocols."

Because so many vendor offerings are available and because these offerings change over time, the following sections list features that we think are useful instead of citing particular products.

## NBP and AEP diagnostic tools

A commonly used set of tools depends on NBP and AEP. AEP tools enable you to send an *echo packet* to a selected device; if the device is live, it returns an echo packet. These tools require AEP software on the clients that you want to *echo*.

NBP tools send out NBP LkUp (lookup) packets for various types of AppleTalk devices and processes. These devices then return a set of information to the re-questing tool. The term for a network device or process within a node is a *socket*. Each node on the network has sockets within it that further address each network-aware process in the node. The format of an AppleTalk address is **net.node.socket.** In the address 3.128.142, for example, 3 is the network number, 128 is the node number, and 142 is the socket number.

A Macintosh can have several sockets. The Mac may, for example, have one socket for sending and receiving e-mail and another socket for System 7's personal file-sharing feature. An NBP tool returns information regarding the type, quantity, and names of devices in a particular zone. An NBP tool may tell you, for example, that a zone has one FastPath router, two Apple LaserWriters, and ten Macintoshes.

Some NBP diagnostic tools enable you to send a query at specified intervals and also to maintain a log of *events*. (An event may be the addition or deletion of net-work services.) You can, for example, ask the NBP diagnostic tool to produce a report that shows you when any of the FastPaths changed status. Some tools even send you such a report instantly via modem or e-mail. Inter•Poll, made by Apple, is a popular tool that uses both NBP and AEP. (See the sidebar "About Inter•Poll" in the section and "The faulty cable disaster," later in this chapter.)

Like the AEP tools, NBP tools require that the devices you query have applications that respond to NBP LkUp packets. These applications are called NVEs, or *Net-work Visible Entities.* AppleShare, for example, is an NVE and thus responds to an NBP LkUp.

Because NBP is an essential part of the AppleTalk operation, most network ser-vices are NVEs. The router, however, is an exception because it does not *always* behave as an NVE. As a result, NBP-based diagnostic tools are currently not effi-cient at monitoring router activity.

Some routers behave as NVEs only off one port; other routers do not behave as NVEs off any port. If, for example, you have a LocalTalk-to-EtherTalk router that is an NVE only on its LocalTalk port address but is not an NVE on its Ethernet port address, any NBP query sent by a diagnostic tool to the zones on the Ethernet do not include this router in the reported list of EtherTalk devices.

## Router diagnostic tools

One favorite tool set for monitoring the activity of a medium- to large-sized AppleTalk internet is the set that comes with AppleTalk routers. These tools can be found in routers that join two LocalTalk networks, as well as in routers that join an EtherTalk network to a LocalTalk network or to another EtherTalk network. Most router tools enable the network manager to set the tool to monitor the network for almost every action or to monitor for only very serious actions. The tools can also provide messages that warn of unusual activity, according to the level of monitoring set. Such messages may warn you about unusual occurrences, such as a multitude of ZIP (Zone Information Protocol) GetNetInfoReply packets; ATP (AppleTalk Transaction Protocol) packet time-outs; or routes to networks going away or coming on-line.

Such messages should supply another important item of data — the time these events occur. Many router diagnostic tool sets also include diagnostics that tell about network misconfiguration, including the Ethernet address of the misconfigured router and the specific nature of the misconfiguration. As you use these tools, you see the network from the router's perspective. You may need to look at the diagnostic messages from other routers on your network, as well as look at the network with other types of tools to gain a full perspective of the problem. Router diagnostics are great for quick checkups on your AppleTalk internet to see whether anything is going haywire.

## Bridge and repeater diagnostic tools

Many vendors' bridges and repeaters that are used to expand LocalTalk networks come with diagnostics. One difference between the diagnostics supplied with bridges and repeaters and diagnostics offered with routers reflects a primary functional difference of these devices. Bridges and repeaters, unlike routers, do not keep track of network numbers or zone names. Notice that bridges and repeaters come into play only in the first and second layers of the protocol stack — repeaters operating at the physical layer and bridges at both the physical and the data link layers. These layers are concerned with the physical representation and formation of data packets, not with network numbering. Network numbering is part of the network layer and, therefore, is a concern of router diagnostics.

For more information on how bridges and repeaters work, see Chapter 2, "Understanding Networks." For information about protocol layers, refer to Chapter 3, "Understanding AppleTalk Protocols."

Bridges differ from repeaters in that they maintain tables of addresses for each cable attached to a port. This table helps the bridging software decide whether a packet should be forwarded to a destination address across the bridge, from one port of the bridge to another. Bridge diagnostics, therefore, can tell you things about the addresses on each port, and some diagnostics send NBP LkUps to compile a list of all devices by name.

Bridges and repeaters can tell you whether they have shut down a port — a process called *jamming a port* — due to a bad signal. A bridge or repeater jams a port so that a bad signal coming from a faulty end node does not propagate across the entire cable and take up the cable's bandwidth. Or the diagnostics may tell you about a faulty physical cable on a particular port. So, if several users seem to be pushed off the network, check the diagnostic messages from your bridge or repeater to see whether the users are all on the same port. If so, see whether something is wrong with that port.

Another consideration for diagnostic tools, whether for repeaters, bridges, or routers, is the distinction between *in-band* and *out-of-band*. *Out-of-band* means that the diagnostics tool doesn't need to use the AppleTalk network to perform its diagnosis. Having some of the diagnostic information obtainable out-of-band is important if the network is malfunctioning. You can usually obtain out-of-band reports by plugging a Macintosh loaded with the diagnostic software into a special serial port on the repeater, bridge, or router.

### SNMP tools

A third set of tools uses *SNMP*, the Simple Network Management Protocol. SNMP is a protocol to help manage networks that have several different protocol suites running. SNMP is discussed in greater detail earlier in this chapter.

## Troubleshooting the network

Suppose that you've been monitoring your network with your network diagnostics tool set and you've discovered a network failure — or worse yet, a user has discovered one first. Now *you're* on the defensive with the clock ticking. In the accompanying box is a series of troubleshooting steps that can help you step through the problem.

These steps can be viewed in two parts. The first part, composed of steps 1, 2, and 3, is the phase of gathering information from the user to narrow your search by putting it within boundaries. In the second part, covered in steps 4 and 5, you use diagnostic tools to start looking at the components and relationships of the network. You start at the top layer of the protocol stack, where you look for possible problems with applications on a user's machine, and work your way down to the bottom layer of the protocol stack, where you look for problems with the cabling or other hardware components that make up the network.

STEP-BY-STEP

### Problem Solving Without Panic

Here's a good technique for approaching and solving network problems. Start by heeding Douglas Adam's advice: "Don't Panic." Then work through the problem, step-by-step. This technique works for us, and it can work for you.

1. **Write down the user's statements regarding the problem in your notebook, or, if you discovered the problem yourself, write down the symptoms of the problem.**

2. **Write down all the components that could be involved.**

   Don't forget application items, such as client/server software and the Chooser. And don't forget such simple physical items as transceivers and PhoneNET or AppleTalk connectors.

3. **Break the symptoms, or the user's statements, into small segments. Next, develop a series of either/or questions for each segment based on the user's statement (or your discovery notes) and the components of the network.**

These questions should give you the groundwork to begin either at, or close to, the top layer of the protocol stack as you use your diagnostics tools in the next series of steps.

4. **Try to establish *what changed*.**

   If the network was functioning before, something changed to cause the failure. Sometimes you can't establish this immediately but must ask yourself constantly as you work through the problem: "What has changed here?" Remember to refer to your monitoring tool set. If you have been monitoring the network, you should have some idea about what the tools told you previously as opposed to what they are telling you now.

5. **Use your diagnostics tools to work through your list of questions.**

   Continue to make new questions. This stage should be like stepping through a flow chart.

As mentioned, steps 4 and 5 of the accompanying steps involve using the OSI Reference Model (see Figure 13-9). We believe that protocol layers provide an excellent mechanism for stepping through your network logically. Although disciplining your thinking according to the protocol layers may take a little effort, if you stay with it, it becomes a natural process.

After you use the first three steps to gather information, you should be able to narrow the problem to a group of devices — or even to a single device. If the problem seems to be narrowed down to an end node or a set of end nodes, begin at the top with Layer 7, the application layer.

A problem may be occurring with an application's interface to a network driver, which means that the problem is within the operating system of the end node and not actually out on the network. The Scores virus, for example, can cause print jobs to abort from within several applications. If the Scores virus is corrupting the system software and preventing the user from using network services, you must reinstall the operating system and any affected applications.

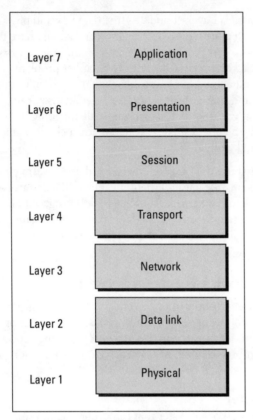

**Figure 13-9: The OSI Reference Model.**

Look next at Layer 6, the presentation Layer, if a user is experiencing printing or file-sharing problems — the AFP (Apple Filing Protocol) and PostScript are located in that layer. A problem at the presentation layer may be caused by a misconfigured AppleShare server; perhaps a user's account was not entered correctly in the server or the user's AppleShare client driver on the user's end node was not installed correctly. Another example of a problem at the presentation layer occurs with the use of fonts, in which a user did not select a PostScript font that the printer had in its memory; as a result, the user's file printed out in bitmap format.

Look in the network, transport, and session layers (Layers 3, 4, and 5) for problems that stem from misconfigured routers, traffic overloads that don't enable sessions to be established, and problems with NBP (Name Binding Protocol). An example of difficulty at these layers is the problem discussed in Appendix B, "Converting Phase 1 AppleTalk Networks to Phase 2," in which an NBP forward packet is sent to a router that recognizes only Phase 1 NBP LkUp packets. At this level, you can use the Chooser as a diagnostics tool for a perspective of what is visible on the network, because the Chooser uses the NBP process.

Finally, work your way down to Layers 1 and 2 — the data link and physical layers. By this time, you've gathered quite a bit of information and should have the problem fairly well narrowed down. At the data link layer, you can use network packet analyzers to examine the packets on your network to decipher problems with the three layers just above the data link layer — problems that you didn't find with tools such as the Chooser and router diagnostics. A packet analyzer can also help point to the physical layer if you find that no packets at all are going between two points on your network. At the physical layer, you look for such mechanical problems as loose connectors and faulty cables.

Examining the network by using the OSI Reference Model may seem cumbersome at first, but the model does provide a useful theoretical base to help put boundaries around your network problems and attack them in a logical progression. Troubleshooting is often easier if you start from the top layers, where the examination techniques and tools are simpler to use, and then move down to the more technically difficult lower layers.

# Examples of network disaster recoveries

The troubleshooting process we outlined may seem confusing at this point. So, to help clarify these steps, the following section walks you through a network failure caused by a faulty cable. You see how the five-step troubleshooting process leads the troubleshooter to the problem cable. Afterward, we offer some short narratives of network disaster recoveries.

### The faulty cable disaster

What follows is a walk-through of a disaster that can occur even on small LocalTalk networks. In this example, the user reports a network failure by making the following statement:

"No one can print in zone Alpha!"

After the manager completes the first step — receiving the user's complaint — the next step is to identify the components of the network this user is on. In this case, the base of the network is a LocalTalk network created by a daisy-chain of AppleTalk shielded wires and connectors (see Figure 13-10). The AppleTalk connectors have built-in resistors, and the network includes ten Macintoshes, one Apple LaserWriter, and one Shiva FastPath 4, a LocalTalk-to-Ethernet router. The Shiva FastPath 4 is connected to an Ethernet cable with a 10BASE5 (thick-wire) AUI connector. The Ethernet network is based on a standard 10BASE-T Ethernet hub. Two other LocalTalk networks, each with its own zone name, are connected to this Ethernet hub. All the Macintoshes in zone Alpha are supposed to be running the same version of System 7's LaserWriter software.

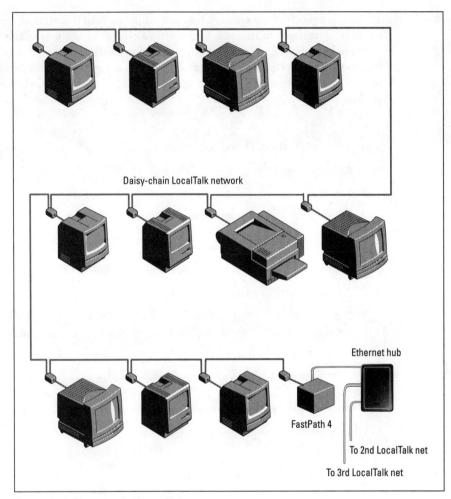

**Figure 13-10: The network of zone Alpha.**

Following the third step of our five-step process, the network manager divides the user's statement to form several questions for each part:

". . . in zone Alpha"

**A.** Is the user who reported this statement located on the same network cable as the Alpha zone?

Or

**B.** Is the reporting user accessing the printer from another zone?

These questions lead the network manager to the parts of the network that are involved. The larger the portion of the network involved, the more likely is the problem to be caused by a single component that touches all the sections. Remember, too, that components can be software as well as hardware. In this example, the components that affect everyone on the network are the set of LaserWriter drivers and the cable.

"No one . . ."

This phrase always needs to be examined closely.

**A.** Is this a true statement?

    **1.** For all users in Alpha?

    **2.** For users of Alpha's printer from another zone?

Or

**B.** Does *no one* include only a group of related users, but not all the users?

    **1.** Are these users in a row on the daisy-chain?

    **2.** Is one of the users who could print actually on the other side of this row, sending packets across this section of daisy-chain to get to the printer?

    **3.** Or is just one user involved?

". . . can print . . ."

This is probably the most important part of the statement to decipher.

**A.** Can the users see the printer in the Chooser?

    **1.** Never?

    **2.** Sometimes?

    **3.** Always?

**B.** If always, what happens when the user sends a print job?

    **1.** The light blinks on the LaserWriter, but no paper comes out?

    **2.** The print job aborts, and the bomb icon appears on the Macintosh screen?

By asking these questions, the network manager covers a great deal of territory in attempting to pinpoint the problem, working from the network as a total entity and proceeding down to each end-user's machine.

Next, we look at how the questions are answered and how the network manager uses the information to expose the problem.

"... in zone Alpha"

The user reporting the problem has one of the ten Macintoshes located on the Alpha network. This step locates the problem within the LocalTalk zone, thus ruling out a malfunction with the LocalTalk-to-EtherTalk router or with the Ethernet hub. If the user had been on another network, the equipment between the two networks — and problems with the routers that use the protocols ZIP, RTMP, and DDP, from the network, transport, and session layers (Layers 3, 4, and 5) — would also be suspect.

"No one . . ."

In this case, all ten Macintosh users on the network reply that they cannot print either. If only one user had been unable to print, the next list of questions would focus first on the operating system of that particular Macintosh. If the manager found no application trouble in the system, the manager would next check the physical layer — the LocalTalk connector. If only a certain segment of users, but not *all* users, could not print, the list of questions would possibly have traced the problem to the physical wiring, such as reflection caused by missing resistors.

"... can print . . ."

In this case, no one can see the printer in their Choosers. If the users could see the printer appearing and disappearing, a resistor problem would be a strong possibility.

Always remember that, even if you suspect that you know what the problem is, stepping through the analysis is still important. If the printer were appearing and disappearing in the Chooser, the problem could have been caused by a system virus. You would have found any virus problems while looking for application layer problems.

After working through a series of questions based on the user's initial complaint, the next step is for the network manager to see what changed. In this example, the network manager, who was unfamiliar with the day-to-day operations of this particular building's network, did not know of anything that had changed.

This brings the manager to step 5, where the manager is ready to select diagnostic tools to search for the problem. In this case, the network manager selects Inter•Poll, Apple's software diagnostics tool, to examine the problem at Layer 4 — the transport layer. The network manager starts at this layer because the user's inability to see the printer in the Chooser indicates no NBP traffic between the end nodes and the printer. Problems at the upper layers, therefore, are highly unlikely. The network manager selects Inter•Poll to confirm suspicions of trouble at the transport layer.

### About Inter•Poll

Inter•Poll, a software diagnostics tool sold by Apple, should be a staple item in your troubleshooting arsenal. For Macintoshes running operating systems prior to System 7, the Inter•Poll tool requires an INIT called *Responder* to be placed into the system folder of all Macintoshes on the network where you want to use this tool. In System 7, the Responder code is already built into the operating system.

The Responder INIT and Inter•Poll work as a team. Inter•Poll sends out a query in the form of an NBP LkUp to a selected zone. All devices with the Responder INIT reply with some basic information about their status, such as the name that is in the Chooser window and what type of machine it is. In addition, Inter•Poll enables you to send echo packets to each device with the Responder INIT. The INIT returns the echo packet. Apple LaserWriters have a built-in Responder that also replies to an Inter•Poll query.

Using one of the ten Macintoshes, the manager tries to select the Alpha zone in the Chooser to see whether the LaserWriter responds over the network. But no zones show up at all. The view from other Macintoshes show the same result. This is indeed a dead network. The network users, of course, have determined the viability of the network based only on the printing feature. But results from Inter•Poll show that other network features, such as file-transfer applications, don't work either.

At this point, the network manager has the following two options:

❖ Use packet analyzer tools to examine Layer 2 — the data link layer.

 Or

❖ Use tools that examine Layer 1 — the physical layer.

The network manager decides that, if nothing can be determined by the Chooser, which uses the NBP (Name Binding Protocol), or by Inter•Poll, which uses the AEP (AppleTalk Echo Protocol), a good chance exists that no packets are to be seen. The analysis strongly suggests a physical problem with either a component (in this case, the printer) or the cabling.

The LaserWriter is an easy place to begin looking. A built-in diagnostic feature of the LaserWriter is contained in a cover sheet that is printed whenever the LaserWriter starts. If this sheet prints after the printer is restarted, you know that the internal mechanisms of the machine are working. In this case, the cover sheet does print. (Notice that you can send a software command to the LaserWriter to prevent it from printing the cover page. If this command has been issued, printing the cover sheet to check the operations of the printer doesn't work for you.) The LaserWriter therefore appears to be functioning perfectly.

The network manager next must choose a method for examining the cabling and cabling components, such as the transceivers and AppleTalk connectors. Using an ohmmeter is appropriate if the problem appears to be caused by incorrect placement or breakage of resistors. But a resistance problem usually reveals itself as an intermittent network failure, with devices such as LaserWriters appearing and disappearing from the Chooser. Because this is not the case, the network manager chooses another approach to examine the physical layer — the divide-and-conquer method.

The network manager splits up the network into two small islands of users and moves the LaserWriter back and forth between the islands. At this point, the LaserWriter shows up in the Chooser for one group but not for another. By continuing to split the network this way, the manager finds a faulty section of cable between the last Macintosh and the FastPath. Replacement of this cable restores the network back to full functioning.

Although this network failure and resurrection took several pages to describe, it took only a couple of hours to perform. One of the main reasons for quick success was a logical step-by-step analysis of the situation. All components were carefully considered. The diagnostic approach was top-down, working from the upper layers of the protocol stack down, and in this case, all the way down to the bottom — the physical layer.

This detailed example took you through the troubleshooting process to locate a faulty cable. The following sections show you some additional problems for which you can look.

## Overloaded printers

Overloading an Apple LaserWriter is a common problem. With the profusion of sophisticated drawing packages that send huge files to the printer, network managers are seeing "hung" LaserWriters more often. The problem can often be traced to insufficient memory in the LaserWriter. Upgrading to a LaserWriter NTX or replacing the printer with a high-end PostScript printer can solve the memory deficit.

Keep an eye, too, on applications that send files to the printer in bitmap format. Bitmapped images require that each pixel on the page be given a definition of black or white. As a result, very large files are sent to the printer. The immediate solution is to shut off both the Macintosh and the LaserWriter to clear their memory buffers.

## ZIP storms

*ZIP storm* problems have been experienced on several large AppleTalk internets that are still using AppleTalk Phase 1. We cite the problem here as an example of how a network crash can be caused not by the failure of a component but by the complex AppleTalk relationships among several components.

Even if you don't run AppleTalk Phase 1, this problem still can plague you. We recently saw a problem, very similar to the ZIP storm discussed in this section, on a network that hadn't run AppleTalk Phase 1 in years. The cause? A public-domain UNIX-based AppleTalk program that was sloppily implemented and did not fully support AppleTalk Phase 2.

The disaster in this example is called a ZIP storm because a malfunction on the network causes an inordinate number of ZIP (Zone Information Protocol) request packets to enter and flood the network. A ZIP storm can flood an entire Ethernet backbone, halting processes by other protocols, including TCP/IP, DECnet, or any other protocol running on the network.

ZIP storms normally occur only in networks that contain more than a hundred zones and have all the following devices in combination: LocalTalk-to-EtherTalk routers, EtherTalk-to-EtherTalk routers, and a Phase 1 Ethernet server/router.

The ZIP storm in this example was traced to a *runt* RTMP (Routing Table Maintenance Protocol) Data packet that also had a strange listing of network numbers. (A *runt* packet on Ethernet is a packet that is smaller than 64 bytes, an illegal size in the Ethernet specification.) The strange network numbers turned out to be random garbage and did not identify actual networks on the internet. Because of their invalid structure, these runt RTMP packets with their bad network numbers were thrown away by both the LocalTalk-to-EtherTalk routers and the EtherTalk-to-EtherTalk routers. The Ethernet server/router, however, placed these invalid network numbers into a special holding buffer. In Figure 13-11, this buffer is labeled as "Reserve."

The Ethernet server/router then broadcasted its next RTMP Data packet. The RTMP Data packet coming from the Ethernet server/router had a valid structure, but it also now contained numbers (obtained from the runt packet and stored in the buffer) for routes to nonexistent networks.

All routers use the RTMP packet broadcasted from the Ethernet server/router to create new entries in their routing tables. Because the invalid network numbers are also now found within the valid RTMP packet, however, all the routers broadcast RTMP packets with the bad numbers until the routes are timed-out (see Figure 13-12).

Notice that timing-out routes in Phase 1 takes a long time because each router continues to validate the route until it is incrementally set to 15 hops. (The process of deleting routes is described in Chapter 11, "Designing an AppleTalk LAN.")

On finding the new route in the routing table, the ZIP process in the example network's router sent out ZIP Query packets to determine the zone name for these nonexistent networks. So many of these ZIP Query packets were sent out that layer 2, the data link layer of the Ethernet, was flooded (see Figure 13-13).

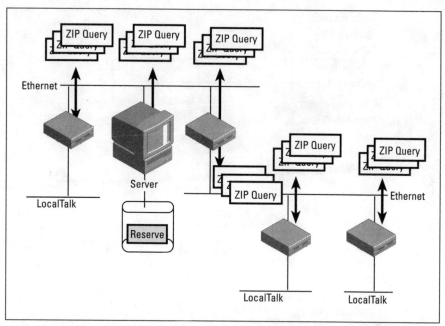

**Figure 13-11: Routers send out ZIP Query packets requesting the zone name for the nonexistent zone.**

The network managers found the problem by isolating the network into segments and running network packet analyzers to discover what all the ZIP packets wanted and where the strange network numbers were originating.

The networks in this example were down for several weeks. A calm step-by-step approach by some top-notch network managers and vendor technical support teams was required, but they eventually found the problem and got the network up and running again.

Notice that this type of ZIP storm cannot easily occur in a Phase 2 network. In Phase 1, every router broadcasts an RTMP Data packet with all the network numbers it knows about — even those that are invalid.

In Phase 2, however, a router broadcasts an RTMP Data packet containing only the network numbers that are directly connected to it (split horizon). For a typical backbone network configuration, the packet contains two network numbers — the LocalTalk network number and the EtherTalk network range. (For more information on split-horizon routing in Phase 2, see Chapter 11, "Designing an AppleTalk LAN.")

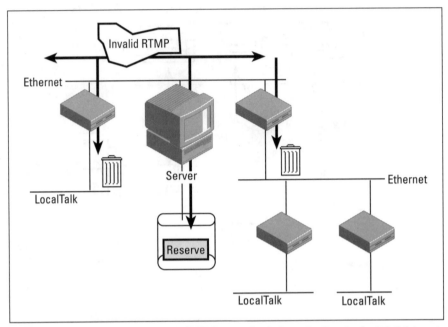

Figure 13-12: An invalid structure for an RTMP Data packet is transmitted on the AppleTalk internet.

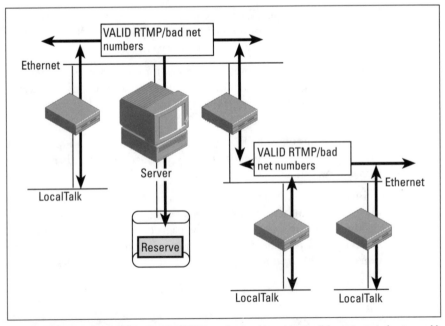

Figure 13-13: The valid structure for the RTMP packet is sent out by the Ethernet server/router and is absorbed into all routers' routing tables.

## Black holes

*Black holes* are a network problem that can occur on an AppleTalk internet of any size. Black holes are caused whenever the network is misconfigured — specifically, whenever two or more routers have a different network number for the same cable. Routers can send packets only to networks to which they are directly connected or to which they have a route. If network 3 sees a packet from network 2, for example, network 3 discards that packet if it doesn't have a route for it. This procedure helps maintain legitimate route tables, preventing the ZIP storms described in the previous example. What happens is that the two routers build completely separate internets with no knowledge of the other's existence. If a user is on one of these networks, it seems as though the zones on the misconfigured router have simply disappeared into a black hole.

In Figure 13-14, the middle router has been misconfigured with net range 2-2 instead of net range 3-3. The other two routers have no route to network 2, so devices on the networks behind them, networks 27 and 25, do not see any devices on the network behind the misconfigured router, network 26. This problem is further compounded if one of the Macintoshes on the Ethernet takes its startup configuration (GNI/GNIR) from the misconfigured router and becomes a node in network 2.

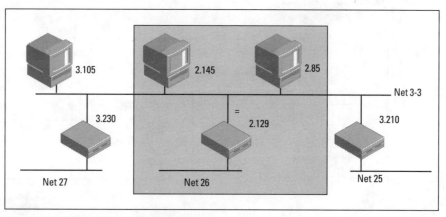

Figure 13-14: A black hole in the network.

## Ethernet storms

Another common problem is an *Ethernet broadcast storm* caused by a malfunctioning device on the Ethernet. (The device can be either an AppleTalk device or any other type of node, such as TCP/IP or Novell.) In an Ethernet broadcast storm, the malfunctioning device floods the Ethernet with packets that are destined for the broadcast address. A router limits the extent of an Ethernet broadcast storm because a router does not forward packets destined for the broadcast address.

A bridge, however, does not limit the flood because a bridge passes packets that are destined for the broadcast address across to any of the bridge's other attached cables.

Misconfigured Sun Microsystems computers commonly cause TCP/IP Ethernet storms. This fault is caused by a bug in the original implementation of Sun's TCP/IP kernel involving the multicast address for TCP/IP packets. The best cure for this problem is to ensure that all TCP/IP systems are running the "standard" broadcast address.

In Figure 13-15, notice that the broadcast packets are passed across the bridge but are not passed across the router. The figure shows that the router effectively serves as a *firewall* to prevent the storm of packets coming from the offending device.

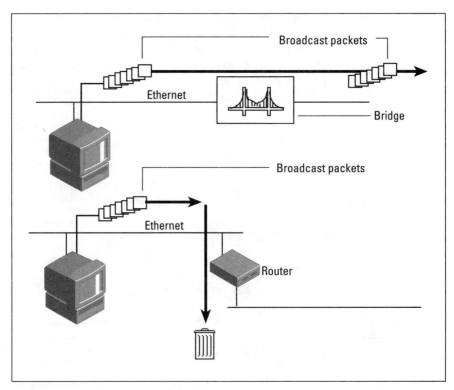

**Figure 13-15: Ethernet broadcast storms.**

If you detect an Ethernet storm, remove the offending machine from the network. You must perform some additional troubleshooting to find the malfunction, which can result from hardware failure or software misconfiguration. So that you can quickly isolate the offending device, a good idea is to maintain a list of Ethernet addresses and their locations. Otherwise, you must use the divide-and-conquer approach and separate your network into smaller and smaller islands until you find the malfunctioning device.

# CHAPTER *13* CONCEPTS AND TERMS

- Larger LocalTalk networks require a consistent and well thought-out design. Growing an AppleTalk network by simply adding stations to the end of an existing daisy-chain is not a good idea.

- Configuration monitoring and management tools such as NetWORKS and LANsurveyor can be a great help to network managers trying to watch over a large multiprotocol network.

- SNMP management is an emerging standard for protocol and vendor independent system management. Although many Macintosh-based network products support an SNMP agent, no good SNMP management station that runs on the Macintosh currently exists.

- Every network manager needs a network protocol analyzer to bolster evidence whenever the smoking gun of incompatibility is discovered.

- Network managers should monitor network performance over time to plan for configuration and expansion without service disruption.

- Diagnosing and repairing network faults in the world of AppleTalk requires a well thought-out and thorough approach to problem solving.

## agents

Agents are pieces of software located in each network device. The agent software responds to requests sent by the management station to retrieve information from MIB variables for its device. The agent acts as a translator, peering into the inside of a proprietary device to pass status information out using an open protocol.

## backbone

A central network that connects a number of networks, usually of lower capacity. The lower-capacity networks can pass data to each other over the backbone network.

## big endian

Network byte order usually specifies that the most significant byte (or octet) of an integer is transmitted first on the LAN. This ordering is called *big endian*. Some machines, however, don't represent data internally in the same way the data is transmitted. These machines are know as *little endian* machines.

## black holes

*Black holes* are a network problem that can occur on an AppleTalk internet of any size. Black holes are caused whenever the network is misconfigured — specifically, whenever two or more routers have a different network number for the same cable.

## collision

A situation that occurs when two devices on a network try to transmit at the same time and their transmissions "run into" each other. The signals are crossed, causing the data to become garbled.

## datagram

In the Internet protocols, a datagram is a packet containing destination address and data.

## debugging (or diagnostic error reporting)

Debugging tools enable you to view the condition of the network router at any time. These tools perceive and report certain errors or unusual conditions.

## echo packet

AEP (AppleTalk Echo Protocol) tools enable you to send an *echo packet* to a selected device; if the device is live, it returns an echo packet. These tools require AEP software on the clients that you want to *echo*.

## Ethernet broadcast storm

A common problem is an *Ethernet broadcast storm*, which is caused by a malfunctioning device on the Ethernet. (The device can be either an AppleTalk device or any other type of node, such as TCP/IP or Novell.) In an Ethernet broadcast storm, the malfunctioning device floods the Ethernet with packets that are destined for the broadcast address. A router limits the extent of an Ethernet broadcast storm because a router does not forward packets destined for the broadcast address.

## filtering bridge

An Ethernet filtering bridge lets you filter the flow of packets between two (or sometimes more) Ethernet segments based on protocol type. The bridge discards any packets of a type you specify to be filtered. If you establish AppleTalk filtering, for example, no AppleTalk connectivity exists over that bridge. Some bridges also enable you to establish priority settings that take effect whenever their buffers become full and overflow packets must be discarded. A low-priority packet type is discarded first.

## leg

An internet, a collection of AppleTalk networks joined by routers, can be configured in either of two ways: combining two or more networks serially in a row (a *serial configuration*) or connecting them in a star layout with a *center hub* and one or more *legs*. We recommend the star topology if your LAN internet is a collection of networks at one physical site (an Ethernet or fiber optic internet located in one or multiple buildings rather than extended across a city).

## management stations

A management station is where the network management software runs. Management stations, also called *consoles*, are usually UNIX-

*(continued on the next page)*

*(continued from previous page)*

based workstations. Think of the management stations as the control seats for the entire network; using a management station, the network manager can watch over, troubleshoot, and configure any SNMP-capable device in the network. Depending on your network management style, you may have a single management station or a more than one.

**MIB (Management Information Base)**
Information used by SNMP for maintaining status and control of a network device. MIBs are specific to each type of device; information within the MIB is relayed by a SNMP agent to network management software either on request or when a problem occurs within the device.

**multicasting**
In AppleTalk, this is a critical part of the functioning of the AppleTalk protocol (RTMP, for example). For this reason, we also suggest that you don't assign AppleTalk packets a low priority. Assigning AppleTalk a low priority can cause zones to disappear and reappear on the network because of the RTMP time-out procedure.

**open system**
In network terminology, an *Open system* is the opposite of *proprietary*. It refers to a set, published standard to which everyone has access and can implement. But open network management software tools for AppleTalk are still merely chalk on the drawing boards, voices in meeting rooms, and bits on e-mail systems.

AppleTalk network managers must continue to manage their network configuration primarily by using *proprietary* software tools.

**proactive**
This term is of critical importance for network managers. A proactive network manager has the right tools and skills to stay on top of a disaster. The best fault-management plan enables the network manager to avoid noticeable network

downtime by catching the problem before the users do. To do so, you must monitor your network.

**protocol analyzers**
Tools for looking at networks. They "watch" a wire, capture all the data that passes over the wire, and can display (and sometimes explain) each bit of data. Protocol analyzers exist both for LAN links, such as Ethernet and token ring, and for WAN links, such as RS-232 lines. Protocol analyzers are the last word in network diagnostic tools. With an analyzer in place, the network to which it is applied holds no secrets. Every frame, every packet, can be viewed and reviewed. If a serious problem exists on a network, a protocol analyzer is the tool to use to find it.

**protocol decoding**
The most important function of a protocol analyzer and the one by which a protocol analyzer can really make your life easy. Decoders such as EtherPeek can display the basic information of items like an AppleTalk RTMP packet.

**saying**
Saying is different from a sound. Saying implies you type in text and out come the sounds of words. Recorded sounds are simply recordings. With networks, you could have it actually say the name of the router without having to have pre-recorded each router name using a microphone.

**seed router**
Seed routers seed, or initialize, the internet with the configuration information the administrator enters (network number and range, zone name and list). Nonseed routers wait and listen for a seed router and then take this configuration initialization information from the first seed router they hear. After a nonseed router obtains a network configuration, it begins to participate in the routing of the network. This participation effectively makes that router a seed router for any new nonseed routers coming on line. Seed and nonseed determinations, therefore apply only as a router starts up.

**SNMP (Simple Network Management Protocol)**
A protocol in the TCP/IP suite for managing objects on the network. SNMP uses agents on managed devices to maintain a MIB (Management Information Base) and transmit MIB data to the management software on request.

**traps**
Notifications sent by a network device's agent after some event occurs. Traps help to keep an eye on the network without constantly asking every device for status information. One kind of trap, for example, is the *Cold Start trap*. A router that speaks SNMP sends out a Cold Start trap every time it boots up. A management station that receives that trap could simply log the information to a file, notify a network manager via e-mail or a pocket pager or set up that trap to trigger some other action, such as downloading device-configuration information.

**triggering**
Triggers are used to begin capturing frames only after a specific event occurs, such as after a particular type of packet goes by ("Next time the Jan router sends an RTMP update packet, start capturing") or after a certain time has passed ("Start capturing at 1:17 a.m.").

**ZIP storms**
When a malfunction on the network causes an inordinate number of ZIP (Zone Information Protocol) request packets to enter and flood the network. A ZIP storm can flood an entire Ethernet backbone, halting processes by other protocols, including TCP/IP, DECnet, or any other protocol running on the network.

# Managing AppleTalk Networks for Management

IN THIS CHAPTER

- Preparing for network disasters

- Accounting for network resources

- Keeping track of network hardware and software

- Making strategies for dealing with customer service from your software and hardware vendors

- Balancing user privacy and network management

**M**ost computer managers like to think of themselves as pretty pragmatic individuals. A good network manager cares most about keeping the users happy, keeping things running smoothly, and making sure that any problems are fixed promptly. About half of this job is rather technical, as a look at Chapter 3, "Understanding AppleTalk Protocols" shows you. Most of the other half is what we call *people skills*. A good network manager needs to have a lot of both to be really effective.

But there also is a third part to being a successful manager — keeping *your* management happy. Sometimes network managers feel that the needs of upper management are not congruent with getting their job done. Upper management usually disagrees with this assessment, and because your managers are responsible for approving budgets and personnel requests, they have a pretty powerful stick to wield if they don't like what you're doing. It is your job to cover both bases: meeting the technical needs of the users you were hired to serve *and* meeting the non-technical needs of your corporate management.

The topics covered in this chapter are ones that very technical managers may feel aren't very important. But these topics are also the ones that high-level managers often think of as most important. We think that you'll be better off in the long run if you provide a quality technical answer to a management question like, "What do we do when a hurricane hits?" It's for these reasons that we included this chapter — it represents our best advice on how to manage for management.

QUOTABLES

"Convenants without swords are but words."
— Thomas Hobbes

# Preparing a Disaster Recovery Chart

The network disaster recovery chart has several purposes. After you draw up a list of features and users, you'll be ready to achieve an important goal of the chart, which is establishing priorities. For example, setting priorities is important when you are working on two or more hot projects and some part of the network fails. Your chart indicates which project takes priority. For such a plan to be effective, it's a good idea to have management in agreement on these priority settings. You may even decide that you need authorized signatures at the bottom of your chart.

## Identifying the group

To create the network disaster recovery chart shown in Figure 14-1, you first need to know what features are in use on your network and who uses them. By *network features*, we mean applications such as e-mail, AppleShare, file-transfer applications, or workflow-database applications. Don't confuse network features with the topology and internetworking products that make up your network, such as bridges and routers. On the network disaster recovery chart, the combination of a feature and the users of that feature is called a *group*.

| Network manager | Group (Feature Users) | Reaction time | Components | Repaired by |
|---|---|---|---|---|
| Nancy Jones | Program Office E-Mail Users | One hour | Wiring<br>StarController<br>Router<br>E-Mail Svr HW<br>E-Mail Svr SW<br>E-Mail Node SW | B. Turner<br>N. Jones<br>N. Jones<br>J. Tice<br>J. Maleski<br>J. Maleski |
| Dave Kosiur | 3rd Floor AppleShare Users | Five hours | Wiring<br>StarController<br>AShare Svr HW<br>AShare Svr SW<br>AShare Node SW | B. Turner<br>N. Jones<br>J. Tice<br>J. Maleski<br>J. Maleski |

Group: Program Office E-Mail Users   Representative signature:     *L. L. Bartkowski*

Group: 3rd floor AppleShare Users   Representative signature:     *Jean Harrison*

**Figure 14-1: The network disaster recovery chart.**

## Identifying the network's users

The next step is to identify who is using the features that you have identified. In a large network, it is probably adequate to identify the users by departments and activity groups rather than as individuals. Yet even in a large network, it's important to keep in mind who the high-demand users are. Office politics is often an unavoidable part of the network manager's life. Our philosophy is to grin and bear it by balancing the needs of the high-demand users against the needs in the critical business arenas. After completing this chart, you should have an idea of how to apply this compromise to your situation and avoid the pendulum effect that the combination of politics and crises can create.

Remember that each feature and its set of users make up a group. You can come up with descriptive names to label these groups. One group could be the "xyz program office e-mail users" and another group the "executive e-mail users." The division into groups should be made along organizational-chart lines and take into consideration who will require different levels of priority.

## Determining downtime and reaction time

Next, you need to assign acceptable downtimes for each group. Determining downtime can be tricky, because downtime is not truly controllable. A network failure may be caused by a loose cable that you quickly locate, or it may be caused by a misconfigured router, which may take hours or even days to hunt down. Perhaps a better term than downtime is your *reaction* time. The question you are really asking is more like this: "How fast should you and your organization *react* to a failure of a particular group's network, such as the "executive e-mail users?"

To determine an acceptable reaction time, ask yourself questions such as these:

❖ What impact will downtime have on the company's revenue?

❖ How will downtime affect the normal work flow of the office?

❖ What, if any, are the alternative methods, commonly referred to as *redundant paths*, for the user to reach the desired feature?

## Obtaining authorized approval

Once a reaction time is established, it's best to get approval from a key person in that group. Again, it may be prudent to have this person's signature on your network disaster recovery chart.

### Planning a Redundant Communications Path to Solve a Problem

How can using a redundant communications path help resolve a problem? Suppose that a particular program office's server fails. On this server is an application that the office depends on to plan meetings efficiently. A redundant communications path is in place if the program office can use its voice mail as an alternative method of scheduling meetings until the server is repaired. Of course, the program office won't be as satisfied with this method as with its primary tool, but the alternative method gets the office by until the repair is made.

## Establishing network support

You now have a list of groups that make up, or define, your network; each group has an assigned reaction time; and redundant paths are identified. Are you finished? Not by a long shot. You still need to do the planning that will get your organization ready to meet these goals.

Identify which organizations and individuals play a part in the repair of your network. Don't stop at the hardware level of the network, but cover support all the way up to the people who support the end-node network feature applications.

The larger your AppleTalk internet gets, the more complex it becomes. Recall the Second Law of Thermodynamics: the universe constantly moves from order toward chaos. With the right planning, and a heap of diligence and responsibility, you can alter this course and avoid chaos on your network. In a small network, you may be the master of all: cabling, bridges, routers, and servers and their specialized applications. In larger networks, these tasks are more likely to be split among many individuals and organizations. So you need a well-constructed plan to keep all these people on an orderly course.

Finding the individuals responsible for repairing the various components of the network is the next critical step in your disaster recovery and fault management plan. You are responsible for staying on top of organizational changes that affect delegation of responsibilities. Get to know these people. They will be your lifeline. We suggest also getting to know the people in your human relations department so that they'll provide you with timely organizational charts.

At this stage of the planning, take some time to look over the list of network groups (features and users) that you have compiled. Then you need to establish who is responsible for the repair of the feature within the group. Although each company has a different organizational plan, the following is an example of what this list may look like.

❖ Physical repair: cabling and wiring

❖ Hardware repair: servers and network devices such as bridges and routers

❖ Software repair: Macintosh servers

❖ Software repair: OpenVMS/AppleTalk Pathworks servers

❖ Software repair: UNIX/AppleTalk servers

❖ Software repair: network devices, such as bridges and routers

For each group on your chart, you can identify individuals, such as those who *own* the areas mentioned in the preceding list. When someone owns an area it means he or she is responsible for the repair of the hardware and software of individual features.

For example, in Figure 14-1, the group called "3rd Floor AppleShare Users," managed by Dave Kosiur, has different persons identified for various repairs. For example, J. Maleski is responsible for software repair on the Macintosh node and on the AppleShare server; J. Tice is responsible for hardware repair of the AppleShare server; N. Jones is responsible for hardware repair of the network device (the StarController), and B. Turner is responsible for repair of the wiring that goes to the 3rd Floor AppleShare server.

Be sure to include on your chart all the responsibilities needed for each group. You can then work with these individuals so that they agree to support the identified reaction times for each group and understand the importance of their roles.

## Reviewing the completed chart

Your chart will look complete now. You've identified features and users and split them into groups. You've found a key individual for each group, and you've agreed on specified reaction times. You've also made a list of all possible persons and organizations that may be called on for repair. Are you finished? Not yet.

One more item is needed for your list. Someone must be responsible for that first step — the discovery and inspection of the failure. This person will decide whether the disaster is more likely the result of a software crash or a broken-cable connection.

We believe that this person should be the network manager. In some companies, the person responsible for the wiring looks at all problems first and then hands the task off to another person, who manages the software. We believe that this approach has two major flaws:

❖ No one owns the network failure and assumes responsibility from discovery to repair.

❖ No one takes a systems approach to look at the whole network and decide the most logical place to begin.

### Who Wants to Own a Problem?

You do. In any problem solving situation, we think it's very important to have a single individual responsible for making sure that the problem gets fixed. You may think you don't want to "own" a problem, but you'll find that things get solved — and you get a better reputation in your organization — if you do. "The buck stops here" is a good approach. When you take on a problem, taking it all the way to its complete conclusion is both personally satisfying and good for your organization.

How many times have you seen problems linger on and on, never getting completely fixed, because no one would take reponsibility for finishing the job? The best-functioning organizations parcel out problems to the individual best equipped to solve them.

The network manager must remain knowledgeable, at least at some level, about all elements of the network, because that person is involved in how the network is designed and installed. The network manager is therefore the best person to look at the whole network to decide where to begin.

The network manager should also own the problem and take responsibility for another key process in fault management — escalation. If a network repair looks like it is going to exceed an acceptable downtime, or if you're having difficulties getting the right people to work on the problem (perhaps because of other commitments), you need to escalate the issues to appropriate layers of management and to the key users. Keeping others informed of the progress of repairs can calm many nerves. Most users and managers simply want to know that something is being done and that someone has taken ownership of the problem.

## Accounting Management

There comes a time in every network's life when you have to pay the piper. You just spent a lot of money setting up a network, buying computers, and installing software, and maybe everything's running smoothly. Now someone with a ledger or spreadsheet in hand wants to know how much it cost. Was it worth it? How often will you have to upgrade the network hardware and software? Are you planning to enlarge the network? Are the departments being properly charged for their use of special printers and slide makers? And so on...

Accounting management is simply a means of answering these and other questions that may relate to network usage. Sometimes, pertinent questions don't have a dollar sign in front of them. You'll find, however, that the tools of accounting management help you plan for future network expansion and perhaps even help sell company management on the effectiveness of current and future network plans.

Should you really bother with the accounting management of your network? If your network is small and you can see all your network users by looking down the hall or glancing around the room, maybe not. You know the costs of your network, probably because you installed it yourself, you put paper and toner in the laser printer, and you're the one who sees requisitions for new Macs and software.

But if you have a larger network, one comprised of a few workgroups or possibly one extending across several buildings — if not counties or states — you may have no choice but to try accounting management for your network. Under these circumstances, you may well be asked for usage statistics on laser printer output, perhaps even broken down by department or workgroup so that the costs of the network (particularly the operating costs) are properly distributed among profit centers. Or, if your phone bills go through the roof, you may need to determine who's using the networked modems or fax modems so often.

Unfortunately, there aren't many tools available to handle the accounting management of AppleTalk networks. Perhaps this stems from the individualism of microcomputer users in general, and Mac users specifically. But there are a few steps you can take to audit resource usage on your network. We'll cover these in the following sections.

## Auditing printers

The most commonly audited device is a networked printer. We're not talking here about tracking the amount of paper or toner used. Printer auditing involves keeping track of print jobs according to the paper used (plain paper vs. transparencies, for example), the number of pages, and who printed the file. Armed with that type of information, you can bill the appropriate department in your company for using a specific printer. This type of auditing can be especially important when you've installed costly printers, such as those for large page sizes, special paper, or color output.

QUICK TIPS

### Accounting Isn't Just for Bean Counters

As mentioned, accounting management can provide you with ammunition for network expansion. By auditing usage of laser printers, modems, or file servers, you may be able to spot problem areas and point out what network equipment needs to be upgraded or replaced, or what new equipment might help. Having usage statistics (and perhaps even related costs — don't forget how much your co-workers' time is costing the company) can help determine if your network is maxed out and needs to be expanded.

Ordinary print spoolers (including Apple's own AppleShare Print Server) don't tell you much about usage, especially on a user account basis. Instead, you have to devote a machine to act as a print server for one or more printers and run special spooling and auditing software to track the jobs sent to each printer. We use an OpenVMS workstation running Digital's Pathworks software, which provides very detailed accounting logs. Another noteworthy program that includes audit logs as well as calculation of printing costs per user is Print Central (Compumation, Inc.).

## Auditing file servers

You wouldn't normally think of monitoring file usage on a file server in the same way as auditing a printer. What may be more important is tracking the amount of disk storage that each person is taking up on the server. Discovering that a person hasn't used any of the files he or she has stored on the server in six months is a good reason to talk to the user about removing the files and freeing some of that space for others. Or you may wish to monitor disk-space usage by department in order to justify a new server specifically for one department's use.

None of the Mac-based file servers offers much of anything in auditing. Apple's own AppleShare has a pitifully small report that shows little detail about server usage. It doesn't, for instance, break down file usage by users or by age of the oldest files or folders. AppleShare 3 does at least include the hooks so that developers can write their own report generators — although we haven't seen any yet. Distributed, or peer-to-peer, file servers like System 7's File Sharing feature stress the individual's control of the sharing process and offer no logs at all.

## Auditing telecommunications devices

Telecommunications costs are a significant item in most every company's budget. Call-tracking on an employee-by-employee basis is common, but how do you handle a phone line used for a modem shared by networked users? That's when you turn to network tools for logging modem usage. Maintaining logs of modem usage for outgoing calls can tell you who is using the modems; you can then use the information for billing purposes. Logging incoming calls to a modem will also tell you if an unauthorized user is attempting to call into the network.

Most AppleTalk Remote Access (ARA) servers offer a logging facility to keep track of who logs in and for how long. Most keep this on the server, where you must take pains to download it occasionally for reporting purposes. ARA servers which run on the Macintosh, including Apple's Personal and Multiport servers, will keep logs on local hard disks, which is more convenient.

Auditing the usage of networked modems and other telecommunications devices on AppleTalk systems is a mixed bag. Most e-mail systems that offer telecommunications links don't offer auditing of calls, either incoming or outgoing; QuickMail is the exception. And if you're connecting two remote networks with half-routers (see Chapter 12, "Designing an AppleTalk WAN"), the routers don't support call logging either.

At any rate, auditing the device usage on an AppleTalk network is problematic. You can get some reports, but for now, you're on your own when it comes to compiling those reports into a spreadsheet to calculate usage and charge back costs for various users.

# The Elements of Asset Management

Asset management typically isn't included in the definition of network management. Yet asset management makes extensive use of the network and often falls within the job description of the network manager, so we include this management concern as part of our coverage of network management.

Varied activities fall under the heading of asset management. You may be concerned with installing the proper system files on everyone's Mac or checking that everyone is using the latest version of a software package. Ensuring that all copies of the software are properly licensed is another aspect of asset management. So is updating software over the network.

Asset management has become one of the fastest growing areas of Mac application development over the past two years. Thanks to that fast growth, you can now pick and choose among a variety of programs to cover every aspect of asset management.

Our opinion of asset management is that it's good for some environments, but nearly useless in others. Small networks probably don't need specialized asset management. Even some large networks of over 100 Macs cannot use asset management effectively. Some companies don't have a centralized person or department for maintaining software upgrades and the like. In such systems, individuals order their own upgrades. We don't condone this approach, but some companies still operate this way.

The way you manage your network and related assets is a matter of personal and corporate style. The tools we'll describe offer varying degrees of flexibility, allowing you to customize them to your own needs. This flexibility applies both to collecting information and to reporting it.

The data that you collect to maintain users on the network falls into two basic categories (see Figure 14-2). First, you need data about the hardware and software for each computer. Second, you need location or user data, such as where the machine is located and who the user is. The slate of programs currently offered can all use Apple's built-in system support, now called Gestalt, to learn which NuBus cards and monitors are installed, as well as how much RAM and disk storage are available.

## When to Manage and When to Ignore

Any accounting or asset management system absolutely must take into account its cost-benefit ratio. There is a tendency in organizations to make excuses for hiring more "overhead" people — the ones who support the people actually getting the job done — as this tends to increase the power base of managers who don't really have much of a reason to live anyway.

For example, if your company has 100 Macintoshes and you have a full-time person handling both accounting and asset management, you're probably wasting your money. The benefits of knowing exactly what software is running on what machines with what configuration for how many seconds each day have to be balanced across the cost of gathering that knowledge.

Over a decade ago, the computing center for an august Southwestern land-grant University decided to "account" for every nanosecond of usage on their large and expensive mainframe computers. After several highly-paid man-years of labor, the end result was that 70 percent of the disk space was consumed by accounting data and 10 percent was left over for the poor users!

Providing this kind of information in microscopic view is itself harmful because it encourages myopic accountants to spend enormous amounts of time groveling over infinitesimal particles of data. On the other hand, as the erudite Aaron Leonard has observed, "It could be well argued that people so inclined [to want accounting information] are better occupied entangled in makework than what they might be doing otherwise." (From "Received Bytes Accounting," Aaron Leonard, 1992.)

Any time someone asks you for this kind of information, you should ask yourself — and them — if the benefits to the organization really outweigh the costs of gathering.

[Reprinted with permission]

## Defining asset management tasks

Before we review the programs for collecting system and application data over the network, we've put together some illustrations of how these tools can be used.

**Situation 1:** Users have more than one Laser Prep file.

**Problem:** Users are complaining that they're always resetting the laser printer when they print because someone on the network is using a different Laser Prep file.

**Solution:** Use software such as InterPoll, GraceLAN, or Status*Mac to scan the users' disks. Find out who has an out-of-date Laser Prep file or who has installed a new one that other users don't have yet. Decide which version should be used, and either update the problem Macs manually or use network-wide software-updating software like NetDistributor or File Ware.

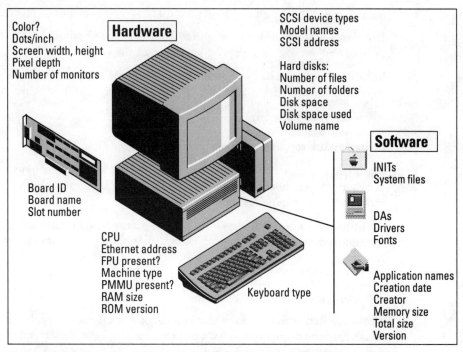

**Figure 14-2: The types of data that you can acquire with resource management programs.**

**Situation 2:** You need to distribute fonts for desktop publishing.

**Problem:** Not all the users have the proper fonts for printing their reports.

**Solution:** If you already know which fonts are needed, use software-updating software to distribute the missing fonts. If you don't know who has which fonts, scan the users' disks with a program like GraceLAN or Status*Mac to identify the fonts each user has, and then update the users' Macs.

**Situation 3:** You're planning to upgrade to a newer version of System 7.

**Problem:** It's time to upgrade all your Macs to some new release of System 7, such as System 7 Pro, but not everyone has sufficient RAM or the right hardware (such as adequate disk space) to use all its features.

**Solution:** Use GraceLAN or Status*Mac to scan each user's Mac for RAM; check to see if users have sufficient disk space for added files. Then either use Apple's Installer program and the System 7 Pro files on a file server, or use updating software like NetDistributor or File Ware to update each Mac over the network.

**Situation 4:** You're planning to integrate a new version of a word processor.

**Problem:** This is similar to the System 7 Pro upgrade situation, but this time you need to find out who has the program and what the version is.

**Solution:** Use GraceLAN or Status*Mac to scan each user's disk for the program to be upgraded. Then use a program like NetDistributor or File Ware to update each user's version.

**Situation 5:** Users have multiple system files on the same Mac.

**Problem:** Some users may complain that they don't see the same fonts or desk accessories when they use their programs. This may be because they've installed more than one system file on their Mac.

**Solution:** Use a program like GraceLAN or Status*Mac to scan the users' disks for multiple system files; then ask your users with multiple system files to remove all but one.

**Situation 6:** The company is moving to centralized control of licensed software.

**Problem:** Rather than let each user keep a copy of a particular application on the Mac's hard disk, your company wants to keep a copy on a file server and control access according to the site license.

**Solution:** Scan everyone's hard disk to see which users have a copy of the program; then work with them to remove it. Now install KeyServer or Quota on the file server and use it to keep track of the number of legal simultaneous users for the licensed application now installed on the server. Or, if you have an AppleShare 3 server or newer, use the built-in features of AppleShare to limit the maximum simultaneous users.

QUICK TIPS

## License Control Using a Server?

An easy way to handle license control for software is to put the software on a file server and control access using one of the programs described here. Unfortunately, there are significant downsides to this approach. First, you may find that performance slows to a crawl when 20 or 30 users try and run a program like Microsoft Word from the same hard disk. Second, the server itself becomes a weak link in the network. If that goes down, no on can use software you're storing there. Balance these problems with the benefits of this approach.

**Situation 7:** Management wants an audit of all Mac hardware.

**Problem:** Your company management wants to know the serial numbers of all Macs and what hardware is installed in or attached to them.

**Solution:** Use a program like GraceLAN or Status*Mac to scan each user's Mac for the hardware configuration. Unfortunately, the Mac doesn't electronically encode its serial number anywhere. If you planned ahead, you entered the serial numbers when you installed the GraceLAN or Status*Mac responders; if not, each user will have to relay the serial number to you. With the data in hand, create a custom report.

## Collecting system data

What kinds of information can you acquire with asset management programs? The simplest programs, such as InterPoll, Radar, and TalkManage collect the version of each Mac's System and the Finder and LaserWriter files, as well as the zone, network, and node numbers.

The more sophisticated programs, such as GraceLAN, Status*Mac, and Network SuperVisor, collect much more information about a Mac, including the types of cards and disks installed, type of monitor, the desk accessories, the fonts and INITs installed, as well as the applications residing on each hard disk. GraceLAN can also acquire data from MS-DOS computers that have an AppleTalk-compatible adapter installed — in this case, GraceLAN lists the type of processor, the version of DOS, the amount of regular and extended memory, and other information about hard disks and video adapters, as well as serial and parallel ports. Table 14-1 shows several vendors and features of their programs.

How do you collect and store all of this information? The amount of information you can collect from a node is directly related to the software that you install on that node. InterPoll and TalkManage depend solely on Apple's Responder INIT to get their information. Remember, in System 7, the functions of the Responder INIT are now handled directly by the System file; there is no longer a separate Responder file.

All other programs require you to install a special cdev on each Mac for obtaining more than just the basic system information. Using the master program (or administration program), you then query each Mac on the network for its information and wait for the answers. Figure 14-3 shows how this is done. Some queries can be issued and stored for later processing on the Mac at the user's convenience, and the results are forwarded later. Status*Mac and Network SuperVisor require you to import the results into their databases. GraceLAN, on the other hand, stores the data internally while the program is active. If you want to store the data for analysis at a later date, you must export the data to a text file, which can then be imported into any database of your choosing.

Table 14-1
Overview of Features in Resource Management Programs

| Product | Vendor | Software Updating | Printed Reports | Saved File Reports | Custom Reports | Logs | Internal Database | Data Exportable | Special Workstation Software Required |
|---|---|---|---|---|---|---|---|---|---|
| GraceLAN | Technology Works | | * | * | * | | | * | * |
| GraceLAN Updater | | * | * | * | | * | | | * |
| Inter*Poll | Apple | | * | * | * | | | | * |
| NetDistributor | TriK, Inc. | * | * | * | * | * | | | * |
| NetOctopus | MacVONK | * | * | * | * | * | * | * | * |
| NetUpdater | MDG Comp. Serv. | * | | | | * | | | |
| Network Supervisor | CSG Technologies | | * | * | * | | * | * | * |
| Radar | Sonic Systems | | * | * | * | | | * | |
| Status*Mac | ON Technology | * | * | * | * | * | * | * | * |

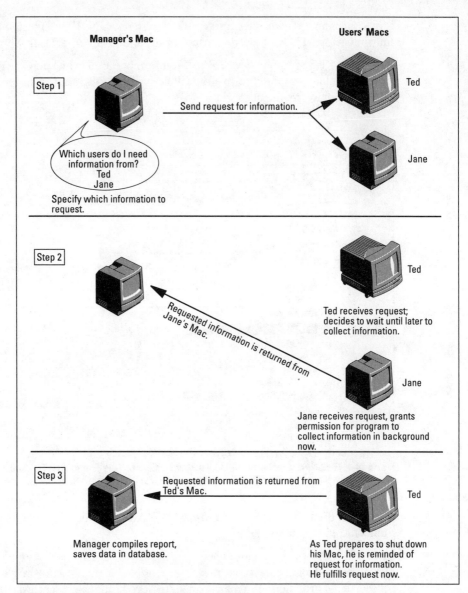

**Figure 14-3: Resource management programs acquire and store data.**

Apple's new AppleTalk Connection for Macintosh and newer versions of TCP/IP Connection for Macintosh (which includes the MacTCP TCP/IP network protocol stack) include an SNMP (Simple Network Management Protocol) agent, which can provide all of the information needed by a good asset management program. The advantage of using SNMP is that non-Macintosh applications, such as UNIX-based SNMP network management stations, could be used to handle the asset management program and that the program could be unified across multiple platforms, including Macintoshes and MS-DOS systems. (SNMP is discussed more fully in Chapter 13, "Configuring, Monitoring, and Fixing AppleTalk Networks.")

Figure 14-4 shows Apple's MacSNMP Admin application, which lets the network manager define just what information will be available to an asset management program running on the network.

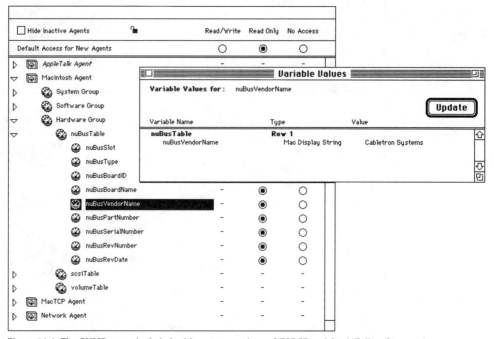

**Figure 14-4: The SNMP agent included with newer versions of TCP/IP and AppleTalk software gives the network manager the capability of looking inside a Macintosh from across the network.**

Table 14-2 displays the new Macintosh SNMP MIB variables available from Macs running Apple's MacSNMP.

The success of these programs depends on the active participation of each network user. Usually, the individual Mac user is responsible for running the profiler that collects the information. As a management tool, you can make users aware that if they don't send a profile to the network manager, they risk not receiving an update to a needed software program. The network manager may not know that the program is there.

## Tracking software licenses

Controlling access to properly licensed program copies is another facet of facilities management. KeyServer (from Sassafras Software) and Quota (from Proteus Technology) are two programs designed to control networked access to applications.

KeyServer can be especially useful because it maintains a queue of users waiting to use an application that's already been signed out for use. Furthermore, because KeyServer passes only a key from the license server to the user for legitimate program use, the amount of network traffic generated by this form of access control is small.

Quota differs from KeyServer in its design because Quota depends on an INIT on the user's workstation for authentication and permission to use an application. Application usage is then relayed to a status database on a file server. The database is accessible to every user, but modifications such as changing access rights can be made only by the Quota Admin application.

| Table 14-2 New Macintosh SNMP MIB variables | |
|---|---|
| **MacSNMP Variable Name** | **Comments** |
| **System Group** | Identifies the Mac computer for SNMP operations. |
| General | General information about the Macintosh, such as its Chooser name and the location. |
| MIBs | Which MIBs have been implemented in this SNMP agent. |
| Trap Configuration | Where to send trap messages (such as "user in trouble"). |
| **Software Group** | Identifies the versions of software on the system, the chosen printer, and all files in the System folder. |
| General | The entire Gestalt table, including RAM size, ROM version, system version, and AppleTalk version. |
| Printer | Selected printer name, zone, and type. |
| System Folder | Contains a list of all files in the System folder and all subfolders, including name, creator, size, creation and modification dates, version, directory name, and file type. |
| Applications | Contains a list of all applications on all mounted volumes, including name, creator, size, creation and modification dates, and version. |
| **Hardware Group** | Describes the physical parts of the Macintosh, including each expansion card in the NuBus and each device plugged into the SCSI bus (and each mounted volume). |
| General | Anything in Gestalt not covered below or in the Software Group. |
| NuBus | Contains a list of all the NuBus cards contained in the Macintosh, including slot, type, board ID, vendor name, board name, part number, serial number, revision number, and date. |
| SCSI | Contains a list of all SCSI devices in the Mac, including SCSI ID, type, vendor, product name, and version. |
| Volumes | Contains a list of all the volumes directly connected to the Macintosh, including name, kind, location, bytes used, and bytes free. |

Both programs maintain logs of application usage so that you can determine who's been using what software. You can review the logs to see if you need more copies of a particular program. Conversely, if a licensed program is not heavily used, you may want to reduce the number of licensed copies when the next version is ordered.

AppleShare, Apple's file-server program, also includes a software control feature. As long as the program you want to control has been written as a multilaunch program, you can set AppleShare to allow a maximum number of simultaneous users for that program. For example, if you're licensed for ten users of FileMaker Pro, you can install one copy on the server and set the limit to ten. When the eleventh user tries to launch FileMaker Pro from the AppleShare server, the user is informed by an AppleShare message that the program is unavailable at this time. Unlike KeyServer, however, AppleShare does not log all uses, legal or otherwise, of the program.

## Updating software

Merely being able to collect system and application data isn't enough to solve workstation- or usage-related problems. If possible, you want to correct conflicts caused by different versions of software. You can do this by upgrading software over the network. For instance, you may want to send a new version of the LaserWriter Prep file to certain users. GraceLAN Updater (Technology Works), NetDistributor (TriK Inc.), NetUpdater (MDG Computer Services), and VersionTerritory (SoftWriters, Inc) are designed with this form of management in mind.

NetUpdater uses HyperCard and a custom stack to define scripts for certain actions, such as "update QuickMail address books" or "delete Compactor 1.0." You can apply these scripts to selected Macs on the network. Any file can be replaced on the user's workstation. But all replacement files and installation scripts must be located on a file server that the users can access.

VersionTerritory follows a similar procedure, but it is a stand-alone application, not a HyperCard stack. After sets of update instructions are created, they can be executed in the background from the administrator's workstation. You can also choose to monitor the progress of an upgrade on a user-by-user basis. In this way, you can learn important things like someone's hard disk doesn't have enough room for the new software.

GraceLAN has a complementary program — GraceLAN Updater — which gathers data about software and hardware installed on everyone's Mac; the program also can poll DOS machines for certain configuration information. GraceLAN Updater uses some of the data acquired by the GraceLAN Responder to determine whether software updates can be installed on the user's Mac. For instance, a user's hard disk may have insufficient space, or the Mac may be lacking a memory-management unit, even though the user wants to run System 7's virtual memory.

## Counting Program Copies for Site Licenses

You might think that programs like GraceLAN or Status*Mac are perfect for counting the number of copies of a program so that you can order a site license. However, you'll soon discover that most, if not all, vendors will not accept a number from these utility programs as an accurate count for site licensing.

Vendors commonly view these numbers as suspect because users often think nothing of copying an upgrade from someone else if they already have an older version. Vendors frown on this practice because they charge for such upgrades on a copy-by-copy basis.

One possible solution to this problem is for the program vendors and the developers of GraceLAN and Status*Mac to cooperate on using registration numbers to track legitimate copies of each program.

NetDistributor performs in a similar fashion. It can also use information from the GraceLAN Responder to determine whether all installation rules, as set by the network manager within NetDistributor, are met prior to installation.

# User Privacy and Network Management

How much information should be private? The currently accepted guideline for asset management programs apparently is to leave user files alone. Therefore, these programs focus on data collection about fonts, desktop accessories, INITs, cdevs, and applications, but not about an individual user's files. Application data usually includes the version number, which is handy for tracking upgrades. The latest versions of these programs give the user control over what information is sent back to the administrator. For instance, you can choose not to have information on your DAs or fonts relayed back to Status*Mac or Network SuperVisor.

User education is an important part of any privacy and security policy. People hate surprises, especially when they feel that their privacy is being violated. For example, if you intend to read everyone's e-mail, make sure you tell them that from the beginning. This practice can avoid nasty situations or lawsuits later on. If you don't have a privacy policy, you should talk to your management about writing one. It's much better to have a restrictive policy spelled out because it lets people know what their responsibilities and rights are — even if you intend to claim they have none.

Although each user may feel more comfortable with individual control, administrators and users must reach an understanding about what this control means to system maintenance. If the users don't relay information on their INITs, for example, they cannot expect the network administrator to solve the problem easily when their Macs crash, especially when it's due to an INIT conflict.

How you collect data is something that affects both the network administrator and the users on the network. Two factors are involved. First, there's the question of how quickly and how often you want data from the users. Second, do the users you support want to be interrupted from their own work to provide system information? Or would they rather do it at their own convenience?

Our opinion is that if you're going to monitor the network and the users' workstations at regular intervals for any reason, inform the users of that activity. Set the ground rules up front.

If your users object to any type of monitoring, we offer the following points as ammunition in favor of monitoring and *intrusive* network management. By providing answers to these questions you may convince the users that monitoring offers them a benefit as well:

❖ Does the monitoring ensure continuous or improved uptime of the network?

❖ Does the monitoring ensure that the users receive software updates in a timely fashion?

❖ Can you solve the users' problems more easily because of the added information you have?

And this question relates to secure networks:

❖ If the systems are not secure from unauthorized use, how much time (and corporate funds) would the users have to spend in order to get back to square one?

QUICK TIPS

### Network Management Versus Privacy

A raging controversy continues about the seemingly irresolvable problem of network management versus the users' perception of the privacy of their computers. After all, don't we still call them "personal computers?"

The central issues are these: How much information should a network manager, or boss, be able to obtain about what's on your Mac or about how you use your Mac? Further, how much of that information should this person be able to acquire without your consent?

We offer no easy solution for this dilemma. We bring up the issue here because it's likely to involve you at one time or another if you're a network manager, even if you're only monitoring traffic and analyzing packets.

# Customer Service from Technical Hotlines

Suppose that you've tried everything you know about. You've carefully worked through the problem step by step. Now you're stuck, the network is still down, and your eye is twitching. It's time to call the folks who made the network products and sold them to your company. An important consideration in purchasing a product is the quality of service that the company provides. Investigate this service by asking the sales people specific questions and asking people in local Apple user groups about their experiences with different vendors.

However, good service is not completely the responsibility of the vendor. Some of that responsibility is yours. For best results, be sure that you are prepared before you call. Have available the serial number of the product or the maintenance contract number, and remember that you will also need to provide configuration information. You also need to have a way for the vendor to get back in touch with you. If you have a beeper number, leave that for the vendor.

Every network is unique. Maintaining an accessible list of components on your network is invaluable. Many vendors will request a packet trace (from a network packet analyzer). They will also request reports from their product's diagnostics. Don't make any assumptions. After all, you were stuck, so be prepared to let someone else take a fresh look at the problem. Carefully explain to the vendor the events that you have seen on the network and the specifics of the failure. The vendor should then work with you to step through the problem.

## Calling the vendor

Here are some things that you should expect from your vendor:

❖ **Courteous service:** Number one is courteous service. You should never be treated as if you are too ignorant to understand the problem or the solution. The vendor should always take the time to explain everything to you.

❖ **Prompt reply:** The vendor should return your call within a reasonable amount of time. Same-day response is reasonable for most calls, but calls that are flagged as emergencies should be returned even more quickly.

❖ **Knowledgeable technical support:** The vendor should have knowledgeable people answering the hotline. These people may not know the immediate answer to your question, but they should have the assets available to find out. Realize that some problems are tricky and must be fielded back to the programmer who wrote the code.

❖ **No excuses:** You should never be asked to accept inferior service because of a vendor's internal problems. If everyone is on vacation that week, this is not your problem.

## Vendors working with other vendors

A vendor should be willing to work with you on a problem that may be caused by relationships between products from different vendors. For example, many networks of over 20 zones have different router types. If a vendor determines that the problem is caused by someone else's product. The vendor you call should help you explain this to another vendor. Many companies will even look at your problem with a team composed of people from several companies. The repair of the ZIP storm we described in the last chapter was done with such a team.

Some vendors have regional sales engineers who can come to your site to help out. If this is important to you, ask whether this service is available. All vendors should be willing to send someone to assist you if the problem goes *ballistic*. The slang word ballistic means that you and the vendor have been pounding your heads against the problem for some time and your company is losing serious amounts of money from having the network down.

With these suggestions in mind, look closely at the hotlines that support the components you have. Call the vendor in advance of a network failure and find out how much support the vendor can give you and what is expected from you when you call with a problem. Some vendors even provide 24-hour support contracts. Also, many vendors prefer that you call their hotline before you make a major change or upgrade to your network so that the vendor's staff can review the configuration with you, especially if you are moving from Phase 1 to Phase 2 AppleTalk. A good relationship between you and the hotline staff is critical to your fault management plans.

QUICK TIPS

### Apple Is at Your Service, Too

Apple Computer can be an unexpected ally in the finger-pointing fighting which can occur in these situations. Apple works with third-party software vendors to maintain lists of compatible software. These lists are compiled into an application called the Compatibility Checker, which is available with system software upgrade kits (such as the System 7 Pro kit) from your Apple dealer, on-line services, and the Internet. The figure shows a part of a compatibility check on a Macintosh with lots of applications.

Compatibility Report – 5/8/94

**Disk Copy** Version 4.2  Apple Computer, Inc. (Assistance Center)
Compatible except for the following limitations:
• Should not be used with Virtual Memory turned on.
(Named "DiskCopy" on the disk "jms++")

**DiskFit Pro** Version 1.1  Dantz Development Corp.
Your version of this software is earlier than the versions for which we have compatibility information.
The latest version of this software is version 1.1a.  Contact Dantz Development Corp. for upgrade information.
The upgrade is free.
(On the disk "jms++")

**Dyno Notepad** Version 1.0.3  Portfolio Software, Inc.
Compatible
(Named "Acta 7™ 1.0.3" on the disk "jms++")

**Edit Add/Strip™ 2.9.2** Version 2.9.2
Compatibility information currently unavailable
(On the disk "jms++")

**Apple's Compatibility Checker can help identify software which won't work with the current version of the Macintosh System Software.**

# CHAPTER 14 CONCEPTS AND TERMS

- Preparing a disaster recovery plan is an important step. Disasters come from all quarters, not just floods, fires, and hurricanes.

- Accounting for resources such as printers, file servers, and modems, cannot be easily done in an AppleTalk network without additional software.

- Keeping track of systems and software is easy with one of many third-party applications. Apple's new Macintosh SNMP MIB can also extend your asset management program across the network.

- The network manager must walk a fine line between intrusion into user privacy and proper management control over systems and networks. Working with users is the best approach.

**ballistic**
When a minor or medium problem becomes very serious, meaning that a great amount of downtime or loss of critical services may occur.

**cdevs (control panel device)**
A utility program for the Macintosh. The cdev is found in the System Folder and appears as an option in the Macintosh Control Panel.

**cost/benefit analysis**
This is an important component of accounting management. By auditing usage of laser printers, modems, or file servers, you may be able to spot problem areas and point out what network equipment needs to be upgraded or replaced, or what new equipment might help. Having usage statistics and related costs — don't forget how much your co-workers' time is costing the company — can help determine if your network is maxed out and needs to be expanded.

Beware, though, that you don't expend too many resources on accounting. The "bean counting" has to outweigh the advantages of doing so.

**disaster recovery plan**
This chart has several purposes. It establishes priorities in the event of a disaster, natural or electronic. For such a plan to be effective, it's a good idea to have management in agreement on these priority settings. You may even decide that you need authorized signatures at the bottom of your chart.

**downtime**
The time a network or a functioning unit of a network cannot be used because of a fault within the unit or network environment.

**group**
On the network disaster recovery chart, the combination of a feature and the users of that feature is called a *group*.

**INITs**
Another term for extension, which is a miniprogram that you install by dropping it into your System Folder. From that moment on, the extension will run itself when you turn on the Mac. It will be on all the time.

**intrusive management**
An issue in network management where there is a system of monitoring the activities of users. It is important to emphasize to the users that monitoring offers them benefits as well.

**network features**
Applications such as e-mail, AppleShare, file-transfer applications, or workflow-database applications. Don't confuse network features with the topology and internetworking products that make up your network, such as bridges and routers.

**reaction times**
Amount of time required to initially respond to a network problem. Should also include a parameter for amount of time problem may persist.

**redundant paths**
A second path that a network packet may use to travel from its source to its destination. The redundant path is used when the primary path between two nodes is disrupted.

CHAPTER FIFTEEN

# Securing an AppleTalk Network

IN THIS CHAPTER

- Security management of AppleTalk networks
- Controlling access to network resources
- Dealing with viruses

M any casually designed AppleTalk LANs now exist, mainly because small AppleTalk networks are relatively easy to install. But as these LANs grow larger or are incorporated into standard corporate networks, the network manager soon discovers the need to treat these networks as corporate information assets.

Managing security for larger internets also is more complicated than managing security for a small network. Some companies have long practiced some measure of computer security; if you've ever worked with a mainframe computer, you undoubtedly remember *logging in* with a password. This step of logging into shared resources can extend to networks as well.

Two areas of security must be managed on networks. The first area is at the level of network management. This level involves restricting LAN access to network managers for such activities as configuring routers and assigning file-server passwords. A second level involves maintaining the security of the users and their data. This chapter examines both of these security areas.

QUOTABLES

"Just because you're paranoid doesn't mean they're not out to get you."

— Ray Kaplan, Kaplan & Kovara Associates [printed with permission]

Another important part of security in the 1990s is protection against the STDs (Sexually Transmitted Diseases) of computerdom — *viruses*. The last section of this chapter discusses techniques for managing computer viruses in your environment and offers some tips on how to inexpensively keep your network bug-free.

# Security Management

Network security is an important aspect in managing a network, whether its purpose is to limit the usage of certain network devices or to prevent unauthorized traffic on the network. Currently, no overall security application exists for AppleTalk networks, nor is it an easy task to monitor your network's security. One reason for this difficulty is the variety of services that a network can provide. Little has been done to standardize all the security features needed to encompass networks that involve more than one type of service to which access needs to be controlled (for example, printing, file-sharing, and telecommunications). Many Macintosh users also tend to be casual with their computing resources, both hardware and software, and think nothing of sharing those resources. Such users may resent having security restrictions placed on them.

QUICK TIPS

## Security Techniques: Part 1

Security experts tend to identify five major areas of security for networks. The following list describes those areas as well as some security techniques associated with each area:

**1. Physical security:**

Techniques that emphasize physical security include locating your file servers in locked rooms, using TEMPEST technology to prevent the broadcasting of errant data signals, and keeping high-risk network activities within a shielded room.

**2. Authentication of users:**

Using passwords, magnetic cards, voice prints, or other technology are ways to control access to resources.

**3. Definition of privileges for users:**

You can define user privileges by assigning only the basic access rights to each user as needed and not providing network management rights to all users.

**4. Encryption of data:**

You can secure data by using private key or public key encryption schemes for the transmission of electronic messages or other confidential files.

**5. Maintenance of audit trails:**

Logs that track attempts to dial into a network modem or to track usage of secure files on a user-by-user basis are effective ways to maintain audit trails for future reference.

QUICK TIPS

### Security Techniques: Part II

The following are some additional practices that can help you maintain network security on AppleTalk LANs:

❖ Restrict users from routinely using certain output devices, such as high-resolution imagesetters or slide makers.

❖ Subdivide the network so that one workgroup's resources cannot be accessed by users in another workgroup.

❖ Permit only certain users to send faxes or to use special e-mail services (MCI Mail or CompuServe, for example).

❖ Limit dial-in access to the network via modem to certain callers.

❖ Control user privileges on shared workstations.

❖ Conscientiously apply passwords to file server and e-mail accounts.

## Controlling zone and device access

An effective method of managing security involves restricting certain areas of your AppleTalk internet. Just as areas of your company or university may be off-limits to certain users, you can restrict access to certain areas in your LAN.

Of course, to provide the ultimate in security, you must physically disconnect the designated area from the rest of your internet — and in extreme cases, put this physically disconnected network into a shielded room so that radio frequency signals from the computers cannot be detected (Did you know that each tap on your keyboard emits a signal that powerful spy technology receivers can pick up?)

For most AppleTalk security needs, however, you can use a technology called *filtering* to restrict access.

Filtering is accomplished by the use of optional software provided with most *routers*. The implementation of filters from each vendor all vary somewhat, but the three basic methods used by router vendors are as follows:

❖ GetZoneList packet restriction

❖ NBP LkUp-Reply packet restriction

❖ RTMP packet restriction

Filters can be further subdivided into the following two types of access restrictions:

❖ One-way access restriction

❖ Two-way access restriction

Additional security techniques are discussed in the following sections.

NBP and GetZoneList filters restrict access in one direction and permit access in the other direction, while RTMP filters provide *two-way access* restrictions. *One-way access* restricts either incoming access or outgoing access. In a one-way access restriction, for example, a filter restricts all users of Zone A from accessing any network services outside their zone. The filter, however, allows all incoming traffic into Zone A. With an RTMP filter's two-way access restriction, users from one network are restricted from accessing services in a second network — and users from the second network are restricted from accessing services in the first.

## GetZoneList

A *GetZoneList filter* is useful if you want to restrict a certain set of users from accessing your internet. Suppose that you want to set up a zone for visitors' use, but do not want visitors able to access your AppleTalk internet. You can set up a GetZoneList filter to restrict the visitors' use of the network. This setup is depicted in Figure 15-1.

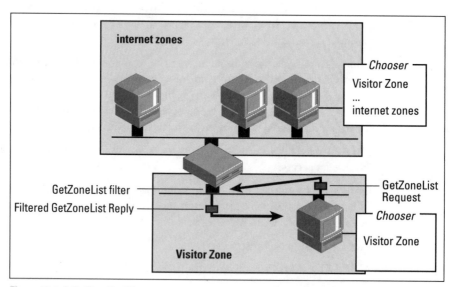

**Figure 15-1: A GetZoneList filter.**

In Figure 15-1, the GetZoneList filter is set up in the configuration of the router's port attached to the Visitor Zone. Whenever any Mac from within the Visitor Zone boots up and sends a GetZoneList packet to the router (to obtain the internet zone list to display in the Chooser), the router returns a filtered zone list, and the Chooser displays only the zone lists available in the Visitor Zone. Because the visitor sees only the filtered zone rather than the complete list of internet zones in the Chooser, the visitor is less likely to become frustrated in being unable to access services in other zones.

The router, however, sends out the full zone list to any Macintoshes that request the GetZoneList through the router's other port (refer to Figure 15-1). Users on the internet, therefore, can also access any services set up for the visitors in the Visitor Zone. This situation may be desirable if you installed expensive special services, such as high-speed printers, for visitors' use.

## NBP LkUp filters

*NBP filters* work by restricting the passage of NBP packets across the router. Although setting up a filter that restricts NBP BrRq (Broadcast Request) packets is possible, most router vendors implement an NBP filter that uses *NBP LkUp-Reply packet restriction*. With this type of restriction, some implementations enable the filter to search all NBP LkUp-Reply packets for a particular type of reply.

Consider the example shown in Figure 15-2. Suppose that you set up a zone for desktop publications (the Publication Zone) and that the LaserWriters in the Publication Zone are all heavily used. You can set up an NBP filter that restricts users who are in zones outside the Publication Zone from accessing the LaserWriters in the Publication Zone. In the example in Figure 15-2, the router checks all packets against the filter and then discards any NBP LkUp-Reply packet that uses the NBP device type of LaserWriter. Any users from outside the Publication Zone, such as users from the Engineering Zone, receive no entries in the Chooser for LaserWriters in the Publication Zone.

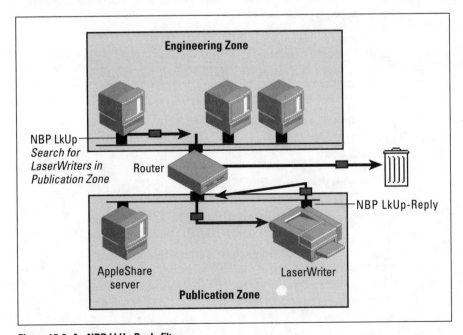

**Figure 15-2: An NBP LkUp-Reply filter.**

## Speed Versus security

NBP LkUp-Reply packet restriction is an intensive operation for a router to perform. The operation seriously affects the router's capability to quickly switch data packets. Other filter types also affect the performance of a router. With today's technology, speed and security do not necessarily go hand in hand.

The NBP filter still permits partial communication to a network area. Because the filter restricts only a particular device type, users still can access other device types in the restricted area. Users in an Engineering Zone, for example, can log onto an AppleShare server in the Publication Zone to send rough drafts to the editors.

Figure 15-3 shows the configuration panel for a multiport router made by Webster Computer Corp. This device has four LocalTalk channels, two EtherTalk channels, and can also support remote users through ARA (AppleTalk Remote Access). In this example, users on LocalTalk channels 1 and 2 cannot see any device not in their own zone. On LocalTalk channel 3, no LaserWriters are available to systems on other ports, and no devices at all are available outside their own zone. If anyone tries to access those LaserWriters, the router doesn't hide them but instead labels each such device as an "Inaccessible Printer." The configuration depicted here is complex, but it is also powerful enough to solve most security needs.

```
"MultiPort/LT S/N 2756":Filter Config

General  AppleTalk  DECnet  TCP/IP  SNMP  Filters  ARA  Help  Cancel  OK
```

| Filter Selection | Macintosh (Stay In) | | | Device (Stay Out) | | |
|---|---|---|---|---|---|---|
| | Laser | Tilde | Zone | Laser | Tilde | Zone |
| LocalTalk Channel 0: | ☐ | ☐ | ☐ | ☐ | ☐ | ☐ |
| LocalTalk Channel 1: | ☐ | ☐ | ☒ | ☐ | ☐ | ☐ |
| LocalTalk Channel 2: | ☐ | ☐ | ☒ | ☐ | ☐ | ☐ |
| LocalTalk Channel 3: | ☐ | ☐ | ☐ | ☒ | ☐ | ☒ |
| IPTalk: | ☐ | ☐ | ☐ | ☐ | ☐ | ☐ |
| EtherTalk Phase 1: | ☐ | ☐ | ☐ | ☐ | ☐ | ☐ |
| EtherTalk Phase 2: | ☐ | ☐ | ☐ | ☐ | ☐ | ☐ |
| Remote Access Users: | ☐ | ☐ | ☐ | ☒ | ☐ | ☐ |

Filter Notification
○ Hide    ● Substitute    ○ Overwrite    ○ Prefix
Notification Message: Inaccessible Printer

Figure 15-3: The configuration panel for this multiport router helps solve important security needs.

# RTMP filters

*RTMP filters* are useful for segregating your AppleTalk internet into restricted areas. Suppose, for example, that you have three separate areas in your internet: Marketing and Sales, Engineering and Development, and a shared area with AppleShare servers. In this example, you do not want the users in the Marketing and Sales zones to access the Macintosh file servers in the Engineering and Development zones. Figure 15-4 illustrates this type of RTMP filtering process in an example network.

In Figure 15-4, an RTMP filter is used to set up the three distinct areas. First, a separate network cable is installed; the AppleShare file servers are installed on this cable. In the example, this zone is called the Share Zone. Then two routers are set up; one router is placed between the Marketing and Sales Zone and the Share Zone. Notice in Figure 15-4 that port A of router 1 is attached to the Marketing and Sales networks, and port B is attached to the Share Zone.

The second router is placed between the Share Zone and the Engineering and Development Zones. Notice that port C of router 2 attaches to the Share Zone, while port D attaches to the Engineering and Development networks.

With this physical configuration in place, RTMP filters are set up in the router's configuration software. All zones associated with Engineering and Development are listed and placed into the configuration file of port A, where the router requests "which zones to discard/filter?" (This request can come in many variations depending on the router manufacturer's implementation; "deny . . ." or "don't listen to . . ." are two possible wordings.)

The same process is repeated for port D: All zones associated with Marketing and Sales are listed and placed into the filter for port D. These actions correctly set up a two-way RTMP filter.

The RTMP filter looks at the zone names and matches the names to their network numbers. (Remember that routers use network numbers for routing packets; the zone names are for user convenience.) In composing the RTMP Data packet that the router broadcasts out of the port, the router filters out the *routing tuples* associated with the zones to be restricted. Without these routing tuples, any routers that are also attached to the same network cannot learn about routes to the restricted areas. Because they do not learn about the routes, the ZIP processes in these routers never request the zone names for these routes. Because the users cannot see the zone names for the restricted areas in their Choosers, the users do not search for services in the restricted zones.

In addition to the RTMP filter, the router should also run a GetZoneList packet filter. That way, any Macintoshes that are directly attached to the same network as the port with the filter (rather than behind another router) receive a filtered zone list that does not include the restricted zones.

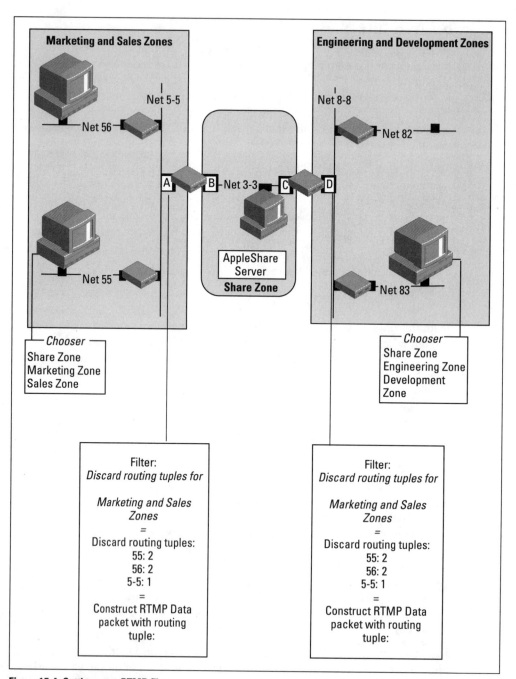

**Figure 15-4: Setting up an RTMP filter.**

Setting up any RTMP filter on two ports, as described in the preceding example, is important. But even if the filter is not set up this way, the AppleTalk protocol still prevents communication from flowing in both directions. The result of such a setup, however, is not very user-friendly. Figure 15-5 depicts such a situation.

In this example, the RTMP filter is set up only on port A to discard routing tuples related to Engineering and Development; no RTMP filter is set up on port D to discard routing tuples associated with Marketing and Sales. With this setup, you may think that Engineering and Development can still reach services in the Marketing and Sales network areas. After all, access here is restricted only from Marketing and Sales to Engineering and Development — whether Engineering and Development can access Marketing and Sales doesn't really seem to matter. In fact, Engineering and Development users can see zones in the Marketing and Sales network area, because their routers receive full routing and zone information.

Suppose, however, that an NBP search (NBP BrRq packet) is sent from a Macintosh in the Engineering and Development network area to a zone in Marketing and Sales. The NBP LkUp-Reply packet never returns. The routers in the Marketing and Sales network area do not have a route to return the NBP LkUp-Reply packet, because these routers did not receive routing tuples for the Engineering and Development network areas.

As Figure 15-5 shows, the router does not know where to switch a NBP LkUp-Reply packet destined for return to network 82; the router has no "next address" for network 82. The router, therefore, discards the NBP LkUp-Reply packet. The users in the Engineering and Development network areas end up with a list of zones in their Chooser in which *no* services are reachable on the other side of the router — not a very friendly situation.

## Controlling telecommunications access

Another important area of network security involves telecommunications access. If you permit remote access to the network by modem, you can choose either of two levels of access control (or both): *password security* and *call-back control*.

The simplest level to set up is password security. In such a system, each user is assigned a password that must be entered correctly as part of the dial-in process. Older dial-in access devices such as Shiva's NetModem and NetSerial use simple password access. Remote access via AppleTalk Remote Access (ARA) requires both user name and password access. (Nonsecurity aspects of ARA are discussed in greater detail in Chapter 10, "Using Modems with Networks.")

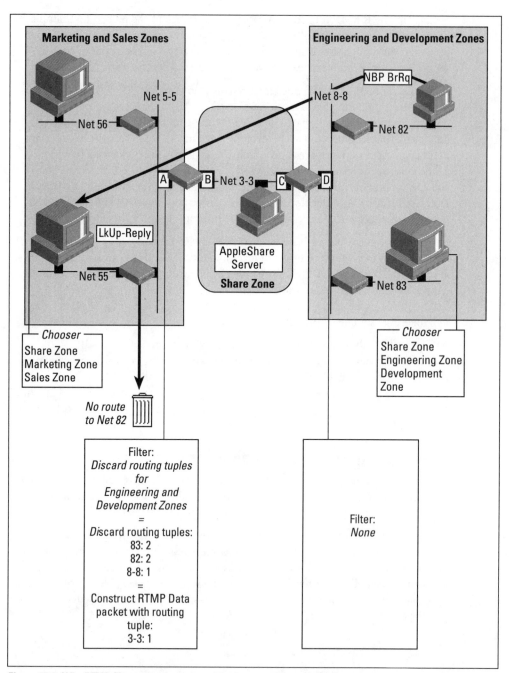

Figure 15-5: Why RTMP filters must be set up with two-way access restriction.

# ARA 2 Offers Security Advantages

ARA security in version 1 of ARA was simple: Users had both user names and passwords and needed to enter them to access remote AppleTalk networks. In ARA Version 2, released in early 1994, this security scheme is extended considerably. Now, users can change their passwords at any time. System managers also have at their disposal a wide variety of options for detecting and avoiding system break-ins. The figure shows one configuration screen available for Global Village's ARA server. As shown in this control panel, a network manager has configured this server to do the following:

❖ Enable users to change their passwords

❖ Require a minimum password length of at least eight characters on all new passwords

❖ Require users to change their passwords at least once every six months

❖ Disconnect a user after three consecutive failed log-in attempts (to frustrate anyone trying to break in by requiring them to redial your remote access numbers after trying three passwords)

❖ Completely disable a user's account after 10 consecutive failed log-in attempts

This last technique is particularly valuable for *break-in evasion.* Suppose, for example, that a malicious person discovers the correct password to an account simply by entering many different words, one after another. After the tenth incorrect password, the intruder is shut out of the system without even knowing that he had figured out the password — unless, of course, he does so in fewer than 10 attempts.

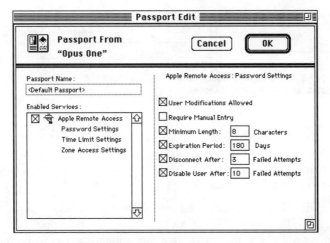

If a simple password scheme isn't secure enough for your purposes, you can use what's called *dial-back*, or *callback control*. With callback control, you call the device and give it your name. After you do so, the device breaks the connection. The device then looks for your name on its list of permitted callers and calls you back at the phone number it has listed for you. The one difficulty with this type of security lies in its assumption that you always use the same phone number from which to call in. If you're on the road or call from a variety of regional offices, you must list a separate entry for each phone number, including different names for each one.

Most ARA server products can be configured for dial-back security, usually on a per-user basis. Figure 15-6 shows a user set up for dial-back on an ARA server. Whenever "Romeo Julieta" dials in and correctly validates herself, the system immediately calls her back (in this case, at the American Embassy in Moscow).

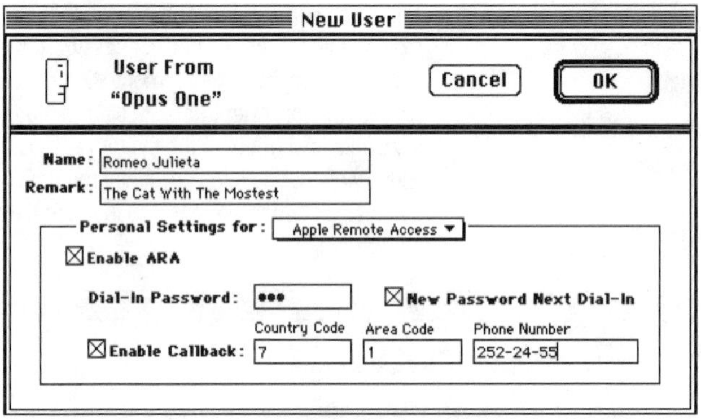

Figure 15-6: This is an ARA configured to "callback" the user
(at the American Embassy in Moscow).

If you use e-mail gateways with your LAN-based e-mail package, you may also have control over which e-mail accounts can use the gateway services. This control covers such options as access to MCI Mail and CompuServe via modem, as well as the capability to send faxes.

So far, this chapter has discussed only those products developed specifically for use with AppleTalk networks. You also need to be aware, however, of other modem security products on the market that function independently of the network protocols. Such products usually take the form of some modem-related hardware device that includes authentication and dial-back features (a multiplexer, for example).

A new technology that is becoming increasingly popular is the use of *personal authentication devices*. A personal authentication device is about the size of a pocket calculator and is programmed with a secure encryption key. If a user tries to log onto a network that has implemented this type of security, the user does not enter a password. Instead, the personal authentication device is used to generate a one-time key for that session only. The advantage of this type of setup is that the user's password changes with every log in. No password can be stolen because, in effect, none exists.

Two types of personal authentication systems are commonly in use. The *event synchronous* style of hardware was first made famous by Security Dynamics Corp. when it created the SecurID personal authentication device. In this type of system, after logging on, the user simply types the number displayed at that moment on the SecurID card, which is that user's current password. Every 60 seconds, the SecurID card generates a new number. The SecurID card and its host computer are time-synchronized (hence the term *event synchronous*) so that the host knows what number *should* be showing on the SecurID card at any moment. Security Dynamics works with most computing manufacturers so that these companies' operating systems and telecommunications software are compatible with the SecurID hardware. Many newer ARA servers, for example, can be used with SecurID instead of the standard user password.

A slightly different authentication strategy uses a *challenge/response system*. In this style, the host system issues a "challenge" to the user that must be entered into the user's authentication device. The device then computes some function on the challenge and displays a response, which the user enters as a password. One company that offers this approach is CRYPTOCard, Inc. Table 15-1 lists and compares the sequence of events that occur in using both event synchronous and challenge/response security devices.

| Table 15-1 | |
|---|---|
| **Sequence of Events, Challenge/Response vs. Event Synchronous Security Devices** | |
| *Challenge/Response* | *Event Synchronous* |
| User starts up communications package (such as ARA). | User starts up communications package (such as ARA). |
| Communications package sends user ID ("Julieta") to server. | Communications package sends user ID ("Julieta") to server. |
| Server issues a random number challenge ("3255092"). | NA |
| User enters random number challenge into authentication device ("3255092"). | NA |
| Personal authentication device displays answer to random challenge ("3240494"). | Personal authentication device displays currently valid password ("3240494"). |
| User enters answer (and possibly other information, such as a PIN) for transmission to server. | User enters answer (and possibly other information, such as a PIN) for transmission to server. |
| User is successfully logged on. | User is successfully logged on. |

Some better-quality modems now include security features such as the capability to store user passwords and callback numbers within the modem itself so that you don't need special software on a Mac to use these features; the CXR Telcom/Anderson Jaconson 9653-MM2, MultiTech Systems MultiModem series, and Telcor Systems Accelerator series are examples of such modems. Other modems, including some of those from NEC America and Telenetics, also offer *audit trails* to display all authorized and unauthorized attempts to access the system. The NEC America modems can also be programmed to restrict access to specific times of the day or specific days of the week.

Unfortunately, very few modems offer built-in data encryption, which greatly improves the security of your transmissions. Cylink, however, offers the STM-9600 modem, while Racal-Datacom markets the Omnimode and RM series of encrypted modems.

## Controlling file access

File server software, such as Apple's AppleShare, Digital's Pathworks, Banyan's VINES, and Novell's Netware, normally includes simple security provisions such as passwords for user accounts. Users are owners of either the disks or the folders on disks that make up the file server. But the security of the data is only as secure as the passwords. If you, as the server administrator, want a secure server, you must make sure that users guard their passwords and routinely change them to prevent unauthorized file use — and assigning blank passwords is never a good idea for any reason.

BACKGROUNDER

### Public Key or Secret Key Encryption?

Encryption and authentication almost always use an *encryption algorithm* of some sort. The two most common types of encryption algorithms are *public key* and *secret key*. The RSA encryption algorithm (Rivest, Shamir, and Adleman, named after its discoverers) is an example of the most popular public key systems; Apple has chosen this algorithm for its AOCE encryption services. DES, the Data Encryption Standard, is the most popular private key encryption algorithm. This algorithm currently is a federal standard that is now under review for possible replacement.

The primary advantage of using public key cryptography over secret key is the increased security the former affords; the private part of the public key need never be transmitted or revealed to anyone. In a secret key system, however, both parties must have access to the secret key — which means that the key must have been transmitted, either on paper or electronically, at some time. The main disadvantage of public key cryptography is its speed. Several popular DES devices exist that are significantly faster than any currently available RSA implementation.

Most file server systems do not encrypt passwords as the passwords go through the network. Anyone using even inexpensive protocol analyzer software, therefore, can easily grab passwords off the network and use them. (Protocol analyzers are discussed in greater detail in Chapter 13, "Configuring, Monitoring, and Fixing AppleTalk Networks.") If your file server does not encrypt passwords, you may want to use bridges and routers to keep traffic for local file servers off of easily accessible backbones.

AppleShare 3 offers a feature to enhance its password security. You can now set up AppleShare to require a minimum password length, and you can *age* passwords — a system that requires users to choose a new password after a set time period.

Password security takes on a more personal face in System 7's file sharing; users take responsibility themselves for creating accounts and passwords for others with whom they want to share files. Because System 7 file sharing is so easy to set up, users may not realize that they've turned their personal Macintosh into a corporate information leak. It's your job as network manager to help educate people about what personal file sharing actually entails and how dangerous that can be.

Users must be informed of the danger of activating file sharing in which all users can access their files. Users, in fact, should implement file sharing only if they specifically need to share files with another user or group of users; they should also keep to a minimum the number of users with access to their Macs.

Whenever possible, do not enable guest logins under System 7's file sharing. *Especially* do not enable guest privileges for your entire hard disk. If you do, anyone who logs in as a guest can delete any or all of your files.

## Controlling shared workstations

Although many of us enjoy offices in which we have our own Macs, many schools and companies must use shared workstations. The shared workstation is especially prevalent in schools, where sharing resources in classrooms and labs is desirable. But many companies also set up special workrooms for communal use by members of a group. Inevitably, users store their files on these workstations instead of keeping the files on floppies or removable cartridges. As a network manager, your problem is ensuring the privacy of those files left on the Mac. Another concern arises if not all users merit the same printing privileges or use of such network resources as modems.

Quite a few programs on the market now require users to log onto a Mac before using it. Folders also are locked to all but their rightful owners. Among such programs are AtEase, Advanced Security, A.M.E., Camouflage, DiskLock, EmPower, FileGuard, MacSafe, and Sentinel. Many programs even maintain an encrypted audit trail to log both legal and illegal access, but few go beyond file and folder protection to restrict access to network resources. One program that does restrict network access is Access Managed Environment, or AME. Not only does this program enable you to set different levels of protection for users or groups of users, but you can also control access to desk accessories and network resources on a user-by-user basis. Another program, Authenticator, originally developed for Harvard University, also contains features such as controlled access to a workstation and both controlled and logged printer usage on a user-by-user basis.

Recognizing that Apple's File Sharing feature does not adequately monitor remote user access, TriK Inc. offers Nok-Nok as an added security product for file sharing. Nok-Nok notifies you any time a remote user connects to your computer; the product also can maintain an activity log. Each entry in the log contains information about the user who attempted to connect, including the time and date of the attempt. Nok-Nok also enables you to decide how long a connection can be maintained.

# Dealing with Viruses

Viruses of any kind can be nasty. Certainly, enough has been written about computer viruses in the last few years to convince people that viruses are a problem. Whether or not viruses actually disrupt your daily work, you should guard against them. Some viruses, such as the WDEF virus, attempt to infect other workstations over the network and can lead to extremely poor workstation and network performance.

Like their biological counterparts, computer viruses are designed to spread easily. A virus contains software instructions that enable it to copy itself into legitimate files. Some viruses infect only application files, but others can invade document files or even the Mac's system files. In addition to replicating itself, a virus can also inflict unique symptoms on the infected computer. Often these symptoms are relatively harmless and just a nuisance, but some viruses are maliciously designed and cause serious trouble to your Mac.

How can you combat viruses? The best bet is a three-pronged approach — education, isolation, and eradication. First, educate the users on your network about the potential problems viruses can cause and how they spread through software sharing (and, in some cases, data sharing). Take care before any new software is run on a networked Mac.

Second, create an isolated workstation — one not connected to the network — to test run any new program before you distribute the program to others. Run the program while using one of the available virus detection/prevention programs. You may also choose a virus-scanning program that runs after the suspect program to search your system for viruses. If your virus detection/prevention programs are up to date and they don't detect any viruses, you can go ahead and distribute the program.

Keep your original software on locked floppies even before you discover that it is virus-free. Be aware that the presence of shrink wrapping on a package is no guarantee that the software vendor has not inadvertently shipped a virus with the software. After you obtain a new piece of software, immediately lock the original disks. (If we're feeling exceptionally paranoid, which is always, we actually pry out the little write-lock sliders so that the disks can't ever be unlocked.) Use only copies of the originals. Remember that a virus cannot infect a locked floppy disk.

Using an isolated workstation, however, doesn't always work. This approach has its best chance of succeeding if your company strictly enforces a centralized method for distributing software to employees. Even then, you need to remember the *personal* in personal computers — users often like to acquire and install their own software, either for business or nonbusiness uses. If you can't be sure that only company purchased and distributed software is installed on each Mac, make sure that each Mac has its own virus detection programs and that the users know how to use them. This leads into the third step in fighting viruses — eradication.

Several effective commercial antivirus programs are available (SAM and Virex among others), as are several excellent public-domain packages (such as Disinfectant and Gatekeeper). All are kept up to date for detecting viruses and preventing them from infecting your machine. Every Mac should have at least one such program installed.

Not only is installing an antivirus INIT such as Disinfectant on every system extremely important, but keeping the program up to date also is vital. Older versions of antiviral software are often ineffective against new viruses. If you lack access to a reliable source of information about new viruses, your best course is to use a commercial antiviral product that offers an update service. And then make sure that all updates are sent directly to you and that you read them as soon as they come in.

If you want to learn more about Macintosh viruses, the best source is John Norstad's Disinfectant documentation. You can obtain a copy of Disinfectant from most on-line services (and off the Internet) or by sending a formatted high-density floppy and a self-addressed, stamped mailer to Norstad at the following address:

Academic Computing and Network Services
Northwestern University
2129 North Campus Drive
Evanston, IL 60208 USA

Table 15-2 lists all known Macintosh viruses and is based on John Norstad's documentation.

| | Table 15-2 Known Macintosh Viruses | |
|---|---|
| **Virus Name** | **Comments** |
| Scores | Infects system files and applications. Does not intentionally do damage, but does conflict with System 6. Creates an invisible file called SCORES in your system folder. |
| nVIR | Infects system files and applications. Not malicious, but can cause crashes. Creates nVIR resources in infected files. Many clones of nVIR have been found. |
| INIT 29 | Infects system files and applications. Applications need not be run to be infected. Not malicious, but can cause crashes. Creates INIT resource with ID 29 in infected files. |
| ANTI | Infects applications. Does not spread at all in System 7. Not malicious, but can cause problems. |
| MacMag | The original Mac virus. Infects system files only. Waits until March 2, 1988, and then displays a message on your Mac. Not often found. |
| WDEF | Infects Desktop files used by the Finder, but not under System 7. Causes crashes on most newer Macs. |
| ZUC | Infects applications, and the applications do not need to be run to become infected. |
| MDEF | Infects both applications and system files, as well as documents. Applications need not be run to be infected. |
| Frankie | Rare. Attacks Macintosh emulators running on Atari computers. |
| CDEF | Similar to WDEF. System 7 is immune to CDEF. |
| MBDF | Infects system files and applications. Applications are infected as soon as they are run. |
| INIT 1984 | Malicious virus. Damages files on any Friday the 13th. Infects only INITs. |
| CODE 252 | Malicious. Triggers any time a system is started after June 6. Infects applications and system files (but only system files under System 7). |
| T4 | Infects applications, system files, and the Finder. Infected applications cannot be repaired. Attempts to masquerade itself as Disinfectant. |
| INIT 17 | Infects both system files and applications. Displays message on infected systems after October 31, 1993. |
| INIT-M | Malicious virus, designed to trigger on any Friday the 13th. Infects all kinds of files. |
| CODE 1 | Infects system files and applications but not documents. Renames hard drive to "Trent Saburo" if restarted on October 31. |
| INIT 9403 | Very destructive. Alters Finder and inserts copies in various compaction, compression, and archive programs. |

A final comment about viruses: Users often mistake other system problems for those caused by viruses. This often happens if viruses are foremost in their minds, which usually occurs just after another new virus article appears in the press. The number of ordinary, everyday problems for which viruses have been blamed is simply amazing. The best way to counteract such paranoia is through training. Make sure that your users know exactly what viruses do; make sure, too, that users understand what causes other problems, such as INIT conflicts, insufficient system heaps, and so on. The more you educate your users, the fewer such problems you — and they — are likely to experience.

QUICK TIPS

## A Virus Protection Tip

You can never be completely certain that your users aren't installing their own software, for business or personal use, on the workstations on your network.

Providing each Mac with its own set of virus-detection programs, therefore, is always an excellent practice.

## CHAPTER *15*   CONCEPTS AND TERMS

- Security management requires that you consider physical security, authentication, privileges, encryption, and audit trails as parts of a well-rounded security policy.

- Most routers have some technique available to keep devices on different sides of the router from each other. These aren't foolproof, but they are an excellent start.

- Passwords are an important part of dial-in security. Newer ARA servers feature especially good password protection capabilities.

- Other security techniques, such as dial-back and personal authentication devices, are appropriate in a higher-security environment or if your company has much valuable information at stake.

- Viruses are a constant source of problems in network environments. Common sense, education, and a good set of tools, both hardware and software, enable the network manager to provide a safe and flexible environment for users.

### audit trails
Logs that track attempts to dial into a network modem or to track usage of secure files on a user-by-user basis are effective ways to maintain audit trails for future reference.

### challenge/response system
An authentication strategy where the host system issues a "challenge" to the user that must be entered into the user's authentication device. The device then computes some function on the challenge and displays a response, which the user enters as a password.

### dial-back/callback control
A security technique for remote access which requires a user to call the device and give it a name. After that, the device breaks the connection. The device then looks for your name on its list of permitted callers and calls you back at the phone number it has listed for you. The one difficulty with this type of security lies in its assumption that you always use the same phone number from which to call in. If you're on the road or call from a variety of regional offices, you must list a separate entry for each phone number, including different names for each one.

### encryption algorithm
Encryption and authentication almost always use an encryption algorithm of some sort. The two most common types of encryption algorithms are *public key* and *secret key*. The RSA encryption algorithm is an example of the most popular public key systems; Apple has chosen this algorithm for its AOCE encryption services. DES, the Data Encryption Standard, is the most popular private key encryption algorithm. This algorithm currently is a federal standard that is now under review for possible replacement.

### encryption key
A personal authentication device is about the size of a pocket calculator and is programmed with a secure encryption key. If a user tries to log onto a network that has implemented this type of security, the user does not enter a password. Instead, the personal authentication device is used to generate a one-time key for that session only. The advantage of this type of setup is that the user's password changes with every log in. No password can be stolen because, in effect, none exists.

### event synchronous (time-synchronized)
Two types of personal authentication systems are commonly in use. The event synchronous style of hardware was first made famous by Security Dynamics Corp. In this type of system, after logging on, the user simply types the number displayed at that moment on the SecurID card, which is that user's current password. Every 60 seconds, the SecurID card generates a new number. The SecurID card and its host computer are time-synchronized (hence the term *event synchronous*) so that the host knows what number *should* be showing on the SecurID card at any moment.

### filtering
For most AppleTalk security needs, you can use a technology called *filtering* to restrict access. It is accomplished by the use of optional software provided with most *routers*.

### personal authentication devices
A device about the size of a pocket calculator that is programmed with a secure encryption key. See *encryption key*.

### password
Like saying "Open Sesame" to a Mac on a network. A password is usually required to access certain parts of a network. You may also need a password to gain access via a remote server.

### public key cryptography
The RSA encryption algorithm is an example of the most popular public key systems; Apple has chosen this algorithm for its AOCE encryption services.

The primary advantage of using public key cryptography over secret key is the increased security the former affords; the private part of the public key need never be transmitted or revealed to anyone. In a secret key system, however, both parties must have access to the secret key — which means that the key must have been transmitted, either on paper or electronically, at some time.

*(continued on the next page)*

*(continued from previous page)*

The main disadvantage of public key cryptography is its speed. Several popular DES devices exist that are significantly faster than any currently available RSA implementation.

**routing tuples**
A type of data in which two values are paired with each other because the two items are related; for example, in the routing table, the two items are a network number and the distance a network is away, measured in hops.

**secret key cryptography**
See public key cryptography.

**virus**
A program capable of replicating itself and doing severe damage to the content of the user's personal computer.

# PART FOUR

# Integrating Macs into Other Networks

CHAPTER SIXTEEN

# Bringing AppleTalk to the Masses

IN THIS CHAPTER

- Using AppleTalk in non-Macintosh computers

- Bringing MS-DOS into an existing AppleTalk network

- Bringing non-Apple file servers into an AppleTalk network

- Managing a heterogeneous AppleTalk network

In this section, we will show you how to integrate Macintosh computers into larger networks — networks that may use MS-DOS, OS/2, UNIX, OpenVMS, and even IBM mainframes as their primary operating system.

We'll discuss integration approaches that will bring Macintosh users onto equal footing with other MS-DOS, workstation, minicomputer, and even mainframe users. This chapter focuses on keeping the Macintosh on its home turf. As opposed to showing what Macs must do to operate on non-Apple networks, we focus on bringing AppleTalk services to non-Macintosh computers and using non-Macintosh computers to host AppleTalk services. If you want to see the other side of the coin, read Chapters 18, 19, and 20, to learn how to move Macs into TCP/IP, SNA, and OSI.

QUOTABLES

The duck hunter trained his retriever to walk on water. Eager to show off this amazing accomplishment, he asked a friend to go along on his next hunting trip. Saying nothing, he fired his first shot and, as the duck fell, the dog walked on the surface of the water, retrieved the duck, and returned it to his master.

"Notice anything?" the owner asked eagerly.

"Yes," said his friend, "I see that fool dog of yours can't swim."

— Anonymous

Integrating a network of Macintosh systems isn't difficult, but it does stretch across a broad range of services, starting with simple terminal access at one end all the way to elaborate cooperative processing applications at the other (see Figure 16-1). We believe you should start bringing Macintoshes into heterogeneous networks in the middle of this broad range, with file and print services. These services let Macintosh users share disk and printer resources — transparently — with other network users. As our anecdote in the "Quotables" points out, though, your focus should be on the broad range of systems an AppleTalk network can link, even if your less-enlightened colleagues can't see a network without a NetWare server at its center.

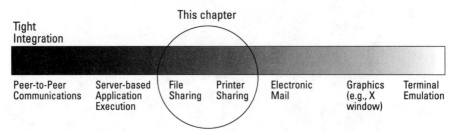

Figure 16-1: Network and system integration ranges across a broad spectrum. This chapter concentrates on the middle.

# Learning about Architectures

In order to talk about integrating Macintosh networks into larger networks, we have to think about the different approaches to the problem. Initially, we'll look at ways of handling file services. (Print services usually go hand-in-hand with file services, but keeping them out of the picture to start will simplify things.)

When you make a choice about Macintosh file server architectures, you have options ranging from high-end, multiprotocol solutions down to low-end, single protocol servers.

## Using multiple protocols

To handle hundreds of systems, we recommend choosing a multiprotocol approach. In this architecture, a file server provides access to clients running different operating systems and different file server protocols. This system is beneficial because it allows both personal computer and minicomputer clients to use the most convenient protocol for each client when working on the same servers.

In the Macintosh world, the most convenient protocol is AFP, the AppleTalk Filing Protocol. Apple purposely built AFP into every Macintosh so that all Macintosh users can access files stored on a file server running AFP without installing any additional software. So when you go into the Chooser and select an AppleShare server, you're using the built-in (and free) AFP client.

The multiprotocol approach puts a burden on the server, but it makes life much easier for clients. In Figure 16-2, you can see an example of how this multiprotocol system works. This figure shows the normal Chooser selecting a file server. To the Macintosh, it looks like any other AFP server. Except it's not; it's an OpenVMS system running Digital's Pathworks for Macintosh.

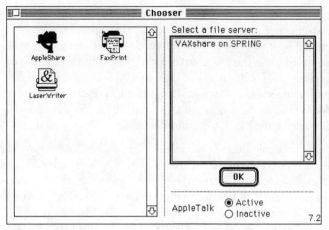

Figure 16-2: The Chooser is used to select all AppleTalk Filing Protocol (AFP) servers, regardless of operating system or platform. All look the same to the Macintosh.

A multiprotocol architecture helps ensure low-cost and high-performance client / server software. Even though a multiprotocol architecture may sound chaotic, it's really not. If you take the time to think through your multiprotocol architecture, you'll have the ability to do the following:

❖ Scale up quickly as your network grows.

❖ Be compatible with new architectures and operating systems.

❖ Obtain better performance than is available using only Macintosh hardware.

It is also important to note that in certain situations, multiprotocol is your only realistic option. For example, if you have an existing multiprotocol network with hundreds or thousands of NetWare, AppleTalk, TCP/IP, and VINES clients, it's much easier to use a multiprotocol server to link to them than it is to change all of the clients to a single protocol. If you have existing servers which will not be re-placed, then multiprotocol is certainly the only compatible solution.

Because of the potential complexity, multiple protocols do mean network manage-ment headaches and higher capital costs. It's harder to route five protocols than two, which makes multiprotocol routers more complex and expensive than their simpler cousins.

## Using a single file sharing protocol

If your goal is to minimize the number of file sharing protocols, several single-protocol solutions work with the world of Macintosh.

For networks that already have a significant number of Macintosh users, the easiest and most cost-effective approach is bringing UNIX and MS-DOS systems into the Macintosh world by installing AFP clients on those platforms. Unfortunately, your choices of software to do this are pretty limited. For example, there is only a single UNIX AFP client (IPT's Partner) and only four MS-DOS oriented AFP clients: Farallon Computing's Timbuktu for MS-DOS and Windows, Miramar's Personal MacLAN for Windows, CoOperative's COPSTalk for Windows, and CoActive's CoActive Connector for MS-DOS and Windows.

Another single protocol option is NFS. The *Network File System* was developed by Sun Microsystems to bind together clusters of its UNIX-based workstations. NFS has become so popular that it's now available for every major computer, from Macintoshes and MS-DOS PCs up to multimillion dollar IBM mainframes. Like AppleShare, NFS uses both server and client systems. The language is also similar to AppleShare: AppleShare advertises volumes which Macintosh users access via the Chooser; NFS exports file systems for client users to mount on their workstations.

Many network managers have chosen NFS, particularly when they have an existing pure *TCP/IP network* — a network which only runs TCP/IP and no other protocol. NFS offers the greatest number of client and server implementations of any file server architecture. Macintoshes can participate in pure NFS networks by using NFS client software and in pure Novell NetWare networks with NetWare client software.

The down side of a single protocol solution is that some clients will be excluded, and choices for others may be restricted to a small number of suppliers. For example, there is no AFP client for OpenVMS and there are only a handful of AFP clients for MS-DOS.

## Using gateways between different protocols

Another approach you may want to consider is one designed to minimize complexity by using gateways between AFP and other file server protocols. For example, some vendors offer hardware and software solutions that will translate between the Network File System (NFS) and AFP. If a network is primarily based on NFS, installing a gateway keeps the number of protocols to a minimum, and reduces management hassles. Also, by using a gateway, neither the server nor any of the clients need to install any additional software.

In any environment, making Macintoshes work with other clients like MS-DOS is tricky. Here are some of the problems that make it difficult:

❖ Macintosh file names are longer than MS-DOS names.

❖ Macintosh files have *resource forks* that MS-DOS servers can lose.

❖ The Macintosh standard for storing text files is substantially different from the way files are stored in MS-DOS.

As you've probably discovered, Macintosh users are often a religious bunch. Asking them to give up long file names for compatibility with their MS-DOS coworkers may provoke a palace revolt. No matter what the server does, no MS-DOS user is going to be able to access the Macintosh file "My Summer Vacation in Tucson" easily.

At any rate, integrating Macintosh users into enterprise networks means picking a preferred architecture. First and foremost. Macintoshes can be clients in AFP, NFS, IPX, and VINES networks (among others). But which protocol will MS-DOS, OS/2, UNIX, and OpenVMS clients use when they want to share data with Macintosh clients? Your hardest choice is making the architectural decision. After you have made the decision, you'll be able to use features such as security, management, performance, and pricing to figure out which products to buy.

# Selecting an Architecture

In the sections below, we'll discuss some solutions for the different architectures. Table 16-1 provides a description and comparison of the products considered in this discussion.

## Solutions supporting multiple protocols

If you decide on a multiple protocol architecture, you have a lot of flexibility in file server hardware and software. There is a great deal of competition and alternatives. For example, all of the major file server vendors in the MS-DOS world have added AFP to their product lines. This lets MS-DOS clients and Macintosh clients access the same files on the same server, but using different protocol stacks. After you've established the architecture, you can mix and match different servers on the same network.

In a UNIX or OpenVMS environment, Macs can also be added easily, as many vendors are ready to export the local file systems over AFP to Macintosh clients. There is an additional advantage to choosing an open operating system like UNIX or OpenVMS — doing so opens up even several more choices for servers. For example, there are five AFP servers which run on UNIX, but there is only one each for Banyan's VINES, Novell's NetWare, Microsoft's LAN Manager, AT&T/NCR's StarGROUP, and Artisoft's LANtastic.

Table 16-2 shows a summary of some of the products available for each common hardware and software platform.

## Table 16-1
## Solutions for AppleTalk-Centric Integration

| Product | Type | Protocols | Platforms | Print Service | Password Features | Access Control Features | Security Features |
|---|---|---|---|---|---|---|---|
| StarGROUP Server for Macintosh (NCR/AT&T) | Server | AFP | UNIX | Included | | File, Folder | Access logging |
| VINES Option for Macintosh (Banyan) | Server | AFP | Dedicated | Included | Aging, Encryption | File, FOlder, Date/Time | |
| AppleShare | Client/Server | AFP | Macintosh | Included | Aging | Folder | Break-in Detection |
| LANtastic for Macintosh (Artisoft) | Gateway | AFP/ LANtastic | MS-DOS | Included | | Folder | |
| Pathway Client NFS for Macintosh (Wollongong Group) | Client | NFS | Macintosh | Included | | | |
| GatorShare (Cayman Systems) | Gateway | AFP/ NFS | Proprietary | Included | | File, Folder | |
| Windows NT Services for Macintosh (Microsoft) | Server | AFP | Windows-NT | Included | Encryption | File, Folder | |
| LAN Manager Services for Macintosh (Microsoft) | Server | AFP | Dedicated | Included | | File, Folder | |
| NFS/Share (InterCon Systems) | Client | NFS | Macintosh | none | | File, Folder | |
| NetWare for Macintosh (Novell) | Server | AFP | Dedicated | none | | File, Folder | |
| Pathworks for Macintosh (Digital Equipment) | Server | AFP | OpenVMS | Included | Aging, Encryption | File, Folder, Control lists | Detection, Break-in Access Logging |

| Product | Type | Protocols | Platforms | Print Service | Password Features | Access Control Features | Security Features |
|---|---|---|---|---|---|---|---|
| DOS Mounter Plus (Dayna Communications) | Client | IPX | Macintosh | None | Encryption | | |
| EtherShare (HELIOS, USA) | Server | AFP | UNIX | Included | Encryption, Volume-level | File, Folder | |
| COPS Easy Server (CoOperative Printing Solutions) | Server | AFP | Dedicated | None | Encryption | File, Folder | |
| uShare (Information Presentation Technologies) | Server | AFP | UNIX | Optional | | File, Folder | Access Logging |
| Partner (IPT) | Client/ Server | AFP | UNIX | Optional | | File, Folder | Access Logging |
| PacerShare (Pacer Software) | Server | AFP | UNIX, VMS | Included | Aging, Encryption | Folder | |
| K-AShare (Xinet) | Server | AFP | UNIX | Optional | Encryption | File, Folder | |
| SoftNode (Insignia Solutions) | Client | IPX | Macintosh | None | | | |
| Waterloo MacJANET (WATNET Technologies) | Server | AFP | Macintosh | Included | Volume | Control Lists | Access Logging, Launch quotas |
| COPSTalk for Windows (CoOperative Printing Solutions) | Client | AFP | MS-DOS | Included | | Folder | |
| Timbuktu (Farallon Computing) | Client | AFP | MS-DOS | Included | | Folder | |

| Table 16-2 | |
|---|---|
| **Products Available for Each Operating System/Hardware** | |
| *Operating System/Hardware* | *AFP Servers* |
| Macintosh | AppleShare Server 3; AppleShare 4; AppleShare Pro; System 7; MacJANET |
| Intel 80x86 (no DOS) | COPS Easy Server |
| Sun/SunOS | EtherShare; uShare; Partner; PacerShare; K-AShare |
| NeXT | uShare |
| IBM AIX (RS/6000) | EtherShare |
| Data General (Aviion) | EtherShare |
| HP 9000/series | EtherShare; PacerShare; K-AShare |
| Silicon Graphics IRIX | K-AShare |
| Digital Ultrix | EtherShare; PacerShare |
| Digital OpenVMS | PacerShare; Pathworks |
| Windows NT | Windows NT Services for Macintosh |
| Banyan VINES | VINES Option for Macintosh |
| Novell NetWare | NetWare for Macintosh 3.1 |
| Artisoft LANtastic | LANtastic for Macintosh |
| Microsoft LAN Manager | LAN Manager Services for Macintosh |
| AT&T/NCR UNIX System V | StarGROUP Server for Macintosh (AT&T 63xx, NCR 3000) |

To a Macintosh user, all AFP servers look the same, and all of them are only a mouse click away. Macintosh clients can even be set to automatically log in and mount multiple file systems every time they're booted, thereby making the operation completely transparent to the end user. AFP server disks also have security and protection, something that local disks don't.

Choosing AFP as the protocol for bringing file services to the Macintosh has a tremendous advantage: Macintosh clients don't have to install anything to use it. Banyan's VINES, Novell's NetWare, Artisoft's LANtastic, and Microsoft's LAN Manager all offer AFP as an extra-cost add-on to products which are aimed primarily at the MS-DOS market. We tend to think of these as a second, rather than a first choice. If you were starting from scratch, you wouldn't want to put in a Novell NetWare server and add an AFP module. That's for folks who already have a lot of NetWare and want to integrate Macs.

Multiprotocol architectures based on multiuser operating systems like UNIX and OpenVMS are alternatives which provide the most powerful connectivity architecture. These systems can run multiple file server products on the same disk volume at the same time.

OpenVMS is an excellent example of this approach, and is our first choice for a multiprotocol Macintosh file sharing solution. The same OpenVMS file system can be advertised to:

❖ Macintosh users (by Pathworks for Macintosh)

❖ MS-DOS users running LAN Manager, Windows for Workgroups, or Pathworks/DOS (by Pathworks for MS-DOS)

❖ Any NetWare IPX clients (by NetWare servers from TGV, Digital, and InterConnections)

❖ Any NFS clients (by NFS servers from TGV, Digital, Process Software, and The Wollongong Group)

❖ Other OpenVMS systems (by Digital's VAXcluster or Distributed File System software)

Of course, Digital doesn't have a lock on this technology. There are AFP, NetWare, and NFS servers from other vendors for many UNIX implementations as well.

Multiuser operating systems have another advantage. Their AFP servers don't require a dedicated server platform. You can put together an OpenVMS or Sun workstation for the same price as a high-end NetWare server, but it's not stuck in a closet doing only file service. You may even find performance better with one of these environments than with a dedicated file server that costs the same amount.

Even in a Macintosh-only world, there might be reasons to pick a multiprotocol server. If you want to work on a real shoestring, you may want to look at Artisoft's LANtastic product line. It runs on very inexpensive MS-DOS systems, costs less than any AppleShare AFP server, and can support a mostly-Macintosh network fairly well. Of course, this isn't as inexpensive as simply turning on System 7's Personal File Sharing option on an existing Macintosh — if you've got a Mac fast enough to both do its job *and* handle file services.

## Solutions based on the Network File System (NFS)

You may discover that your organization has a pure NFS policy. Many companies are choosing pure NFS for religious, rather than technical, reasons. If pure NFS is a corporate network strategy, Macintoshes can run an NFS client application, similar to Apple's AppleShare, which lets them mount NFS volumes on a Macintosh desktop. The Wollongong Group and InterCon Systems have been battling over

## Why Would You Use NFS?

NFS has two major advantages over all of the other client/server distributed file systems. First, it's been implemented on every major computing platform. Microcomputer, minicomputer, and mainframe all support NFS client, and many support NFS server. Second, it's cheap. Not only is the client software inexpensive, but it's also cheap to install, cheap to maintain, and cheap to manage. NFS was designed to be simple to implement and simple to operate, and it lives up to that very well. Once you've got a TCP/IP network installed, adding NFS to most servers takes only a few minutes.

NFS also has some disadvantages. NFS normally runs on top of Sun's RPC (Remote Procedure Call) software, and RPC normally runs over the UDP (User Datagram Protocol) protocol in a TCP/IP network. Although most users don't care about such things, there is an important implication — most TCP/IP networks don't checksum UDP packets. This means that any data which is corrupted in passing over a network won't be discovered as *bad* by NFS. If your application calls for high levels of data reliability, you'll probably want to think twice before choosing NFS.

NFS also doesn't support sophisticated file organizations and operations, such as indexed files or record locking. In the NFS world, these operations are left to higher-level application packages. Security in NFS is limited to UNIX-style user- and group-id mapping.

Nevertheless, NFS makes a lot of sense for many environments. It provides broad access to file-based data across all significant computing platforms. It's designed for distributed operation, which makes it easy to build very large networks. And it uses TCP/IP, which is better supported than transports such as Novell's IPX or Digital's DECnet.

the NFS client market for several years. Wollongong's Pathway Client NFS and InterCon's NFS/Share offer the same basic functionality. In other words, they mount NFS-exported file systems onto Macintoshes. For UNIX managers who have been using NFS to build large computing resources for years, Wollongong's Pathway Access for Macintosh and InterCon's NFS/Share can bring Macintosh computers into the UNIX fold very easily.

NFS has a problem that most other file sharing architectures don't have. NFS doesn't have any concept of printing. NFS is only a file system sharing protocol. Neither Pathway Client NFS nor NFS/Share do anything to help Macintosh users access printers on systems which are also NFS servers. However, Pathway Client NFS does offer an LPR (line printer) server, which lets users on remote TCP/IP systems print to Macintosh-connected printers using the TCP/IP LPR/LPD (line printer/line printer daemon) protocols.

Gateway products provide an alternative to installing NFS client software on every Macintosh. For Macintosh networks with many Macintoshes and many NFS servers, an entirely different approach is needed. Cayman Systems, Inc. offers a stand-alone gateway product called Cayman's GatorShare that acts as a translator between NFS and AFP. GatorShare makes NFS volumes appear as normal AFP volumes in the Macintosh Chooser. Users can mount file systems without knowing or caring whether they originate on NFS servers or AFP servers.

GatorShare runs on Cayman's Gatorbox products as an extra-cost option that adds to the existing functionality of the router/gateways. GatorShare offers a cost-effective way to add NFS-to-AFP translation to an existing Cayman router or gateway. Cayman offers GatorShare as a solution for environments where up to 20 Macintosh users need to access NFS file systems.

Cayman also offers GatorPrint, an LPD-to-PAP gateway. The GatorPrint gateway allows Macintosh users to select printers which are accessible through TCP/IP's LPD (Line Printer Daemon) protocol using the Chooser

The attractive thing about GatorShare is that Macintosh users don't need to install additional software. From a wider perspective, management is also simpler. Managing a gateway can be easier than either adding a new protocol to an existing server or adding new software to every client in the network.

## Why NFS May Crash and Burn

The headlong rush to open systems has left many personal computer LAN systems far behind. When supporting remote access, we are always tempted to settle on a non-proprietary solution such as NFS to reduce costs and multiplying systems. Unfortunately, that may be the worst choice.

At one of the authors' consulting clients, the presence of a corporate TCP/IP backbone suggested that LAN access via TCP/IP would be the best choice. To handle the multiprotocol environment, the NFS (Network File System) protocol was chosen. Ideally, MS-DOS systems and Macs could dial in to TCP/IP routers, bring up the SLIP (Serial Line IP) protocol, and use NFS to access shared disk drives. The disks were located on OpenVMS systems which were running Digital's Pathworks for MS-DOS, Pathworks for Macintosh, and TGV's Multinet NFS server.

In the LAN testbed, everything worked fine. Macintosh users saw their data through both Pathworks for Macintosh and NFS; PC users saw the same information through both Pathworks for MS-DOS and NFS. When the experiment was ex-

tended to include dial-in access, all heck broke loose for the Macintosh users.

The Macintosh operating system occasionally checks the status of each disk drive it has mounted to see if some data have changed. In this case, the checks were occurring about once every 10 seconds. The NFS protocol, being blind to the proprietary systems it was supporting, passed along these status requests from the remote users to the corporate disk servers. In a true high-speed LAN environment, the checks wouldn't be a big deal. Even though nothing was changing, the overhead of requesting status and receiving a response used up all the bandwidth available (in this case, 19.2K bps).

When Macintosh users switched to the not-open proprietary AppleTalk Remote Access (ARA) protocol, all the problems went away. Because ARA knows about the internals of the Macintosh file system, it was able actively reduce the extraneous requests for information and provide good response time over the 19.2K bps line.

# Solutions based on AppleShare

In a single protocol environment, pure AFP is the solution with the largest set of products. Apple has broadened its product line to include three different versions of its AppleShare Server software: AppleShare Pro, AppleShare 4, and the venerable AppleShare 3, the great granddaddy of all AFP servers. AppleShare Server 3, the low-end of this line, isn't designed as a high-performance product. That's just as well because you may want to use older Macintosh systems with AppleShare 3 as file servers, turning otherwise useless hardware into medium-speed and medium-capacity servers. AppleShare 3 is perfect for this design.

AFP, unlike some of its older MS-DOS cousins, doesn't restrict users to a single server. Macintoshes can log in and use as many servers as their memory will allow. Also, each server may have many disk services. However, there are limits on the number of simultaneous clients that an AppleShare server can handle. Up to 120 users can be logged in to an AppleShare 3 server, but no server could handle all of them accessing the disk at the same time. According to Apple, a realistic maximum for an AppleShare 3 server is 15 simultaneous users.

AppleShare 4, which is only supported on select high-end Macintosh hardware platforms, offers between two and three times the performance of AppleShare 3 on the same hardware. AppleShare 4 also doubles Apple's recommended number of active clients to 30 users who can be pounding on the file server at the same time.

AppleShare Pro takes the Macintosh hardware platform to the limit, running only over Apple's A/UX operating system (a System V UNIX). AppleShare Pro runs on the new Apple Workgroup Servers, designed from the ground up to be file servers. AppleShare Pro offers four times the performance of AppleShare 3, and triples Apple's recommended maximum active users to 45.

Because AppleShare Pro runs on A/UX, there are additional benefits:

❖ Up to four SCSI adapters can be connected, which quadruples the maximum disk capacity of the server to a theoretical 28 drives.

❖ AppleShare Pro also increases the maximum number of files which can be open simultaneously, from 346 to 5,000.

❖ Both of the newer AppleShare products have another significant architectural difference and benefit. They'll use all available memory for disk caching, which can yield significant performance improvements in memory-rich systems.

Of course, there's always the very low-end of AppleShare services. System 7's Personal File Sharing is a built-in peer-to-peer networking for small workgroups, which lets any Macintosh be both client and server. If a large, centralized server isn't required, you may want to look at the Macintosh file sharing supported by System 7 as an inexpensive alternative for connecting very small numbers of systems with low-level performance.

Apple only has one competitor at providing AFP services on the Macintosh hardware platform — WATNET Technologies. WATNET created MacJANET which bundles together file, print, and mail servers with a management system designed for educational and business environments of less than 100 clients. The additional security and control MacJANET provides mean that Macintosh users can't use the Macintosh Chooser to select resources. However, for a network manager who wants an integrated package to handle disk quotas, application quotas, and other management issues on a Macintosh platform, MacJANET's relatively restricted environment may be a suitable option.

# Handling MS-DOS and UNIX in a Single Protocol Environment

If you've chosen to run with a single protocol solution, you will probably have to deal with MS-DOS and UNIX clients who need access to file services. Although the AFP environment is a natural for Macintoshes, it is possible to add MS-DOS and UNIX clients to an AFP-oriented network. (If you never have to deal with them, then consider yourself lucky!)

CoOperative Printing Solutions, Farallon Computing, Miramar, and CoActive all offer AFP client software for MS-DOS computers running Windows. Using CoOperative's COPSTalk for Windows, Farallon's Timbuktu for Windows, Miramar's Personal MacLAN, or CoActive's Connector, MS-DOS users can access volumes stored on AFP servers.

There's even an AFP client for UNIX. Although most UNIX-based AFP products allow Macintosh users to mount local and remote UNIX volumes, only Information Presentation Technology, Inc.'s (IPT) Partner lets local UNIX users become clients to an AFP server running elsewhere on the network.

The flip side of this is what Macintosh managers fear the most — a single protocol environment where the protocol isn't AFP. Although Novell's NetWare can support an AFP server, Dayna Communications lets the NetWare server run in its pure and unadulterated form. Dayna's DOS Mounter Plus lets Macintosh users mount NetWare file server volumes without installing AFP server software on the NetWare server. For sites which are committed to an all-NetWare, single protocol solution, Dayna provides a cost-effective way of bringing small, isolated Macintosh networks into a corporate LAN backbone.

If you really want to go crazy, you can try using Insignia Solutions' unusual single protocol approach. Insignia's Softnode product, when used in conjunction with SoftPC, provides a virtual MS-DOS personal computer inside of a Macintosh — complete with the ability to mount Novell NetWare volumes. Why run Lotus 1-2-3 for the Mac, when you can use the original, complete with NetWare access? Of course, this kind of solution runs so slowly as to make it almost useless. The performance penalty of emulating MS-DOS on a Macintosh keeps Softnode out of the high-end solution set, but for occasional use, the MS-DOS-in-a-Mac style of networking provides an innovative and powerful connectivity tool.

# Choosing Between File Server Solutions

If you've chosen an architecture, you still have to sort through products which can help implement that architecture. All AFP servers are not alike, and you will want to look at features such as printing, security, management, additional services, and price, in order to differentiate between the products.

## Printing

Printer services are bundled by most vendors, but broken out as separate products by IPT, Kinet, and SunSelect. Normally, printers in Macintosh networks provide their own *print service*. A server is only needed in heavy usage environments to provide queue management. One of the key features provided by some servers, such as Pacer Software, Inc.'s PacerShare, is the ability to attach printers directly to the server, through serial or parallel lines, instead of going over the AppleTalk network.

When a server takes control of a printer, the server can also offer printing services in non-AFP environments, such as to local users (on a multiuser system) or through some other protocol the server supports. Banyan's VINES, for example, lets MS-DOS users print to Macintosh printers either in native PostScript, or by automatically translating plain text to print on PostScript printers.

Printing, though, is a perennial problem child. PostScript generated by Macintosh applications is notoriously fragile (although System 7 has done a lot to help this), and the hassles of using a print server could outweigh the benefits. In environments where print service is important, you should be sure to stress test the printing software because this area is where you hear the most complaints, no matter what architecture is chosen.

## Security

Security is one area where the Apple corporate style regarding security and data sharing may collide with your company's security needs. Apple's simple security model just isn't powerful enough for large networks. Because Apple has not set strong standards for how security in file servers should be engineered, server vendors have had to invent their own schemes, or rely on the host operating system. This last option brings power and flexibility, but at a cost — management time is increased.

Macintosh file servers provide very different security and access control schemes. Every server uses passwords as a starting point to control access. After access to a volume has been granted, the security features start with the individual folder protections of Apple's System 7 File Sharing, and work their way up from there.

Some servers, such as EtherShare, MacJANET, and the NFS clients allow an administrator to specify individual passwords for each volume on the server. For AFP servers, this means that users will have to add additional software because basic AFP doesn't support volume level passwords. Microsoft lets you have it either way in their Windows NT Services for Macintosh — use the standard Chooser for basic security, or add in its client software for advanced security features. Many of the servers also allow the administrator to age passwords and have minimum password lengths.

Access control at the high end includes sophisticated access control lists, such as those provided in Digital's OpenVMS, and time-of-day restrictions, such as those in Novell's NetWare and Banyan's VINES. Some servers based on multiuser operating systems, such as Pathworks, allow the network manager to map each Macintosh user into a different local username. Then access to individual files requires that both the standard AFP protection scheme and the host operating system scheme be satisfied. Others, such as K-AShare, map AFP permissions directly to the local protection scheme, providing simpler management.

Other security and access management features provided by some servers include break-in detection, break-in avoidance, access logging, disk quotas, and application launch quotas. This latter feature can be a useful tool because it restricts the number of users who can use an application simultaneously, which is a great help in license management.

## Management

Server management is an integral part of a file sharing network — although it's an extra cost option for some servers. You will need to set up volumes, add users, establish security, and reset passwords as people forget them with alarming frequency. Management systems range from the Macintosh-based point-and-click of Apple's AppleShare, Helios' EtherShare, COPS' Easy Server, and Novell's NetWare for Macintosh to arcane command-line management on UNIX and OpenVMS systems. Digital's Pathworks users don't have to put up with OpenVMS, though, because third party vendors offer Macintosh-based interfaces for server management.

SNMP has not come to file servers yet. (We talk about SNMP more fully in Chapter 13, "Configuring, Monitoring, and Fixing AppleTalk Networks.") A few of the products allow SNMP-based management stations to view information about the server and its performance. With SNMP emerging as a common management standard in large networks, this could be an important feature to look for. But don't expect full SNMP management for a while — SNMP may be *simple*, but molding it to handle the complexity of a file server is like fitting a round peg into a square hole.

## Additional Services

Many of the products available in the Macintosh file sharing market provide additional services, either as an integral part of the package, or as an extra-cost add-on. You may find these important in large networks if your Macintosh users need to do more than just share files and printers.

Electronic mail and terminal emulation packages are popular additional features. For example, Helios includes a Macintosh terminal emulation package that uses ADSP (AppleTalk Data Stream Protocol) to let Macintosh users log onto UNIX systems, and a Macintosh mail user agent which works with the UNIX server to provide electronic mail services. Digital's Pathworks for Macintosh is the leader in additional features: aside from electronic mail and terminal emulation, it includes a conferencing system client, an AppleTalk-to-DECnet gateway, an AppleTalk-to-LAT gateway, a full X window system server, a database server, and a full DECnet for Macintosh protocol stack.

These additional features can either help or hinder. If the corporate standard electronic mail system isn't compatible with a package bundled with the file server, you've just bought something you don't want, and risk having a fragmented electronic mail network. On the other hand, if distributing a full suite of services to Macintosh users is the goal, built-in conferencing and electronic mail can be a cost advantage.

# CHAPTER 16 CONCEPTS AND TERMS

- Choosing a file and print services architecture is the first step before you ever look at a product.

- Approaches to integrating Macs and other computer platforms include multiprotocol environments, single protocol environments, and file sharing gateways.

- The two most common single protocol solutions in the Mac world include AFP (AppleShare's Filing Protocol) and NFS (the Network File System).

- A multiprotocol solution based on Digital's OpenVMS architecture gives you the greatest opportunities for serving the largest number of users.

- Gateways can be used to handle environments with only two protocols, such as NFS and AFP or AFP and LANtastic.

- Once you've chosen an architecture, other issues, such as price, performance, printing, security, and management will help you decide the best way to go.

**AppleShare**
Apple's Mac-based file server and printer sharing software using the AFP protocol. AppleShare is available as AppleShare 3, AppleShare 4, and AppleShare Pro.

**AppleTalk Filing Protocol (AFP)**
The presentation-level protocol that governs remote file access in an AppleTalk network.

**backbone**
A central network that connects a number of networks, usually of lower capacity. Those lower-capacity networks can pass data to each other over the backbone network. The backbone network normally is built with a high-capacity medium, such as an Ethernet or fiber-optic cable. The lower-capacity networks connect to the backbone using routers. Information sent from one device to another within a network stays in that network, but data sent from one network to another travels over the backbone. Individual devices can also connect directly to the backbone network; they do not have to be part of one of the lower-capacity networks.

**file-locking**
A method of network data management in which a file is reserved for the first user who requests it. Other users are locked out of access to the file and thus prevented from altering the file at the same time another user is modifying the file.

**file server**
A computer specifically intended for storing files that people can share over the network. The computer being used as the file server might not be able to be used for other common workstation tasks. Workstations used for a single purpose like a file server are called *dedicated* devices because they are dedicated to a single function. Often a dedicated file server is kept away from work areas for security reasons and to prevent accidental or malicious use. However, not all file servers must be dedicated. Some networking software allows any workstation to handle file server tasks and still function as a workstation.

**gateway**
A network device that connects two networks, each of which operate with a different set of protocols, such as TCP/IP and AppleTalk. The gateway translates all the protocols of one network into those of the other network so that workstations and other devices on the two networks can communicate with one another. Some gateways translate all the protocols from the physical layer up to the applications layer. Others translate only the protocols above the data link layer or the transport layer.

**interoperability**
The capability to operate computers and exchange information in a heterogeneous network.

**IP (Internet Protocol)**
A protocol located in Layer 3 of the TCP/IP protocol suite, used to provide connectionless transmissions of data packets over a TCP/IP network.

**IPX (Internetwork Packet Exchange)**
A network layer protocol used by Novell NetWare to provide functions for addressing, routing, and switching packets.

**multiprotocol environment**
A network which supports multiple protocols on the same physical medium. Not all systems on the network need to "speak" all protocols on the medium.

**Network File System (NFS)**
A Sun Microsystems' developed protocol for sharing file services over a TCP/IP network. NFS allows files on remote nodes of a network to appear as if they were stored on the local workstation.

**OpenVMS**
Digital Equipment Corporation's multiuser operating system for VAX and Alpha computers.

**print server**
A device (usually an additional workstation) that acts as a large buffer for files being sent to the printer. When users send data to the printer, the data is actually sent to the server and stored there until the printer is available. Then, the print server automatically sends the data to the printer to be printed.

*(continued on the next page)*

*(continued from previous page)*

A print server enables network users to send data to a printer even if the printer is busy with another job. Thus, users do not need to wait for an available printer on the network. If more than one print job is waiting on the server, the print-server software keeps track of the jobs and prints them in order. Some software allows for the reassignment of priorities to print jobs as well as job cancellation so that some people can get their work printed ahead of others.

### print spooler
An application program or combination of hardware and software that allows users to print at the same time they are working on some other task.

The print spooler acts as a buffer for the files to be printed. The files are stored in the spooler until a printer is free for printing. The spooler then sends the file to the printer.

### single protocol environment
A network in which only a single protocol is allowed. Contrast with multiprotocol environment. There are few, if any, true single protocol networks out there.

### resource fork
One of the two parts of a file in the Macintosh file system. Files are divided into two parts, resource and data forks. Different kinds of information are stored in different parts of a file, depending on the application which created the file.

### TCP (Transmission Control Protocol)
The transport layer protocol of the TCP/IP protocol suite. TCP provides connection-oriented, end-to-end transport of packets between workstations.

### TCP/IP (Transmission Control Protocol/Internet Protocol)
A set of protocols designed to let many networks interconnect.

TCP/IP is the standard for internetwork communication established in the U.S. Department of Defense network known as ARPAnet. ARPA, also called DARPA, stands for the Advanced Research Projects Agency. ARPAnet is the research and development arm of the Department of Defense.

TCP/IP is rapidly becoming a de facto standard for network interconnections for universities and research organizations. It has been associated with UNIX networks because various companies selling UNIX devices have built the TCP/IP protocols into the devices.

# The World of Protocols

IN THIS CHAPTER

- The protocols used by the DECnet, SNA, TCP/IP, NetWare, VINES, and LAN Manager networks

- How Macs can be set up to use non-AppleTalk protocols

- The differences between routers and gateways

- How MacIP and IPTalk work

As you recall, Chapter 3 introduced the OSI Reference Model for network protocols. So far, this book has concentrated on how the various AppleTalk protocols work within that layered model. Now it's time to see what other networking protocols are available and how Macs can be used on these other networks.

Many network protocols currently are in use. Books that simply summarize all the protocols get thick quickly or even turn into multivolume sets, and wall charts covering more than a few network operating systems look like cat's cradles gone awry. Such expansive treatments make interoperability look like the quest for the Holy Grail.

But don't despair — the interoperability scene has been improving over the past few years. Macs are becoming usable clients for many of the popular network operating systems, as you'll see in the various chapters of this part of the book.

This chapter provides an overview of the wide world of protocols. Each topic mentioned in this chapter is discussed in detail in other Part IV chapters.

## Protocols, Protocols, and More Protocols

QUOTABLES

"There's nothing funny about protocols. Computers talking to each other behind our backs, 24 hours a day. That's a conspiracy, not a network."

— Anonymous

We won't attempt to cover all the networking protocols that currently are available; rather, we'll summarize some of the most important protocols so that you'll have some understanding of how they relate to one another when we start talking about Macs.

We chose to subdivide the networking protocols into two groups. In the first group are the *large-system protocols*: those often used in creating large networks that include mainframes and minicomputers (what some network snobs would call "real protocols"). In the second group are the *LAN protocols*: those used for setting up a LAN of MS-DOS computers and/or Macs.

The dominant large-system protocols are Digital Equipment Corporation's DECnet (or DNA, for Digital Network Architecture); IBM's SNA (System Network Architecture); the International Organization for Standardization (ISO) and International Telecommunications Union (ITU, formerly CCITT) protocols; and TCP/IP (named for the dominant protocols in the suite: TCP, or Transmission Control Protocol; and IP, or Internet Protocol).

Figures 17-1 through 17-4 show how some of the major networking protocols fit into the ISO model. Figure 17-5 gives you a rough idea of how some of the major LAN protocols fit together — not very well! AppleTalk is not included here because Chapter 3 covered AppleTalk in detail. The LAN operating systems of interest in this chapter are Microsoft's LAN Manager, Novell's NetWare, and Banyan's VINES.

One thing that you'll notice right away in Figures 17-1 and 17-2 is the fact that these protocols often can use the same data link and physical layers: the interface boards and transmission media. This capability is available partly because the ISO (International Organization for Standardization) and IEEE (Institute of Electrical and Electronics Engineers) have created a series of standards for the physical and data-link layers (see Figure 17-6), and it's hardly necessary to reinvent this wheel. Each protocol stack usually includes options for other transmission media and interfaces (such as ARCnet) as well.

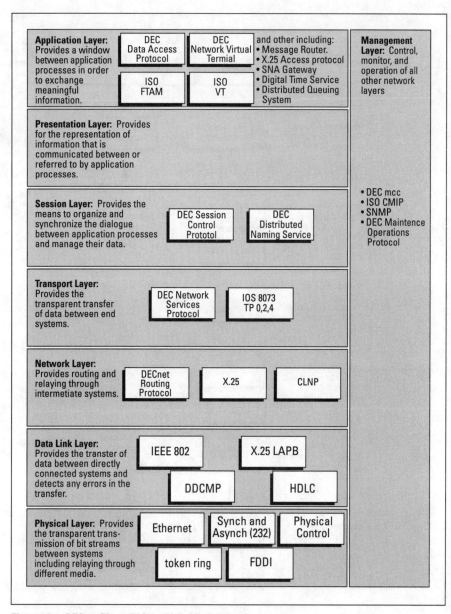

**Figure 17-1: DECnet Phase IV from Digital Equipment Corporation.**

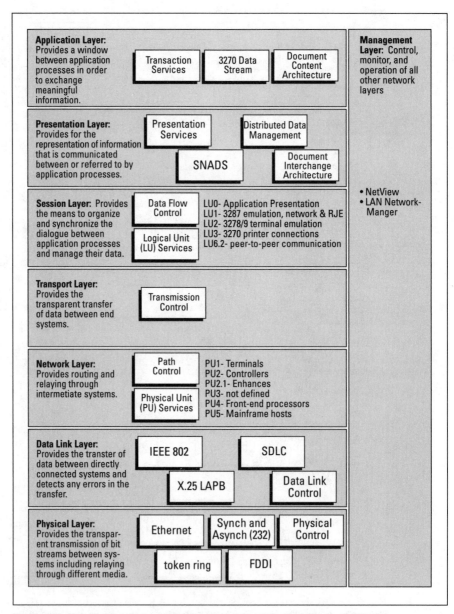

Figure 17-2: SNA (Systems Network Architecture) from International Business Machines.

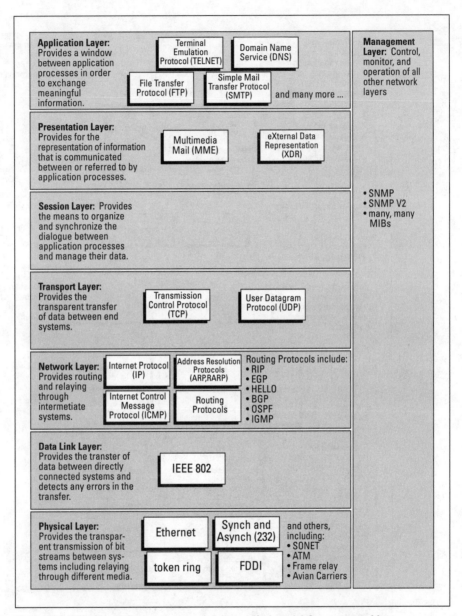

**Application Layer:** Provides a window between application processes in order to exchange meaningful information.

Terminal Emulation Protocol (TELNET)

Domain Name Service (DNS)

File Transfer Protocol (FTP)

Simple Mail Transfer Protocol (SMTP)

and many more ...

**Management Layer:** Control, monitor, and operation of all other network layers

**Presentation Layer:** Provides for the representation of information that is communicated between or referred to by application processes.

Multimedia Mail (MME)

eXternal Data Representation (XDR)

**Session Layer:** Provides the means to organize and synchronize the dialogue between application processes and manage their data.

- SNMP
- SNMP V2
- many, many MIBs

**Transport Layer:** Provides the transparent transfer of data between end systems.

Transmission Control Protocol (TCP)

User Datagram Protocol (UDP)

**Network Layer:** Provides routing and relaying through intermetiate systems.

Internet Protocol (IP)

Address Resolution Protocols (ARP,RARP)

Internet Control Message Protocol (ICMP)

Routing Protocols

Routing Protocols include:
- RIP
- EGP
- HELLO
- BGP
- OSPF
- IGMP

**Data Link Layer:** Provides the transfer of data between directly connected systems and detects any errors in the transfer.

IEEE 802

**Physical Layer:** Provides the transparent transmission of bit streams between systems including relaying through different media.

Ethernet

Synch and Asynch (232)

token ring

FDDI

and others, including:
- SONET
- ATM
- Frame relay
- Avian Carriers

**Figure 17-3: TCP/IP's architecture grew out of the academic and defense communities.**

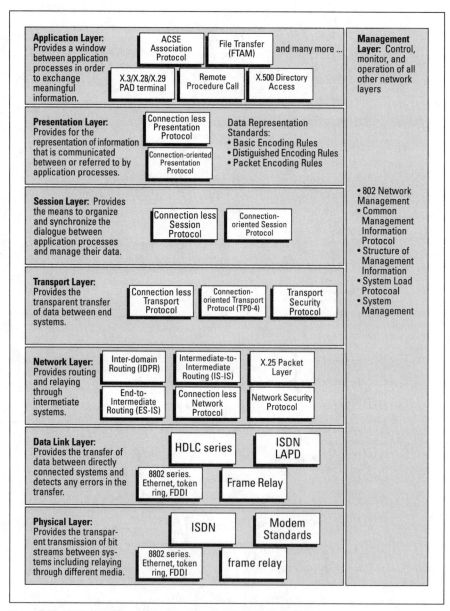

Figure 17-4: ITU-T and ISO networks based on the OSI Reference Model.

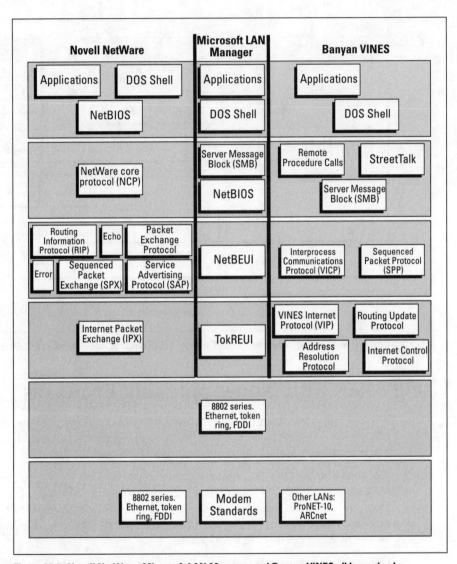

**Figure 17-5:** Novell NetWare, Microsoft LAN Manager, and Banyan VINES all have simpler architectures than DECnet, SNA, TCP/IP, or ISO networks.

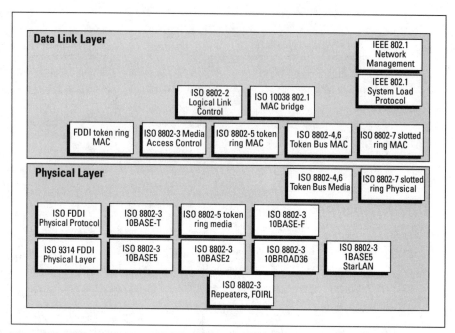

**Figure 17-6: LAN standards from the IEEE cover a broad range of media, speeds, and distances.**

# Using Macs with Non-AppleTalk Protocols

You can link a Mac to any of these networking systems in either of two ways: you can run the protocols native to the other networking system on your Mac, or use a gateway between AppleTalk protocols and the foreign-protocol suite.

A limited number of protocol suites can be run on the Mac. Of particular note are DECnet (also called DNA, or Digital Network Architecture) and TCP/IP. Both of these protocol suites can run on your Mac simultaneously with AppleTalk, allowing you to use your LaserWriter or AppleShare server at the same time you access an OpenVMS VAX or UNIX computer.

Gateways can provide even more flexibility for your network, because they don't require you to install the second protocol suite on each user's Mac. These devices operate on the lowest layers of the OSI model. A gateway, however, uses four to seven layers of the OSI model because it must handle translations among more protocols in each suite (see Figure 17-7). We'll say more about the various types of gateways soon.

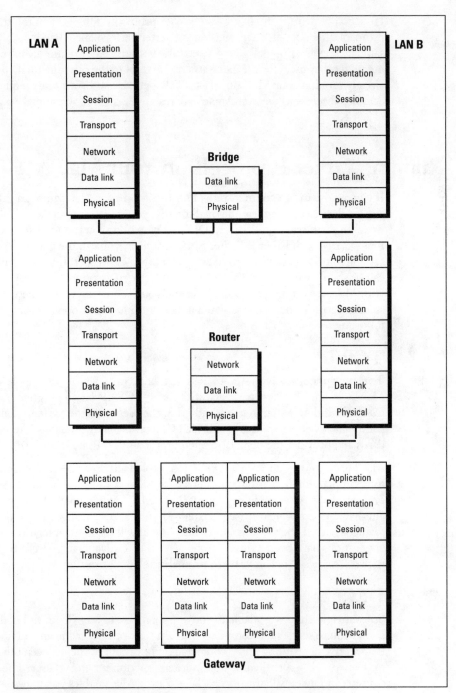

Figure 17-7: The functions of a bridge, router, and gateway are compared here.

How do the two approaches to using other protocols differ? If you run the foreign-protocol suite on your Mac, you can get better performance than by running the same protocols through a gateway, because with the latter method you're competing with other users for the gateway's resources. On the other hand, if you're already running your Macs on a LocalTalk network and your users require only occasional access to the non-AppleTalk resources, a gateway can make a great deal of sense.

# Running Other Protocols on Your Mac

If you choose to run another suite of protocols on your Mac without a gateway, you almost always can use the same medium that you'd use for your AppleTalk network. In the case of TCP/IP and DECnet networks, you can use Ethernet cabling that's shared with EtherTalk. For SNA protocols, you can use either coaxial cabling for direct connections to an SNA host or controller, token-ring cabling that can be shared with TokenTalk, or the same Ethernet you use for everything else. If your Macs are running on LocalTalk, and you want to use one of these protocol suites over the same network, you'll have to turn to a transport gateway, as the following section explains.

## TCP/IP

The most popular way to run TCP/IP protocols on a Mac is with Apple's MacTCP. This driver is packaged with many TCP/IP-based programs (such as *telnet*, X window system servers, and NFS, the Network File System) that provide additional services to a Mac user. MacTCP conforms with various Internet standards and provides the basic IP-related protocols (TCP, UDP, and IP).

MacTCP allows you to run TCP/IP and AppleTalk processes at the same time — for example, simultaneously running a *telnet* session and printing to a LaserWriter on LocalTalk. All versions of MacTCP since 1.1 (quite an old release) support alternate *link access protocols* (see Chapter 3), such as token ring, PPP, and SLIP; formerly, only Ethernet was supported. As you will see in Chapter 18, a number of applications have been written for the Mac to take advantage of TCP/IP-based network services, such as virtual-terminal emulation, printing, and file services.

## DECnet

Software currently is available to convert your Mac to a DECnet end node, which allows you to send and receive data over the network. By being an end node rather than a DECnet routing node, your Mac cannot route traffic between other nodes in the network — usually not an important function for an end user. The basic software in Digital's Pathworks package for the Mac enables you to use serial communications, AppleTalk, or Ethernet to access a DECnet network. All DECnet network applications are layered atop the selected communications interface.

We won't go into detail on running DECnet except to note that the Pathworks package includes not only a DECnet protocol stack, but also a license to use an OpenVMS system as a file and print server, a terminal-emulation package, an X window system server (MacX), and other goodies — a very cost-effective package. Chapter 16 discusses using OpenVMS as a Macintosh file server.

## SNA

You run a subset of SNA protocols on your Mac when you're using terminal-emulation software with an associated interface board to emulate either IBM 3270- or 5250-style terminals (and associated local printers). In such cases, you may not be using the same cable as for AppleTalk, because the SNA protocols most often are run on non-Ethernet networks: coax, twinax, or SDLC (Synchronous Data Link Control) networks.

Normally, a 3270 emulator board attaches to a coaxial cable that feeds into an IBM communications controller. (A 5250 emulator usually uses *twinax cable*, which is a coaxial cable with two conductors in the center.) Emulator boards that also come in token ring varieties allow you to run SNA and TokenTalk sessions on the same cable. Chapter 19 covers running SNA on your Macintosh.

## OSI

The OSI protocol stack is supported by Apple's MacOSI, MacX.400, MacODA, and MacX25 products. There isn't a lot of interest in these products in the United States right now; most OSI work is focused in Western Europe. MacOSI is especially useful if you want to run X.400 electronic mail or X.500 directory services (see Chapter 20 for a detailed look at X.400 in the Macintosh environment). You also can use MacX25 to connect remote Macintoshes to network resources across an X.25 public data network.

MacODA implements the Open Document Architecture (ODA) standard for the interchange of documents created with different applications. Documents converted with MacODA retain text formatting and graphics, even for applications functioning under different operating systems.

# Using a Gateway

What is a gateway? The word *gateway* actually encompasses more than one type of networking device. In networking today, three devices are routinely called gateways; to distinguish among them, we'll refer to them as encapsulating routers, transport-level gateways, and application-level gateways.

*Encapsulating routers* do just what their name implies. They take packets from one network system and enclose them in packet formats for transmission on a second network system. These routers also perform the reverse process — that is, they can process the encapsulated packets, stripping away the second system's packet information and sending the packets to the first network (see Figure 17-8). Some common examples of encapsulating routers are Shiva FastPath and Cayman Gatorbox when they're set up to connect AppleTalk and TCP/IP networks by using MacIP (discussed later in this section).

*Transport-level gateways* perform a function similar to that of encapsulating routers. The distinguishing factor between the two types of devices is that a transport-level gateway uses protocols at layers higher in the OSI Reference Model (see Chapter 3). For a detailed example, see the section on IPTalk later in this chapter.

Notice that Digital uses the term *transport gateway* for the gateway between AppleTalk and DECnet provided with Pathworks. This gateway is not simply a *transport-level* gateway, because the Pathworks AppleTalk-DECnet gateway uses protocols above those in the OSI transport layer (namely, ADSP in the AppleTalk stack).

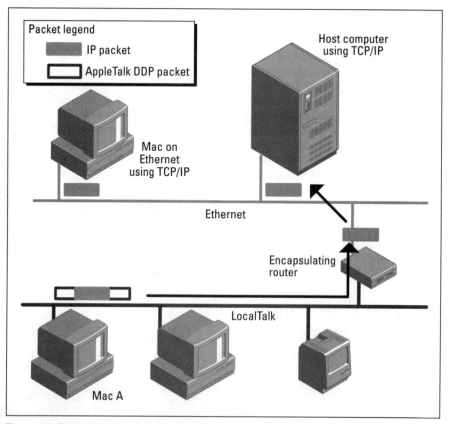

**Figure 17-8: Packet encapsulation using MacIP.**

*Application-layer gateways* are the type of gateways we briefly described when we said that all seven layers of the OSI Reference Model are needed to translate data between two network systems (refer to Figure 17-7). A good example of an application-level gateway is an e-mail gateway, such as the gateways offered for CE Software's QuickMail and Microsoft Mail to exchange messages with X.400 (Touch Communications), VAXMail (Alisa Systems), and PROFS (SoftSwitch Inc.).

Gateways (the generic, all-encompassing term here) exist between AppleTalk and all four major protocol suites: DECnet, TCP/IP, ISO/OSI, and SNA. In some cases, such as for DECnet and TCP/IP, the gateways usually are stand-alone hardware devices (like FastPath and Gatorbox) that can translate between AppleTalk and the desired protocol suite. Software gateways are available for DECnet and TCP/IP as well. Many SNA gateways are software packages installed on another computer on the network — either a Mac or a DOS-based computer — that provide SNA services to the Macs over AppleTalk.

## TCP/IP

Perhaps because of the large number of TCP/IP networks throughout the world, there's been a great deal of interest in connecting Mac networks via TCP/IP backbone networks. Gateways are a good way to accomplish this task — a fact that the various AppleTalk-TCP/IP gateway manufacturers recognize by offering two ways of tying AppleTalk and TCP/IP networks together. MacIP is meant primarily for providing IP services on LocalTalk networks, whereas IPTalk helps Mac users communicate with other AppleTalk networks over a TCP/IP backbone network without putting AppleTalk directly on the IP cables.

### MacIP

Although IP packets cannot be transmitted directly on LocalTalk, they can be encapsulated in AppleTalk DDP packets. Adding and removing the DDP headers is accomplished by both the MacTCP driver (on the Mac) and the IP router (refer to Figure 17-8), which also provides many supporting services. For example, the router manages a block of IP addresses and assigns them, either dynamically or statically, to the client Macs. The router also can perform a proxy ARP (TCP/IP's Address Resolution Protocol, similar to AARP, AppleTalk's Address Resolution Protocol) so that the rest of the IP network thinks that the Macs are directly attached to Ethernet. (This is *KIP-style* IP addressing, named for the Kinetics [now Shiva] Internet Protocol.) In addition, the router can be used to create an IP subnet for each LocalTalk network, which is a better approach.

We noted earlier that devices supporting MacIP should be called encapsulating routers because the process of encapsulating the packets occurs at the network layer in the OSI Reference Model. Figure 17-9 shows the flow of packet data through the protocols of the AppleTalk and IP stacks during encapsulation.

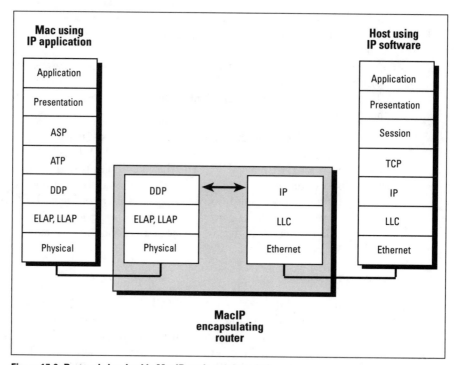

Figure 17-9: Protocols involved in MacIP packet encapsulation.

## IPTalk

The IPTalk service is the opposite of MacIP. IPTalk encapsulates AppleTalk packets in UDP headers, which can be useful for sites that are IP-only and do not allow other protocols on the internetwork (see Figure 17-10). The router can convert all LocalTalk traffic to IPTalk instead of EtherTalk, although there is a performance penalty because of the additional processing that the router must perform. Chapter 12 describes in detail ways of encapsulating AppleTalk packets in TCP/IP.

Devices that supporting IPTalk packet encapsulation should be called transport-level gateways, in keeping with the definition earlier in this chapter. Figure 17-11 makes the reason clear: the UDP protocol used to encapsulate the AppleTalk packets is located in the transport layer of the OSI Reference Model.

## DECnet

Some of the same hardware routers that provide access to TCP/IP networks can become DECnet routers. In these cases, Macs running DECnet software on LocalTalk networks use LocalTalk as the transport mechanism to the router, which in turn connects to Ethernet and maintains a connection with DECnet. Encapsulation here uses the same approach as MacIP. Compatible Systems and

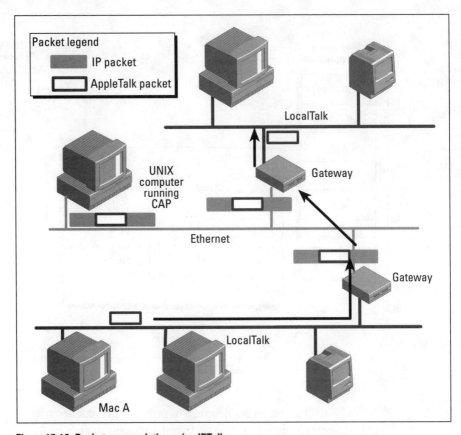

**Figure 17-10: Packet encapsulation using IPTalk.**

Webster Computer make products that handle DECnet translation to and from LocalTalk and Ethernet networks.

Digital's Pathworks for Macintosh includes software that provides gateway functions between AppleTalk and DECnet networks. With this software, the gateway process runs on an OpenVMS computer, and AppleTalk users access the router via AppleTalk for VMS (also part of Pathworks). As this gateway exists only at the transport and session layers (see Figure 17-12), applications on the Mac need to use the same higher-layer protocols as those on their VAX servers.

## SNA/SAA

As mentioned earlier in this chapter, most SNA gateways are combined hardware/ software packages. These products include an appropriate network interface board for the Mac or DOS computer that serves as the gateway machine, as well as the software that controls the gateway processes.

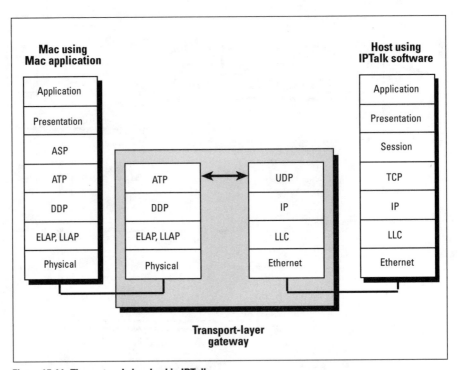

**Figure 17-11: The protocols involved in IPTalk.**

The majority of gateways are designed to provide SNA connectivity — that is, 3270-terminal emulation, and Type 1- and Type 3-printer emulation — to Macs running on AppleTalk networks. IBM's major direction in distributed computing and networking, however, revolves around a strategy called SAA (Systems Application Architecture), which includes an interface defined for peer-to-peer communications, called APPC (Advanced Program-to-Program Communications). APPC runs on the LU6.2 protocol (see Figure 17-13).

You can expect many of IBM's future network services to concentrate on APPC and LU6.2. Apple's gateway, SNA*ps, provides SNA and SAA/APPC connectivity in the same product and runs on a Macintosh. Chapter 19 examines these solutions in detail.

# Using Other LAN Protocols

This chapter has concentrated on the large-system protocols: DECnet, TCP/IP, and SNA. As mentioned at the beginning of this chapter, however, a whole series of LAN protocols should be considered for integrating Macs into heterogeneous (multiprotocol) networks. These network operating systems include Microsoft's LAN Manager, Novell's NetWare, 3Com's 3+, and Banyan's VINES.

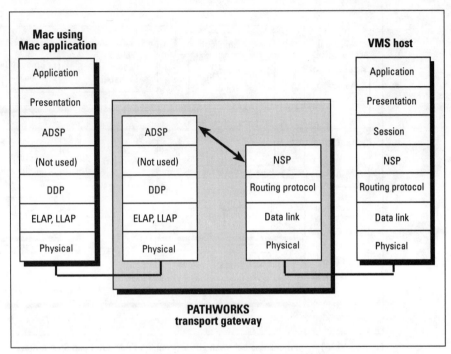

**Figure 17-12: The protocols involved in a Pathworks AppleTalk-DECnet gateway.**

One rarely sees protocols that are native to a non-AppleTalk network operating system running on a Mac. The original version of 3Com's 3+ ran some of the 3+ protocols on the Mac, but when 3Com switched to 3+Open (which has since reverted to Microsoft as part of LAN Manager), the system was redesigned to support the AppleTalk stack on the Mac.

One program that does provide non-AppleTalk LAN protocols on the Mac is the SoftNode module for the SoftPC DOS emulator package. This module handles normal IPX and SPX protocols through an Ethernet card and runs simultaneously with AppleTalk protocols on the same Mac.

The standard approach to supporting Macs on non-AppleTalk LAN systems is incorporating the AppleTalk stack within the server. Thus, systems such as NetWare (Novell) LAN Manager (Microsoft), and Pathworks (Digital) run multiple protocol stacks in parallel on the server, handling translations between the protocol stacks according to the client's needs (see Figure 17-14).

This method enables the server to be the integrator for multiprotocol networks and allows each client computer to run the protocol suite best suited to it. A DOS computer, therefore, would run NetWare's IPX/SPX protocols, but a Mac would continue to use AppleTalk. Chapter 16 looks at the issues in mixing Macintosh and non-Macintosh computers.

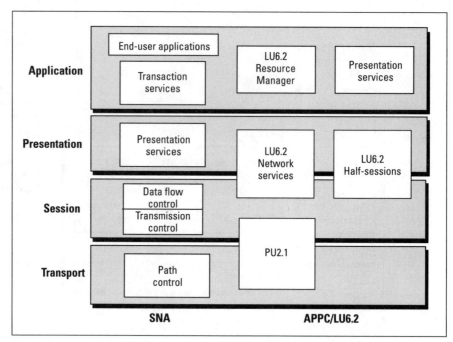

Figure 17-13: The relationships between LU6.2 (from the SAA suite) and SNA protocols.

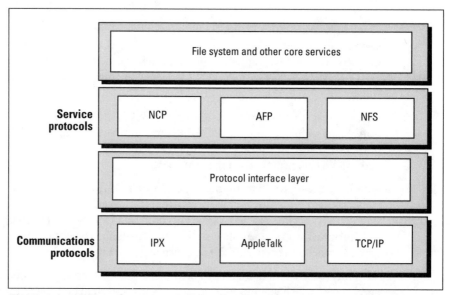

Figure 17-14: NetWare support for multiple protocols is an example of parallel handling of protocol stacks on a server.

# CHAPTER 17 CONCEPTS AND TERMS

- An encapsulating router doesn't change the contents of your AppleTalk packets.

- A gateway most likely will alter the contents of packets to conform to the other network system's requirements.

- Macs can run DECnet and TCP/IP (and some SNA) protocols either directly or via a gateway.

- MacIP encapsulates IP packets within AppleTalk DDP packets for transmission on LocalTalk networks.

- IPTalk encapsulates AppleTalk packets within TCP/IP UDP packets for transmission on TCP/IP networks.

- DEC's Pathworks gateway can convert between AppleTalk ADSP packets and DECnet NSP packets.

- NetWare and other network systems provide access to more than one protocol stack.

**KIP-style IP addressing**
A technique for linking LocalTalk-only Macintoshes to TCP/IP by routing them from the Ethernet (typically) LAN onto the LocalTalk LAN and encapsulating them in AppleTalk DDP packets.

**transport-level gateways**
Link two networks by translating between two (or more) types of protocols at Layers 3 and 4 of the OSI Reference Model.

**twinax cable**
A type of coaxial cable with two center conductors, hence the name "twin-coaxial" cable.

**application-level gateways**
Link two networks by translating between two (or more) types of protocols at layers above Layer 4 of the OSI Reference Model.

**encapsulating routers**
Link two different networks by taking packets from one type of network (such as AppleTalk) and enclosing them in another (such as TCP/IP).

# Macs in the World of TCP/IP

IN THIS CHAPTER

- The Macintosh Communications Toolbox
- The place of MacTCP
- Commercial applications that help bring TCP/IP to the Macintosh
- Freeware and share-ware pointers for the Macintosh

TCP/IP is the common language of networking. If you have to connect Macintoshes to the wide world of corporate computers, we think that TCP/IP is your best choice. With TCP/IP network software, Mac users can log on to a mainframe in London, send files to a VAX in Frankfurt, read mail from a PC in Moscow, and catch up on the news from a UNIX system in Naples. If you've got a computer, someone's got a TCP/IP for it. TCP/IP won't always be the most elegant solution, but it's the one universal solution for connecting systems and networks.

Putting TCP/IP on your Macintosh is like building a house. Start with a foundation, add supporting walls, cap it with a roof, and you've got a full-scale TCP/IP networked workstation. In the land of Macintosh, the hard part is making sure that you have all the pieces you need.

If you want to know more about the networking protocols in TCP/IP, consult *Internetworking with TCP/IP*, by Douglas Comer (Prentice-Hall). You may also want to refer to *Network Security SECRETS* by David J. Stang and Sylvia Moon (IDG Books Worldwide).

## Building a TCP/IP House

QUOTABLES

"We shall never understand each other until we reduce the language to seven words."

— Kahlil Gibran

The blueprints for the Macintosh TCP/IP house come from Apple, in the form of the Communications Toolbox. Apple introduced the Communications Toolbox as an option in System 6 and built it into System 7. If you're running System 7, you've got the Communications Toolbox whether you know it or not. The Communications Toolbox allows you to mix and match pieces to meet your networking needs.

### Three Pillars of Wisdom

The Communications Toolbox has three parts: connection managers, terminal managers, and file-transfer managers.

*Connection managers* enable applications to make connections to other hosts. Apple's Serial Tool, for example, is a simple connection manager that enables applications to use the Mac's serial port to talk to modems and hosts. In the TCP/IP world, the equivalent is a Telnet Tool — something between an application and MacTCP that handles the telnet protocol. Apple provides Modem, ADSP (AppleTalk Data Stream Protocol), and Serial tools as part of the basic Communications Toolbox.

*Terminal managers* emulate a kind of terminal, such as a DEC VT100 or an IBM 3270. Apple provides DEC VT102, DEC VT320, and "dumb" TTY tools as part of the basic Communications Toolbox.

*File-transfer managers* enable applications to transfer files without having to know about protocols such as XModem, YModem, ZModem, and Kermit. In the TCP/IP world, the relevant file-transfer tool would support FTP, the File Transfer Protocol. Apple provides XModem and Text tools as part of the basic Communications Toolbox.

Not every TCP/IP application has to use the Communications Toolbox. Many older applications have their own equivalents of the terminal, connection, and file-transfer tools built into a single application.

But an application that fully supports the Communications Toolbox is more flexible and easier to expand.

Suppose that you're working with a communications application that supports TCP/IP and standard modems but doesn't use the Communications Toolbox. If you suddenly need to talk to a DEC host using DECnet or an IBM host using SNA, you have to buy and learn a new communications program. But if you're already using the Communications Toolbox, you can simply plug in a new manager.

This solution sounds like a great idea, and it is — in theory. In practice, only a few communications applications fully support the Communications Toolbox, and only a few companies (ASC, Synergy Software, and InterCon) sell tools to extend the Communications Toolbox itself. Most communications-applications vendors have just begun to see the benefits of working with the Communications Toolbox and are using only the Connection Manager part of the Toolbox.

If you're working with a terminal emulator that doesn't support TCP/IP but does support the Communications Toolbox (MacTerminal is a good example), you can add TCP/IP support simply by buying ASC's TCPack, Synergy's Versatilities, or InterCon's TCP/Toolz & Toyz.

## Learning about MacTCP

The foundation of the TCP/IP house also comes from Apple, as MacTCP. The Macintosh TCP/IP software world can be divided into halves: before MacTCP and after MacTCP. Before MacTCP is an ugly, dark time of incompatible solutions, hard-to-configure software, and sorrowful network managers. Before MacTCP also is before the Communications Toolbox. Before MacTCP, if you wanted to write a TCP/IP application, you also had to implement the entire TCP/IP protocol stack. Early TCP/IP applications, such as Stanford University's MacIP and the NCSA (National Center for Supercomputing Applications) Telnet included their own protocol stacks.

So what is MacTCP? MacTCP is the standard platform that Apple provides for building applications and services over the TCP/IP protocols. MacTCP is the piece in the middle. It talks to the hardware, it talks to the applications, and it takes care of everything in between.

MacTCP provides the basic TCP/IP protocol stack on which everything rests (see Figure 18-1). MacTCP works with LocalTalk, EtherTalk, and TokenTalk networks out of the box, and you can purchase extensions that use SLIP or PPP protocols to work over modems. With MacTCP out there, application designers can concentrate on the task at hand — terminal emulation, file transfer, or whatever — instead of worrying about writing network software.

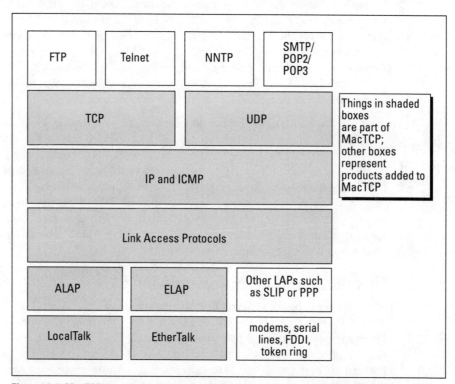

**Figure 18-1: MacTCP is part of the bigger networking picture when running TCP/IP applications on a Macintosh.**

All the commercial products come with a copy of MacTCP, although you probably will want the latest version (2.0.4, as of summer 1994). If you choose freeware, you will have to buy a copy from Apple or APDA for about $50.

The next time you hear an MS-DOS user cursing about how this Ethernet board won't work with that software or how he can't run five different network packages at the same time, snicker softly: MacTCP and the Communications Toolbox mean that Mac users need never worry about such things. (Stand up, turn toward Cupertino, and say, "Thank you, Apple.")

Configuring MacTCP is simple. More important, Apple has provided a flexible tool kit that allows administrators to restrict user options as much as necessary when they are configuring systems. Apple's tool kit doesn't provide any true security, but it does lessen the chance that a misconfigured system will be unable to communicate with the rest of the world.

Figure 18-2 shows the basic configuration control panel in MacTCP, and Figure 18-3 shows the extended configuration controls. If you plan to support a network of systems running MacTCP, a copy of the developer's kit would be a good investment. This kit includes both the locked and unlocked MacTCP control panels, plus a well-written manual that describes many of the possible scenarios for handling user configuration of MacTCP systems. The manual also comes in Microsoft Word format, which can be helpful for developing your own end-user documentation.

After you lay the MacTCP foundation, it's time to go shopping. What do you need? VT100 terminal emulation to talk to the UNIX systems in Engineering? IBM 3270 terminal emulation for the mainframes in MIS? File transfer to keep databases synchronized? Electronic-mail gateways to link Mac networks to the rest of the company? Network management tools? Or just more network toys and gadgets? No problem. All these products are available, and your selection is limited only by your budget and the size of your hard disk. More important, you don't have to worry about finding one program to do everything; MacTCP enables you to run multiple TCP/IP applications at the same time.

## Installing and configuring MacTCP

We really don't have to tell you how to install and configure MacTCP. With the MacTCP Developer's Kit (available from APDA, the Apple Programmer's and Developer's Association), Apple includes manuals that each developer can distribute to explain how to install and configure MacTCP in a variety of environments. Rather than duplicate Apple's excellent manual, we'll simply remind you that you probably already have good instructions sitting on your shelf; they came with whatever TCP/IP product you bought.

If you bought MacTCP directly from Apple (or got it for free with System 7.5), the MacTCP kit also includes instructions on how to install and configure the software. If you are a system manager who is responsible for many Macintoshes, you should get at least one copy of the MacTCP Administrator's Kit from Apple, even if you buy all your TCP/IP software commercially. This package includes some software and documentation that Apple and most vendors don't send out with the basic MacTCP package. This material can be very helpful if you manage a multi-Macintosh TCP/IP network.

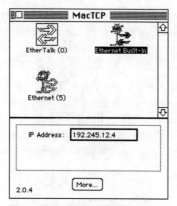

Figure 18-2: Configuring MacTCP can be as simple as picking a network interface and entering an IP address...

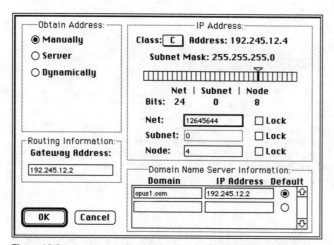

Figure 18-3: ...or may require that you set additional options, such as TCP/IP gateway routers and domain name system (DNS) servers.

# Choosing TCP/IP Network Applications

Dozens of TCP/IP network applications for the Macintosh are available, all of them compatible with MacTCP. There are more than 40 TCP/IP-based applications.

The four most popular TCP/IP applications are terminal emulation (*telnet*), file transfer (*ftp*), electronic mail (SMTP and POP2/POP3), and news (NNTP). These applications cover almost everything that almost everyone does all day long: log in, read mail, move files back and forth, and read news.

You can find many good commercial and shareware/freeware applications. We spend most of our time, however, on two applications. At home, on the big-screen Macintosh, we use InterCon's TCP/Connect II; on the road, on the PowerBook, we use Synergy Software's VersaTerm.

VersaTerm's complete Communications Toolbox compatibility (see Figure 18-4 to see just how flexible VersaTerm is) makes good sense when we're on the road and don't know whether we're going to need SLIP, PPP, DECnet, AppleTalk, or TCP/IP to communicate. We don't need that flexibility at home, when other features of TCP/Connect II (such as the ability to have multiple windows open at the same time) are more important.

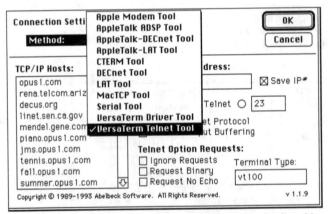

**Figure 18-4: Because VersaTerm uses the Communications Toolbox, it's easy to have many different kinds of network connections, including TCP/IP, DECnet, and modem.**

Why two packages? Because we have different needs at different times. That doesn't mean that the other packages aren't as good (or even better); these packages are simply what we use. Many of our colleagues use NCSA Telnet not because it's better, but because it's free.

## Terminal emulation and file transfer

All TCP/IP emulators start with the basics: DEC VT-series terminal emulation, and file transfer. Terminal emulation in the TCP/IP world is the same as it is everywhere else: the Mac looks like a terminal to a minicomputer or mainframe. Instead of going over a modem or serial connection, the traffic flows over a LAN. By using TCP/IP, Macintoshes, and terminal-emulation software, you can connect without buying additional terminal servers, asynchronous ports, modems, or phone lines. In addition, the same Macintosh can participate in client/server applications and file sharing, as well as run normal Mac applications simultaneously.

Not all VT-emulators are created equal. The most difficult and featureless ones you'll find are the VT102 and VT320 Display Managers built into the basic Communications Toolbox. But that makes sense; these emulators are free, so they shouldn't be the best. If all you want is a terminal that does nothing more than a VT102, you'll be happy with those display managers, even though we don't think they're very powerful. If you want to make use of that 21-inch color screen by having a nice big terminal window of 48 lines with a light gray background, you're out of luck; Apple's VT320 can't do it.

Most of the other commercial communications applications do a better job of terminal emulation than Apple's freebies. You will find, however, that many of the seldom-used features of DEC terminals, such as downloadable character sets and color-graphics options, aren't included in the base price of the commercial packages. If you need something unusual, such as ReGIS support, make sure that the package you pick has the feature you need, and take the cost difference seriously.

File transfer in the TCP/IP world is handled through the FTP protocol. FTP has two parts: a server and a client. The client on one machine initiates a transfer with a server on another. Some packages support file transfer as an FTP server only; in a configuration of this type, the Mac cannot initiate file transfers. Other packages support only client FTP, in which the Mac initiates the file transfer but can't act as a server to some other client. Some packages include both client and server FTP, either built-in or as an extra-cost option. Table 18-1 identifies the FTP client and server features of several packages.

An FTP server can open your Mac so that anyone can read — or write — any file. That fact makes security an important part of FTP service. If you choose to install an FTP server on a Macintosh, make sure that the Mac is password-protected. Early versions of NCSA Telnet either couldn't set the password or made it very hard to do so. You may be vulnerable.

You need not depend solely on the FTP capabilities of your communications application. Several excellent stand-alone FTP clients and servers are available, and all of them are simple to use. The easiest-to-use FTP clients are the shareware programs Xfer It and Fetch. To set your Mac up as an FTP server, ASC's commercial FTPshare or Peter Lewis's shareware FTPd would be a good choice.

## Terminal emulation bells and whistles

After basic terminal emulation and file transfer, many more things can be jammed into a communications application. If you need to do more than just log on as a VT100 and transfer files, these features will narrow down your buying choices.

IBM mainframes require more than DEC VT100 emulation. To connect a Mac to an IBM mainframe over TCP/IP, you need 3270 emulation. If you want IBM's

| | | Uses Comm Toolbox Connection Mgrs | Uses Comm Toolbox File Transfer Mgrs | Uses Comm Toolbox Display Mgrs | Supports Serial/Modems | IBM 3270 Emulation (tn3270) | Tektronix 4014 Emulation | Scripting/Command Language | SLIP | FTP Client | FTP Server |
|---|---|---|---|---|---|---|---|---|---|---|---|
| | | | | | | | | | | | |
| **Product** | **Company** | | | | | | | | | | |
| Pathway Access | The Wollongong Group | | | | | • | • | • | | • | • |
| PacerTerm | Pacer Software | • | • | • | • | | | • | | • | |
| Mac 320 | White Pines Software | • | | | • | | • | | | | • |
| TCP Connect II Basic | InterCon Systems Corp | | | | • | | | | • | • | • |
| VersaTerm with Versatilities | Synergy Software | • | | | • | | • | • | • | • | • |
| Reflection 2+ and Telnet Connection | Walker Richer and Quinn | • | | | • | | | | | | • |
| 5PM, asc420, FTPack, and TCPack | Helios USA or OpenConnect Systems | • | • | • | • | • | | • | | • | • |
| LAN Workplace | Novell | | | | | | | | | • | |
| NCSA Telnet/tn3270 | (not sold commercially) | | | | • | • | • | | • | • | • |

Table 18-1
**FTC Product's Client and Server Features**

### Notes

| | |
|---|---|
| Pathway Access | Includes Graphical Keyboard remapping and LPD/LPR printing support. IBM 3179G, Tektronix 4014, and Mail (SMTP/POP/IMAP/NNTP) Optional. |
| Mac 320 | Tektronix 4014 Optional. VT340 Graphics Optional. QuickKeys Lite bundled |
| TCP Connect II Basic | Mail (POP/SMTP), News (NNTP), 3270, LPR, VT240 graphics, and SLIP all optional. PH Client. |
| VersaTerm with Versatilities | Terminal Server; Network Time. Tektronix 4105 available. MAIL, News included. |
| Reflection 2+ and Telnet Connection | VT340 graphics, HP 700/92, and HP 2393A graphics optional |
| 5PM, asc420, FTPack, and TCPack | Supports MacWorkstation. Optional SNA and IBM terminal support (work with Apple SNA•ps), TN3270, and IBM 5250 emulation. |
| LAN Workplace | Includes Whois and Finger |
| NCSA Telnet/tn3270 | TN3270 different application from regular telnet |

color-graphics terminal emulation, you also have to have 3179G. Most newer applications display directly on personal computers or graphics workstations, but many older mainframe and minicomputer graphics applications are designed to work with the workhorse Tektronix 4014 graphics terminal or the color Textronix 4105. Table 18-1 identifies the terminal-emulation features of several packages.

Scripting and command languages are popular features. Most users will be happy with basic scripting features: automating the process of logging on, checking electronic mail, and performing simple file transfers. But if you have the time to write communications scripts, you may want to use some of the very powerful tools that are available. ASC's 5PM is the leader in this area. The program's strangely named features called Vamps, Palettes, and Esmerelda enable you to build Macintosh-style applications so that users need never see what a mainframe looks like. This automated application style is often used in the IBM mainframe world. If you'd like to build applications which talk to back-end servers but don't make end-users wade through log-on screens and terminal emulators, read "Cooperative Processing" in Chapter 19, "Macs in the world of SNA."

Close behind the ASC product are WRQ's Reflection, Pacer's PacerTerm, and Wollongong's Pathway Access. Synergy's VersaTerm and White Pine's Mac300 series also have more restrained scripting capabilities. All these products have sophisticated scripting capabilities that allow you to automate many routine communications tasks.

Many communications applications support common TCP/IP applications besides terminal emulation and file transfer. Wollongong's Pathway Access is the only package that includes LPR/LPD software; InterCon's add-on Interprint supports LPR. LPD enables your Macintosh to act as a line printer server to other TCP/IP systems; LPR enables you to use LPD printers on other systems. If you don't want to install an AppleTalk package on each of your minicomputers, Pathway Access or Interprint can help bridge the gap.

Both InterCon and Synergy have tried to put together all-in-one packages that solve all of your TCP/IP needs, such as TCP/IP mail (SMTP), news readers, and directory services. Figure 18-5 provides a glimpse of InterCon's News Reader. As the Internet gets larger and more popular, you should expect more and more software to be released with the goal of a unified interface to TCP/IP services, rather than the current pick-and-choose style of Macintosh TCP/IP.

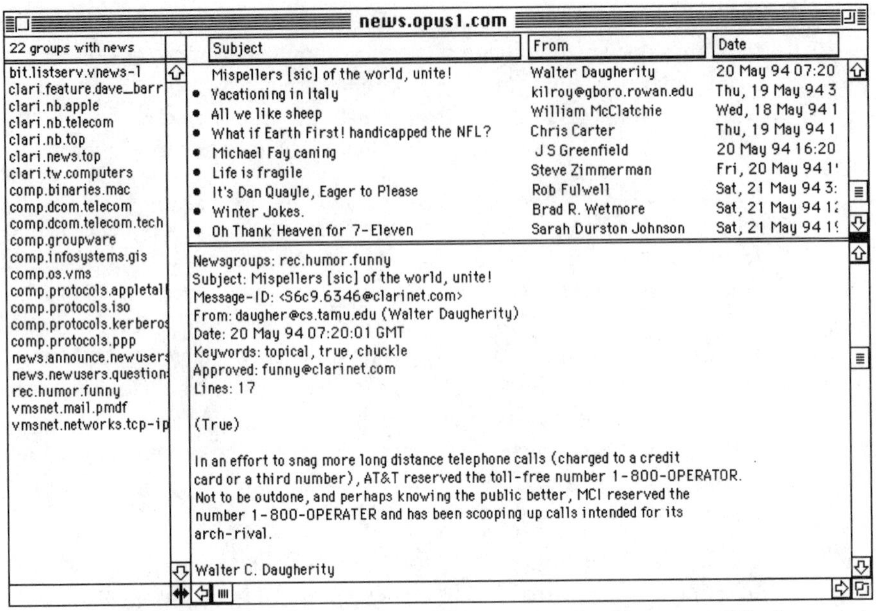

```
┌──────────────────────────── news.opus1.com ──────────────────────────────┐
│ 22 groups with news │ Subject              │ From              │ Date          │
│ bit.listserv.vnews-1│  Mispellers [sic] of the world, unite! │ Walter Daugherity     │ 20 May 94 07:20 │
│ clari.feature.dave_barr│ • Vacationing in Italy│ kilroy@gboro.rowan.edu │ Thu, 19 May 94 3 │
│ clari.nb.apple      │ • All we like sheep   │ William McClatchie │ Wed, 18 May 94 1 │
│ clari.nb.telecom    │ • What if Earth First! handicapped the NFL? │ Chris Carter │ Thu, 19 May 94 1 │
│ clari.nb.top        │ • Michael Fay caning  │ J S Greenfield    │ 20 May 94 16:20 │
│ clari.news.top      │ • Life is fragile     │ Steve Zimmerman   │ Fri, 20 May 94 1 │
│ clari.tw.computers  │ • It's Dan Quayle, Eager to Please │ Rob Fulwell │ Sat, 21 May 94 3: │
│ comp.binaries.mac   │ • Winter Jokes.       │ Brad R. Wetmore   │ Sat, 21 May 94 1: │
│ comp.dcom.telecom   │ • Oh Thank Heaven for 7-Eleven │ Sarah Durston Johnson │ Sat, 21 May 94 1 │
│ comp.dcom.telecom.tech│─────────────────────────────────────────────────────│
│ comp.groupware      │ Newsgroups: rec.humor.funny                           │
│ comp.infosystems.gis│ Subject: Mispellers [sic] of the world, unite!        │
│ comp.os.vms         │ Message-ID: <S6c9.6346@clarinet.com>                  │
│ comp.protocols.appletal│ From: daugher@cs.tamu.edu (Walter Daugherity)      │
│ comp.protocols.iso  │ Date: 20 May 94 07:20:01 GMT                          │
│ comp.protocols.kerberos│ Keywords: topical, true, chuckle                   │
│ comp.protocols.ppp  │ Approved: funny@clarinet.com                          │
│ news.announce.newusers│ Lines: 17                                           │
│ news.newusers.questions│                                                    │
│ rec.humor.funny     │ (True)                                                │
│ vmsnet.mail.pmdf    │                                                       │
│ vmsnet.networks.tcp-ip│ In an effort to snag more long distance telephone calls (charged to a credit │
│                     │ card or a third number), AT&T reserved the toll-free number 1-800-OPERATOR. │
│                     │ Not to be outdone, and perhaps knowing the public better, MCI reserved the │
│                     │ number 1-800-OPERATER and has been scooping up calls intended for its │
│                     │ arch-rival.                                           │
│                     │                                                       │
│                     │ Walter C. Daugherity                                  │
└───────────────────────────────────────────────────────────────────────────┘
```

Figure 18-5: The Usenet news reader in TCP/Connect II provides abundant opportunities for wasted time.

Chapter 16 discusses another important part of TCP/IP for the Macintosh: dial-up access with SLIP and PPP protocols.

# Finding and Using TCP/IP Freeware and Shareware

A great deal of freeware and shareware is available for Macintosh TCP/IP. Most of this software is available on CompuServe or via anonymous FTP on the Internet to major sites such as *mac.archive.umich.edu* and *sumex.stanford.edu*. See Table 18-2 for a list of popular anonymous FTP sites for Macintosh files. The following sections describe our picks and pans for the TCP/IP world.

### Terminal emulators

NCSA Telnet, along with TN3270, is definitely the most popular. Another freeware contender, Termy (by Tim Endres), depends on Communications Toolbox tools, so you're stuck with Apple's VT320.

## Table 18-2
## Popular Macintosh Freeware/Shareware FTP Sites

| Site Name | Mac Files Start Here |
|---|---|
| ezinfo.ethz.ch | /mac |
| ftp.apple.com | /dts |
| ftp.cso.uiuc.edu | /mac/MUG |
| ftp.funet.fi | /pub/mac |
| irisa.irisa.fr | /News/comp.binaries.mac |
| mac.archive.umich.edu | /mac |
| nic.switch.ch | /software/mac |
| sumex-aim.stanford.edu | /info-mac |
| toklab.ics.osaka-u.ac.jp | /mac/info-mac/info-mac |

### Toolbox tools
TGE TCP Tool (also by Tim Endres) is the missing piece you need to make a Communications Toolbox-aware emulator work over MacTCP. If you already have MacTerminal, you can plug in TGE TCP, which isn't of commercial quality but is freeware.

### Transport
If MacSLIP's $50 price tag is too much, you can try PPP (from the Merit networking support group at the University of Michigan), which is a freeware PPP LAP for MacTCP, or try InterSLIP, a freeware SLIP LAP from InterCon. PPP isn't as widely supported as SLIP, but it is destined to replace SLIP eventually.

### File transfer
For an FTP server, FTPd (by Peter Lewis) is a sophisticated application that uses AppleShare permissions to handle FTP service. Xfer It (shareware by Steve Falkenburg), HyperFTP (freeware by Douglas Hornig), and Fetch (freeware/shareware by Jim Matthews) are all easy to use.

### Mail
Using POP and SMTP to read mail over TCP/IP is very popular at universities. Eudora (freeware by Steve Dorner), POPmail (freeware by the University of Minnesota), and Mews (freeware by Charles Lakos) are available; we liked Eudora's interface the best. Eudora has been taken over by Qualcomm, which turned it into a commercial-strength (and nonfreeware) product. If you use Eudora, make sure

that you're passing around the free version — and upgrade to the commercial version if you like what you see. To build an entire freeware Macintosh-to-TCP/IP mail network, MacPost (by Lund University) is a client/server application for a network of Macs. Leemail (shareware by Lee Fyock) handles a single Macintosh.

### News

USENET news is a popular way to while away a boring day. If you're lucky enough to have a news server on your network, you can take advantage of four NNTP news readers for the Macintosh. Nuntius (freeware by Peter Speck), TheNews (shareware by Bill Cramer), and Stacked News (freeware by Georg Gollmann) are good, but our favorite is NewsWatcher (freeware originally by Steve Falkenburg, now supported by John Norstad).

### Toys and tools

The Macintosh is a favorite platform for all sorts of TCP/IP tools and toys. Mosaic, Archie, Gopher, and WAIS clients are must-haves for anyone who is connected to the Internet. Other fun possibilities include *finger* (user information query) and *talk* (interactive person-to-person communications) programs, Internet Chat (multiuser person-to-person communications) and MUD (MultiUser Dungeon) clients, and the ever-popular Net Cookie, which retrieves a fortune cookie from far, far away. Our vote for most useful shareware, though, is Pete Resnick's Network Time, a shareware program that will keep your Macintosh's time in sync with other TCP/IP systems on the network.

# CHAPTER *18* CONCEPTS AND TERMS

- The Communications Toolbox is the architecture for communications tools in the Macintosh. The Toolbox includes AppleTalk and "foreign" protocols such as TCP/IP.

- MacTCP is the core TCP/IP protocol stack that Apple provides. All vendors use this stack and build value on top.

- Various commercial applications support terminal emulation and file transfer. Applications are distinguished by their features.

- A large, important body of shareware and freeware is available to help budget-minded managers provide TCP/IP communications on the Macintosh.

### Archie
A protocol (and application) is used on the Internet to search directory lists of sites which allow Anonymous FTP.

### connection managers
Part of the Apple Communications Toolbox, these enable applications to make connections to other hosts. For example, Apple's Serial Tool is a simple connection manager that enables applications to use the Mac's serial port to talk to modems and hosts.

### chat
A TCP/IP application which enables two or more users to connect their work-stations over a TCP/IP network so that everything one user types is seen by all other users.

### file-transfer managers
Part of the Apple Communications Toolbox, these enable applications to transfer files. Some typical file-transfer managers include Kermit and XModem, which implement popular file transfer protocols.

### finger
A user information protocol (and the name of the application which usually runs it) commonly used in TCP/IP networks.

### FTP
File Transfer Protocol, the protocol (and the name of the application which runs it, usually) used in TCP/IP networks for file transfer.

### IRC
The Internet Relay Chat, a network of chat servers.

### MacTCP
Apple's TCP/IP protocol stack. This includes all of the TCP/IP stack up to TCP and UDP, but does not include applications like *telnet* or *ftp*. These must be acquired from third-parties.

### Mosaic
An application packaged developed by the National Center for Supercomputing Applications (NCSA) at the University of Illinois Urbana-Champaign. Mosaic, available for the Macintosh, MS-DOS systems running Microsoft Windows, and any minicomputer which supports the X window system, is a client to multiple TCP/IP information resources, including WWW servers, gopher servers, and FTP servers.

### MUD
MultiUser Dungeon (the D in the acronym changes depending on the speaker, but the original meaning was "Dungeon"). MUDs are multiplayer, real-time games which operate over TCP/IP networks. Users *telnet* to a MUD server which operates the "Dungeon" and users move about, interact, and modify their environment.

### NNTP
The Network News Transfer Protocol, a simple protocol which enables news servers to pass articles around and news clients to read articles from servers in the Usenet news system.

### POP2/POP3
Post Office Protocol versions 2 and 3. These are client/server e-mail protocols used in TCP/IP networks. In the POP model, a server delivers messages to a

client which is then responsible for all storage of the message.

### SMTP
Simple Mail Transfer Protocol. A protocol in TCP/IP networks used to transfer mail between post offices and from clients to servers for later delivery. SMTP has only a very limited feature set compared to many other common mail systems.

### talk
A protocol (and the name of the application which usually includes it) which enables two users to connect their workstations over a TCP/IP network so that everything one user types is seen on the other's screen, and *vice versa*.

### telnet
The name of the protocol (and the application which usually runs it) in TCP/IP networks used for virtual terminal traffic. In a Macintosh, a *telnet* program must include both the protocol *and* a terminal emulator capability.

### terminal managers
Part of the Apple Communications Toolbox, these emulate terminals, such as the DEC VT100 or IBM's 3270.

### Usenet News
An enormous, loosely organized network of news servers which pass around "articles" written by participants in the network on a variety of topics. There are thousands of different discussion topics registered in the network and each day tens of thousands of articles are added to these topics.

### VT100
A terminal designed and marketed by Digital Equipment Corporation. The VT100 uses escape (control) commands based on the ANSI X3.64 standard and has become the industry standard for terminal emulation.

### WWW
The World Wide Web is a term used to encompass a protocol (HTTP, HyperText Transfer Protocol) and a hypertext authoring language (HTML, HyperText Markup Language) used as an information service technology for TCP/IP networks.

# CHAPTER NINETEEN

# Macs in the World of SNA

- How the pieces of SNA networks fit together

- Software and hardware tools that connect Macintosh computers to IBM mainframes

- Software that extends the life of existing applications

- Client/server computing

**B**ig iron is the opposite of *personal computer*. *Big iron* means *mainframes:* huge, powerful, and expensive; disk farms; tape drives; operators; air conditioning and power conditioning; rooms with big glass windows. When big iron hiccups, 23,000 travel agents stop taking calls. When big iron is sick, a team of customer engineers comes in (at 3 in the morning, if necessary) and makes it all better. *Big iron* means *IBM*.

IBM computers normally use SNA (Systems Network Architecture), a network architecture originally developed by IBM more than 20 years ago. SNA has a different word for everything, and this makes it very confusing for the poor Macintosh manager who has to link Macintoshes to SNA. This chapter presents just enough SNA architecture to get you started and discusses some existing products that you can use to make the Macintosh-to-SNA link.

## Understanding SNA

"Es geht, geht alles durcheinander wie mäusedreck und coriander."

("It goes, goes all into confusion like mouse droppings and coriander seeds.")

— J.W. von Goethe
from *Peter Brey*

Understanding micro–mainframe links means learning a little bit about IBM networking — and many model numbers and acronyms. IBM (and compatibles, such as those made by Amdahl and Fujitsu) mainframes don't actually handle networking themselves. IBM mainframes connect to communications *Front-End Processors* (FEPs), such as the 3725 and 3745, through channels. *Channels* are very high-speed interfaces direct to the CPU. Channels are similar to slots in PCs and Macin-tosh systems: direct links to the guts of the computers themselves.

FEPs are powerful computers in their own right. These machines offload the work of handling communications and networking from the mainframes to which they're attached. FEPs manage terminals, printers, modems, local area networks (LANs), and most other communications functions in an SNA network. FEPs can connect directly to local area networks such as token ring and Ethernet.

If your network includes multiple mainframes, the systems can communicate with one another directly by using channel-to-channel links, which bypass the FEP. Multiple mainframes also can link through a single FEP or through multiple FEPs connected with leased data-communications lines or token ring LANs.

Attaching terminals is another thing entirely. For one thing, terminals are considered to be part of the network. Terminals are called 3270 devices, named for the oldest member of the family. 3270s don't resemble the simple asynchronous terminals with the RS-232 ports that you're used to on UNIX and OpenVMS systems. These devices attach with a coaxial cable or a synchronous communications line to a cluster controller. A *cluster controller* handles multiple terminals, and attaches to the communications FEP directly, with a coaxial cable; over a token ring LAN; over a telephone line, using synchronous modems and a protocol called *SDLC* (Synchronous Data Link Control); or over an X.25 network, such as USSprint, BT Tymnet, or CompuServe.

Naturally, everything has a model number, and IBM networking terminology throws these numbers around constantly. The cluster controllers usually are designated 3174, 3274, or 3276. Terminals have many name possibilities; the newest terminals are various 3278 and 3279 models. These models differ from the 3270 because they can have color, larger screens, and other options, such as light pens and multiple fonts. To do graphics work, you need what IBM calls an *All-Points-Addressable* (APA) terminal, such as the 3179 or 3192.

In some of IBM's smaller systems (such as the AS/400) and in low-end configurations (such as the ES/9370), the communications functions are built into the basic system unit. This arrangement means no FEP and possibly no cluster controller. Figure 19-1 shows an example of a typical SNA network.

# Understanding Micro-to-Mainframe Options

Most IBM mainframes use SNA, the granddaddy of all networks, for communications. IBM, however, has long understood the importance of TCP/IP (Transmission Control Protocol/Internet Protocol) networks, as well as the evolving OSI (Open Systems Interconnection) network standards being developed by the ISO (International Organization for Standardization) and the ITU (International Telecommunications Union). IBM supports both TCP/IP and OSI networks for mainframe-to-mainframe and microcomputer-to-mainframe communications.

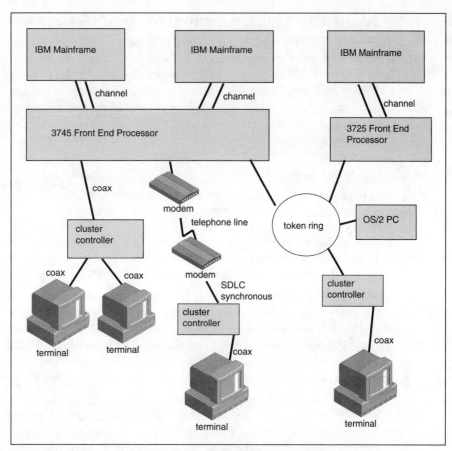

**Figure 19-1: SNA networks built from IBM mainframes can mix and match different hardware, including coaxial cable, token ring networks, and telephone lines.**

(Chapter 18 discusses TCP/IP on the Macintosh, and Chapter 20 discusses OSI on the Macintosh.)

IBM mainframes also can act as disk servers for personal computers. Although more cost-effective ways of providing disk service for Macintosh systems exist, excess capacity on mainframe disk drives can be made available to Macintosh and MS-DOS systems. One advantage of this approach is the superior backup, restore, and archiving systems that are commonly available on mainframe systems. Because mainframes often are tended by 24-hour-a-day operation staffs, adding a few hundred megabytes of personal-computer backup to an existing schedule is not much of a burden. You can read more about AppleTalk Filing Protocol (AFP) servers in Chapter 16 — even if we haven't found any AFP servers for IBM mainframes.

## Making the Mac a terminal in an SNA network

Terminals on IBM mainframes may seem to be primitive, but the power of IBM networking means that a terminal can be much more than just a single window on a host. When a Macintosh acts as an SNA terminal, it gains multiple-session capability. This capability allows the Macintosh user to open more than one session on more than one host. Because IBM applications each may have their own log-in and log-out sequences, having multiple sessions open allows you to switch between applications quickly and easily. Macintosh Clipboard copy-and-paste capability is an additional benefit; getting data from one application to another by using the Clipboard is fast and efficient.

Macintosh personal computers have been connecting to IBM mainframes since 1984, emulating 3270-type terminals. In the years since, software and hardware products that support this connection have multiplied and matured. Unfortunately, though, such connections really ignore the power of the personal computer; the PC acts only as a glorified terminal. The vast majority of products available work in some way to connect your Macintosh as a terminal via SNA to an IBM mainframe.

Most Macintosh 3270-type emulators also support printing functions (usually called 3287), enabling mainframe data to be "printed" directly to a Macintosh hard disk or on a nearby laser printer. A third benefit of 3270-type emulators is IBM's de-facto standard for mainframe-to-micro file transfer, called IND$FILE. The IND$FILE software on the mainframe side works with the 3270-type emulator to copy files to and from Macintosh hard disks, floppies, and network file servers.

In addition, innovative software on the Macintosh called *frontware* can be used to hide the 3270 screens and automate common tasks such as report generation (see the section on frontware later in this chapter). With most frontware, the main-frame application remains the same, but the user sees a Macintosh-style application. All these benefits add up to a powerful way to bring IBM mainframe power to Macintosh users.

As the oldest method of connecting Macintosh systems to IBM mainframes, making a Macintosh look like a terminal (and a printer) can be accomplished in different ways. The first thing you need to do is to decide whether you want to connect a stand-alone Macintosh directly to the mainframe or use a gateway. Table 19-1 summarizes the main differences between gateways and dedicated systems.

The following two sections provide more detail on architectural and product options.

| Table 19-1 | |
|---|---|
| **IBM/Macintosh Gateways *versus* Dedicated Systems** | |
| ***Issue*** | ***Pros and Cons*** |
| Mixed platform | Gateways can support mixed platforms (MS-DOS, UNIX, Windows, and Macintosh) and multiple networks. It may be easier to buy one gateway from one vendor than to buy ten different stand-alone products. When a network is in place, adding a gateway will be easier. |
| Security | Stand-alone systems can be isolated, and access to them can be controlled. Gateways usually have some security, but they open larger windows of opportunity for security problems. |
| Performance | Stand-alone can be faster, especially compared with a 128-user gateway, but you won't see much difference in small configurations. |
| Remote access | Gateways make remote access easier. A stand-alone connection over a synchronous line works but can require specialized hardware and modems. Gateways make better use of limited host resources by letting multiple users share a small number of connections — especially when coaxial connections are the rule. |
| Management | Managing one gateway is easier than managing multiple stand-alone connections. If you have to change the client software, however, the task is just as difficult. Some gateways (Apple and Novell) have NetView support; none of the stand-alone products does. |
| Cost | A gateway costs more than a single stand-alone connection, but every gateway has a break-even point (usually, about eight users) that you can calculate. Your mileage may vary considerably here. |

## Using stand-alone Macs

In a stand-alone environment, a single Macintosh is connected to a mainframe. Figure 19-2 summarizes some of the possibilities. Swap a 3270-type terminal attached to the end of a coaxial cable for a Macintosh, and you have the simplest possible situation.

Three vendors dominate the market: Apple Computer, Avatar Corp., and Digital Communications Associates (DCA). Banyan and Novell also have released SNA gateway products. Apple will be happy to sell you the Apple Coax/Twinax Card, which plugs into any Macintosh II NuBus slot. Alternatively, you can turn to Avatar's MacMainFrame II or DCA's MacIRMA NuBus. Avatar and DCA both support Macintosh SE and SE/30 systems with coaxial cards; Macintosh LC users can get a MacMainFrame LC from Avatar. If you're using something really old, Avatar offers the MacMainFrame DX, a coaxial adapter that connects to the serial port of a Macintosh.

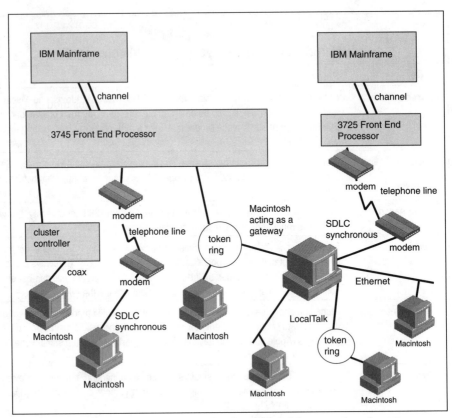

Figure 19-2: Macintosh systems can connect directly to IBM mainframes or through a gateway.

When a Macintosh is connected to a cluster controller, it can serve as a *control-unit terminal* (CUT), which allows for a single session per host, or as a *distributed-function terminal* (DFT), which allows up to five simultaneous sessions. Apple's SNA*ps 3270, Avatar's MacMainFrame and DCA's IRMA Workstation for Macintosh have similar functionality: up to five sessions, 3287 printer emulation, file transfer with IBM's IND$FILE, and support for most 3278/3729 terminals. All programs support a 3270 Application Programming Interface (API), which can be used to build customized 3270 applications. Some products also have optional support for All Points Addressable high-resolution graphics displays through the MacMainFrame Graphics and IRMA Graphics for Macintosh products.

If coaxial connections aren't your cup of tea, you can use synchronous connections or token ring networks to connect a stand-alone Macintosh to an IBM FEP. A synchronous connection uses SDLC (Synchronous Data Link Control) protocols to connect the Macintosh directly to the IBM FEP, bypassing the cluster controller.

One key benefit of an SDLC connection over a coaxial connection (aside from getting rid of that old coaxial cable) is that the maximum number of simultaneous sessions that IBM allows on a single cable goes up to 255. Because most users won't need that many sessions, the software limits the number of simultaneous sessions to eight (depending on the product you choose). SDLC connections also provide an opportunity for dial-in or leased-line access via synchronous modem. Speeds can range from 1200 bps to 64,000 bps. Apple supports the Serial NuBus card, with its own 68000 and 512K of memory. Avatar prefers its MacMainFrame II (NuBus) or SE/30 card.

For maximum performance and the latest technology, you can use IBM's own token ring to connect. Token ring (at 4M bps or 16M bps) attachments can be made through a 3174 or 3172 cluster controller, or directly to the FEP (often referred to as a TIC connection). Like SDLC, IBM allows up to 255 simultaneous sessions over one token ring board. Token ring boards are available from several sources besides Apple, DCA, and Avatar; ask your current network-equipment vendor to help you find them.

These three solutions (token ring, SDLC over coax, and synchronous connections) aren't the only possibilities. Simware's SimMac supports some of the traditional connections discussed earlier in this chapter, as well as an asynchronous-style connection. SimMac allows a user who has a more traditional modem (such as an off-the-shelf PowerBook 180) to dial in to an IBM front end. Simware provides proprietary software to run on the IBM side; this software fools the mainframe into thinking that it's talking to a standard 3270-type terminal. SimMac also falls into the frontware category, discussed later in this chapter.

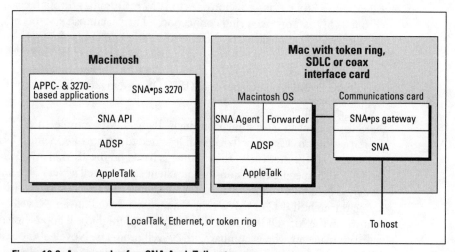

**Figure 19-3: An example of an SNA-AppleTalk gateway.**

## Using a gateway

In a gateway environment, a Macintosh connects to the IBM in one of the ways described earlier (see Figure 19-3). Any other Macs that need access to SNA services (the clients) attach to the gateway through a local area network: LocalTalk, Ethernet, or token ring. The gateway doesn't have to be a Macintosh; vendors offer both dedicated hardware and Intel-based PC solutions.

Depending on the number of users you have to support, you can dedicate a Macintosh to the gateway function, share a file server, or (for light loads) have the gateway run on someone's Mac. Most gateways support multiple boards and multiple communications methods, so the gateway can be quite busy.

With an SNA gateway, mixing and matching client and gateway software can be a problem; not every vendor supports every client. Before trying a mixed environment, make sure that you test carefully.

Apple's SNA*ps product has both gateway and client versions. SNA*ps Gateway is sized by the maximum number of simultaneous sessions through the gateway: 8, 32, or 64. You can mix coaxial, SDLC, and token ring connections, with multiple adapters per gateway. A coaxial connection can contribute up to 5 sessions; a token ring can contribute up to 8; and an SDLC connection can support 18 (64, with additional memory). On the client side, Apple supports LocalTalk, Ethernet, and token ring networks. Clients must have a copy of SNA*ps 3270 (which can connect directly or through a gateway) or SNA*ps GC (which can connect only through a gateway) on each system.

DCA's MacIRMALAN and IRMALAN/EP are typical of DOS-based gateways. With MacIRMALAN, an IBM PC/XT (or better) can gateway LocalTalk, Ethernet, and token ring Macintoshes to IBM mainframes through coaxial, synchronous SDLC, or token ring connections. The Macintosh systems have to run DCA-provided client software. MacIRMALAN comes in 8-, 32-, 64-, and 128-session versions (fewer, if you're using coaxial connections). IRMALAN/EP is a similar product, except that *EP* (Extended Platform) means that it supports client connections from Macintoshes and MS-DOS systems running straight DOS or Windows.

Novell and Banyan have similar products. Banyan, for example, offers the VINES Communications Gateway for 3270. Designed to support DOS and Macintosh clients on VINES networks, the product is based on the IRMALAN/EP platform, with VINES-specific extensions on the client side. Novell's NetWare for SAA is designed to handle all the usual NetWare clients and attaches to the IBM mainframe through SDLC or token ring connections. Like Banyan, Novell is most mature on the MS-DOS side, and either product might be a good choice for a network manager who is familiar with Novell products. Novell also boasts the highest-capacity gateway in the market, supporting up to 254 simultaneous sessions (if you can find a PC that fast).

Avatar's Netway series of SNA gateways is a good example of a dedicated hardware product. The Netway is a SPARC CPU dedicated to routing and gateway functions. Available in 8-, 16-, 32-, 64-, and 128-session versions, the product supports Macintosh, MS-DOS, and MS-DOS Windows clients. Netway attaches to IBM mainframes via SDLC synchronous or token ring connections. As a router, Netway also supports AppleTalk, IPX, AppleTalk-to-TCP/IP, and token ring source routing across multiple LocalTalk, Ethernet, and token ring networks.

For networks with Digital Equipment Corp.'s DECnet/SNA gateway, Avatar also supports MacMainFrame for Pathworks. Digital's DECnet/SNA gateway attaches to the IBM mainframe through an SDLC synchronous connection or directly as a channel-attached peripheral. Macintoshes on Ethernet or LocalTalk networks then can connect up to eight sessions per user through the gateway to the IBM mainframe.

You also can use Apple's AppleTalk Remote Access (ARA) for an inexpensive asynchronous connection. In this scenario, PowerBooks dial up an ARA server, using their ARA client software. If the ARA server is on a network served by an SNA gateway such as those described in this section, the PowerBook user can use the SNA client software to connect through the ARA server and the SNA gateway to the IBM mainframe. Other dial-up AppleTalk connections, such as a Shiva NetModem, offer the same functionality.

## Using cooperative processing techniques between Macintosh and IBM

*Cooperative processing* is the buzzword used to describe applications that wish they were client/server but aren't. In a client/server application, two or more independent entities communicate over a network to accomplish some task. When you are dealing with IBM mainframes, changing from terminal-based applications to client/server can be a difficult step. The interim solution has been dubbed cooperative processing, or frontware.

With frontware, a personal computer such as a Macintosh sits between a user and the ugly old mainframe application. The mainframe application thinks that it's talking to a terminal; the user thinks that he's talking to a Macintosh. Frontware provides a friendly front end to old application. Early versions of frontware, such as Apple's MacWorkstation, required changes in the mainframe application. It turns out that most organizations don't want to touch their applications, lest they break those applications and have to spend zillions of dollars for repairs. With that reluctance to change existing code, nonintrusive frontware came to the foreground.

Macintosh users are free to write their own applications on top of the 3270-type emulators mentioned earlier. All frontware vendors support a 3270 API (Application Programming Interface); some also support a HyperCard-based API. The difficulty of writing Macintosh applications, however, suggests that using a programming library is a better idea (see Figure 19-4).

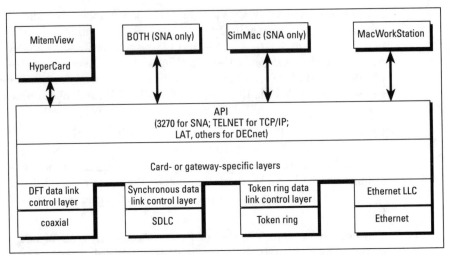

**Figure 19-4: The relationships between the different front-ends and the underlying APIs.**

## Frontware tool kits and products

Connectivité's *Both* is one example of this type of product: a tool kit for building frontware applications. Both runs over any of the 3270-type terminal emulators discussed earlier. The goal is to make mainframe applications palatable and easier to use. Both's approach to frontware couples a proprietary Automatic Screen Recognition algorithm with a Mac-style event-driven approach to application development. This approach keeps the Macintosh application relatively stable when changes occur on the host side. Other features to look for in frontware products include multiple-platform compatibility and the capability to run identical personal-computer code on Macintosh, MS-DOS, and Windows systems.

Other frontware-application generators have different features. MitemView (from Mitem Corp.) works with hypertext and database applications such as HyperCard and 4th Dimension, giving the developer additional tools and flexibility.

## Simpler technologies

Some environments don't need all the power of an application generator. For example, Office Vision (which replaces PROFS, the Professional Office System) is a popular IBM office-automation application, providing electronic mail, scheduling, and related tasks in a unified application package. For an organization that uses Office Vision heavily, an application front end such as Simware's SimVision or MacPROFF from Mariette Systems might be appropriate. MacPROFF is a Hyper-Card-based front end to Office Vision. Building on someone else's HyperCard API, MacPROFF brings office-automation functions from an IBM mainframe to a Macintosh. At the same time, the Macintosh adds functionality. In MacPROFF, the user can store local nicknames, save messages, and automate some common functions.

There are many other approaches to handling electronic mail in a mixed environment. Most of those approaches are discussed in chapters 20 and 24.

## Learning about IBM's peer-to-peer networking

One of the key changes in IBM's network architecture during the early 1980s was the transition from a very hierarchical network — terminals connected to hosts — to a peer-to-peer network. The mechanism used to facilitate this transition is a piece of SNA called LU6.2. *LU* stands for *Logical Unit;* it represents an abstract thing inside a computer attached to an SNA network. An LU6.2 entity can communicate with other LU6.2 entities. This concept may sound obvious if you're from a TCP/IP or DECnet environment, but to IBM, it was revolutionary. With LU6.2, a lowly, humble Macintosh could hope to talk directly to a god-like IBM mainframe as a peer for the first time.

To be conversant in an IBM peer-to-peer environment, you need to learn a few more acronyms. The enhanced connectivity is made possible by *Systems Application Architecture* (SAA), an overriding architecture of which SNA is part. Within SNA, peer communications are handled through *Advanced Program-to-Program Communications* (APPC), a combination of logical and physical parts of an SNA network: LU6.2 and PU2.1 (*PU* stands for *Physical Unit*).

Conflicts exist, however. IBM's SAA includes a *Common User Access* (CUA). If you're running CUA, your application looks a lot like Microsoft Windows. Apple believes that it understands user interfaces better than IBM does, so Apple is not so hot to stick Windows applications into the Macintosh Desktop. Most Mac users probably feel just fine about their user interface. The real goal is for Mac programmers to build applications that empower existing users and make them more comfortable (at least, that's what Apple thinks).

The earliest version of Apple's LU6.2 library was MacAPPC. When SNA*ps came out, the Apple Programmers and Developers Association (APDA) released the SNA*ps APPC developer's kit. SNA*ps APPC gives programmers the tools to write Macintosh APPC applications that participate in peer-to-peer communications in mainstream SNA environments and to distribute APPC services to networks attached to SNA*ps Gateways: LocalTalk, Ethernet, and token ring.

APPC's style is subtly different from the 3270 APIs discussed earlier. A 3270 API gives programs access to applications that talk to 3270-type terminals, whereas an APPC API gives programs direct access to other applications. The level of integration in APPC is much higher; it's not for casual programmers. An SAA application that uses APPC means you will have to write code on the IBM mainframe and on the Macintosh, and not just few lines of HyperCard.

## Using database access tools

If all these front-end technologies sound like too much for you, check out DAL, the Data Access Language (formerly from Apple, and now available from ITI). Apple developed a superset of SQL (a common query language for databases), originally called CL/1 and now DAL. Written to work within a client/server architecture, DAL enables you to formulate queries on your Mac and have those queries sent over the network to the appropriate databases on other, larger computers (see Figure 19-5). The amount of network traffic is minimized, because you're not attempting to transmit the entire database over the network.

*Query languages* are special programming languages that enable users to construct requests for data from relational databases. In addition to allowing users to select columns and rows from tables, query languages include conditional statements, such as IF...THEN and WHILE..., and many of the other control statements in programming languages. Such statements enable users to construct complex procedures for retrieving data.

If you're going to work with DAL, you should understand that the DAL query language is based on SQL. You still need to provide some type of front end, or interface, for constructing the queries. Many programs, such as 4th Dimension, Omnis (Blyth), Excel (Microsoft), and Wingz (Informix), offer DAL support so that you can create queries within them and then view the reported data in the same application. Other products, such as DataPrism (Brio Technology), GQL (Andyne), and ClearAccess (Fairfield Software), are designed to make query construction easier; these products do not demand extensive knowledge of either SQL or DAL.

Last, remember that you usually need a DAL server on the mainframe or minicomputer for each type of database that you want to support (some servers, such as those from ITI and Pacer, can support more than one type of database on the same hardware/operating system platform). This requirement isn't limited to IBM mainframes: DAL servers are available for databases running on eight different UNIX systems (including Apple's A/UX), Digital's VAX/VMS, Data General's AOS/VS, Tandem's Guardian, and IBM's VM/CMS, MVS/TSO, MVS/VTAM, and DOS/VSE.

Apple has extended the capabilities of DAL by including many of the client capabilities in System 7, in the form of the Data Access Manager (DAM). The major change is Apple's definition of a system resource that can store any DAL query. By supporting queries at the system level as a resource, System 7 allows you to create and share any query. You can create special queries within DataPrism, GQL, or ClearAccess, for example, and then transfer those queries as resources to someone who is using Excel with DAL to gather data. Even better, you can use these query resources within a program that by itself cannot create queries but that does accept and manipulate data — for example, a word processing program with a table function (see Figure 19-6).

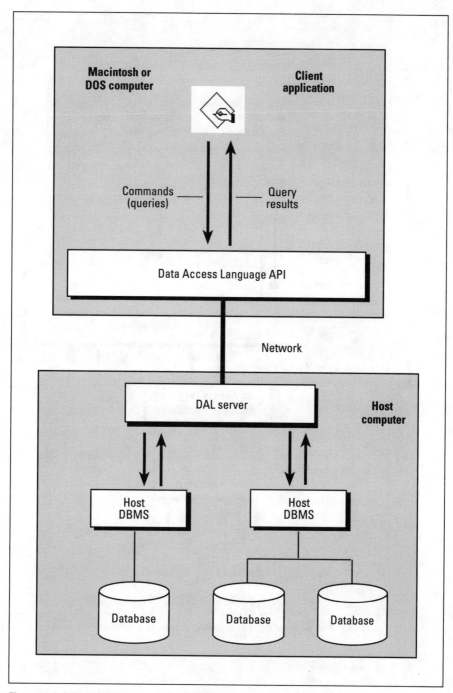

**Figure 19-5: DAL and the client-server architecture.**

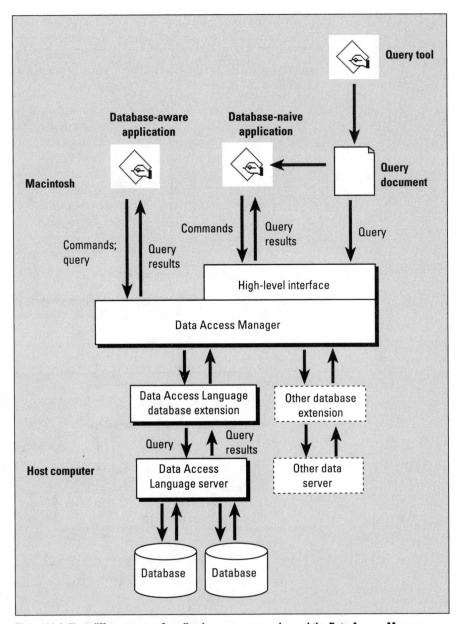

Figure 19-6: How different types of applications can use queries and the Data Access Manager.

You see that DAL can be used as a common query language for a variety of host-based databases. Therein also lies the problem with DAL: DAL incorporates the query commands common to all the databases and doesn't include database-specific commands. Thus, if you want to use some specific features of your database, such as special query controls, DAL may not support them.

To get around the problem of database-specific command support, you can use any of the other client/server database systems for the Mac. The design of SequeLink (TechGnosis) is similar to that of DAL, but the SequeLink servers are written specifically for each database that the product supports, including all the database's special features. This approach gives you all the database features that you paid for, but it can cause problems on the client side, because you now need to know what kind of database you're querying. Other databases — notably, Oracle, Ingres, and Sybase — offer client software specifically for the Mac, but in each case, the software is designed to communicate only with that particular vendor's database.

# CHAPTER *19* CONCEPTS AND TERMS

- SNA networks are less peer-to-peer and more hierarchical than Macintosh networks.
- Attaching Macintoshes to IBM mainframes means choosing among terminals, cooperative processing, and true client/server applications.
- Terminal connections to IBMs can be direct from the Macintosh, over a direct or LAN connection, or through a gateway connecting AppleTalk and SNA networks.
- Cooperative-processing frontware makes old IBM applications more familiar to Macintosh users.
- Client/server and database access techniques give Macintosh users the greatest control and the most power.

**Advanced Program-to-Program Communications (APPC)**
IBM's protocol and standards for peer-to-peer communications in an SNA network.

**All-Points-Addressable (APA) terminal**
IBM's term for a graphics terminal in which each pixel is individually addressable. A Macintosh might be said to be an APA device.

**channels**
In IBM's architecture, a channel is a direct attachment to the internal registers of a CPU. "Channel attached" devices are the fastest possible linkages between a peripheral and a CPU in any computing architecture.

**cluster controller**
A communications controller attached to an IBM mainframe which manages the communications with terminals.

**Common User Access (CUA)**
IBM's standards for application user interfaces. Similar in concept (but not execution) to the Macintosh user interface.

**Control-Unit Terminal (CUT)**
A type of terminal device attached to an IBM SNA cluster controller. A CUT only allows for a single session from the terminal to the host.

**cooperative processing**
See frontware.

**Distributed-Function Terminal (DFT)**
A type of terminal device attached to an IBM SNA cluster controller. A DFT allows for multiple sessions from the terminal to the host.

**front-end processors**
In IBM's networking world, front end processors are attached to mainframe CPUs to handle the work of communications.

**frontware**
Software installed on a client microcomputer which interacts with an existing minicomputer or mainframe application and yet still provides a very different interface to the end-user. Frontware is an alternative to true client-server application development.

**logical unit**
A type of entity within an SNA network. An LU represents an abstract thing inside of a computer attached to an SNA network.

**physical unit**
A type of entity within an SNA network. A PU represents a physical thing (such as a printer) attached to an SNA network.

**query languages**
Special programming languages that enable users to construct requests for data from databases.

**SDLC (Synchronous Data Link Control)**
IBM's data link layer (Layer 2) protocol in SNA.

**Systems Application Architecture (SAA)**
IBM's architecture for both networking and distributed applications.

# Macs in the World of OSI

IN THIS CHAPTER

- Linking Macintosh computers to an OSI network by using the MacOSI Transport and MacX25 protocol stacks

- Converting between document formats by using the standardized Open Document Architecture

- Using X.400 electronic mail to reduce complexity as a corporate e-mail backbone

- Bringing X.400 electronic mail directly to the Macintosh Desktop

You probably will choose to read this chapter after you've read everything else. Macintosh computers are, by and large, not major players in the world of OSI networking; in fact, no personal computers are. The complexity of the OSI stack and the relatively simple needs of microcomputers have left the world of OSI networks to minicomputers, servers, and mainframes.

Before we get started, let's take a moment to define our terms. When we say OSI networking, we're stepping on some toes. The world of the OSI model usually is said to include networks built on standards from the ISO (International Organization for Standardization) and the ITU (International Telecommunications Union). In the same sentence, most networkers then dismiss both organization's efforts by saying, "...and we don't use that stuff." Of course, those networkers are wrong; almost all modems are products of ITU standards. The phone company, ISDN, and networks such as frame relay and ATM are all products of the ISO and the ITU. Ethernet, token ring, and all the connectors we use are standardized by the ISO and ITU.

For the sake of convenience, we'll lump together the ISO and ITU standards for the network layer and for everything above that, and call it ISO networking. It's a bit like Humpty Dumpty's profoundly whimsical discourse on semantics: "When *I* use a word, it means just what I choose it to mean — neither more nor less." So we'll play a bit sloppy with the rules and see where it takes us.

# Learning about Apple's OSI Protocol Stacks

As in the world of TCP/IP, Apple divides networking on the Macintosh into two parts: the part that Apple provides, and the parts that third-party vendors provide. In the OSI world, Apple has declared that it will provide the network and transport layers and that everyone else can play above those layers. Apple has two products about which you may not have heard: MacX25 and MacOSI transport. Figure 20-1 shows where those products fit into the OSI model.

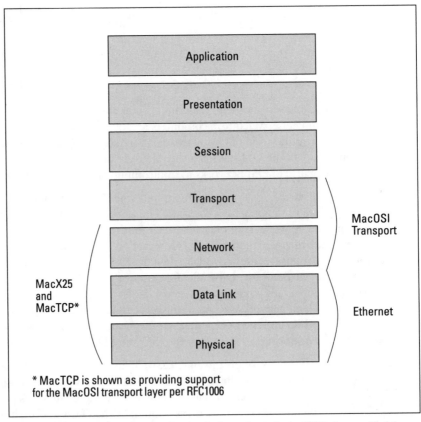

Figure 20-1: Apple's OSI products implement the lower layers in the OSI Reference Model.

## MacOSI transport

MacOSI transport is Apple's implementation of the ISO and ITU connectionless network-layer protocol and connection-oriented transport-layer protocol. ISO 8073 (also published as ITU X.224) is the transport protocol definition. Classes 0 and 4 of that protocol are supported by MacOSI transport.

## Transport-Layer Protocol Classes

The ISO-defined transport protocol contains several classes of protocol. Which one you use depends on what service your application needs and what service the underlying network provides. Despite the presence of five classes of transport service, though, almost everyone uses Class 0 or Class 4, which are the classes that MacOSI Transport provides.

**Class 0:** This class is used when a highly reliable network is available, such as an X.25 packet-switching network. Class 0 provides minimal additional services and refers to network-layer functions whenever possible. Thus, if the network connection is lost, so is the transport connection; no error-recovery mechanism or multiplexing exist. MacOSI Transport uses a transport provider based on this class when running over an X.25 or TCP/IP network.

**Class 1:** This class provides a basic transport connection with a simple mechanism to recover from errors signaled by the network layer. Class 1 is used with networks that are less reliable than those used with Class 0 and Class 2; no multiplexing exists.

**Class 2:** Used with reliable networks, this class provides the same functionality as Class 0 plus the options of multiplexing several transport-layer connections onto a single network-layer connection and of using flow control for transport-layer messages (PDUs, or *Protocol Data Units*).

**Class 3:** This class provides the same functions as Class 2, including flow control and multiplexing, plus disconnect and error-recovery mechanisms. Class 3 is used with the same level of network reliability as Class 1.

**Class 4:** This class is used for highly unreliable networks, such as those that use a connectionless service (like Ethernet). Class 4 service provides full error recovery from any error by using various timers and sequencing mechanisms. Class 4 also provides detection of lost, duplicated, and corrupted data. MacOSI Transport uses a transport provider based on this class when running over Ethernet.

MacOSI transport can participate in the ISO routing system by acting as an end system. An *End System* (usually abbreviated *ES*) is one that does not route messages; an *intermediate system* participates fully in routing traffic. MacOSI includes the ISO ES-IS routing protocol (ISO 9542).

At the network layer, MacOSI Transport includes the ISO *Connectionless Network Protocol* (CLNP, also known by its standard number ISO 8473). MacOSI Transport also operates over TCP/IP (per RFC1006) or MacX25. Figure 20-2 shows the allowable protocol stacks for MacOSI Transport.

# MacX25

Apple's MacX25 software links Macintosh computers to packet-switched data networks (PSDNs) by using ITU Recommendation X.25.

## Routing in the ISO World

In the ISO world, routing is far more stable and well thought out than in the TCP/IP world. ISO recognizes two main classes of systems: end systems (ES), which have no routing function and simply send messages to the nearest router when they need to leave their local network, and intermediate systems (IS), which handle the routing. To make all this work, the ISO defined three routing protocols: ES-IS, IS-IS, and IDRP.

**ES-IS:** This extremely simple protocol is used between end systems and intermediate systems. The main function of this protocol is to enable an end system to proclaim its presence to the intermediate system router, which lets it figure out which IS the end system should use.

**IS-IS:** This workhorse routing protocol is used by intermediate systems to communicate routing information. Intermediate systems talk about which

end systems they serve and how to get from one IS to another IS across the intervening network. You may see this protocol called Intra-Domain Routing Protocol, although that term can cause more confusion than it's worth, because another protocol (see the following paragraph) has the same initials.

**IDRP:** This protocol — the Inter-Domain Routing Protocol — is used by entire networks to communicate information about routing. IDRP would be used when two corporate networks join. IDRP is more complex than IS-IS because it handles more difficult situations, called *policy routing*. An example of a policy-routing issue that IDRP might have to support is "Send traffic from Opus One, Inc., to ACES Research, Inc., over the Internet unless it's marked *Confidential*, in which case it should go over the CompuServe network."

MacX25 server software allows a Macintosh computer to be set up as a single entry point to the PSDN. Access to host computers and end-user services on the PSDN is distributed from the server to other Macintosh computers using AppleTalk over a network such as LocalTalk or Ethernet.

MacPAD software (part of MacX25) works in conjunction with the server software and provides Packet Assembler and Disassembler (PAD) connections to the PSDN. MacPAD is used as a connection tool for the Communications Toolbox; it enables terminal applications that use the toolbox to connect to host systems on the PSDN. This means that you can use a terminal application such as VersaTerm (which supports the Communications Toolbox) to connect to a host computer over an X.25 network without any additional software.

MacX25's administrator's application also allows network administrators to maintain a list of X.25 hosts with matching aliases. This feature means that MacPAD users don't have to know X.25 host addresses (such as "31320602000493.05") and can use names (such as "Opus One") instead.

MacX25 can support up to 64 virtual circuits and multiple connections at speeds up to 64K bps.

| | | | | |
|---|---|---|---|---|
| **Application** | | | | |
| **Presentation** | | | | |
| **Session** | | | | |
| **Transport** | MacOSI TP0 | MacOSI TP0 | MacOSI TP4 (ES-IS optional) | MacOSI TP4 |
| **Network** | MacX25 | TCP/IP per RFC1006 | MacOSI CLNP | (empty) |
| **Data Link** | MacX25 | any legal IP-supporting layer | Ethernet | Ethernet |
| **Physical** | either X.21bis or V.35 | any legal IP-supporting layer | Ethernet | Ethernet |

Figure 20-2: MacOSI Transport allows the application to select from several different "stacks" of protocol layers to meet different data transmission needs.

# Using ISO's Open Document Architecture

Apple's MacODA is a software translator that implements the Open Document Architecture (ODA) standard. ODA is a document-interchange standard established by the ISO that facilitates the interchange of documents among different applications and platforms, including documents that contain complex formatting and graphics.

Using MacODA, users can exchange complex documents (including graphics) with users who work with different word processors or on different platforms, and preserve the original format of the documents.

MacODA converts ODA documents to and from the Claris XTND format, a Claris translation system. With XTND integrated into an application and the appropriate translator installed, users can open documents that were created in another application. MacODA gives XTND-compatible applications the capability to open ODA documents and to save documents in ODA format. Unfortunately, the set of XTND-compatible applications is rather small. Microsoft Word, for example, does not include XTND support.

# Using ISO's Message-Handling Systems

*X.400* is the common name of a set of standards for electronic mail systems. You may hear X.400 electronic mail referred to by some of its common aliases: MHS (Message Handling System), MOTIS (Message Oriented Text Interchange System), and IPM (Inter Personal Messaging).

ITU-T Recommendation X.400 (formerly CCITT Recommendation X.400) actually is just one of a set of more than two dozen international standards that describe how to build interoperable electronic mail systems. More than 1,000 pages in the X.400 series handle everything: from protocols, testing, even the way you link X.400 e-mail systems to the telex network.

Although the first usable X.400 standards were published in 1984, software that links X.400 networks with personal computer electronic mail systems has just become available. In the past few years, no fewer than 11 companies have introduced almost 30 new products designed around X.400 electronic mail. X.400 has become most popular in Western Europe. In North America, X.400 is overshadowed by SMTP (Simple Mail Transfer Protocol), the TCP/IP-based electronic mail system used in the Internet.

X.400 can be an efficient way of building a mail backbone. Figure 20-3 shows the traditional way of linking electronic mail systems; Figure 20-4 shows how an X.400 backbone can ease the stress.

## Understanding message-handling systems

The X.400 model of an electronic mail system is based on a distributed client/server model. Note that the X.400 series was substantially revised in 1988. The model shown here is from the 1988 Recommendations. In the X.400 world, a user (that's you) uses a *User Agent* (UA) to access the e-mail system. The UA is responsible for helping the user compose, send, receive, and manage electronic mail. The UA connects to a big network, usually represented as a cloud, called a *Message Transfer System* (MTS), that is responsible for transferring e-mail messages.

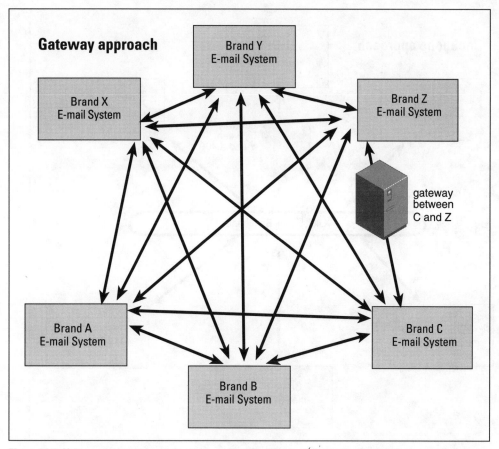

**Figure 20-3:** Using a gateway approach, you'd need to have 15 translating gateways to link six e-mail systems.

If this explanation is getting confusing, look at Figure 20-5. E-mail messages get shoveled into and out of the MTS by the UA. If the MTS does its job, the messages pop out the other side for someone to read.

An MTS is made up of many smaller pieces called message transfer agents and message stores. *Message Transfer Agents* (MTAs) are the individual systems that run the e-mail backbone. MTAs handle the routing of messages, format conversions, the generation of receipts, and the management of the e-mail backbone.

*Message Stores* (MSs), which are new in the 1988 X.400 standards, sit between a particular UA and the rest of the MTS. An MS provides secure, continuously available storage. If your UA ran on a Macintosh, you probably would want an MS to receive and hold mail for you. That way, if your Mac was turned off, your mail wouldn't get bounced back to the sender. Also, by storing your e-mail on the MS, you could read your mail when you're in someone else's office or on the road.

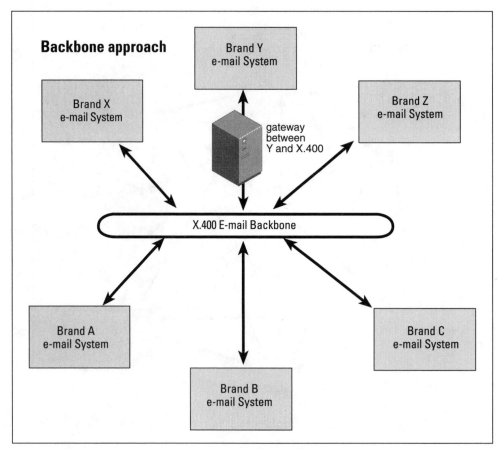

**Figure 20-4: Using a backbone approach, six gateways (and an X.400 backbone) can link six e-mail systems.**

A UA is one way of getting e-mail into and out of an X.400 backbone. Another method is via *Access Units* (AUs). When the connection to the X.400 backbone isn't a single person running UA software, an AU is used. Some AUs are delivery-oriented. For example, a FAX AU could be plugged into an X.400 network to allow users to send mail to recipients who have only fax machines. X.400 also has a physical-delivery AU that connects an X.400 to a real post office (remember back before there was electronic mail?). Most important for purposes of this discussion are gateway AUs, which connect non-X.400 e-mail systems to X.400 backbones.

The X.400 standards define 93 options, attributes, and characteristics that can be selected for a particular X.400 message. These elements range from simple things, such as whether distribution lists are expanded when the message is delivered, to complex attributes, such as authentication information guaranteeing that after you

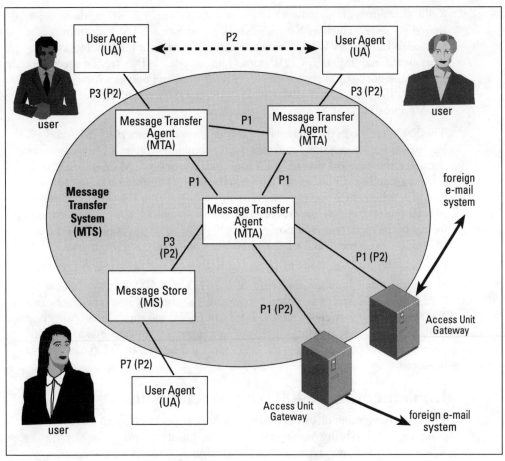

Figure 20-5: The model of an e-mail system used in the X.400 standards allows for considerable flexibility in putting together different parts from different vendors.

read a message, you can't claim that you didn't see it (a feature called, in X.400 terms, *nonrepudiation of delivery*). X.400 is a feature-rich e-mail system. X.400 is richer than any micro-based e-mail system.

To do the grungy work of shuttling e-mail around the world, X.400 defines a set of high-level protocols that transfer messages among UAs, AUs, MSs, and MTAs. X.400 usually is run over an ISO-based network, but that's not the only way to go. In the TCP/IP world, RFC1006 describes how X.400 can be run over TCP. Several X.400 vendors, including Apple, have added TCP/IP compatibility so that you can retain your investment in TCP/IP networking.

X.400 also allows for no network link. For example, many X.400 products use a shared file system (such as Novell's NetWare or Sun's NFS) to communicate between a UA and an MTA. That approach is proprietary, but it reduces the requirement for an ISO or TCP/IP stack. The reasons: (1) PCs are not smart enough and too memory-shy to have room for real software and network software, and (2) not many ISO stacks are available (although MacOSI Transport fills this need in the Macintosh world).

The X.400 protocols themselves have the imaginative names *P1*, *P2*, *P3*, and *P7*. Pay attention, because there's no easy way to remember them. P1 (*message-transfer protocol*) is the protocol that an MTA uses to talk to another MTA or to an AU, such as a gateway. P3 (*submission-and-delivery protocol*) is what a UA uses to talk to an MTA, whereas P7 (*message-store access protocol*) is what a UA uses to talk to an MS. P2 (*interpersonal-message protocol*) is a pseudo-protocol of sorts; it describes the format of the electronic mail carried in each of the other protocols. P2 is the end-to-end X.400 protocol, and P1, P3, and P7 are point-to-point protocols.

Electronic mail goes hand in hand with directory services, which is why X.400 often is mentioned in the same breath as X.500. The X.500 directory standards (like X.400, X.500 really is a family of documents) are used in several places in X.400 to store user-friendly names, distribution lists, and capabilities of user agents. X.400 also has a very strong security and authentication model, and X.500 is one place where public keys used in the encryption and signing of X.400 messages can be stored.

# Implementing X.400 with Macintoshes

The client/server and distributed nature of X.400 networks means that several good ways exist to bring Macintosh computers into the world of X.400: pure X.400, split X.400 user agent, and X.400 gateway.

## Pure X.400

In a pure X.400 world, Macintosh users would use a native X.400-based User Agent. The X.400 agent would communicate over a network to an X.400 MTA (using P3 protocol) or an X.400 MS (using P7 protocol). This approach has some significant advantages. Because the Macintosh-to-X.400 link is a standardized one, different users could have different user agents to meet different needs, yet all users would connect to the same MTA. Alternatively, the MTA could be changed, upgraded, expanded, or replaced without affecting end users.

Unfortunately, no pure X.400 world for the Macintosh exists right now. Both ISOCOR and Enterprise Solutions Ltd. have announced their intentions to market pure X.400 UAs for the Macintosh. Neither company had begun shipping software as of early 1994.

Even if a real X.400 user agent were available for the Macintosh, purists might insist that the user agent run over an ISO network — an arrangement that is unlikely for the first releases of these products. Because most X.400 MTA software is designed to run on UNIX systems, TCP/IP will be a much more common transport. Macintosh users shouldn't care much: Apple's TCP/IP Connection and MacOSI Transport solve the problem either way.

## Split X.400 user agent

Many companies believe that the effort of running a full X.400 UA on a personal computer isn't worth the benefit — that it would be a little like giving a Formula One race car to someone who drives at 10 miles per hour. One popular approach to X.400 electronic mail splits the UA in two parts: one on the personal computer and one on a server system.

This split seems to invite chaos, eliminating the gains that a standardized e-mail system would provide. That's almost the case. Vendors agreed that the two parts of an X.400 user agent can communicate via a standardized Application Programming Interface (API); then the vendors went out and defined many such APIs. X/Open's API is aimed straight at X.400. Microsoft's MAPI, Lotus' VIM, and Apple's AOCE all provide different models of the way that a user agent can be put together across a network. These models are not specific to X.400; they are general solutions to the problem of splitting e-mail user agents into client and server pieces. Notice that this e-mail user agent is not necessarily an X.400 UA.

Standard interfaces mean that you will be able to buy the two halves of your X.400 UA from different vendors and to mix and match to your heart's content. The operative word, however, is *will*; these interfaces are a few years down the road.

Digital's TeamLinks software is the only Macintosh product that splits an X.400 UA. TeamLinks Mail is half of an X.400 user agent; the other half resides on a minicomputer running OpenVMS or OSF/1. The two pieces talk by using Digital's DECnet protocol family or AppleTalk. Several MS-DOS products that split the X.400 UA also are available.

TeamLinks is a family of applications that run on Macintosh, MS-DOS (Windows), OpenVMS, and several UNIX-flavored operating systems. TeamLinks actually is a suite of groupware applications. A conferencing system, document routing, and electronic mail are the main elements.

TeamLinks brings X.400 features to the Macintosh (and to Windows), but only in conjunction with Digital's Mailworks server. In the next release of TeamLinks for Macintosh, Digital intends to replace the MAPI-like interface internal to TeamLinks with one that conforms to Apple's AOCE (Apple Open Collaboration Environment). Chapter 23 discusses AOCE.

TeamLinks handles X.400 addresses in a user-friendly way. Addressing in the X.400 world always is a sore point, particularly among TCP/IP users, who are accustomed to short and easy-to-remember addresses such as "president@whitehouse.gov." X.400 user addresses, called *O/R names* (Originator/Recipient names) have highly structured fields that get verbose fast. An equivalent X.400 address for Bill Clinton probably would look something like this: C = "US", ADMD = "ATTMAIL", PRMD = "USGOV", O = "WHITEHOUSE", OU = "PRESIDENT", S = "Clinton."

TeamLinks helps users deal with this electronic diarrhea by including an address-book function that reduces addresses of any type to user-selected nicknames, such as "The Prez."

The Wollongong Group's (TWG) PathWay Messaging is a hybrid of X.400 and proprietary technologies. The PathWay Messaging approach to X.400 connectivity is similar to Digital's: split the user agent between a personal computer (PC, Mac, or workstations running X/Motif) and a server.

PathWay Messaging uses vendor-proprietary extensions to standard TCP/IP e-mail protocols to bridge the two parts of the user agent. In PathWay Messaging, the client part is called PathWay Messenger and the server is called PathWay Messaging Services. Because TWG has extended the TCP/IP connection, many X.400 features are available to PathWay Messaging users, including receipt notification, expiration time, importance, and sensitivity. The PathWay Messaging Services server (which runs on several UNIX platforms) includes a full X.400 MTA.

## X.400 gateway

Existing Macintosh electronic mail networks have another alternative: a gateway between the existing e-mail system and an X.400 network. Suppose that your task is to connect an existing QuickMail for a Macintosh network to X.400. WorldTalk Corp. offers a software product that runs on the QuickMail server to transmit QuickMail messages to WorldTalk's WorldTalk 400 server, a full X.400 MTA that runs HP 9000 UNIX and SCO UNIX (Intel) computers.

Retix also offers a compatible solution: QuickMail to any of its OS/2, MS-DOS, or UNIX-platform X.400 MTAs. Isocor, StarNine, and InterCon also can make the QuickMail-to-X.400 connection.

Most gateway products are intimately tied to a particular server. WorldTalk, for example, sells only gateways that work with its own server software. ISOCOR and Retix take the same approach, whereas StarNine and InterCon work only with the Apple X.400 server. That situation is not as strange as it seems. Remember that an e-mail gateway to an X.400 network must appear to the network to be a full MTA itself; the gateway has to use the P1 protocol to talk to some other MTA. An X.400 MTA doesn't fit into an INIT on a 1M Macintosh Plus running the mail-server software.

The most popular Macintosh mail packages are well covered when it comes to connections to X.400. Microsoft Mail, Lotus cc:Mail, and CE Software's QuickMail all have several paths into X.400 networks (see Table 20-1). Lotus and Microsoft also have announced plans to support their own gateways into X.400 networks. Lotus cc:Mail Router X.400, and Microsoft Enterprise Messaging Server have been discussed for several months, but the products hadn't shipped as of summer 1994.

Unless you delight in testing new software, consider sticking with the companies listed in Table 20-1.

| Table 20-1 X.400 and Macintosh E-Mail System Connectivity Map | | | | | | |
|---|---|---|---|---|---|---|
| **Vendor** | **Connects to** | **MS Mail** | **QuickMail** | **cc:Mail** | **SMTP** | **Comments** |
| StarNine | Apple MacX.400 | • | • | | | |
| InterCon | Apple MacX.400 | | • | | | |
| Innosoft | any X.400 MTA | | • | • | | |
| Wollongong | any X.400 MTA | | | • | | Mac UA |
| Digital | any X.400 MTA | | | | • | Mac UA |
| ISOCOR | own MTA | • | • | • | • | |
| SoftSwitch | own MTA | • | | • | • | |
| Retix | own MTA | • | • | • | • | |
| WorldTalk | own MTA | • | • | • | • | |
| Lotus | any X.400 MTA | | | • | | not yet released |
| Microsoft | any X.400 MTA | • | | | | not yet released |

In some TCP/IP-dominated environments, Macintosh users may be using SMTP (Simple Mail Transfer Protocol), POP (Post Office Protocol), and IMAP (Interactive Mail Access Protocol) protocols to build an e-mail system. Because most X.400 MTAs run on UNIX platforms, the best way to link TCP/IP-based mail systems into X.400 is at the X.400 MTA itself. Most X.400 MTA manufacturers have SMTP gateways available. Pure-SMTP users can connect directly to that system. POP and IMAP users can't throw away their POP/IMAP server system just yet; no X.400 MTA offers POP and IMAP as alternatives to the X.400 P7 protocol.

## Integrating e-mail with Apple's MacX.400

If you are uneasy about the prospect of diving into a UNIX-based X.400 gateway, turn to your old friend, Apple, and look into MacX.400. MacX.400 works entirely in the Macintosh hardware and software environment, and a solution based on MacX.400 and a third-party gateway can be thousands of dollars less expensive than competing solutions.

MacX.400 comes in two flavors: a low-cost single-domain version, which can connect only to a single X.400 MTA, and a more expensive multiple-domain version, which can connect to more than one MTA. MacX.400 does not require a dedicated Macintosh. Depending on the traffic load, you could run MacX.400 on the same Macintosh that already is serving as the e-mail post office and gateway. MacX.400 also supports ISO and TCP/IP transports, for a wider range of connection options.

MacX.400 is not a full partner in the X.400 backbone. For example, MacX.400 will not act as a pass-through gateway, routing e-mail messages from one MTA to another. The multiple-domain version will route outgoing messages to multiple adjacent MTAs, though, based on any O/R name attribute.

By itself, MacX.400 doesn't do anything. To make the product useful in an e-mail network, third-party gateways and user agents are required. InterCon Systems and StarNine Technologies, Inc. offer applications that link QuickMail and Microsoft Mail networks to X.400 via the MacX.400 server.

InterCon's Dispatcher/MacX.400 for QuickMail installs on the QuickMail server and routes QuickMail messages into and out of the X.400 environment. StarNine's Mail*Link for MacX.400/MS runs on the MacX.400 server and works with Microsoft's MS Mail Gateway (included with Microsoft Mail). StarNine also offers a QuickMail version of its Mail*Link software.

## Making your X.400 choice

The task of linking Macintosh e-mail users to an X.400 network has many potential solutions. With all this flexibility, how can you decide which product to select? If your goal is connectivity, you should ask four main questions in comparing different solutions.

❖ **"How does it handle addresses?"** Extended electronic mail systems of any type have a serious directory problem. Users at one end of the system want to be able to send messages to users at the other end without worrying about incorrect addresses and without having to make a telephone call ahead of time to figure out the address at the other end.

Directory services based on X.500 can help. X.400-based systems such as TeamLinks and PathWay Messaging have built-in support for large directory services. X.500, however, doesn't easily penetrate the veil of an X.400-to-proprietary mail gateway. If your network is large, pay particular attention to the way that different gateways propagate addressing information in and out. Is address propagation done manually? Is addressing information easy to update? Are rule-based or table-based translations used?

Addresses aren't limited to single users; distribution lists have become an important tool in the e-mail user's toolbox. X.400 supports many kinds of distribution lists and distribution-list attributes. You need to know, however, whether distribution lists on one side of a gateway will be available to users on the other side.

❖ **"How does it handle attachments?"** The age of the simple-text electronic mail message has passed. People now use electronic mail to pass more than just text messages. Word-processor files with text attributes, graphics files of all sorts, multimedia sound and video clips, and executable programs are all considered to be fair game for electronic mail.

The Macintosh, with its strange file format with resource and data forks, is a perennial problem for electronic mail systems. Apple Single and Apple Double formats are a way to handle this problem, but not every package handles either format (or both). Before considering any solution, make sure that Macintosh users can send documents across the backbone and have those documents arrive intact.

X.400 defines a binary message part, and industry and national standards exist for platform-specific message parts, such as MacBinary. These parts are used to transfer nontext information. Can the different gateways work with the backbone to make sure that standard and nonstandard message parts don't get garbled? How will conversion of parts occur during transfers from Macintosh to MS-DOS, UNIX, and OpenVMS users?

❖ **"Is everyone compatible?"** X.400 is a large set of standards, and the release of 1984 and 1988 versions didn't help. Most X.400 MTA vendors have undergone specific compatibility testing to make sure that their products work with one another. Because X.400 networks often are multivendor monstrosities, keep a list of what software is running to check for compatibility and configuration issues. Did you choose TCP/IP even though your vendor supports ISO?

Even if everything is compatible on paper, X.400 still is a new ball game. The parts are *supposed* to work together, but tweaking, shimming (adding a small translation layer), tuning, and adjustments often are necessary. Is your vendor committed to making the software work in your environment? Is the vendor asking the right questions? Do you have complete answers?

❖ **"Can it be managed?"** One e-mail system isn't hard to manage; 100 e-mail systems are. When you select a connection, consider how you will manage the world of X.400. What may be cost-effective for one far, dark corner of the network may cost more in the long run because it can't be managed from afar.

# CHAPTER 20 CONCEPTS AND TERMS

- Apple's MacOSI Transport and MacX25 fill your need for an OSI-compatible protocol stack. You also can run OSI transport protocol over TCP/IP or directly over Ethernet.

- Open Document Architecture is a way of converting document and graphics formats between different applications. ODA is not well supported in the Macintosh world.

- X.400 is the ISO- and ITU-defined electronic mail system. X.400 is compatible with Macintosh e-mail systems.

- You can link Macintoshes to X.400 networks either directly or through a gateway.

### Apple Single and Apple Double format
The Macintosh, with its strange file format with resource and data forks, is a perennial problem for electronic mail systems. Apple Single and Apple Double formats are a way to handle this problem, but not every package handles either format (or both).

### Access Units (AUs)
A method of getting e-mail out of an X.400 backbone is via Access Units (AUs). When the connection to the X.400 backbone isn't a single person running UA software, an AU is used. Some AUs are delivery-oriented. For example, a FAX AU could be plugged into an X.400 network to allow users to send mail to recipients who have only fax machines. X.400 also has a physical-delivery AU that connects an X.400 to a real post office.

### end system
A system that does not route messages. By contrast, an *intermediate system* participates fully in routing traffic.

### ES-IS
This extremely simple protocol is used between end systems and intermediate systems. The main function of this protocol is to enable an end system to proclaim its presence to the intermediate system router, which lets it figure out which IS the end system should use.

### IS-IS
This workhorse routing protocol is used by intermediate systems to communicate routing information. Intermediate systems talk about which end systems they serve and how to get from one IS to another IS across the intervening network. You may see this protocol called Intra-Domain Routing Protocol.

### IDRP
This protocol — the Inter-Domain Routing Protocol — is used by entire networks to communicate information about routing. IDRP would be used when two corporate networks join. IDRP is more complex than IS-IS because it handles more difficult situations, called *policy routing*.

### intermediate system
See end system.

### Message Stores (MSs)
For use with e-mail, this is a new feature in the 1988 X.400 standards. They sit between a particular UA and the rest of the MTS. An MS provides secure, continuously available storage. If your UA ran on a Macintosh, you probably would want an MS to receive and hold mail for you. That way, if your Mac was turned off, your mail wouldn't get bounced back to the sender. Also, by storing your e-mail on the MS, you could read your mail when you're in someone else's office or on the road.

### Message Transfer Agents (MTA)
The individual systems that run the e-mail backbone. MTAs handle the routing of messages, format conversions, the generation of receipts, and the management of the e-mail backbone.

### OSI
The world of the OSI model includes networks built on standards from the ISO (International Organization for Standardization) and the ITU (International Telecommunications Union).

### policy routing
See IDRP.

### User Agent (UA)
The UA is responsible for helping the user compose, send, receive, and manage electronic mail. The UA connects to a big network, usually represented as a cloud, called a *Message Transfer System* (MTS), that is responsible for transferring e-mail messages.

### X.400
The common name of a set of standards for electronic mail systems. You may hear X.400 electronic mail referred to by some of its common aliases: MHS (Message Handling System), MOTIS (Message Oriented Text Interchange System), and IPM (Inter Personal Messaging).

ITU-T Recommendation X.400 (formerly CCITT Recommendation X.400) actually is just one of a set of more than two dozen international standards that describe how to build interoperable electronic mail systems. More than 1,000 pages in the X.400 series handle everything: from protocols, testing, even the way you link X.400 e-mail systems to the telex network.

# Using Networks

# Printing on AppleTalk Networks

IN THIS CHAPTER

- How the Macintosh sets up a printing job
- The differences between print spoolers and print servers
- Ways to connect serial and parallel printers to the network for sharing

Originally, AppleTalk networking assumed that a laser printer would be shared over a network. In fact, a shared printer service is still a common task on AppleTalk networks. After all, you don't see LaserWriters on everyone's desk, even if prices have dropped dramatically since their introduction.

Setting up laser printers and other shared printing devices — such as imagesetters and slide makers — on a network requires a balance of wants and requirements. Users demand printing speed and expect minimal interference on their Macs and network traffic. In this chapter, we'll discuss these issues.

## Reviewing the Mac Printing Process

As you work with a file on your Mac, the document is represented internally as a series of QuickDraw commands. QuickDraw is Apple's imaging model and is built into the Mac's ToolBox, a part of the operating system.

When you select the print command from your application, the QuickDraw representation is sent to the printer driver that you select in the Chooser. When you select the LaserWriter icon, you indicate to your application that you ultimately want to print to a PostScript printer. The printer driver has the task of translating the QuickDraw page description into the PostScript commands required by the printer (see Figure 21-1). Some applications under- stand PostScript themselves, so they may also pay attention to the type of printer you have selected; the type of printer may change how these PostScript-savvy applications behave.

QUOTABLES

"He who first shortened the labor of Copyists by device of Movable Types was disbanding hired Armies and chiering most Kings and Senates, and creating a whole new Democratic world; he had invented the art of printing."

—Thomas Carlyle

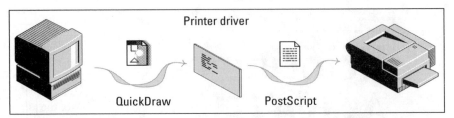

Figure 21-1: A page destined for a PostScript printer follows this route in the Mac printing process.

If you've turned off Background Printing, you're stuck for a while. Background Printing is an option in the Chooser when you select the LaserWriter icon (In Figure 21-2, we've turned on Background Printing because we don't like to wait). You now wait for the Mac and the printer to complete their cycle of exchanging data and printing all the pages you requested. Only when the laser printer has completed your job will it relinquish control to your Mac so that you can go to your next job.

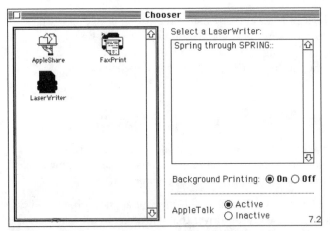

Figure 21-2: The Chooser lets you select which network services you want, whether or not you want Background Printing, and whether or not you want AppleTalk at all.

If you're on a network with a busy laser printer, your wait may be long. That's because laser printers can deal with only one job at a time; they can't store information for other jobs which might be waiting to print. If someone is already printing on the printer, your Mac simply sits there, polling the printer to find out when it's ready to print your job. And you can't do anything else with the Mac while it's waiting.

But there are ways to deal with this problem and get back to using your Mac. Two solutions ease those seemingly interminable waits for the printer: *print spoolers* and *print servers.*

A print spooler is software that intercepts your print job and stores it on your Mac. When the laser printer is ready for your job, the spooler sends the printing commands to the printer, just as your Mac would normally control the job. This process works without interfering with whatever you're doing at the time. Apple's PrintMonitor in System 6.0.x and System 7 and Fifth Generation's Super LaserSpool are two examples of such spoolers.

Print servers operate similarly to print spoolers, except that they're run exclusively on another computer. One reason for using a print server is that it can process print jobs from a number of users, sending them to more than one printer. Another advantage of print servers over spoolers is their more sophisticated logging and queue control, as you'll see shortly.

# Using Print Spoolers

Although all print spoolers accomplish the same end, they differ by the manner in which they intercept printing commands on your Mac (see Figure 21-3). Some spoolers, like Apple's own PrintMonitor, grab the QuickDraw output directly from your application. Others, like TurboSpool (Peripheral Land Inc.), wait for the printer driver to perform its translations and then intercept the resulting data, either as a PostScript or a bitmap file.

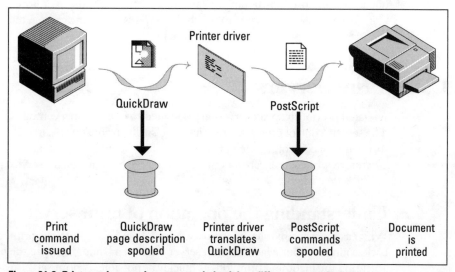

Figure 21-3: Print spoolers can intercept a printing job at different stages in the process.

In the first case, with output taken directly from the application, the spooler takes less time to create the printing file, so control is returned to your Mac sooner. The second approach tends to take a bit longer because the printer driver must make its translations before the spooler file is created. In both cases, remember that you'll need some spare room on your hard disk for the spooler to store its temporary files.

After the spoolers create their spool file, they work in the background to send the file to the printer. This background process can be bothersome at times because communications between the spooler and the printer occasionally require extensive data transfers and take almost full control of your Mac before finishing. Erratic cursor movement in any program and slow character drawing in a word processor are examples of the background spooler exerting control over your Mac.

What are the benefits and drawbacks of print spoolers? The main advantage is obvious — you can work on your Mac while the spooler sends your print file to the printer. Also, without the spooler, you'd wait for the laser printer to finish another job before you could send yours. The spooler patiently waits for the printer to become available, allowing you to do other work.

The spooler's disadvantages are relatively minor. First, the spooler does require some RAM to function (usually less than 100K), and it also requires disk space for storing the spool files. From a management viewpoint, spoolers are meant for individual Macs. The spooler won't allow you to control the printer's queue. So there's nothing you can do if someone is printing the latest revision of his book while you're waiting to print a rush two-page memo.

In Figure 21-4, you can see some of the features of the standard PrintMonitor (built into your Macintosh System 7 software). It lets you manage an internal queue of print jobs, postponing or canceling them before they get printed. PrintMonitor also allows you to watch the progress of your printing, telling you its status as it processes and sends data to the printer.

# Using Print Servers

As stated previously, print servers are designed to operate on a central computer. The servers control one or more printers. Usually, print servers also offer some sort of queue control for each printer, as well as the logging of all print jobs. Therefore, print servers are a network-wide service, rather than a service designed for individual Macs.

## Understanding the operation of print servers

Whereas the print spooler intercepts a print job and sends it to the printer in the background on your Mac, the print server acts just as though it were the printer, accepting the incoming print jobs as quickly as possible. A print server usually receives print files and stores them on a hard disk, directing them to the appropriate printers as the printers become available.

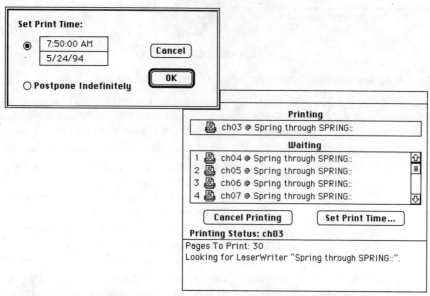

**Figure 21-4: The PrintMonitor application lets you see which jobs are waiting to print and which are printing. You can also schedule jobs to print at a later time.**

Because print files are stored on the server before they're printed, a manager or a user can review the queue of waiting jobs and alter the order or even delete certain waiting jobs. Of course, the capability to change the status of other users' print jobs is in the hands of the server's manager and is subject to some type of security control. Users, however, can review their own queue of jobs and delete some of their own files if they want to.

Because print servers can service more than one printer, they often can be instructed to redirect jobs automatically to the next available printer (as long as paper and other requirements are identical). Also, print servers usually can handle serial, parallel, and AppleTalk interfaces to printers, making available some printers that normally aren't available on networks.

In Chapter 14, "Managing AppleTalk Networks for Management," we discussed aspects of accounting management. Print servers help with accounting because they normally maintain a log of all jobs processed through the server. Full-featured print servers enable you to assign users' names by department or category, as well as to sort out costs for each printer. These options make cost control and charge backs easier.

Because print servers are rapidly writing your print file to their disk and not actually processing the print commands until later, they are faster than a laser printer at receiving your print file and turning control back to your Mac.

## Spooler or Server?

Spoolers are best for individual Macs, where you are controlling your own print jobs.

Print servers work well as a network-wide service because they are designed to queue print jobs from a

number of computers.

You can use both! Figure 21-4 is actually a picture of a Macintosh PrintMonitor Spooler sending jobs to Digital's Pathworks for Macintosh printer server.

The main disadvantage with a print server is that it can actually increase network traffic if it's improperly located on the network with respect to the printer that it serves. This is more important in AppleTalk networks than Ethernet networks. (See Chapter 13 and the following section for some tips regarding layout.) Another possible disadvantage is that a print server requires a computer to perform the server's functions, although sometimes this computer can provide more than one network service, such as acting both as a file server and a print server.

## Setting up a print server

If you're going to use a print server with a networkable printer (such as a LaserWriter), you should locate the server and the printer carefully. In particular, if you're using an AppleTalk network, don't place a router between the server and the printer (or printers).

Consider the role the server plays in handling your print job (see Figure 21-5). First, you send a print file over the network to the print server. Then the print server sends the file to the designated printer. If the printer is networked rather than directly attached to the server, this represents a second transmission of the file on the network. So the print server just doubled the amount of network traffic associated with printing. Not exactly what you had in mind, is it?

If you're using a print server with a networked printer, try to keep the server-to-printer traffic isolated from the user-to-server traffic. Segregating traffic is not always possible, but one approach is installing a LocalTalk bridge (such as the LocalSwitch) and placing the print server and its printers on one port of the bridge. With this layout, users send their jobs through the bridge to the print server, but any traffic between the server and its associated printers is isolated from the rest of the network.

The only problem with this arrangement can be with throughput — if a number of users are sending jobs to the server, the bridge can turn into a bottleneck. However, most modern bridges are designed to work at *wire speed*, which is to say that they can handle the maximum possible number of packets on your LocalTalk or Ethernet network without dropping any.

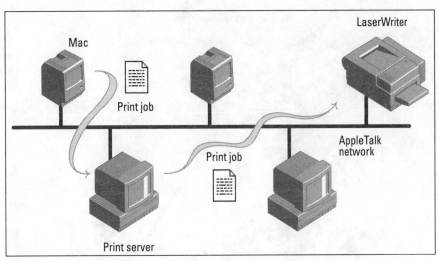

**Figure 21-5: Note that the print job is transmitted on the network twice in order to get to the networked printer.**

Another remedy is to keep *all* the printers off the network. Although most of us think of LaserWriters as printers that are networked via AppleTalk, such printers also have a serial port. Other PostScript printers also have parallel ports for faster data transfers than a serial port provides. In these cases, you can use the serial or parallel ports to attach the laser printers to the server and thereby eliminate some network traffic (see Figure 21-6).

The problem with this strategy is that you can slow down the printer from its 230K bps LocalTalk rate to a 9.6K bps serial port rate, and that will slow down your print jobs. This technique also works when a computer running a different operating system acts as the print server, which we described in Chapter 16, "Bringing AppleTalk to the Masses."

# Using Non-AppleTalk Printers

Attaching a LaserWriter (or other AppleTalk-aware printer) to an AppleTalk network has always been a relatively simple task because of the LaserWriter's built-in networking support, first for LocalTalk and now for Ethernet. The problem, as we said before, is to get the print job done and off your Mac so that you can turn to other tasks.

But what about other printers that don't have built-in networking support? A great many printers have only serial or parallel ports. If these printers offer features that you can't find in networkable printers, such as high-speed multiform printing, you can still set them up for sharing among networked users.

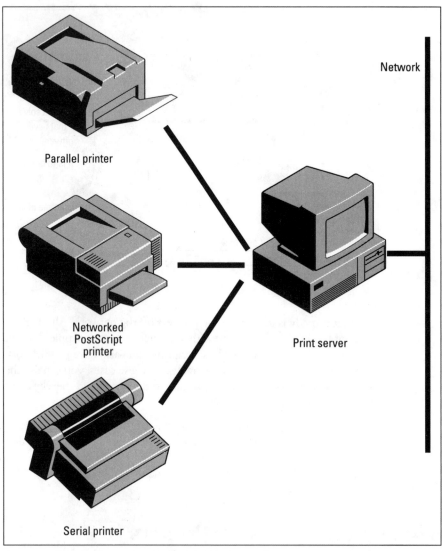

Network

Parallel printer

Networked
PostScript
printer

Print server

Serial printer

**Figure 21-6: Print servers can handle print jobs for both serial and parallel printers, as well as for networked printers.**

As described previously, one way to do this is to attach these printers to a print server that is part of the network. Another approach is possible (see Figure 21-7). You can install a device like the NetSerial (Shiva) to act as the interface between your serial printer (or plotter) and the AppleTalk network (a parallel printer will not work with Shiva's NetSerial). You may need a special printer driver to make this work, but most of the drivers necessary for serial and parallel printers are available from either Insight Development Corp. or GDT Softworks, Inc.

## Making the Link Between LocalTalk and Ethernet

If you've chosen Ethernet as your network media, then you may find your printers out in the weeds, so to speak, and unavailable to your Ethernet Macintoshes.

There are several solutions available, including software routers between LocalTalk and Ethernet. Our favorites are the printer-specific mini-routers available from Dayna and Compatible Systems. The EtherPrint Plus (Dayna) connects up to four LocalTalk devices (such as printers or networked modems) to

an Ethernet. The EtherWrite (Compatible Systems) connects up to six. With a street price of less than $500 for the EtherWrite, you can solve a lot of headaches with a tiny box that never needs attention, configuration, new software, or even a cleaning.

Of course, the other option is to only buy printers which have Ethernet ports on them. For many mid-range and high-end printers, that's not much more money and gives you the ultimate in flexibility.

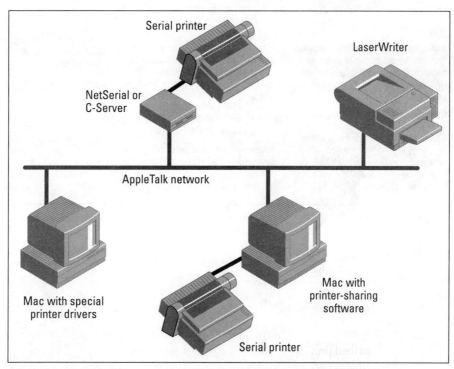

**Figure 21-7: Use either hardware or software to make a non-networked printer or plotter available to networked users. Special printer drivers must be installed on the user's Macintosh.**

# CHAPTER *21* CONCEPTS AND TERMS

- A print spooler operates on an individual Mac, whereas a print server works on another networked computer.

- Some print spoolers work with the QuickDraw representation of a print file, but others work with a PostScript representation of the file.

- Users can track the progress of or delete their print jobs, even when using a print server.

- Print servers can accommodate many different interfaces to printers — AppleTalk and serial, as well as parallel. Moving printers off of LocalTalk onto serial ports will slow them down tremendously.

- A LocalTalk-to-Ethernet adapter can connect LocalTalk printers to an Ethernet network and reduce network manager headaches.

- You can keep a print server and its associated printers on the same network side of a router to reduce traffic.

on the network. If more than one print job is waiting on the server, the print-server software keeps track of the jobs and prints them in order. Some software allows for the reassignment of priorities to print jobs as well as job cancellation so that some people can get their work printed ahead of others.

**print spooler**
An application program or combination of hardware and software that allows users to print at the same time they are working on some other task.

The print spooler acts as a buffer for the files to be printed. The files are stored in the spooler until a printer is free for printing. The spooler then sends the file to the printer.

**PostScript**
A page description language from Adobe. PostScript is used in Apple's laser printers.

**buffer**
A temporary storage location in memory that provides uninterrupted data flow between devices, such as printers and keyboards, with fewer interruptions or pauses.

**Chooser**
A desk accessory included with the Macintosh system software. The desk accessory is used to select network services by service type (such as LaserWriter or AppleShare), device name, and zone name.

**print server**
A device (usually an additional workstation) that acts as a large buffer for files being sent to the printer. When users send data to the printer, the data is actually sent to the server and stored there until the printer is available. Then, the print server automatically sends the data to the printer to be printed.

A print server enables network users to send data to a printer even if the printer is busy with another job. Thus, users do not need to wait for an available printer

# Sharing Files on AppleTalk Networks

- The difference between file transfers and file sharing
- When to use file-transfer utilities instead of file servers
- The difference between centralized and distributed file servers
- Details of Apple's AppleTalk Filing Protocol (AFP) for standardizing file sharing
- How to set up an AppleShare file server
- How to set up fault-tolerant file servers
- How to develop server backup strategies

Information justifies the network. More precisely, sharing information is the prime reason for installing a network. Most of us deal with information on our Macs in chunks called *files*. Whether they come from a word processor, page-layout program, spreadsheet, or drawing program, the least common denominator in all these applications is the file.

So how do we share file-based information on a network? Two basic methods for sharing files are available to upgrade the old sneakernet system of trading floppies between machines. One way is to move a file from one Mac to another Mac over the network. To illustrate, one user sends you a copy of a file, whereupon you can hack away at it to your heart's content. If you want the original user to see what you've done with the file, you can return a copy of the modified file to him or her. We refer to this process as the *file-transfer method* throughout the book.

The second method for sharing information is to use a file server to share files. In this system, a user can put a file of interest on the server so other users can see the file without copying it to their Macs. We refer to this process as *file sharing*. If users do want to copy a file from the server to their Macs to modify it, they can do this as well.

The two methods may sound fairly similar — after all, isn't the file server just another means of transferring the file to other users? Not exactly. The file server can be used that way, but file servers incorporate features for protecting and controlling access to the files that file-transfer programs don't have. When you use a file-transfer program to send a file to other users, you lose all control over what happens to that file once it's sent. On the other hand, when you copy a file to a server, you can set access privileges for the file so that it cannot be modified or copied.

In this chapter, we focus on file sharing in a mostly Macintosh world. If you are interested in file sharing in a cross-platform environment, you should also read Chapter 16, "Bringing AppleTalk to the Masses."

# Moving Files on the Network

There are a few file-transfer utilities that work on AppleTalk networks, such as Flash (Beagle Bros.), LapLink Mac (Traveling Software), Timbuktu (Farallon), and Mac-to-Mac (Caravelle Networks). Using one of these utilities is similar to the sneakernet method of putting the file on a floppy and taking that floppy over to the other user, except that with the networked versions you don't have to get out of your chair (see Figure 22-1).

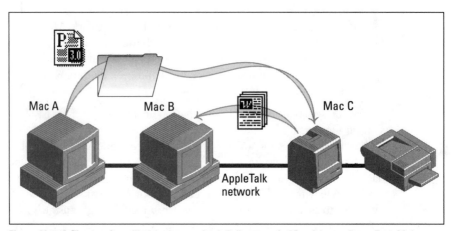

**Figure 22-1: A file-transfer utility used on an AppleTalk network. Mac A is sending a PageMaker document to Mac C. Mac C is sending a Word document to Mac B.**

These utilities require that both machines be up and running at the same time for the transfer to be completed; if not, the destination Mac cannot receive the files that you're sending to it. Apple's Personal File Sharing, an integral part of System 7, can do away with the need for separate file-transfer utilities, since setting up an AppleShare server is just as simple as installing a file-transfer program.

File-transfer utilities are a quick and easy way to share files or entire folders over an AppleTalk network. However, they do not permit simultaneous multiuser access to a file. Note that in Figure 20-1, Mac A is sending a PageMaker document and folder to Mac C. Mac C, meanwhile, is sending a Word document to Mac B.

You can also use any of these network programs when you need to distribute files to more than one other co-worker. Many of the file-transfer programs allow you to define groups of users as named workgroups. You just select the name of the desired workgroup when you're sending a file, and a copy will go to everyone in that list. But watch out: When you're working with more than one person, problems can arise with keeping track of files and their changes.

When you transfer files around the network using a file-transfer program and expect to get the files back (after changes are made, for example), you'd better set up some kind of system for renaming the returned files. This is especially crucial if you want to keep track of both the old and new versions. For instance, you might call your original file "JAN92 REPORT(original)," and then call the edited one that comes back from Jane "JAN92 REPORT(Jane)", and the one that comes back from Don "JAN92 REPORT(Don)."

Even if Jane sends you the edited file back with the original name of "JAN92 REPORT(original)," the file-transfer programs we've discussed here don't automatically overwrite your copy of the file with the incoming file. Each of the programs allows you to select where these files are to be stored (in a different folder, for instance) and how they're to be named — this is the point when you can rename the incoming file from Jane as "JAN92 REPORT(Jane)."

If all of this sounds like a good way to lose data, we agree! In Chapter 23, "Groupware," we talk about several software products which can help you manage the task of passing around documents. However, all of these products depend on a file server, rather than file-transfer technology.

### QUICK TIPS

### Using E-Mail as Your File-Transfer System

Note that you can use an electronic mail system in much the same way as any of these file-transfer programs. You simply enclose the files in a mail message and send the message off to the desired recipients. We discuss electronic mail in greater detail in Chapter 24.

E-mail has a distinct capability over most of the file-transfer programs. This capability is called *store-and-forward.* Many of the file-transfer programs require that both Macs be running at the same time in order to send or receive a file. But, because most e-mail systems store all messages on an e-mail server, you need only a connection between your Mac and the server to send or receive a file.

Because of the store-and-forward architecture of an e-mail server, a user can send a message or file to you even when you're not on the network; the server stores the message until the next time you're on the network. Then, when you log on to the e-mail system, the message (or file) will be transferred to your Mac, even if the original user is no longer on the network. This makes information exchange much easier.

File-transfer programs are good for very small workgroups where you need to occasionally transfer a file between users. We wouldn't recommend using a file-transfer program to send a copy of a file to 100 users, for instance. Nor would we recommend that you use one of these programs to send a copy of something like the stock inventory report every day.

# Sharing Files on the Network

Whereas file-transfer utilities are good for transferring a small number of files among small workgroups, file servers are better suited for sharing files among large workgroups. File servers also have built-in mechanisms to assist you in controlling multiuser access to folders and files on the server, making use of items like databases much easier. We now look at what kinds of file servers are available and how they differ.

## Understanding file servers

Because file-transfer programs perform a very basic action — moving a copy of a file from one Mac to another — these programs don't require any special understanding of new concepts, such as folder- and file-access rights. On the other hand, file servers offer services that make use of some new concepts.

File servers are comprised of a main processor unit (a computer) connected to a series of one or more hard disks or similar storage media (such as a CD-ROM drive). Each disk is usually called a *volume*, which is mounted by the file server. The file server then controls access to each of the mounted volumes, first at the level of the entire volume, then at the level of individual directories (or *folders*, with the Mac interface), or in some systems, at the level of individual files.

### What's a WORM?

WORM — the acronym stands for Write Once, Read Many — drives are used as archival and security storage in a variety of environments. A WORM drive is usually based on some optical medium, similar to a CD-ROM, which can be written only once, but read many times. For archival purposes, WORM platters can then be placed in a jukebox for occasional access. WORM drives are also used in some high-security environments to ensure that transaction or security logs can not be erased by software bugs — intentional or accidental.

Each user of the file server has a designated log-in name/password pair. A file server stores this name/password pair in a special file on the main server volume and relates access privileges to that name. On the simplest file server, the access privileges define your ability to use a given volume and what you can do with files on that volume — whether, for example, you can add or delete files or copy files.

One of the file servers that we'll concentrate on in this chapter is AppleShare, which controls access to files in a slightly different way from file servers found on other networks.

AppleShare (and other servers using the AppleTalk Filing Protocol) controls access to files at the folder level, rather than at the individual file level. This means that all files within a folder are treated equally; they can all be copied or deleted, for example. If you want different controls for the various files, you must place these files in folders with separately defined access privileges.

Furthermore, AppleShare's control over access privileges isn't limited to folders at the level of individual users. AppleShare uses the concept of *groups of users* and allows owners of folders to grant access to those folders to a group, rather than to an individual. This means that when you create a folder on an AppleShare file server, you can allow another person to use that folder if this user is also a member of an AppleShare group to which you belong. All members of that group will have the same access to the folder. If you want only one other user to have access to a folder, your only choice is to create a group of two, comprised of you and the other user, and allow access privileges to this group. You can also sidestep the group-based security and allow everyone to have access to the folder.

Because servers can control single-user and multiuser access to files in different ways, developers can use these access features to create *multilaunch applications*. These applications allow more than one person to use the program at the same time. The relations between single-user and multiuser applications are categorized in Table 22-1.

## Classifying servers

The field of file servers is far more complicated than that of file-transfer programs. That's because servers can be either *centralized* or *distributed*, which means that they can function either within a *client/server* or a *peer-to-peer* framework. We'll take a brief look at what all this means before we head on to the specific uses and features of each kind of server.

Centralized servers are reminiscent of the earlier days of mainframes, with all data of interest stored on one computer in a central location. You log on to the server whenever you want to access the data there or to add files to those already stored there. This is a relatively convenient setup, especially for large workgroups, where administration of the server is centralized and can be handled by one person (at least in theory). Also, this setup makes security a bit easier — you can lock up the server machine in a closet or computer room to prevent unauthorized access to the hardware.

| Table 22-1<br>**Network File Sharing Applications** | | |
|---|---|---|
| *File sharing mode center* | | |
| | Single-user mode | Multiuser mode |
| Single launch | ❖ One user per application<br><br>❖ Only one user at a time can modify a file | ❖ Only one user per application<br><br>❖ Two or more users at a time can modify a file |
| Multilaunch | ❖ Two or more users per application<br><br>❖ Only one user at a time can modify a file | ❖ Two or more users per application<br><br>❖ Two or more users at a time can modify a file. |

Centralized servers are usually computers dedicated to the task of file services. In most cases, the centralized server is the best choice for such access-intensive applications as multiuser databases. For these situations, you want only one copy of the file to exist on the network, but you want more than one user to be working with the database at one time (see Figure 22-2). The security- and file-access options of a server make this possible, and the dedicated resources of a centralized server allow most databases to perform better than if they were installed on a distributed, or non-dedicated, server.

In this centralized scheme, Macs other than the server can act only as clients. In Figure 22-2, three types of files are stored on the centralized server. Mac A, running PageMaker, is working with a PageMaker file on the server as if it were on a local disk. Mac B and Mac E, both running 4th Dimension, are simultaneously accessing the same 4D database file from the server. This is possible because both 4D and the server support multiuser access. Mac C and Mac D (both running Microsoft Word — an application that doesn't support multiuser access) are working with two different Word files on the server.

*Distributed servers* are a newer networking concept. Rather than storing all shared files a single computer, distributed servers permit users to store files on their own Macs and allow other users on the network to have access to those files. This kind of file sharing is also called *peer-to-peer* sharing. Each Mac can function both as a file server and as the client of other file servers. The administration of such a system is more of a headache, however, because it requires that each "owner," or individual user, of a file server be responsible for that server. Also, finding files can be a hassle when a user isn't certain which server contains which files. However, there are ways around this difficulty, as you'll see later in this chapter.

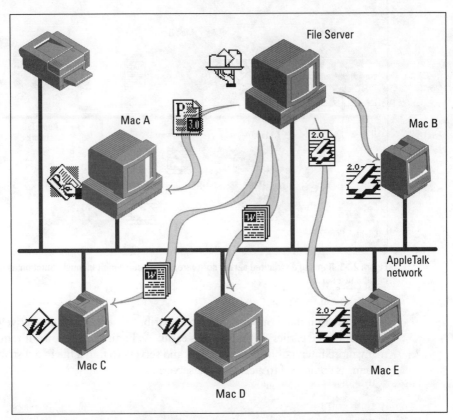

**Figure 22-2: A centralized server system, with one computer (labeled File Server) dedicated to holding shared files and information for all users on the network.**

Distributed servers, such as Apple's File Sharing feature in System 7, seem to work best for small workgroups. One reason for this limitation is that your Mac is operating both as your personal workstation as well as a file server to other users. There's bound to be competition for your Mac's resources in this situation, and you don't want too many people using your Mac's disk space and processor just for sharing information (see Figure 22-3). Under such conditions, you wouldn't get much work done on your own Mac. As a rule of thumb, Apple recommends no more than 10 users for System 7's File Sharing feature.

In Figure 22-3, Mac D, running PageMaker, is a client of Mac A. Mac D is also acting as a server to both Mac E and Mac C (both running 4th Dimension, a multiuser application). If the distributed server supports multiuser access, Mac E and Mac C can be accessing the same 4D file on Mac D. Mac C is also a server for Mac B (running Microsoft Word).

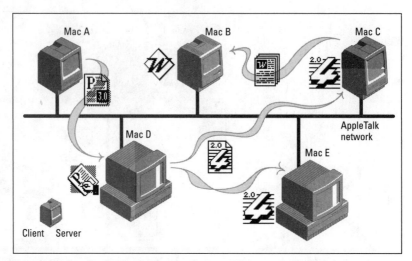

Figure 22-3: Running distributed server software, a Mac can simultaneously function as a client and a server.

Another reason that you want to keep a distributed server system relatively small is one mentioned earlier — finding files easily. As Figure 22-4 shows, it requires many more interactions between users and servers to find a file in a distributed system, as compared to a centralized server.

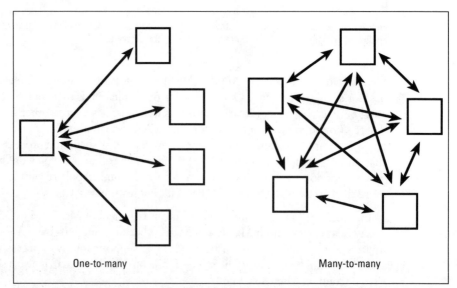

Figure 22-4: This schematic shows how the number of interactions increases dramatically when you change from a centralized server to a distributed server.

## Using System 7's File Sharing feature

With the introduction of System 7, Apple has made network-wide file sharing a part of the Mac's operating system. Apple offers a feature called File Sharing that allows you, as the owner of your Mac, to make folders available for use by other users on the network. These folders hold files that users can modify or delete, or they can add new files, according to the privileges you grant each user.

While your Mac with the File Sharing option is acting as a file server to other users, you can use the AppleShare client software on your Mac to access files on other Macs also running File Sharing. As your Mac is now acting as a file server and a client, we call this a *peer-to-peer*, or *distributed*, file server system.

How does the System 7 File Sharing feature work? The setup of File Sharing is covered in detail in the Networking Manual of the System 7 documentation, so we'll only summarize here.

System 7 File Sharing is managed with three control panels (see Figure 22-5) and the "Sharing..." menu item on the File menu.

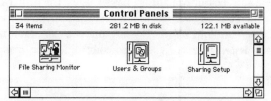

**Figure 22-5: The File Sharing Monitor, Users & Groups, and Sharing Setup control panels are used to control System 7 Personal File Sharing.**

The contents of any folder on your Mac can be shared with other network users. This is a two-sided process; you enable File Sharing on your Mac to make it a background file server, and the other users each log on to your Mac to see which folders and files you've made available for their use. To control access to the folders, you must add the names of users who should use your files. For added security, you can create passwords for each user.

You don't have to install special software to use File Sharing; it's part of the system software installed on your Mac along with System 7. All you need to do is turn on File Sharing and create your list of users. To turn on file sharing, select the "Sharing Setup" control panel and press the Start button in the File Sharing section. In Figure 22-6, you can see what the Sharing Setup control panel will look like after you have started it; before starting, the button would be labeled "Start." Don't start Program Linking unless you have been told you need it. Once you start File Sharing, it will automatically start up every time you restart your Macintosh. If you don't want to use File Sharing, turn it off because it takes up memory and processor cycles.

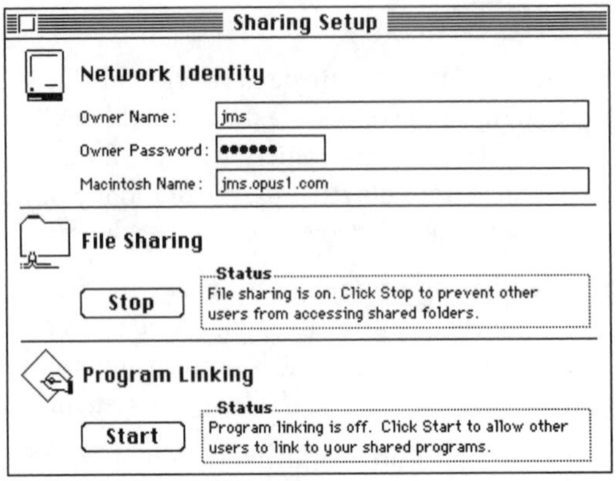

Figure 22-6: The Sharing Setup control panel shows that this Mac is already running File Sharing, but not Program Linking.

To allow users to connect to your Macintosh, use the "Users & Groups" control panel. In Figure 22-7, you can see our Macintosh has six users: the owner named *jms*; a *<Guest>* account, which can be used without a password (if you allow it); and some users named *Keri, Jan, Face,* and *Julieta*. If you want, you can organize your users into groups and then assign access privileges to your folders for groups rather than for individuals.

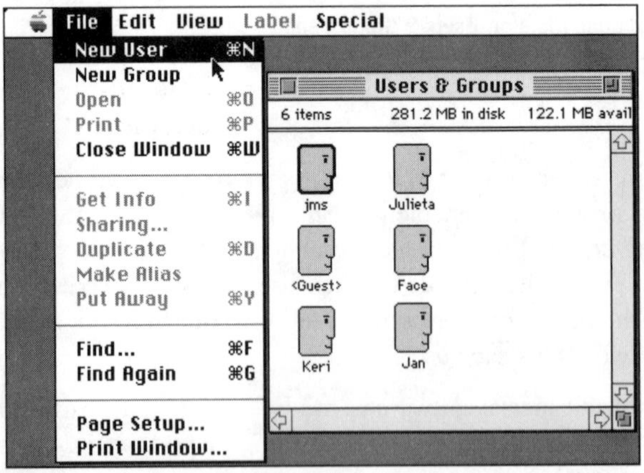

Figure 22-7: The Users & Groups control panel lets you add and delete users to System 7 File Sharing.

Once you've set up sharing and users, you must enable the disks connected to your Macintosh for file sharing. To do that, select the disk you want to share, pull down the "Sharing..." menu item from the File menu, and click in the box labeled "Share this item and its contents." See Figure 22-8 for an illustration.

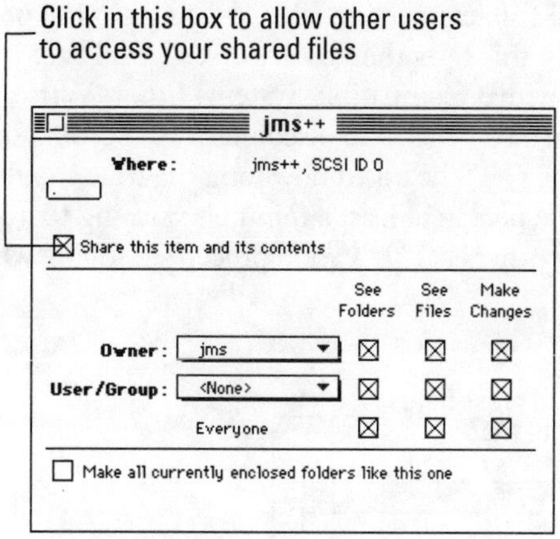

Click in this box to allow other users
to access your shared files

| jms++ |
|---|
| **Where:** jms++, SCSI ID 0 |

☒ Share this item and its contents

|  | | See<br>Folders | See<br>Files | Make<br>Changes |
|---|---|---|---|---|
| **Owner:** | jms ▼ | ☒ | ☒ | ☒ |
| **User/Group:** | <None> ▼ | ☒ | ☒ | ☒ |
|  | Everyone | ☒ | ☒ | ☒ |

☐ Make all currently enclosed folders like this one

**Figure 22-8: Personal file sharing lets you specify different access privileges for different users and groups to your disks and folders.**

The sharing options for any folder on your Mac allow you to set the access to **Everyone**, so that all users have access to your files. (See Chapter 15, "Securing an AppleTalk Network," for a discussion of the related security problems of this situation.) Or you can restrict folder use to one group or to an individual. If you want more than one individual to have access to a folder, you must define a group made up of those individuals.

The desktop in System 7 offers visual feedback about shared folders and shows whether they are currently being accessed. If a folder is set up for sharing but is not in use by someone on the network, its icon looks like the left-hand icon in Figure 22-9. But if someone is using a file within the folder, the icon changes to the right-hand icon in Figure 22-9.

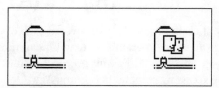

**Figure 22-9: Folder icons change when users are accessing folders with System 7 File Sharing.**

You can also monitor the file sharing activities with the "File Sharing Monitor" control panel. The Monitor window includes an activity bar and a list of shared folders and connected users. In Figure 22-10, you can see that Keri (a PowerBook) has connected to the server "jms.opus1.com" and can access the disk named "jms++."

You can also see that Keri's LocalTalk connection isn't stressing out the powerful Quadra 800's Ethernet adapter. In this case, the PowerBook's LocalTalk is connected to the Quadra's Ethernet with a Compatible Systems Ether•Write. The File Sharing Monitor window can also be used to disconnect users from your Mac. If you choose to disconnect a user, you'll be asked how long the Mac should wait before the disconnection. Give the person at least a minute's warning to make a clean exit from the file. "Do unto others . . ." is a good precept to follow when sharing files.

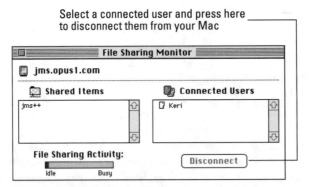

Figure 22-10: The File Sharing Monitor shows what's being shared on your Mac, who's using it, and how much of the Mac is being taken up.

Next we'll look at the AppleTalk protocol that is crucial to the workings of both AppleShare file servers and System 7's File Sharing — the AppleTalk Filing Protocol.

# Examining the AppleTalk Filing Protocol (AFP)

In Chapter 3, "Understanding AppleTalk Protocols," we covered each of the protocols that Apple has defined for its network operating system. One of those protocols is the AppleTalk Filing Protocol, or AFP. This protocol defines how file servers are supposed to handle file access by computers running Mac OS, MS-DOS, or ProDOS (the Apple II file system). The first implementation of AFP was Apple's own AppleShare file server; many other servers, including ones running on Intel 80x86, DEC VAX, and UNIX computers, are now available with AFP support. You can turn to Chapter 16, "Bringing AppleTalk to the Masses" to read more about these products.

The AFP specifications are concerned primarily with user access privileges at the folder (that is, directory) level and how these privileges are presented to the user at the desktop level. Another important feature of AFP is its control of how file names are mapped between the supported operating systems — Mac OS, MS-DOS, or ProDOS.

As noted previously, AppleShare employs the concept of groups in defining access privileges. AppleShare has three user categories for assigning access — **Owner, Group,** and **Everyone.** As owner of a folder on an AppleShare server, you can assign to each user category any combination of the following privileges: **See Folders, See Files,** and **Make Changes.** The first privilege lets someone see what other folders, if any, are contained within the folder you created. The second privilege allows users to not only see files within the folder, but also to open or copy any of those files. **Make Changes** allows users to create, move, or delete files and folders located in the folder you created. File Sharing within System 7 and AppleShare offer the same user categories and access privileges.

The combination of these access privileges can lead to a unique folder, called the *drop folder.* To create a drop folder, you allow users (a group or everyone) to make changes, but not to see folders or files. Your users can add files to the folder, but they do not see what's in the folder. This is a simple way to enable users to send files to you and ensure the privacy of what they send you, as only you as the owner of the folder can manipulate the files within a drop folder.

On a Mac, AppleShare uses icons to display your access rights to each folder on the desktop (see Figure 22-11). In addition, every folder that you can open on an AppleShare file server has a set of small icons in the upper-left corner of the folder's window to indicate your access privileges within that folder (see Figure 22-12).

In Figure 22-11, note the AFP folder icons; these icons are generated by AppleShare, System 7's File Sharing feature, or any AFP-compatible file server. The differences in the folder icons depend on whether you're using the AppleShare client software under System 6.0.x or System 7.

Apple included two unique features in the Mac's file structures when it designed the Macintosh operating system. One is the capability for 31-character file names; the other is the division of a file's contents between the *data fork* and *resource fork.* Both of these file attributes can cause problems when you're trying to exchange information with other non-Mac systems, which is a capability AppleShare is designed to have. You can communicate between operating systems with Apple's AFP, but you have to be careful. We'll show you what the pitfalls are in the following section.

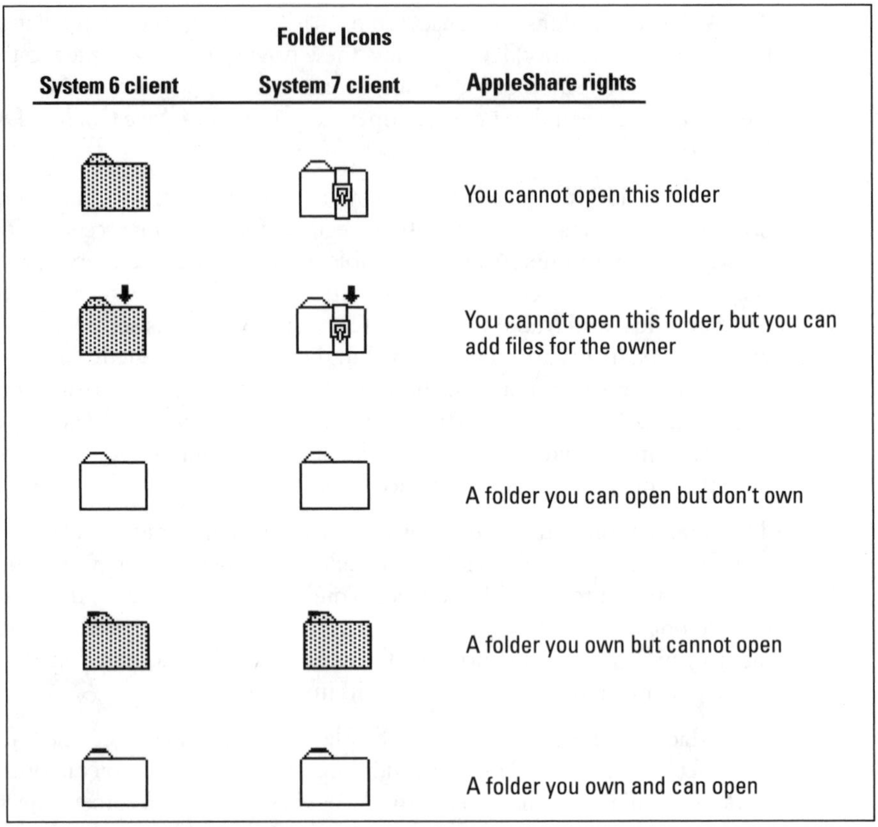

Figure 22-11: The AFP folder icons and the access rights they represent.

The Macintosh operating system lets you assign file and folder names of up to 31 characters; you can use any character except a colon in those names. On the other hand, MS-DOS limits file names and directory names (the equivalent of a Mac folder) to a maximum of eight characters, followed by a period, then followed by one to three additional characters for the file extension. Many special characters — such as [ , ] , / , " — cannot be used in MS-DOS file names.

The AFP specifications include rules that define how file names are mapped between the three supported operating systems: Mac OS, MS-DOS, or ProDOS (for Apple II computers). Here we'll be concerned only with the Mac and MS-DOS operating systems — Apple II systems are really too rare nowadays to worry about.

AFP deals with these naming problems by maintaining multiple names for each directory and each file on the server and by following special rules for converting one name into another. To support Mac and MS-DOS, an AFP server stores both

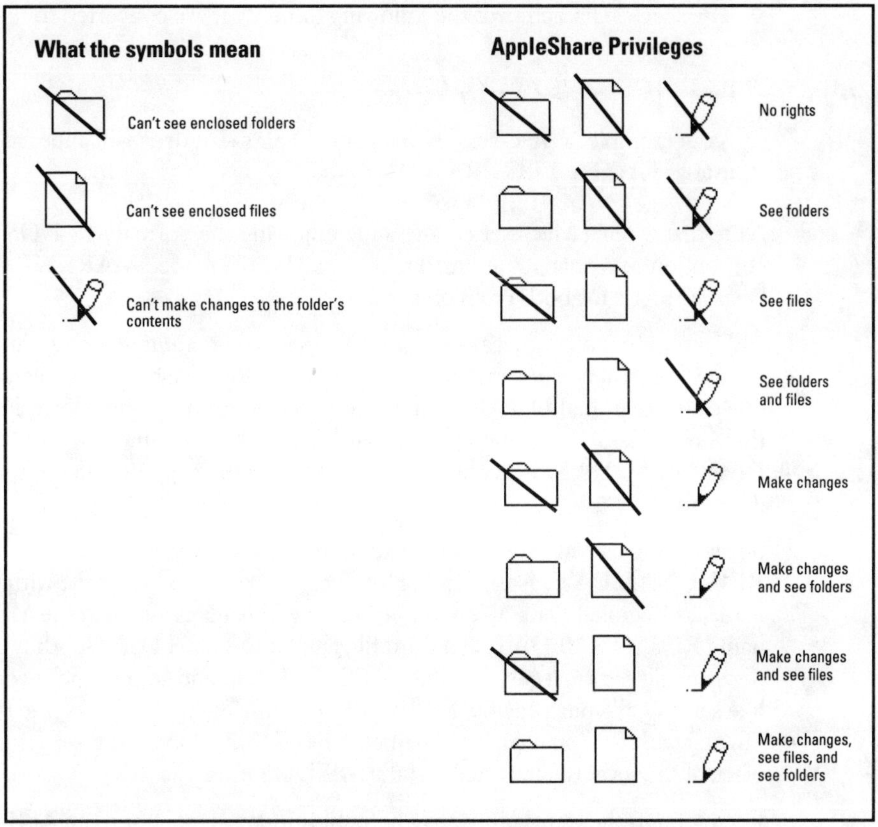

**What the symbols mean**                    **AppleShare Privileges**

Can't see enclosed folders

Can't see enclosed files

Can't make changes to the folder's contents

No rights

See folders

See files

See folders and files

Make changes

Make changes and see folders

Make changes and see files

Make changes, see files, and see folders

**Figure 22-12: These AFP icons are used within a folder's window to indicate a user's access privileges.**

a long name of up to 31 characters and a short name of up to 12 characters for a file. The manner in which file names are translated depends on which operating system (Mac or MS-DOS) was used to create the file on the server.

If a Mac user creates a file name more than 12 characters long, AFP translates the file name for an MS-DOS user with the following changes and adjustments:

❖ Spaces and periods are removed.

❖ All alphabetic characters are changed to uppercase.

❖ The first 11 characters are used to create the DOS file name.

As an example, the Mac file name **Project Overview**, which includes a space and upper- and lowercase letters, changes to **PROJECTO.VER.** Likewise, the Mac file name **junk.c.o.,** with its mix of periods and lowercase letters, becomes **JUNK.CO.**

❖ The special characters of the following limited set are converted to the underline character:

( = + [ ] ; " * , < > / ? \ | )

As an example, a Mac-created file named **Facts+Figures** will appear to a DOS user as **FACTS_FI.GUR.**

Note that when a Mac user creates a file following the normal MS-DOS naming conventions, no changes are made. Thus, a Mac file named **MARKET.WKS** will keep the name for both types of users.

AFP introduces one other translation rule to avoid creating files with duplicate names. For instance, it would be a simple matter for a Mac user to create two files, one called Regional Data-East and one called Regional Data-West. Following the above rules, both names will be translated to the DOS file name of **REGIONAL.DAT,** which won't work if you try to keep both files in the same directory.

So according to AFP, the first file stored in the directory is named **REGIONAL.DAT,** as expected. However, if you save another file with a similar name, as Regional Data-West in our example, this file is assigned the MS-DOS name **REGIONA0.DAT.** If a third file named Regional Data-South is created in the same directory, it becomes **REGIONA1.DAT,** and so on. And if you really like starting all your Mac file names with the same eight characters, the twelfth file starting with Regional will be renamed **REGION0L.DAT** (the zero is inserted in place of the seventh character) for the MS-DOS user.

Even though the translations may be straightforward (at least to an AFP server), the rules can make it difficult if Mac and MS-DOS users want to communicate with each other. MS-DOS users actually have it easier because the files that they create on a server will display the same name for the Mac users. On the other hand, if a Mac user creates a file for MS-DOS users to access on the server, the user should keep in mind these translation rules and try to name the shared files according to the MS-DOS conventions.

The file-access model that is part of the AppleTalk Filing Protocol is designed so that a user's application program issues file-system calls found in the native operating system, but an AFP translator on the user's workstation translates these calls into AFP file-system calls that the AFP file server understands. This approach allows the user to access both local disks and any AFP file-server volumes as if they were all local disks (see Figure 22-13).

A program can directly issue AFP calls, or the AFP Translator can translate the native file system calls to AFP calls. However, only AFP calls are transmitted on the network to the AFP server.

## File Types in the Macintosh's Operating System

The Macintosh operating system is unique among microcomputer operating systems in that files are composed of two parts rather than the more traditional single part. These two parts are known as the *data fork* and the *resource fork*. The data fork usually stores only the ASCII text and format information, such as you'd find in any regular word processing file on other systems. Mac applications store their program code in the resource fork, where you find such items as window and menu definition, as well as the program's icons.

To allow the same application to run on both Motorola 68xxx-based Macintoshes and the newer Power Mac systems, some application developers have included *FAT binaries*, which store the Power Mac application code in the data fork.

When you transfer a Macintosh file to non-Mac system, there's no easy way to keep the two forks separate and you can end up either losing information, having two files (one for each fork), or something in between.

On the receiving end — at the file server — another AFP translator takes over and converts the AFP File System calls into file-system calls of the file server's operating system. This conversion is necessary because AFP servers now run on a variety of operating systems (NetWare, UNIX, and OpenVMS, for example). The workstation-based AFP translators are needed because Mac, MS-DOS, and Apple II workstations can use an AFP-based file server.

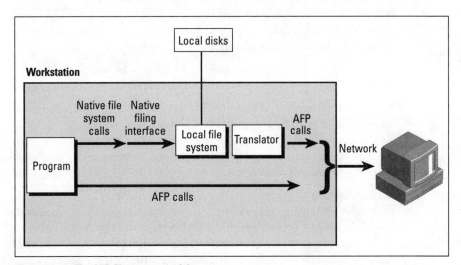

Figure 22-13: The AFP file access model.

# Managing a File Server

If you look back to our discussion of System 7's File Sharing feature in this chapter, you'll see that the administration of a distributed file-server system such as File Sharing is mostly left up to the individual. Centralized file servers not only offer more power for networked applications, such as databases and e-mail, but also consolidate management responsibilities. Usually only one person needs to take the responsibility of maintaining a centralized server.

Because centralized servers are so important to networks, we'll give you some tips next for setting up and maintaining a centralized AFP server. We'll also use this example server to illustrate some server features and cover two issues that can be applied to all types of servers — fault-tolerant server design and making server backups.

## Setting up a server

Apple has worked hard to make installation of the AppleShare software as simple as possible. AppleShare uses the same Installer program you find with system upgrades and other programs from third-party vendors. So it's familiar to many network managers and individual users. All you have to do is select the Mac hard disk that you want the AppleShare software installed on and click the Install button. The server will be ready to run the next time you restart that Mac. To help decide which version of AppleShare you should use, consult Table 22-2.

In order for users to access any files on the AppleShare server, you have to create accounts for them. Partly because both AppleShare and System 7's File Sharing are based on the AppleTalk Filing Protocol, the procedures for setting up users and groups of users are almost identical.

Rather than merely repeating Apple's instructions for installing the software, we'll explain some ways to make your AppleShare server more efficient.

First, use as powerful a Mac as possible for the AppleShare server. Remember that a centralized file server is going to be accessed by many users at the same time, and a more powerful Mac, such as the Quadra or Apple's new Workgroup Server series, is better equipped to process the server's requests because of the faster microprocessor found on those machines.

Second, buy a big (1 gigabyte or larger) and fast hard disk for your server. Again, remember that many users will store files on this system, so you'll need the larger hard disk. And a faster access time will also make the server more efficient when many users are accessing it. Disk prices are dropping rapidly. (You can buy disks of that size for about 70 cents per megabyte right now. By the time you read this, it will be cheaper.) So you have to balance your desire to not keep buying more disks every week with fiscal sense of not buying a lot of expensive disk when you won't need it for many months. Or, in simpler terms, you may want to wait to buy disk space because it will be cheaper soon.

## Table 22-2
### AppleShare Specifications and Recommendations

|  | AppleShare 3 | AppleShare 4 | AppleShare Pro |
|---|---|---|---|
| Concurrent logons | 120 | 150 | 200 |
| Open Files | 346 | 346 | 5,000 |
| Number of hard disks | 7 | 7 | 20 |
| Users | 8,192 | 8,192 | 8,192 |
| Groups | 8,192 | 8,192 | 8,192 |
| Users in group | 8,191 | 8,191 | 8,191 |
| Recommended Active Users | 15 | 30 | 50 |
| Max Concurrent Connections | 120 | 150 | 200 |
| Apple II logon | yes | yes | no |
| Apple II network startups | 40 | n/a | n/a |
| Minimum RAM | 4 M | 8 M | 16 M |
| Minimum System Software | 7.0 | 7.1 | A/UX 3.0.1 |
| Supported Platforms | Any Mac Centris 610, Quadra 700, 800, 950; Apple Workgroup Server 60, 80, 6150, 8150, 9150 Apple Workgroup Server 95 | | |

Note: The sum of users and groups cannot exceed 8192, and the recommended limit is 2000.

Finally, allocate the RAM on your server wisely. With AppleShare 2.0.1, the server software used up to a maximum of 2.5M of RAM for a RAM cache to improve performance. Installing more RAM than that on an AppleShare server didn't make sense because the software wouldn't use the extra RAM. You should add more than 2.5M of RAM to a server only when you plan to install other server-based software, such as electronic mail or a print server.

Things have changed with the introduction of AppleShare 3, 4, and AppleShare Pro. With this software, AppleShare can and will use as much memory as you have in your machine. Give it lots because memory is very cheap, and make sure that AppleShare can get at it. With newer versions of AppleShare, you can increase the amount of memory allocated for the File Server program by selecting the program icon, choosing Get Info from the File menu, and increasing the number in the Preferred Size box.

## Creating fault-tolerant servers

We discussed fault tolerance previously in the context of network design (see Chapter 5, "Network Design 101"). For file servers, the concept is the same: Fault tolerance means that the system can continue functioning when a component fails.

If you're dealing with a single file server, fault tolerance focuses on the hard disks attached to your server. A new technology, called RAID (Redundant Arrays of Inexpensive Disks) is designed to increase both performance and reliability.

RAID subsystems are arrays of disk drives along with controllers and firmware (see Figure 22-14). They combine two different concepts to achieve their goals. *Disk striping* transparently distributes data across multiple disks to make them appear as a single, larger and faster disk. Striping speeds up disks by allowing multiple I/O operations to occur in parallel. The problem with disk striping is that it greatly decreases reliability. If you stripe eight disks together to form a single virtual drive, then your reliability is only ⅛ as high as with any one drive.

To solve this problem, RAID uses a second concept, called *redundancy*. With redundant operation (called *disk mirroring, shadowing,* or *duplexing* before RAID became popular), the same information is written to multiple disk drives. At its extreme, one could write everything to two sets of drives, thereby turning the eight disk *stripe set* into a 16 disk *stripe and shadow set*.

The goal of RAID is to balance different performance, reliability, and budget criteria to fit your needs. RAID was first described in a 1988 paper by three faculty members — David Patterson and Randy Katz of the University of California, Berkeley, and Garth Gibson, now at Carnegie-Mellon University. At that time, they listed five levels of RAID, numbered 1 through 5. Since then, these researchers and their colleagues have refined their views and now offer seven levels, numbered 0 to 6.

Apple's newer Workgroup Servers, such as the 9150, include Apple RAID software (an OEM product originally from Conley, Inc.), which supports RAID levels 1 and 0. Ciprico's Rimfire, Conley's SR1 and SR2, CORE International's CORE, FWB's SledgeHammer, Mass Microsystems's MASSterArray, and MicroNet Technology's RAVEN all offer Apple-compatible RAID disk storage subsystems.

RAID level 5 arrays are your best bet for fault-tolerant server configurations. These balance performance with fault tolerance. In a RAID 5 array, any one of the disks can be removed while the array is operating and no loss of data will occur. A RAID 5 array typically has between four and eight disk drives integrated into a single volume. Typically, the capacity of the volume is 80 percent or more of the total aggregate capacity of the drives without RAID technology. This is a big improvement on disk shadowing, where half of your disk space is wasted!

If you're willing to treat power outages as a "fault" that needs to be guarded against — and we suggest you do — you should consider purchasing an uninterruptible power supply (UPS) for your file server.

The UPS is designed to provide battery power when the normal power in the building is disrupted. UPS battery life is a consideration when shopping for a

UPS — shorter UPS lives are designed to give your server enough time for a standard shutdown; a longer life UPS lets you keep on working with the server as if nothing happened. But we must warn that if you do install a UPS for your server, make it a regular practice to check the battery. There's nothing more embarrassing than to find out that the battery is dead when the building power dies.

When shopping for a UPS, don't immediately buy the most expensive one. Many UPSes have expensive circuitry to handle special kinds of power failures that you may or may not have in your area. For example, if you suffer from brownouts, you will probably have to pay a lot more for the same level of UPS than if you only suffer from occasional blackouts. Don't be bamboozled into buying more UPS than you need.

## Backing up servers

The more often people use a server to store their crucial files and applications, the more they expect the data to be undamaged. But let's face it — no computer's perfect, and they do crash occasionally. Also, there are users who occasionally delete the wrong files. A solution to all these problems is the habit of making regular backups of the server.

The following are the most common ways to back up a file server:

❖ You can select all the files on the server disk and use the Mac's drag-and-copy procedure to copy all the files to another disk attached to the server.

❖ You can select all the files on the server disk and use the Mac's drag-and-copy procedure to copy all the files to a disk attached to your own Mac.

❖ You can copy all, or selected, files from the server to another disk or tape drive attached to the server, using software that backs up files at preprogrammed intervals.

❖ You can copy the files from the server to your own Mac, using software that backs up files at preprogrammed intervals.

Each approach has advantages and disadvantages.

The drag-and-copy approach is the simplest method, and it has the advantage of preserving the native format of the Mac files. No encoding or compression of the files into special proprietary formats are involved. However, there are two potential problems with this approach. First, unless you're the network manager or another user with access privileges to all files on the server, you won't be able to copy all the files from the server. Second, if you want to also copy the server's system folder, you'll have to disconnect all the users from the server, shut down the server, and then restart the server before making the copy.

BACKGROUNDER

## RAID Levels

The seven RAID levels are shown in Figure 22-14, a variation on one prepared by the original RAID researchers. We describe the RAID levels below in words to help you see the subtle differences. You will probably want to have the diagram close at hand.

RAID 0: This is simple disk striping, where no data is written redundantly. This has the best write performance of any RAID level. Different blocks of data are written to different drives in parallel to speed writes.

RAID 1: All data is written redundantly to two disk drives. This is often called mirroring or shadowing, especially when only two disks are used. This gives the best read performance of any RAID level (and the worst storage efficiency).

RAID 2: This level applies memory-style ECC (error correcting codes) to disk systems. RAID 2 can detect and correct any error where any disk (or subset of a disk) goes bad. It requires fewer disks than RAID 1, and can tolerate the greatest range of disasters.

RAID 3: Because it is easy to see when a disk has failed, the complex ECC scheme isn't necessary for most classes of disk problems. Using this scheme, a single disk is used for a parity bit and can tolerate any single disk failure. RAID 4 is a variation on RAID 3, which uses blocks as the level of parity, rather than bits. Although RAID 3 and RAID 4 can both recover from any single disk failing, they have inherent performance limitations built into their architecture.

RAID 5: This scheme uses block-level parity (rather than the bit-level parity of RAID 3) but spreads the parity information across all disks rather than centralizing it on a single disk. This has performance advantages over both RAID 3 and RAID 4 and loses none of the reliability.

RAID 6: A variation on RAID 5, this scheme uses an additional disk for additional parity information. The performance will be slightly slower than RAID 5, but this level will be able to tolerate a greater range of errors than RAID 5 (although not as many as RAID 1).

The second approach is basically the same as the first; you're just copying to a different hard disk. This method has three disadvantages. The first disadvantage is the same as for dragging and copying to a disk attached to the server: You may not be able to access all the files. The second disadvantage is that the system folder on an AppleShare server is invisible and cannot be selected for copying on the Mac desktop. This means that if you have special files or INITs in the server's system folder, they won't be backed up. Third, copying files from the server to your Mac's disk will create a great deal of network traffic — the only time you may be able to back up an entire server is at night, which is no fun. That's why backup systems that can be preprogrammed to run on their own are better, as you'll see next.

One of the most popular ways to back up a file server is to use a tape drive with special backup software, such as NetStream (PCPC, Inc.) or Retrospect (Dantz Software). These systems can be programmed to run in the wee hours of the night, when no one else is likely to be using the server. And even if someone is using the server, these systems usually are capable of recognizing a file in use and will skip that file in the backup.

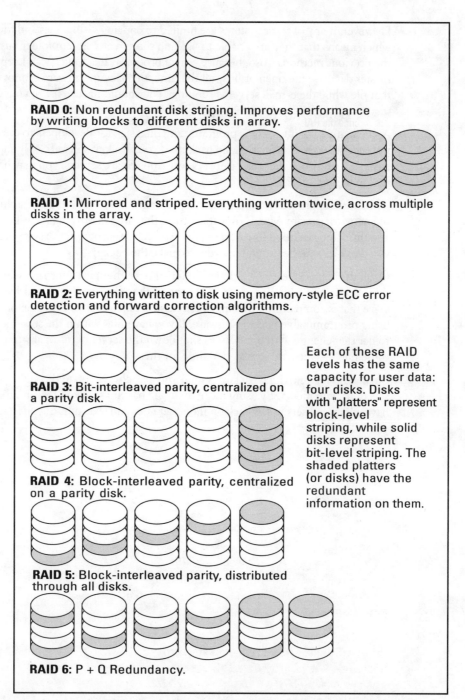

**RAID 0:** Non redundant disk striping. Improves performance by writing blocks to different disks in array.

**RAID 1:** Mirrored and striped. Everything written twice, across multiple disks in the array.

**RAID 2:** Everything written to disk using memory-style ECC error detection and forward correction algorithms.

**RAID 3:** Bit-interleaved parity, centralized on a parity disk.

**RAID 4:** Block-interleaved parity, centralized on a parity disk.

**RAID 5:** Block-interleaved parity, distributed through all disks.

**RAID 6:** P + Q Redundancy.

Each of these RAID levels has the same capacity for user data: four disks. Disks with "platters" represent block-level striping, while solid disks represent bit-level striping. The shaded platters (or disks) have the redundant information on them.

Figure 22-14: RAID configurations can provide both increased performance and fault tolerance

However, many of these systems are limited to copying visible files and folders, which means that they are unable to back up the server's system folder, just as with the previous methods. Also, because e-mail programs like QuickMail keep the master database file open or busy all the time, the backup software cannot back up that file while the e-mail server is running. You should make a list of your file server applications and use that to qualify your backup program.

AppleShare 3 includes a new programming interface for developers to create software for such tasks as unattended backup. If your backup software only supports advanced features when run against newer AppleShare servers, you may have a reason to upgrade.

The fourth approach listed is to have a preprogrammed system copying files over the network to your Mac. This suffers from the same disadvantages as the second and third approaches. However, because you can preprogram the system, at least you don't have to be around in order to make the backup.

Of all the approaches, which do we prefer? To us, the third approach seems the best. When you're planning your file server, try to buy another disk drive or tape drive that is compatible with AppleShare and set up a regular schedule of backups using programmable backup software. If you have files within the server's system folder that change with use, plan to shut down the server occasionally to back up those files — weekends are a good time for this.

Finally, no matter which backup system you use, always rotate through multiple sets of backup media. By using more than one backup set, you'll ensure that you have additional sets to fall back on if one set goes bad (backups of your backup, if you will).

# CHAPTER 22 CONCEPTS AND TERMS

- File-transfer utilities may be adequate tools for sharing files when you're working in a small workgroup.

- Distributed (or peer-to-peer) file servers are good for small workgroups, but they bog down with usage of more than 10-12 users.

- Centralized file servers are best for large databases and groups.

- The AppleTalk Filing Protocol includes rules for translating file names between the Mac OS, MS-DOS, and ProDOS conventions.

- RAID arrays are a good way to protect your data on a file server because this technique duplicates the data automatically.

- File servers should have uninterruptible power supplies.

- Not all files on an AppleShare server can be backed up while the server is running. You must verify carefully that your backup utility works with all your file-server applications.

**centralized file server**

This type of file server offers more power for networked applications, such as databases and e-mail. It also consolidates management responsibilities. Usually only one person needs to take the responsibility of maintaining a centralized server.

**disk striping**

Transparently distributes data across multiple disks to make them appear as a single, larger, and faster disk. Striping speeds up disks by allowing multiple I/O operations to occur in parallel. The problem with disk striping is that it greatly decreases reliability. If you stripe eight disks together to form a single virtual drive, then your reliability is only ⅛ as high as with any one drive.

**drop folder**

To create a drop folder, you allow users (a group or everyone) to make changes, but not to see folders or files. Your users can add files to the folder, but they do not see what's in the folder. This is a simple way to enable users to send files to you and ensure the privacy of what they send you, as only you as the owner of the folder can manipulate the files within a drop folder.

**file sharing method**

This method of sharing files uses a file server. In this system, a user can put a file of interest on the server so other users can see the file without copying it to their Macs.

**file-transfer method**

A method to transfer files. To illustrate, one user sends you a copy of a file, whereupon you can hack away at it to your heart's content. If you want the original user to see what you did with the file, you can return a copy of the modified file to him or her.

**folders**

See volume.

**RAID (Redundant Arrays of Inexpensive Disks)**

The goal of RAID is to balance different performance, reliability, and budget criteria to fit your needs. RAID was first described in a 1988 paper by three faculty members — David Patterson and Randy Katz of the University of California, Berkeley, and Garth Gibson, now at Carnegie-Mellon University. At that time, they listed five levels of RAID, numbered 1 through 5. Since then, these researchers and their colleagues have refined their views and now offer seven levels, numbered 0 to 6.

**redundancy**

RAID uses redundancy to write the same information to multiple disk drives. At its extreme, one could write everything to two sets of drives.

**store-and-forward**

A distinct characteristic of e-mail. A user can send a message or file to you even when you're not on the network; the server stores the message until the next time you're on the network. Then, when you log on to the e-mail system, the message (or file) will be transferred to your Mac, even if the original user is no longer on the network. This makes information exchange much easier.

**volume**

Each disk in a file server system is usually called a *volume,* which is mounted by the file server. The file server then controls access to each of the mounted volumes, first at the level of the entire volume, then at the level of individual directories (or *folders,* with the Mac interface), or in some systems, at the level of individual files.

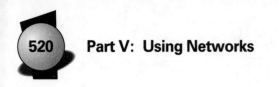

# Using Groupware

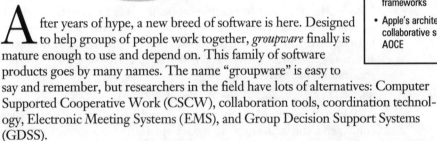

**IN THIS CHAPTER**

- Understanding what groupware is and how it can help your organization

- A model that helps you compare groupware products in a consistent way

- A survey of groupware products for the Macintosh, including Lotus Notes, group schedulers, electronic meeting systems, conferencing systems, and groupware frameworks

- Apple's architecture for collaborative software: AOCE

After years of hype, a new breed of software is here. Designed to help groups of people work together, *groupware* finally is mature enough to use and depend on. This family of software products goes by many names. The name "groupware" is easy to say and remember, but researchers in the field have lots of alternatives: Computer Supported Cooperative Work (CSCW), collaboration tools, coordination technology, Electronic Meeting Systems (EMS), and Group Decision Support Systems (GDSS).

The names are confusing because no one can agree on a definition. Is electronic mail a form of groupware? Maybe. What about an airline reservation system? Probably not. A multiuser sales and inventory database? If you insist. A real-time conferencing package? Almost certainly. The debate continues.

Groupware has long been the stomping ground of universities. Who else would describe how a product had been used to "contextualize" information? Like artificial intelligence, groupware has moved gradually from the research and academic communities to the real world of business workgroups. The natural crossover point always has been big organizations with lots of money, including the U.S. Department of Defense, Big Six accounting firms (including Arthur Andersen and Price Waterhouse), IBM, and General Motors.

Now groupware has begun to filter down to small organizations. Software vendors have started to build tools that can be useful to organizations that don't have $100,000 and 20 man-years to spend.

**QUOTABLES**

"Toto, I don't think we're in Kansas anymore."

— L. Frank Baum,
*The Wizard of OZ*

# Understanding Groupware

At the root of groupware is the late-1960s work of Peter Drucker, who was one of the first to notice that the United States was changing from a nation of farmers and manufacturers to a nation of "knowledge workers." As soon as it became obvious that Drucker was right, people such as Douglas Engelbart starting trying to figure out how to make these knowledge workers more efficient. Remember Doug Engelbart? He helped invent the mouse, the workstation, graphical user interfaces, and remote procedure calls. From those inventions, it was a short step to making groups of knowledge workers more efficient — as groups.

While researchers and experimenters began to flesh out the idea of groupware, ARPAnet — the Internet's great granddaddy — began to spread its tendrils into universities and think tanks across the United States. (See Chapter 26, "Exploring Mac LANs and the Internet," for a brief introduction to the Internet.)

Initially, the ARPAnet was justified as being a way to share expensive resources such as big CPUs, disks, and other special-purpose hardware. When people got onto the ARPAnet, though, they found other applications, including conferencing systems (sometimes called bulletin boards) and electronic mail. The first groupware applications had arrived.

The explosive growth of electronic mail and conferencing wasn't due just to the ARPAnet, however. Many technologies (and a good dose of government funding) combined to make the first groupware applications a roaring success. Among those technologies were interactive timesharing, inexpensive computers, and local and wide area networks.

The obvious benefits of groupware for businesses have led to a massive amount of hype. Vendors have renamed products "groupware" simply to attract attention. And vaporware is ever-present. A recent Groupware study by International Data Group listed 17 Macintosh groupware applications; we could find only 12 that were real products.

Meanwhile, the real innovators in the groupware world have begun to bring mature products into the playing field. University researchers and corporate R&D centers are slowly commercializing the fruits of their labors through large software houses (such as Lotus Development Corporation, with its mammoth Notes product) and tiny startup firms.

## A model for groupware

When you dive into the wild world of groupware, you'll find a perplexing pile of products and pronouncements. To make sense of it all, we suggest using a framework to help group the products. We followed the lead of other researchers and divided the field along three axes: time, place, and structure (see Figure 23-1)

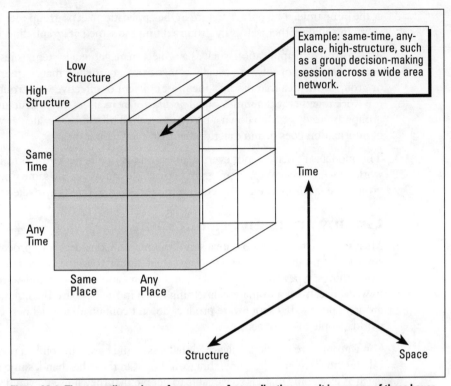

Example: same-time, any-place, high-structure, such as a group decision-making session across a wide area network.

**Figure 23-1: The many dimensions of groupware. Any application can sit in any one of these boxes. New "smart" electronic-mail systems are any-time, any-place, and high-structure, whereas video conferencing is same-time, any-place, and low-structure.**

In this model, *time* is when the group works together. *Same time* means that the group activity happens simultaneously. Screen-sharing applications, such as Farallon Computing's Timbuktu, are same-time groupware. The opposite of same time is any time. Electronic mail (*e-mail*) is any-time groupware; it works just as well spread across time.

*Place* is where the group works. A meeting in a single conference room is a same-place meeting. Groupware for that kind of meeting is same-place groupware. A package that helps members of a group vote anonymously on items in a meeting is same-time, same-place groupware. Most groupware applications, though, are any-place applications. They don't care whether you're at your desk or on the road, as long as you can dial in. A bulletin-board system is a good example of any-place groupware.

*Structure* divides applications based on how they view information. A low-structure application, such as a group text editor, doesn't care what kind of information you put in it; a group text editor just lets multiple people write text in the same document at the same time. The only structure in the application keeps group members from stomping all over themselves by group-editing the same paragraph, line, or word.

A high-structure application, such as a project management system, is just the opposite. This kind of software usually comes from a particular management theory or group-work idea that predicts the most efficient or effective way group members can work together. Sometimes called *fascistware* by its users, high-structure groupware leads a group down a particular path. The software manages what kind of information goes in and exactly what that information means.

This model isn't perfect; not every application fits in one neat little box. But in a world in which virtually any program two people can use at the same time is called groupware, it's important to categorize the products so that they make sense.

## Groupware in an organization

Most software tries to automate a single operation. Consider word processing and spreadsheet programs. These programs are designed to imitate very simple real-world things: typewriters, calculators, and graph paper. Good group-ware is harder to write, because it automates something much more complex: the interactions of a group of people. If a groupware product doesn't contain all the richness of the real world, people may not accept it.

Some groupware developers learned that lesson the hard way: build a poor graphical user interface, and the whole thing will flop. On the other hand, some groupware (such as electronic mail) is so valuable to people that they'll use it even if it looks like it was designed by a 12-year-old.

Picking out good groupware sounds pretty easy. You needs to answer only a few questions:

❖ Does the package fit well with my group's view of the world?

❖ Can it be adapted to work with my group's schedule and work flows?

❖ Is it available on all the platforms my group needs?

❖ Can it handle the group's pace without choking or collapsing?

Unfortunately, you can't answer any of these questions until you use the groupware package in a real group. Evaluating groupware isn't like evaluating a database; to determine whether groupware will work, you have to try it in a group. Nothing less will do.

Many products that look great in a technical evaluation fail miserably when used by some groups. The reason? Group interactions are so complex that users are unwilling to compromise for the sake of automation. Group scheduling and calendar systems are a good example. If the software can't emulate the subtle, behind-the-scenes negotiations that setting up a meeting can involve, people just won't use it.

# Groupware for the Macintosh

Groupware as vaporware is a familiar sight. This section gives you a whirlwind tour of groupware products for the Macintosh.

Mainframes are bad. Everyone knows that; it's drilled into us by every publication we read. A lot of rhetoric — "rightsizing," "getting rid of the glass house," and "re-engineering," for example — is putting the mainframe manufacturers out of business. When a mainframe application can be replaced by a single accountant running a spreadsheet program, getting rid of the mainframe is obviously a good idea.

Groups and mainframes, though, have a special affinity. It's a lot easier for a group of people to coordinate their work when all the data is stored in one place and computing is done on a central resource. "Distributed systems" sound good, but they're genuinely hard to develop and deploy. An intermediate step, however, exists between mainframes and fully distributed systems: *client/server computing*. Many client/server applications are being billed as groupware.

The connection isn't hard to make. Group members run the same application, but they look at the same data in different ways. The server-based databases help coordinate the group members' actions, and that function sounds like groupware. In a market in which "groupware" is a prime label, why not?

The developers of the new family of client/server applications have reinvented the mainframe. These developers have created a virtual mainframe, incorporating some of the best attributes of the behemoths that users worked so hard to get rid of. Fortunately, client/server groupware is politically correct.

## Lotus Notes

The authors of client/server groupware application authors have recreated the shared space of the mainframe. Users get the power of a shared database without giving up the friendliness of their desktop microcomputers.

In the client/server groupware business, there is a single dominant player: Lotus, the company that brought the word "groupware" to everyone's lips. With half a million Lotus Notes licenses out there, Notes has become the standard by which client/server applications are measured.

When Lotus introduced Release 3 of Notes in early 1993, it jumped into the Macintosh groupware business with both feet. Well, maybe with one foot: it took Lotus until 1994 to come up with a version of the Macintosh Notes client that worked with most existing Notes servers. In 1994, Lotus began shipping UNIX and NetWare NLM Notes servers to complement the existing MS-DOS and OS/2 platforms.

## What is Notes?

Notes itself is not an application — Notes is somewhere between a programming language and an operating system, with a database thrown in. As an off-the-shelf software product, Notes is completely useless out of the box. If you want Notes to do anything useful, you've got to build (or buy) a Notes application. Building an application is both more and less work than you're used to. Writing the application's "code" is simple; the hard part is figuring out what to write.

Notes is a true client/server system. The server (or servers) keeps all the data, handles the security, and, most important, performs all the database processing. The client is responsible for user interface: presenting Notes information to the user.

The Notes server not only responds to Notes client requests but also performs tasks of its own, independent of any client requests. These loosely coupled tasks are an important part of Notes, enabling the Notes server do things that the Notes developers didn't have to think of in advance.

One Notes database, for example, acts as the catalog of all databases. Once a day, each Notes server updates this catalog as a separate task. By breaking the link between creation of a database and building the database catalog, the Notes developers got a simpler and stronger product. The developers didn't have to think of everything and consequently build one huge program; they just had to make room for others to build programs that run in the Notes environment.

Notes servers talk to Notes clients by using a variety of different network protocols. Depending on the platform (Windows, OS/2, or Macintosh), Notes clients can use Banyan VINES, NetBIOS, NetWare SPX, dial-up connections (called XPC), AppleTalk, and TCP/IP. A Notes network doesn't have to select one protocol exclusively; multiple protocols can be loaded at the same time.

### Notes building blocks

Notes divides the world into *databases*. Every bit of data in a Notes environment, including electronic mail, is stored in a Notes database. Most Notes applications need no traditional programming; the database itself contains all the code needed to operate the application.

The basic element of information in a Notes database is called a *document*. A document in Notes is roughly the same as a tuple, row, or record in a relational database; it's the basic unit of manipulation, and all the parts (called *fields*) of a single document are related to one another. Notes uses the term "document" instead of "record" to emphasize the freeform nature of a document.

Documents are divided into nine types of fields. Some subset of the fields in a database can be grouped in a *form*, and databases can contain many different kinds of forms. A form is used to present the information to the Notes user or to gather information from a Notes user for storage in the database.

When a single Notes document is shown to a user, a form is used. When multiple Notes documents are shown, a *view* is used. Views are designed to help users navigate the database. Databases often have many different views.

Notes has a very flexible security model, which can apply at all levels of database access. The database itself can contain *access control lists* showing who can and cannot open the database. At the document level, Notes maintains lists of users who can update or even read a particular document. Within a document, each field can be encrypted.

Although most of the action occurs when a document is added or updated, Notes also supports *background macros*, the equivalent of batch processing. These macros can handle reporting, alarm conditions, and nightly synchronization of multiserver databases.

## Notes application programming

The beauty of Notes is what you don't have to worry about. Every part of Notes is automatically maintained as a multiuser database. A Notes developer doesn't have to explicitly lock and unlock records, worry about propagating updates, or care whether the application is distributed across one or a thousand servers. In many ways, Notes takes programmers back to the days of mainframe- and minicomputer-applications development. Notes makes a distributed set of microcomputers and servers appear as a monolithic platform for developing applications, without requiring much application-programming expertise.

In Notes, electronic mail also is tightly integrated into every application's environment. Any document can be sent via electronic mail at almost any stage.

Notes clients use a windowing user interface to provide a uniform look and feel to all Notes applications. When a user starts a Notes client on a Macintosh, OS/2, or Microsoft Windows personal computer, the client brings up a screen of icons that represent database applications. To start an application, the user just clicks the application's icon.

Notes doesn't make much distinction between application users and application programmers. Any Notes user is free to create database applications on a local workstation (although administrator privileges are required to make an application available on a server).

The Notes client/server architecture is built for heavy-duty environments, with dozens of servers spanning multiple companies and handling thousands of users.

Beyond responding to client requests and running asynchronous tasks, Notes servers can perform sophisticated security and database functions, as you learn in the following section.

### Notes security and database features

Notes is prepared to be as secure as you need it to be, offering a strong set of built-in encryption tools. Notes uses the RSA public key cryptosystem. (RSA encryption is discussed in Chapter 15, "Securing an AppleTalk Network.") With public key encryption, Notes not only can keep information confidential, but also can provide electronic signatures on documents and data-integrity controls (which ensure that a document has not been tampered with).

Notes lets you encrypt electronic-mail messages, documents in databases, and even individual fields within documents. You could use this last feature to keep an employee's salary a secret; you wouldn't have to worry whether every application that accesses the information is enforcing data security.

Notes security enables you to build intercompany networks for departments that don't necessarily trust one another, restricting access to particular databases. Linking two companies through a Notes network also links the electronic mail systems.

When two (or more) Notes systems can communicate, the Notes software can replicate the systems' databases automatically. *Replication* is the process of applying database updates and changes so that copies of the same database remain consistent. Notes can replicate databases between servers or between a client and a server. If your company has a sales force in the field, for example, each salesperson could carry a PowerBook with a copy of the sales database. Every time a salesperson dials into Notes to send and receive mail, Notes automatically (and transparently) updates the databases to upload new order and customer information and to download new additions to the corporate database.

Database replication also occurs among servers. Distributing copies of commonly used databases among multiple Notes servers can speed retrieval time significantly.

### Notes in the organization

Notes itself isn't a groupware application at all, in the same way that COBOL isn't a business data processing application. Notes is a platform for building groupware applications; it takes care of much of the hard stuff that groupware developers need to handle.

For the groupware *buyer*, Notes is almost completely useless out of the box. For a groupware *developer*, Notes can form the operating system, database, communications subsystem, and programming language, all rolled into one package. Notes' all-in-one architecture makes developers very happy. Most Notes users are running custom-written applications — a fact that translates into dollars for the corps of Notes consultants and VARs (Value-Added Resellers) that have sprung up.

Although a few Notes applications can be purchased off the shelf for immediate use, the great majority of Notes installations are heavily customized. Notes customizations don't necessarily tie you to a single software vendor, though. Notes' architecture encourages applications and users to communicate — and makes that communication easy.

The ideas behind Notes applications are familiar to Macintosh users: make every application look the same; bring functions like electronic mail to every application; have each application use the same conventions in forms and dialog boxes; and make sure that the system automatically takes care of the details of management, rather than burdening end users or network managers. Like the Macintosh itself, Notes is based on the idea of one training session for all applications — even ones that haven't been written yet. Good Notes applications work together without much stress on developers or, more important, end users.

# Group scheduling systems

People spend an awful lot of time in meetings. In many organizations, the job of manager means going from one meeting to the next, all day long. The demand for some sort of groupware to ease the pain of continuous meetings is high.

Unfortunately, the developers of electronic meeting systems haven't chosen the Macintosh as a platform. Products such as Ventana Corporation's GroupSystems, which brings 16 meeting-management and support tools into the meeting room itself, don't have commercial Macintosh-based brethren. Instead, Macintosh developers have concentrated on another aspect of meetings: scheduling them.

## Meeting Maker XP

The acknowledged king of multiuser scheduling programs is Meeting Maker XP from ON Technology. The "XP" stands for cross-platform: Meeting Maker supports both Macintosh and Windows clients. To handle the network issues of connecting Mac and Windows systems to the same server, ON Technology includes an IPX (NetWare) protocol stack. Meeting Maker coordinates calendars, handling the scheduling of meetings, conference rooms, and resources (such as slide projectors).

Using Meeting Maker, you can propose a meeting with a series of guests. Meeting Maker finds an appropriate time slot by comparing guests' calendars and sends out invitations, along with any agenda you provide. Guests receive notifications of the proposed meeting and can agree or refuse to attend the meeting (or put off making a decision).

Meeting Maker's calendars also can be used for other activities, such as private appointments. Any entry in your calendar can have an associated reminder to help keep you on time. In addition, Meeting Maker supports both private and group to-do lists, handling them in much the same way it does calendars.

Meeting Maker doesn't have all the bells and whistles of its mainframe precursors, but it makes up for that in ease of use. The product doesn't require user training, and it uses the visual representation of a calendar in a very natural way. Handling your calendar is simple and intuitive.

ON Technology also thought about people who move around a lot. Meeting Maker doesn't require you to sit at your own workstation to check your calendar, and it doesn't require you to be in contact with the server. This arrangement is ideal for PowerBook users. Sign on to Meeting Maker at least once before you leave the office; the program automatically grabs a copy of your calendar, and you can hit the road. While you're out of touch with the office, you can propose and respond to meetings. These actions are queued up until the next time you connect to the server. Meeting Maker then synchronizes your calendar and sends and receives all pending actions — all without any special thought on your part.

### Other group scheduling groupware

Group scheduling is such an obvious application that Meeting Maker has lots of competition, including Milum Corporation's Office Tracker Pro, Now Software's Now Up To Date, Microsoft Schedule+, and WordPerfect Symmetry (formerly WordPerfect Office).

Milum Corporation's Office Tracker Pro takes a slightly different approach from Meeting Maker. Office Tracker Pro has evolved from an automated "in/out board" package to a product designed for a different kind of office environment, one in which the scheduling of meetings is not quite so contentious.

Now's Up To Date takes the portable features available in Meeting Maker XP one step further. With this product, you can export calendar and scheduling information to a variety of personal schedulers, including the popular Sharp Wizard. (At this time, none of the group scheduling software packages supports the Newton PDAs (Personal Digital Assistants), but that support is sure to come very soon.)

Microsoft and WordPerfect both provide group scheduling capabilities in their larger office-automation packages. Schedule+, from Microsoft, works only as part of a Microsoft Mail network. Schedule+ uses Microsoft Mail messages as a way of scheduling meetings; requests for meetings arrive as mail messages. WordPerfect Symmetry (formerly WordPerfect Office) works the same way. Calendar and meeting-scheduling functions are an integral part of the whole WordPerfect Symmetry system, which also includes facilities for electronic mail, reminders, phone messages, group notices, and to-do lists.

## Virtual-meeting groupware

Virtual meetings take place in the cybernetic ether. In a virtual meeting, people talking to one another in real time across a computer network. Groupware, sometimes combined with multimedia hardware, pulls these meetings together.

QUICK TIPS

## The Computer Is Your Friend

Tools like Meeting Maker can be used for more than just group coordination; a group member can manipulate these products to support a personal agenda. With Meeting Maker, someone calling a meeting can attach an agenda. A colleague of the authors' has long been known for hating to go to meetings — and uses this feature to his own advantage. When this fellow is invited to a meeting, he has only two responses. If the meeting scheduler fails to attach an agenda, the man's immediate reply (and refusal of the invitation to attend) is that anyone who calls a meeting without taking the time to prepare an agenda is wasting time. On the other hand, if the scheduler *does* attach an agenda, the reply is different: "I have reviewed your agenda and can see that I can add nothing to this meeting." Invitation refused.

---

The oldest company in the Macintosh virtual-meeting business is Farallon Computing. Farallon's Timbuktu package was designed as a way for two Macintosh users to share a single screen; the product later became widely accepted as a way to manage AppleShare servers remotely. Farallon has extended Timbuktu to create a build-it-yourself virtual-meeting environment.

With Timbuktu, multiple networked Macintosh (or Windows) users can view one another's screens. Timbuktu distinguishes between observers, who can only see what's happening, and controllers, who can drive the remote Macintosh as though it were local. A shared screen is called a *host;* observers and controllers together are called *guests.*

Using Timbuktu, the members of a networked workgroup could edit a word processing document, draw in a drawing package, chart data from a spreadsheet, and pull information out of a corporate database. Because Timbuktu is logically independent of the application on the shared screen, users can continue working in the programs with which they feel most comfortable.

Aspects, from Group Technologies, is virtual-meeting software with lots of groupware support built in. With Aspects, a group of Macintoshes can be linked in a virtual meeting that supports shared editing, painting, and drawing programs. Aspects' shared tools are part of the Aspects product, so you can't use your normal word processing program in the shared environment. Because Aspects shares at the application level instead of at Timbuktu's screen level, however, conference members don't have to view the same part of the same document at the same time. Aspects' shared documents (both text and graphics) can be tightly linked in "What You See Is What I See" views (*WYSIWIS*, pronounced "wizzy-wiz"), and participants can see different parts of the same document at the same time.

Aspects supports different types of *mediation* — the process of choosing who will draw or write next. With Aspects, the conference manager can choose to open a document in a free-for-all environment in which multiple participants can write at the same time, or the manager can restrict access so that only one person can edit at a time. In its one-at-a-time mode, Aspects enforces a round-robin style of editing. To edit something, you electronically raise your hand. If no one is editing at that time, you get editing control. If someone else is editing, you'll be put in a queue. When the current editor releases control, the first person in the queue gets editing control of the document.

A big difference between Aspects and Timbuktu is how each product uses the network. Because Timbuktu thinks in terms of screens, sharing large screens or color screens can use a lot of network bandwidth. For someone who is trying to join a conference by means of a dial-up modem, Timbuktu probably will be intolerably slow. Aspects has to handle only individual documents, however, so it transfers document-update information as things change, not entire screens of information. Aspects' update feature makes remote use via modem a lot more practical.

Timbuktu is a general-purpose screen-sharing application and is a good choice for environments in which small groups may want to share all sorts of applications in an impromptu way. Aspects has much more structure and a good set of meeting-specific tools; this product fits better in environments in which drawing, painting, and editing are typical group tasks.

## Any-time, any-place groupware

By far the most popular category of groupware is any-time, any-place products, also known as *asynchronous groupware*. One reason for the popularity of these products is that they permit almost anything to occur any time and any place. Electronic mail, for example, is the original groupware product — and the most successful. Chapter 24 covers e-mail in detail.

QUICK TIPS

### Another View of Group Editing

If you've ever tried to have a group edit a document, you know that keeping track of who's got what when and where can be a nightmare. Although group editing tools such as Aspects and Timbuktu are useful for simultaneous editing, the more pedestrian style of group writing also has software solutions. We really like ON Technology's Instant Update. All that Instant Update does is manage the process of group editing. Managing editing doesn't sound like much, but when members of a geographically dispersed team have to work together on a single document, Instant Update can be a life saver.

## Digital's TeamLinks

At the high end of the groupware/electronic-mail line are products such as WordPerfect Symmetry and Digital's TeamLinks.

WordPerfect Symmetry integrates into one package electronic-mail, calendar, and time-management functions, group scheduling, simple project management, and reminders.

TeamLinks, from Digital Equipment Corporation, is an office-automation product that combines many groupware products in a single package. Digital's entry is an attempt to move existing OpenVMS users to a user-friendly personal-computer interface. For that reason, TeamLinks still depends on server software running on minicomputers — software that's not very easy for a new installation to get up and running.

Nevertheless, TeamLinks is one of the few packages that really aims at enterprise-wide solutions. TeamLinks combines electronic mail, shared document libraries (*group memory*, in groupware terms), conferencing/bulletin-board software, and document routing in a single package. TeamLinks works with multiple clients, including OpenVMS, Ultrix (Digital's UNIX), and OSF/1 terminal and workstation users, as well as Macintosh and Microsoft Windows users.

Most TeamLinks applications are pretty familiar. The exception is TeamLinks Routing, which simplifies the process of routing forms and documents in organizations. This product allows you to create a form and then route it to a list of people who can update, approve, and sign it electronically. With a form-routing package such as TeamLinks Routing, you always know where a document is. No more losing things on crowded desks — TeamLinks Routing lets you lose them in crowded e-mail directories.

Digital is replacing TeamLinks with a new system, TeamWorks, which has better integration of tools and provides a unified view of a group's memory.

## Conferencing and bulletin-board systems

The groupware community likes to draw lines between the pedestrian and oh-so-common bulletin boards and sophisticated collaborative conferencing systems. Both systems are based on the same premise: users engaging in group discussion, spread across time and space. The issue of whether a particular package is a bulletin board or a conferencing system really isn't important. As with any groupware, the most important questions are "How well will my group accept and use this?" and "How does this software meet the needs of my group?" With the tremendous popularity of Internet news groups, CompuServe Forums, and PC bulletin-board systems all over the world, conferencing has become a national sport.

Most conferencing has been the domain of minicomputers and mainframes, but there are alternatives in the Macintosh world. ResNova's NovaLink is the most professional of the Macintosh-based bulletin-board systems, bringing together a host of bulletin-board features in a single *information server*.

NovaLink is a client/server application. End users connect over AppleTalk, TCP/IP, or X.25 networks or over modems. The information server supports electronic mail, file libraries, conference discussion groups, voting, real-time conferencing, and links to the Internet. NovaLink clients run one of ResNova's two Macintosh user interfaces or (for clients who don't have Macintoshes) a terminal-based user interface.

PacerForum, from Pacer Software, is a conferencing system aimed at small workgroups. A PacerForum system is divided into bulletin boards that contain various discussion-topics areas. PacerForum users post messages in discussion topics, using the full spectrum of Macintosh capabilities. A message can have attached documents from any other Macintosh application: spreadsheets, graphics, charts, and even sounds. PacerForum lets users indicate their level of interest in each bulletin board. For boards of high interest, PacerForum sends a notification every time a new response is posted on the board.

# Apple's Architecture for Collaboration

Macintosh software packages have one fundamental difference from their MS-DOS and Windows cousins: they all look about the same. That's a design goal. For example, every well-designed Macintosh application lets you leave the application ("quit" is the Macintosh term) by pressing Command-Q or by selecting the last entry in the File menu. In turn, the File menu always is the leftmost application menu on-screen. One key idea behind Apple's Macintosh System software and the Macintosh ROMs is to make software uniform enough from package to package that users don't have to remember different commands to do the same thing. Apple has helped this similarity along by providing guidelines, tools, and routines to direct the interactions between users, applications, and the Macintosh operating system.

Every few years, Apple's designers carve out another piece of technology, standardize it, and document it in a series of manuals called *Inside Macintosh*. You saw (in Chapter 18) what Apple did with communications when it introduced the Communications Toolbox. More recently, Apple took on collaboration, and the architecture is called *Apple Open Collaboration Environment* (AOCE).

The brain behind the plan is Gursharan Sidhu, the fellow who designed the original AppleTalk. Sidhu brought together families of products in a unified architecture that can be used by collaborative applications and collaborating people. AOCE isn't the answer to every application writer's dreams, but it does provide a wide range of services that are common to lots of collaborative applications.

The first AOCE software to be released is called PowerTalk, available as part of Apple's System 7 Pro product. PowerTalk brings the functions of the AOCE environment to your desktop Macintosh, and it includes some basic client features that facilitate the interface between you and any AOCE applications.

Along with PowerTalk, Apple has shipped two products under the PowerShare name: a PowerShare mail and message server, and a PowerShare catalog and authentication server. PowerShare is to AOCE as AppleShare is to files: servers for collaboration information. PowerShare servers act as mail servers and information gateways, and otherwise broker the AOCE information.

System 7 Pro essentially is Apple's System 7 (version 7.1.1), along with the PowerTalk client software, support for AppleScript (Apple's scripting language), and a new version of QuickTime (Apple's multimedia file format). Apple is aiming System 7 Pro at business and professional communities; standard System 7 including system 7.5, which comes with every new Macintosh, is the company's choice for personal use.

## PowerTalk client software

Apple picked out five capabilities that it believed collaborative applications would need, and it concentrated on those. Not surprisingly, two of the capabilities are communications-based: *interapplication messages* and *interuser electronic mail*. Messages are a further refinement of the Apple Events technology introduced with System 7: a way for applications to talk to each other by using *store-and-forward* technology rather than direct communication.

The AOCE view of electronic mail also is a logical extension of existing technology. With AOCE electronic mail, users send documents to each other without concern about network topology, addressing, or document format. AOCE still doesn't solve the problem of sending a Lotus 1-2-3 worksheet to a Microsoft Excel user, but it should let the 1-2-3 user drop the worksheet in the mail while working in 1-2-3, rather than invoking a separate electronic-mail application.

The third AOCE capability is a uniform way of representing network resources: as entries in a *catalog*. Almost anything can go in a catalog. Electronic-mail addresses are obvious, as are things like AppleShare servers. AOCE also lets application developers build gateways between the AOCE catalog and other directories, such as an X.500 directory or a real phone book on a CD-ROM. Catalogs are represented as hierarchical sets of people, places, and things. All AOCE users share a single *global* catalog and may have their own private catalogs to store frequently accessed objects. For example, you might use a private catalog to store e-mail address entries for people with whom you correspond frequently. That setup saves the effort of browsing through the global catalog every time you want to send a message.

Authentication and privacy capabilities in PowerTalk can be used to enhance security at the same time they make security less intrusive. The first visible manifestation of this is the Apple keychain. A *keychain* is a place where you put keys — the passwords. Then you lock the keychain with yet another password. The passwords on the keychain are encrypted and protected. When you unlock the keychain by using its password, all the keys you stored there are available for AOCE to use in accessing resources. If your users commonly have to log on to three different AppleShare servers with three different passwords, they'll appreciate this capability; they won't have to type those passwords anymore. AOCE stores each user's server name and password on the keychain and uses those items automatically thereafter.

If you change your password on the server, of course, you'll have to manually change the password on the keychain. And if someone discovers the password to your keychain, he has access to all the resources you added to it.

A final security capability is *digital signatures*. Without diving into the math, AOCE digital signatures are elements you apply to a document that offer two guarantees. First, you are the person who signed the document, and no one else could have (unless you gave away your password). Second, digital signatures guarantee that any changes to the document will be detectable as part of the analysis of the signature.

The PowerTalk digital signature is based on RSA's *public key cryptosystem* algorithms. To get your digital *signer*, which is the piece of data which PowerTalk needs to digitally sign a document, you go through a goofy but fun procedure. First, you run a Mac application that generates a form on your laser printer. Then you take that form, along with three pieces of identification, to your friendly notary public. The notary verifies that you are who you say you are, and RSA then registers your digital signature. The intent of this procedure is that your digital signature becomes as legal as your written signature. You can take a digital signature to RSA and verify that you are indeed who you say you are (or at least who your IDs say you are). Apple includes a certificate for a free signer with each copy of the PowerTalk software.

You can, of course, use digital signatures without going through RSA. The point of getting involved with RSA is to build a digital signature that is useful in doing business that requires a real signature.

# The AOCE model

The AOCE model has five layers. Apple's architecture for AOCE is shown in Figure 23-2. The following sections describe the layers as they appear today.

## AOCE Applications

At the very top are applications that use the services. Apple includes only a couple of sample applications with AOCE: a very, very simple mail system and a simple digital-signature application. Even though Apple is providing the architecture, it expects third parties to provide the applications. To prove its commitment, Apple lined up 36 companies on AOCE-announcement day; all those companies committed to shipping products. Amazingly, products that work with PowerTalk were available from the very start, and more are shipping every month.

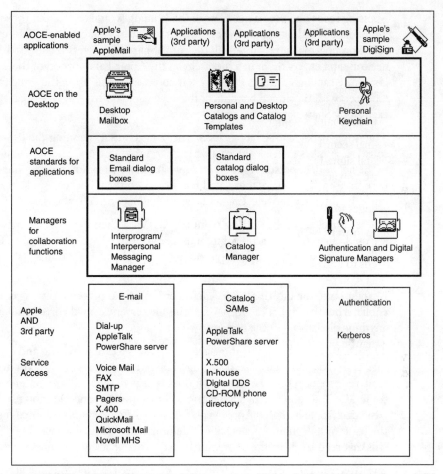

**Figure 23-2: The AOCE architecture includes a core, provided by Apple, that third parties can build on and around.**

## AOCE Desktop layer

Below the application layer is the Desktop layer. This layer includes simple interfaces to the Catalog (which stores network resources), the mailbox, and your PowerTalk keychain. The Catalog is the Finder of AOCE; it does for AOCE resources what the Macintosh Finder does for files and applications. You can pick things up, move them around, and look at them, more or less, but applications do the really interesting work. The mailbox and keychain also are Finder-like interfaces, but they have little power in the AOCE world. In the resources that the mailbox and keychain allow you to view, most of the work is done by AOCE-savvy applications.

Apple includes one access manager in the Catalog (you'll read about those in a few moments) for linking AppleTalk networks to PowerTalk catalogs. The AppleTalk catalog access manager gathers all the AppleShare file servers on an AppleTalk network and enters them in a hierarchy in the AppleTalk portion of the catalog. Using the catalog to access file servers is about as easy as using the standard Chooser, with the added benefits of the keychain: you have to type a password for each AppleShare server only once!

The AppleTalk Catalog has another type of entry: users running the PowerTalk software. Apple's goal for the catalog is clear: providing one interface to any object in the network (a person, file server, or whatever). Instead of having a file system here, an e-mail directory there, and file servers on the Chooser, Apple has tried to unify the interface for selecting and organizing network resources.

These entries are just a starting point for AOCE. When PowerShare mail servers are used, the artificial partitioning of users into AppleTalk zones can be eliminated. When third-party applications put things in AOCE catalogs, things will be even easier.

In addition to the global catalog, each user can have a personal catalog of entries copied from the global catalog — favorite file servers, e-mail correspondents, and anything else stored in the network-wide catalog.

The Desktop-layer mailbox interface allows users to see incoming and outgoing mail and to do some basic mail sorting. The interface doesn't allow you to actually read, receive, or reply to e-mail; all it does is display the mailbox contents, which some AOCE-enabled mail application will manipulate. The Desktop mailbox is so basic that Apple included AppleMail, a mail package that adds minimal functions to the basic AOCE mail. AppleMail just demonstrates electronic-mail capabilities; you will have to use one of the many third-party e-mail packages to do any real work.

Similarly, the PowerTalk keychain does little more than let you look at the keys you stored on the key chain. Actually putting keys on the chain is the responsibility of applications such as the Catalog. When you double-click an AppleShare file server in the Catalog, for example, an extra dialog box appears after you enter your file-server password, asking whether you want to put a new key (to unlock that server) on your keychain (see Figure 23-3). After you do, you won't have to type your password on that server again unless you change it.

**Figure 23-3: Dialog boxes like this one are part of AOCE. They let developers bring collaboration functionality to the Desktop in a consistent way across applications and vendors.**

## AOCE standards for applications

The dialog box shown in Figure 23-3 is part of the next layer of the AOCE architecture. The standards for applications layer is where Apple provides a set of higher-layer functions that the company feels are commonly used by collaborative applications. This layer makes the application designer's job easier, and, more important, it makes applications easier to learn, because all AOCE applications use the same user interface to perform the same function. This interface feature is an extension of the basic Macintosh philosophy: do the same thing the same way everywhere, and users have to learn it only once. This layer provides standard dialog boxes and other user-interface elements to "allow users to select addresses, add attachments, and approve documents in a consistent, intuitive way from within any application." (from Apple's product announcement for AOCE).

## AOCE managers for collaboration

AOCE managers for collaboration functions are below the application-standards layer. These managers present services to the AOCE applications above them: catalogs, messages, and security operations. Developers add services by calling the AOCE managers through an Apple-defined API. The managers shield application developers (and users) from the different technologies that AOCE managers bring together. The AOCE managers are linked to a series of access modules (the lowest layer in the AOCE architecture), which actually implement the services.

Consider the example of an AOCE electronic-mail user who wants to find someone's address. The e-mail application calls the catalog manager, which (in this hypothetical system) has links to a QuickMail *Service Access Module* (SAM), an X.500 SAM, and a SAM that reads a CD-ROM that contains the city telephone directory. All these kinds of addresses appear to the user in a uniform format, because the application uses the same dialog and selection boxes and because the application uses the catalog manager API to get the information. The directory databases may look very different, but it's the responsibility of the different SAMs to present the information to the catalog manager in the same format.

# CHAPTER  23    CONCEPTS AND TERMS

- Groupware is hard to define. You can think of groupware as being software that helps groups coordinate their activities.

- Good groupware is very hard to find and can't be evaluated in the same way as most other software; it has to be tested in your own environment.

- Many groupware products are available for the Macintosh, and these products fill different needs.

- Apple's AOCE architecture, PowerTalk client software, and PowerShare servers are Apple's building blocks for collaborative tools. Third-party vendors are expected to build software based on AOCE and to integrate AOCE into their existing products.

**Apple Open Collaboration Environment (AOCE)**
Apple's architecture for groupware in the Macintosh world.

**asynchronous groupware**
Any-time, any-place groupware.

**catalog**
In AOCE, catalogs are places where lists of objects are stored. These are similar to directories.

**client/server computing, client/server applications**
A networked computing system in which the two participating computers each use their own on-board processing capabilities to perform part of the task. In client/server systems, one of the two computers exerts more control over the transactions.

**database**
A collection of inter-related data that is created and managed by a database management system (DBMS).

**document**
In Lotus Notes, a document is a single record in a Notes database.

**fascistware**
Groupware which insists you do everything exactly the way it wants you to.

**fields**
A field is the physical unit of data in a record. Name, address, city, state, zip, and amount due are examples of fields in a record. A field is one or more bytes in size, and the collection of fields make up a record.

**form**
In Lotus Notes, a form is a subset of the fields in a particular document, arranged much like a paper form.

**group memory**
As group members gain knowledge individually, some organizations attempt to capture this knowledge in a single place for future use by the whole group. This is known as the group memory.

**interapplication messages**
Peer-to-peer data transmission.

**keychain**
In AOCE, multiple security authenticators (such as passwords) are gathered together and protected as a unit on a keychain.

**mediation**
The process by which a meeting or other gathering is kept orderly and on-track.

**public key cryptosystem**
An encryption/decryption system which does not depend on prior key exchange by participants. Instead, an encrypting party uses a publicly known key announced by the recipient to encrypt a message which only the decrypting party can decode.

**replication**
In Lotus Notes, databases automatically synchronize themselves so that the same database located on different systems is kept consistent. This process is called replication.

**signer**
In AOCE, a signer is the private key of a public key encryption system. Documents processed using the signer can then be decrypted using the public half of the encryption key and give assurance that only the possessor of the signer could have encrypted them. In effect, the signer allows for a digital signature.

**view**
In database management, a view is a special display of data that is created as needed. A view temporarily ties one or more records together so that the combined records can be displayed, printed, or queried as a single unit. Database managers normally give different users different views of the same database.

**WYSIWIS**
What You See Is What I See, an acronym often used in the groupware world to indicate a system which offers identical views of the same information to all participants.

CHAPTER TWENTY-FOUR

# Using Electronic Mail

IN THIS CHAPTER

- What features to look for when shopping for electronic mail

- How electronic mail stores and processes your messages

- How to link LAN-based electronic mail to other mail systems

- How to use facsimiles with e-mail

E lectronic mail, or *e-mail*, is rapidly becoming one of the major uses of networked Macs. This chapter first looks at the features that make up a good e-mail product and then explains some of the things you can do with e-mail.

## What Is E-Mail?

Simply put, electronic mail is a network application that enables you to send messages to other users over your network. These messages may include text, graphics, or sound and may have other files enclosed with them.

Every e-mail user has a unique name or address. This address is used for routing messages, just as the U.S. Postal Service uses your home address to deliver mail to you. The network equivalent of the post office, where postal workers store and sort your mail, is the *e-mail server*.

Just as with a letter sent through the postal service, when you want to send something to someone via e-mail, you decide on the format for your letter, write the letter, and then address it to the intended recipient. Clicking the Send button is the same as taking your letter to the nearest mailbox. The similarity between the postal service and e-mail probably is what has made e-mail so popular. The basic concepts are easy to grasp, making it simple for users to become comfortable with e-mail.

QUOTABLES

"Evil communications corrupt good manners."

— I Corinthians 15:33

Another reason for the popularity of e-mail is its convenience. This convenience is primarily because of *store-and-forward* architecture. This capability allows you to compose e-mail messages at your Mac and then send them to your list of addressees, even if the intended recipients are not part of the network (see Figure 24-1). Using store-and-forward, e-mail servers store pending messages until the intended recipients log on to the network, at which time the server can send, or *forward*, the mail.

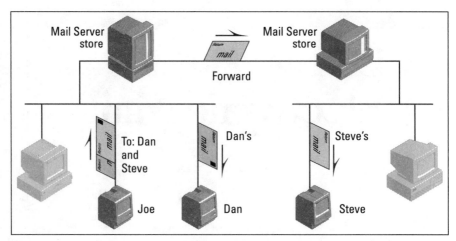

**Figure 24-1: Store-and-forward electronic mail means that Steve's copy must go through two post offices before Steve will get it.**

Imagine a postal system in which the post office refuses to accept a letter unless you guarantee that the recipient will be home when the postman plans to deliver the letter. That's what would happen *without* store-and-forward architecture.

We'll offer an example to take a closer look at how the store-and-forward system works (see Figure 24-1). Joe, who is logged on to Mail Server A, sends mail to Dan and Steve. In a store-and-forward e-mail system, Server A stores mail for Dan and Steve until it can deliver that mail. Dan receives his mail when he logs on to the network and Server A. Steve's copy gets forwarded from Server A to Server B whenever Server A connects to Server B. That final forwarding could happen immediately, if both servers are on the same network, or later, if the connection is made by modem. Server B then stores Steve's copy until Steve logs on to that server.

# Choosing an E-Mail Model

Most Macintosh users think of electronic mail as being a very localized product for communications within a group or perhaps a whole company. With the rise of the global Internet, however, e-mail has come to mean true *any-to-any communication*: anyone on any e-mail system should be able to communicate with anyone on any other e-mail system.

Three styles of electronic-mail systems are commonly in use:

❖ With *LAN-based* e-mail, you build an e-mail network of personal-computer clients and servers, usually running MS-DOS or the Macintosh operating system. Any link to the outside world is through an e-mail gateway (see Figure 24-2).

## Is It a Phone Call, or Is It a Letter?

People treat electronic mail as casually as they do telephone calls. Because e-mail is so easy to send and receive, users jot short notes to one another, confirming lunch dates or commenting on a recent message. In an organization, electronic mail can take on a very informal aspect. When that happens, people tend to think of e-mail in the same way that they think of telephone calls: ephemeral, private, and unofficial.

However informal e-mail is, though, a phone call isn't a good analogy. E-mail is not ephemeral; depending on your system-management policies, e-mail messages could end up being archived forever. (And look at what trouble *that* got Ollie North into.) E-mail is

not private; any system administrator can read e-mail, either stored in mailboxes or in transit through the network. These two characteristics deny the third: e-mail is official communication. When the going gets tough and the subpoenas or grievance hearings start, e-mail suddenly becomes much more formal and important than it was intended to be.

These facts don't mean, however, that e-mail isn't one of the most valuable tools for interoffice (and intraoffice) communication ever designed. What is important is that you and your correspondents remind yourselves periodically of the real nature of electronic mail — and of the consequences of your use of it.

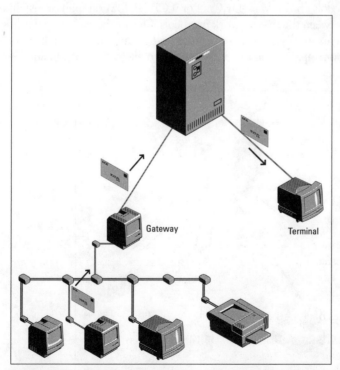

Figure 24-2: In the LAN-based mail system, an e-mail gateway converts message formats and addresses between the LAN-based e-mail and the host-based e-mail.

❖ With *host-centric* e-mail, you use the host computer's e-mail with some connection between the Macs and the host (see Figure 24-3).

❖ With *mixed client/server* e-mail, a host computer runs an e-mail server application, and client Macs on the LAN communicate with the host server (see Figure 24-4).

When you use a host-based e-mail system exclusively, each Mac user needs to have an appropriate terminal emulator to communicate with the host. In these cases, the Mac is little more than a *dumb terminal*, and the user has to learn the procedures of the host's operating system. In Figure 24-5, you see a dumb terminal on a Macintosh using ALL-IN-ONE, a very popular host-based electronic-mail system.

Another way of using the host's intelligence to process mail is to share the tasks, as in a client/server mode. In this case, the host acts as the mail server and also performs some of the mail processing, such as notifying users of pending mail. But the Macs on the network also perform some processing tasks, such as creating and storing mail. This approach doesn't limit you to the use of a terminal emulator and provides more Mac-like front ends to the host's mail service.

Usually, setting up a mixed client/server system requires running the host's network protocols on the Mac (DECnet or TCP/IP, for example) or installing a gateway between the two network protocols. One of the most popular host-centric e-mail applications is Eudora (see Figure 24-6) from Qualcomm. Eudora originally was a freeware application that was destined to die for lack of a maintainer.

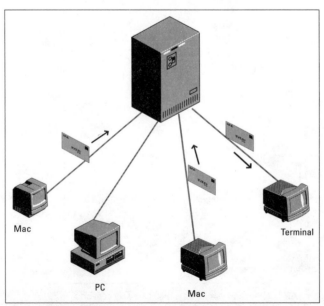

**Figure 24-3: In the host-centric mail system, mail is processed on the host and the messages are read by the clients, usually acting as terminals.**

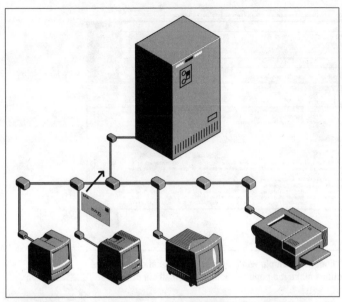

**Figure 24-4: In the mixed client/server e-mail system, both the host post office and the client workstations share in the processing of messages.**

**Figure 24-5: A terminal on a host-based mail system (like this ALL-IN-ONE office automation system) does not offer the same ease of use which a Mac user interface can.**

Qualcomm hired Steve Dorner, the author of Eudora, and turned Eudora into a commercial product supporting both Macintosh and Microsoft Windows users. Eudora uses POP and SMTP over a TCP/IP network to transfer mail from a server to the Eudora client.

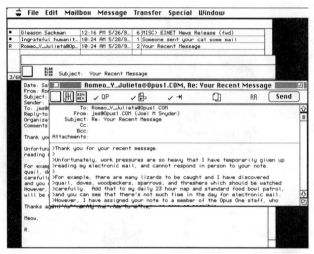

**Figure 24-6: Eudora's multiple window user interface and icon-based option selections make it a popular client/server mail client.**

A LAN-based system also lets you use more of the Mac's interface and intelligence to process e-mail. Figures 24-7 and 24-8 show the user interface of two popular LAN-based e-mail systems: Microsoft Mail and QuickMail.

## Two Models for Mixed E-Mail

POP and IMAP are the most popular technologies used for mixed client/server electronic-mail systems. In the world of *POP* (Post Office Protocol), a Macintosh is responsible for keeping track of its own e-mail. The responsibility of the POP server is to receive e-mail for the user and dump it to the user's Mac whenever asked. In this case, the POP model severely restricts your options for reading and receiving electronic mail. You can use only e-mail packages that are compatible with the POP format, and if your Macintosh e-mail box is inaccessible, you can't get your e-mail.

With *IMAP* (Interactive Mail Access Protocol), the server has greater responsibility: it also must store your electronic mail. This protocol is a much more powerful way to handle electronic mail, because it gives users more options and greater accessibility. Because the e-mail is always accessible through a standardized interface, different e-mail applications (called *user agents*) can be used to access the same electronic mail. IMAP-stored electronic mail also is more accessible from a greater number of locations than POP-stored electronic mail.

Figure 24-7: The user interface for QuickMail is more involved, with icon buttons for message types (labeled "New") as well as actions for any message. Messages are stored in folders, with waiting mail in the MailBox. The front-most window shows a typical message form, in this case for recording a phone message — note the large number of options available on the form, represented by the row of icons.

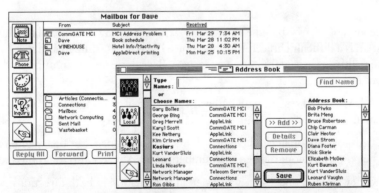

Figure 24-8: Microsoft Mail uses icons (left-hand side of rear window) to indicate what forms are available. Messages are shown in the upper-half of the window, while folders for storing those messages are in the bottom half. The front-most window shows the user's address list, which, in this case, includes addresses for the network (Connections), MCI (CommGATE MCI), and AppleLink (AppleLINK).

The crucial link here is the e-mail gateway. This gateway provides translations of both addresses and messages between the formats used by the e-mail systems on the host computer and on the LAN. Gateways also can be used to provide translations between different LAN-based e-mail systems. In Figure 24-9, you see the configuration screen for a gateway between Microsoft Mail and SMTP (the Internet). Some other gateway technologies are discussed in Chapter 26, "Mac LANs and the Internet."

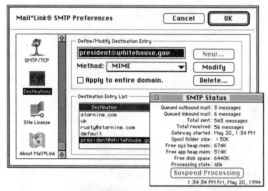

**Figure 24-9: StarNine's Mail*Link SMTP lets Microsoft Mail send and receive messages into an SMTP mail network, such as the Internet.**

Selection of a LAN-based e-mail system with a gateway as opposed to a host-based system is a difficult choice. And this choice often is determined as much by corporate politics as by suitability to your needs. Bear these factors in mind while you're planning:

❖ A LAN-based system with gateways gives the user a single interface to multiple mail systems.

❖ LAN-based e-mail can help distribute the e-mail load, but the system may not be powerful enough when the numbers of users reach into the thousands.

❖ Gateways don't necessarily transfer all information in both directions; some may not forward or translate enclosures, or handle graphics and sound.

❖ Host-based systems usually carry with them company-supported automatic archiving and backup of files.

❖ In the absence of universal directory services (still on the horizon), employment of varied e-mail systems usually means maintaining redundant user directories.

# Selecting E-Mail Features

Although most e-mail products have nearly the same architecture with respect to store-and-forward capability, each e-mail package has a variety of distinguishing features. Some of these features substantially affect the way you use your e-mail service. The following sections consider the most important choices to be made.

## User-related features

Personal tastes get involved in the user interface on the Mac; individual customization is as much the rule as the exception. All currently available e-mail programs for the Mac have reasonable user interfaces, but they do vary in complexity (refer to Figure 24-7). Some programs display all their bells and whistles at once. Other programs, such as cc:Mail (Lotus), keep the fancier user options — custom forms and the like — to a minimum so that the interface can remain simple. What is food to one program is poison to others, and so it is with e-mail interfaces (although none has been found to be poisonous yet).

If you're in the process of selecting an e-mail program, you have an array of user-related features to consider. Most of these features focus either on message sending and receiving or on handling address lists.

Sending messages is at the heart of any e-mail system. First, you want a program that makes it easy to compose a message and find the proper addressees. Then you probably want a program that lets you send multiple file enclosures along with the message. You shouldn't need a program like StuffIt to create a single package of the many files you want to send just because your e-mail program has a single-enclosure limit.

Users may not always be connected to the network, yet want to prepare messages to be sent at a later time. For these occasions, it's important that your program provide off-line support, either within the e-mail application or by importing files into the message. You should be able to compose your messages in a word processing program, for example, and import them later. Few programs work off-line. QuickMail, WordPerfect Symmetry (formerly WordPerfect Office), and cc:Mail allow you to compose and address messages if you're not connected to the server.

Received messages may call for either formulating a reply or forwarding the message to other readers. The best programs let you send a reply to a subset of the original address list (a selected few on the cc: list, for example). Also, a good e-mail program lets you add comments to a received message before you forward it to someone else.

Two further issues pertain to organizing the received messages: filing the messages in the native e-mail format for creating later replies, and saving the messages as files on your disk. Almost all e-mail vendors have adopted a folder-like paradigm for filing messages. Some applications let you drag messages to the folders just as you would on the Mac Desktop, but others require you to choose the folder's name from a pop-up menu.

More important is where these messages actually reside once they're filed. Programs like Microsoft Mail, cc:Mail, and WordPerfect Symmetry have you file messages on the server. QuickMail is the only program that files messages on your local hard disk (cc:Mail and WordPerfect Symmetry have an archive function that also works this way). Filing on your local hard disk saves the server's hard disk space, which most mail administrators will appreciate. But local hard disk filing does make it more difficult for users who are on the road, or those who are accessing mail through more than one computer, to review past mail.

Every e-mail program lets you save the contents of a message to the disk of your choice, so that's not a distinguishing factor. But a related feature that we've found to be useful is the capability to append a message to a stored message. This feature is a great way to maintain the history — often called the *thread* — of an important series of communications.

As mentioned earlier in this chapter, you want to make it easy for users to find and use e-mail addresses when they need to send a message. One way to simplify this routine is to allow all users to create and maintain their own address books. All Mac e-mail programs let you create at least one personal address book, which can contain a subset of the master directory maintained on the server, as well as individually entered custom addresses (more about this shortly). Personal address books are especially handy when you're working on a large e-mail system that may contain a networkwide directory of 10,000 or more names.

Selecting each addressee's name from a list can be a pain when the number of intended recipients reaches 10 or more. And if you mail messages to the same group more than once, you'll appreciate a mechanism that saves this group list for later use. E-mail programs usually offer two options to assist with group lists. First, the e-mail administrator can set up groups of addressees on the server for everyone's use. Second, you should be able to create your own groups much as you would your personal address book.

While we're on the subject of creating personal address books and groups, the procedure for updating these addresses is worth noting. E-mail systems customarily offer some mechanism for exchanging the directories on each mail server to maintain a network-wide directory. In some cases, you must purchase additional software to compile this global directory. The next step is to propagate any changes to the user. In applications such as Microsoft Mail, the updating is done automatically; in other applications, such as QuickMail, you're prompted to verify the changes manually for each altered address.

These updates don't apply to the custom addresses that you create in your personal address book. Suppose that you know the address for Joe Sender, a special correspondent who uses MCI Mail. Rather than have the mail administrator insert Joe's address into the MCI Mail gateway for your system, you can enter it in your own address book. But this address won't be updated by the mail system's directory service, because the service doesn't know about Joe. Most LAN-based mail systems propagate all addresses to all servers. Although this arrangement works well for small to medium-size organizations, it is unwieldy in large ones.

Another user feature deserves mention: custom message forms. QuickMail started the trend toward user-defined forms that can include both graphics and text; Microsoft Mail and WordPerfect Symmetry also support custom forms. Notice that these forms are defined within the e-mail system, not by a forms-based front end to a database. Using custom e-mail forms is much like using personalized stationery; the form helps get a point across effectively and also says something about you.

One last user-related feature is the option of remote access to the server. With the increased popularity of laptop and notebook computers, more users are taking their computers with them on the road. While they are away, they want to communicate with the home office and use the e-mail system as well. Being able to make direct calls to the mail server with a modem is an attractive feature. This option usually includes basic security measures, such as a password-based log-on procedure.

An alternative plan does not rely on direct dial-in to the mail server; it offers users dial-in access to the network. If you maintain multiple modems or a modem server for the network, more than one remote user can join the network and access the mail server. While on the network, this user can access other network services, such as printing and file servers.

## Server-related features

Until now, this chapter has discussed the features that keep users satisfied with their e-mail service. But these features are all for naught if the e-mail server isn't reliable or lacks some important features. This section guides you through some server-related features.

As mentioned earlier in the chapter, store-and-forward architecture is very important to today's e-mail systems. Store-and-forward architecture not only is useful for client-to-server communications to send mail to someone who's not connected, but also enhances server-to-server communications. If you're on a network that's large enough for more than one server, the e-mail system needs a channel for passing messages to users of other servers. Again, just as it does for users, store-and-forward architecture lets servers hold messages meant for other servers that may be down or disconnected. Message storage is particularly valuable if you have e-mail servers that are connected by modem lines. Each server can hold messages destined for the other and exchange those messages when the modem link is established.

Two further aspects of server architecture come into play in e-mail systems: the method that the server uses to store messages, and the location of most of the server's intelligence.

An e-mail server can store one copy of a message for each of the intended recipients; or it can store a single copy of the message independent of the number of addressees. The latter approach is preferred because it reduces the space required on the server's hard disk. Naturally, this method also applies to enclosures included with a message.

With respect to the location of the server's intelligence, the early e-mail programs use a file-based system. This system relies on a file server to store files containing all e-mail messages, directories, and other necessary files. The e-mail application on the user's computer contains all the intelligence needed to store a message in the appropriate file on the file server, as well as to retrieve messages addressed to the user (see Figure 24-10). The computer acting as the file server doesn't hold an additional application designed specifically to assist the e-mail program; the server's operating system handles multiuser access to e-mail files just as it would control a multiuser database file — which is essentially what an e-mail server's main file is.

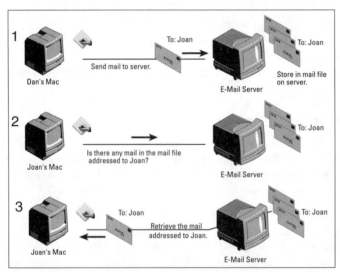

**Figure 24-10: In a file-based e-mail system, all of the intelligence is on the client workstation. The e-mail server only acts as a file server.**

More advanced e-mail systems use a client/server architecture that distributes the system's intelligence between the user's computer and the server (see Figure 24-11). Thus, when you use a program such as QuickMail or Microsoft Mail, you have to install a program on the mail server to make everything work. This program usually assumes the tasks of notifying each user when mail is waiting, monitoring each log-on to the system, and updating directories. The client software (your e-mail application) has only to worry about composing, sending, and receiving messages, as well as responding to the server's alerts.

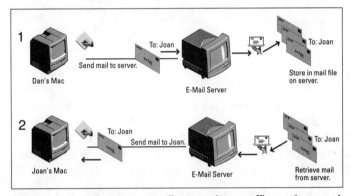

1 Dan's Mac · Send mail to server. · To: Joan · E-Mail Server · Store in mail file on server. · To: Joan

2 Joan's Mac · To: Joan · Send mail to Joan. · E-Mail Server · Retrieve mail from server. · To: Joan

**Figure 24-11: In a client-server e-mail system, the post office on the server is an integral partner in delivering electronic mail.**

For most environments, the client/server architecture is preferred. Yet there is an advantage to the file-based system: this system can be used on a variety of file servers and doesn't require specially written server software for each server's operating system.

cc:Mail lets you install its system files on practically any file server, and only the client software is system-specific. But when you get to complicated multiserver systems, you must purchase additional software to get the servers to exchange e-mail. That problem is less common with client/server architecture.

# The Administrative Issues of E-Mail

Each e-mail system depends on a centralized e-mail server, so e-mail requires some administration. At the most basic level, administration means assigning names and passwords to the users and perhaps assigning dial-in privileges. More complicated systems may require you to determine routes between servers, diagnose server problems, set times for server-directory updates, and select gateway configurations (discussed later in this chapter). And don't forget backing up the mail server's files.

Diagnosing e-mail problems perhaps is the one administrative area that most e-mail programs have not adequately addressed. The reporting options available to server administrators are quite limited, offering data on disk use, number of messages transmitted, date last used, and the like. Microsoft Mail does include more options in its reports, some of which can be used to gauge server-to-server traffic and other performance issues that may prove useful for reconfiguring your e-mail system.

You must exercise some care when you're ready to back up a mail server. Most vendors advise you to be sure that all mail users are logged off before you back up the server files; otherwise, the files may be altered and subsequently damaged during the backup process.

# Other Gateways

A diverse assortment of e-mail gateways is available beyond those meant for connecting host-based e-mail. Various other gateway designs hook up to national or international service providers, such as AppleLink, CompuServe, GEnie, MCI Mail, EasyLink, and the Internet. These gateways usually connect to the larger system via modem.

Should you plan to use a gateway to connect to one of these services, be aware of the limitations that these services may impose on your e-mail. For example, some services don't provide for file enclosures; some services do, but permit only one per message, which is not the norm for most LAN-based e-mail systems. If a service provider does not support multiple file enclosures, make certain that your gateway can translate a message containing multiple enclosures into multiple messages, each with one enclosure.

Many foreign (that is, non-LAN) mail systems use such complex addressing schemes that a gateway must map to the LAN-based e-mail scheme. A good technique for coping with complicated addresses is to have them created and stored on the server that includes the gateway and then to designate simpler aliases for these addresses.

The X.400 messaging standard put forth by the ISO (International Organization for Standardization) promises to reduce many of the problems in current e-mail gateways. Just bear in mind that few, if any, current mail systems use X.400 as their native protocol and thus are translating between their own proprietary protocols and X.400. When e-mail systems switch over to X.400, the number of translations (of messages, addresses, and enclosures) will be reduced, making interoperability between mail systems simpler. X.400 is discussed in greater detail in Chapter 20, "Macs in the World of OSI."

# Using Facsimiles with E-Mail

Facsimile (or *fax*) transmission currently enjoys international popularity that over-shadows that of e-mail. The primary reason is that more people have fax machines than have computers. But it's possible to combine e-mail and fax transmissions to expand the reach of both technologies.

All LAN-based e-mail systems offer some type of gateway to fax-transmission fa-cilities. The normal procedure is for you, as an e-mail user, to select the address of an intended fax recipient and then to create your message. The gateway converts your message to a form suitable for fax transmission and dials the phone number of the addressee's fax machine. You usually can specify a cover sheet, stored electroni-cally on the server, for use with the outgoing fax. One nice feature of a fax gateway is that it can dial the phone numbers of all addressees automatically, even though you created only a single message (with an address list) in your e-mail program.

Whether you use the fax system alone on the network or via an e-mail interface (that is, a gateway), you should be aware of a few things. First, fax images are bitmapped images. Standard resolution for a Group 3 fax is approximately 200 dots per inch, which can create large files that must be stored on your fax or e-mail server. (For a quick review on fax standards like Group 3, see "The Facts on Fax" in Chapter 10, "Using Modems with Networks" or turn to Tina Rathbone's *Modems For Dummies*, published by IDG Books Worldwide). Second, the time it takes to convert text and/or graphics to a bitmapped fax image can be extensive. Good fax systems let you perform the conversion at your Mac or at the server. The better procedure is to schedule the conversion at the server; locating conversion there reduces the amount of data to be transmitted over the network and also releases the Mac to the user faster.

When you set up a suitable configuration for a fax server, the size of the stored images will be a paramount consideration. For example, a 10-page MacWrite file (text only, no graphics) takes up 24K on a hard disk, whereas the fax image created from that MacWrite file requires 737K of disk storage. Similarly, a scanned image saved as a PICT file took up 450K of storage on the disk, but the fax image created from that PICT file occupied 1.2M. Most sites that the authors have consulted prefer to devote a Mac with a large hard disk to act solely as a fax server, with a gateway in the case of an e-mail connection.

For the time being, you'll find that it's much easier to use a fax gateway to send faxes than to receive faxes, especially over a network. Incoming faxes aren't like e-mail; they don't contain any electronic addressing information. Fax gateways usually deal with this situation by accepting all incoming faxes and sending them to one designated user — perhaps the mail administrator. That person then is respon-sible for reviewing each fax and forwarding it to the appropriate e-mail user. Technologies for overcoming this problem are being developed. One such technology is Direct Inward Dial (DID), which requires a special phone line and phone number for each user. Another method encodes the address of the recipient in the fax-message header itself but requires matching systems. Other approaches append a user ID (via touch tones) after the fax modem's number is dialed. Fax vendors, however, haven't accepted a single solution.

Actually, you don't need a fax gateway to send and receive faxes; service providers such as CompuServe, EasyLink, and MCI Mail offer fax transmission to their users. Of course, this service is limited to text-only faxes, but these may be sufficient for some users' needs. You can use an e-mail gateway to these services to send e-mail transmissions to other computer users and fax transmissions to customers who don't have a computer.

We'll offer here a few last thoughts about working with faxes on computers. Combining a fax modem and fax gateway with e-mail is a good way for your users to send faxes, but this method often is not optimal for receiving faxes. If a fax has to be signed and re-sent, you'll go through the bother of printing the received fax, signing it, and then scanning it back in or sending it via a regular fax machine. Remember that a fax is a bitmapped image and that many faxes take a long time to print. Also, faxes are received as (at best) 200-dpi bitmapped images, so they're not high-quality documents. If you intend to use artwork that is to be faxed to you, you'd be better off arranging for the other party to send the file to you via a regular modem.

# Expanding the E-Mail Interface

Even though e-mail already offers great communications flexibility for networked users, the marketplace promises even more changes and advantages in the not-too-distant future. Many of these improvements derive from the idea that e-mail's message-handling system can be used for more than personally generated messages, particularly for application-to-application transfers of data and commands. Thus, we'll see new systems that use message-handling and directory services as e-mail does, but with different interfaces on the front end.

The first move in this direction offers *Application Programming Interfaces*, or APIs, to existing e-mail systems. These APIs allow developers to provide direct support for e-mail within their applications. Microsoft Word and Excel, for example, enable you to send and receive documents via Microsoft Mail while you're working within those applications; Aldus PageMaker lets you place received mail documents as stories within a page-layout file.

Apple already is moving up to the next step by developing what it calls the *Apple Open Collaboration Environment* (AOCE), which is discussed in detail in Chapter 23, "Using Groupware." Coupling AOCE with some of Apple's new features in the versions of System 7, such as Apple Events, should make it easier for Mac applications to exchange data and commands over the network.

QUICK TIPS

### Fax or Modem?

When two computers communicate with each other over a modem, they arrange to transfer electronic files. If the other person doesn't have a computer, use a fax. If you need to send a computer-generated document, the document almost always will look better if you send it through a fax gateway or modem than if you print it and then scan it in through a fax machine. A fax machine never has perfect registration of the scanned image, whereas a computer-generated fax does.

And what about multiplatform support? Most popular LAN-based e-mail systems offer support for both Mac and DOS clients, as well as for Mac and DOS servers. In some cases, the problem is simply deciding which products are appropriate; working your way through the list of selections is like ordering a meal at a Chinese restaurant. But the process can be rewarding.

These new steps toward message handling within applications are even crossing platform boundaries. Of possible significance is Lotus' development of Vendor-Independent Messaging (VIM) and Microsoft's development of Messaging Application Programming Interface (MAPI). Both interfaces are designed to provide APIs for using common message-handling services across computing platforms. Only time will tell which — if either — of these interfaces will be the dominant one.

# CHAPTER 24 CONCEPTS AND TERMS

---

- File-based e-mail is good for multiplatform server networks.

- Client-server e-mail systems reduce the amount of processing over the network.

- An e-mail gateway is useful for exchanging mail between LANs and larger host computers.

- Networked fax systems (with or without e-mail support) require large amounts of storage and are better suited for sending faxes than for receiving them.

---

**Application Programming Interfaces (APIs)**
An interface to a network application is an API. This is used by programmers who wish to use services provided by that network application.

**dumb terminal**
A character-based device which is used to connect to a host. On a microcomputer, we use a terminal emulator program to emulate a dumb terminal.

**e-mail server**
A system which is responsible for receiving and processing e-mail messages on behalf of one or more clients.

**host-centric e-mail**
A system built around a host computer. Personal computer access to e-mail is through a terminal interface to the host using a dumb terminal emulation program.

**IMAP**
The Interactive (sometimes referred to as Interim) Mail Access Protocol, a client/server mail protocol. In IMAP, the server receives and stores messages on behalf of the client.

**LAN-based e-mail**
A system built of personal computer clients and servers, usually running MS-DOS or the Macintosh operating system. Any link to the outside world is through an e-mail gateway.

**mixed client/server e-mail**
A system built around a host computer running an e-mail server application (similar to LAN-based e-mail) with client users on the LAN. Mixed client/server is similar to LAN-based e-mail; the differences are mainly in the scale of things. LAN-based e-mail is for smaller networks than client/server e-mail.

**POP**
The Post Office Protocol, a client/server mail access protocol. In POP, the server receives messages on behalf of the client. When the client connects to the POP server, the server transfers the messages to the client.

**store-and-forward architecture**
Most electronic mail systems use a store-and-forward architecture where e-mail messages are sent from one server to another in distinct hops. Any break in the chain delays the message, but does not keep it from being delivered.

**thread**
An e-mail thread is a chain of messages linked by a common subject. Thus, a thread contains an original message and all replies to that, as well as replies to the replies, and so on.

**user agents**
In a client/server application, the user agent is the client side. The user agent handles the "user" issues of the mail system. User agents connect to mailers, message transfer systems, or message handling systems (the name varies depending on the model you are using), which actually do the work of moving the mail around.

# Using the X Window System

As a grandfather in the world of windows, it's only reasonable that the Macintosh should be a full peer in the network window system that has taken over the world of minicomputers: the X window system.

X is a combination of programming interfaces and protocols that allows CPUs to display graphics and text on bitmapped displays. In X, a computer running an application is called the *client;* the screen, keyboard, and mouse are called the *server.* The terms are a trifle confusing if you've thought of your Macintosh as being a client of an AppleShare disk server, but in X, they make sense: the server provides a service to the client. In X, that service is the display of graphics, text, and any sort of image information. See Figure 25-1 for a brief schematic of the X window system.

Most microcomputer applications are anchored firmly on the same CPU as their display. You run Excel or Word on a Mac; the program displays on the same Mac. In X, the link the display and the CPU can occur over the network (or it may be entirely local to a single system). Further, X doesn't bind a single server to a single client; a server can display applications that are running on many clients. For example, a UNIX workstation might display a CAD drawing on an X server at the same time that an IBM mainframe performs structural analysis in a 3270 terminal window.

As X servers, few personal computers — the Macintosh included — can match the performance of a minicomputer workstation. Nevertheless, you may find situations in which it makes good sense to bring Macintoshes into the world of the networked X window system.

QUOTABLES

"And storied windows rightly dight, Casting a dim religious light."

— John Milton, *Il Penseroso*

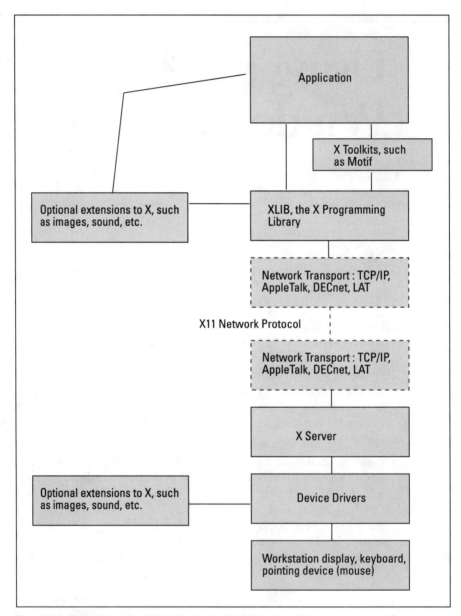

Figure 25-1: The architecture of the client/server X window system.

A final note: don't ever call it "X Windows." The name of the software is just plain X. As the folks at the X Consortium are fond of reminding people, "It's a window system called 'X,' not a system called 'X Windows.'" Calling a software package X may seem a little odd, but that's par for the course in a business in which the most popular text editor is called Word and two different integrated packages are called Works.

# X Server Software for the Macintosh

Two packages dominate the world of X on the Macintosh: Apple Computer's MacX and White Pine Software's eXodus. MacX also is available from Digital as part of that company's Pathworks for Macintosh product.

In the world of X window system servers, performance has become the most significant reason to choose an X server package. Because the X window system applications handle the user interface, the X server becomes little more than a fancy terminal, and X server software is little more than a commodity. Issues of compatibility and integration, however, may swing the balance from one package to the other.

MacX and eXodus offer the same basic feature. They allow X clients to display windows on the Macintosh over TCP/IP, DECnet, or AppleTalk's ADSP (AppleTalk Data Stream Protocol).

Apple's MacX is an austere X11R4 server that offers excellent performance and a high level of reliability. MacX does not have a lot of bells and whistles. White Pine Software's eXodus is a feature-rich X11R5 server that has seen active development. The product has grown into a mature server with good performance and many user-selectable options.

Bells, whistles, and features are nice to have, but users of X servers end up focusing on performance and reliability. You should test any X server that you select to see whether its performance will be acceptable to end users.

# The Mac as an X Client

Although the Macintosh most often is thought of as an X window system server, it also can act as an X window system client. In this case, the Macintosh Finder is the application. Put an X client on the Macintosh, and you can control that client from any X window server, such as a UNIX or OpenVMS workstation. An X client provides access to a Macintosh without requiring physical access. Planet X (from InterCon Systems Corporation) does just that: it lets you display Macintosh applications on any X server, including another Macintosh. The Mac-based applications still run on a Macintosh, but you control them from any X display device.

# Why would you want to do that?

An X client is a good idea for the user who needs only occasional access to a Macintosh — perhaps two to four hours a day. Heavier use probably would call for a different solution. We see lots of applications for this style of product, above and beyond sharing of screens. As a tool for the system manager, these products allow remote support and management of Macintoshes without running around buildings, finding keys to locked offices, or disturbing users. A system manager could use these tools to install new software, change network configurations, and even reboot systems remotely.

Help desks and user training groups also could take advantage of an X client on a Macintosh. Because the local display and mouse are not disabled, a help desk could connect to a user's Macintosh, demonstrate an application feature, or try to debug a problem, all remotely and under the eye of the user. Outstanding potential for user support exists here.

# Using a Mac as an X client

After you install and configure a system like InterCon's Planet X (a.k.a., X), using it is easy — just *telnet* to the Macintosh. (*Telnet* is a TCP/IP-based protocol which supports terminal emulation. Often the command to invoke a terminal emulator and use the telnet protocol is, simply enough, *telnet*.) Planet X asks for a user name and password, and then gives you the IP address of the system from which you're telneting. If the display is the one you want to use, press Return. Assuming that you remembered to use *xhost* to make connections, the Mac screen will pop up in a window on your display in about five seconds. Stick the Macintosh in a computer room or telephone closet, and no one needs to touch it again.

You also can start Planet X from the Macintosh side, using the Planet X control panel. This panel allows you to specify an X display to connect to and (optionally) to specify that this connection should occur every time the Macintosh is rebooted, without further intervention.

From there, using the Mac is just as easy (or hard) as if you were sitting in front of it. Cutting and pasting between Macintosh and X applications isn't perfect, however; a special tool is required to move data between the X and Macintosh Clipboards.

Performance is the biggest problem area. Screen updates and animations aren't as fast as on the Macintosh, but they can be quite acceptable. Color is another story; it's painfully slow in some cases. Monochrome performance is between three and eight times faster, leaving color in the (multicolored) dust. We suggest that you restrict your use of an X client in monochrome or 2-bit color; trying 8-bit (or more) color probably will be quite disappointing.

QUICK TIPS

### Share and Share Alike

Another way to handle the problem of sharing Macintosh resources exists. Farallon Computing's Timbuktu is the original remote-control application, letting Macintosh and MS-DOS users drive around each other's machines over AppleTalk and TCP/IP networks. Timbuktu is more a micro-to-micro application, but it solves some of the same kinds of problems that Macintosh X clients and servers have. For more information on screen sharing and group editing, see Chapter 23, "Using Groupware."

# UNIX on a Macintosh

Any talk of X client and server software on the Macintosh would be incomplete without a discussion of UNIX on the Macintosh. Two vendors — Apple Computer and Tenon Intersystems — provide UNIX implementations on the Macintosh.

Apple and Tenon took different approaches to putting UNIX on the Macintosh. Both companies aim to maintain compatibility with existing Mac applications, but Apple's A/UX replaces the standard Macintosh operating system and provides a compatibility layer to let native Mac applications work. Tenon's MachTen takes the alternative approach, running a whole UNIX virtual machine as a single task under the Macintosh operating system. Neither approach is perfect, but both products accomplish the same thing: a fully functional UNIX on a Macintosh.

## A/UX

A/UX is a complete replacement for the Macintosh operating system. When you install A/UX, it formats the hard disk into a set of UNIX partitions and one small Macintosh partition. From there, the Macintosh always boots up in the standard Macintosh operating system. The user double-clicks A/UX Startup, and A/UX takes over, effectively rebooting the Macintosh into UNIX. After about a minute, a log-in screen appears, and the system becomes a UNIX workstation. Going back to the normal Macintosh operating system requires a complete reboot.

A/UX has three main user interfaces. When logging in, you choose either the familiar Mac Finder, an X11 window manager, or a TTY-like console. The Finder interface looks like a Macintosh: double-click an icon, and you're running the application. UNIX is hiding: there's a disk on the Desktop labeled /. Click it, then click the Bin folder, and then click the *ls* icon, and up pops a window with lots of little buttons and boxes, each corresponding to an *ls* option. When you finish setting options, you confirm the box, and A/UX brings up a terminal window (called a Command Shell) and performs the *ls* operation, leaving you in the window. If you want to go directly to a terminal window, you can open a Command Shell or two from the Apple menu; it's there as a desk accessory.

The window that comes up when you click a UNIX command is brought to you by a slick program called Commando. Commando is an instant refresher course on each command's options. Can't remember how to list a *cpio* archive? Type **cpio** in a Command Shell and press Command-K, and up pops instant help. This program is very helpful addition to UNIX for Mac users.

An alternative interface is standard X11, which is fully supported, as is Apple's MacX product. You also can hook up a terminal or log in through a terminal server: A/UX supports up to 16 simultaneous users; a 32-user version is available as well.

A/UX is a full System V R2V2 implementation, POSIX-compliant, with Berkeley extensions. This means that A/UX has everything you'd expect from a good UNIX: *man* pages, TCP/IP (with streams and Berkeley r-utilities), NFS client and server, NIS, X and Motif, cc, f77, SCCS, C, Bourne, and Korn shells, and even Adobe's TranScript for PostScript printer support. (If you don't know what all that means, don't worry about it. You probably won't need all these items.) Also, you can run most Macintosh applications, except for those that require direct hardware control.

## MachTen

Tenon's MachTen takes an entirely different approach from Apple's A/UX, appearing as a regular Mac application, with Mac files, on a Mac disk — no partitioning or new layout of your hard disk is required. To start MachTen, click the MachTen icon, which launches UNIX as an application. At any time, you can move back to the Finder and launch Macintosh applications, too.

MachTen appears to the Macintosh operating system to be a single application, but inside, Tenon provides a real UNIX implementation. Version 2.1 of MachTen also includes UNIX-style virtual memory.

MachTen's standard user interface is a command shell. Based on Carnegie-Mellon's Mach microkernel version of UNIX, and using the Berkeley 4.3BSD-Reno code as a base, MachTen lacks some of the features of A/UX but does have most of what you'd need to build a respectable system: TCP/IP networking, X and Motif, NFS client and server, and the GNU C compiler. MachTen omits the standard C or f77 compilers and some less critical programs. MachTen takes up about 30M of disk space, without the X window system server.

MachTen's manuals (20 pounds, compared with A/UX's back-breaking 60 pounds) follow the traditional Berkeley style: a few short tutorials, some version-specific information, and standard *man* pages. Tenon also includes ManTen, a HyperCard stack that contains all the manual pages.

## Choosing between A/UX and MachTen

Don't buy A/UX or MachTen and expect to get much off-the-shelf software. Quite a bit of freeware has been ported to both A/UX and MachTen, but none of the popular UNIX applications has an A/UX or MachTen version. That's not much of a problem, however — why buy the UNIX version of Lotus 1-2-3 when the Mac version is cheaper and easier to find, too?

A/UX and MachTen are excellent products that fill different needs in the market. A/UX is a big UNIX with more documentation than even IBM's AIX system; it feels, and is, complete. Any single-user UNIX workstation that has a shell script to add users clearly is thinking big thoughts. Some users might even accuse Apple of overkill in A/UX: is the market really large enough to justify the resources required to maintain such a complex product? Regardless, UNIX users will enjoy the luxury of A/UX, a fully featured UNIX that includes complete Mac compatibility.

MachTen is a much more modest endeavor. The MachTen Personal UNIX, which lacks virtual memory, lets you enjoy the horrors of manually configuring sendmail (the world's most difficult-to-configure program, standard on most UNIX platforms) for not too much money on a less expensive Macintosh than A/UX requires. MachTen is the better product for someone who is interested in learning about UNIX. For students, hobbyists, and anyone who just wants to work with UNIX on a Macintosh, MachTen is an excellent solution. With MachTen Professional, you even can conceive of using a PowerBook as a software-development station!

- The X window system is a client/server-based display graphics system. In X, the client runs the application, and the server displays the graphics.

- A Macintosh can act as an X server and display applications running on other computer systems.

- A Macintosh can be an X client, which lets workstations remotely control a Macintosh.

- A/UX and MachTen are versions of the UNIX operating system that run on the Macintosh. These products serve different markets and different sets of needs.

**server**
See client.

**UNIX**
An operating system developed by Bell Laboratories that features multiprogramming in a multiuser environment. The UNIX operating system was originally developed for use on minicomputers but has been adapted for mainframes and personal computers. It is a trademark of AT&T Bell Laboratories.

**X window system**
X is a combination of programming interfaces and protocols that allow CPUs to display graphics and text on bitmapped displays.

**client**
In X, a computer running an application is called the *client;* the screen, keyboard, and mouse are called the *server*. The terms are a trifle confusing if you've thought of your Macintosh as being a client of an AppleShare disk server, but in X, they make sense: the server provides a service to the client. In X, that service is the display of graphics, text, and any sort of image information.

# Exploring Mac LANs and the Internet

IN THIS CHAPTER

- A brief introduction to the Internet, how big it is, and what goes on there.

- Electronic mail, discussion groups, file transfer, and client/server information servers on the Internet

- How to connect to the Internet

- Issues in connecting to the Internet, including security, training, electronic mail, and directory services

Only if you've been sequestered in Mongolia can you have missed all the hoopla about the Internet. The 1990s will be remembered as the decade when the Internet rose — and possibly fell — to the center of public attention. At newspapers from Tijuana to Bangor, goggle-eyed reporters have been stumbling over the complexity of the Internet. The Internet has been featured on television, in comic strips, on the radio, and in magazine article after magazine article.

How big is the Internet? It's big enough that no one knows — and no one can know. The last person who tried to check figured that the Internet consists of about 20 million people using a couple of million computers. Think of the Internet as being the combined populations of Belgium, Benin, Bermuda, Bhutan, Bolivia, Botswana, and the British Virgin Islands, able to communicate whenever they want. Figure 26-1 shows how the number of networks joined to the Internet has grown. Figure 26-2 shows the growth of Internet traffic over time.

The Internet itself defies exact description. It's not a single entity; instead, the Internet is a network of networks. Internet gurus disagree on exactly where the core stops and where the unfashionable backwaters begin. All the experts agree, though, that the center is the 45M bps TCP/IP backbone that stretches across North America and into Europe and Asia. This backbone links the main service providers — organizations that connect various networks with the Internet.

Of the tens of thousands of networks linked directly to the backbone, about half are in the United States. The backbone passes more and more data among Internet users each month. When we were writing this book, in the summer of 1994, the figure was about 14 terabytes a month. A terabyte, if you hadn't thought about it, is a million megabytes. Think of it as representing roughly 18,000 stacks of paper, each as high as the Statue of Liberty (more or less).

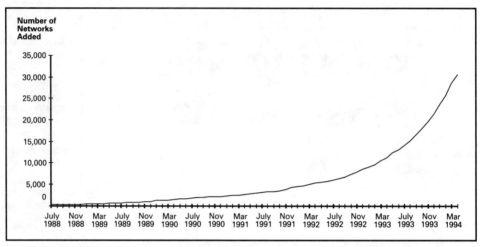

**Figure 26-1: The number of different networks which have connected to the Internet has grown dramatically in the past two years.**

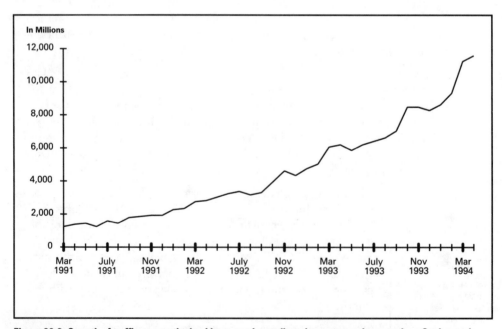

**Figure 26-2: Growth of traffic across the backbone can be attributed to new services, such as Gopher and WWW, as well as millions of new users.**

The service providers, and their customers, link many other networks and protocols. Many of the 60,000 active nodes that participate in the Usenet network use the UNIX UUCP (UNIX-to-UNIX *cp*, or UNIX-to-UNIX copy) protocol; BITNET's 2,900 nodes run IBM's RSCS (Remote Spooling and Communications Subsystem); Fidonet's 20,000 nodes use their own protocol; and the 50,000 nodes in SPAN use Digital's DECnet. Some links to the Internet hide the internal structure of the connecting network. CompuServe's 2 million subscribers don't know how many computers CompuServe has, but they know that the Internet is just an e-mail message away.

In this chapter, we'll only be able to give you a whirlwind tour of the Internet and some of the issues surrounding how you connect your corporate network to the Internet. If you want more information, you should refer to these excellent guides: *Internet For Dummies* by John Levine and Carol Baroudi and *More Internet For Dummies* by John Levine and Margaret Levine Young (published by IDG Books Worldwide).

# Information Resources on the Internet

A wide variety of information resources are available to you through the Internet, ranging from electronic mail to file transfer to client/server applications such as Gopher and the World Wide Web (WWW). Figure 26-3 breaks down the most popular uses for the Internet in April 1994, and Figure 26-4 shows how the proportion of use has changed over time.

## Electronic mail on the Internet

Almost 10 percent of all Internet traffic is electronic mail, using the *simple mail transfer protocol* (SMTP). (See Chapter 18, "Macs in the World of TCP/IP," to learn more about SMTP and Chapter 24, "Using Electronic Mail," to learn more about electronic mail on the Macintosh.) Electronic mail is the smallest common denominator of the Internet — the one thing that links every user. Need to get in touch with a cement supplier in St. Petersburg? Want to discuss a problem with an engineer at Novell (or any other major hardware or software manufacturer)? If you can figure out an e-mail address, you can communicate with almost anyone.

Internet gateways pass electronic mail from suppliers like MCI Mail and CompuServe back and forth. With telex and FAX gateways, you can reach an almost unlimited number of people without picking up a telephone.

If you already have electronic mail on your Macintosh LAN, linking to the Internet is a must. To remain competitive, you have to have electronic mail service between organizations. A supplier who isn't available to clients via electronic mail can't

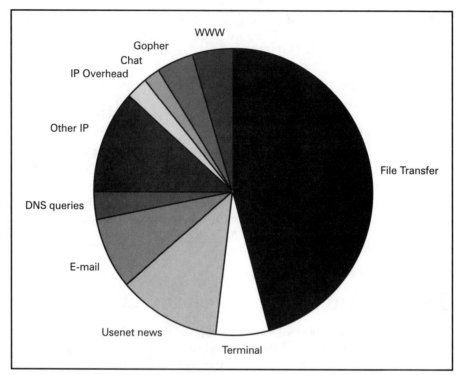

**Figure 26-3: Even though new services such as Gopher and WWW are very popular, file transfer remains the most popular service on the Internet.**

provide the same level of service as one who is. Electronic mail no longer is a curiosity; it is becoming an expectation. Connecting to the Internet is an excellent way to link your electronic mail system to the world and to open lines of communication.

## Discussion groups on the Internet

One of the richest assets of the Internet is the news service. Again, people argue over the service's name and boundaries, but what most folks call Usenet is a distributed bulletin board/conferencing system with more than 5,000 separate conferences (called *groups*) on every imaginable topic, ranging from alien visitors and alcoholism to molecular biology, cold fusion, and neural networks.

Usenet originally ran exclusively over the UNIX UUCP protocols and was one of the prime motivations for the UUCP network. Now Usenet news is passed over a variety of networks using many different protocols.

The most popular of these Usenet news groups are read by 200,000 people a day. A more esoteric group, such as one on current research directions in Japan, finds a mere 15,000 readers.

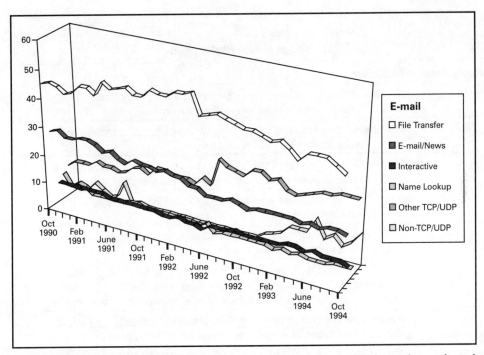

**Figure 26-4: The mix of Internet services has changed over time as the goals of the Internet's users have changed.**

Although a good portion of Usenet is devoted to recreation and nonprofessional issues, the availability of information on computing systems and applications is unmatched anywhere. (See Table 26-1 for a rough idea of the general areas covered in Usenet conferences.) The level of discussions and quality of advice on Usenet is substantially better than on local bulletin boards, and the access to people with good problem-solving capabilities is unmatched.

The 350-plus computer groups, which are aimed at computer professionals and hobbyists, cover every major and minor application package, networking technology, and topic of interest to system managers and users. To find out the latest before it appears in *Computerworld*, or to get in direct touch with users and programmers all over the world, you will want to explore the more than 20 different groups that distribute advice, freeware, and shareware for Macintosh users and programmers. (See Table 26-2 for a list of the current Macintosh-oriented news groups.) These groups really are just a start, as the Internet has dozens of other groups that discuss all sorts of data communications and networking issues, system-management concerns, and specific networking products (such as Cisco routers in comp.dcom.cisco and AppleTalk in comp.protocols.appletalk).

## Table 26-1
### Major Usenet News Hierarchies

| Hierarchy Name | Description |
| --- | --- |
| comp | More than 300 groups covering computer science, software, and hardware. Groups distribute freeware and shareware for every operating system. |
| sci | More than 50 groups covering science research. Groups include astronomy, cryptography, economics, electronics, medicine, and space. |
| misc | More than 30 groups on topics that cannot be easily classified, such as buying and selling computer systems, employment, investments and taxes, and legal issues. |
| soc and talk | Groups that primarily address social issues and socialization in cultures around the world. Debates and discussions fill these 100 groups. |
| rec | About 225 groups oriented toward hobbies and recreational activities. Groups include antiques, science fiction, television, audio, sports, cooking, games, and music. |
| alt | A collection of newsgroups that take the anarchy of Usenet to its limit: the Internet places no restrictions on alt groups, and there are more than 1,200 of them. Some groups discuss cutting-edge topics too new to have a home in the other categories. |
| biz | Twenty-five newsgroups that cover the world of business products — in particular, computer products and services. Groups include product announcements, announcements of fixes and enhancements, product reviews, and postings of demo software. |
| ClariNet | The commercial side of Usenet. Each site pays to receive ClariNet postings, which include stock quotes and reports, news from the major wire services, local news in the United States and Canada, and other newspaper-style information. |

A particularly interesting part of Usenet is ClariNet, which costs money but brings machine-readable news of the world to your computer. If knowing what's going on in the world is important for you, if you want to watch your competitors, or if you need to keep up on the latest developments in more than two dozen fields, ClariNet is a powerful and surprisingly inexpensive tool, with subscription rates for a small company beginning at less than $100 a month.

## File transfer on the Internet

Need some software? Patches and bug fixes from your application and operating-system vendors? The latest security alerts? Papers on electromagnetic engineering? Back issues of the *Biosphere* newsletter? Almost half the traffic on the Internet is file transfers — people and machines busily moving information around. If Usenet is the dynamic part of the Internet, file-transfer archives are the static part. Almost everything that goes into Usenet is archived somewhere, and these archives are only a small percentage of the tremendous information resources available.

**Table 26-2**
**The comp.sys.mac Hierarchy**

| Group Name | Description |
|---|---|
| comp.sys.mac.advocacy | The Macintosh computer family, compared with others. |
| comp.sys.mac.announce | Important notices for Macintosh users (moderated). |
| comp.sys.mac.apps | Discussions of Macintosh applications. |
| comp.sys.mac.comm | Discussions of Macintosh communications. |
| comp.sys.mac.databases | Database systems for the Macintosh. |
| comp.sys.mac.digest | Macintosh information and uses, but no programs (moderated). |
| comp.sys.mac.games | Discussions of games on the Macintosh. |
| comp.sys.mac.graphics | Macintosh graphics: paint, draw, 3-D, CAD, and animation. |
| comp.sys.mac.hardware | Macintosh hardware issues and discussions. |
| comp.sys.mac.hypercard | Macintosh HyperCard information and uses. |
| comp.sys.mac.misc | General discussions about the Macintosh. |
| comp.sys.mac.oop.macapp3 | Version 3 of the MacApp object-oriented system. |
| comp.sys.mac.oop.misc | Issues of object-oriented programming on the Macintosh. |
| comp.sys.mac.oop.tcl | Symantec's THINK Class Library for object programming. |
| comp.sys.mac.portables | Discussions of laptop Macintoshes. |
| comp.sys.mac.programmer | Discussions of programming the Macintosh. |
| comp.sys.mac.scitech | Discussions of using the Macintosh in scientific and technological work |
| comp.sys.mac.system | Discussions of Macintosh System software. |
| comp.sys.mac.wanted | Postings, such as "I want XYZ for my Mac". |

To get access to archives, you usually use a technique called *anonymous ftp*. *FTP* is File Transfer Protocol, a TCP/IP utility that allows you to move files from one system to another. *Anonymous* means that you don't need to prearrange your access with anyone; through a network-wide convention, you can use the user name "anonymous" without any password to access whatever the system administrator has made available. Normally, you run the *ftp* program to do file transfers, but many Gopher and WWW client programs can do anonymous file transfers as well.

No one knows how many sites are willing to allow anyone to log in and download interesting software — like the rest of the Internet, trying to count things is always futile. McGill University's Archie program tries to keep track of anonymous *ftp* sites: it indexes 600 sites with more than 2 million files.

What's available? You name it; it's there. Interested in downloading the entire source code of the X window system? It's there. Want a high-quality C (or C++) compiler for every machine in your shop? It's there. Need documentation on U.S. Supreme Court decisions? How about a copy of the open version of the Central Intelligence Agency database on every country in the world, or a complete set of digital maps, State Department travel advisories, or a thesaurus? The list goes on and on.

## Information services on the Internet

Electronic mail, the news service, and file transfer are the three largest services available on the Internet. As a wide area network, the Internet offers remote terminal access (usually called *telnet* and *rlogin*) from host to host. *Telnet* allows you to log in to any of the timesharing systems connected to the Internet — if you have a user name and password, of course. (If you need to know more about what *telnet* and *rlogin* are, turn to Chapter 18, "Macs in the World of TCP/IP.")

The Internet also is home to hundreds of smaller, special-purpose information services. It's impossible to know about all these services. Don't even try. The only current listings are the on-line ones. Internet services range from small databases of very local information (such as the campus-wide information system at the University of Arizona) to extremely sophisticated collections (such as NASA's data on nuclear decay and radiation). WAIS, the Wide Area Information Service, uses the ANSI Z39.50 information retrieval protocols to make many of these databases available.

Almost everyone who has ever tried to find something on the Internet ends up being frustrated by the massive quantities of information and poor indexing. To help solve this problem, groups are working on tools for navigating through the Internet. The Internet Gopher and the World Wide Web (WWW) are two tools that build an interface on top of the Internet. Gopher is similar to a card catalog, enabling you to find and retrieve resources by topic. WWW provides a trendy hypertext interface to the Internet, enabling users to follow links and find resources — if they're part of the web.

Some of the resources are extremely valuable. If you're worried about security issues, the Internet is the fastest method of disseminating information about problems and fixes. The security-incident reporting and management teams from all major vendors (and for the Internet itself) are all connected to the Internet, and their bulletins about problems and fixes for software and operating systems are available. Manufacturers such as Digital and Sun also are connected, and the latest information and patches to these companies' operating systems can be delivered over the Internet.

Apple also is a significant contributor to the Internet, housing an FTP site where you can get the most recent copies of system add-ons such as CD-ROM drivers, updaters for the Macintosh System software, and other nifty tidbits and tools.

# How to connect to the Internet

Connecting to the Internet means finding a service provider. Providers will walk you through software and hardware installation; they will install phone lines and serve as your point of contact in the Internet. Before you find a provider, though, you have to decide what kind of service you want. For most organizations, the decision comes down to finances: how much service can I buy on my current budget? Naturally, the more money you have to throw at the problem, the better class of service you will get.

Your choice of service provider has another important effect: it determines the side of the Internet to which you get connected. Because large parts of the Internet are funded by the U.S. government, there are restrictions on the kinds of commercial activities that can pass over those parts. If you are connecting to the Internet "in support of research or education," (from the original NSFnet charter) you can hop on pretty much anywhere. If you want to use the Internet for purely commercial purposes, you need to choose a service provider attached to the commercial side of the Internet (called CIX, for Commercial Internet Exchange). Your choice of service provider won't necessarily change the list of people you can communicate with; the restriction simply ensures that commercial traffic doesn't use the federally-funded research backbone.

Over time, the commercial backbones are growing larger than the non-commercial ones, so restrictions on what the Internet can be used for mean less and less each day. Nevertheless, you should be careful to understand what restrictions your service provider places on the uses you can make of the Internet.

The next step in getting connected is bringing the Internet into your organization. If you're already running TCP/IP internally, you're all set. But if you're working with a simple disk/printer operating system like NetWare or AppleShare, you have work to do (discussed in detail later in this chapter in "Issues in Connecting to the Internet").

Bringing TCP/IP access to personal computers for network news, file transfer, remote terminal, and other services (such as Gopher, WAIS, Archie, and the WWW) means adding software. For detailed information, make sure that you read Chapter 18.

Most medium-size to large companies will want to have a dedicated gateway system that serves as the portal to their Internet connection. Gateway systems running either OpenVMS or UNIX are more flexible than their MS-DOS and Macintosh counterparts; these systems give the network manager greater control of security, mail forwarding and gateway service, access, and network management. The gateway system doesn't necessarily have to be a large system; in fact, many organizations find that old, slow hardware makes an especially cost-effective network server.

To find out how to join the Internet, you should refer to Susan Estrada's *Connecting to the Internet* (O'Reilly & Associates, Inc.), which will walk you through the steps.

# Issues in Connecting to the Internet

After you physically link your network to the Internet, you will have to answer many questions about making the upper-level connection between your corporate network and the Internet. The following sections discuss the most important issues you need to consider when connecting the corporation (not just the network) to the Internet.

## Security

The first concern of anyone who has just connected to the Internet is security. Notice that we use the word *concern*; security should not be an obsession. Before you make the final connection between your corporate network and the Internet, you need to decide what level of risk you're willing to take and contrast that with the inconvenience to both corporate and external users. At one end of the spectrum, your Internet-connected computers are disconnected from the corporate networks, with no physical link (an "air gap") between the two. Air gap security is sure to please paranoid security managers, but it will annoy and inconvenience everyone who wants to join the Internet community.

At the other end of the security spectrum is a complete merger of your corporate network with the Internet. Unless you have security tightly wrapped up on every system on the corporate wires, merging your corporate network with the Internet is equally inadvisable. Besides, little or no reason exists for every single Macintosh in your company to have direct peer-to-peer communications over the Internet.

A more reasoned approach to security combines multiple tools with a common-sense policy. Packet filters are a good start. *Packet filtering* is a capability in well-designed TCP/IP routers that allows you to specify conditions for filtering out packets to and from the Internet. Make sure that the router between your network and the Internet has these filters. To use packet filters effectively, you need to characterize Internet communications based on TCP/IP address and traffic type.

If you anticipate that your only connection to the Internet will be for electronic mail, for example, you can use packet filters to allow only SMTP TCP traffic to enter and leave your network. Similarly, you may want to allow management traffic to enter your network, but only from your Internet network provider. In this case, you would filter out all SNMP (*Simple Network Management Protocol*) UDP traffic except that coming from known addresses at your provider. If you plan to have a Gopher or WWW server, you want only incoming connections to TCP port 70 (the gopher port) or 80 (the WWW port) to be allowed on that particular server.

The key to secure use of packet filters is starting with the most restrictive situation and working your way out. Don't ignore a port just because no service is assigned to it; you never know what problems future bugs will create.

Depending on packet filters makes your router the weak link in the security scheme, so protecting it from intrusion or manipulation is especially crucial. If possible, have your Internet provider apply filters on your incoming connection to block all attempts to talk directly to your router.

Some Internet service providers consider the router to be part of their management domain, and they will refuse to give you the configuration passwords or will insist on sharing them. In such a situation, you should consider adding a second router — which only you control — to minimize risks.

A larger network or a particularly security-sensitive organization may want to build an electronic firewall between the Internet and internal networks. Many configurations are possible, but a typical one includes a routing system with a tightly configured set of packet and address filters. The next step beyond packet filtering — connection filtering — is a common firewall service. In connection filtering, TCP connections are allowed only in certain directions. An interactive-terminal session (telnet), for example, might be allowed only if the session originated within the corporate network; the firewall would deny any attempt to telnet into the corporate network from the Internet.

Firewalls can be built from dedicated routers or can be part of a gateway computer that forms the bridge between the Internet and corporate networks. A gateway computer offers services to the Internet and has limited capability to connect to the corporate network. These gateway systems, kept separate from other corporate information assets, can be used as electronic mail, file-transfer, and information servers that link corporate users and public information to the Internet.

No matter how much confidence you have in the security of your Internet connection, planning for a compromise of security is prudent. Take advantage of the configuration capabilities of your minicomputer networking software by activating its own port-filtering capabilities. If your organization uses a small set of Class B or Class C IP network numbers, for example, configure your minicomputers to allow only TCP connects from those network numbers. Although this configuration technique is not as comprehensive as those offered by firewall routers, any good minicomputer TCP/IP package permits broad restrictions on access. Publish a set of guidelines to help minicomputer and mainframe managers add this extra ounce of prevention.

For microcomputer users, education is your primary tool. Any Macintosh with an FTP server is a potential hole leading directly into your corporate LAN-based data. Make sure that the default TCP/IP configuration is distributed with FTP service disabled and passwords enabled.

# Training

You can't just dump your network users into the world of the Internet and expect them to make effective use of the resources. Your organization is paying for the connection, the hardware, and the people to support both; the organization has a right to expect some return on its investment. Plan from the start to make a wide variety of training services available to internal users.

Short courses of two to four hours for beginners should be a basic part of your training package. Plan for a snowball effect. Little interest and low turnout will turn to overwhelming demand for training when word gets out about your new connection and the services it offers. Many training companies now offer Internet training courses. Your network provider probably can help you find good teachers nearby. If you can afford it, have a trainer who is familiar with your organization give several on-site classes. Internal users relate best to training given in the context of their own responsibilities and interests.

Classroom-lecture training should be supplemented with generous doses of information in both on-line and hard-copy format. A good Internet curriculum might have multiple short courses in it, including:

❖ Technical aspects of the TCP/IP protocol suite itself (only needed in some organizations).

❖ An introduction to the Internet and its resources — very brief discussion, an hour at most.

❖ Extending the existing tools, such as electronic mail, of an organization across the Internet.

❖ Beginning client tools, such as *telnet*, *ftp*, Gopher, and WWW.

❖ Beginning search techniques; how to find the information you want on the Internet.

❖ Advanced search techniques.

❖ Bringing internal information resources to the Internet — how your company can be a server.

Each of these should be kept short and distinct. We have found that trying to do all of these in one mammoth all-day training session doesn't work very well.

# Electronic mail

Most organizations have a variety of electronic mail systems that reflect a combination of history, hierarchy, and politics. If possible, you should avoid spreading the chaos of your e-mail systems to the Internet. Many organizations joining the Internet use an electronic mail gateway system to accept e-mail from the Internet and translate that e-mail to the appropriate internal formats. At the same time, an e-mail gateway can provide a uniform addressing scheme that simplifies connections between an organization and the rest of the world.

Consider one of the authors' companies, Opus One, which has PC, minicomputer, and mainframe e-mail systems. Rather than ask outsiders to remember and recreate addresses like "snydjo%venus.mis%mhs@opus1.com," which might work to actually route the e-mail, Opus One's Internet e-mail gateway allows a much simpler format: "Joel_Snyder@Opus1.COM."

A well-configured gateway accepts aliased e-mail and properly generates aliases for outgoing mail. Thus, mail sent by "snydjo" will appear to come from "Joel_Snyder." This format ensures that random, confusing addresses don't get propagated into the Internet.

The exact format of the e-mail addresses that you use isn't important as long as you enforce a consistent approach. Table 26-3 shows some of the common formats in use.

| Table 26-3 E-Mail Addressing Styles | |
|---|---|
| **Format** | **Example** |
| First.Last | Ronald.Reagan |
| First_Last | Ronald_Reagan |
| First_M_Last | Ronald_W_Reagan |
| FLast | RReagan |
| FMLast | RWReagan |
| LastF | ReaganR |
| FirstLast | RonaldReagan |
| FirstMLast | RonaldWReagan |
| FML | RWR |

Gateways can have other features. By requiring that all e-mail pass through a gateway, a network manager has access to a single choke point in case of problems. A gateway also can reject or reroute e-mail that needs special handling. Some e-mail gateways include heuristics that try to deliver misaddressed e-mail by matching a partial or ambiguous address. E-mail sent to "Snyder@Opus1.COM," for example, would be delivered if only one Snyder existed or would be returned with a list of all the Snyders if more than one existed. (Heaven forbid such a calamity!)

The "Sendmail" package, which is part of most standard UNIX systems, commonly is used to manage an e-mail gateway. Unfortunately, Sendmail is one of the worst choices. The program is difficult to configure, has cryptic and misleading error messages, and usually leaves few traces when a problem needs to be tracked down. The main reasons for sendmail's popularity are its price (free) and wide availability.

Commercial vendors have played to Sendmail's weakness by introducing a variety of enterprise-wide e-mail gateways. Retix and SoftSwitch are two popular, if comparatively expensive, solutions that can run on UNIX platforms. SoftSwitch's roots lie in the mainframe IBM world, bringing together enterprise e-mail systems with thousands of users. Retix approached the market from the other direction by being first with ISO-standard-based networking and electronic mail products, such as ITU-T X.400 electronic mail. Other UNIX-based vendors include The Wollongong Group, ISOCOR, and WorldTalk.

For a combination of economy, performance, and strength under load, Digital's OpenVMS platform is difficult to beat, particularly on the new Alpha hardware. An organization that is interested in a truly robust e-mail gateway should consider packages such as Innosoft International's PMDF running on OpenVMS. For a hardware-and-software investment of less than $15,000, you can assemble a gateway that will transfer messages between popular PC e-mail systems, along with Internet (SMTP) mail and ITU-T X.400 e-mail.

## Directory services

Going hand in hand with electronic mail services are automated directory systems. The absolute best way to discover someone's e-mail address is through what datageeks like us like to call "out-of-band *a priori* knowledge," which means calling them on the phone, but Internet correspondents have a curious reluctance to use this tried-and-true approach; instead, they seek out on-line directory information. The hope of these users, we conjecture, is to get the electronic jump on their quarry — the rough equivalent of showing up, uninvited and unannounced, at the home of a high-school sweetheart simply to see the look on his or her face.

Toward this end, Internet-connected organizations have used a number of redundant directory-services technologies. These technologies range from the simple *finger* and *whois* commands, with their simple syntax and limited capabilities, to packages and experiments such as the CSO "ph" (phone book) protocol, PSI White Pages, whois++, and the long-awaited ITU-T X.500-based directory databases.

Even if you have a full-featured internal electronic directory, making that corporate database fully available on the Internet may not be wise. Information that employees and other users consider to be reasonable to divulge to their co-workers (home addresses and phone numbers, for example) may not be reasonable to publish to the entire network community.

We suggest picking a common technology, such as the finger or whois command, and using it as a primary directory tool. Other, less-common directory channels should be activated, but they return only information about how to use the real directory. If you chose to use finger as the interface from the Internet to your electronic directory, someone attempting a whois command would get a polite message to try "finger" instead.

As X.500-based servers and, more important, clients become more widely deployed on the Internet, you probably will want to change to an X.500-based directory server.

A finger or whois-based directory server does not easily provide the capability to search based on personal attributes — something that the newer directory services (such as CSO's "ph" and X.500) do with ease. It would be difficult to request the e-mail address or phone number of anyone in Accounts Payable in Chicago through the simple finger protocol. Searches based on more normal criteria, such as last or first name, are quite easy.

For most organizations, though, the additional flexibility of X.500 does not justify the risk and difficulty of being an early adopter. Even with the relatively limited finger and whois protocols, more specialized information can be distributed with only a little ingenuity. The California State Senate has installed a finger server, which, given a California zip code, returns the counties that the zip code covers; the names, addresses, and phone numbers of the senators who are responsible for the area; and the legislative committees to which those senators belong.

## Your face on the Internet

Organizations that are in the computer business should use their Internet connection as an opportunity to make better contact with their customers and users. One prime technique is using a Usenet news group that deals with products and services. A news group can provide a forum for users of your products to discuss issues, problems, rumors, and solutions. Eavesdropping on these discussions is a valuable form of market research. Of even greater value is participation: actively responding to questions and problems, providing information about features and product changes, and keeping in touch with your most loquacious users.

Proper participation in a Usenet news group does not require huge investments of either engineering or support staff. Your participation will be a valuable marketing edge, however, when those customers make their repurchase decisions. Companies that have good reputations on the Internet are finding those reputations to be more and more valuable in distinguishing themselves in the global marketplace.

If a news group seems to be too large a step, mailing lists are a good way to get your feet wet (without a huge shock). Some corporations, such as Digital Equipment Corp. and Sun Microsystems, have created mailing lists that are used solely to broadcast corporate information and press releases. Other companies use mailing lists as part of two-way communication between vendor and customer — all done over the Internet.

Any organization with links to the Internet should expect potential customers to come knocking at their electronic doors in search of marketing information. Although blatant advertising on the net is considered to be poor *netiquette* (that's *network etiquette*, for you *newbies* out there), making comprehensive information about products and services available over the wires is praiseworthy. Organizations that have other information to share, such as locally developed public-domain software, databases, or random musings by the company president, also will want to establish an anonymous FTP area as part of their Internet connection.

Anonymous FTP should be limited to a small number (perhaps a number as small as one) of well-known computers. Internal network users must consider any bit of data on the anonymous FTP system to be available, even if that data hasn't been explicitly placed in normal anonymous FTP directories. Similarly, the anonymous FTP computers should not have any access to organizational data stored on the network. That means that every computer in the network should know that the FTP server is on the "unsecure" side of the network. Similarly, the FTP server should have its network software configured to restrict access from it to internal systems. If NFS (Network File System) disks are shared between corporate computers, for example, the anonymous FTP system should not have these disks mounted or even accessible. Other disk-sharing systems, including any AppleShare service, should have similar restrictions on their access from the Anonymous FTP server.

Anonymous FTP goes hand in hand with an organizational policy on what kinds of information can be made available, how files will move from internal systems to the Anonymous FTP system, and who will be responsible for keeping the data up to date.

Other information-based services, such as Gopher servers, WWW servers, and WAIS servers, are admirable goals for organizations seeking to take part in the Internet's current information obesity. So long as these services are well maintained, they also convey a favorable impression of their sponsoring organizations. On the other hand, nothing looks sloppier than a Gopher server from which most of the links jump off to electronic never-never land. Before embarking on an information-publishing expedition, make sure that you have management support to keep the information current — or be prepared to pull the service off-line at any time.

## Names for your Internet services

When you set up Internet services, use some good sense about how people will find you. Putting your Gopher service on a computer called Boombox, for example, is not nearly as useful as putting it on a computer named Gopher. Remember, too, that the DNS (*Domain Name System*) allows a single system to have an unlimited number of names. Even if everything is packed on a single computer, it's better to tell people to access Gopher on "gopher.opus1.com," FTP on "ftp.opus1.com," and WWW on "www.opus1.com." This arrangement gives you flexibility to move things around as needs and capacities change, without confusing the world at large.

The only exception to this strategy that we advise is in the area of electronic mail. Although making people send mail to "mail.opus1.com" is perfectly acceptable, those extra five characters will simply frustrate frequent correspondents and clutter already-crowded business cards. (You were planning to have your new e-mail address on all your business cards, weren't you?)

## Management issues

When planning your Internet e-mail gateway, be sure to plan for the additional time it will take to manage the resource and to respond to random queries from the world at large. The Internet cabal highly recommends that every e-mail destination have a user *postmaster* who is responsible for smooth operation and troubleshooting. The omnipresent postmaster often turns into a corporate-communications officer. Every Internet postmaster has stories of random questions and demands that float in over the wires. Many novice network researchers have mass-mailed surveys and announcements to every domain that they can discover, usually addressed to the attention of the poor postmasters.

Despite the interruptions caused by unsolicited e-mail transmissions, conscientious gateway managers should create a wide range of e-mail destinations to help hapless citizens who are searching for a contact. Good starting points, in addition to "postmaster," include "root," "system," "operator," and "hostmaster," as well as customer-oriented addresses such as "sales," "support," "service," "info," and (of course) "complaints." Missives need not flow directly from Internet to the heart of the organization; it's simply a good idea to have someone listening should anyone come knocking.

Keeping track of problems and questions should be an integral part of your postmaster's job. When outsiders make contact with an organization, they expect that their communications will be taken at least as seriously as a letter, even if you think of those communications as casually as you would a telephone call. Having a system that tracks incoming messages to make sure that timely replies go back out is a good idea; you don't want anything to fall through the cracks.

The postmaster also needs to have the right attitude about handling incoming queries. Many correspondents will be confused or beginners at the e-mail game and may need some special hand-holding. Some system managers, while technically supportive, may not have the people skills to represent your organization to the outside world properly. In the world of electronic mail, in which most of our normal communications cues are missing, even an innocuous message can be interpreted as being hostile or insulting. If your network and system managers don't have diplomatic writing skills, you should find a good spokesperson to read and respond to mail sent to the corporate postmaster.

# CHAPTER 26   CONCEPTS AND TERMS

- The Internet is an anarchic collection of networks that have chosen to band together. The Internet has no central authority whatsoever.

- The Internet is really, really, really big — and growing.

- The Internet hosts many services, including electronic mail, file transfer, news and discussion groups, and client/server information applications.

- You can use many technologies to connect to the Internet. Your choice is limited only by geography and budget.

- Security should be an important concern for anyone who is connecting to the Internet. A proper gateway firewall is the most appropriate technology.

- Services such as electronic mail can be managed flexibly through the use of a minicomputer server, rather than a Macintosh or MS-DOS server.

- Organizations can contribute to the Internet by making information available in many ways. Organizations also can link their electronic mail networks to improve contact between customer and supplier.

which allows distributed authority for names. DNS is used to map from names to addresses in TCP/IP.

**news groups**
A convenient heading for a discussion topic in the Usenet news system

**packet filtering**
Gateway technique used to create a firewall between your network and another (like the Internet). Packet filtering means that the firewall gateway will not pass packets except those which conform to a narrowly defined rule set designed by the network security manager.

**anonymous FTP**
Internet file transfer which does not require prior authorization.

**DNS (Domain Name System)**
Internet naming and addressing system. The DNS is a hierarchical naming system

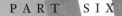

PART SIX

# Appendixes

# AppleTalk
# Packet Formats

This appendix contains drawings representing the formats of the various packet types used in AppleTalk. Figure A-1 is a layer-by-layer map of the AppleTalk packets described in this appendix. For further information on packet contents and program calls to the protocols, refer to *Inside AppleTalk*, 2nd Edition (Addison-Wesley, 1991).

List of figures in Appendix A:

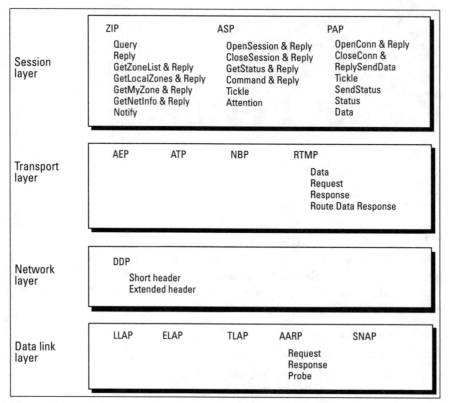

Figure A-1: Layer-by-layer map of AppleTalk packets included in Appendix A.

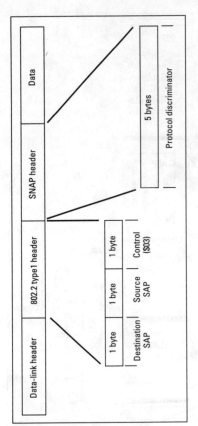

Figure A-3: Sub-Network Access Protocol (SNAP).

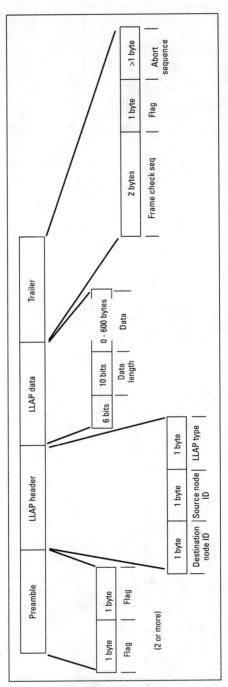

Figure A-2: LocalTalk Link Access Protocol (LLAP).

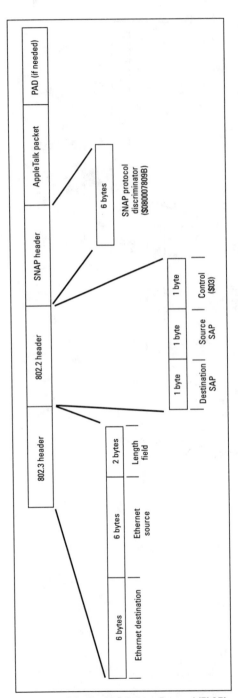

**Figure A-4: Ethernet Link Access Protocol (ELAP).**

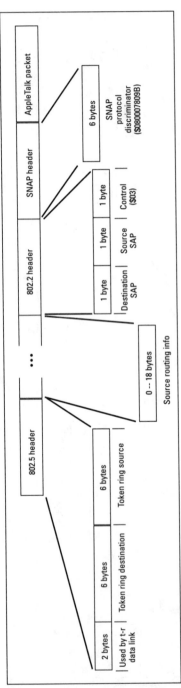

**Figure A-5: Token Ring Link Access Protocol (TLAP).**

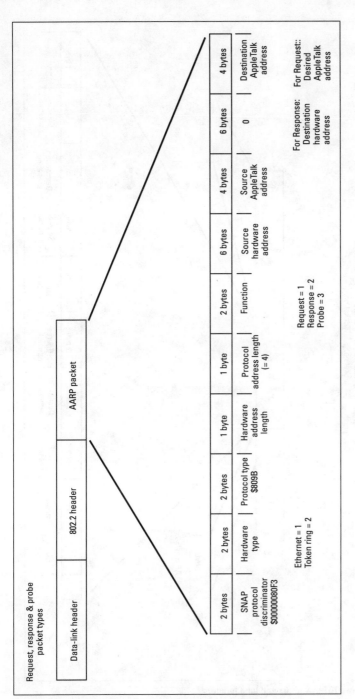

**Figure A-6: AppleTalk Address Resolution Protocol (AARP).**

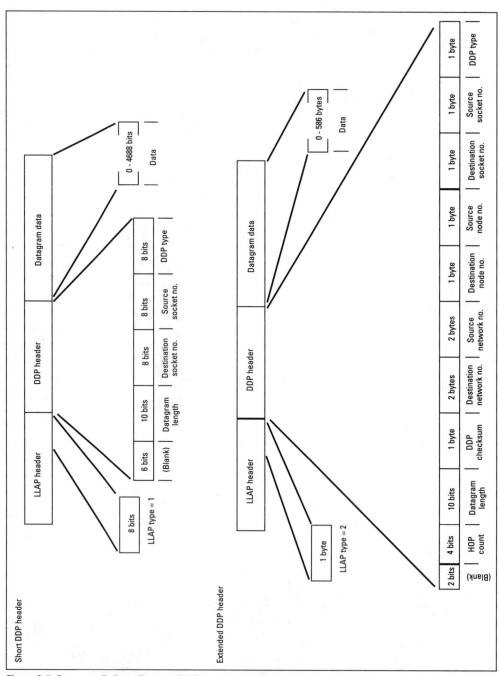

**Figure A-7: Datagram Delivery Protocol (DDP) — short and long headers.**

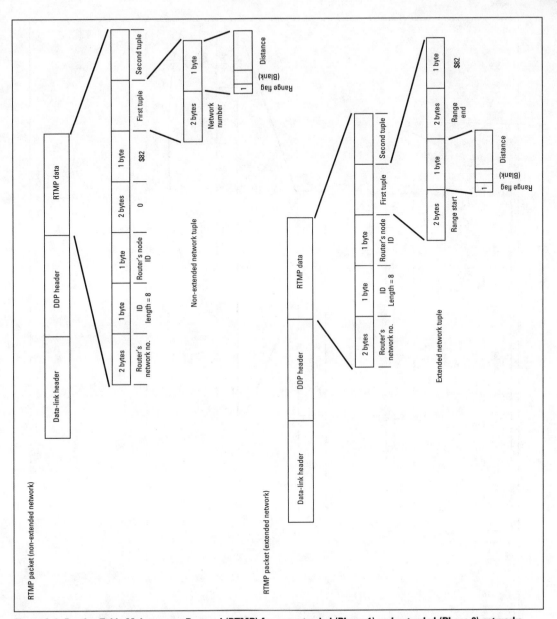

**Figure A-8: Routing Table Maintenance Protocol (RTMP) for nonextended (Phase 1) and extended (Phase 2) networks.**

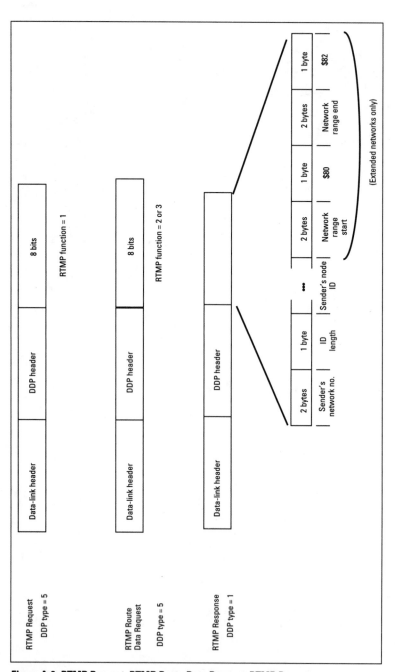

**Figure A-9: RTMP Request, RTMP Route Data Request, RTMP Response.**

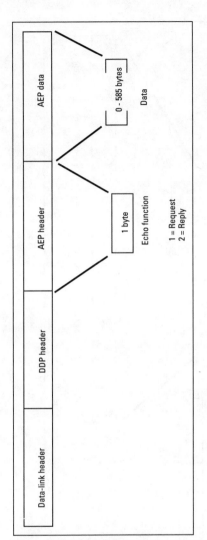

**Figure A-10: AppleTalk Echo Protocol (AEP).**

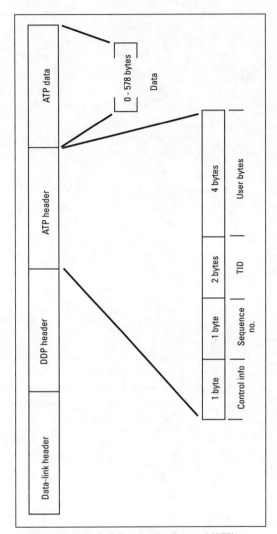

**Figure A-11: AppleTalk Transaction Protocol (ATP).**

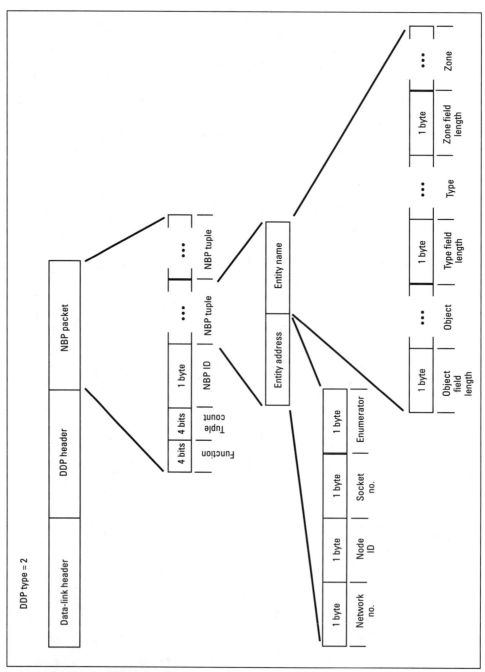

**Figure A-12: Name Binding Protocol (NBP).**

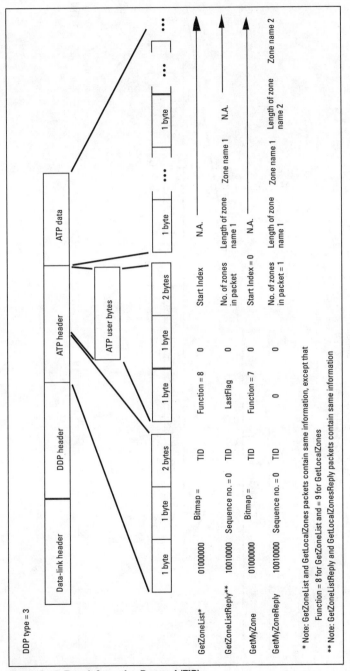

**Figure A-13: Zone Information Protocol (ZIP).**

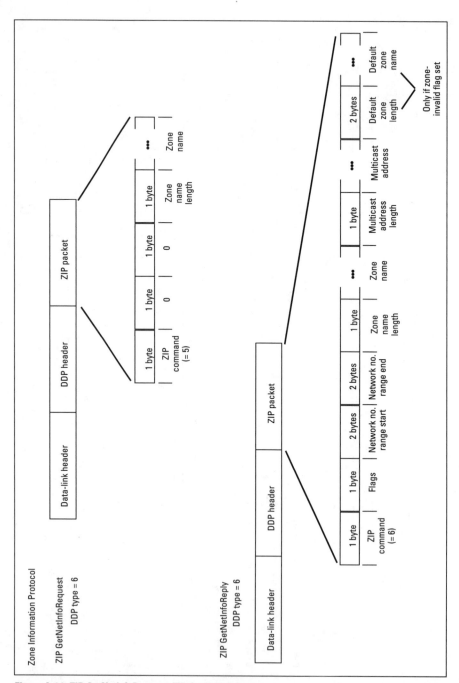

**Figure A-14: ZIP GetNetInfoRequest, ZIP GetNetInfoReply.**

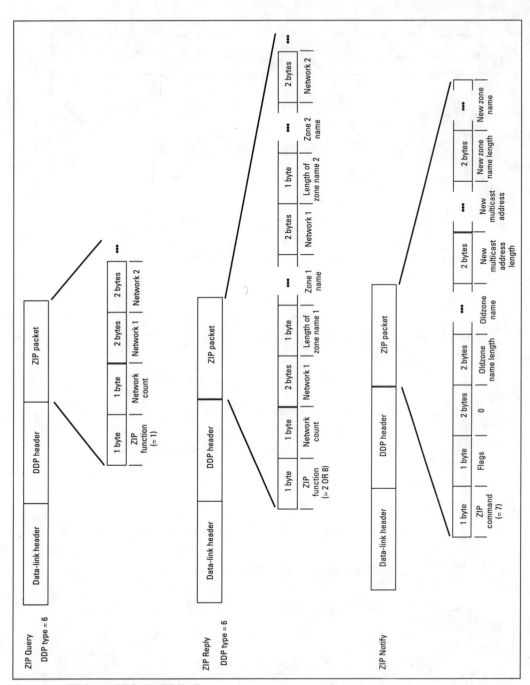

**Figure A-15: ZIP Query, ZIP Reply, ZIP Notify.**

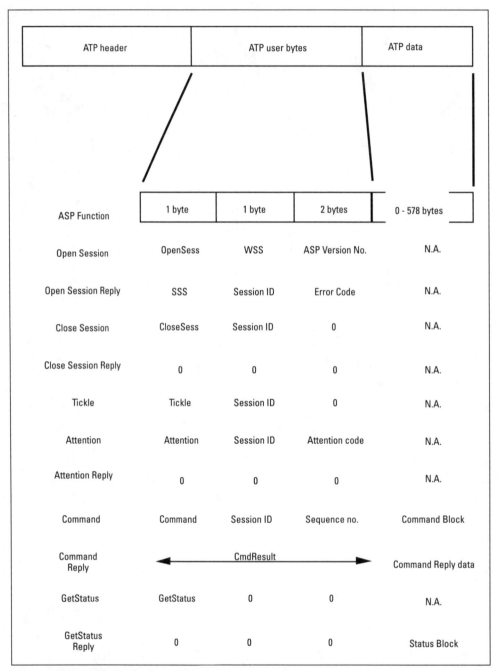

| ASP Function | 1 byte | 1 byte | 2 bytes | 0 - 578 bytes |
|---|---|---|---|---|
| Open Session | OpenSess | WSS | ASP Version No. | N.A. |
| Open Session Reply | SSS | Session ID | Error Code | N.A. |
| Close Session | CloseSess | Session ID | 0 | N.A. |
| Close Session Reply | 0 | 0 | 0 | N.A. |
| Tickle | Tickle | Session ID | 0 | N.A. |
| Attention | Attention | Session ID | Attention code | N.A. |
| Attention Reply | 0 | 0 | 0 | N.A. |
| Command | Command | Session ID | Sequence no. | Command Block |
| Command Reply | ← CmdResult → | | | Command Reply data |
| GetStatus | GetStatus | 0 | 0 | N.A. |
| GetStatus Reply | 0 | 0 | 0 | Status Block |

Header row (top): ATP header | ATP user bytes | ATP data

**Figure A-16: AppleTalk Session Protocol (ASP).**

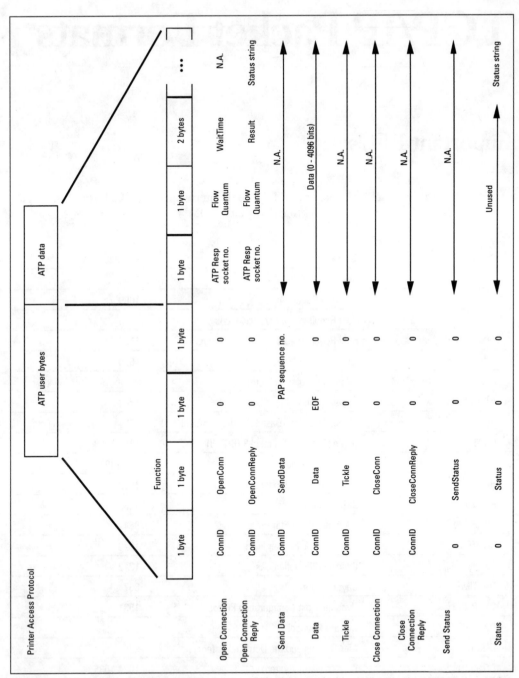

**Figure A-17: Printer Access Protocol (PAP).**

# TCP/IP Packet Formats

## Important RFCs

(All are available via Anonymous FTP to ds.internic.net or on CD from InfoMagic, Inc, 800-800-6613 on their "Standards CD-ROM")

| Category | Name | RFC No. |
|----------|------|---------|
| | Assigned Numbers | 1340 |
| | Gateway Requirements | 1009 |
| | Host Requirements - Applications | 1123 |
| | Host Requirements - Communications | 1122 |
| | Internet Official Protocol Standards | 1600 |
| ARP | Address Resolution Protocol | 826 |
| AT-MIB | Appletalk MIB | 1243 |
| AURP | Appletalk Update-Based Routing Protocol | 1504 |
| BGP3 | Border Gateway Protocol 3 (BGP-3) | 1267,1268 |
| BOOTP | Bootstrap Protocol | 951,1497 |
| BOOTP | Clarifications and Extensions BOOTP | 1532 |
| BSD Login | BSD Login | 1282 |
| CHARGEN | Character Generator Protocol | 864 |
| CONTENT | Content Type Header Field | 1049 |
| Concise-MIB | Concise MIB Definitions | 1212 |
| DAYTIME | Daytime Protocol | 867 |
| DHCP | Dynamic Host Configuration Protocol | 1531 |
| DISCARD | Discard Protocol | 863 |
| DNS-MX | Mail Routing and the Domain System | 974 |
| DOMAIN | Domain Name System | 1034,1035 |
| ECHO | Echo Protocol | 862 |
| EGP | Exterior Gateway Protocol | 904 |
| FINGER | Finger Protocol | 1288 |

| Category | Name | RFC No. |
|---|---|---|
| FTP | File Transfer Protocol | 959 |
| GOPHER | The Internet Gopher Protocol | 1436 |
| IARP | Inverse Address Resolution Protocol | 1293 |
| ICMP | Internet Control Message Protocol | 792 |
| IDPR | Inter-Domain Policy Routing Protocol | 1479 |
| IDPR-ARCH | Architecture for IDPR | 1478 |
| IGMP | Internet Group Multicast Protocol | 1112 |
| IP | Internet Protocol | 791 |
| IP-CMPRS | Compressing TCP/IP Headers | 1144 |
| KERBEROS | Kerberos Network Authentication Ser (V5) | 1510 |
| LISTSERV | Listserv Distribute Protocol | 1429 |
| MAIL | Format of Electronic Mail Messages | 822 |
| MIB-II | Management Information Base-II | 1213 |
| MIME | Multipurpose Internet Mail Extensions | 1521 |
| NETBIOS | NetBIOS Service Protocols | 1001,1002 |
| NICNAME | WhoIs Protocol | 954 |
| NNTP | Network News Transfer Protocol | 977 |
| NTPV2 | Network Time Protocol (Version 2) | 1119 |
| NTPV3 | Network Time Protocol (Version 3) | 1305 |
| OSPF2 | Open Shortest Path First Routing V2 | 1247 |
| PCMAIL | Pcmail Transport Protocol | 1056 |
| PEM-ALG | PEM - Algorithms, Modes, and Identifiers | 1423 |
| PEM-CKM | PEM - Certificate-Based Key Management | 1422 |
| PEM-ENC | PEM - Message Encryption and Auth | 1421 |
| PEM-KEY | PEM - Key Certification | 1424 |
| POP3 | Post Office Protocol, Version 3 | 1460 |
| PPP | Point-to-Point Protocol (PPP) | 1548 |
| PPP-ATCP | PPP AppleTalk Control Protocol | 1378 |
| PPP-AUTH | PPP Authentication | 1334 |
| PPP-DNCP | PPP DECnet Phase IV Control Protocol | 1376 |
| PPP-EXT | PPP Extensions for Bridging | 1220 |
| PPP-IPCP | PPP Control Protocol | 1332 |
| PPP-LINK | PPP Link Quality Monitoring | 1333 |
| PPP-OSINLCP | PPP OSI Network Layer Control Protocol | 1377 |

*(continued on the next page)*

| Category | Name | RFC No. |
| --- | --- | --- |
| QUOTE | Quote of the Day Protocol | 865 |
| RARP | A Reverse Address Resolution Protocol | 903 |
| RIP | Routing Information Protocol | 1058 |
| SMI | Structure of Management Information | 1155 |
| SMTP | Simple Mail Transfer Protocol | 821 |
| SNMP | Simple Network Management Protocol | 1157 |
| SNMP-AT | SNMP over AppleTalk | 1419 |
| SNMP-IPX | SNMP over IPX | 1420 |
| SNMP-OSI | SNMP over OSI | 1418 |
| SNMPv2 | Administrative Model for SNMPv2 | 1445 |
| SNMPv2 | Coexistence between SNMPv1 and SNMPv2 | 1452 |
| SNMPv2 | Conformance Statements for SNMPv2 | 1444 |
| SNMPv2 | Introduction to SNMPv2 | 1441 |
| SNMPv2 | Management Information Base for SNMPv2 | 1450 |
| SNMPv2 | Manager-to-Manager MIB | 1451 |
| SNMPv2 | Party MIB for SNMPv2 | 1447 |
| SNMPv2 | Protocol Operations for SNMPv2 | 1448 |
| SNMPv2 | SMI for SNMPv2 | 1442 |
| SNMPv2 | Security Protocols for SNMPv2 | 1446 |
| SNMPv2 | Textual Conventions for SNMPv2 | 1443 |
| SNMPv2 | Transport Mappings for SNMPv2 | 1449 |
| SUN-NFS | Network File System Protocol | 1094 |
| SUN-RPC | Remote Procedure Call Protocol Version 2 | 1057 |
| TACACS | Terminal Access Control Protocol | 1492 |
| TCP | Transmission Control Protocol | 793 |
| TELNET | Telnet Protocol | 854,855 |
| TFTP | Trivial File Transfer Protocol | 1350 |
| TIME | Time Server Protocol | 868 |
| TP-TCP | ISO Transport Service on top of the TCP | 1006 |
| UDP | User Datagram Protocol | 768 |
| USERS | Active Users Protocol | 866 |

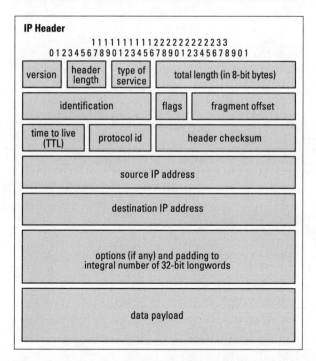

## IP Header Fields

| | |
|---|---|
| ***Version*** | *: IP version number (normally 4)* |
| Header Length: | Length of the header, in 32-bit longwords |
| Type of Service: | Not often used, fields which specify priority, throughput, and precedence |
| Total Length: | Length of the entire IP datagram, in 8-bit bytes (octets), including the IP header |
| Identification: | A unique identification number for this datagram |

*(continued on the next page)*

| IP Header Fields *(continued)* | |
|---|---|
| *Version* | *: IP version number (normally 4)* |
| Flags: | Used for fragmentation |
| Fragment Offset: | Indicates where this fragment belongs in a fragmented IP datagram in unites of 64-bit quadwords |
| Time to live: | A counter which is decremented by every router this datagram passes through. When it reaches 0, the datagram must be discarded |
| Protocol ID: | Identifies which protocol is in this IP datagram. Values are taken from RFC1340. Typical ones include:<br>1 : ICMP<br>6 : TCP<br>17 : UDP |
| Header Checksum: | Used to verify that the header of this packet has been passed undamaged. Must be recomputed at each router because of change in TTL. |
| Source, Destination IP addresses: | IP addresses (32-bit values) of sending and receiving end systems |
| Options | Optional IP extensions which may be included. This field is always padded to an integral number of 32-bit longwords. |
| Data | The whole point of the packet. In integral 8-bit bytes (octets). |

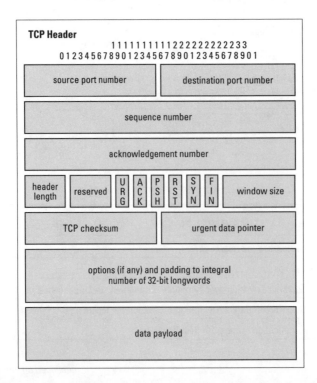

| TCP Headers Defined | |
|---|---|
| Source, Destination Port | Identifies a particular port (or higher level protocol) within the end system for this packet. See table below. |
| Sequence Number | The sequence number of the first byte (octet) in this packet. The sequence number is incremented by one for each octet and increases monotonically for the life of the connection |
| Acknowledgement Number | Piggyback acknowledgement of last correctly received sequence number +1 coming from the other direction |
| Header length | Length of the header, in 32-bit longwords. Also called "data offset" |
| Flags | 6 flags which are used in connection setup and management |
| | URG : Urgent data pointer is significant |
| | ACK : Acknowledgement number is significant |
| | PSH : Push function |
| | RST : Reset connection (1-way close) |
| | SYN : Synchronize sequence numbers |
| | FIN : Connection to be torn down (3-way close) |
| Window size | Indicates how much data the sender of this packet is willing to receive from the receiver |
| Checksum | Computed once; this is the checksum over both the header AND the data |
| Urgent Data Pointer | Points to end of urgent data (length) |
| Options | Not often used |

# Port numbers

These are defined in RFC 1340 (Assigned Numbers RFC), which is periodically updated. Most defined numbers are seldom used, but some common ones are:

| | | | |
|---|---|---|---|
| | 0 | Reserved | |
| echo | 7 | Echo | |
| discard | 9 | Discard | |
| systat | 11 | Active Users | |
| daytime | 13 | Daytime | |
| qotd | 17 | Quote of the Day | |
| chargen | 19 | Character | Generator |
| ftp-data | 20 | File Transfer | |

| | | | |
|---|---|---|---|
| ftp | 21 | File Transfer | |
| telnet | 23 | Telnet | |
| smtp | 25 | Simple Mail Transfer | |
| time | 37 | Time | |
| nicname | 43 | Who Is | |
| domain | 53 | Domain Name Server | |
| bootps | 67 | Bootstrap | Protocol Server |
| bootpc | 68 | Bootstrap | Protocol Client |
| tftp | 69 | Trivial File Transfer | |
| gopher | 70 | Gopher | |
| finger | 79 | Finger | |
| www | 80 | World Wide Web HTTP | |
| kerberos | 88 | Kerberos | |
| pop2 | 109 | Post Office Protocol - Version 2 | |
| pop3 | 110 | Post Office Protocol - Version 3 | |
| sunrpc | 111 | SUN Remote Procedure Call | |
| nntp | 119 | Network News Transfer Protocol | |
| ntp | 123 | Network Time Protocol | |
| netbios-ns | 137 | NETBIOS Name Service | |
| netbios-dgm | 138 | NETBIOS Datagram Service | |
| netbios-ssn | 139 | NETBIOS Session Service | |
| imap2 | 143 | Interim Mail Access Protocol v2 | |
| snmp | 161 | SNMP | |
| snmptrap | 162 | SNMPTRAP | |
| bgp | 179 | Border Gateway Protocol | |
| irc | 194 | Internet Relay Chat Protocol | |
| at-rtmp | 201 | AppleTalk | Routing Maintenance |
| at-nbp | 202 | AppleTalk | Name Binding |
| at-3 | 203 | AppleTalk | Unused |
| at-echo | 204 | AppleTalk | Echo |
| at-5 | 205 | AppleTalk | Unused |
| at-zis | 206 | AppleTalk | Zone Information |

| at-7 | 207 | AppleTalk | Unused |
|------|-----|-----------|--------|
| at-8 | 208 | AppleTalk | Unused |
| z39.50 | 210 | ANSI Z39.50 | |
| ipx | 213 | IPX | |
| softpc | 215 | Insignia Solutions | |
| imap3 | 220 | Interactive Mail Access Protocol v3 | |
| ulistserv | 372 | Unix Listserv | |
| ntalk | 518 | | |
| lotusnote | 1352 | Lotus Note | |

TCP state table for connection establishment and tear-down

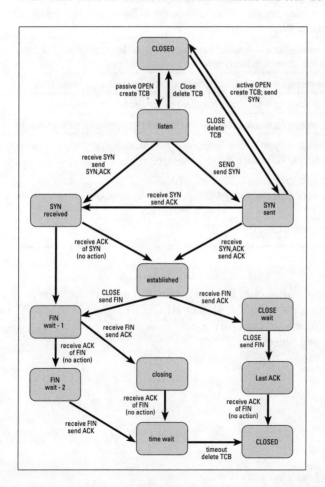

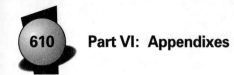

A TCP connection progresses through a series of states during its lifetime. The states are: LISTEN, SYN-SENT, SYN-RECEIVED, ESTABLISHED, FIN-WAIT-1, FIN-WAIT-2, CLOSE-WAIT, CLOSING, LAST-ACK, TIME-WAIT, and the fictional state CLOSED.  CLOSED is fictional because it represents the state when there is no TCB, and therefore, no connection.  Briefly the meanings of the states are:

| TCP Connection Phases | |
|---|---|
| LISTEN | represents waiting for a connection request from any remote TCP and port. |
| SYN-SENT | represents waiting for a matching connection request after having sent a connection request. |
| SYN-RECEIVED | represents waiting for a confirming connection request acknowledgment after having both received and sent a connection request. |
| ESTABLISHED | represents an open connection, data received can be delivered to the user. The normal state for the data transfer phase of the connection. |
| FIN-WAIT-1 | represents waiting for a connection termination request from the remote TCP, or an acknowledgment of the connection termination request previously sent. |
| FIN-WAIT-2 | represents waiting for a connection termination request from the remote TCP. |
| CLOSE-WAIT | represents waiting for a connection termination request from the local user. |
| CLOSING | represents waiting for a connection termination request acknowledgment from the remote TCP. |
| LAST-ACK | represents waiting for an acknowledgment of the connection termination request previously sent to the remote TCP (which includes an acknowledgment of its connection termination request). |
| TIME-WAIT | represents waiting for enough time to pass to be sure the remote TCP received the acknowledgment of its connection termination request. |
| CLOSED | represents no connection state at all. |

A TCP connection progresses from one state to another in response to events. The events are the user calls, OPEN, SEND, RECEIVE, CLOSE, ABORT, and STATUS; the incoming segments, particularly those containing the SYN, ACK, RST and FIN flags; and timeouts.

# ICMP Packet Formats

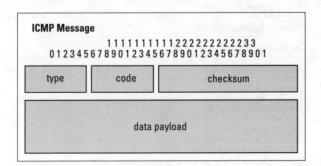

| Parts of ICMP Message | |
| --- | --- |
| Type | Type of the ICMP message. These are defined in RFC 792. |
| Code | Codes specific to each message. Defined in RFC 792. |
| Checksum | The 16-bit ones complement of the ones complement of the sum of the ICMP message starting with the ICMP type. |
| Data | Varies, depending on type of message (see RFC 792) |

| ICMP Messager Types and Legal Codes | |
|---|---|
| **Message Type (value)** | **Legal Codes (values)** |
| Destination Unreachable (3) | Network Unreachable (0) |
| | Host Unreachable (1) |
| | Protocol Unreachable (2) |
| | Port Unreachable (3) |
| | Fragmentation Needed and DF set (4) |
| | Source Route Failed (5) |
| Time Exceeded (11) | TTL exceeded in transit (0) |
| | Fragment reassembly time exceeded (1) |
| Parameter Problem (12) | Pointer indicates error (0) |
| Source Quench (4) | (none) (0) |
| Redirect (5) | Redirect datagrams for the Network (0) |
| | Redirect datagrams for the Host (1) |
| | Redirect datagrams for the TOS and Network (2) |
| | Redirect datagrams for the TOS and Host (3) |
| Echo (8) | (none) (0) |
| Echo Reply (8) | (none) (0) |
| Timestamp (13) | (none) (0) |
| Timestamp Reply (14) | (none) (0) |
| Information Request (15) | (none) (0) |
| Information Reply (16) | (none) (0) |

# Converting Phase 1 AppleTalk Networks to Phase 2

In this Appendix, you learn various strategies for the transition of a network from AppleTalk Phase 1 to AppleTalk Phase 2. Beyond explaining techniques and options, we'll list some problems that can occur during the transition. Some talented network managers unexpectedly experienced the seven technical problems described in this chapter, and we hope their experiences will sharpen your sense of caution.

We'll concentrate in this chapter on strategies for making a transition from Phase 1 to Phase 2 — not on the basics of how extended networking in Phase 2 works. Before reading this chapter, you need a clear understanding of the AppleTalk Routing Protocol, GetNetInfo packets, default zones, RTMP packets, network ranges, zone lists, and split-horizon routing. If you're not familiar with the concepts used in extended AppleTalk networks, refer to Chapter 3, "Understanding AppleTalk Protocols," and Chapter 11, "Designing an AppleTalk LAN."

Although this book primarily covers LocalTalk and EtherTalk networks, many of the EtherTalk concepts for Phase 2 apply to other types of extended AppleTalk networks, such as TokenTalk.

We believe that network administrators should move their networks over to AppleTalk Phase 2. Phase 2 offers many advantages, such as split-horizon routing, and Phase 2 is the building block of many exciting new networking products. Just be careful and thorough in your transition plans. We can't emphasize too strongly that you should test all products before releasing them on your production network.

# The Basics of Moving to Phase 2

The basic task in changing your internet from Phase 1 to Phase 2 is actually quite simple — you change the configuration files of all your EtherTalk routers from nonextended network configurations to extended network configurations. (No change is needed for bridges, which don't have network numbers.) Then you re-load any EtherTalk devices with Phase 2 drivers.

Recall that you cannot make a LocalTalk network into an extended network. When Apple wrote the protocol, the company decided that multiple zone names and networks were unnecessary on such a slow network. So, for LocalTalk-to-EtherTalk routers, you only need to change the configuration files of the ports that are attached to EtherTalk networks.

To change the ports configuration file to an extended format, you must change the routers format for information in the ports configuration file. The format will change from a network number to a network range and from a zone name to a zone list. A network range is an extended numbering scheme, and a zone list is an extended zone-naming scheme.

## Defining Phase 1 and Phase 2

Before going further, we need to clarify some terminology. As much as possible, we try to use extended and Phase 2 together to avoid confusion. To be absolutely precise, there are Phase 1 routers and Phase 2 routers, and there are extended networks and nonextended networks. But there are no Phase 1 or Phase 2 networks.

If this seems confusing, bear in mind that Phase 1 and Phase 2 are not networks — Phase 1 and Phase 2 are *specifications* for how to route and form packets. Routers *route* packets over and between either extended or nonextended networks. Software drivers *form* packets and then put them out over extended or nonextended networks.

The following critical distinction is most important to the network manager:

Phase 1 routers can route packets across nonextended networks but *not* across extended networks.

Phase 2 routers can route packets across *both* extended *and* nonextended networks.

Note that many Phase 1 routers, such as the older Shiva FastPaths (Model 2), were built before the release of the Phase 2 specification. Phase 2 routers can recognize both the Phase 1 and Phase 2 specifications. A Phase 2 router can tell whether a packet is being sent from a Phase 1 or a Phase 2 router by looking at an embedded version number in the RTMP Data packet. In a later section of this chapter, you'll see that these routing decisions can sometimes lead to problems.

Moreover, some Phase 2 routers implement a portion of the Phase 2 specification even on ports the administrator has configured for Phase 1 routing on a nonextended network. For example, some vendors have chosen to implement split-horizon routing on both extended and nonextended networks. So even if you believe your internet is totally Phase 1 because you selected Phase 1 in your configuration files dialog box, you may in fact have something other than Phase 1 on your internet. Unless you have only older routers on the internet, what you probably have is an internet that is using some newer Phase 2 technology to route packets over nonextended (Phase 1) networks.

As you can see, this terminology can be confusing. You don't want to be a slave to terminology, however, and for the most part the two sets of terms — Phase 1, nonextended, and Phase 2, extended — are used interchangeably. We'll continue to use the terms together when precise distinctions are not required.

## Choosing an extended network configuration

In the next section, you learn four methods for changing your internet from nonextended (Phase 1) to extended (Phase 2). With any of these methods, you have to devise a new numbering and zone-naming scheme.

To keep the implementation of the extended network configuration simple, you can even use the same network number and zone name you used for your nonextended (Phase 1) network. If, for example, your EtherTalks network number is 45, the new network range can be 45-45, which is a network range of one network. Furthermore, the zone list can be a zone list of one, consisting of the same zone name you used before.

The rules for network numbers are the same for Phase 2 as they are for Phase 1. You cannot duplicate a network number on another network, even if the number falls within a range of numbers. If your nonextended (Phase 1) network number is 45, and this nonextended network is connected with a transition router to an extended (then Phase 2) network, then you cannot use the number 45 to make the Phase 2 networks range 45-45 or even 43-46. As long as two or more networks are connected, each network number can be used only once.

As you select network numbers for your extended (Phase 2) internet, remember to plan for the growth of your network. Try to estimate how many users you will have over the next five years and how many additional networks you expect to connect to your current AppleTalk internet. Is there a good possibility that you will be connecting more buildings or more remote sites to your internet? If so, plan a numbering scheme you can grow with.

For example, many large companies use a code, based on their building and floor numbers, for establishing network numbers. In such a system, the network range 1014-1014 can stand for Building 101, Floor 4. This type of code allows easy addition of networks to your internet numbering scheme.

QUICK TIPS

### Assigning Zone Names

Remember that zone names are intended as a reference for the user. As a result, zone names that simply match up with network numbers are of no help to the user who is trying to determine what is available in a zone.

Don't give each network its own zone name: This is not necessary and, in most cases, not desirable. In larger internets, such a numbers-oriented manage-ment strategy often results in huge lists of zone names that mean little to the user. Zone names like Building 101 Floor 4 to match a network range of 1014-1014 do not indicate what network resources and devices can be found in the zone. As you choose zone names, also keep in mind that multiple network cables can share a zone name.

When choosing a network-number range for a particular network cable, also consider how many users you'll have on the cable. Recall that in Phase 2, each network number allows 253 AppleTalk devices to be attached to an Ethernet cable. If you have selected a network range of 4-6 for a particular cable, for example, you have created networks numbered 4, 5, and 6 — three networks of 253 nodes each. You can therefore attach 759 AppleTalk devices to that Ethernet cable.

Most networks don't have more than 253 devices and therefore require only a one-number range, such as 4-4. This type of numbering means that a particular cable is identified by each attached router as network 4. In fact, we advise you never to set up more than one network for each cable. If more than 253 users are on a cable, we suggest that you install an EtherTalk-to-EtherTalk router to facilitate manage-ment control over your network.

Although we recommend only one network number per network cable, we do advise the use of multiple zone names. Wise selection of zone names helps users navigate their way around the internet. Select descriptive zone names that will help users locate file servers, mail servers, and other multiple-user devices. Where ap-propriate, select zone names that describe the type of users who will have their Macs connected to the Ethernet. If your zone list includes an Engineering zone and a Marketing zone, for example, users who want to share engineering data can select to be in the Engineering zone, and users who want to share marketing data files can locate their Macintoshes in the Marketing zone.

The following example illustrates the use of helpful zone names. An AppleTalk internet at a certain company had an engineering program office, with Macintoshes on a LocalTalk network and file services on an EtherTalk network. (The network was set up in this way because the AppleTalk file server was on a VAX multiprotocol host.) To make it easy for Mac users on the LocalTalk network to find their server on the EtherTalk network, the zone name for the LocalTalk network was included in the EtherTalk networks zone list. In this configuration, a

LocalTalk Macintosh would display both its LocalTalk zones services and the EtherTalk file server in the same Chooser list because both LocalTalk and EtherTalk services were in the same zone. The user didn't need to be aware that two networks were involved.

# Four Phase 2 Transition Methods

After you carefully choose a configuration for your extended network, you're ready to select a method for changing your nonextended (Phase 1) internet to an extended (Phase 2) internet. With any of the methods discussed in the next sections, be sure that all your devices and software drivers are Phase 2 functional and that you are prepared to install the new software at the same time you change the routers. If you still have devices or software drivers that can operate only as Phase 1 nonextended network nodes, you can use any of the first three methods to retain some Phase 1 functionality on your internet.

You can use any of several methods to accomplish the Phase 1 to Phase 2 configuration change. In the following sections, you learn four of these methods:

1. The logical separation method

2. The physical separation method

3. The transition router method

4. The go-for-broke method

Each method has its advantages and hazards, and the size and complexity of your AppleTalk internet is a factor in deciding which is best for you. Keep in mind that the logical separation and the transition router methods are by far the most dangerous, especially in networks that have routers from two or more vendors. In fact, the logical separation and transition router methods lead to most of the seven problems described later in this chapter. Yet hazardous as they are, the logical separation and transition router methods remain the most convenient for many network managers — especially those who need to quickly establish Phase 2 routing or who do not have enough personnel resources to use the physical separation or go-for-broke methods. We don't recommend the use of the logical separation or transition router methods, but the two methods are used so commonly that we are including them in our list of procedures so that you can be informed of all your options.

## The logical separation method

With the logical separation method, you break your AppleTalk internet into two permanently separate, logically unconnected (no data throughput) internets. You do not have to physically separate the cables. With this method, the two internets operate independently of each other, even though both are attached to the same physical cable.

The steps for the logical separation method are fairly straightforward. First, you choose the network cables that you want to upgrade — you may select, for example, one floor of a building to do first. Then you shut off the routers that attach those networks to your original (Phase 1) internet and reconfigure their EtherTalk ports with an extended network format. When you reboot the newly configured routers, the networks attached to their ports will now make up a new Phase 2 internet.

If you plan at a later time to connect these logical internets with a transition router (described shortly), you must change the network numbers so that no duplication occurs. The logical separation method assumes that you will never connect the Phase 1 nonextended networks to the new, extended (Phase 2) networks. But if you do need to connect these internets at a later date as circumstances warrant, choosing new network numbers now will prevent potential duplications of network numbers later.

Each router you reconfigure to an extended (Phase 2) network format will function as if it were on a second and completely different cable running in a totally separate internet. Remember that an AppleTalk internet can be defined as a collection of networks joined with routers. Each separate internet is called a *logical internet*. The term *logical* differentiates between the functional type of network separation, which happens at the software level, and the *physical* type of network separation, where actual cables are separated. With logically separated networks, the routers remain connected to the same physical Ethernet cable.

The Phase 1 EtherTalk network has a separate identity from the Phase 2 EtherTalk network because its Ethernet header is different. A device, such as a Macintosh running an AppleTalk Phase 1 driver (Ethernet 2), ignores a packet with a Phase 2 header (Ethernet 802.3). Likewise, a Phase 2 device ignores packets with Phase 1 Ethernet headers.

Figure B-1 shows two separate logical networks that exist on the same physical cable. The two Macintoshes are on separate networks even though they are attached to the same Ethernet cable. No router connects one network to another, so these Macs have no path to each other and cannot communicate with each other for services, such as transferring files.

*Note:* In the figures of this section, a thick horizontal line represents the logical networks, and a vertical dashed line indicates the ports that are associated with each logical network.

Any LocalTalk network configuration stays the same because you do not reconfigure the port that attaches to the LocalTalk network — LocalTalk cannot be an extended (Phase 2) network. A LocalTalk network will be a part of whichever of the two internets (extended or nonextended) the EtherTalk port of the LocalTalk-to-EtherTalk router is configured for. If the EtherTalk port of the

LocalTalk-to-EtherTalk router is configured for Phase 2 routing and is therefore attached to the extended network, any network attached to the other ports of the router, such as a LocalTalk network, will also be a part of the extended networks internet.

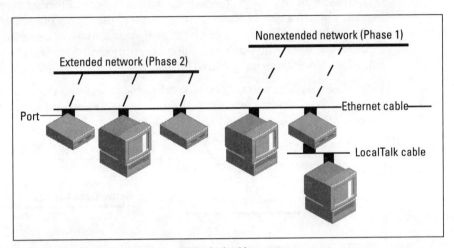

**Figure B-1: Two logical networks on one physical cable.**

Refer again to Figure B-1, which shows a LocalTalk-to-EtherTalk router with a LocalTalk network attached. The EtherTalk port of the router is configured to attach to the nonextended (Phase 1) internet. Therefore, the LocalTalk network is also a part of the nonextended internet. Any devices attached to the LocalTalk network are *not* able to communicate with devices that are part of the extended (Phase 2) network.

An advantage of the logical separation method is that you can complete the transition in stages, while your internet continues to run. You can pace yourself, devoting only a few hours at a time to the task of network transition. You may also find the extra time advantageous when you are caught in between trying to obtain upgrades for some of your network products that still run only Phase 1 software and having to use other, newer products that only run Phase 2.

The logical separation method does have disadvantages, however. During the transition period, a device on the nonextended (Phase 1) internet cannot send files or communicate with devices on the extended (Phase 2) internet. If you have an e-mail system, for example, you need two servers — one for each internet. Again, no mail will pass between these two internets. Another potential problem is that your router types leak packets between Phase 1 and Phase 2. This problem is described later under the heading, "Routers that leak packets from Phase 1 to Phase 2."

## The physical separation method

A second method is to physically separate your Ethernet networks and make the Phase 2 transition one network at a time. With this method, you reformat one router at a time to your new, extended (Phase 2) configuration. You do not, however, connect the newly configured router back to the same Ethernet segment. Instead, you start a new Ethernet segment that is physically disconnected from the Phase 1 Ethernet segment and attach the newly configured routers to the new segment. Of course, you won't have full connectivity until every one of your EtherTalk routers is reconfigured to Phase 2.

Figure B-2 is an illustration of two physically divided networks during a transition to Phase 2. Note that the two networks do not share the same Ethernet cable as the logically separated networks in Figure B-1 do.

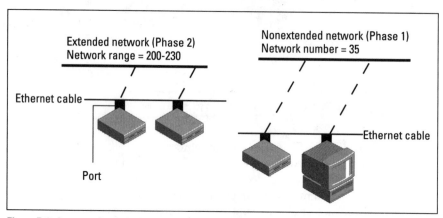

**Figure B-2: An example of physically divided networks.**

A word of caution: Because you'll eventually connect all your networks back together, you must be careful during the transition to not duplicate your network numbers.

The physical separation method is similar to the logical separation method, but it is more cumbersome. You must be careful not to attach Phase 1 internet cables or routers to your Phase 2 internet. You have the same disadvantage as with the logical separation method in that you lose communication between the two internets, for the obvious reason that the cables are physically disconnected. But just as with the logical separation method, you have the advantage of more time to upgrade your Phase 1 products to Phase 2.

The physical separation method does have several advantages over the logical separation method. You don't have to worry about any routers leaking packets, for example. In fact, the physical separation method, even though it is cumbersome and time consuming, is one of the safest ways to move your AppleTalk internet to Phase 2. Also, with the physical separation method, Phase 1 packets never pass into your Phase 2 internet. You can therefore safely use the extended features of Phase 2 and configure the new networks with network ranges of multiple networks (such as 4-6) and zone lists with multiple zones.

## The transition router method

In the transition router method, you establish a connection between a Phase 1 and a Phase 2 internet by using a special router, commonly called a *transition router*. The transition router can route traffic between a nonextended (Phase 1) network and an extended (Phase 2) network.

To connect a Phase 1 internet to a Phase 2 internet with a transition router, you first need to create two separate logical internets, just as with the logical separation method. Then, when you configure the transition router, the router will have two logical ports attached to the same physical Ethernet cable. Both of these *logical* ports attach through just one *physical* connection.

Configure one port so that it attaches as a router node to your Phase 1 internet, and configure the second port so that it attaches as a router node to your Phase 2 internet. The transition router now routes between these two logical internets, making them one internet.

The transition router sends out RTMP and ZIP packets in both an extended and a nonextended format, so that both Phase 1 and Phase 2 routers receive a complete picture of the internets route structure. The transition router also translates data packets into the appropriate format. In other words, if the router receives a Phase 1 packet, the router translates the packet headers into 802.3 Ethernet format so that the Phase 2 routers can receive the packet.

If you plan to use a transition router, carefully observe the following rule: Configure your Phase 2 routers with a network range of one network number and a zone list of one zone name.

Recall that a single network range, such as 4-4, allows devices to select network 4 to reside in. On the other hand, with a multiple-net range, such as 4-6, devices can choose network 4, 5, or 6 to reside in. Because Phase 1 routers cannot map a route to a cable that has more than one network on it, a multiple-item network range is not allowed anywhere on an internet that has a transition router. The same logic applies to the zone list.

The following discussion may help you understand this important transition rule. Each entry in a Phase 1 router's routing table can hold only one number for identifying a network. The Phase 1 routing table has no capability for storing a range of numbers (number-number) as is the format of a Phase 2 router's routing table.

Figure B-3 shows the type of network numbering that you need to use with the transition router method. In this setup, the transition router has one physical port connection to the Ethernet cable and two logical network ports. Notice that the extended (Phase 2) network has a single-number network range of 200-200, whereas the nonextended (Phase 1) network has a net number of 35. Multiple-number network ranges are not allowed anywhere on this internet because of the presence of the transition router.

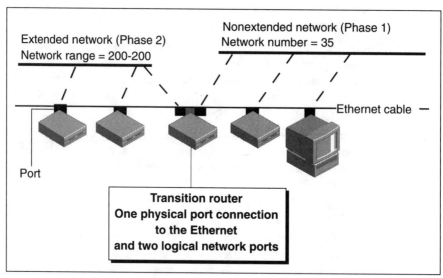

**Figure B-3: An internet configured with a transition router.**

Suppose that you have an Ethernet segment on the network that is all Phase 2. If this Ethernet segment is connected to a mixed Phase 1/ Phase 2 transition network, you must observe the transition rule of one net number per range and one zone name per list because a Phase 1 router on one side of the EtherTalk-to-EtherTalk router must have a listing in its routing table of the networks on the other side. The transition router must be able to translate this listing into the single-number format that the Phase 1 router can use.

If you need more than one zone name in the zone list, which is quite likely on a large network, you cannot use the transition router method. You must change the network over all at once (the go-for-broke method described in the next section). Otherwise, your other option is to face loss of connectivity between network sections, as with the physical separation method.

# The go-for-broke method

A fourth method for transition is to shut the entire internet down — in other words, "go-for-broke." With this method, you turn off AppleTalk on all of the routers and then bring the internet back up, one router at a time, with the new Phase 2 configuration.

Although the go-for-broke method requires the most cooperation from your users because they will have to endure an extended downtime period, we recommend the go-for-broke method over the other three. If all of your routers and software drivers are Phase 2 capable, the go-for-broke method is the fastest, safest, and most efficient way of moving your entire internet to Phase 2.

If you are using multiprotocol routers, such as those from Cisco Systems, you need only to turn off the AppleTalk routing. The other protocols, such as TCP/IP or DECnet, are not affected by this operation. Its also a good idea to shut down the rest of the AppleTalk nodes. Once you have all the routers on-line, you can bring these nodes back up again.

Shutting off all AppleTalk devices prevents any of the nodes from becoming confused by the change in zones. If you need to keep the devices running, you probably won't have problems, but shutting the devices off before you make the transition and then rebooting them after the new internet is up is a much cleaner process. With the routers turned off, devices won't be able to connect to devices on other cables.

With the go-for-broke method, be sure to schedule three times the amount of time you think the process will take. Turning off all of your routers, reconfiguring them, and then restarting them may take longer than you expect.

When planning how long the go-for-broke method will take, you may want to consider some of the following questions:

❖ How many *knowledgeable* people can help you?

❖ How long will it take you to walk from one router to the next?

❖ Do you have keys or access to all the locations of the routers?

❖ How long will it take you and your colleagues to reconfigure a router?

For example, ten minutes is a good estimate for the amount of time it will take you to reconfigure a router you are familiar with. As with any new configuration, we strongly suggest that you try out the configuration on a test network first so that you can iron out any difficulties with the use of the router's interface.

In a fast-paced weekend, a team of two colleagues (both of whom are familiar with configuring your types of routers) should be able to shut down and bring back up an AppleTalk internet of about 35 routers. We recommend, however, that you make contingency plans for Monday morning in case you run into problems. You should determine in advance whether you will switch back to Phase 1 or whether you will leave the internet down and continue working on the transition.

We feel that for many large networks, the go-for-broke plan is the only one that makes sense. The method allows you to take full advantage of the extended zone-list feature of Phase 2, and, if you complete the transition over a fast-paced weekend, you'll suffer the least duration of lost connectivity time. Also, as you'll see in the following sections, the go-for-broke method can help you avoid several problems that may crop up in a transition environment.

# Seven Phase 2 Transition Problems

Somehow things went awry with Apple's first dreams of its Phase 2 specification. Apple envisioned an easy and quick transition for everyone; administrators who need a little extra time to gather up the new code for all their devices would use Apples internet routers upgrade utility. The utility would act as a transition router, allowing administrators to maintain both Phase 1 and Phase 2 networks in the same internet. Apple believed that developers would quickly turn out their new Phase 2 products, and any router developers that had questions about implementation could observe Apples example with the Apple Internet Router.

Now, years after Phase 2 was introduced, some networks are still not running in extended (Phase 2) network mode. Implementations of the Phase 2 specification were all a bit different from one another. Some vendors had trouble getting their new Phase 2 products to pass the stress test of busy or large networks, and network administrators were often forced to make large capital expenditures in order to upgrade their Phase 1 products to Phase 2 before they could complete the transition. Because of budget restraints, many administrators had to put off Phase 2 completely or try to live with a mixed Phase 1/Phase 2 transition internet.

The following sections describe seven technical problems network managers have encountered over the past few years. Software revisions fixed many of these difficulties, so be sure to check with your vendors to get the latest versions. We present these problems so that you can see what types of things can go wrong and how important it is to test products and configurations before you put them on your production internet.

## Routers that leak packets from Phase 1 to Phase 2

One of the first transition problems to be discovered was that certain routers *leak* packets. The leakage occurs when a router configured for a Phase 1 nonextended network sees a Phase 2 extended network packet and fails to ignore it as it should. Instead, the Phase 1 router accepts the Phase 2 packet and begins leaking the Phase 2 packet. In the worst cases, the router converts itself to a Phase 2 extended network router. In such a case, the router that formerly sent and received Phase 1 packets no longer acknowledges the Phase 1 packets and simply drops them.

Because of this potential leakage risk, it is not a straightforward task to create two logically separated networks, with one network running in nonextended mode and the other in extended mode (as in the logical separation method). Theoretically, the logical separation method, which looks fine on paper, should work. In reality, routers that leak packets may not stay in the logical network where you put them.

After a leak, certain Macintoshes — those on the Ethernet or those that are behind the routers that were receiving zone information from the router that switched to become a Phase 2 extended network router — can no longer reach the services they could reach before the switch. The switched router not only changes its network routing to an extended (Phase 2) format, but it also begins sending out 802.3 rather than Ethernet 2 packets.

Note the example shown in Figure B-4. The original nonextended (Phase 1) network was configured with the network number 4, and an extended (Phase 2) network was configured with the network range 6-6. The switched router adds an extended network configuration of the range 4-4. When the switched router forwards a data packet from a node on its directly attached LocalTalk network (network 22) to any other node or network destination, the data packet is formatted into an 802.3 packet type.

When the data packet is destined to go to a node in network 38 or network 6, the switched router looks in its routing table and determines that the next router for networks 38-38 and 6-6 is reachable via node 4.220. (Remember that a node in AppleTalk has only a single number, but that AppleTalk routing uses network ranges, which is why we refer to routing entries for a single network as 6-6 or 38-38.)

When the data packet is destined for a node in network 21, the switched router follows the same process and forwards the packet to node 4.215. Likewise, when the data packet is destined to a node in network 4, the switched router sends the packet directly to node 4. In all three cases, the receiving nodes (nodes 4.220, 4.215, or 4.x) are set up as nonextended (Phase 1) end nodes and should only receive packets in Ethernet 2 format. These nodes throw away any packets sent to them in 802.3 format. Because of the packet type incompatibility, any nodes that are in networks behind the switched router (in this example, network 22) lose connection to any devices beyond the switched router.

## Servers that turn into routers

The problem discussed in this section certainly caught many AppleTalk administrators by surprise. Several manufacturers of AppleTalk Ethernet file-share servers changed their implementation dramatically when they added Phase 2 drivers. Instead of simply providing EtherTalk Phase 2 drivers for their servers, they added built-in AppleTalk routers as well. This situation was seen on AppleTalk servers that reside on non-Macintosh platforms.

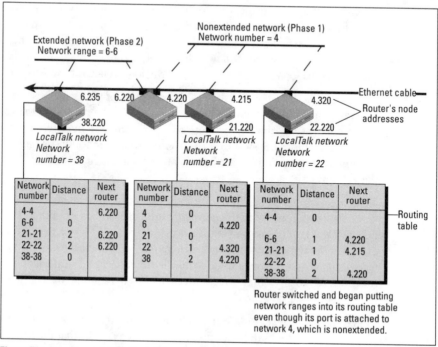

Figure B-4: A router switching from Phase 1 to Phase 2.

Some vendors gave their new routers both seed and non-seed start-up modes, but others provided seed mode only. When you reconfigure the seed-only router/ servers for Phase 2, you also must add a network range and a zone list. The servers (which are now also routers) participate in the routing scheme of your internet by issuing RTMP packets and answering ZIP queries.

The server-turned-to-router turns into a problem when the server administrator, who in many companies is *not* the same person as the network manager, must configure the router properly to coexist on the network. The server administrator must be aware of the correct network range and zone list to use. At an even more fundamental level, the server administrator must know to ask the network manager for the correct network range and zone list. Experience shows that the server administrator often does not understand the importance of the addition of a router and merely types in the numbers provided by examples in the server's installation manual.

Incorrect network number and zone name entries cause the server to conflict with routers on the internet. The result is loss of connectivity. The users on the Ethernet, whose Macs obtain their zone lists from the router in the file-share server, find that the Chooser list of zones that other users see (from properly configured routers) is gone. These unfortunate users see only the zone that the server administrator entered from the example in the installation manual. The users whose Macs are receiving the invalid zone list from the file-share server/router are not able to connect to any of the network services that are in the real internet.

An added problem occurs if non-seed routers are coming on-line after the misconfigured file-share server/router is up. A non-seed router obtains its network range and zone-list configuration from the first router that answers the non-seed routers query. Because the misconfigured file-share server/router is not busy with real routing (unlike the properly configured routers), the misconfigured router will most likely be the first router to answer the new non-seed router. When a non-seed router takes its routing and zone information from the misconfigured file-share server/router, the connectivity problem is further compounded because the new non-seed router displays the invalid zone list to any networks that are behind the new routers.

Why *did* the vendors of AppleTalk file-share servers add routing capabilities to their servers? One reason may be historical. Because Phase 1 Ethernet networks were nonextended and allowed only one zone name per cable, several vendors' servers implemented an internal logical network to go along with their services as a convenience to users. This internal logical network, which had its own zone name, allowed the server to be found on a zone separate from the other devices. Many Ethernet servers had other services, such as spooled printers, and all services could be grouped together within one easily identifiable zone. But there was no longer a need for an internal, logical network of this type when Phase 2 was introduced. An extended (Phase 2) network allowed the administrator to add a special zone to the zone list for the Ethernet server and its services.

If you are a network manager, we advise you to monitor the installation of all AppleTalk servers on your internet, especially those that reside on non-Macintosh platforms. For example, we know of two non-Macintosh-platform servers that originally added routing to their Phase 2 implementations: TOPS on its Sun platform and Novell NetWare on its PC platform. Make it your responsibility to manage the installation of servers. Verify the placement of the servers for best performance and whether each servers configuration files do or do not require routing information (such as net-number or zone name).

## Routers that send Phase 2 packets to Phase 1 routers

Under some conditions, routers can send Phase 2 packets to Phase 1 routers. This problem occurs on internets that have multiple Ethernet networks still using the old Phase 1-only routers. Suspect this problem when devices behind the older router don't show up in the Chooser for nodes on the other side of an EtherTalk-to-EtherTalk router (nodes on a different Ethernet cable).

When a router receives a packet type that it doesn't know about, it drops that packet as unreadable. Some Phase 2 routers send a new Phase 2 packet type called an NBP FwdReq (the Name Binding Protocol Forward Request) packet to Phase 1 routers. Because the code of the Phase 1 routers predates the existence of the NBP FwdReq packet type, the Phase 1 router throws the packet away. Because the Phase

1 router is unable to process the NBP FwdReq, any devices from the zone behind the Phase 1 router never respond. Note that these devices are invisible to the users behind the Phase 2 router. When a user clicks on that zone in the Chooser in order to see a device such as a LaserWriter, the user does not see the LaserWriter or any other device. In fact, the user will tell you that the zone is dead. The zone isn't really dead, however. The problem instead is with certain routers' interpretation of the new Phase 2 specification.

On a Phase 2 internet, when you open the Chooser and select a zone and the LaserWriter icon, you see a list of LaserWriters because the Phase 2 router for that zone is responding to an NBP FwdReq. In the original Phase 1 specification, however, NBP requests over an internet were made with an NBP LkUp (lookup) packet type. A Phase 1-only router expects to see the LkUp packet rather than the FwdReq. If the FwdReq is discarded, the list of available LaserWriters never appears in the Chooser. You can't see, or select, any devices from that zone.

The router type that exhibits this behavior decides that because it is attached to an Ethernet network in which all routers are newer, Phase 2-capable routers, all routers on the entire internet must be Phase 2-capable as well. The router therefore uses the new Phase 2 NBP FwdReq packet to send out NBP requests over the internet. The router does this even if you select Phase 1 in all your routers configuration files.

The router's assumption is incorrect. The router decides that if all routers on its Ethernet are Phase 2-capable, all the routers on the other Ethernets in the internet are also Phase 2-capable. Recall that the router determines whether all devices on its own Ethernet backbone are Phase 1 or Phase 2 by checking an embedded code in the broadcasted RTMP Data packets. But RTMP information from a second Ethernet backbone is regenerated by the EtherTalk-to-EtherTalk router. (RTMP information is regenerated at each hop because broadcasts are not forwarded across routers). Therefore, if a Phase 1 router is on the other side of the EtherTalk-to-EtherTalk router, the router that is deciding whether or not all of the routers on the internet are Phase 2-capable does not know about the existence of the Phase 1 router. The RTMP information from the Phase 1 router is regenerated by an EtherTalk-to-EtherTalk Phase 2 router. Therefore the embedded code is in a RTMP Data packet coming from a Phase 2-capable router.

So why doesn't the EtherTalk-to-EtherTalk router catch the NBP FwdReq packet and change it to a Phase 1 LkUp? At each hop, the NBP FwdReq is merely switched. The intervening routers only regenerate RTMP and ZIP information because this information is sent to the broadcast address. All other data packets, NBP packets included, are simply routed according to the destination address inside the packet. The router looks at the destination address, which is in the network.node format, checks its port files to see which port file has a route for that network, and then sends the packet out that port. Checking each packet type to find those that are NBP packets would mean checking deeper within the packet structure, which would considerably slow down any router.

This process is illustrated in Figure B-5. The Macintosh shown at the top of the figure sends an NBP BrRq (Broadcast Request) to a Phase 2-capable router (Router A in the figure) that has been configured to route packets over a nonextended (Phase 1) network. The network manager selected this configuration — having the Phase 2-capable router route packets over a nonextended network — by selecting Phase 1 in the routers configuration dialog box.

When the Phase 2-capable router (Router A) receives the NBP BrRq, it forwards the packet toward its destination in the form of an NBP FwdReq packet. Recall that the NBP FwdReq packet is new to the Phase 2 specification and is used to forward an NBP request over an extended (Phase 2) network rather than over a nonextended (Phase 1) network. The Phase 2-capable router (Router A) has made the decision that all routers on the internet are Phase 2-capable because there are no Phase 1 routers on its network. Note that the Phase 1-only router is two networks away.

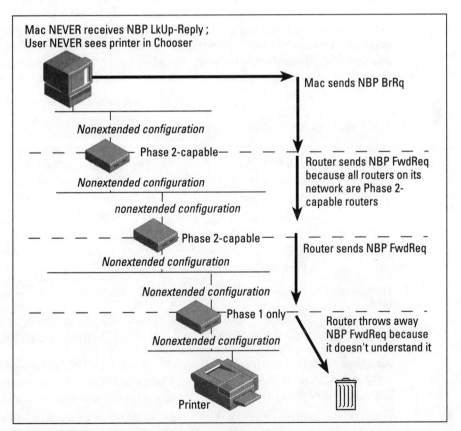

Figure B-5: How an NBP FwdReq can fail on a multitiered internet.

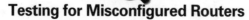

## Testing for Misconfigured Routers

You can test for a router that sends NBP FwdReq packets when configured as a nonextended network node. Attach to an isolated Ethernet cable one port of the router to be tested and a second Phase 2-capable router along with a network packet analyzer. Select Phase 1 (nonextended) mode for both routers network configuration files. Attach a Macintosh to the other port of the router you are testing — usually the LocalTalk port. Attach a printer to the second (LocalTalk) port of the second router. While capturing packets with the network packet analyzer, open the Chooser and look for printers in the second zone. If the analyzer shows that the router sent an NBP FwdReq instead of an NBP LkUp packet, you've found a misconfigured router.

The next router (Router B) receives the NBP FwdReq packets and forwards it toward the destination. Unfortunately, the next router in line is a Phase 1-only router which does not recognize the NBP FwdReq (Router C) packet type. The packet is discarded, and the LkUp-Reply is never returned to the original Macintosh. Without the LkUp-Reply, the Macintosh will never see the printer from the network behind the Phase 1-only router, and the user will never see the printer in the Chooser.

## Default zones that change

Another problem involves default zones that change. A default zone is set by the administrator in the router configuration file. Devices that don't select a zone to reside in from the zone list are placed in this default zone. Some server implementations are not zone-configurable and therefore always reside in the default zone.

With early implementations of Phase 2, some routers did not use the default zone that the administrator selected in the routers configuration file. These routers disregarded the administrators configuration information and used either the last or the first zone in the zone list as the default zone.

If you are using a router model of this type, your only problem is that your default zone won't be the one you select, although it will be a stable zone. But if you use router types from several vendors, one defaulting to the last zone in the list, and another model using the default zone you select, you can have further difficulties.

One problem is that a device such as a server may reboot into a different default zone each time, depending on which router it heard from. Users are left playing a game of "where did the server go?"

A second problem occurs when you use seed routers that verify the network configuration before coming on-line to route. The routers will discover the conflict of two or more different default zones when they receive mismatched GNIRs

(GetNetInfoReply) and won't route until the conflict is resolved. The zones that are behind them won't be visible in the Chooser. Although this process may sound unfriendly, having the seed router not come up and route unless the network is properly configured has its advantages. The system alerts you to the conflict *before* users complain that network devices are down. In this case, the devices are just rebooted into the other default zone.

An administrator can spend valuable time troubleshooting the specific operations of a device that keeps "disappearing." The administrator may, for instance, go through the routine of troubleshooting a servers operating system, only to find out that the disappearance resulted from the existence of two conflicting default zones.

## Routers that restrict the number of zones

Several router vendors have developed Phase 2 routing software that allows only a limited number of zones. With these routers, the limit has been anywhere from 120 to 150 zones, although the AppleTalk Phase 2 specifications state that Phase 2 zone tables can include up to 255 zones.

With these routers, only a limited number of zones can be held in the ZIT (Zone Information Table). A network administrator may go over this limit when placing a large number of zones in the EtherTalk zone list, and the number of zones in the ZIT already includes many zones from other nonextended networks, such as LocalTalk. Also, in larger internets, the administrator sometimes has more than one extended network and tries to give each one of these a large zone list, again adding to the number of zones in any of the internet routers' ZITs.

The problem takes a strange twist in an unstable internet, where routers restart themselves, or in a changing internet, where new routers are coming on-line. In this situation, a Mac receives a zone list from a router and selects one of the zones. But then the Mac is told that the zone is invalid for use when it sends a GNI (GetNetInfo) packet back to confirm the zone and receive the zone's multicast address. How does this happen?

Between the time the router sent the zone list to the Macintosh and the time it receives the Macintosh's GNI packet, its ZIT has changed. Because of its limitations, the router deleted the zone that the end node requested in favor of another new zone coming from a new router (recall that the router can hold only a limited number of zones). Two other signs of this problem are Macintoshes mysteriously moving back into the default network or entire zones appearing and disappearing from the Chooser list.

### Testing for Routers That Limit the Number of Zones

To find out whether a router limits the number of zones in its zone information table, place the router and a Macintosh with an Ethernet card on an isolated test Ethernet cable. Configure the router with 250 zones in the zone list. Bring up the router first; then turn on the Macintosh. If the Macintosh is able to select from all 250 of the zones, the router does not have this problem.

## Devices that don't respond to a zone multicast

Another problem occurs with some early implementations of Phase 2 software device drivers that do not recognize a specific zones multicast address. These devices recognize only those packets sent directly to their **net.node** address or those sent to the AppleTalk broadcast address, $09:00:07:ff:ff:ff, which is where all AppleTalk nodes respond. However, when an NBP LkUp packet is sent to a zone, it is addressed to the zone's specific multicast address, which is different from the overall broadcast address for the entire EtherTalk network. These devices do not respond to NBP LkUps and therefore are invisible to the network user.

If several devices are on an EtherTalk network before a router is installed, and if one of these devices is of the type that doesn't recognize a zone's specific multicast address, the following events occur. At first, the devices see each other. But none of these devices are using a zone multicast address, as this address is given out by a router; these devices are sending their NBP LkUps to the AppleTalk broadcast address. If a router is placed on this network, the nodes notify their users/administrators that they need to be rebooted. When the nodes are rebooted, they send out a GNI (GetNetInfo) packet, and the router returns a GNIR (GetNetInfoReply) packet containing the zone multicast address for the chosen zone.

The malfunctioning device, however, ignores the GNIR information and continues to respond only to LkUp packets sent to the broadcast address. Devices that previously could communicate are no longer able to do so because they are sending their NBP LkUps to the new zone multicast address that the malfunctioning device is ignoring. This problem may be mistakenly diagnosed as bugs in the router because the problem with network connectivity appears when a new router is brought on-line.

## Start-up nodes that initiate a GNIR flood

The final Phase 2 transition problem we discuss involves a flood of GNIR (GetNetInfoReply) packets. The flood results from an implementation of an end nodes Phase 2 driver that flushes its **net.node** address from its memory each time the end node starts. Normally, a Phase 2 end node retains its **net.node** address in nonvolatile memory and uses this stored number in the AARP probes that it issues upon startup. (AARP probes are used to verify that the **net.node** is unique. Please refer to Chapter 11 for a more thorough discussion of how AARP and GNI packets are used in Phase 2 end node startup.)

Because the driver flushed its **net.node** number, it must use a number from the startup range. After verifying that it has a unique address within the startup range, the end node sends out a GNI packet to obtain zone verification. Because routers do not have a route to the startup range network and therefore cannot respond directly to this end node, routers respond to the GNI by sending a GNIR to the broadcast address.

When the device broadcasts its GNI packet, every other device on the cable is interrupted once. Now, with every router replying to the device at the broadcast address, every AppleTalk device on the cable is interrupted as many times as the internet has routers.

If you are using a software driver, end nodes are not moved from one extended network to another. However, if you are using a software driver for an extended network that doesn't maintain the **net.node** in its memory, every time that node is restarted, your internet receives a flood of broadcast GNIR packets. If you use this software driver on many nodes, your problem compounds by the number of nodes that are restarting, a number that increases dramatically if the problem software driver is installed on your Macs and your users habitually turn off their Macs at night and restart them in the morning all at about the same time. The more Macs with this forgetful software driver that are restarting, the more likely it is to be a problem.

BACKGROUNDER

### EtherTalk Zone Multicast Addresses

An EtherTalk zone multicast address is computed by the ZIP process in a router and can range anywhere from \$09:00:07:00:00:00 to \$09:00:07:00:00:fc. The EtherTalk multicast address that is sent to all Ether-Talk devices is \$09:00:07:ff:ff:ff. This address is used by RTMP Data packets and AARP probe packets.

### Testing for GNIR Flooding

An Ethernet packet monitor can help you detect the problem of GNIR flooding. Set up a test network with an Ethernet packet monitor, a router, and a Macintosh (or whatever platform the driver is on). Configure the router with a network range and zone list different from the internet where the Mac was located. Start the router. Load any of the drivers you want to test onto this Macintosh. Reboot the Macintosh once. The Macintosh comes up with an invalid net number; reselect an appropriate address. Then reboot again and watch to see if it selects the same address.

# Is Phase 2 Worth It?

Is all this trouble worth it? Yes. There are potential hiccups and bugs in the implementation of a new Phase 2 network. But after you work through these difficulties, your internet will run much more efficiently than it did before. Split-horizon routing alone is reason enough to justify a move to Phase 2. Also, a zone-multicast system that restricts NBP LkUps to devices in a particular zone reduces unnecessary traffic. Perhaps the most important reason of all is to be able to use new networking products built on the Phase 2 specification, such as System 7's file sharing features. So go for it, and good luck.

# List of Vendors

The following list of vendors is not intended as a comprehensive guide to all the vendors listed in this book. Rather, it is offered as a starting point for gathering information.

Note that the descriptions are organized as follows:

Company Name
A description of pertinent products offered by the company
The company address and phone number

## List of Vendors

| Company Name | Product Information | Address | Phone Number |
|---|---|---|---|
| 3Com Corp. | Supplier of 3+/3+Open network operating system and associated server hardware. | 5400 Bayfront Plaza Santa Clara, CA 95052-8145 | 408-764-5000 |
| ACI US, Inc. | Developer and supplier of 4th Dimension relational database for the Macintosh. | 20883 Stevens Creek Blvd. Cupertino, CA 95014 | 408-252-4444 |
| AESP Inc. | Wiring and wire-accessory supplier, especially for LocalTalk and PhoneNET. | 1810 NE 144th St. N. Miami, FL 33181 | 305-944-7710 |
| The AG Group | Developer of LocalPeek and EtherPeek packet analysis software; NetWatchMan device-monitoring software. | 2540 Camino Diablo, Suite 200 Walnut Creek, CA 94596 | 510-937-7900 |
| Aldus Pre-Press Division | Developer of Print Central print server software; also ColorCentral, Presswise, and Trapwise. | 411 First Ave. South Seattle, WA 98104 | 800-685-OPEN |

| Company Name | Product Information | Address | Phone Number |
|---|---|---|---|
| Alisa Systems Inc. | Developer and supplier of AlisaTalk, AlisaShare and AlisaPrint VAX and UNIX-based file servers, AlisaMail, VMS-based e-mail server, and MailMate/QM and MailMate/MM Mail, bridges for QuickMail and Microsoft Mail. | 221 E. Walnut St., Ste. 175 Pasadena, CA 91101 | 818-792-9474 |
| ANDREW Corp. | Source for IBM 5250 terminal emulation software and associated interface hardware for Macs and PCs. | 4301 Westbank Dr., Ste. A-100 Austin, TX 78746 | 512-314-3000 |
| Andyne Computing Ltd. | Developer of GQL, query construction tool for DAL and SQL; also PaBLO client-server software. | 552 Princess St. Kingston, Ontario K7L 1C7 Canada | 613-548-4355 |
| Apple Computer, Inc. | Developer and supplier of the Macintosh and LaserWriter II. | 1 Infinite Loop Cupertino, CA 95014 | 800-776-2333 |
| Asante Technologies, Inc. | Source for Ethernet and token ring interface cards for Macintosh computers. | 821  Fox Ln. San Jose, CA 95131 | 408-435-8388 |
| ASD Software, Inc. | Developer of FileGuard security software and WindowWatch. | 4650 Arrow Hwy., Ste. E-6 Montclair, CA 91763 | 909-624-2594 |
| AT&T | Telecommunications service providers. | 295 N. Maple Ave. Basking Ridge, NJ 07920 | 800-CALL-NCR |
| Banyan Systems, Inc. | Developer and supplier of VINES network operating system; also ENS for Netware, HPUX, and ScoUNIX. | 120 Flanders Rd. Westboro, MA 01581 | 508-898-1000 |
| Belkin Components | General network wiring source. | 1303 Walnut Pkwy. Compton, CA 90220 | 310-898-1100; 800-223-5546 |
| Blyth Software | Developer of Omnis 5 and Omnis 7 relational databases, as well as DAL tool for DOS, Windows, and OS/2. | 989 E. Hillsdale Blvd., Ste. 400 Foster City, CA 94404 | 415-571-0222 |
| Brio Technology, Inc. | Developer of DataPrism SQL/DAL query construction tool and DataPivot data-viewing tool. | 444 Castro St., Ste. 700 Mountain View, CA 94041 | 415-961-4110 |
| Cabletron Systems | Source for SPECTRUM network management software, intelligent wiring hubs, interface modules, and DNI Ethernet, token ring, and FDDI cards for Macintosh computers. | 35 Industrial Way Rochester, NH 03867 | 603-332-9400 |
| Caravelle Network | Developer of NetWORKS for Macs and NetWORKS/PC network monitoring software; also PagerPro paging software. | 301 Moodie Dr., Ste. 306 Nepean, Ontario K2H 9C4 Canada | 613-596-2802 |

| Company Name | Product Information | Address | Phone Number |
|---|---|---|---|
| Cayman Systems, Inc. | Source of GatorBox EtherTalk routers, GatorRoute and GatorStar multiprotocol routers, and GatorLink, an AppleTalk Remote Access server for Ethernet. | 400 Unicorn Park Dr. Woburn, MA 08101 | 617-932-1100 |
| cc:Mail, Div. of Lotus Corp. | Developer of cc:Mail e-mail products for DOS and Macintosh computers. | 800 El Camino Real Mountain View, CA 94040 | 415-961-8800 |
| CE Software, Inc. | Developer of QuickMail e-mail products for DOS and Macintosh computers. | P. O. Box 65580 W. Des Moines, IA 50265 | 515-221-1801 |
| Cisco Systems Inc. | Source for Ethernet routers and WAN-related products. | 170 W. Tasman Dr. San Jose, CA 95134 | 408-526-4000 |
| ClientSoft Inc. | Source for BOTH front-end software for IBM 3270 communication sessions. | Talleyrand II, 220 WhitePlains Rd. Tarrytown, NY 10591 | 914-631-5365 |
| Compatible Systems Corp. | Developer of RiscRouter, a multiprotocol Ethernet to Ethernet router, MicroRouter, a multiprotocol remote router, EtherRoute II EtherTalk router, EtherRoute TCPII AppleTalk/EtherTalk router, EtherWrite and EtherWrite LTR interface for Laser-Writers. | P. O. Drawer 17220 Boulder, CO 80308-7220 | 303-444-9532; 800-356-0283 |
| CoOperative Printing Solutions | Source for LocalTalk interface card for 80286 and 80386 PCs and PS/2s. | 5950 Live Oak Pkwy., Ste. 175 Norcross, GA 30093 | 404-840-0810 |
| CSG Division, Management Science Associates | Developer of Network Supervisor resource-management software and utilities software. | 530 William Penn Place, Ste. 329 Pittsburg, PA 15219 | 412-471-7170; 800-366-4622 |
| Cypress Research Corp. | Developer of FaxPro, networked fax for server hardware and software Macintosh clients; also PhonePro, a telephony application builder for the Mac. | 240 E. Caribbean Dr. Sunnyvale, CA 94089 | 408-752-2700 |
| DataViz Inc. | Supplier of MacLink Plus file-translation software. | 55 Corporate Dr.Trumbull, CT 06611 | 203-268-0030; 800-733-0030 |
| Dayna Communications Inc. | Source for EtherPrint interface for Laser-Writers, as well as external adapters, hubs, routers, Ethernet and Ethernet interface cards for the Mac. | 849 W. Levoy Dr. Inc. Salt Lake City, UT 84123 | 801-269-7200 |
| Distributed Technologies Corp. | Supplier of PATHTracker, client/server asset management software, and Talk-Manage network management software. | 275 Wyman St. Waltham, MA 02154 | 617-684-0060 |

| Company Name | Product Information | Address | Phone Number |
|---|---|---|---|
| EDI Communications Corp. | Developer of MacToken token-ring diagnostic software for the Mac and IBM PC. | 20440 Town Center Ln., Ste. 4E Cupertino, CA 95014 | 408-996-1343 |
| Farallon Computing, Inc. | Offers the award-winning EtherWave product family: daisychainable 10Base-T Ethernet for Macintosh, PCs and printers. Farallon also provides EtherMac products, a complete line of simple Ethernet connectivity products for Macintosh and printers; Ethernet and LocalTalk hubs and routers — including the award-winning InterRoute/5; and Timbuktu remote control and file transfer software for Macintosh and Windows computers. | Alameda, CA | 510-814-5000 |
| Focus Enhancements, Inc. | Supplier of TurboNet PhoneNET-clone connectors, TurboStar LocalTalk multiport repeater, EtherLan Ethernet interface cards and hubs for the Mac, and FOCUS FaxModems. | 800 W. Cummings Park, Ste. 4500 Woburn, MA 08101 | 617-938-8088 |
| Hayes Microcomputer Products, Inc. | Source for high-speed modems and Hayes InterBridge LocalTalk router. | P. O. Box 105203 Atlanta, GA 30348 | 404-840-9200 |
| Helios USA | Supplier of EtherShare UNIX-based file- and print-server software. | 10495 Bandley Dr. Cupertino, CA 95014 | 408-864-0690 |
| Information Presentation Technologies, Inc. | Developer of uShare UNIX-based file- and print-server and SunPartner file-exchange software. | 555 Chorro St. San Luis Obispo, CA 93405 | 805-541-3000 |
| Insight Development Corp. | Developer of print drivers for Mac use of non-AppleTalk printers. | 2420 Camino Ramon San Ramon, CA 94583 | 510-244-2000; 800-825-4115 |
| Insignia Solutions | Developer of SoftWindows DOS-emulation software for the Mac. | 1300 Charleston Rd. Mountain View, CA 94043 | 800-848-7677 |
| InterCon Systems Corp. | Source for WorldLink for DOS and Mac computers. | 950 Herndon Pkwy., Ste 420 Herndon, VA 22070 | 703-709-5500 |
| International Transware Inc. | Developer of InterTalk AppleTalk router line, TransTalk WAN network connectors, SerialWay Mac serial servers, and Ether-Way multiprotocol LocalTalk-Ethernet router/gateway. | 1503 Grant Rd., Ste. 155 Mountain View, CA 94040 | 415-903-2300; 800-999-NETS |
| Mainstay | Developer of Marco Polo document-retrieval software and MarkUp group-editing software for the Mac. | 591-A Constitution Ave. Camarillo, CA 93012 | 805-484-9400 |

| Company Name | Product Information | Address | Phone Number |
|---|---|---|---|
| MCI Mail | Telecommunications service providers. | 1133 19th St. NW, Ste. 700 Washington, DC 20036 | 800-444-6245 |
| MDG Computer Services | Supplier of QM Log Translator, a 4th dimension database that summarizes QuickMail logs. | | 708-622-0220 |
| Microcom Inc. | Source for high-speed modems. | 500 River Ridge Dr. Norwood, MA 02062-5028 | 800-822-8224; FAX 617-551-1021 |
| MicroDynamics, Ltd. | Developer of MARS document archive system. | 8555 16th St., Ste. 700 Silver Spring, MD 20910 | 301-589-6300 |
| Microsoft Corp. | Developer of Mail for Macs and PCs, MS Schedule+ group scheduler, and LAN Manager network operating system. | One Microsoft Way Redmond, WA 98052-6399 | 800-426-9400 |
| Miramar Systems | Developer of cross-platform file- and client-server software. | 121 Gray Ave., Ste. 200-B Santa Barbara, CA 93101 | 805-966-2432 |
| MITEM Corp. | Source for Mitem*View*, a mission critical client/server application that integrates data from multiple sources. | 640 Menlo Ave. Menlo Park, CA 94025 | 415-323-6164 |
| Neon Software, Inc. | Developer of NetMinder LocalTalk and Ethernet packet analysis software for Macs, RouterCheck router-monitoring software, LANsurveyor, a network mapping tool, and TrafficWatch II, a network monitor. | 3685 Mt. Diablo Blvd., Ste. 203 Lafayette, CA 94549 | 510-283-9771; 800-334-6366 |
| Network General Corp. | Developer and supplier of Sniffer hardware for network packet analysis; distributed Sniffer system for enterprise-wide network analysis; and Foundation Manager console with cornerstone agent probe, a module for standards-based monitoring. | 4200 Bohannon Dr. Menlo Park, CA 94025 | 415-473-2000; 800-SNIFFER |
| Network Resources Corp. | Developer and supplier of MultiGate Ethernet routers. | 61 Daggett Dr. San Jose, CA 95134 | 408-383-9300 |
| Odesta Systems Corp. | Developer of Open ODMS, Odesta Workflow, and ProposalWorks, workflow and document management software. | 4083 Commercial Ave. Northbrook, IL 60062 | 708-498-5615; 800-676-ODMS |
| Oracle Corp. | Developer of Oracle multiplatform databases and OracleCard front-end databases. | 500 Oracle Pkwy. Redwood Shores, CA 94065 | 415-506-7000 |

| *Company Name* | *Product Information* | *Address* | *Phone Number* |
|---|---|---|---|
| Pacer Software Inc. | Developer of PacerShare AFP-compatible file-server software for VMS and UNIX systems, PacerTerm terminal emulator software, PacerForum networked bulletin board system, PacerLink network software for VMS and UNIX systems, and DAL servers for UNIX systems. | 7911 Herschel Ave., Ste. 402 La Jolla, CA 92037 | 619-454-0565; 800-722-3702 |
| Penril Datability Networks | Developer of RAF and MacRAF disk server software that runs on the VMS operating system; also AppleTalk routers that support multiple Ethernet and WAN ports, modems, and DSU/CSU and TI channel bank equipment. | One Palmer Terrace Carlstadt, NJ 07072 | 201-438-2400 |
| Photonics Corp. | Supplier of Cooperative, an external transceiver that enables AppleTalk/LocalTalk-compatible devices. | 2940 N. First St. San Jose, CA 95134 | 408-955-7930; 800-628-3033 |
| Proteus Technology | Developer of Quota license server software for networks. | 9919 68th St. Edmonton, Alberta T6A 2S6 Canada | 403-448-1970 |
| Racal-Interlan, Inc. | Supplier of Ethernet interface cards for Macs and PCs, transceivers for Ethernet, pocket adapters for Ethernet and token ring, and stackable hubs for the Ethernet. | 155 Swanson Rd. Boxborough, MA 01719 | 508-263-9929 |
| Sassafras Software | Developer of KeyServer license management software. | Box 150 Hanover, NH 03755 | 603-643-3351 |
| Shiva Corp. | Source of FastPath 5 EtherTalk router, NetBridge WAN device, NetModem V.32 shareable modems, TeleBridge network modem server, LanRouter/L ARA server, and LanRover/E Ethernet ARA multiline server. | 63 Third Ave. Burlington, MA 01803 | 617-270-8400 |
| Simware | Developer of SimMac, IBM 3270 terminal emulation software for Macs (also A2B for Windows and SimPC for DOS computers). | 2 Gurdwara Rd. Ottawa, Ontario K2E 1A2 Canada | 613-727-1779 |
| Soft Switch, Inc. | Source for backbone switches, gateways, directory services, e-mail management tools, and application programming interfaces. | 640 Lee Rd., Ste. 200 Wayne, PA 19087-5698 | 610-640-9600 |

| Company Name | Product Information | Address | Phone Number |
|---|---|---|---|
| Sonic Systems, Inc. | Supplier of Ethernet transceivers, cards, hubs external SCSI devices, Radar network management software, Server Sentry file-management software, and Bridge Series, a LocalTalk to extended network software bridge. | 1150 Kifer Rd., Ste. 201 Sunnyvale, CA 94086 | 408-738-1900; 800-535-0725 |
| Spider Island Software | Developer of TeleFinder graphical bulletin board and NetConnect option for use on networks. | 4790 Irvine Blvd., Ste. 105-347 Irvine, CA 92720 | 714-669-9260 |
| StarNine Technologies, Inc. | Developer of numerous gateways between Mac-based e-mail programs and other e-mail system and the Internet. | 2550 Ninth St., Ste. 112 Berkeley, CA 94710 | 510-649-4949 |
| Symantec Corp. | Supplier of SAM virus checker; also Installer Pro and Net Distributor Pro, Mac networking software. | 175 W. Broadway Eugene, OR 97401 | 800-441-7234 |
| Synergy Software | Developer and supplier of VersaTerm and VersaTerm-PRO terminal emulators; also Versatilities, providing TCP/IP connectivity and access to the Internet. | 2457 Perkiomen Ave. Reading, PA 19606 | 610-779-0522; order line 800-876-8376 |
| Talaris Systems Inc. | Supplier of various laser printers, including some with Ethernet interfaces. | P. O. Box 261580 San Diego, CA 92196 | 619-587-0787; 800-934-3345 |
| TechGnosis Inc. | Developer of SequeLink SQL interface between Mac and SQL databases. | 5 Burlington Woods Dr., Ste. 202 Burlington, MA 01803 | 617-229-6100 |
| Technology Works | Source for Ethernet interface cards for Macs and GraceLAN resource management products. | 4030 W. Braker Ln., Ste. 350 Austin, TX 78759 | 512-794-8533; 800-688-7466 |
| Traveling Software Inc. | Codeveloper of Newton connection kit to Windows. | 18702 N. Creek Pkwy. Bothell, WA 98011 | 206-483-8088; 800-343-8080 |
| Trik, Inc. | Developer of NokNok, monitoring software for System 7 file sharing, and Lookout, AppleShare protector for the Chooser. | 400 W. Cummings Park, Ste. 2350 Woburn, MA 08101 | 617-933-8810; 800-466-8745 |
| Ungermann-Bass, Inc. | Source for concentrators, routers, and WAN devices for many types of networks; also network management software. | 3990 Freedom Circle Santa Clara, CA 95054-1263 | 408-496-0111 |

| Company Name | Product Information | Address | Phone Number |
|---|---|---|---|
| United Data Corp. | Source for ALAC for the Mac, a developer's toolkit. | 3755 Balboa St., Ste. 203 San Francisco, CA 94121 | 415-750-8068 |
| US Sprint Communications Co. | Telecommunications service provider. | 8140 Ward Pkwy. Kansas City, MO 64114 | 800-877-2000 |
| Walker, Richer & Quinn, Inc. | Developer of Reflection series of VT1xx, VT2xx terminal emulation software, and NS Connection and 3000 Connection for the Mac. | 1500 Dexter Ave. N. Seattle, WA 98109 | 206-217-7500; 800-872-2829 |
| Webster Computer Corp. | Source for MultiPort/LT, a five-port Apple-Talk router and Ethernet gateway and Apple remote access server. | 2109 O'Toole Ave., Ste. J San Jose, CA 95131-1338 | 408-954-8054; 800-457-0903 |
| White Pine Software, Inc. | Source for complete line of DEC and Tektronix emulation software, X-server software for Mac, Windows, and DOS platforms, and workgroup productivity solutions. | 40 Simon St. Nashua, NH 03060 | 603-886-9050; sales hotline 800-241-PINE |
| WilTel | Telecommunications service provider. | P. O. Box 21348 Tulsa, OK 74121 | 800-642-2299 |
| The Wollongong Group Inc. | Supplier of TCP/IP-based internetworking software for the enterprise, with a wide range of applications including terminal emulation, file transfer, printing services, e-mail, newsreader, NFS client, and a developer's toolkit for Mac and Windows platforms. | 1129 San Antonio Rd. Palo Alto, CA 94303 | 415-962-7100 |
| WordPerfect Corp. | Developer of WordPerfect Office for Mac and DOS computers. | 1555 N. Technology Way Orem, UT 84057 | 801-225-5000; 800-451-5151 |
| Xinet Inc. | Source for UNIX-based K-AShare file-server software for Macs; also K-Spool, print spooling software for networks using Apple file protocol, and K-FS, file-sharing software between UNIX and the Mac. | 2560 Ninth St., Ste. 312 Berkeley, CA 94710 | 510-845-0555 |

# Glossary of Networking Terms

**10BASE2**

An implementation of the Ethernet IEEE standard on thin coaxial cable, a baseband medium, at 10 megabits per second. The maximum segment length is just under 200 meters.

**10BASE5**

The original Ethernet medium, an implementation of the Ethernet IEEE standard on twinaxial cable, a baseband medium, at 20 megabits per second. The maximum segment length is 500 meters.

**10BASE-T**

An implementation of the Ethernet IEEE standard on 24 gauge unshielded, twisted-pair wiring, a baseband medium, at 10 megabits per second.

**802.2**

The third layer defined in the IEEE 802 LAN specifications, overlaying the 802.8, 802.4, 802.5, and FDDI protocols. 802.2, or Logical Link Control (LLC), is responsible for addressing and data link control and is independent of the topology, transmission medium, and medium access control technique chosen.

**802.3**

Defined by the IEEE, these standards govern the use of the **CSMA/CD** (Carrier Sense Multiple Access/Collision Detection) network access method used by Ethernet networks.

**802.4**

Defined by the IEEE, these standards govern the use of the token bus network access method.

**802.5**

Defined by the IEEE, these standards govern the use of the token ring network access method.

**AAUI (Apple Attachment Unit Interface)**

The name used for Apple's new Ethernet physical interface, which uses a special connector and requires an external transceiver to complete a connection to the network.

**access line**

A circuit between a device, such as a router, and a network, such as a frame relay, .X25, or ATM network.

**active star**

A network wired in a star topology with a concentrator or multiport *repeater* located at the center of the star. All wiring runs lead to the *concentrator*, which is responsible for retransmitting the network signal from one wiring run to the rest of the wiring runs attached to it.

**address**
A name, set of numbers, or sequence of bits used to identify devices on a network. Each computer, printer, server, or other device on the network must have a unique address. Addresses are necessary so that information transmitted on the network will get to the right destination. The network software keeps track of the addresses.

**AFP (AppleTalk Filing Protocol)**
The presentation-level protocol that governs remote file access in an AppleTalk network.

**agents**
Agents are pieces of software located in each network device that respond to requests by the management station to retrieve information from MIB variables for its device. The agent acts as a translator, peering inside a proprietary device to pass status information out by using an open protocol.

**aging process**
A technique in which routes that have not been updated are moved progressively from suspect status to bad status and are then deleted.

**amplitude**
The difference between the maximum and minimum voltage of an electrical signal.

**analog**
A form of transmission in which the waveform is continually varied over an infinite range of voltage.

**ANSI (American National Standards Institute)**
The principal organization in the United States dedicated to the development of voluntary standards for American industry.

**API (Application Program Interface)**
A series of specifications describing the types of data and commands that can be relayed from a program to other software or a software-controlled device, such as a network interface card.

**APPC (Advanced Program-to-Program Communications)**
Specifications for peer-to-peer communications in an IBM SNA network. See *LU6.2* and *SNA*.

**AppleDouble**
A file format specified by Apple for storing the data fork and resource fork of a Macintosh file in separate files on another computing system. Many file servers support the AppleDouble method for storing Mac files. The method allows you to share files with non-Mac users. With AppleDouble, other users simply access the data fork of a Mac file stored in the AppleDouble format.

**AppleShare**
Apple Computer's Mac-based file server software, using the AFP protocol.

**AppleSingle**
A file format specified by Apple for storing both the data fork and resource fork of a Macintosh file in a single file on another computing system.

**AppleTalk**
Apple Computer's networking software and protocols that provide the capabilities for communications and resource sharing among the computers, printers, and other peripherals attached to the network.

**AppleTalk address**
A number that uniquely identifies software processes in an AppleTalk network. For example, if the networking software includes a process that sends and receives a certain type of data, that process receives its own AppleTalk address. Processes of that type are called *socket clients*.

The address is composed of the socket number and the identification number of the node (the node ID) containing that socket number. This combination makes the address unique for each socket. See *socket*.

**application layer**
The layer of the OSI Reference Model that defines protocols for user or application programs. See *OSI Reference Model*.

**application-level gateways**
Link two networks by translating between two (or more) types of protocols at layers above layer 4 of the OSI Reference Model.

**Archie**
A protocol (and an application) that is used on the Internet to search directory lists of sites that allow Anonymous FTP.

**ARCnet (Attached Resource Computer Network)**
First developed by Datapoint Corporation, ARCnet is a local area network for IBM personal computers and compatibles. ARCnet uses the token-passing method.

**ARP (Address Resolution Protocol)**
A protocol in the TCP/IP protocol suite, ARP is responsible for translating an IP address into a physical address, such as an Ethernet address.

**ARPAnet (Advanced Research Projects Agency)**
See *TCP/IP*.

**ASCII (American Standard Code for Information Interchange)**
The ASCII code represents keyboard characters, control characters, and some graphics elements as an on/off pattern of 7 bits plus one more bit for an error-checking process known as *parity checking*. For example, the ASCII code for the letter "a" is 01100001 in binary, 61 in hexadecimal, and 97 in decimal.

Although initially developed as the code for representing text in a file on a single computer, the ASCII code is now also one of the most common codes used for transmitting data on networks of personal computers or between pieces of data processing equipment, such as a computer and a printer. The ASCII code can represent 128 characters.

**asynchronous communication**
A method for transmitting data that sends one character at a time. Asynchronous also refers to commands, as in a windowing environment, that may be sent without waiting for a response from the previous command. See *synchronous communication*.

**attenuation**
The loss of signal strength that occurs as a signal is transmitted through a cable.

**AWG (American Wire Gauge)**
A standard for specifying the diameter of a wire. Larger AWG numbers represent wires with smaller diameters.

**backbone network**
A central network that connects a number of networks, usually of lower capacity. Those lower-capacity networks can pass data to each other over the backbone network. The backbone network normally is built with a high-capacity medium, such as an Ethernet or fiber-optic cable. The lower-capacity networks connect to the backbone using routers, half routers, or modems. Information sent from one device to another within a network stays in that network, but data sent from one network to another travels over the backbone. Individual devices can also connect directly to the backbone network; they do not have to be part of one of the lower-capacity networks.

**balun**
A device that connects a balanced line to an unbalanced line, for example, a twisted wire

pair to coaxial cable. A balanced line is one in which both wires are electrically equal. In an unbalanced line, such as coaxial cable, one line (the central conductor) has different physical properties from the other (the surrounding concentric conductor).

**bandwidth**
The capacity of a network to carry information using a particular type of cable, as measured by the maximum number of bits per second (bps) the network can transmit. In a network, the higher the bandwidth, the greater the information-carrying capacity of the network, and the faster data can be transmitted from one device to another.

**baseband**
A type of network transmission that uses the entire bandwidth of a network to transmit a digital signal. The cables of a baseband network only carry one set of signals at a time. (See *broadband*, a type of transmission that can send multiple signals simultaneously.)

**baud rate**
The transmission speed of a communications channel. Baud rate is commonly used to represent bits per second. Baud rate is technically the switching speed of a line.

**big endian**
Network byte order usually specifies that the most significant byte (or octet) of an integer is transmitted first on the LAN. This ordering is called big endian. Machines that don't represent data internally in the same way that the data is transmitted are known as little endian machines.

**black hole**
A network problem that occurs whenever an AppleTalk internet is misconfigured — specifically, whenever two or more routers have a different network number for the same cable.

**blind transfer**
A SCSI transfer in which the SCSI master sends the data without explicit acknowledgement of each byte.

**bridge**
An electronic device that connects two networks so that devices on one network can communicate with devices on the other network. Bridges connect only networks that operate under the same communications protocols.

**broadband**
A method of transmitting data so that a single wire or cable can simultaneously carry many different channels of information. Cable television uses the broadband method to carry as many as 100 channels on a single coaxial cable. (Compare with *baseband*.)

**broadcast transmission**
A message sent over the network to all network devices. A network administrator planning to shut down the network for maintenance may send a broadcast transmission so that everyone on the network will know when the interruption will occur. Without the ability to send a broadcast transmission, the administrator would have to send messages to each user individually.

**brouter**
A device that can route specific protocols and bridge others, thus combining the capabilities of bridges and routers.

**buffer**
A temporary storage location in memory that provides uninterrupted data flow between devices, such as printers and keyboards, with fewer interruptions or pauses.

**bus topology**
A network topology in which a single cable is used to carry the network's signals. Computing devices are attached to the central cable (also known as a *backbone cable*) via taps.

**carrier sense multiple access**
See *CSMA*.

**CCITT (Consultative Committee for International Telegraphy and Telephony)**
An international standards-making body

consisting of national telecommunications authorities.

**cdev (Control Panel Device)**
A utility program for the Macintosh. The cdev is found in the System Folder and appears as an option in the Macintosh Control Panel.

**centralized server**
A computer dedicated to providing network services to users or clients. Often called a *dedicated server*.

**challenge/response system**
An authentication strategy in which the host system issues a "challenge" to the user that must be entered into the user's authentication device. The device then computes some function on the challenge and displays a response, which the user enters as a password

**channel**
In IBM's architecture, a channel is a direct attachment to the internal registers of a CPU. "Channel attached" devices are the fastest possible linkages between a peripheral and a CPU in any computing architecture.

**chat**
A TCP/IP application that enables two or more users to connect their workstations over a TCP/IP network so that everything one user types is seen by all other users.

**cheapernet**
See *Thinnet*.

**checksum**
A simple method used for detecting errors in transmission of data. The bytes comprising the data are added together; this sum is appended to the end of the data packet. The receiver recomputes the sum of the bytes in the packet and compares it to the sum received from the sender to determine if any data has been garbled.

**circuit-switched service**
A network in which the end-user has a clear channel between two network entities without visible processing by the network. Compare to packet-switched.

**Chooser**
A desk accessory included with the Macintosh system software. The desk accessory is used to select network services by service type (such as LaserWriter or AppleShare), device name, and zone name.

**client**
A relationship in which one device or program is dedicated to serving another device or program. For example, a workstation that requests services from a file server is a client of the server.

**client/server**
A networked computing system in which the two participating computers each use their own on-board processing capabilities to perform part of the task. In client/server systems, one of the two computers exerts more control over the transactions.

**cluster controller**
A communications controller attached to an IBM mainframe that manages the communications with terminals.

**coaxial cable**
An electrical cable that contains two separate wires. One wire is solid, and the other is a tube. The solid wire is inside the tube. Both wires have the same center point, or axis, which is why the cable is named *coaxial*. The solid wire carries data while the tube wire acts as a shield for the solid wire. The solid wire is surrounded by insulation to isolate it from the tube wire. The tube wire, which is made of a braided mesh, screen material, is in turn surrounded by insulation. Coaxial cables, also called *coax*, are the familiar wires used for cable television connections. Terminals used

on IBM networks frequently have coaxial cables for their connections; many Ethernet networks also use coaxial cables.

**collapsed backbone**
A new network topology in which the backbone of the network is collapsed into a single multiport transceiver or router backplane.

**collision**
A situation that occurs when two devices on a network try to transmit at the same time, and their transmissions "run into" each other. The signals are crossed, causing the data to become garbled. When a collision occurs, the data of each transmission is ruined and must be retransmitted. See *CSMA*.

**connection managers**
Part of the Apple Communications Toolbox, these enable applications to make connections to other hosts. For example, Apple's Serial Tool is a simple connection manager that enables applications to use the Mac's serial port to talk to modems and hosts.

**cookie**
A protocol in TCP/IP networks that allows a client to query a server for a "fortune cookie" message.

**crosstalk**
The electrical interference between signals transmitted on wires.

**CSMA (Carrier Sense Multiple Access)**
A method used by network devices to gain access to a single channel on the network. Each device "listens" to the traffic on the network (or *senses the carrier*) and thus detects whether the network is clear, whether signals are already passing on the cables, or whether signals are about to pass. If the network is clear, a device signals its intent to begin transmitting.

Two refinements of CSMA are Collision Avoidance (CA) and Collision Detection (CD). Collision Avoidance (CSMA/CA) is the process for resolving contention for the channel. *Contention* occurs when two devices both signal their intent to begin transmitting at the same time. When contention occurs, the transmitting workstations wait a random time interval, and then retransmit. The time interval is random so that when the devices begin retransmitting, chances are exceedingly small that they will start at the same time. An AppleTalk network system with LocalTalk cables uses the CSMA/CA technique.

The Collision Detection technique (CSMA/CD) senses when two transmissions occur on the same channel simultaneously. The main difference between the Collision Avoidance and Collision Detection methods is that transmitting devices using Collision Detection *listen* while transmitting. If the devices hear different signals than the ones transmitted, a *collision* is known to have occurred. Also, the receiving device doesn't send an acknowledgment character to the transmitting device. As with the Collision Avoidance method, the devices will wait a random amount of time before beginning to retransmit. Ethernet networks use the CSMA/CD technique.

**CTERM (Communications Terminal Protocol)**
Part of the virtual terminal service defined in layer 6 of the DECnet architecture.

**daemon**
A program running in the background on a UNIX system. A daemon performs a single task the entire time that it is running.

**daisy-chain network**
A topology in which the network wiring of a single branch "chains" from one station to another. Any failure of a station to pass on

network signals causes all systems down-stream of that station to lose network connectivity.

**data compression**
A process in which data are coded to require fewer bits of information to carry the same information.

**data link layer**
The layer of the OSI Reference Model that defines protocols governing data packets and transmissions. See *OSI Reference Model*.

**datagram**
In the Internet Protocols, a *datagram* is a packet containing destination address and data.

**DDCMP (Digital Data Communications Message Protocol)**
A data link protocol used in the DECnet architecture. DDCMP is used for point-to-point links between nodes in either asynchronous or synchronous modes. See *asynchronous communication* and *synchronous communication*.

**DDP (Datagram Delivery Protocol)**
The AppleTalk Datagram Delivery Protocol (DDP) is responsible for ensuring delivery of datagrams between AppleTalk sockets.

**DECnet/DNA**
The series of network protocols defined by Digital Computer, Inc. DNA, or Digital Network Architecture, contains the definitions of the protocols. DECnet is Digital's implementation of DNA.

**demodulate**
Demodulate is to recover a modulated signal back into its original form by filtering the data out of the carrier.

**directed broadcasting**
AppleTalk nodes register to receive packets from a multicast address (defined by DDP). Non-AppleTalk nodes do not register on that

address, so they cannot receive or be inter-rupted by AppleTalk broadcasts.

**disk server**
Software that allows a user to treat a partition of another computer's hard disk as if it were a locally attached disk drive. The contents of that partition cannot be shared with other users, a characteristic that distinguishes a disk server from a file server, which does allow sharing.

**distributed server**
A server system in which computers can be both clients and servers at the same time. Distributed servers do not require the full resources of the computer and are often run in the background. Also commonly called a *peer-to-peer* system. See *peer-to-peer*.

**DOS (Disk Operating System)**
Single-user operating system developed by Microsoft. Primarily used on IBM and IBM-compatible computers but sometimes ported to other systems.

**downtime**
The time during which the network and/or its services are unavailable to users.

**driver**
Software for using a peripheral hardware device attached to a computer. For example, to control a printer from a Macintosh computer, the print driver program for that type of printer has to be added to the Macintosh's System Folder.

**dynamic acquisition**
A technique in which information is gathered dynamically from the running network rather than requiring pre-configuration by the net-work manager.

**dynamically assigned socket**
A socket that is allocated to the software whenever it is required. A *socket* is an address-able memory location in a node on the

**Part VI: Appendixes**

network. Transmissions are sent directly to a socket in a node rather than to the node in general. Nodes can have more than one socket. See *DDP*.

**EBCDIC (Extended Binary Coded Decimal Interchange Code)**
An 8-bit code for representing letters, numerals, punctuation marks, and other symbols. Primarily used in IBM equipment, EBCDIC defines 256 character codes. The other, more commonly used code for representing characters is *ASCII* (American Standard Code for Information Interchange).

**electronic mail (e-mail)**
The use of electronic data communications to exchange information with other users. Electronic mail uses personal addresses for each recipient to determine to whom mail should be sent.

**emulation**
See *terminal emulation*.

**encapsulating routers**
Link two different networks by taking packets from one type of network (such as AppleTalk) and enclosing them in another (such as TCP/IP).

**encapsulation**
A generic networking concept in which one protocol is contained within another. For example, AppleTalk can be encapsulated inside of IP.

**encryption algorithm**
Encryption and authentication almost always use an encryption algorithm of some sort. The two most common types of encryption algorithms are public key and secret key.

**enterprise computing**
The term currently used to describe corporate networks, which are composed

of different types of computers running different operating systems and probably also using different network protocols. The goal of enterprise computing is inter-operability.

**Ethernet**
A data link protocol jointly developed by Intel, Xerox, and DEC and subsequently adopted by the IEEE as a standard.

**Ethernet broadcast storm**
A common problem is an Ethernet broadcast storm, which is caused by a malfunctioning device on the Ethernet. (The device can be either an AppleTalk device or any other type of node, such as TCP/IP or Novell.) In an Ethernet broadcast storm, the malfunctioning device floods the Ethernet with packets that are destined for the broadcast address. A router limits the extent of an Ethernet broadcast storm because a router does not forward packets destined for the broadcast address.

**EtherTalk**
The name given to AppleTalk protocols transmitted over Ethernet media.

**event synchronous (time-synchronized)**
Two types of personal authentication systems that are commonly in use. The event synchronous style of hardware was first made famous by Security Dynamics Corp., which makes the SecurID personal authentication device. In this type of system, after loggin on, the user simply types the number displayed at that moment on the SecurID card. Every 60 seconds, the SecurID card generates a new number. The SecurID card and its host computer are time-synchronized so that the host knows what number is showing on the SecurID card at any given moment.

**fault tolerance**
A design principle that includes the analysis of probable system, human, and equipment

failure and procedures, hardware, and software to keep the system running (even in degraded operation) while a component fails.

**FDDI (Fiber Distributed Data Interface)**
A 100-megabit/sec LAN standard based on the token ring system. Currently designed to be used with fiber-optic cabling.

**fiber-optic cable**
See *Optical fiber*.

**file-locking**
A method of network data management in which a file is reserved for the first user who requests it. Other users are locked out of access to the file and thus prevented from altering the file at the same time another user is modifying the file.

**file server**
A computer specifically intended for storing files that people can share over the network. The computer being used as the file server might not be able to be used for other common workstation tasks. Workstations used for a single purpose like a file server are called *dedicated* devices because they are dedicated to a single function. Often a dedicated file server is kept away from work areas for security reasons and to prevent accidental or malicious use. However, not all file servers must be dedicated. Some networking software allows any workstation to handle file server tasks and still function as a work-station.

**file-transer managers**
Part of the Apple Communications Toolbox, these enable applications to transfer files. Some typical file-transfer managers include Kermit and XModem, which implement popular file transfer protocols.

**filtering**
For most AppleTalk security needs, you can use a technology called filtering to restrict access. It is accomplished by the use of optional software provided with most routers.

**filtering bridge**
An Ethernet filtering bridge lets you filter the flow of packets between two (or sometimes more) Ethernet segments based on protocol type.

**finger**
A user information protocol (and the name of the application which usually runs it) commonly used in TCP/IP networks.

**frame**
A series of bytes of data encapsulated with a header. The data link layer sends frames back and forth. The term *frame* is often used interchangeably with the term *packet*. See *packet*.

**frequency**
The number of times per second an electrical signal cycles from maximum to minimum voltage and back again.

**frontware**
Software installed on a client microcomputer which interacts with an existing minicomputer or mainframe application yet provides a very different interface to the end-user. Frontware is an alternative to true client/ server application development.

**FTP (File Transfer Protocol)**
An upper-layer protocol in the TCP/IP suite that provides services for copying files across the network.

**full block**
A punchdown block (Type 66) in which all four punch positions in a horizontal row are electrically connected.

**full-duplex**
A data communications term that indicates that both ends of a communications link can transmit data at the same time. See *half-duplex*.

**gateway**
An electronic device that connects two networks, each of which operate with a different set of protocols, such as AppleTalk and EtherTalk. The gateway translates all the protocols of one network into those of the other network so that workstations and other devices on the two networks can communicate with one another. Some gateways translate all the protocols from the physical layer up to the applications layer. Others translate only the protocols above the data link layer or the transport layer.

**groupware**
Also called *collaborative computing*. Groupware includes programs designed to handle group-related tasks such as scheduling meetings, sending messages and other information, and coauthoring documents. Other programs include networked bulletin board systems and group decision support systems.

**half bridge**
A device that connects a network to a communications link, such as the telephone lines. Often the half bridge connects to a modem that then connects to the communications link. Workstations on the network can then transmit through the half bridge, then to the modem, over telephone lines, and to another network. The other network may also be attached to telephone lines with a modem and a half bridge.

Because half bridges do not deal with any addressing information, messages sent through half bridges are sent to the network, not to a particular workstation. The networking software then has to route the message to its proper destination. Half bridges can also connect a network to other dedicated circuits, such as a PBX.

Whereas a half bridge connects a network to an intermediate communications link, a *full bridge* connects one network to another. Conceptually, two half bridges, two modems, and the telephone lines create a full bridge between two networks.

**half duplex**
A data communications term that indicates that only one end of a communications link can transmit data at the same time. One end must wait for acknowledgment of its data transmission from the other end before it can continue with transmitting another data packet. See *full duplex*.

**half router**
A device that connects a network to a communications link, often using a modem. Unlike a half bridge, a half router maintains addressing information about the networks. Workstations on the network can send messages through the half router, then through the modem, over the telephone lines, through another modem and another half router, and then on to a workstation.

Because the router maintains the addressing information for both networks, messages can be properly routed to the correct workstations with a minimum of additional processing. See *router*.

**hardware handshake**
A flow control technique that uses out-of-band signals to start and stop modem transmission.

**harmonica block**
Used to convert a 50-pin Amphenol-style connector on the end of a 25-pair phone cable to one or more RJ-style jacks.

**HDLC (High-Level Data Link Control)**
An ISO protocol for the data link layer. HDLC is used in both X.25 and OSI networks.

**header**
A listing of control information that is found at the front of a packet. A packet header usually includes an identification of packet type, source and destination addresses, sequence numbers, and other indicators of priority levels. See *frame* and *packet*.

**hop**
A pass of data through a router. Routers connect the networks physically and maintain addressing information for each network. By going through the router, data leaves one network and passes to another, or "hops" from one network to the other. See *router*.

**ICMP (Internet Control Message Protocol)**
The protocol used by the IP layer of TCP/IP stacks for exchanging messages that control routing.

**IEEE (Institute of Electronic and Electrical Engineers)**
A major standards-setting group in the United States. Part of the ISO.

**IETF (Internet Engineering Task Force)**
A group of network engineers and users responsible for controlling the implementation of protocols on the Internet. See *Internet*.

**impedance**
Measurement of a transmission medium's resistance to an alternating current. Impedance is measured in ohms. See *ohms*.

**INITs**
Another term for extension, which is a miniprogram that you install by dropping it into your System Folder.

**Internet**
Called "The Internet." A collection of networks with a common routing backbone which encompasses such public networks as NSFnet (National Science Foundation Network) as well as private networks such as those at various universities. Not to be confused with the generic term *internet*.

**internet**
Two or more networks that are connected. Workstations in each network can share data and devices with other parts of the internet. Also called an *internetwork*.

The networks on an internet are connected through routers. A *router* is a device that physically connects the network cables and maintains network addresses. Data passing from one network to another passes through the router on its way to nodes on another network. See *router*.

**interoperability**
The capability to operate computers and exchange information in a heterogenous network.

**intrusive management**
An issue in network management in which there is a system monitoring the activities of users.

**IP (Internet Protocol)**
A protocol located in layer 3 of the TCP/IP protocol suite, used to provide connectionless transmissions of data packets over a TCP/IP network.

**IPX (Internetwork Packet Exchange)**
A network layer protocol used by Novell NetWare to provide functions for addressing, routing, and switching packets.

### ISDN (Integrated Services Digital Network)

An international communications standard that allows the integration of voice and data on a common transport mechanism.

### ISO (International Standards Organization)

An international standards-making body responsible for the OSI network standards and the OSI Reference Model.

### Kip-style addressing

A technique for linking LocalTalk-only Macintoshes to TCP/IP by routing the Macs from the Ethernet (typically) LAN onto the LocalTalk LAN and encapsulating them in AppleTalk DDP packets.

### layer

One set of networking protocols that is part of a complete group or *suite* of protocols. Processing at each layer performs one or more major functions necessary for transmitting data over a network.

One of the most common models of networking layers is the Open Systems Interconnection (OSI) Reference Model put forth by the International Standards Organization (ISO). In that model, seven layers of protocols dictate the processing of data before it can be transmitted to a receiving workstation. See *OSI Reference Model*.

### LAN (Local Area Network)

A network in one location. The size of the location can vary; for example, a network on one floor of an office building is a LAN. So is a network connecting all the buildings of a college campus. Networks connected by modems and telephone lines, however, are not LANs. Thus, a network connecting buildings in different cities is not a LAN (although the networks in each of the buildings probably are).

LANs provide the connections between workstations and peripherals such as printers and disk servers. Unlike telephone networks, in which all the lines and much of the equipment is owned by a telephone company, a LAN is typically owned by the company that uses it.

### LAP (Link Access Protocol)

AppleTalk protocols for controlling the hardware interface to different network media, including ELAP for Ethernet and LLap for LocalTalk.

### LAT (Local Area Transport)

A proprietary architecture developed by Digital Computer for terminal servers on Ethernet networks. LAT is designed to conserve network bandwidth and off-load processing from host computers.

### link

See *data link*.

### LLC (Logical Link Control)

Part of the IEEE LAN model (IEEE 802 standards). The logical link control layer presents a uniform interface to the user of the data link service, usually a network layer, and therefore reduces the need for the user to know what network medium is being used.

### LocalTalk

The name for Apple Computer's low-cost connectivity products consisting of cables, connection boxes, cable extenders, and other cabling equipment for connecting computers and other devices. LocalTalk was formerly called the AppleTalk Personal Network Cabling System.

Sometimes the term *LocalTalk environment* is used to describe the capabilities of an AppleTalk network. A LocalTalk environment is merely an AppleTalk network connected with LocalTalk cabling and connectors. Calling the system a LocalTalk environment differentiates it from an AppleTalk network connected with some other type of media and having different capabilities, such as EtherTalk.

**LU (Logical Unit)**
An IBM term in SNA (Systems Network Architecture) networks to describe the software that uses the network.

**LU 6.2**
A logical unit (LU) used on networks that use the Systems Network Architecture (SNA) protocols. LU 6.2 is being implemented as part of APPC. APPC allows peer-to-peer communications so that computers with the same processing capabilities will be able to communicate with each other directly as peers. This, in turn, means that processing loads can be more evenly distributed on the network and that computers need not resort to terminal emulation in order to talk to mainframes.

**mail server**
A network computer that acts as an electronic post office. People using the network transmit a message to the mail server, where the message is stored until the addressee checks the server and reads the message. Thus, a mail server has the electronic equivalent of post office boxes. With some mail servers, users can also store the messages after reading them.

**MAN (Metropolitan Area Network)**
A network capable of data communications over distances from a few miles to one hundred miles. Normally, a MAN is thought of as a network consisting of fewer than 1,000 nodes and using very high data rates (100 Mbps or higher).

**Manchester encoding**
A digital, self-clocking method of encoding that describes a bit value by the transition between two signals.

**mapping**
The redirection of local resources to network resources.

**management station**
A management station (also called consoles) is where the network management software runs.

**MIB (Management Information Base)**
Information used by SNMP for maintaining the status and control of a network device. MIBs are specific to each type of device; information within the MIB is relayed by an SNMP agent to network management software either on request or when a problem occurs within the device.

**modem**
A device that takes digital data from a computer and encodes it in analog form (modulation) for transmission over a phone line. It also performs the opposite process for incoming signals (demodulation). The term modem is derived from the terms *mo*dulator/*dem*odulator.

**modulate**
Modulate is to mix a voice or data signal onto a carrier for transmission in a communications network.

**multicast address**
A term used in network addressing. A multicast address is a group address that is meant for a certain subset of devices on the network. See *address*.

**multiprotocol environment**
A network that supports multiple protocols on the same physical medium. Not all systems

on the network need to "speak" to all protocols on the same medium.

### NBP (Name Binding Protocol)

An AppleTalk protocol used for translating
device names to addresses.

### network

A collection of individually controlled computers, printers, modems, and other
electronic devices which are interconnected
so that they can all communicate with each
other. Networks also include all the software
needed to run the network as well as the
wires, cables, connection boxes, and other
hardware that make the physical connections.
Using a network, people can share data, programs, and send messages to each other.
Networks also let people share resources,
such as printers and disk storage units.

### Network Interface Controller (NIC)

A card (or set of chips) that fits inside a computer so that the computer can connect to a
network. The card has a connector for attaching the network cable. Sometimes the
network interface controller (or NIC) is
called simply the *interface card*.

Different types of networks require different
interface cards. The connectors are different
sizes to accommodate the cables of different
networks, and the chips on the card contain
the hardware and software needed to implement the various protocols for a specific type
of network.

### network layer

The layer of the OSI Reference Model that
defines protocols governing data routing.

### NFS (Network File System)

A protocol defined by Sun Microsystems to
extend TCP/IP network file services. NFS
allows files on remote nodes of a network to
appear as if they were stored on the local
workstation.

### network number

A 16-bit number used to indicate the Apple-
Talk network a node is connected to. Nodes
choose their network number from within the
network number range assigned to their network.

### node

An addressable device on a network, such as a
LaserWriter or a Macintosh. Network processes running within a node are called *sockets*
and are assigned *socket numbers*.

### NVE (Network-Visible Entity)

Any computing node or socket that can communicate with a network and be seen by other
nodes or sockets. Your Mac, PC, Laser-
Writer, or file server are all network-visible
entities.

### ohm

An electrical unit of measurement used to
measure the resistance of a transmission medium to the flow of electrons (that is, a
current) through the medium. If the current
is a direct current (DC), the term *resistance* is
used. If the current is an alternating current
(AC), the term *impedance* is used. Both resistance and impedance are measured in ohms.

### ohmmeter

An electrical measuring device. Ohmmeters
include a series of wiring posts with insulated
wires for connecting to the circuit or electrical device to be measured and also include
either an analog display (a meter) or a digital
display for showing the value of the measured
quantity. Ohmmeters can also be used to
measure voltages and/or electrical current.

### optical fiber

A type of network cabling composed of thin
glass fibers. In order for optical fibers to be
used on a network, electrical signals are converted into pulses of light to be sent through
the fibers. A receiving device then transforms

the light pulses back into electrical signals and passes those signals on to the appropriate destination.

Fiber optics have an extremely high bandwidth for carrying information. Thus, they can transmit information at very high rates and can also carry many channels. Other benefits include maximum protection from eavesdropping and virtually no susceptibility to electromagnetic interference or atmospheric disturbances, such as rain or lightning.

### OSI Reference Model

A model for the modularization of network protocols and their functions. Each layer communicates only with the layer immediately above and below it. The OSI Reference Model has seven layers: physical layer, data link layer, network layer, transport layer, session layer, presentation layer, and application layer. OSI stands for *Open Systems Interconnection*.

### packet

A group of bits, including address, data, and control elements, that are switched and transmitted together. See *frame*.

### packet-switched service

A network technology in which data are broken up into units called packets. Compare with circuit switched service.

### passive star

A network topology in which each wiring run is connected together at a common end. Each wiring run is called a *branch*, or *leg*, of the star. Unlike the active star, a passive star has no concentrator at the center. See *star topology*.

### peer

A device treated as the equal of another device on the network. Networks that let workstations and other nodes communicate with each other as equals are called *peer-to-peer networks*.

### port descriptor file

A file maintained by a router for network-related information for each of the router's ports. The port descriptor file includes the *port ID*, a number that designates the identity of the port for the internal processing use of the router; the *network number*, a number that labels the cable that is attached to the port with a unique number that identifies it as a separate network; and the *network address*, a number that designates the port's address on the network.

### PPP (Point-to-Point Protocol)

A replacement protocol for SLIP, designed to provide router-to-router as well as host-to-network connections over asynchronous and synchronous links. See *asynchronous communication* and *synchronous communication*.

### presentation layer

The layer of the OSI Reference Model that defines protocols governing data formats and conversions.

### print server

A device (usually an additional workstation) that acts as a large buffer for files being sent to the printer. When users send data to the printer, the data is actually sent to the server and stored there until the printer is available. Then, the print server automatically sends the data to the printer to be printed.

A print server enables network users to send data to a printer even if the printer is busy with another job. Thus, users do not need to wait for an available printer on the network. If more than one print job is waiting on the server, the print-server software keeps track of the jobs and prints them in order. Some software allows for the reassignment of priorities to print jobs as well as job cancellation so that some people can get their work printed ahead of others.

**print spooler**

An application program or combination of hardware and software that allows users to print at the same time that they are working on some other task.

The print spooler acts as a buffer for the files to be printed. The files are stored in the spooler until a printer is free for printing. The spooler then sends the file to the printer.

**protocol**

A procedural rule or convention for sending information over a network. Each network has its own way of transmitting data and divides the entire process into a series of specific functions. Each function requires a complete set of operating rules, or *protocols*.

The OSI Reference Model has become one of the primary models for network protocols. If companies developing communications protocols follow the OSI model, their networks can probably (with minor conversion routines) interconnect with most other networking protocols in use today.

The entire set of protocols used by a particular network is called its *family* or *suite* of protocols. A particular implementation of a protocol family in a computer is called that computer's *protocol stack*.

The protocols themselves are small programs that control a specific set of communications functions. However, none of the protocols can carry out full communications from start to finish. The protocols all have to work together in sequence.

**protocol analyzer**

A tool for looking at networks. It watches a wire, captures all the data that passes over the wire, and can display (and sometimes explain) each bit of data.

**protocol layers**

The functional divisions of processing to send and receive data on a network. The layers refer to the main tasks the networking software has to accomplish to transmit and receive data.

**protocol stack**

The implementation of a specific protocol family in a computer or other node on the network. The protocol stack refers to the visual analogy of all of the layers of a set of protocols — a stack of protocols being implemented on a node.

**punchdown block**

A wiring device used by phone companies and network installers for connecting many wires together in one location. A typical punchdown block (type 66 block) has fifty rows of four contacts, or pins. Wires are pushed, or "punched down," onto a pin to make electrical contact using a special tool called a *punchdown tool*.

**public key cryptography**

One of the two most common types of encryption algorithms, the other being secret key. The RSA algorithm is an example of the most popular public key system. The primary advantage of using public key over secret key cryptography is the increased security that public key provides. The main disadvantage of public key is its speed.

**redundant path**

A second path that a network packet may use to travel from its source to its destination. The redundant path is used when the primary path between two nodes is disrupted.

**repeater**

A hardware device that repeats the signals on a network. As signals pass over a line, they lose some of their power and pick up static. A repeater amplifies and conditions the signals on a network line.

Repeating a digital signal is sometimes called *regenerating the signal* because the repeater device removes static (line noise) and boosts the signal strength so that it becomes louder as it passes over the line. By improving a signal, repeaters reduce the possibility of error when a workstation has to interpret the signal. Repeaters also enable the signals to be sent greater distances and therefore essentially extend the length of the network.

A repeater acts only at the physical layer of the network's protocols and therefore can only connect two networks with identical physical links.

### ring topology

A network arrangement in which all the devices are connected in a circle, or ring. Data passes around the ring from node to node, always in the same direction. Each node essentially acts as a repeater and retransmits the messages to the next node.

IBM's token ring network uses the ring topology. In that system, a sequence of bits — the token — is passed around the network, and the node that has the token can have access to the network. When the node is through, it releases the token to be passed to the next node that wants access.

### RIP (Routing Information Protocol)

A protocol for updating routing tables in TCP/IP networks.

### router

A device that connects two networks together and maintains addressing information for each network. Workstations can pass information from one network to another by sending the information through the router.

Routers are often confused with bridges. A bridge physically connects two networks, but a bridge does not maintain the network addressing information. The router maintains a table of network addresses and is more effective in sending data to nodes on the different networks. See *bridge*.

### routing tuple

A type of data in which two values are paired with each other because the two items are related. For example, in the routing table, the two items are a network number and the distance a network is away, measured in hops.

### SAA (Systems Application Architecture)

A set of network operating procedures developed by IBM that attempts to let nodes use different programming languages and applications on an IBM network. SAA is IBM's attempt to solve the problem of software incompatibility among its computers.

Prior to SAA, programs written for one type of IBM computer were not usable on other IBM computers. SAA's basic premise is that software for one IBM computer should work on any other IBM computer. The concept is called *device independence* for the software.

### SDLC (Synchronous Data Link Control)

A data link protocol used in IBM's SNA networks. See *asynchronous communication* and *synchronous communication*.

### seed router

Seed routers seed, or initialize, the internet with the configuration information the administrator enters (network number and range, zone name and list).

### segment

Any section of cable that is attached to a port of a repeater, bridge, or router.

### server

A computer, workstation, or similar device that provides a service to network users or other devices on the network. The three most common types of servers on local area networks are the print server, file server, and mail server.

**session**
A term used to refer to the logical stream of data flowing between two programs that are communicating over the network. There are usually many different sessions originating from one particular node of a network. In AppleTalk, each session in a node has its own socket. See *socket.*

**session layer**
The layer of the OSI Reference Model that defines protocols that govern communications between applications. See *OSI Reference Model.*

**shielded cable**
A wire or circuit enclosed by a grounded metallic material. Shielding serves two purposes. First, it keeps outside electrical disturbances from reaching the wire and disrupting the signals passing over it. Second, shielding keeps the cable from emitting radiation that can disrupt radio and television reception or that can be captured and interpreted by some unauthorized person.

**single protocol environment**
A network in which only a single protocol is allowed. There are few, if any, true single protocol networks out there.

**SLIP (Serial Line Internet Protocol)**
A TCP/IP-based protocol used to run IP over serial lines such as telephone circuits. See *TCP/IP* and *IP.*

**SMDS (Switched Multimegabit Data Service)**
A high-speed networking technology offered by telephone companies.

**SMTP (Simple Mail Transfer Protocol)**
The electronic mail protocol defined for TCP/IP networks.

**SNA (Systems Network Architecture)**
A set of communications protocols developed by IBM for synchronous transmission of data.

SNA is popular on networks that include an IBM mainframe computer. SNA includes protocol layers for the data structures, formats, control of the data links, and maintaining data transmission.

A key purpose of SNA is to allow different types of computers to communicate over the network. Users of the SNA network are unaffected by the way the network provides its services, or by the equipment necessary to maintain the network. See *asynchronous communication* and *synchronous communication.*

**SNADS (SNA Distribution Services)**
Part of the SNA networking architecture, designed for transferring messages within SNA.

**SNMP (Simple Network Management Protocol)**
A protocol in the TCP/IP suite for managing objects on the network. SNMP uses agents on managed devices to maintain a MIB (Management Information Base) and transmit MIB data to the management software upon request.

**sneakernet**
Common term denoting a non-network method for transferring files between computers. With sneakernet, you transfer the files by walking — in your sneakers — from computer to computer with a floppy disk that contains the files.

**socket**
Any addressable entity in a node on an AppleTalk network. Sockets are "owned" by the software processes that create them. For example, if a communications program ob-

tains a socket for receiving messages, that socket can only be used to receive messages for that program. Messages that arrive for some other program arrive through their own sockets. The software processes that own the sockets are called the *socket clients*.

### socket number
The number that identifies a particular socket. Each node may have the capability to allocate many sockets. The socket number identifies which one is being used by a particular software process.

### software handshake
A system for flow control that uses in-band characters (such as the ASCII XOFF [control-S] and XON [control-Q]) to stop and start data transmission.

### split block
A punchdown block in which each half of the block, divided vertically, is independent. On a split block (sometimes called a "half block"), the leftmost two connectors on each horizontal row are connected to each other, and the rightmost two connectors are also connnected to each other. Connecting the left half to the right half requires an external connection.

### split-horizon routing
A technique for maintaining routing tables of individual routers. If a router A is attached (via a network) to one port of another router (B), then router B only informs router A of networks that are reachable through the other ports of router B. Router A is thus not informed of networks that are attached to the same port of Router B as the one router A is attached to.

### SPX (Sequenced Packet Exchange)
The transport Layer protocol used by Novell NetWare. Provides a connection-oriented, guaranteed delivery link between workstations.

### SQL (Structured Query Language)
A data manipulation language standardized by ANSI and used in most relational database systems.

### star topology
A centralized network with the main computer in the center and all the nodes connected to it. For LANs, a device known as an *active hub*, *concentrator*, or *star controller* replaces the main computer at the center of the network.

The central device controls each workstation. For one workstation to communicate with another, the message passes through the central device, also called the *hub*. The hub controls access and transmission along all of the connecting lines. For example, the part of a telephone network that includes a local telephone exchange is a star network because communications between any two telephones must first pass through the local exchange. The exchange is, essentially, the hub of that star network.

Star networks are simple to control because all control takes place at one point. Also, problems are easy to isolate because the workstations are not directly connected to one another. However, the two disadvantages of the star network are the cost of the central computer and the vulnerability of the overall network if the hub fails. Unlike bus networks that can still operate if a device fails, star networks fail completely if the hub fails. See *hub* and *ring topology*.

### store-and-forward
A message-passing technique in which messages are temporarily stored at intermediate points before being retransmitted to the next destination.

**synchronous communication**
A data transmission method in which a packet of data is sent, and the sender and receiver stations resynchronize their clocks. See *asynchronous communication*.

**tap**
Used to connect a station to a network (usually a bus network, such as 10BASE5 Ethernet).

**TCP (Transmission Control Protocol)**
The transport layer protocol of the TCP/IP protocol suite. TCP provides connection-oriented, end-to-end transport of packets between workstations.

**TCP/IP (Transmission Control Protocol/Internet Protocol)**
A set of protocols designed to let many networks interconnect.

TCP/IP is the standard for internetwork communication established in the U.S. Department of Defense network known as ARPAnet. ARPA, also called DARPA, stands for the Advanced Research Projects Agency. ARPAnet is the research and development arm of the Department of Defense.

TCP/IP is rapidly becoming a de facto standard for network interconnections for universities and research organizations. It has been associated with UNIX networks because various companies selling UNIX devices have built the TCP/IP protocols into the devices.

**TELNET**
An upper-layer TCP/IP protocol that provides virtual terminal services and allows users to log onto remote nodes.

**terminal emulation**
The process of making a personal computer imitate a terminal, often a "dumb" terminal.

Terminal emulation is necessary in certain systems because mainframes expect all the terminals on a network to have similar input/output requirements. Specifically, the terminals need to use and understand the same control characters that indicate different processing procedures. Programs called *emulators* allow a personal computer to emulate a terminal. The programs store the meaning of the control characters and the various procedures in the personal computer's memory. When the computer receives the control character over the network from the mainframe, the computer responds with the proper procedure. Similarly, the personal computer translates its input characters and control keys into the form the mainframe expects and understands. To the mainframe, it appears as if the personal computer is the proper type of terminal.

**terminator**
A device attached to the end of a cable to prevent unwanted signals from being transmitted on the line or link. A terminator resistance matches the characteristic impedance of the line so that signals arriving at the end of the cable do not find an impedance discontinuity and are not reflected.

**Thicknet**
Cabling scheme using 50-ohm coaxial cable with N-type connectors. Thicknet uses a 50-ohm coaxial cable as the backbone for the network. The cable has an outer diameter of 0.37 to 0.41 inches, depending on the type of insulation. Also note that Thicknet cable has two layers of shielding.

**Thinnet**
Cabling scheme using 50-ohm coaxial cable with BNC-type connectors — thinnet coax is 0.20 inches in outer diameter and has a single layer of shielding. Sometimes called *cheapernet*.

**throughput**
In data communication, the total traffic between stations per unit of time.

**timeout**
The process by which a computing task determines if a connection is still active or valid. The task maintains a clock counter to determine if a packet is delivered properly within a predetermined period of time. If the receiver does not acknowledge receipt of the packet within that time period, the sender either tries again or closes the connection.

**token passing**
Involves sending an electronic token packet on the network from one station to the next. This token gives the receiving station permission to transmit data. When that station is finished sending its data, it passes the token on to the next station.

**token ring**
A network that connects workstations in a closed ring and that uses token passing to enable nodes to use the network. A token is a set of bits that the networking software uses to grant access to the network. Token passing refers to the process of passing the token from node to node on the network until one node wants to use the network. That node then keeps the token while it is using the network. See *ring topology*.

**topology**
The physical layout of a network, including the cables and devices. The topology of a network is its roadmap and can show which devices can communicate directly and which cannot because they don't share a connection path. Typical topologies used on local area networks are the bus, star, and ring.

Topology can also mean the possible logical connections along the network. Logical connections are those that permit nodes to communicate through some additional software processing instead of directly through physical connections.

**transceiver**
A device used as an interface between a workstation and the network to which it is attached. The transceiver performs the task of transmitting frames onto the cable and receiving them from it. It also monitors signal levels on the medium and detects collisions and other error conditions.

**transport layer**
The layer of the OSI Reference Model that defines protocols that govern message structure. Provides some error checking. See *OSI Reference Model*.

**transport-level gateways**
Link two networks by translating between two (or more) types of protocols at layers 3 and 4 of the OSI Reference Model.

**trap**
Notification sent by a network device's agent after some event occurs. Traps help to keep an eye on the network without constantly asking every device for status information

**tunneling**
A technique for networking that involves packing the packets of one protocol into the packets of another protocol (or the same protocol) for passage over a backbone network.

**tuple**
A type of data in which two values are paired with each other because the two items are related. For example, in the routing table, the two items are a network number and the distance the network is away, measured in hops.

**twinax cable**
A type of coaxial cable with two center conductors.

**twisted-pair cable**

Ordinary telephone wire consisting of two insulated copper strands twisted about each other to reduce outside interference of their signals. Twisted-pair wiring is relatively inexpensive, easy to install, easy to modify, and may already exist in many installations as part of the telephone network. See *shielded cable*.

**Type 66 block**

An older type of punchdown block, very common in buildings wired before 1988 (and many wired after). The Type 66 block is distinguished by a relatively low density and low cost.

**UDP (User Datagram Protocol)**

Part of the TCP/IP protocol suite. The protocol is used as an alternative to TCP for unacknowledged datagrams.

**VAX (Virtual Address Extension)**

A series of computers manufactured by Digital Computer.

**Vines (Virtual Network Software)**

Banyan's network operating system based on UNIX and its protocols.

**virtual terminal**

A definition of a standardized terminal for a network that can accommodate different type of terminals. Protocols are used to prevent incompatibilities among the different types of terminals. Signals to and from the nonstandard terminals are converted into signals that would come from the standard terminal. Therefore, all the terminals appear to be the same to the host computer.

**VMS (Virtual Memory System)**

A proprietary operating system used by Digital Computer for its VAX computers.

**WAN (Wide Area Network)**

A network that spans many geographically separated locations. The WAN links between each local network are provided by a telecom-munications service, such as leased line, SMDS, or other long-distance carriers. See *SMDS*.

**workstation**

A computer on a network, usually reserved for end users.

**ZIP (Zone Information Protocol)**

The AppleTalk protocol used to exchange information on zone names and locations between routers.

**ZIP storms**

When a malfunction on the network causes an inordinate number of ZIP (Zone Information Protocol) request packets to enter and flood the network. A ZIP storm can flood an entire Ethernet backbone, halting processes by other protocols, including TCP/IP, DECnet, or any other protocol running on the network.

**ZIT (Zone Information Table)**

Table maintained within an AppleTalk router, relating zone names to the router's ports.

**zone**

A collection of networks on an AppleTalk internet. A zone can consist of a single network or a number of networks.

One of the main reasons for breaking a network into zones is to reduce the amount of searching a user has to do to find a resource on the network. For example, to use a particular printer on the network, the user can search various zones instead of searching the entire network.

Although grouping an internet into zones is usually done on some logical basis such as work loads or business departments, the zones do not have to be physically contiguous. A network in one building might be part of the same zone as a network in another building.

# Networking Acronyms

This appendix lists common networking acronyms and their meanings.

| | |
|---|---|
| AARP | AppleTalk Address Resolution Protocol |
| AAUI | Apple Attachment Unit Interface |
| ADSP | AppleTalk Data Stream Protocol |
| AEP | AppleTalk Echo Protocol |
| AFP | AppleTalk Filing Protocol |
| ALAP | AppleTalk Link Access Protocol |
| ALOE | AppleTalk Low Overhead Encapsulation |
| ANSI | American National Standards Institute |
| AOCE | Apple Open Collaborative Environment |
| API | Application Program Interface |
| APPC | Advanced Program-to-Program Communication |
| ARA | AppleTalk Remote Access |
| ARP | Address Resolution Protocol |
| ASCII | American Standard Code for Information Interchange |
| ASP | AppleTalk Session Protocol |
| ATM | Asynchronous Transfer Mode |
| ATP | AppleTalk Transaction Protocol |
| AURP | AppleTalk Update-Based Routing Protocol |
| AUI | Attachment Unit Interface |
| AWG | American Wire Gauge |
| BSI | Basic Rate Interference |
| CCITT | Consultative Committee for International Telegraphy and Telephony |
| CDDI | Copper Distributed Data Interface |
| CIX | Commercial Internet Exchange |
| CLNP | Connectionless Network Protocol |

| | |
|---|---|
| CRC | Cyclic Redundancy Check |
| CSMA/CA | Carrier Sense Multiple Access/Collision Avoidance |
| CSMA/CD | Carrier Sense Multiple Access/Collision Detection |
| CSU/DSU | Channel Service Unit/Data Service Unit |
| CTS | Clear to Send |
| DAMQAM | Dynamically Adaptive Multicarrier Quadrature Amplitude Modulation |
| DCE | Data Circuit-terminating Equipment |
| DDP | Datagram Delivery Protocol |
| DNA | Digital Networking Architecture |
| DOS | Disk Operating System |
| DSP | Digital Signal Processors |
| DTE | Data Terminal Equipment |
| ELAP | Ethernet Link Access Protocol |
| EIA | Electronic Industry Association |
| ES | End Systems |
| FCS | Frame Check Sequence |
| FDDI | Fiber Distributed Data Interface |
| FOIRL | Fiber Optic Inter-Repeater Link |
| FTP | File Transfer Protocol |
| GNI | GetNetInfo |
| GNIR | GetNetInfoReply |
| HDLC | High-Level Data Link Control |
| HTML | HyperText Markup Language |
| HTTP | HyperText Transfer Protocol |
| IDG | Interdialog Gap |
| IDRP | Inter-Domain Routing Protocol |
| IEEE | Institute of Electronic and Electrical Engineers |
| IETF | Internet Engineering Task Force |
| IFG | Interframe Gap |
| IMAP | Interactive Mail Access Protocol |
| IP | Internet Protocol |
| IPM | Inter Personal Messaging |
| IPX | Internet Package Exchange |
| IRC | Internet Relay Chat |
| IS | Intermediate Systems |
| ISDN | Integrated Services Digital Network |
| ISO | International Standards Organization |
| ITU | International Telecommications Union |

| | |
|---|---|
| LADA | Local Area Data Access |
| LAN | Local Area Network |
| LAP | Link Access Protocol |
| LAPM | Link Access Protocol Modem |
| LLAP | LocalTalk Link Access Protocol |
| MAN | Metropolitan Area Network |
| MAU | Medium Attachment Unit |
| MDI | Medium Dependent Interface |
| MHS | Message Handling Service (System) |
| MIB | Management Information Base |
| MNP | Microcom Networking Protocol |
| MOTIS | Message Oriented Text Interchange System |
| MS | Message Store |
| MTA | Message Transfer Agent |
| MTS | Message Transfer System |
| MUD | MultiUser Dungeon |
| NBP | Name Binding Protocol |
| NFS | Network File System |
| NIC | Network Interface Controller (Card) |
| NIU | Network Interface Unit |
| NNTP | Network News Transfer Protocol |
| NRZ | Non-Return to Zero |
| NVE | Network-Visible Entity |
| ODA | Open Document Architecture |
| OSI | Open Systems Interconnection |
| PAD | Packet Assembler and Disassembler |
| PAP | Printer Access Protocol |
| PEP | Packetized Ensemble Protocol |
| PMA | Physical Medium Attachment |
| POP2/POP3 | Post Office Protocol versions 2 and 3 |
| PPP | Point-to-Point Protocol |
| PSDN | Packet-Switched Data Networks |
| PSN | Packet-Switched Network |
| PSTN | Public Switched Telephone Network |
| QAM | Quadrature Amplitude Modulations |
| RAID | Redundant Arrays of Inexpensive Disks |
| RAM | Random Access Memory |
| ROM | Read-Only Memory |
| RPC | Remote Procedure Call |
| RTMP | Routing Table Maintenance Protocol |
| RTS | Ready to Send |

| | |
|---|---|
| SAA | Systems Application Architecture |
| SCSI | Small Computer Systems Interface |
| SEDI | Simple Encapsulation of DDP in IP |
| SLIP | Serial Line Internet Protocol |
| SMDS | Switched Multimegabit Data Service |
| SMTP | Simple Mail Transfer Protocol |
| SNA | Systems Network Architecture |
| SNAP | Sub-Network Access Point |
| SNMP | Simple Network Management Protocol |
| SONET | Synchronous Optical Network |
| SPX | Sequenced Packet Exchange |
| SQL | Structured Query Language |
| SCC | Serial Communications Controller |
| SVC | Switched Virtual Circuit |
| TCP/IP | Transmission Control Protocol/Internet Protocol |
| TCM | Trellis Coded Modulation |
| TDR | Time Domain Reflectometer |
| TIA | Telecommunications Industry Association |
| TID | Transaction ID |
| TRLAP | Token Ring Link Access Protocol |
| TREDI | Traffic Reduced Encapsulation of DDP in IP |
| UA | User Agent |
| UDP | User Datagram Protocol |
| UPS | Uninterruptible Power Supply |
| UTP | Unshielded Twisted Pair |
| UUCP | UNIX-to-UNIX CP |
| VAX | Virtual Address Extension |
| WAN | Wide Area Network |
| WORM | Write Once, Read Many |
| WWW | World Wide Web |
| ZIP | Zone Information Protocol |
| ZIT | Zone Information Table |

# Index

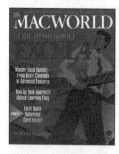

# Order Form

**Order Center: (800) 762-2974** (8 a.m.-5 p.m., PST, weekdays) or (415) 312-0650

**For Fastest Service:** Photocopy This Order Form and FAX it to: (415) 358-1260

| Quantity | ISBN | Title | Price | Total |
|---|---|---|---|---|
| | | | | |
| | | | | |
| | | | | |
| | | | | |
| | | | | |
| | | | | |
| | | | | |
| | | | | |
| | | | | |
| | | | | |
| | | | | |
| | | | | |

## Shipping & Handling Charges

| Subtotal | U.S. | Canada & International | International Air Mail |
|---|---|---|---|
| Up to $20.00 | Add $3.00 | Add $4.00 | Add $10.00 |
| $20.01-40.00 | $4.00 | $5.00 | $20.00 |
| $40.01-60.00 | $5.00 | $6.00 | $25.00 |
| $60.01-80.00 | $6.00 | $8.00 | $35.00 |
| Over $80.00 | $7.00 | $10.00 | $50.00 |

In U.S. and Canada, shipping is UPS ground or equivalent.
For Rush shipping call (800) 762-2974.

Subtotal

CA residents add
applicable sales tax

IN and MA residents add
5% sales tax

IL residents add
6.25% sales tax

RI residents add
7% sales tax

Shipping

Total

## Ship to:

Name _____

Company _____

Address _____

City/State/Zip_____

Daytime Phone _____

**Payment:** ❑ Check to IDG Books (US Funds Only)   ❑ Visa   ❑ Mastercard   ❑ American Express

Card# _____ Exp._____ Signature_____

Please send this order form to: IDG Books, 155 Bovet Road, Suite 310, San Mateo, CA 94402.

Allow up to 3 weeks for delivery. Thank you!

# IDG BOOKS WORLDWIDE REGISTRATION CARD

**RETURN THIS REGISTRATION CARD FOR FREE CATALOG**

**Title of this book:** **Macworld Networking Bible, 2E**

**My overall rating of this book:** ☐ Very good [1] ☐ Good [2] ☐ Satisfactory [3] ☐ Fair [4] ☐ Poor [5]

**How I first heard about this book:**

☐ Found in bookstore; name: [6]      ☐ Book review: [7]

☐ Advertisement: [8]      ☐ Catalog: [9]

☐ Word of mouth; heard about book from friend, co-worker, etc.: [10]      ☐ Other: [11]

**What I liked most about this book:**

**What I would change, add, delete, etc., in future editions of this book:**

**Other comments:**

**Number of computer books I purchase in a year:** ☐ 1 [12] ☐ 2-5 [13] ☐ 6-10 [14] ☐ More than 10 [15]

**I would characterize my computer skills as:** ☐ Beginner [16] ☐ Intermediate [17] ☐ Advanced [18] ☐ Professional [19]

**I use** ☐ DOS [20] ☐ Windows [21] ☐ OS/2 [22] ☐ Unix [23] ☐ Macintosh [24] ☐ Other: [25] _____ (please specify)

**I would be interested in new books on the following subjects:**
(please check all that apply, and use the spaces provided to identify specific software)

☐ Word processing: [26]      ☐ Spreadsheets: [27]

☐ Data bases: [28]      ☐ Desktop publishing: [29]

☐ File Utilities: [30]      ☐ Money management: [31]

☐ Networking: [32]      ☐ Programming languages: [33]

☐ Other: [34]

**I use a PC at** (please check all that apply): ☐ home [35] ☐ work [36] ☐ school [37] ☐ other: [38] _____

**The disks I prefer to use are** ☐ 5.25 [39] ☐ 3.5 [40] ☐ other: [41] _____

**I have a CD ROM:** ☐ yes [42] ☐ no [43]

**I plan to buy or upgrade computer hardware this year:** ☐ yes [44] ☐ no [45]

**I plan to buy or upgrade computer software this year:** ☐ yes [46] ☐ no [47]

Name:      Business title: [48]      Type of Business: [49]

Address ( ☐ home [50] ☐ work [51] /Company name: _____ )

Street/Suite#

City [52] /State [53] /Zipcode [54]:      Country [55]

☐ **I liked this book!** You may quote me by name in future IDG Books Worldwide promotional materials.

My daytime phone number is _____

**IDG BOOKS**

THE WORLD OF
COMPUTER
KNOWLEDGE